# government

**Walter E. Volkomer**
Hunter College of the City University of New York

**Appleton-Century-Crofts, New York**
Educational Division
Meredith Corporation

# contents

**part three**
# the institutions of national government

**part four**

# government in action: challenge and response

chapter **19**  civil rights:
equal protection under the law    *page 637*

# preface

This text is designed for use in introductory American government courses at the college level. It includes systematic and comprehensive coverage of basic concepts and principles, terminology, important trends in political research, and application of this research. The book also surveys some of the branches of political science so that students who later wish to take advanced courses will be familiar with fields of specialization.

Every textbook writer must realize that there is no right way to teach a course; a good teacher will adapt the material to suit his own special abilities and interests and his students' needs. Limiting a book to only one school of political science—institutional, behavioral, or policy studies—often results in limiting its usefulness. This book therefore includes material from many points of view. Such an inclusive approach seems especially valuable in a field such as political science—a field that is changing and developing rapidly—because it gives the student a broad framework with which to handle new concepts and viewpoints that will arise in the future. A special effort has been made to use many current resources that will help the reader keep abreast of significant recent developments. For example, the book contains material showing the latest trends in the voting behavior of Americans, as well as the latest legislation in the nationwide attempt to control pollution.

Like most introductory textbooks, this volume introduces and discusses many aspects of American government. But it concentrates on its subject matter in a way that involves the student, in a way that makes the study of American government more a part of his world.

## The plan of the book

The first two chapters introduce the student to some important concepts (on politics and democracy) that apply to material throughout the text.

**Part I.**     **The Framework of Government.**     Part I takes up the historical and constitutional framework of the American political system. In addition, this section examines a basic characteristic of that system—federalism—and the problems of contemporary urban America which pose the greatest challenge to the nation's federal system.

**Part II.**     **The Politics of Participation.**     This section deals with the major means by which the American public participates in the nation's political system. Separate chapters examine the formation of public opinion, the voting behavior of Americans, the activities of interest groups, the political party system, and campaigns and elections, with special focus on the nomination and election of the President.

**Part III.**  **The Institutions of the National Government.**  Part III is concerned with the the three branches of the national government. It examines the executive branch of government, especially the powers and limitations of the office of the President and the role of the federal bureaucracy. This section also analyzes the Congress and compares the similarities and differences between the House of Representatives and the Senate. Finally it considers the role of the federal judiciary and the particular significance of the United States Supreme Court.

**Part IV.**  **Government in Action: Challenge and Response.**  The final part of the textbook deals with national policies. It examines the role of the Supreme Court in interpreting the Constitution in the areas of civil liberties and civil rights. The national government's role in foreign policy, national defense, the economy, human welfare, and natural resources are also discussed.

The chapters of the textbook are sufficiently independent so that they may be rearranged to fit the individual professor's curriculum requirements. Several alternative sequences are possible depending on the orientation and objectives of the instructor and the length of the introductory American government course. Sequences I, II, and III are designed for a one-semester course and sequence IV is appropriate for a one-year course.

## I.  A general introductory course (Institutional)

| | |
|---|---|
| *Chapter* 1 | Politics and People |
| *Chapter* 2 | The Democratic Idea |
| *Chapter* 4 | The Constitution: Stability and Change |
| *Chapter* 5 | The Federal System |
| *Chapter* 7 | Opinions and Opinion Making |
| *Chapter* 8 | Voters |
| *Chapter* 9 | Interest Groups in Action |
| *Chapter* 10 | The Politics of Parties |
| *Chapter* 11 | Campaign Dynamics and the Electoral Process |
| *Chapter* 12 | The Presidency: Power and Restraint |
| *Chapter* 13 | The President |
| *Chapter* 14 | Congress: Makers of the Law |
| *Chapter* 15 | The Senate and the House: Separate and Distinct |
| *Chapter* 16 | The Bureaucrats: The Machinery of Government |
| *Chapter* 17 | The Judges: Guardians of the Law |

## II. A course with emphasis on policy

## III. A course with emphasis on behavior

## IV.   A one year general introductory course

**First Semester:** Parts I and II.

Note: Chapters 1, 2, 3, 4, 6, 7, and 9 each can be covered in one week (or three lectures each); chapters 5, 8, 10, and 11 each require two weeks (or six lectures each).

**Second Semester:** Parts III and IV.

Note: Chapters 14, 15, 16, 17, 20, 21, 22, and 23 each can be covered in one week (or three lectures each); Chapters 12, 13, 18, and 19 each require two weeks (or six lectures each).

# Why another political science textbook?

APPLETON-CENTURY-CROFTS is putting this book on the market because they realize that many teachers require an eclectic textbook that satisfies their students' needs for clarity and for up-to-date and relevant resource materials. To improve these areas would make a book that is more interesting and useful to students and a better teaching tool for professors.

**Readability** The only good textbook is one that students can and will read. So a first step in producing this book was to define "readability" in the context of the teaching situation and to determine how it might be achieved. After much discussion and analysis, and with the help of professionals, it was decided that readability depends on organization, language, and relevance.

Good organization makes a book readable. Material should be presented one step at a time, and the presentation should identify important interrelationships. The chapters in this book are separate and virtually self-contained units of study. This style of organization makes the material easy for the student to comprehend and at the same time allows the professor considerable latitude in arranging reading assignments to suit his own curriculum.

Clear and familiar language makes a book readable. A student should not have to learn a whole new vocabulary before he can understand his text. It is often possible to introduce even the most complicated concepts in simple language. This book uses only the amount of technical terminology that a student must know in order to understand the concepts or to be prepared for a more advanced course. When new terms are introduced here, they are set off in italics and clearly defined. Glossaries at the end of each chapter serve as convenient references and study aids.

Relevance makes a book readable because it creates motivation to read. Therefore, in this book, theories and concepts are illustrated not only with the results of published studies, but with examples drawn from contemporary politics. Each example was chosen because of its significance to the subject of the chapter in which it appears and its interest to beginning students of American government. Many examples were suggested by researchers on the basis of their reported effectiveness in the classroom.

**Abstracts and Studies** Each chapter contains several abstracts or studies. (These studies appear within the text, but are distinguished by a colored rule in the margin.) They are introduced by brief explanatory comments and are concerned with important subjects dealt with in the chapter. The studies themselves are quotations drawn from authoritative sources and are sometimes comparative in nature.

**Illustrations**     Modern education is increasingly oriented toward visual aids. This book contains a large number of cartoons, photographs, and line drawings that give visual impact and support to the text. The captions assist the student in relating the meaning of the illustrations to the material in the text.

The importance of the visual is underlined in the text by the addition of four Portfolios. Each Portfolio deals with a specific topic—campaigns, the presidency, and black rights, for example—and these subjects are developed pictorially as well as verbally.

**Tables and Graphs**     Since political science has an empirical base, it is important for the new student to be able to understand how data are organized. All the tables and graphs in this text have been designed to make these data attractive, graphic, and readily comprehensible.

**Suggested Readings**     Each chapter ends with a list of Suggested Readings. Such a list can be of great value to the student. He can turn to it when he wants clarification of an area that he finds difficult or confusing; he can use it as a help in carrying out homework assignments or preparing for a class discussion; when he becomes especially interested in a specific topic, he can locate books for further reading on his own; he can use it as a guide for independent study and work projects.

The first section in each list consists of important texts, both classic and contemporary, that are especially relevant to the chapter under consideration. The titles on the list are annotated to identify for the student their value, use, and specific content. For students who may wish to become familiar with the kind of research that is reported in journals or carried out for advanced degrees, even though these materials are not always readily available, we have included samples of such articles and papers. To stimulate student interest in the subject they are studying and to better relate the subject to their own experience, the Suggested Readings also includes currently popular books.

**Supplements**     The text is supplemented by a Student Workbook and an Instructors Manual. The Workbook includes an outline of each chapter and a series of questions. The questions lead the student from the simple to the complex; the student discovers the answers for himself, and the answers are then reinforced. (This is made possible by ACCESS™, a specially processed marker that is rubbed across a line to make the answers visible.) The Instructors Manual includes brief overviews of the chapter's emphasis, suggested discussion topics, lists of available films and tapes, and test questions. A test item file of additional questions is also available.

# Acknowledgments

I have taught the introductory course in American government for more than a decade. During this period I have been influenced by many people. The students I have taught, primarily at Rutgers, the State University, and at Hunter College, have had a profound effect on my thinking and in shaping my general approach to the teaching of the beginning course in American government. My thanks also extends to the members of the Political Science Department at Rutgers, where I was both a student and, for a time, a member of the teaching staff, and to the faculty of the Political Science Department at Hunter with whom I have worked for almost ten years.

There are several persons to whom I would like to express my particular gratitude: Frederick L. Zimmermann, Professor Emeritus and former Chairman of the Political Science Department at Hunter, and Miss Pauline Roth, the former secretary of the Department, initially recognized my talents and encouraged their further development and in these ways helped launch my career at Hunter College.

W.E.V.

*Hunter College of the City University of New York*

# 1 politics and people

THIS YEAR, for the first time in American history, the majority of college students are also voters. For many, access to the voting booth will not be the first experience in American politics. Students traditionally, have manned the campaign quarters of candidates they support; canvassed their neighborhoods in voter registration drives; petitioned their congressmen; berated their newspapers; and exercised their privilege of dissent, in assembly, in print, and on the street corner.

This year, however, the participation of the eighteen- to twenty-one-year-old American is especially meaningful. It marks the formal entrance into a political system of that system's most serious critics. It enlarges the prior commitment with responsibility.

Certainly we, as a people, are committed to self-examination. National introspection is a political pastime. Our uses of democracy are continually under attack from thoughtful Americans of all ages. The response of government to popular demands is called into question. The relationship between the individual and his government is cause for constructive anxiety. The political needs of the majority, and the very composition of the majority, are differently identified.

None of the answers to our current questions may be found in this book. But a perspective for consideration—a strategy for inquiry—is developed here. An understanding of the nature of American government, and the politics that sustains it, are fundamental tools for participation, and indispensable weapons for reform.

## Politics

Broadly speaking, *politics* is the process of seeking and effectively using power. Politics is concerned with the distribution of advantages and disadvantages among people.[1]

Each of us employs politics to some extent in his daily activities. A man who performs small favors for his boss in order to climb the executive ladder is practicing politics. He is seeking power, the power a promotion will provide him, and he is concerned with the distribution of advantages and disadvantages within his company. Similarly, the son who appeals to his mother to influence his father's decision on the use of the family car is practicing a kind of politics. He is trying to use power—in this case, the power his mother holds over his father—to influence the distribution of one of the family's resources, the automobile. Virtually all personal interactions (including the good-night kiss, Kate Millet would point out) may be political in some sense. The political scientist, of course, addresses himself to a more precisely drawn area of inquiry when he refers to political activities.

## Political activities

The political scientist does not deal with the politics we employ in daily associations; office politics, school politics, politics of family management do not explicitly interest him. These are the areas in which ordinary people compete for personal advantage; but the power at stake in such contests is usually limited, and the size of the group affected is relatively small. Political activities, on the other hand, encompass large groups of people and broad powers. These activities can affect society as a whole, and for this reason, they are the important subject matter of political science.

An activity becomes political and, consequently, of interest to political scientists, when public concern over that activity reaches a certain level. Any activity or group, even one so noncontroversial as the Young Men's Christian Association (YMCA), is capable of exercising political influence. For example, the YMCA normally organizes fund-raising activities, dances, and other social get-togethers. If, however, all the YMCAs in the United States unite and pledge to use their resources (money, prestige, and so on) to further the campaign to end the war in Vietnam (as they recently did), then the normally nonpolitical activity of a social group becomes political.[2] In principle, no segment of society is incapable of initiating a political activity.

## The popular views of politics

"Politics, ill understood, have been defined as the art of governing mankind by deceiving them," wrote Benjamin Disraeli, a prime minister of England in the late nineteenth century.[3] Early in the twentieth century, the American satirist Ambrose Bierce defined politics as "a strife of interests masquerading as a contest of principles. The conduct of public affairs for private advantages."[4] Both these definitions reflect a stereotype of politics: to many peo-

[1] Harold D. Lasswell, *Politics: Who Gets What, When, How* (New York: McGraw-Hill Book Co., 1958), p. 13.

[2] The social club might decide to *lobby* (work to influence legislators), as described in Abraham Holtzman, *The Townsend Movement* (New York: Twayne Publishers, Inc., 1962).

[3] Quoted in Bernard Crick, *In Defense of Politics* (Chicago: University of Chicago Press, 1962), p. 12.

[4] Ambrose Bierce, *The Devil's Dictionary* (New York: Hill and Wang, Inc., 1965), p. 143.

"Which side of the fence are you on?
Politically speaking, I mean."

Drawing by H. Martin; © 1969
The New Yorker Magazine, Inc.

5 Crick, *In Defense of Politics*, p. 12.

6 Since the public's demands often outweigh available resources, solutions are often partial. The dissatisfied become cynical and attach their cynicism to the politicians who are trying (but not successfully) to meet their demands. See Robert A. Dahl and Charles E. Lindblom, *Politics, Economics and Welfare* (New York: Harper and Brothers, 1953), p. 32.

ple, politics has become synonymous with deception and dishonesty. In their opinion, politics is "muddled, contradictory, self-defeatingly recurrent, unprogressive, unpatriotic, inefficient, mere compromise, or even a sham or conspiracy."5

Those who hold this unhappy view tend to confuse politics with the activities of politicians they dislike. To such people, all political motives are necessarily suspect. Politics then becomes a handy receptacle for the ills of society.

Ironically, politicians themselves have done much to foster this notion of politics. In the 1958 French elections, for example, General de Gaulle's supporters proclaimed that the general was saving the nation from the politicians! After his takeover in Cuba, Fidel Castro announced: "We are not politicians. We made our revolution to get the politicians out."6

Not everyone, however, is cynical about politics. Many concerned people feel that there is cause for a more optimistic view. Their idealism has been sparked in the recent past, perhaps most notably by men such as John and Robert Kennedy, George McGovern, Eugene McCarthy, and Barry Gold-

water; and the hopes of many are kept alive today by the vigor of such men as Edmund Muskie and John Lindsay, political leaders whose "images" suggest that they are genuinely interested in bringing about needed changes and promoting the general welfare of all society's members. Individuals not in political office—for example, Ralph Nader, a prominent lawyer working to protect consumer interests—can also be sources of inspiration. Such men, by demonstrating that one person can affect the social and political environment, have encouraged many young people to view political participation, or a political career, as personally meaningful.

# Political power

Those who choose to participate in politics, or to study those who do, are concerned with the process by which men seek and effectively use power. By definition, *power* is the influence that a person or group has on the behavior of others.[7] Political power refers to the wielding of influence within a particular sphere of activity—that of politics.

Congress is a group of men and women possessing enormous political power. It can pass a law, thereby seriously influencing the behavior of everyone in the country; lack of compliance, after all, results in punishment. Similarly, a county sheriff possesses political power, for he can order disruptive citizens from another community to leave his town, on the grounds or on the pretext that they have violated a law that he has the authority to enforce. For better or worse, groups and individuals occupying positions of political power exercise considerable influence where they have jurisdiction.

[7] Harold D. Lasswell and Abraham Kaplan, *Power and Society* (New Haven, Conn.: Yale University Press, 1950), p. 75.

# The distribution of political power

Political power is never evenly distributed in any society. In all societies there can be found elite groups that hold most of the political power at their level.[8] In our society, members of these elite groups have been labeled everything from "crooked politicians" to "statesmen." But the actual membership of these groups, the identification of the men and women who exercise political power, remains a question of great interest to political scientists.

A study of men who have held great political power in history—Napoleon in France, Hitler in Germany, Churchill in England—would show that these men had little in common, except that they possessed great personal drive and appeared during a period of history that demanded strong national leadership. They came from dissimilar backgrounds and social classes, employed different resources, and displayed vastly different personalities. Why, then, did Napoleon Bonaparte come to power rather than Michel Ney, Adolf Hitler rather than Rudolf Hess, Winston Churchill rather than William Beaverbrook? Robert A. Dahl, the noted political scientist, has advanced three reasons for the uneven distribution of political power.[9]

[8] See C. Wright Mills, *The Power Elite* (New York: Oxford University Press, Inc., 1956), Robert A. Dahl, *Who Governs: Democracy and Power in an American City* (New Haven, Conn.: Yale University Press, 1961), and Lasswell, *Politics.*

[9] Robert A. Dahl, *Modern Political Analysis* (Englewood Cliffs, N.J.: Prentice-Hall, Inc., 1963), p. 17.

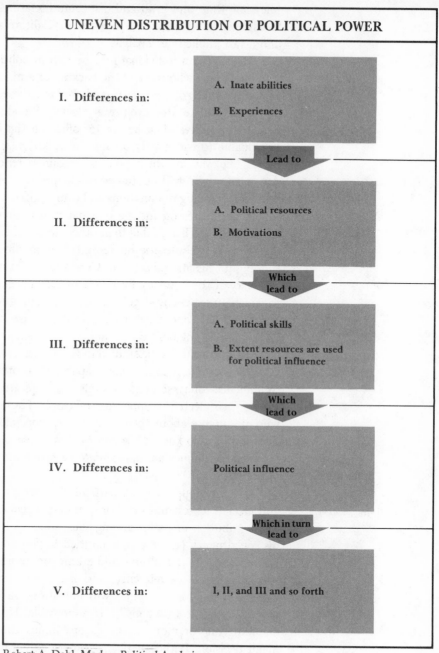

## UNEVEN DISTRIBUTION OF POLITICAL POWER

I. Differences in:
- A. Inate abilities
- B. Experiences

*Lead to*

II. Differences in:
- A. Political resources
- B. Motivations

*Which lead to*

III. Differences in:
- A. Political skills
- B. Extent resources are used for political influence

*Which lead to*

IV. Differences in:
Political influence

*Which in turn lead to*

V. Differences in:
I, II, and III and so forth

Robert A. Dahl, *Modern Political Analysis*,
Prentice-Hall, Inc., 1963; 17.

First, resources are unequally distributed. A rich man has greater potential for political power than a poor man. The wealthier person can use his own money, up to a point, to commandeer talented assistants, purchase television time, and print and distribute literature. Rockefeller in New York, Goldwater in Arizona, and Reagan in California, for example, could well afford vast publicity campaigns.

Moreover, an individual may be rich in political as well as economic resources. A man who receives the backing of a major political party has access to the resources of that party and can use these resources to gain political power. Theodore Roosevelt was elected President as a candidate of the Republican party; when he ran for office on the Progressive party ticket, he was unable to win, partly because he lacked support from a major political party. The way in which political resources tend to be distributed in the American system will be studied in Chapter 11, which describes the electoral process (including nominations and campaigns).

A second reason for the unequal distribution of political power is that some people are better able than others to use their resources. An experienced politician is likely to use his resources more effectively than is a newcomer running for his first office. John Connally of Texas (before he was appointed Secretary of the Treasury by President Nixon) demonstrated well the extent to which an experienced politician, campaigning in his home state, may best overcome old- and newcomers through wise management of resources. (The meaning of political resources, and their effective application in campaign politics will also be studied in Chapter 11.)

Just as some men are more capable than others of using their resources to influence voters, some individuals or groups are especially effective in influencing their elected or appointed officials. "Those people who are *organized*, who are *intense* about their preferences, who make their preferences known *persistently*, who know *to whom to make their preferences known and what kinds of techniques are appropriate in given situations* are likely to be the most successful."[10]

[10] Lewis A. Froman, Jr., *People and Politics* (Englewood Cliffs, N.J.: Prentice-Hall, Inc., 1963), p. 12.

Interest groups may be particularly effective in influencing bureaucrats and elected representatives. For example, a senator must be concerned with the distribution of power among the various political interest groups within his constituency (those people entitled to vote for a candidate to his office). Labor, business, agricultural, and ethnic groups assess his performance from a particular frame of reference, and make different demands upon him. Of course the senator's decisions will not always satisfy all the individuals and groups of people to whom he is responsible. He must weigh the results of offending one or more of the groups in his constituency before making a major decision. If the offended group is strong enough and intense enough in its interests, the senator's decision could result in the loss of office, his removal from a position of power.[11] If the offended group is intense about its interests, but naive in political maneuvering, the senator simply may lose 5,000 votes in the first ward, while gaining 15,000 votes in the second ward.

[11] See Lester W. Milbrath, *The Washington Lobbyists* (Chicago: Rand McNally and Co., Inc., 1963).

The ways in which interest groups and individuals use political resources to influence public officials and achieve a distribution of power in their favor is considered in Chapter 9.

A third factor that influences the distribution of political power within a society is the variation in the extent to which different individuals choose to use their resources for political purposes. Whereas many of the nation's wealthiest men apply their resources to the pursuit of political power, others prefer to channel their resources into such activities as the prevention of the extinction of the whooping crane, or the consolidation of corporate enterprises. The five Rockefeller brothers are excellent examples of men who utilize their resources for different purposes. Although the Rockefeller family is armed with enormous political resources (the family wealth is estimated at upwards of $4 billion), only two of the Rockefeller brothers, Nelson (the governor of New York) and Winthrop (the ex-governor of Arkansas), have participated in politics directly. David Rockefeller is chairman of the board of the Chase Manhattan Bank; John Rockefeller heads the family business and is a noted philanthropist; and Laurance Rockefeller is a celebrated conservationist and developer of resort projects. It should be noted, however, that from their positions of importance, each of the Rockefellers may indirectly affect the political affairs of the nation.

## The bases of political power

A political official, like paper money, is powerful only in that he is accepted by everyone as what he claims to be. The basis of a President's power, for example, is the belief by those who appointed or elected him, as well as those who opposed him, that he has the authority and right to exercise the powers of his office. Once the people invest an official with the authority of his office, the *legitimacy* to wield that power is established. The official becomes a figure of authority, the man who controls the elements of force—the armed forces if he is President, or the local police department if he is mayor. His authority, however, is not based on these instruments of coercion, but rather on his claim to legitimacy.

As Max Weber, the prominent German sociologist, has written, legitimacy in politics stems from three sources, *tradition*, *charisma*, and *legality*:[12]

*Tradition.* Positions of power become legitimate with the passage of time. They become part of established practice. Authority accrues from "belief in the sanctity of immemorial traditions."

The Constitution contains no mention of a two-party system, or of political parties in general; and yet, a two-party system has existed almost since the beginning of our history. The so-called third parties have never been able to secure a sizable enough percentage of the popular vote to win a national election. This reflects a social consensus "on which political methods are and are not legitimate or acceptable."[13] We shall see that many processes

[12] Max Weber, *The Theory of Social and Economic Organization,* trans. by A. M. Henderson and Talcott Parsons (New York: Oxford University Press, Inc., 1947), p. 328.

[13] Allan P. Sindler, *Political Parties in the United States* (New York: St. Martin's Press, Inc., 1966), p. 57.

in our political system have become legitimate through tradition, rather than forethought. For example, some traditional congressional procedures have become both legitimate and seemingly irreversible, defying the rational attacks of political scientists and the complaints of Congress itself.

*Charisma.* Throughout history, as Weber stated, men have exhibited "devotion to the specific and exceptional sanctity, heroism, or exemplary character of an individual person." The overwhelming popularity of such leaders is due, in part, to their great personal magnetism. Leaders such as Lincoln, Churchill, de Gaulle, Gandhi, Hitler, and so on, have conferred legitimacy on their respective political ideas. Some (Mahatma Gandhi of India, for example) had no formal authority; because of their character, the people believed in such leaders and remained faithful to their policies.

Personal magnetism is not a characteristic confined to national leaders; it operates at the local levels and is, in part, a force in drawing a man or woman to national prominence.

*Legality.* Some political activities are considered legitimate because they are legal; they are based on an established and accepted body of laws. Many activities of the political system of the United States—taxation and the regulation of foreign trade, for example—are considered legitimate because they are specifically granted to the government by the Constitution, an accepted *legal* document. The question of legality and, consequently, the interpretation of the Constitution, is basic to many critical issues in American government. For example, whether or not the national government is legitimately allowed to curtail certain civil liberties has been much debated in our courts, and is fully discussed in Chapter 18.

# Government

Many people who exercise political power operate within a particular sphere of activity—the government.

To political scientists, *government* refers to the structures and systems by which decisions or rules are determined and enforced for all members of a society. The Congress, the Supreme Court, and the President are all parts of the government. They have the power to make and enforce decisions or rules for all members of society. In contrast, the governing bodies of labor unions, schools, churches, and social clubs are far more limited in the range of their jurisdiction.

The key phrase in the definition of government is *determined and enforced for all members of the society.* If a man breaks the rules of his social club, at worst, he may be ostracized or thrown out of the club; and once he has left the club, its rules no longer apply to him. If the same man attempts to break the rules of the government, he can be forced to obey, whether or not he agrees with the position of the government. Similarly, when the student government of a college decides that students will no longer be required to take midterm examinations, the decision does not affect *all the members of society*. It does not even affect the students attending the other 3,000 colleges in the United States. But if the government decides to make all college expenses deductible from federal income taxes, this affects all college students, their families, and other members of society as well.

It is important to understand that government is *not* synonymous with politics. Certain individuals and groups, although deeply involved in politics, are not part of government. A labor union, for instance, can exercise great political power. Although it cannot set down and enforce rules for all the members of society, it can greatly influence government decisions that do affect all members of society. If a railroad union (or "brotherhood") threatens to strike, and if Congress, in the interest of preventing a nationwide transportation crisis, accedes to union demands, the resulting wage hike for railroad employees may result in fare increases that affect most of the population. Although the labor union is not part of the government, a government official, such as the Secretary of Labor, may also be involved in the dispute and may use the powers of his office to effect a compromise settlement. Politics involves nongovernment and government agents, working together or at cross purposes.

# Political behavior

Politics, political power, and government depend for their reality on people. How people behave politically, both as individuals and in groups, how they respond to given political situations, how they are motivated to act in a political fashion—these are serious concerns of the political scientist and citizen.

## The individual

An individual's political behavior is influenced by his environment, his past experiences, and his perception of political events. Groups to which an individual belongs influence his attitudes and opinions. The process by which the individual acquires political attitudes and opinions is called *political socialization*.

Political socialization affects individuals strongly, variously, and at many different periods in their lives. Children are influenced in their political attitudes and opinions by their parents, workers by their co-workers, wives by their husbands, students by their teachers and classmates. Political socialization is an ongoing process; it is subject to modification by environmental and individual factors. A change in income or neighborhood, for example, may affect the direction of political socialization.

## Relationship between Activity in Local Affairs, Interest, Concern, and Information*

| | Extent of Activity (In Percentages) | | | | |
| | Least | Low | Medium | High | Highest |
|---|---|---|---|---|---|
| Highly interested and concerned | 16 | 27 | 47 | 64 | 72 |
| Highly informed | 20 | 17 | 21 | 39 | 62 |
| Total number of cases | 188 | 148 | 89 | 68 | 29 |

* New Haven, Conn., 1959.
Source: V. O. Key, Jr., *Public Opinion and American Democracy* (New York: Alfred A. Knopf, Inc., 1961), p. 185.

Political socialization influences not only the attitudes and opinions of an individual, but also the amount of interest an individual has in politics. A child raised in a family where politics is vigorously discussed is more likely to show a strong interest in political affairs than a child raised in a family where politics holds little or no importance. An examination of American families such as the Adamses, Roosevelts, Tafts, Talmadges, Harrimans, Byrds, Lehmans, Aldrich-Rockefellers, Stevensons, and Fitzgerald-Kennedys, suggests that political interest and the ambition to pursue it are strongly influenced by family.

Political scientists are interested in nonparticipants as well as in participants, for the nonparticipant, the disinterested or politically inexperienced individual, does indeed influence political events. The man who chooses to ignore political issues contributes to the status quo, either because he prefers the existing political situation, or because he feels that he, individually, is ineffective in politics. Similarly, the politically inexperienced man, who may

## Relationship of Political Participation to Level of Issue Familiarity

| Issue Familiarity | | Level of Participation (In Percentages) | | |
| | | Low | Medium | High |
|---|---|---|---|---|
| High | 4 | 16 | 30 | 45 |
| | 3 | 17 | 27 | 27 |
| | 2 | 18 | 19 | 16 |
| Low | 1 | 49 | 24 | 12 |
| Number of Cases | | 394 | 770 | 515 |

Source: V. O. Key, Jr., *Public Opinion and American Democracy*, 5th ed. (New York: Alfred A. Knopf, Inc., 1961), p. 185.

have strong feelings about a certain political issue but does not know how to make his opinions heard, contributes to the existence of the status quo.

## Groups

A person may act individually to influence political events—by voting or writing a letter to his congressman, for example. However, many political activities are performed with, or at least influenced by, a group. Group action is collective action; and collective action greatly increases the individual's effectiveness.[14] With a group voting as somewhat of a unit, the possibility is greatly increased that the candidate it favors will be elected.

The fact that groups tend to vote together and hold similar political opinions can be explained in two ways: First, groups are naturally formed among people who have similar interests, attitudes, backgrounds, and, consequently, similar political ideas. Second, members of a group tend to influence each other's opinions. Especially in groups that are composed of people who live or work in close proximity to each other, members tend to develop similar interests and to exhibit "certain uniformities of behavior and attitude."[15] These similarities are reflected in the group's political behavior.

Political scientists use these behavior patterns to study the influences of group membership and identification on political behavior. Classic studies made in 1954 and 1964, for example, revealed that "men, younger voters, Catholics, Jews, Negroes, other minority groups, those in metropolitan centers, noncollege-educated, skilled and unskilled blue-collar workers, union members, and low-income groups generally support the Democrats"—whereas "women, older voters, Protestants, whites, those in suburban and rural areas, college-educated, professional business or managerial, sales, nonunion, and high-income groups support Republicans."[16] Newer research has shown, however, that behavior is not so rigidly structured as this study indicates.

Political scientists are particularly interested in groups because many groups, due to their size, wealth, and enormous store of political resources, can profoundly influence political decisions. A congressman might take note of a constituent's complaints, but a petition signed by the rank and file of a labor union powerful in his district will most certainly cause him to rethink his position on the issue in question. The effects of group action on political opinion and policy will be studied in Chapters 7 and 9, on the informal groups under which individuals are classified and on the structure and functioning of organized interest groups, respectively.

# The political system

The topics just examined—politics, power, government, and political behavior —are sometimes viewed within the framework of the *political system*. A system is any group of interrelated elements that displays a particular pattern of activities. The circulatory system is a typical system. It is made up of the

[14] Mancur L. Olson, Jr., *The Logic of Collective Action: Public Goods and the Theory of Groups* (Cambridge, Mass.: Harvard University Press, 1965), p. 6.

[15] David B. Truman, *The Governmental Process: Political Interests and Public Opinion* (New York: Alfred A. Knopf, Inc., 1951), p. 21.

[16] Seymour M. Lipset, Paul F. Lazarsfeld, Allen N. Barton, and Juan Linz, "The Psychology of Voting: An Analysis of Political Behavior," ed. by Gardner Lindzey, *The Handbook of Social Psychology* (Reading, Mass.: Addison-Wesley Publishing Co., Inc., 1954), vol. 2, pp. 1124–1177. Quoted in Froman, *Politics and People*, p. 32.

*Politicians seek the favor of influential
groups, primarily by pressing for their needs
in the committees of Congress.*

heart and thousands of arteries, veins, and capillaries. All these elements are
interrelated; they work together to move the oxygen-filled blood to all the
muscles, glands, and organs of the body, and they display a particular pattern
of activities. A basketball team is a system. It is a group of interrelated elements (the five players) that displays a particular pattern of activities (passing, dribbling, scoring points, and so on). The key to defining a system,
whether economic, digestive, or computer, is the particular pattern of activity
it displays.

A *political system* is a particular group of interrelated elements, performing activities resulting first in decision making, and, ultimately, in public policy. *Public policy* includes all the rules of conduct that are formulated and enforced at the various levels of the political system—for example, laws, judicial and administrative decisions, treaties affecting business negotiations with other nations, presidential orders, and local rules. Thus, according to David Easton, "A political system is that system of behavior through which society is able to make decisions that most people accept as authoritative or binding most of the time."[17]

[17] David Easton and Jack Dennis, *Children in the Political System: Origins of Political Legitimacy* (New York: McGraw-Hill Book Co., 1969), p. 4.

There are literally thousands of political systems in the world today. In fact, there are thousands of separate political systems within the American political system. The state of Iowa has a political system: it produces authoritative decisions—laws, ordinances, and administrative decisions—that become public policy for the residents of Iowa. Similarly, the political system of Des Moines, Iowa, makes authoritative decisions that become public policy within that city. No political system operates entirely in isolation; whether it works independently or jointly with other political systems, the activities often overlap.

The activities of the national political system affect the activities of state and local political systems; and each one of these smaller systems, in turn, affects the politics of the larger system to some extent. The degree of importance of any one of the political systems depends on the number of people influenced or affected by its activities, as well as the type of activity under consideration. For example, a judge in Tennessee's supreme court may declare the practices of the local Democratic organization discriminatory, a ruling that may influence judgments throughout the state. Or that judge may rule that all state land east of the Ohio River belongs to the third district, a ruling that will affect only the local politicians elected by popular vote.

The problems of interrelationships among political systems becomes important to an understanding of our federal system of government (which interrelates national and state governments), and to the consideration of urban and suburban problems.

# The political scientist in action

Scientists usually can be identified by the objects or processes they study. A lepidopterist studies butterflies and moths. An orographer studies mountains. An ornithologist studies birds. A political scientist studies and evaluates political behavior and systems. He studies all aspects of political behavior and political systems in order to explain political events: the political behavior and opinions of individuals and groups within the system, the activities of institutions that are part of the system, and the workings of the system

## THE POLITICAL SYSTEM OF THE UNITED STATES

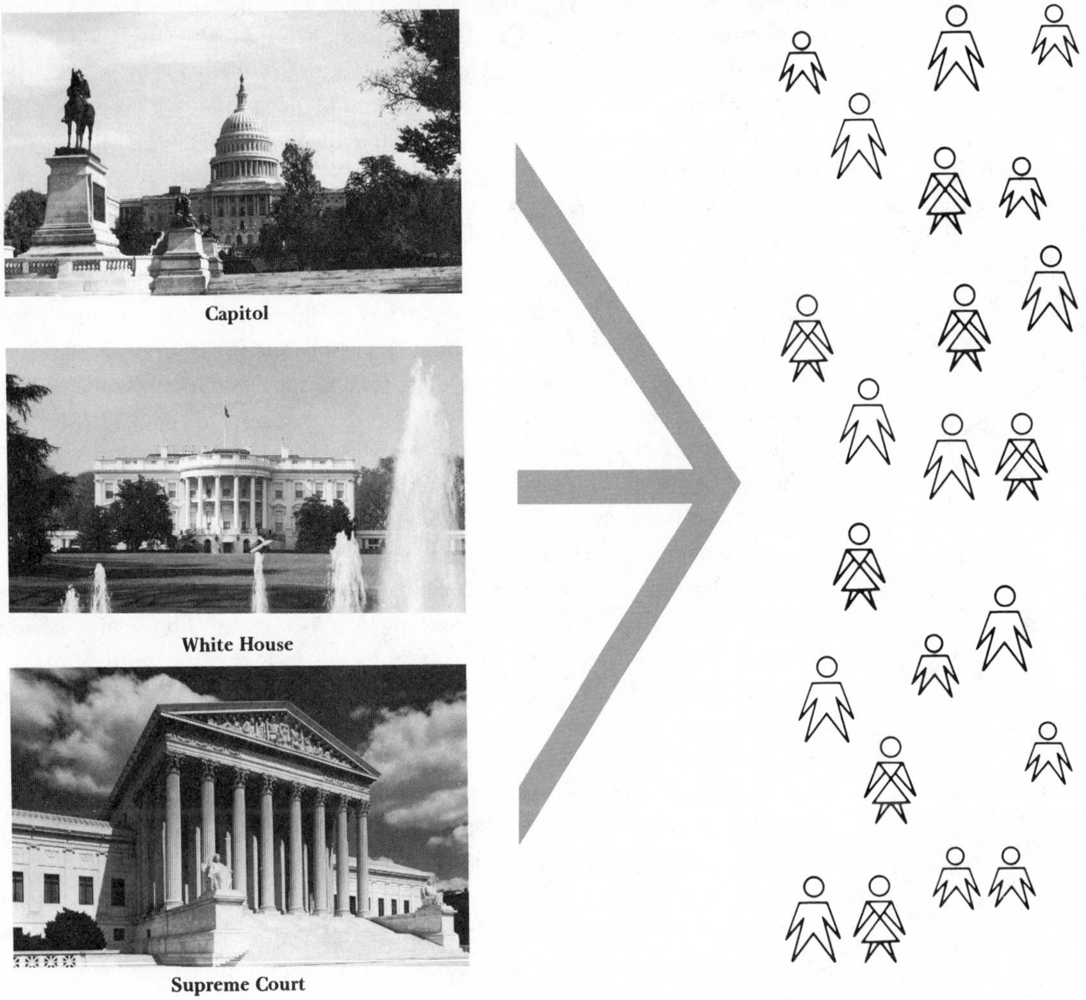

Capitol

White House

Supreme Court

as a whole. He studies public policy, and observes the effect of this policy on the political system, the individuals, groups, and institutions within the political system, and on society as a whole. Finally, he considers the political ideas and doctrines of other men. Correlating this information, he attempts to make generalizations and construct theories about political behavior and political systems.

Political scientists come to grips with certain basic questions, including: What is politics? What conditions make for stability or change? What is the nature of political man? How is power distributed in the society? The ways in which political scientists approach these problems vary with the importance each places on the various aspects of the political system. For example, one political scientist may concentrate on the judicial branch of government and view current problems and institutions in terms of court decisions. Another may employ a purely functional approach and seek to determine how and why the system works; a topic for research in this sphere would be the operations of the Executive Office of the President. In contrast, there are political scientists who seek an international perspective on political institutions in order to identify alternative methods in our own system of government.

In general, several distinct approaches are recognized by political scientists.

**Legalism**

The *legalist* or *institutional* approach to politics stresses the formal institutions of government, their legal rights, and power as defined by law. In the American political system, this law is derived from a written constitution. Thus, political activities are examined against the framework of the Constitution. Congress, the presidency, the bureaucracy, and the court systems; all are discussed in terms of their legal structure, as specified by the Constitution. Much of the material presented in Chapters 14 through 17 on the legislative, executive, and judicial branches of government has benefited from the research of political scientists of a legalist or institutional disposition.

**Behavioralism**

The *behavioralist* approach to politics was initiated in the 1920s and 1930s, at the University of Chicago, by a group of political scientists headed by Charles Merriam. Determined to make political science "scientific," this group adopted many of the methods of the other behavioral sciences— psychology, sociology, and anthropology.

The behavioralists call for theoretical generalizations, based on empirical research, that will explain and predict the behavior of individuals, groups, and governmental institutions within the political system. In order to compile the necessary data, they employ such tools as field studies, survey research, statistics, computer modeling, and systems analysis, to name a few. The behavioralists have used a scientific approach not only in describing the past, but in predicting future events. Through such techniques as opinion polls, surveys, and random sampling, they analyze a particular process and then attempt to predict the future course of the activity. Much of the research cited in Chapters 7 and 8 on political opinions and voting behavior is the work of political scientists who have employed the tools and techniques of behavioralism.

**Post-behavioralism**

In the last decade, a new movement has emerged. *Post-behavioralism,* as David Easton, president of the American Political Science Association, has labeled the new trend, acknowledges the value of the new research techniques

[18] David Easton, "The New Revolution in Political Science," *The American Political Science Review*, LXIII, no. 4 (December 1969): 1051–1061.

developed by the behavioralists. "Only by analysis," writes Easton, "by chopping the world up into manageable units of inquiry, by precision achieved through measurement wherever possible, can political science meet the continuing need of a complex, post-industrial society for more reliable knowledge."[18] Unlike behavioralism, however, the new trend emphasizes the importance of working within the system while simultaneously studying it from without. Going beyond behavioralism, however, the new trend emphasizes the use of behavioral analysis and prediction to find solutions for pressing social and political problems. Most political scientists who take this view advocate working within the present system, while studying it from outside. Some few, going even further, hold that political science must become less "value-free," more *normative*.

## The political scientist in politics

Political scientists of virtually every disposition have endeavored to translate theory into concrete political practice. They have managed political campaigns and have acted as public relations advisers for candidates, parties, and agencies they support. They have helped to establish and staff bureaus of governmental research and institutes of public affairs. Many political scientists have held policy-making positions at the national, state, and local levels. Perhaps the most celebrated political scientist to hold office was Woodrow Wilson, the twenty-eighth President of the United States. Wilson was a professor of political science prior to his entry into political life. Among the more recent political science professors to hold positions of political power are Dean Rusk, McGeorge Bundy, Walther Rostow, Eugene McCarthy, J. William Fulbright, George McGovern, Birch Bayh, Henry Kissinger, and Hans Morgenthau.

The well-known political scientist Harold Lasswell summarizes the activist disposition in political science. He believes that political science should be "policy science," a discipline that is both "scientific" and politically active. The approaches employed are secondary to the primary purpose, that of designing working solutions to the problems confronting the American political system.

Hugh Bone, however, notes:

[19] Hugh A. Bone, "What Direction for Political Science?", remarks delivered at a symposium held during the twenty-third annual meeting of the Pacific Northwest Political Science Association, Billingham, Washington, April 2, 1970.

> Finally, I favor a political science of eclecticism. Our political universe is so vast that no direction, approach, or emphasis will suffice. There is room for all types of endeavor with mutual, though critical, respect for diversity. In political science there is no one true church.[19]

# Glossary

**behavioralism (or behaviorism)**  An approach to political science that utilizes the analytical tools and methods of other behavioral sciences (psychology, sociology, and anthropology) to study political systems and the behavior of individuals, groups, and institutions within those systems.

**constituency**  The people who, by virtue of living in a particular district, are entitled to elect a representative to a legislative body.

**government**  The institutions and processes by which decisions or rules are determined and enforced for all members of the society.

**legalism**  An approach to political science that is concerned with the formal institutions of government, their legal rights and powers.

**legitimacy**  Belief that accepted principles or rules possess a quality of rightness and propriety; defined, according to Weber, as conformity based on tradition, leadership, and legality.

**nonpolitical activities**  Those activities that involve relatively small groups of people and limited power—for example, participating in a dance group.

**political activities**  Those activities that involve large groups of people and large amounts of power, and that can affect the society as a whole—for example, voting in a national or local election.

**political power**  The influence that a person or group has on the political behavior of others.

**political science**  The study of political behavior and political systems.

**political socialization**  The process by which an individual acquires political attitudes and opinions.

**political system**  A particular pattern of relationships, the activities of which result in the authoritative decisions that become public policy.

**politics**  The process of seeking and effectively using power. It is concerned with the distribution of advantages and disadvantages among people.

**post-behavioralism**  A newer trend in the approach to studying political science, emphasizing the importance of working within the system while simultaneously studying it from the outside.

**public policy**  All the rules of conduct (laws, treaties, regulations, and so on) that are enforced within a political system.

# Suggested readings

Almond, Gabriel, and Sidney Verba, *The Civic Culture: Political Attitudes and Democracy in Five Nations* (Boston: Little, Brown and Co., 1965). Theory of political development.

Bentley, Arthur F., *The Process of Government*, ed. by P. H. Odegard, (Cambridge, Mass.: Harvard University Press, 1967). Originally published in 1908. Classic study in political science methodology, including a systematic treatment of the role of interest groups in the political process.

Bluhm, William T., *Theories of the Political System: Classics of Political Thought and Modern Political Analysis* (Englewood Cliffs, N.J.: Prentice-Hall, Inc., 1970). Discussion of classical political thought related to modern political analysis.

Brecht, Arnold, *Political Theory: The Foundations of Twentieth Century Political Thought* (Princeton, N.J.: Princeton University Press, 1959). Analysis of the "theory vs. reality" controversy in politics.

Crick, Bernard, *In Defense of Politics* (Chicago: University of Chicago Press, 1962). Defense of political actions that are responses to maintaining order with tolerance.

Dahl, Robert A., and Charles E. Lindblom, *Politics, Economics and Welfare* (New York: Harper and Brothers, 1953). Analysis of the special relationship between politics and economics.

Dahl, Robert A., *Modern Political Analysis*, 2nd Ed. (Englewood Cliffs, N.J.: Prentice-Hall, Inc., 1970). Excellent short introduction to the systematic study of politics; provides clear, useful definitions of basic terminology.

Davies, James, *Human Nature in Politics: The Dynamics of Political Behavior* (New York: John Wiley and Sons, Inc., 1963). Presentation of the theory that political behavior is founded on man's organic needs.

Deutsch, Karl W., *The Nerves of Government: Models of Political Communication and Control* (New York: The Free Press, 1963). Analysis of politics in terms of communications systems models.

Easton, David, *The Political System: An Inquiry Into the State of Political Science* (New York: Alfred A. Knopf, Inc., 1953). Criticism of methodology of political science; in particular, the recent lack of emphasis on general and systematic theory.

Easton, David, *A Framework of Political Analysis* (Englewood Cliffs, N.J.: Prentice-Hall, Inc., 1965). Attempt to provide a meaningful, general theory of politics.

Edelman, Murray, *The Symbolic Uses of Politics* (Urbana, Ill.: University of Illinois Press, 1967). Interesting analysis of political acts and what these acts can and do mean.

Froman, Lewis A., Jr., *People and Politics* (Englewood Cliffs, N.J.: Prentice-Hall, Inc., 1963). General analysis of the American political system and of the functions of individuals and groups within that system.

Hyneman, Charles S., *The Study of Politics: The Present State of American Political Science* (Urbana, Ill.: University of Illinois Press, 1959). Survey of current research, problems, methods, and data.

Irish, Marian D., ed., *Political Science: Advance of the Discipline* (Englewood Cliffs, N.J.: Prentice-Hall, Inc., 1968). Theory that the fashions in political science tend to follow the concerns and social values of the times.

Lasswell, Harold D., *Politics: Who Gets What, When, How* (New York: McGraw-Hill Book Co., 1958). Analysis of the effective use and acquisition of power in politics.

Lasswell, Harold D., *The Future of Political Science* (New York: Atherton Press, 1963). The evolving trends of study in political science as seen by an eminent social scientist.

McCoy, Charles A., and John Playford, eds., *Apolitical Politics: A Critique of Behavioralism* (New York: Crowell, Collier and Macmillan, Inc., 1968). Collection of essays presenting several criticisms of the behavioral approach to the study of political science.

Meehan, Eugene J., *Contemporary Political Thought* (Homewood, Ill.: Dorsey Press, 1967). The major theories in politics today.

Merriam, Charles E., *History of American Political Theories* (New York: Atheneum Publishers, 1968). Standard classic in the history of political science.

Mills, C. Wright, *The Power Elite* (New York: Oxford University Press, Inc., 1956). Proposition of a theory that government is by layers of elite that often share the same characteristics.

Olson, Mancur L., Jr., *The Logic of Collective Action: Public Goods and the Theory of Groups*, paperback (New York: Schocken Books, Inc., 1968). Analysis of organizations as means of advancing individual interests.

Pye, Lucian W., and Sidney Verba, eds., *Political Culture and Political Development*, 5th ed. (Princeton, N.J.: Princeton University Press, 1965). Development of individual and group political awareness in ten different nations based on the country's political history and political institutions, as well as its mechanisms for political socialization.

Ranney, Austin, ed., *Political Science and Public Policy* (Chicago: Markham Publishing Co., 1968). The role of political science in the analysis and formulation of public policy.

Schweinitz, Karl de, Jr., *Industrialization and Democracy* (New York: The Free Press, 1964). View of the relationship between industrialization and democracy in developed and developing nations.

Somit, Albert, and Joseph Tannenhaus, *American Political Science: A Profile of a Discipline* (New York: Atherton Press, 1964). Study of political science based on questionnaires sent to political scientists.

Somit, Albert, and Joseph Tannenhaus, *The Development of American Political Science: From Burgess to Behavioralism* (Boston: Allyn and Bacon, Inc., 1967). Historical highlights in the development of the discipline during the defined period.

Sorauf, Frank J., *Perspectives on Political Science* (Columbus, Ohio: Charles E. Merrill Publishing Co., 1966). Description of the structure and development of political science, the methods used by political scientists to achieve their goals, and the individual's role in politics.

Storing, Herbert J., ed., *Essays on the Scientific Study of Politics* (New York: Holt, Rinehart and Winston, Inc., 1962). Critical essays on the recent trend in American political science.

Swartz, Marc J., Victor W. Turner, and Arthur Tuden, eds., *Political Anthropology* (Chicago: Aldine Publishing Co., 1966). Seventeen essays on political behavior in primitive, folk, and tribal non-Western societies, emphasizing political process, not the system.

Truman, David B., *The Government Process: Political Interests and Public Opinion* (New York: Alfred A. Knopf, Inc., 1951). Theoretical analysis of the formation and activities of political interest groups and of public opinion.

Van Dyke, Vernon, *Political Science: A Philosophical Analysis* (Stanford, Calif.: Stanford University Press, 1960). Presentation of the essential rules for analyzing political philosophies.

# Topics of further study

Adkins, Roscoe C., *Introduction to Social Sciences* (Harrisburg, Pa.: Stackpole Books, 1956).

Andress, Robert P., "Young Harris College: Its Development, Resources and Programs," (Ph.D. dissertation, Columbia University, 1959).

Black, Gordon S., "Theory of Professionalization in Politics," *American Political Science Review*, September 1970, pp. 865–878.

Brown, Mike, *The Politics and Anti-Politics of the Young* (Beverly Hills, Calif.: Glencoe Press, 1969).

Kramer, Richard H., and Philip H. Barnes, eds., *Texas Government: Readings in Politics, Government and Public Policy* (San Francisco: Chandler Publishing Co., 1971).

Markey, Beatrice, and N. G. Nicolaidis, eds., *Selected Policy-Decision Cases* (Los Angeles: University of Southern California Press, 1960).

Nelson, William H., and F. L. Lowenheim, eds., *Theory and Practice in American Politics* (Chicago: University of Chicago Press, 1967).

Nelson, William R., ed., *The Politics of Science: Readings in Science, Technology and Government* (New York: Oxford University Press, Inc., 1968).

Quade, Q. L., and Thomas T. Bennett, *American Politics: Effective and Responsible?* (New York: Van Nostrand–Reinhold Books, Div. of Litton Educational Publisher, Inc., 1969).

Ulmann, Stephen, *Semantics: An Introduction to the Science of Meaning* (New York: Barnes & Noble, Inc., 1962).

# 2 the democratic idea

To MANY of us, the word "democracy" is associated with the positive elements in the American experience: individualism, civil liberties, and the accommodation of dissent. As long as the United States government pursues policies agreeable to us, we proudly hail it as a "democracy." But as soon as the government adopts policies that offend our idealism, or curtail our freedom of action, we cry out that the government has become "undemocratic," "socialistic," "totalitarian," and even "Fascist."

The truth of the matter is that "democracy," in its most important sense, does not refer to a national value system, but rather, to the way in which values are politically expressed. Democracy does not refer to any specific policies, but rather, to the way in which policy is determined. In short, the term democracy refers to the means by which the distribution of political power is effected in society. A democratic nation is one in which the policy decisions of government rest upon the freely given consent of the governed.

## Direct and representative democracy

The consent of the governed is elicited differently in different democratic systems. America experienced two distinct systems of democracy quite early in her history. One type, *direct democracy*, is illustrated by the New England town government in which all adult males met together to discuss and vote upon matters of community importance. The New England towns initially were political experiments based on the theological doctrines of their Puritan founders. The Puritans, among other things,

"Do you know what this is? A three-hundred-thousand-word manuscript on the breakdown in the democratic dialogue!"

believed that each congregation had the right to govern its own affairs. It followed from this democratic practice in church matters that similar practices might be appropriate in deciding secular matters, such as local taxes and dealings with the local Indians. In many cases, the actual establishment of a town was voted upon prior to the arrival of the settlers at the physical site where the town was to be located. Direct votes were taken on the creation of a compact (or social contract), which clearly defined the rights of the individual and the rights of the town government.

One difficulty of the early Puritan community was its inability to tolerate dissent within its midst, as later democratic governments were to do. However, land was plentiful enough in the New England region, and new communities soon sprang up, formed by the exiles of earlier settlements. The desire to form new compacts, and the relative ease with which this could be accomplished, was unique to colonial New England.[1]

[1] The town meeting variety of direct democracy has practically disappeared in the United States, existing only in some parts of rural, small-town New England.

A distinctly different form of democracy took shape in England's southern colonies. Virginia, the best example, may be characterized as a *representative democracy*, in which certain men were chosen by the colonists to represent them in the governing body, or House of Burgesses.

The Virginia settlements, unlike many of the New England towns, were not originally based upon a compact between men who sought to live together in a social unit. Virginia was the result of a business contract between certain English stock companies and the crown, and between settlers and the companies. The representative system that evolved in Virginia provided for the selection, at two-year intervals, of men who would represent the views of the settlers before the companies' directors, and, in later years, before the royal governor. Because voting was restricted to landowners, however, the more wealthy settlers gained a disproportionate share in the representative assembly.

Direct and representative democracy, as illustrated by the New England and Virginia models, respectively, differ in the means by which they admit the citizen to the decision-making processes of government. In direct democracy, each voter is able to participate directly and personally in the decision-making processes. Because direct democracy presumes a gathering together of all participants, and a general debate and discussion of policy, it must, by nature, be confined to political units of relatively small population. Representative democracy, on the other hand, is a form of government in which individuals delegate their decision-making power to others whom they periodically elect to represent them. This form of democracy (sometimes referred to as *republican* government) is usually found in political and geographical units much larger than those that practice direct democracy. Nevertheless, representative forms of government can also be used in governing smaller units; a small town may elect representatives to sit on a town council, for example.

**Pluralist democracy**

A form of representative democracy is the *pluralist democracy*, in which interest groups (farmers, laborers, Catholics, lawyers, or senior citizens, for example) are represented by leaders who are in a position to influence public policy—by lobbying, by disseminating information, by placing members on governmental regulatory commissions, and so on. In a pluralist democracy the political activity of interest groups influences the choice of candidates and their political behavior after they are elected.

Theoretically, each interest group is operated democratically, and the action of its leaders may be taken to represent the consensus of its members. Thus, when George Meany speaks for the AFL-CIO, he does so only after discussion has taken place at all the locals represented by his alliance. When the representative of the Pennsylvania Chamber of Commerce speaks, he represents the grocer in Loganton, as well as the Philadelphia Savings and

Loan Association. Naturally, it is important that the interest groups that participate in a pluralist democracy remain democratic in operation, just as it is important to all representative democracies that elected officials remain responsive to their constituents.

The political scientists who believe that America is a pluralist democracy speculate that the United States has developed into a pluralist democracy because her population is so diversified in terms of nationality, occupation, and political interest, and because the opportunities for influencing public policy are varied, and exist at several different levels of government.

# Assumptions of democracy

The blossoming of democratic forms of government in America, and the eventual institutionalization of a formal representative democracy in the Constitution, can be understood partly as a response to the seventeenth- and eighteenth-century European experience in government, and more particularly, to the writings of certain social thinkers in England and France.

Montesquieu in France and John Locke in England were two important European philosophers who, in the late seventeenth century and early eighteenth century, attempted to design new political arrangements. Discouraged by the arbitrary practices of the English and French monarchs, these men sought to overcome the abuse of privilege by proposing a government based on the consent of the governed. Their philosophies and political ideas are reflected in our most important political documents, the Declaration of Independence and the Constitution. Their assumptions on the nature and rights of man remain the inspiration of many of our democratic notions.

## Rationality and self-interest

John Locke (1632–1704) was undoubtedly the political philosopher whose writings most strongly influenced the development of democracy in eighteenth-century America. Attempting to justify the "Glorious Revolution" of 1688 in Britain, in which the power of Parliament over that of the King was affirmed, Locke wrote the *Two Treatises* (circa 1690), the second of which became a major inspiration to democratic thinkers.

The basis for Locke's formulation of democratic theory was the belief that man is a rational being who, through the exercise of his reason, is capable of perceiving the higher laws—the immutable laws derived from God or nature—that provide the standard for human conduct. Locke supposed that the perception and understanding of these so-called *natural laws* would lead to a recognition of certain *natural rights* that were derived from these laws. These natural rights, such as the rights to life, liberty, and property, belonged to each man by virtue of his humanity, and, therefore, existed independently of society and the state. As such, these natural rights could not to be abridged by any political state; the state, in fact, existed for the sole purpose of protecting them.

Locke not only believed that natural laws were discoverable through reason; he also believed that each man was capable of knowing self-interest, and, therefore, of exercising his natural rights. As a member of a political state, the man who was capable of reason and of recognizing self-interest was, according to Locke, fully qualified to participate in government, to demand the protection of his rights and those of his fellow man, and to replace governments which failed to protect his rights.

*John Locke, "An Essay Concerning the True Original Extent and End of Civil Government," in* Social Contract, *ed. by Ernest Barker (New York: Oxford University Press, Inc., 1962), pp. 9–10.*

In this essay, John Locke discusses the "self-love" all men inherently possess and the "ill-nature, passion and revenge" that will lead them to punish others too harshly. He advocates the creation of some form of government (but not a monarchy) to regulate man's zealousness.

I easily grant that civil government is the proper remedy for the inconveniences of the state of nature, which must certainly be great where men may be judges in their own case, since 'tis easy to be imagined, that he who was so unjust as to do his brother an injury, will scarce be so just as to condemn himself for it; but I shall desire those who make this objection to remember that absolute monarchs are but men; and if government is to be the remedy of those evils, which necessarily follow from men's being judges in their own cases, and the state of nature is therefore not to be endured, I desire to know what kind of government that is, and how much better it is than the state of nature, where one man commanding a multitude, has the liberty to be judge in his own case, and may do to all his subjects whatever he pleases, without the least question or control of those who execute his pleasure? and in whatsoever he doth, whether led by reason, mistake or passion, must be submitted to? which men in the state of nature are not bound to do one to another. And if he that judges, judges amiss in his own, or any other case, he is answerable for it to the rest of mankind.

Locke, then, emphasized the natural rights of the individual, and saw government as the means of preserving and protecting those rights. Whereas earlier theoreticians believed that the function of government was to establish rules and regulations in order to *restrain* the individual from exercising his liberty in a manner detrimental to the state, Locke believed that it was government's function to *guarantee* the individual natural rights—life, liberty, and property for example. Clearly, Locke's vision is the basis for the democratic conception of government *for* the people, or, more precisely, for the individual.

## Social contract and the right of revolution

[2] Locke's thoughts on the renunciation of government and society were not extraordinary for his times. Various groups had left England (for example, the Puritans, Catholics, and Quakers) and France (the Huguenots), not only to escape religious persecution, but to establish new societies. Even in America, men left to establish new governments when they considered that the prevailing governments had usurped their natural rights.

Integral to Locke's political philosophy was the idea of the *social contract,* an idea popular in both Europe and America during the seventeenth and eighteenth centuries. According to Locke, the formation of society was the first and crucial step in the formation of a government. The decision to form a society, and subsequently, a government, had to be unanimous among all those who were to participate in it, but once it was created, majority decisions controlled the affairs of government. "When any number of men have so consented to make a community," Locke contended, "they are thereby incorporated and make one body politic wherein the majority have a right to act and conclude the rest." Locke believed that each individual, upon reaching maturity, could either accept or renounce the government, and even the society on which it was based.[2]

A government so created, particularly its legislative branch, was regarded by Locke as a trustee of society's rights. As trustee, the government accepts certain obligations to its citizens; this is its sole reason for existence. Should the government fail in its trust to guarantee life, liberty, and property, Locke felt that the people had a legal and moral right to dissolve it. Revolution was a viable alternative when the rights of the individual had been usurped.

Nowhere is this keystone of Locke's philosophy more brilliantly stated than by Jefferson in the Declaration of Independence:

> that, to secure these Rights, Governments are instituted among Men, deriving their just Powers from the Consent of the Governed; that, *whenever any Form of Government becomes destructive of these Ends, it is the Right of the People to alter or abolish it,* and institute new Government, laying its Foundation on such Principles, and organizing its Powers in such Forms, as to them shall seem most likely to effect their Safety and Happiness.

## Majority rule

In describing government as a trustee, Locke argued that government elicits no obligation from its citizens. Still, he noted that the entrance into a political order would signify nothing were the individual to be left free, and subjected to no other ties than he felt prior to his entrance into the state. In fact, the individual is subject to a new tie—that of majority will; for the state, "being only the consent of the individuals of it, and it being one body, must move one way," and, "it is necessary the body should move that way whither the greater force carries it, which is the consent of the majority, or else it is impossible it should act or continue one body, one community, which the consent of every individual that united into it agreed that it should; and so everyone is bound by that consent to be concluded by the majority."

Locke believed that the best manner in which the governed could express their consent or disfavor was through *majority rule,* with each vote having equal weight. Theoretically, the principle of majority rule could work equally well in a direct or representative democracy. In order to insure that

Whitney Darrow, Jr.; © 1969
The New Yorker Magazine, Inc.

*"I think I can safely say
that I speak
for the vast majority
of the American people."*

government is based upon the consent of the people, the majority of citizens must be free to participate directly in government, or to elect those men who will formulate public policy.

Clearly, majority rule is an extension of the idea that man is reasonable and capable of knowing self-interest; it presupposes that man, by virtue of his humanity, has the capacity for making rational decisions and knows what is best for his welfare. Majority rule also assumes that there is a greater chance for the right policy to emerge through a combined decision and exchange of ideas, than through the judgment of the few. Even political theorists who cannot voice an unqualified belief in the judgment of majorities contend that political participation by the greater number of citizens will at least prevent the abuse of power and privilege by a select group.

In short, majority rule sought to replace the arbitrary will of monarchs with the rule of reason. As Harold J. Laski, the English political scientist, has stated:

> Political democracy developed in response to the demand for the abrogation of privilege. In modern European history its cause was the liberation of a commercial middle class from domination by a land-holding aristocracy. To free itself, that middle class formulated a body of liberal generalizations which culminated in the widespread grant of universal suffrage. Their underlying philosophy was the . . . argument, that since each man in a political democracy was to count for one, and not more than one, and since each was, on the whole, the best judge of his own interest, universal suffrage would permit the translation of the majority will into the substance of legislation. Sinister interest, it was urged, belonged only to a few; privilege could not resist the onset of numbers. Representative democracy, on the basis of equal and universal suffrage, would mean the creation of a society in which the equal interest of men in the results of the social process would be swiftly recognized. The rule of democracy was to be the rule of reason. The party which best grasped the purpose of the electorate would win a majority in the legislature, and it would use the normal, constitutional forms to give effect to that purpose.[3]

[3] Harold J. Laski, *Democracy in Crisis* (New York: AMS Press, Inc., 1969), pp. 49–50.

Political theorists who disapprove of the implementation of majority rule have argued, since Plato's time, that one wise and benevolent leader, or a group of such leaders, is infinitely more qualified to decide on policy than is the mass of men. In fact, current studies have shown that the majority is often uninformed about, or uninterested in, political matters. It cannot be denied that a large number of Americans vote for candidates in response to their personalities, physical appearances, or religious and ethnic origins, rather than on the basis of informed political judgment.

*Plato "The Statesman," trans. by J. B. Skemp, in* The Collected Dialogues of Plato, *ed. by Edith Hamilton and Huntington Cairns (Princeton, N.J.: Princeton University Press, 1963), pp. 1073–1074.*

The ancient Greeks, who practiced a form of direct democracy in the small city-state of Athens, produced the first philosophical evaluations of democratic government of "the rule of the many."

In the dialogue, *The Statesman,* Plato compares three forms of government: the rule of one, the rule of the few, and the rule of the many—in terms of their potential for justice or evil. Because he acknowledges that each of the three forms of government may exist in either a law-abiding or a lawless state, he is actually discussing six types of governments. In the following excerpt, the Stranger and young Socrates evaluate the political alternatives:

> *Stranger:* The rule of one man, if it has been kept within the traces, so to speak, by the written rules we call laws, is best of all the six. But when it is lawless it is hard, and the most grievous to have to endure.
>
> *Young Socrates:* So it would seem.
>
> *Stranger:* As for the rule of a few, just as the few constitute a middle term between the one and the many, so we must regard the rule of the few as of middle potency for good or ill. The rule of the many [democracy] is weakest in every way; it is not capable of any real good or any serious evil as compared with the other two. This is because in a democracy sovereignty has been divided out in small portions among a large number of rulers. If therefore all three constitutions are law-abiding, democracy is the worst of the three, but if all three flout the laws, democracy is the best of them. Thus if all constitutions are unprincipled the best thing to do is live in a democracy, but when constitutions are lawful and ordered, democracy is the least desirable, and monarchy, the first of the six is [of the six] by far the best to live under.

Supporters of majority rule do not necessarily refute these points; rather, they argue that the likelihood of continued injustice and errors is, nevertheless, much less likely under democracy than under any totalitarian state. While the public may be uninformed, or even misinformed, about most political issues, it may quickly become involved, and morally outraged if it perceives that an injustice has taken place. After the Kent State incident, for example, many Americans who were far removed from the college protest scene and the Vietnam controversy were quickly led to re-examine, or develop, attitudes on government policy toward protesters and the war in general. Because there seems to be a consensus on what are perceived to be democratic "values," supporters of majority rule maintain that it is likely that the majority will turn against any official or policy that blatantly defies its values and beliefs. The majority may not always be right, but, as Abraham Lincoln once quipped, they cannot be fooled all of the time.

## Minority rights

Although proponents of majority rule argue that this system prevents tyranny by the few, they also recognize that majority rule can establish an equally dangerous type of tyranny: the tyranny of a majority which violates the rights of either individuals or minorites, and which stifles dissent. The British philosopher John Stuart Mill (1806–1897) felt that freedom of individual expression was of prime social value to the democratic state. He held that a repressive, intolerant majority could violate the liberties that government was established to preserve. And, conversely, he stressed the "creative role of unpopular minorities" in the protection of individual liberties.

According to Mill, a political minority can consist of one person or several million persons. The number is unimportant. In his essay *On Liberty* (1859), he argued:

If all mankind minus one were of one opinion, and only one person were of the contrary opinion, mankind would be no more justified in silencing that one person, than he, if he had the power, would be justified in silencing mankind.

*John Stuart Mill*, On Liberty, *ed. by Alburey Castell (New York: Appleton-Century-Crofts, 1947), pp. 111–112.*

In the chapter entitled "Of the Limits to the Authority of Society over the Individual," John Mill professes the view that the individual, given certain rights and privileges by the society in which he lives, is obliged to follow the rules of conduct that will preserve that society. Later in the book, however, Mill notes that the government should be restricted in its power to influence the individual's conduct.

The objections to government interference, when it is not such as to involve infringement of liberty, may be of three kinds.

The first is, when the thing to be done is likely to be better done by individuals than by the government.

The second objection is more nearly allied to our subject. In many cases, though individuals may not do the particular thing so well, on the average, as the officers of government, it is nevertheless desirable that it should be done by them, rather than by the government, as a means to their own mental education—a mode of strengthening their active faculties, exercising their judgment, and giving them a familiar knowledge of the subjects with which they are thus left to deal.

The third, and most cogent reason for restricting the interference of government, is the great evil of adding unnecessarily to its power. Every function superadded to those already exercised by the government, causes its influence over hopes and fears to be more widely diffused, and converts, more and more, the active and ambitious part of the public into hangers-on of the government, or of some party which aims at becoming the government.

[4] Protection of individual and *minority rights* is guaranteed in the United States Constitution's Bill of Rights, in which rights such as equality before the law, freedom of the press, religion, speech, assembly, and the right to petition are extended to all citizens.

This emphasis on the contribution of individual opinion is a powerful argument for the importance of maintaining freedom of speech and intellectual liberty in all areas of endeavor. Mill's argument, in fact, has become a peculiarly American one, notably expressed by the nineteenth-century writer Henry David Thoreau, and invoked by innumerable dissenters throughout our history. In a democracy, majority rule is considered a legitimate and vital expression of the people only when it respects and protects the minority.[4]

"The Minority Be D . . . . d, 1890."

From Allan Nevins, and Frank Weitenkampf (Eds.), *A Century of Political Cartoons, 1914, opp. p. 168.* Drawing by Louis Dalrymple originally appeared in Puck in 1890. Reprinted by permission of Prints Division, The New York Public Library, Astor, Lenox, and Tilden Foundations.

## Constitutionalism and limited government

From the previous discussion, it is clear that Locke and other democratic theorists appreciated the need to set limits on the powers of government, even when that government was a democracy ruled by the majority of its people. American institutions, too, were created by men who harbored deep suspicions of the power of government. Thomas Paine, for example, called government "a necessary evil," and Thoreau is noted for his remark, "That government is best which governs least." Today, Americans who react with distrust to "big government," "government intervention," or the "welfare state" are voicing—intelligently or not—a traditional concern with the limitations on government.

Henry David Thoreau, Walden and Civil Disobedience, *ed. by Sherman Paul (Boston: Houghton Mifflin Co., 1960), pp. 235–256.*

Thoreau, in *Civil Disobedience*, contends that the contract between government and those governed, which Locke defined as a social contract, must recognize that man's individual rights stand above the state, and that it is from man that the state derives its authority. Although Thoreau acknowledges that the American democracy is closer to this ideal than any other form of government, he envisions an even finer state:

The authority of government even such as I am willing to submit to—for I will cheerfully obey those who know and can do better than I, and in many things even those who neither know nor can do so well—is still an impure one: to be strictly just, it must have the sanction and consent of the governed. It can have no pure right over my person and property but what I concede to it. The progress from an absolute to a limited monarchy, from a limited monarchy to a democracy, is a progress toward a true respect for the individual. Even the Chinese philosopher was wise enough to regard the individual as the basis of the empire. Is a democracy, such as we know it, the last improvement possible in government? Is it not possible to take a step further towards recognizing and organizing the rights of man? There will never be a really free and enlightened State until the State comes to recognize the individual as a higher and independent power, from which all its own power and authority are derived, and treats him accordingly. I please myself with imagining a State at least which can afford to be just to all men, and to treat the individual with respect as a neighbor; which even would think it inconsistent with its own repose if a few were to live aloof from it, not meddling with it, nor embraced by it, who fulfilled all the duties of neighbors and fellow-men. A State which bore this kind of fruit, and suffered it to drop off as fast as it ripened, would prepare the way for a still more perfect and glorious State, which also I have imagined, but not yet anywhere seen.

The imperfections in democracy led Thoreau to adhere frequently to his own, rather than to the state's, laws. He subscribed to the theory that one should be able to withdraw from the state, as from any partnership, if that partnership failed to meet his needs.

Although Thoreau obeyed the laws, and paid taxes for government expenditures such as education and highway maintenance, he was imprisoned for refusing to pay a poll tax for six years. In prison for this action of civil disobedience, he decided that the state was "half-witted, that it was as timid as a lone woman with her silver spoons, and that it did not know its friends from its foes. . . ." After his release, he stated, "I lost all my remaining respect for it and pitied it." Certainly, the state could have found a better use for him, writes Thoreau, than confinement.

Considering himself a member of a "just" minority, and contemplating others in this position, Thoreau lends support to all adherents to these theoretical minorities by stating that any "man more right than his neighbors constitutes a majority of one already."

[5] Although the United States Constitution was inspired by the English experience, the English do not have a written constitution, but rely on several great documents, on statutes, and on precedent.

In some democracies, limitations on the government are typically stated in a written constitution, which also outlines the different institutions of government, their relation to each other, and their powers.[5] Because the authority of government can be defined in a constitution and can only be changed or amended through legal processes, no official can exercise any powers except those delegated, expressly or implicitly, to his office. No branch of government can assume authority over an area of life that is not specified to be within its jurisdiction. Furthermore, certain powers (the power to arrest an individual arbitrarily, or convict him without trial, for instance) may be explicitly denied to a government through its constitution. Constitutions seek to assure the citizens of that society that they will not be subject to arbitrary actions—that government will not treat individuals or groups differently if they are weak or hold unpopular opinions. As John Locke specified, a democracy is to have "established laws, not to be varied in particular cases, but to have one rule for rich and poor, for the favourite at Court, and the countryman at plough."

## Equality

[6] Jefferson, according to biographer Merrill Peterson, was unable to affirm the natural equality of the Negro slave, and yet unwilling to deny it. "Whatever be their talent," he declared, "it is no measure of their rights." Merrill D. Peterson, *Thomas Jefferson and The New Nation* (New York: Oxford University Press, Inc., 1970), p. 264.

[7] Sidney Hook, *Political Power and Personal Freedom* (New York: Collier Books, 1962), p. 61.

The concept of *equality* among men is one of the noblest and least-understood concepts in democratic theory. When Locke stressed the equal right of each man to life, liberty, and property—when Jefferson, his American disciple, asserted that "all men are created equal"—it was not to be concluded that Locke believed that men were, in fact or potential, equal in their reasoning power or abilities. Rather, Locke and Jefferson believed that all men were equals in the scheme of nature, having all been created by God.[6]

Believing in the natural equality of man, it is not surprising that Locke and Jefferson argued for political equality among men. According to their assumptions, each man should have equal access to the right of citizenship; each citizen should have a vote of equal weight; and each should be equally protected, by trial by jury, for example, before the law. In no instances might the law establish special punishments or privileges for any individual or group. Clearly, "the principle of equality is not a *description* of fact about man's physical or intellectual natures; it is a *prescription* or policy of treating men."[7]

# The watchdogs of democracy

The assumptions of democracy must be translated into actual institutions and political behaviors, if democracy is to be achieved. Although each democratic system differs in the nature and structure of its institutions, several factors generally contribute to the maintenance of democratic government.

## The dispersion of power

## Separation of powers of government

One of the means by which democratic government is achieved is through the careful dispersion of power; for according to democratic theory, unchecked or concentrated power in any branch of government, in any faction or individual, may imperil the rights of the general public. James Madison, in the famous *Federalist Paper* No. 10, wrote that "ambition must be made to counteract ambition"; much of the energy of any democracy is devoted to making sure that it does.

The idea that power should be dispersed among several branches of government was integral to John Locke's theory of government. Locke was fairly general in his description of governmental organization, perhaps believing that men, through reason, would devise the government best suited to protect their rights. Nevertheless, he did identify three necessary functions in government. First, and most important, he saw the legislative branch as expressing the will of the majority. Second, he saw the need of an executive to perform the will. Finally, government needed a judicial mechanism to decide conflicts arising under the law.

Locke's scheme for the separation of powers of government was rather incomplete. The executive and judiciary were definitely conceived as subordinate to, and serving at the will of, the legislative. Although he advocated the supremacy of legislative power, Locke contended that, if liberty were to be safeguarded, the executive branch could not be in the same hands as the legislative power. Locke did not specify exactly how the separation between legislative and executive powers was to be effected.

The doctrine of the separation of powers and of checks and balances was to be worked out by Montesquieu (1689–1755), who is sometimes referred to as "the godfather of the American Constitution." Montesquieu delineated the division of power in his *The Spirit of the Laws* (*L'Esprit des Lois*), written over a seventeen-year period, and published in 1748. In the eleventh book of his work, he proposed the classic division of government power to be legislative, executive, and judicial. Montesquieu stated that if any two powers—executive and judicial, or judicial and legislative, for example—were held by the same individual or group, then individual rights were imperiled. He also suggested the advantages of checks and balances within government. He believed that the legislative, executive, and judicial powers should have means to control each other (by veto, for instance). Montesquieu praised the English Parliament for its checks and balances: "The legislative body being composed of two parts, they check one another by the privilege of rejecting."[8]

Forty years later, Montesquieu's principles were incorporated into the United States Constitution. The governmental structure of the new nation was based on the separation of powers among the executive, legislative, and judicial branches of government; and each branch of government was given

[8] Baron de Montesquieu, *The Spirit of the Laws* (New York: Hafner Publishing Co., Inc., 1949), Book 11, p. 160; see also Benjamin Fletcher Wright, "The Origins of the Separation of Powers in America," *Economica*, III, May 1933, 169–185.

the authority to check the other two. In addition to incorporating Montesquieu's suggestions, the Constitution, in defining a federal system of government, reflected Madison's contention that the separation of powers geographically—between a central and state governments—would do much to protect individual liberties.

We all know that the pursuit of happiness, the real exercise of personal freedom, is much more difficult for the poor man than for the rich. Similarly, the preservation of individual rights is likely to be more difficult in a society in which economic power is concentrated in a few hands, than in a society in which wealth is more evenly distributed. Strictly speaking, democracy does not presuppose any particular economic system. However, the dispersion of political power, which is fundamental to the success of a democracy, is in reality difficult to achieve if economic and social power are concentrated.

A concern with the issue of the dispersion of economic power in America is an especially common theme today. Political scientists ask, for example, whether or not a few corporations should be allowed to contribute heavily to political campaigns. They ask whether or not the poor defendant gets a fair day in court, whether money and social position, can, in effect, buy leniency from the law. They question the extent to which the underprivileged child is denied the right to adequate education and, consequently, to the larger opportunities that exist in life. All these questions reflect the knowledge that economic inequality is closely related to political inequality, and that democracy has never flourished in a society characterized by the extremes of wealth and power.

## Free and frequent elections

In order that people may voice their political preferences in an orderly and effective manner, democratic nations have established election systems in which each citizen can vote for candidates of his choice. In the United States, elections are regularly scheduled and, by law, are open to all citizens over eighteen-years-old who meet the minimum residency requirements of their state. Nominations are, for the most part, conducted through primaries which allow citizens to choose the candidates who will run in the major election. Primaries are especially important in those areas in which one political party typically dominates. In other areas, the election itself offers important choices between candidates of the two major parties.

Several characteristics of our elections are especially conducive to the realization of democratic goals. First, suffrage, or the right to vote, has been increasingly extended. Elections, at one time decided by the white, male property-owners, were opened to the poor, to blacks and other racial minorities, to women, and, most recently, to eighteen-year-olds. Secondly, the ballot is secret; the voter may sometimes be pressured by certain groups to vote for their candidates, but he cannot be compelled to do so. Every man votes his

## Dispersion of economic and social power

own choice. Thirdly, elections are frequent. Presidential elections are held every fourth year. Senators are elected at six-year intervals, and Congressmen at two-year intervals. This means that elected officials frequently must account to their constituents and respond to the challenge of the opposition. (By contrast, in totalitarian states, the officials of a government may be replaced overnight, not as a response to popular will, but as a result of private conflicts among governmental or party leaders.)

In general, we can conclude that elections, as conducted in the United States, fulfill two essential functions. They give the citizen an opportunity to express his preferences on policy and leadership, and, because elections can be lost, they encourage the elected representative to be responsive to the political wishes of his constituents. Clearly, both functions are basic to representative democracy.

An additional effect of our commitment to the electoral process is the stability and order with which we make changes in governmental personnel. The United States, unlike some representative governments, does not experience major turmoil in attempting to replace governmental leaders. The results of elections are peacefully accepted by those who supported the losing candidate. In our nation, elections confer legitimacy and the general recognition that the winner may indeed exercise those powers that he or she was elected to exercise.

## The organized opposition

Many of the Founding Fathers, George Washington, for example, disapproved of the growth of opposing factions or parties, perhaps fearing that internal political conflicts would be destructive to a young nation seeking to establish a new governmental system. Yet, most political scientists agree today that one distinguishing characteristic of a democracy is the presence of a faction or party that has the full freedom to oppose those in positions of power:

> The essential feature of Western democracy and the feature which alone gives any reality to the choice at an election is the existence within the country of an organized opposition recognized as an element in the country's political life, and left so free to develop its programme, its organization and its resources that it can take over the government at a moment's notice.[9]

9 J. D. Mabbott, *The State and the Citizen* (London: Hutchinson, 1952), p. 176, quoted in H. B. Mayo, *An Introduction to Democratic Theory* (New York: Oxford University Press, Inc., 1960), p. 149.

In the United States, the institution that makes opposition an integral part of the political process is the *political party*, an organized group that supports candidates who go before the public with political alternatives. At the national level of government, when the Republicans are in power (that is, when a Republican President is in office), the Democrats perform the function of the organized opposition; they examine the policies of the men in office and attempt to present attractive alternatives to those policies to the public. So-called third parties have sometimes been successful in performing this function during certain periods of our history.

Some critics of our party system claim that the major parties do not offer real alternatives, and thus, do not truly oppose each other in any ideological sense. Whether or not one feels that the parties differ sharply in their political viewpoints or whether they should do so, one would hardly deny that each performs the valuable service of criticizing the other, especially at election time. The party in office is particularly sensitive to charges made by the opposition. The fact that such charges are answered, rather than silenced, is one of the most commendable features of democracy.

## The open forum

The existence of an "open forum," where people can express their opinions on issues and hear the opinions of others, makes democratic dialogue possible. An open forum exists wherever people gather for discussion of political issues. Forums can range, therefore, from tense presidential press conferences to informal discussions on street corners, trains, and beaches.

In the United States, the principal means for discussion and debate of politics is the mass media—that is, newspapers, magazines, television, radio, and film. The importance of the media in influencing public opinion, and the significance of maintaining an open forum, was underscored in 1971 in the so-called "Pentagon Papers" case, in which the Supreme Court upheld the right of the press to publish a series of controversial, classified documents on our experience in Vietnam.

While discussion about political matters may not determine final truth or bring all the facts out into the open, it serves to furnish people with a factual basis for decisions, forces them to think about issues within new contexts, challenges them to defend their own point of view, and encourages them to develop reasoned opinions. Consequently, an open forum may not only create responsive legislators, but a responsible electorate as well.

As Walter Lippmann has stated:

[10] Walter Lippmann, "The Indispensable Opposition," in *The Norton Reader*, edited by Arthur M. Eastman (New York: W. W. Norton and Co., Inc., 1965), p. 306.

> We must insist that free oratory is only the beginning of free speech; it is not the end, but a means to an end. The end is to find the truth. The practical justification of civil liberty is . . . that the examination of opinion is one of the necessities of man. For experience tells us that it is only when freedom of opinion becomes the compulsion to debate that the seed which our fathers planted has produced its fruit. When that is understood, freedom will be cherished not because it is a vent for our opinions but because it is the surest method of correcting them.[10]

## Universal education

The importance of universal education to democratic government is evident. It is no coincidence that, historically, democracies have experienced a simultaneous expansion of suffrage and education. Recently, for example, the passage of the amendment to extend the vote to eighteen-year-olds was secured, in part, by the argument that today's young adult is better educated than his parents and grandparents at the same age. In fact, many of our original safeguards against mass opinion (the election of senators by the state legislatures, for example) have been removed as education has become more widespread.

The assumption that an educated citizen is better equipped to make political judgments is probably valid. Insofar as education develops analytical skills, it enables one to resist irrational prejudice and propaganda. Insofar as education creates an open mind, it fosters tolerance and respect for the rights of others. Whether or not our present system of public education can prepare Americans for intelligent participation in democracy is a question much debated. The quality of education among the underprivileged is a matter of particular concern, for we have come to regard the right to education as a very critical one. Thomas Jefferson, an early and inspired advocate of public education, claimed that a nation cannot be both ignorant and free. Certainly, the insistence on education for all members of society is an important support for democratic institutions, in argument and in fact.

## Democracy and capitalism: a digression

One often hears catchwords such as "democratic capitalism," and "totalitarian communism," or "imperialistic fascism," and so on. These phrases are actually attempts to link a particular form of government with a particular form of socioeconomic state. There is, however, no necessary relationship between an economic arrangement, such as private ownership of property, or public ownership of property, and particular forms of government, such as democracy or totalitarianism. Rather, we find that nations often adopt governments that express the totality of their social values, history, and even geography—in sum, their culture.

We have seen that the important cultural attributes of the United States are the desire to limit government, and the belief on the part of the vast majority of its citizens that they, and they alone, are capable of defining their self-interest. To be able to define self-interest, Americans expect the freedom to be exposed to the most varied sets of alternatives, and then the freedom to choose among them. Thus, democracy is often compared to the capitalistic marketplace, where a large number of policies and candidates compete for the minds and votes of the people, with a minimum of government regulation.

From this comparison, we can see that capitalism or private ownership in a competitive market reflects certain political views that are characteristic of American democracy. Yet, it would be a mistake to assume that the capitalistic system is the only socioeconomic system in which democracy can be expressed. The Scandinavian countries are headed by monarchs who reign in conjunction with a Parliament, over an economy which combines both private and public ownership of means of production. Nevertheless, these countries are democratic, in that they rely on the freely given consent of the governed in determining public policy, and incorporate many of the features and institutions identified by us as essential to democratic government.

## Eternal vigilance

We have seen that, in setting up a representative democracy formed by a written constitution, our Founding Fathers sought to institute not merely a "new" form of government, but a "better" form. If they did not believe that government by representation would cure all the evils of the past, they did believe that it would protect the rights of individuals that previous governments had violated. They postulated that the separation of powers, the system of checks and balances, and popular elections tempered by elite judgment would guarantee individual liberty and minimize the possibility of tyranny.

In evaluating America as a democracy, we must keep in mind not only the principles of majority rule, minority rights, and equality that inspired our Founding Fathers, but also the problems of applying these principles within the political context of the times. Where our democratic institutions seem to have failed to perpetrate democratic ideas, we must ask ourselves whether this is due to faults in the ideas, faults in the system, or faults in human nature.

As individuals and as a nation we cannot afford to leave unexamined any part of the American political experience if we are to use and retain the gift of freedom.

# Glossary

**democracy**  A system of government in which the policy decisions of government rest upon the freely given consent of the governed.

**direct democracy**  System of governing in which the people themselves meet to discuss and vote upon public policies.

**equality**  Condition of a democratic system in which all men have equal opportunity to pursue their "natural rights" of life, liberty, and happiness, regardless of economic background, social class, or religion.

**majority rule**  Basic premise of a democratic system whereby public policy is set by the freely given consent of the majority, either directly or through elected officials.

**minority rights**  Guarantee of the rights of any individual or group whose beliefs are unpopular with the majority.

**natural law**  An inherent absolute law of higher morality which provides a measure for human conduct, derived from God or nature (rather than the legal system of man).

**natural rights**  Rights presupposed by the existence of "natural law," belonging to man by virtue of his humanity, and existing independently of society. According to John Locke, these rights include "life, liberty, and property."

**pluralist democracy**  Form of democracy in which public officials are elected in free and open elections to represent an electorate with widely diverse interests.

**representative democracy**  A system in which public officials who represent the people are elected by popular majority vote in free and open elections.

**social contract**  Agreement between the ruler and the ruled for mutual protection, of mutual loyalty, and of mutual responsibility.

# Suggested readings

Bachrach, Peter, *The Theory of Democratic Elitism: A Critique* (Boston: Little, Brown and Co., 1967). Discussion of the controversy between elitism and democracy.

Bryce, James B., *The American Commonwealth*, two vols., ed. by Louis M. Hacker (New York: G. P. Putnam's Sons, 1959). First appearing in 1888, this book is a classic analysis of the nature of the American political character; it describes the weaknesses and the strengths of the American political system.

Byrne, Gary C., and Kenneth Pederson, *Politics in Western European Democracies* (New York: John Wiley & Sons, Inc., 1971).

Callinge, Francis Brooks, "The Philosophic Mood and Temper of Walter Lippmann" (Seattle: Ph.D. dissertation, University of Washington, 1964).

Dahl, Robert A., *Preface to Democratic Theory* (Chicago: University of Chicago Press, 1956). Collection of essays dealing with some of the questions of democratic politics.

Dahl, Robert A., *Who Governs? Democracy and Power in an American City* (New Haven, Conn.: Yale University Press, 1961). Study of political power and city government, using New Haven as the basis of study from 1784.

Dewey, John, *The Public and the Problems* (New York: Holt, Rinehart and Winston, Inc., 1927). Examination of the present and future status of democracy in the modern world.

Hartz, Louis, *Liberal Tradition in America* (New York: Harcourt Brace Jovanovich, Inc., 1955). Interpretation of the entire course of American political thinking.

Kendall, Willmoore, *John Locke and the Doctrine of Majority-Rule* (Urbana: University of Illinois Press, 1941). First in a series of monographs dealing with majority rule. Explanation of Locke's doctrine of majority rule as a basis of the American democratic system.

Lindsay, Alexander D., *Modern Democratic State* (New York: Oxford University Press, Inc., 1962). Study of the modern democracy and its problems.

Lippmann, Walter, *The Public Philosophy* (Boston: Little, Brown and Co., 1955). Critical examination of democracy, including the idea that there has been a loss of responsible authority in the western world.

Lowi, Theodore J., *The End of Liberalism: Ideology, Policy, and the Crisis of Public Authority* (New York: W. W. Norton and Co., Inc., 1969). Study of the contemporary "liberal state," including the author's view that we face a crisis of public authority.

Mayo, Henry B., *Introduction to Democratic Theory* (New York: Oxford University Press, Inc., 1960, paper). General introduction to democratic theory.

Mills, C. Wright, *Power Elite* (New York: Oxford University Press, Inc., 1956). Analysis of our society including the author's view that there exists a "power elite" that makes the crucial decisions in the United States.

Pennock, James Roland, *Liberal Democracy: Its Merits and Prospects* (New York: Holt, Rinehart and Winston, Inc., 1950). Defense of liberal democracy in which the author contends that majority rule should be restricted.

Riemen, Neal, *The Revival of Democratic Theory* (New York: Appleton-Century-Crofts, 1962). Analysis of the decline of democratic theory, as well as suggestions of the need for its revival.

Sartori, Giovanni, *Democratic Theory* (Detroit: Wayne State University Press, 1962). Extensive study of democracy, how it functions, and what it is not.

Scanlon, Norman W., Jr., "A Reinterpretation of the Political Philosophy of John Stuart Mill from the Perspective of His Philosophy of History" (Pittsburgh: Ph.D. dissertation, University of Pittsburgh, 1972).

Schattschneider, E. E., *The Semi-sovereign People: A Realist's View of Democracy in America* (New York: Holt, Rinehart and Winston, Inc., 1961). Essays emphasizing the complexity of the American political system and discussing contemporary American democracy.

Thorson, Thomas L., *The Logic of Democracy* (New York: Holt, Rinehart and Winston, Inc., 1962). Discussion of democracy as a political value, and a justification for its existence.

Tocqueville, Alexis de, *Democracy in America*, ed. by Phillips Bradley (New York: Random House, Inc., 1945). Classic analysis of American democracy by a French citizen.

# Topics of further study

Auerbach, Maurice S., "The Political Thought of Spinoza," (Unpublished master's thesis, University of Chicago, 1959).

Bachrach, Peter, *The Theory of Democratic Elitism* (London: University of London Press, 1969).

Davis, Edward, "Cost of Realism: Contemporary Restatement of Democracy," *Western Political Quarterly*, March 1964, pp. 37–46.

Fried, Albert, and Ronald Sanders, eds., *Socialist Thought: A Documentary History* (Chicago: Aldine Press, 1964).

Henderson, Donald, "Minority Response and the Conflict Model," *Phylon*, Spring 1964, pp. 18–26.

Mark, Max, "Reality and Theory," *Ethics*, October 1962, pp. 56–61.

Metz, Joseph G., "Democracy and the Scientific Method in the Philosophy of John Dewey," *Review of Politics*, 31 (April 1969): 242–262.

Payne, Kenneth, "A Consensus on Liberal Values and Democratic Political Development: An Analysis of Authority and Modernization," (Unpublished Ph.D. dissertation, Tufts University, 1971).

Singleton, J. Allen, *A Course Outline for Americanism vs. Communism* (Corvallis, Ore.: Oregon State University Press, 1966).

# part one
# the framework of government

# 3 the political background

ONE OF the first men to examine the American political system closely from the outside was the Frenchman Alexis de Tocqueville, an astute, politically able man who visited America in the early nineteenth century. Speaking of his visit, Tocqueville said, "I confess that in America I saw more than America; I sought there the image of democracy itself, with its inclinations, its character, its prejudices, and its passions, in order to learn what we have to fear or to hope from its progress."[1]

In the last three decades numerous new nations—in Africa, Asia, and Latin America—have attempted to establish political systems resembling the rather idealistic image that Tocqueville described. Many of these new political systems have evolved into forms vastly different from the American one. Some are similar. However, America's journey through colonialism and revolution to a constitutional democracy (a democratic society where government is regulated by law) is a unique historical experience and, as such, has led to the development of a unique, though hardly perfect, political system.

[1] Alexis de Tocqueville, *Democracy in America*, ed. by Phillips Bradley (New York: Vintage Books, 1945), vol. I, p. 15.

## The colonists

The original colonists were mainly Englishmen. They came for a wide variety of reasons and they came in great numbers. In 1641, there were 50,000 English settlers. By 1716, the number had swelled to 435,000. (The French, in comparison, had barely managed to settle 80,000 people from Canada to Louisiana by 1763.) On the eve of the Revolution, the

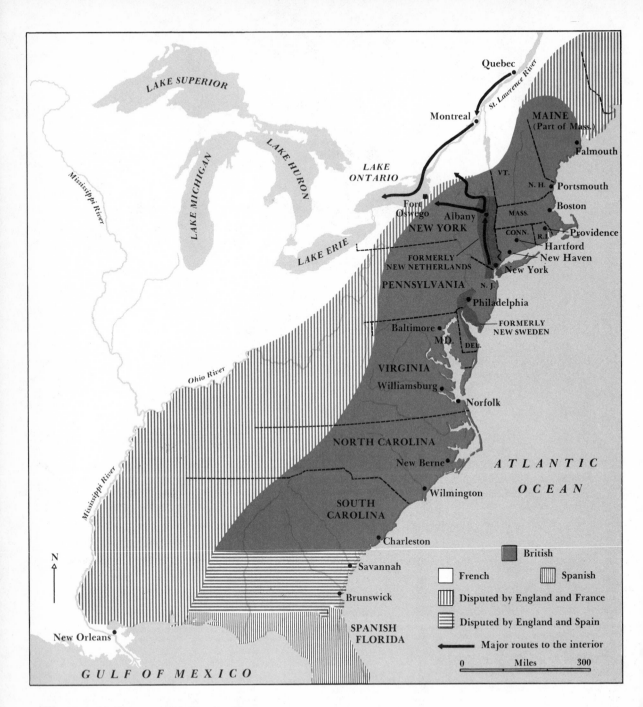

**National Origins of Settlers in the
Original Thirteen Colonies**

2 U.S. Bureau of the Census.

population of the colonies was about 2.5 million, nearly a third that of the mother country.[2]

## English ideas and experiences

Up until the opening shots of the Revolution, the colonists thought of themselves as Englishmen, loyal to the crown. They had come to the colonies with definite ideas—English ideas about politics, religion, law, and human rights. These ideas, which for a time kept them loyal to the mother country and which were based on their earliest experiences with English government, ultimately formed the framework for the new political system.

The colonists brought with them ideas about law, English ideas that are still the basis of the American legal system. For daily concerns—contracts, property and personal damage, basic responsibility—most colonists relied on the *common law*, a body of judicial precedents that dates to the thirteenth century.[3] For taxation guidelines, they readopted the *Confirmation of Charters* (1295). They also brought with them ideas about the powers of judges and the protections provided the individual by the judiciary—the right of an individual to trial by jury, for example. It is interesting that Sir William Blackstone's *Commentaries on the Laws of England* (1765–1769) became the bible of American lawyers from the end of the eighteenth century until well into the nineteenth century.

3 Common law is the basis for the American legal system in all states except Louisiana, where the legal system is based on French law. Louisiana was held by the French from 1682–1762 and again from 1800–1802, when it was finally purchased by Thomas Jefferson, the fourth President of the United States.

England provided the colonists with strong ideas about the *rights of man*, as defined in England's treasured laws and documents. The *Magna Charta* (1215) told them that one's rights are defined by the judgment of his peers, and by the rules of the government; the English *Bill of Rights* (1689) confirmed, among other things, freedom of religion, the right of petition, the right to bear arms, and the right of members of Parliament to debate freely. When the colonists finally demanded their rights, they demanded their rights as Englishmen.

## New arrivals

Because the colonists viewed America as an extension of England, the governments of the individual colonies were modeled after English governments and were affected by decisions within the political system of England.

Each colony was regulated by a charter granted it by the king. There were three types of colonies: proprietary, charter, and royal. Maryland, Pennsylvania, and Delaware were proprietary colonies; Rhode Island and Connecticut were charter colonies; Virginia, Massachusetts, New York, New Jersey, North Carolina, South Carolina, Georgia, and Maine were royal colonies.

The *proprietary colonies* were founded by friends of the king who had been granted the right to establish a colony. These friends, or *proprietors*, sold land to the settlers or charged fees for its use. They controlled the government in their colonies. The proprietors selected the colonial governor and were subject only to the conditions of the charter, the laws of Parliament

*Farm settlement in Salem, North Carolina.*

Depending on the area in which they
settled, the colonists earned their livelihood
as farmers, fishermen, tradesmen, or
shippers. Whether they lived in rural or
urban areas, the colonists, early in the
history of this nation, began to build
educational institutions.

*Fishing in Newfoundland.*

A Westerly View of The Colledges in Cambridge New England
A. Harvard Hall   B. Stoughton   C. Massachusett   D. Hollis   E. Holden Chapel

pertaining to the colonies, and the whims of the king—all two thousand miles away.

The *charter colonies* offered the colonists the greatest voice in their own government. Founded by "king-made" charters that recognized the government set up by the colonists themselves, the charter colonies elected their own governor and were not required to have their domestic laws approved by Parliament. The governments of these colonies, although the most democratic in allowing direct representation, were still not American governments. The charter colonies were required to obey the laws of England, and the Privy Council in London maintained the power to reverse all the colonies' judicial decisions.

The laws of the eight *royal colonies*, on the other hand, came directly from the king. The governor was appointed by the king, and served as his spokesman. The colonists in the royal colonies had virtually no voice in their own government, for although they elected their legislature, the governor had veto power over all legislation. By the second half of the eighteenth century, most of the charter and proprietary colonies were operated as royal colonies, primarily because the king was afraid of their increasing independence and did not want to lose his governmental and financial control of the colonies.

# The road to nationalism

Independence—the idea of a separate nation—hardly occurred to the colonists until just before it was achieved. But the signs of change were evident, even in the early decades of the eighteenth century. Increasingly, the colonists found themselves drawn together. They began to share problems, notably border disputes and the problems of defense against the French and hostile Indians. Personal safety was a major issue to the colonists, and helped to bring them together.

**First attempts at government**

In 1643, the colonists made their first attempt at intercolonial cooperation. Four New England colonies—Massachusetts Bay, Connecticut, Plymouth, and New Haven—banded together to form the *New England Confederation*. They had been plagued with increasing Indian hostilities (in the years before the Confederation, the Indians in New England had made a last effort to keep the colonists from taking over the entire region)—and they were fearful of attacks by the French and Dutch. The New England Confederation functioned for twenty-one years, suppressing the last of the Indian uprisings, returning runaway slaves, and settling boundary disputes. It was dissolved in 1664, and no other serious attempt at intercolonial cooperation was made for more than a century.

*Seaport in Philadelphia.*

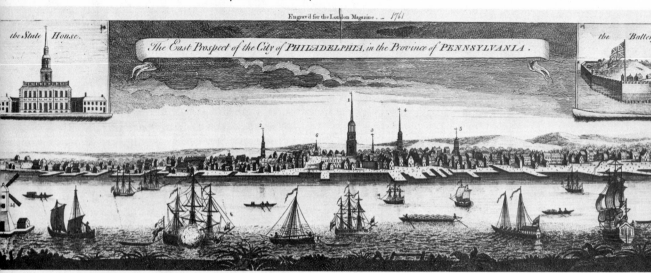

Wooden framed house in Sturbridge
Village, Massachusetts.

Center of New York City.

## The Albany Plan

In 1754, the English Board of Trade and the Privy Council called for a meeting of representatives from the Iroquois nation and representatives from Virginia and the colonies to the north to discuss Indian relations. The negotiations with the Indians, draped in formality and ceremony, centered around thirty wagonloads of gifts—English coats, scissors, tools, silver buttons, and firearms—for the difficult Iroquois chiefs. At the conference Benjamin Franklin, the representative from Pennsylvania, proposed the *Albany Plan*, a new scheme for intercolonial government.

Franklin was familiar with the colonies' Indian problems. He had helped to organize militia in Philadelphia and, after "great drinking of Madeira wine," he had talked the governor of New York into lending cannons to Philadelphia to help the city defend itself against Indian attack. On his way to the Albany Conference Franklin devised his plan. Franklin's scheme for an intercolonial government described a grand council made up of delegates from the colonies and presided over by a president general appointed by the king. The council would be empowered to govern trade with the Indians, tax the member colonies, collect custom duties to finance defense measures, wage war, and contract peace. Many delegates at the Albany Conference saw the need for unification of the colonists against Indian attack and recommended Franklin's Albany Plan to the colonial assemblies. Even though the plan gave the king the power to veto all the Grand Council's decisions, every assembly rejected it. The colonists had problems enough with one strong central government—a government that wanted to tax and legislate for them from two thousand miles across the sea. They were not yet ready to establish another.

## Taxation without representation

It could be said that England taxed the colonists into believing they were no longer Englishmen. The colonists claimed that one of their rights as Englishmen guaranteed that they could be taxed only by their elected representatives, but Parliament taxed them arbitrarily again and again. Although the colonists agreed that Parliament had some power to legislate for them, they protested loudly against its power to tax them.

The colonists drew the distinction between taxation and legislation from the British Constitution. In the British political system only the House of Commons, the representative branch of Parliament, could tax the people. Since the colonists had no representatives in the House of Commons, they believed Parliament had no right to levy taxes on them. That right, they claimed, belonged to their representative colonial assemblies. The *Sugar Act* of 1764 and the Stamp Act, which was to come a year later, directly infringed on this right, which they believed was granted to them by the British Constitution.

The *Stamp Act* of 1765 represented a critical point in colonial relations with England. The Act levied a tax on such items as newspapers, legal documents, almanacs, and playing cards. All these items had to be marked with a stamp to prove that the tax had been collected. Opposition to the Stamp Act was voiced throughout the colonies. Whereas the Sugar Act had affected mainly merchants, the Stamp Act affected anyone who read a newspaper, drafted a legal document, or spent an evening playing cards.

In October 1765, delegates from every colony met in New York to voice their objections to the stamp tax. Called the *Stamp Act Congress*, this gathering of colonial representatives, after proclaiming their subordination to Parliament, declared that this subordination did not include taxation without representation. The Stamp Act Congress demanded the repeal of the Stamp Act, which was revoked in March 1766.

**Rhetoric and violence**

The repeal of the Stamp Act quieted the colonists, but not for long. New legislation and new taxes were introduced, and the fiery words of such men as Samuel Adams and Patrick Henry were heard again. Violence was imminent.

In 1773, England gave the East India Company a monopoly on the tea trade with the colonies. The legislation actually lowered the price of tea in the colonies, but the colonists did not accept what Benjamin Franklin called a "noble piece of chicanery." They resented any kind of monopoly, and their protest turned to violence. On the night of December 16, 1773, a group of Bostonians, dressed as Indians, boarded a ship loaded with tea, and promptly dumped 342 chests of tea into the harbor.

After the so-called *Boston Tea Party*, Parliament passed yet another series of laws, legislation the colonists soon labeled the *Intolerable Acts*. These included a new *Quartering Act* that required the colonists to shelter British soldiers in their homes. The colonists were beginning to feel that they were no longer being governed; they were being occupied.

# Independence

In September of 1774, fifty-five delegates from twelve colonies—Georgia did not send representatives—gathered in Philadelphia. These delegates of the *First Continental Congress* were seeking effective ways to protest the latest infringement on their liberties, the British Intolerable Acts. They decided that all importing, exporting, and consumption of British goods should be halted; and at one of its first sessions, the Congress adopted the *Suffolk Resolves*, presented by Samuel Adams of Boston. This body of resolutions, already adopted by the Massachusetts legislature, recommended open resistance to the Intolerable Acts.

The First Continental Congress had little real power, however. Its decisions were not authoritative—they could not be enforced and no colonial

government was bound to accept them. But the Congress did instill the colonists with a sense of national identity. Here were delegates from twelve different colonies working together toward a popular goal, the resistance of England's oppressive policies. Patrick Henry, while addressing Congress, expressed this emerging sense of nationhood: "The distinctions between Virginians, Pennsylvanians, New Yorkers, and New Englanders are no more. I am not a Virginian, but an American."

The British government, however, was not impressed with the changes that had occurred in the attitudes of the colonists, and Congress seemed too weak to pose a serious threat to British rule. But England's appraisal of the situation proved to be a serious error in judgment. Frustrated by British indifference to their demands, the colonists turned to violent action.

On the morning of April 19, 1775, six companies of British soldiers, or "redcoats," under the command of Major John Pitcairn, traveled west on the road from Boston to Concord. In the little town of Lexington, the road was blocked by a band of Massachusetts militia and minutemen, about sixty in number, carrying muskets. A British officer is reported to have said, "Lay down your arms, you damned rebels, or you are all dead men." John

*The Battle of Lexington, depicted by Amos Doolittle in 1775, illustrates the difference between British and colonial military men. The British were well-organized, immaculately attired, precision marksmen, while the colonists were disorganized, nonuniformed marksmen, who had gained their experience from the fields and woods where they lived.*

Parker, captain of the minutemen, then declared, "Don't fire unless fired upon, but if they want a war let it begin here." Historians cannot determine which side fired the first shot; but shots were fired, and eight minutemen were killed. The war had begun.

The *Second Continental Congress* that assembled in Philadelphia in May of 1775 had been granted no more authority than the first. But the problems of war had persuaded most colonists of the need for at least a temporary centralized government: troops had to be raised, money had to be printed, and channels of communication with foreign powers had to be opened, if the colonists were to emerge as the victors. Congress assumed these governmental responsibilities and at least partially served to coordinate the scattered efforts of the colonists in their fight against the British.

By this time the gravity of the situation had become obvious to the British government; three months after Congress convened, the king declared the colonies to be in a state of rebellion. Yet even then, not all colonists agreed about the future course of the rebellion. The most militant delegates, such men as Patrick Henry and Samuel Adams, saw a complete break with England as the only solution. But the more conservative dele-

## Common Sense

[4] Samuel Eliot Morison and Henry Steele Commager, *The Growth of the American Republic*, 5th ed. (New York: Oxford University Press, Inc., 1962), vol. I, p. 188.

## The formal break

[5] The resolution calling for a permanent confederation formed the basis of the Articles of Confederation, to be discussed later in this chapter.

[6] David Hawke, *A Transaction of Free Man: The Birth and Course of the Declaration of Independence* (New York: Charles Scribner and Sons, Inc., 1964).

gates, Joseph Galloway, for example, still hoped for a reconciliation with the mother country.

The philosopher Thomas Paine, probably more than any other man, finally convinced the colonists to sever their ties with England. In *Common Sense*, a pamphlet printed in January 1776, the British-born Paine labeled the king a "royal brute" and claimed, "Of more worth is one honest man to society, and in the sight of God, than all the crowned ruffians that ever lived." *Common Sense* was enormously popular and was distributed throughout the colonies. It "rallied the undecided and the wavering, and proved a trumpet call to the radicals."[4]

By the summer of 1776, the idea of independence had become popular throughout the country. On June 7, Richard Henry Lee of Virginia submitted two resolutions to the Continental Congress. One called for the establishment of a permanent confederation.[5] The other called for a positive statement of independence, proclaiming that "these United Colonies are, and of right ought to be, Free and Independent States."

The Congress heatedly debated Lee's resolution of independence for nearly a month, finally adopting it on July 2, 1776. John Adams of Massachusetts wrote his wife Abigail that July 2 "ought to be celebrated, as the day of deliverance, by solemn acts of devotion to God Almighty. It ought to be solemnized with pomp and parade, with shows, games, sports, guns, bells, bonfires, and illuminations, from one end of this continent to the other, from this time forward, evermore."[6] But July 2 was not to be the day of "pomp and parade." Congress had asked that a justification for independence be prepared. Jefferson, the eloquent thirty-three-year-old Virginian, prepared the basic text of the public declaration, the formal break with English rule. The Congress adopted the *Declaration of Independence* on July 4, 1776, a day thereafter celebrated with "guns, bells, bonfires, and illuminations."

The Declaration can be examined in three parts: the first, a statement of basic, unalienable rights; the second, a list of grievances suffered by Americans under British rule; and the third, a formal declaration of independence. The first section reflects the American legacy of English political thought—the notion that "all men are created equal, that they are endowed by their Creator with certain unalienable Rights, that among these are Life, Liberty, and the pursuit of Happiness." The Declaration also states Locke's theory that people have a right and a duty to "alter or abolish" those governments that do not protect their natural rights.

The second section of the Declaration lists the "repeated injuries and usurpations" of the king. The drafters of the Declaration purposely aimed their statement of grievances at George III rather than at the Parliament, even though most of the "injuries and usurpations" they suffered came from the halls of Parliament. Their reasoning was simple: an attack on Parliament would be an attack on representative government. An attack against the king —an open rejection of his sovereign power—would be an attack on monarchy, the type of government from which they wished to sever their ties.

The final statement, the formal declaration, served notice to the world that the colonies were no longer under English rule. It states that "these United Colonies are, and of Right ought to be Free and Independent States; that they are Absolved from all Allegiance to the British Crown, and that all political connection between them and the State of Great Britain, is and ought to be totally dissolved; and that as Free and Independent States, they have full power to levy War, conclude Peace, contract Alliances, establish Commerce, and to do all other Acts and Things which Independent States may of right do."

Although the Declaration announced America's independence to the world, much of the world did not care to listen. Only France and the Netherlands recognized ambassadors from the "United Colonies." In the eyes of the rest of the world the United Colonies were English colonies in rebellion. The war was still being fought, and until it was successfully concluded, most foreign powers were not ready to recognize the new nation.

# The Articles of Confederation

One of the resolutions that Virginia's Richard Henry Lee submitted to Congress in June 1776 called for a declaration of independence. The other called for the establishment of a permanent confederation. A year earlier Benjamin Franklin had presented a plan for a "Perpetual Union" to the Congress. And, at Lee's urging, Congress assigned a committee to study Franklin's plan. The committee, realizing the need for some kind of constitutional government, drafted the *Articles of Confederation*, a scenario for a "firm league of friendship" with the states bound together "for their common defence" and to "assist each other." The Articles were not to take effect until they were ratified by all the states and, although twelve states approved the Articles almost immediately, Maryland delayed until 1781. From the adoption of the Declaration of Independence in 1776 until the Articles were ratified in 1781, America had no constitutional government. There were, instead, thirteen independent state governments.

**State governments**

Even before the Declaration of Independence, many states were rewriting their original charters and trying to establish state governments. By 1777, twelve states had constitutions and the remaining state, Massachusetts, adopted a constitution in 1780. The Massachusetts Constitution was notable in that it was drafted by a convention especially elected to produce the docu-

Nineteenth-century painting of the signers
of the Declaration of Independence, with
their signatures.

*Thomas Jefferson, the author of the
Declaration of Independence.*

ment and ratified by a vote of the people themselves, making it a genuine
"social contract." It declared that "the people in this commonwealth have
the sole and exclusive right of governing themselves as a free, sovereign, and
independent state."

The state constitutions were similar in many ways. They were all heavily
influenced by the ideas of Locke and Montesquieu, ideas the colonists had
brought from England. All the constitutions were based on Locke's notion
of "government by consent," the idea that governments are social contracts
among individuals, designed to promote their mutual benefit. Montesquieu's
belief in separation of powers among the executive, legislative, and judicial
branches of government was expressed in several state constitutions.

Almost every state attached a bill of rights to its constitution. The state constitutions ensured such rights as trial by jury and protection against unreasonable search and seizure. These were not new rights, for they were the same rights that Locke had said were derived from "natural law," the same rights that the colonists had been guaranteed by the British Constitution.

Understandably, all the state constitutions concentrated the bulk of political power in the legislature. They had fought for the right to govern themselves, and the legislature was the place they could apply this right. Tired of kings, unchecked governors, the British judges, the states gave their legislatures strong powers over the executive and judicial branches. Most legislatures were given the power to elect governors and veto judicial decisions.

## The national government under the Articles

When Maryland ratified the Articles of Confederation in 1781, the United States finally obtained a national government, a weak national government but a national government nonetheless. Under the Articles, a Congress was established that differed little from the existing Congress. Each state was represented by delegates chosen by their respective legislatures, and each state was allowed one vote, regardless of the size of its population. The delegates were paid by their state legislatures.

The establishment of a formal government under the Articles of Confederation preceded the close of the war by two years. The newly emerging nation had managed to survive the war, but with little help from their new formal government. In addition, the long years of fighting and the collapse of the English colonial system had left their marks. The country underwent an economic depression, and the national ties forged by the Revolution began to loosen. Some states—New York and Georgia, for example—no longer bothered to send representatives to Congress, and most states neglected to meet their financial obligations to the central government. The men who had guided the nation through the Revolution, the men who had established this constitutional government, dispersed—George Washington to rest in Mount Vernon, Thomas Jefferson to represent the new government in Paris, John Adams to represent the new government in London, Alexander Hamilton to oversee his business affairs in New York, James Madison to take his seat in the Virginia House of Delegates. Patrick Henry, John Hancock, and George Clinton became governors in their respective states (Virginia, Massachusetts, and New York). Benjamin Franklin returned to Philadelphia to become the president of Pennsylvania's Executive Council.

The new government lacked the power to give sufficient financial or military aid to its citizens. The country's farmers, shopkeepers, and frontiersmen were discouraged and disillusioned. Even their leaders, such men as John Adams and James Madison, who before the war had been models of talent, education, and wealth, suffered economic setbacks during the post-revolutionary depression. The call for a change in the structure of the national government was loud and insistent. Alexander Hamilton spoke of a "national character" and urged Americans to "think continentally." He wrote, "The republic is sick and wants powerful remedies."

## Troubles at home and abroad

The arguments for a strong central government were many, and all involved protection for the individual citizen: protection against financial losses, protection against foreign thievery and piracy, and protection against domestic insurrection. But Congress, the sole branch of government under the Articles of Confederation, had no power to provide this protection. It could not, for example, enforce any kind of national tariff. And, as supporters of a strong national government pointed out, foreign imports were priced below American products and were draining the profits from American manufacturers. The industrialists needed the tariff to protect their profits.

Champions of a strong central government argued further that concentrated power would salvage the nation's prestige among foreign powers, a prestige that was virtually nonexistent under the Articles. Americans continually broke the provisions of the peace treaty with England by refusing to honor prewar British debts and by confiscating Tory property. Britain retaliated by cutting off American trade to the British West Indies, and Congress had no way to respond short of declaring another war. The eighteenth century English political economist Josiah Tucker called "the future grandeur of America . . . one of the idlest and most visionary notions that ever was conceived by writers of romance." According to Tucker, America had "no center of Union and no common interest. . . . A disunited people till the end of time, suspicious and distrustful of each other, they will be divided and subdivided into little commonwealths or principalities, according to natural boundaries." Another Englishman, Lord Sheffield, wrote, "It will not be an easy matter to bring the American States to act as a nation. They are not to be feared by such as us." Similarly, the French and Spanish paid little attention to the United States government under the Articles. They foresaw few problems with a government as weak as the United States and found it profitable to deal with the individual states. France's foreign minister, Count de Vergennes, wrote in 1784, "The American Confederation has a great tendency toward dissolution."

Congress could not protect Americans abroad or at home. Although the government under the Articles of Confederation had successfully handled the disputes between states over western territories, Congress had no power to protect settlers in these new territories from the everpresent danger of Indian attack.

The main problems facing the government under the Articles sprang from the two powers it lacked—the power to tax and the power to regulate commerce. Unable to tax, the government had virtually no means of obtaining revenue. It could requisition more funds from the individual states, but that approach had proved fruitless in the past. By the end of 1783, Congress had requested some $10 million from the states and had barely collected $1.5 million. The states were troubled enough with their own financial problems. Massachusetts, for example, had taxed heavily and liquidated its debt so quickly, that its own economy had been seriously crippled. Considered a poor risk, Congress could borrow money only at high interest rates, when it could borrow at all. The paper money it printed was never worth more than a fraction of its face value.

Unable to regulate commerce, Congress left the job to the states, and they handled it badly. The states imposed restrictive custom duties on each other, and trade wars broke out. Within the states the economic situation was no better. The legislatures tried to aid the debtors, mainly poor farmers, by extending the lives of mortgages and issuing paper money. But the paper money, which fluctuated in value from state to state, usually was scarce. Many Americans turned to commodities instead. Newspaper subscriptions were purchased with salt pork, North Carolinians paid their bills with whiskey, and Virginians with tobacco.

## Shays's Rebellion

The situation in Massachusetts was particularly bleak. In 1786, mortgage foreclosures were at an all-time high, and the state's prisons were jammed with debtors. Whole towns demanded tax reductions. Advocates in the town of Coxhall announced: "We are almost ready to cry out under the burden of our taxes as the children of Israel did in Egypt when they were required to make bricks without straw." Led by an ex-Revolutionary War captain named Daniel Shays, Massachusetts's delinquent debtors took action. Under Shays's leadership they marched on the courthouse in Northampton and denied entrance to judges who were preparing to foreclose mortgages on their farms. *Shays's Rebellion*, as it was called, lasted for nearly a year, until it was finally quelled by the militia in 1787.

[7] Samuel Eliot Morison, *The Oxford History of the American People* (New York: Oxford University Press, Inc., 1965), p. 304.

[8] Morison and Commager, *The American Republic*, p. 189.

Jefferson, when told of the rebellion, was not seriously disturbed. "I hold it that a little rebellion now and then is a good thing," he wrote. "The tree of liberty must be refreshed from time to time with the blood of patriots and tyrants.[7] But most American leaders were outraged. Washington wrote, "I predict the worst consequences from a half-starved, limping government, always moving on crutches and tottering at every step. I do not conceive we can exist long as a nation without having lodged somewhere a power which will pervade the whole Union in as energetic a manner as the authority of State governments extends over the several states."[8] The rebellion in Massachusetts gave a final push to the movement toward strong national government.

## The Annapolis Conference

In 1785, representatives from Virginia and Maryland had assembled in Alexandria, Virginia to discuss shipping problems on the Potomac River and Chesapeake Bay. In September 1786, another conference was held, this time including representatives from New York, New Jersey, Pennsylvania, Delaware, and Virginia. Meeting in Annapolis, Maryland, the delegates recommended that a convention be convened the following May in Philadelphia "to devise such further provisions as shall appear to them necessary to render the Constitution of the Federal government adequate to the exigencies of the Union." Some states began to select delegates for the convention at once. Congress approved the recommendation in February 1787, and the convention was scheduled to assemble on that date "for the sole and express purpose of revising the Articles of Confederation and reporting to Congress and the several legislatures such alterations and provisions therein as shall when agreed to in Congress and confirmed by the states render the federal constitution adequate to the exigencies of Government and the preservation of the Union."

# Constitution making

The Constitutional Convention was scheduled to begin on May 14, 1787, but, due to bad roads and heavy rains, only the Virginia and Pennsylvania delegations had arrived by that date. Delegates straggled in each day, and by May 29, a quorum of nine states was raised, and the first official session of the Convention was held.

The rule of the Convention granted to each state a single vote under a simple majority rule. The proceedings were closed to the public, and the delegates were forbidden to make copies of the resolutions proposed. (It was thought that if the arguments of the delegates were made public, the individual delegates would feel bound by their original statements and compromise would be impossible.) Fortunately, many of the delegates kept accurate accounts of the Convention, writing in diaries and journals after each session. With the help of these individual records, historians and political scientists have been able to reconstruct a reliable description of the work and the mood of the Convention and the personalities that participated. Without these documents, interpretation and explanation would be even more difficult than it now is. The Constitution by itself gives us no final answers as to the Framers' intentions for the structure and functioning of the constitutional government.

[9] From notes of Major William Pierce in the Federal Convention of 1787, in *Documents Illustrative of the Formation of the Union of the American States* (Washington, D.C.: Government Printing Office, 1927).

**"An assembly of demigods"**

The state legislatures appointed seventy-four delegates to the Convention; fifty-five attended. They were truly an exceptional group of men. William Pierce of Georgia wrote that he was "proud to sit in the wisest council in the world."[9] James Madison called the delegates "the most respectable

10 Clinton Rossiter, *1787: The Grand Convention* (New York: The Macmillan Co., 1966), pp. 79–159.

11 From a letter written to John Adams in London.

characters in the United States . . . the best contribution of talents the states could make for the occasion."[10] Thomas Jefferson, the United States ambassador to France at the time of the Convention, called the delegates "an assembly of demigods."[11]

The delegation from Virginia included George Washington, James Madison, and the state's young governor, Edmund Randolph. Washington, one of the richest men in the nation, four years earlier had announced his retirement from public life. He was reluctant to accept a place in the

*James Madison.*

*William Paterson.*

*George Washingt*

Virginia delegation, but he traveled to Philadelphia to assure the country that he had not lost faith in a strong national government. As commander-in-chief of the revolutionary army, he had become enormously popular. (Washington accepted no payment for his services during the war, and he often paid his soldiers out of his own pocket. Stories of his patriotism and generosity were told throughout the country.) Washington's name bolstered the prestige of the Convention. He was unanimously elected to preside over the proceedings.

James Madison, only thirty-six years old, was the guiding intelligence behind the Virginia delegation. He had served in the Virginia Assembly and had helped to draft Virginia's first constitution. To prepare himself for the Constitutional Convention, Madison studied the governments of ancient Greece and Rome. He examined the administration of the Carthaginian Republic and the political systems of the Italian city states. His detailed notes of the Convention, made public thirty years later, is perhaps the primary source of information about what actually occurred in Philadelphia during the summer of 1787.

Benjamin Franklin headed the Pennsylvania delegation. Eighty-one years old, his health failing, Franklin was still enthusiastic about the future of the United States. When the delegates clashed in heated arguments, he frequently served as a peacemaker.

Many of the patriots who had fought to break the ties with England refused to attend the Convention. Suspicious of a strong central government,

Benjamin Franklin.

Alexander Hamilton.

Edmund Randolph.

**Men of property**

such men as Patrick Henry—who said he "smelt a rat"—and Richard Henry Lee were extremely critical of the proceedings at Philadelphia.

None of the Framers of the Constitution came from the middle, or as it was then called, the *middling* class, which was composed of shopkeepers, artisans, and successful farmers. These men were well represented in the state legislatures but they controlled little power in the national government. Nor could the Framers be identified with the frontiersmen, debt-ridden farmers, and laborers, who made up the base of the society, the lower class.

The men who assembled at Philadelphia to write the Constitution all belonged to the nation's economic and social elite. Forty-two of the fifty-five at one time had served in Congress. Five were or had been state governors. More than half had attended American colleges—Princeton, Yale, Harvard, Columbia, Pennsylvania, and William and Mary—or had received a university education in England. Seven held public securities (government stocks and bonds), twenty-four were moneylenders and investors, all were land speculators (buying up untouched land for the purpose of reselling it at increased value), eight were in commerce or manufacturing, and thirteen owned plantations.

*Charles A. Beard*, An Economic Interpretation of the Constitution of the United States (*New York: The Macmillan Co., 1968*), *p. 188. Originally published in 1913.*

For more than a century after the Convention in Philadelphia, the Constitution and the men who framed it were sacrosanct; their idealism was unchallengeable. Then, in the early years of the twentieth century, the eminent historian Charles A. Beard walked heavily on sacred ground by critically examining the economic situations and professional backgrounds of the Constitution-makers. In this book, Beard observes that most of the Framers were lawyers, that many held government securities that they were eager to protect, that some were slaveholders, and that all were interested in protecting property by establishing a strong national government. Beard calls the Constitution "an economic document drawn with superb skill by men whose property interests were immediately at stake," a document that "appealed directly and unerringly to identical interests in the country at large."

Beard does not claim that the Framers wrote the Constitution *specifically* for personal profit or that the Constitution can be examined only from an economic viewpoint. But he does claim that since the Framers' position as "men of property" was the most important factor in shaping their political philosophies, his economic interpretation of the Constitution was most significant and realistic.

## The issues

Congress had instructed the Framers to assemble "for the sole and express purpose of revising the Articles of Confederation." At the first official session of the Convention, Governor Edmund Randolph of Virginia disregarded those instructions and presented fifteen resolutions, the so-called *Virginia Plan*, one of which declared that "a national government ought to be established consisting of a supreme legislative, executive, and judiciary." This resolution clearly called for more than a revision of the Articles. Yet it was approved for consideration by the Convention with relatively little debate. The Framers had come to Philadelphia to establish a new constitutional system. (Only Connecticut voted against the motion to consider the Virginia proposals.) The decision to scrap the Articles of Confederation and draft a totally new constitution was probably the most significant decision made at Philadelphia.

## Large states and small

The Virginia Plan was debated for many weeks. It was the most controversial proposal considered by the Convention, and the introduction of it at the beginning of the Convention was inspired political strategy. The subsequent proposals, although they also called for a strong central government, were mild in comparison and therefore more easily acceptable to the majority of the delegates.

The Virginia Plan called for a *bicameral*, or two-house, national legislature with representation in both houses determined by population or taxes paid; members of the lower house would be elected by the people and members of the upper house would be appointed by the lower house. The plan gave to the new Congress all the powers that the Articles had given to the old Congress and gave Congress additionally the power "to legislate in all cases in which the separate states are incompetent or in which the harmony of the United States may be interrupted by the exercise of individual legislatures." Under the Virginia Plan the national legislature would be empowered to veto state laws that it considered to be in violation of the Constitution. The legislature also would select a national executive and a national judiciary that would serve as a *council of revision*. This "council" could veto laws passed by the national legislature, but the legislature could reintroduce the law and overrule the veto, if it so wished.

The Virginia Plan clearly favored the large states, such as Virginia, Massachusetts, and Pennsylvania. These states had larger populations and paid more taxes than the smaller states, such as New Jersey, Delaware, and Maryland. Under the Virginia Plan, the large states would control the national legislature, and thus dominate the government. The smaller states objected vigorously and demanded that they be given equal representation in at least one house of the national legislature.

The small states countered the Virginia Plan with a proposal presented by William Paterson of New Jersey—the *New Jersey Plan*. Paterson, who fully understood the need for a strong central government, was concerned about the possible uses of that strength and hoped that the New Jersey plan would force the large states to change their proposals. His plan called for a *unicameral*, or single-house, legislature much like the Congress under the Articles. But this legislature also would have the powers denied to Congress under the Articles, namely the powers to tax and regulate interstate commerce. The New Jersey plan called for a national executive office, to be held by two men, and a national judiciary with broad jurisdiction. Notable in the New Jersey Plan was the *supremacy clause* that was later to make its way into the new Constitution. The clause stated that a law passed by the new government would be "the supreme law of the respective states."

The Framers heatedly debated the virtues of the Virginia and New Jersey Plans. The question at hand was clear: how might the new nation apportion representation in the new Congress so that representatives from both large and small states would be satisfied and would have their desired protection under the law? Should representation be based on population only (as called for in the Virginia Plan) or should it be equal for all states, ignoring the differences in population and taxes paid (as described in the New Jersey Plan)?

The debate between the large and small states ended in a stalemate, and the Convention elected a committee to work out a compromise. The *Connecticut*, or *Great Compromise*, as the resulting proposal was called, established a bicameral legislature in which the seats in the lower house, the *House of Representatives*, would be filled according to population. However in the upper house, the *Senate*, each state would have equal representation. The small states also demanded and obtained a guarantee of equal representation in the Senate, a right to be protected against constitutional amendment. As Article V of the Constitution states, "No State, without its consent, shall be deprived of its equal Suffrage in the Senate."

## North and South

The economic differences between the northern and southern states raised serious questions about the new government's power to regulate trade. The economic systems of the northern states were based on commerce, shipping, and industry. The southern states, on the other hand, based their economic systems on agriculture and slave labor. Since the northern states dominated the Senate (the split was 8–5), the southern states feared interference from and loss of revenue to the more powerful northern states. The southern states feared these losses in three areas: domestic trade, foreign trade, and slave trade. To protect themselves domestically, the southern states successfully argued for the addition to the Constitution of a clause that read "no tax or duty shall be laid on articles exported from any state."

Concerned lest trade agreements with foreign governments, while favorable to the North, would discriminate against southern exporters, the southern states insisted that ratification of all tariffs require a two-thirds majority in the Senate, thus assuring the southern states veto power over agreements that they believed to be discriminatory.

The southern states feared also that the new government would put a stop to the slave trade. As a delegate from South Carolina declared, "meddling with the importation of Negroes" was not the business of government. The Framers reached a compromise on the slave issue. The Congress was to have no power over the slave trade, other than the power to levy a head tax of $10 on each new slave brought into the country, until 1808.

A fourth issue in the North-South controversy also involved the South's slave-holding interests. The southern states believed that slaves should be counted in determining the population of a state—most importantly, to allot seats in the House of Representatives. Northern delegates objected furiously. Elbridge Gerry of Massachusetts asked, "Why then should the blacks, who were property in the South, be the rule of representation more than the cattle and horses of the North?" A compromise, suggested by C. C. Pinckney of South Carolina, provided for three-fifths of the slaves in each state to be counted in determining representation in the House of Representatives.

**Government by consent**

The Framers agreed on the need for a popular government, a government by consent. They did not agree on how this consent was to be obtained, and who was to give it. Delaware's John Dickinson urged that the vote be restricted to property owners. Elbridge Gerry of Massachusetts declared, "The evils we experience flow from the excess of democracy." Benjamin Franklin was one of the few who wanted to give the vote to the mass of men.

The problem of distributing political power was dealt with in the debate over how the Chief Executive was to be selected. The Virginia Plan had called for the President to be chosen by Congress. Pennsylvania's Gouverneur Morris, on the other hand, argued for popular election. He believed that a Chief Executive elected by Congress would be merely a puppet of that legislative body.

The delegates must have realized that George Washington would become the first President, no matter what manner of selection was employed. However, the subject of presidential elections involved many hours of heated debate. The compromise that resulted called for the selection of the President by an *electoral college*. Each state was to choose electors, in any manner they wished, equal to the number of senators and representatives from the state. These electors would vote on two candidates. The candidate who received a majority of electoral votes would become President. The second-place candidate would become Vice-President. If, in the first counting, no candidate received a majority, the House of Representatives—with each state casting a single vote—would make the final decision.

The only delegates who did not sign were Governor Edmund Randolph, Colonel George Mason, and Elbridge Gerry. (Randolph later advocated its passage at the Virginia state ratifying convention.)

## Ratification

The delegates at Philadelphia framed a new constitution. They produced a document that broadly defined the structure of a new government. Thirty-nine of them placed their signatures on it. The problem that the Framers faced in the fall of 1787 was *ratification*. They had to make the document legitimate.

But how was the Constitution to be ratified? Some delegates suggested that ratification be accomplished according to the procedures specified in the Articles of Confederation. An amendment to the Articles had to be approved by Congress and ratified by all thirteen states. If the Framers had adopted these procedures, the Constitution would never have been adopted. Rhode Island had not sent a delegation to the Convention, and there was strong opposition to the Constitution in several other important states. But the Framers had already ignored the instructions of Congress and had written a new constitution, an act Elbridge Gerry of Massachusetts referred to as "that fraudulent usurpation of Philadelphia." They had no reason to follow the amendment procedure laid out by the Articles after the Constitution had been written.

The Framers decided that ratification by nine of the thirteen states would be sufficient to formalize the Constitution. But how would the process of ratification be carried out in the states? The Framers considered submitting the Constitution to the state assemblies for ratification, but they were wise enough to see the danger waiting in the state assemblies. The state legislatures were relieved of considerable power under the Constitution, and they would understandably be hostile to its acceptance. The Framers called for popular conventions—the delegates to be elected specifically for the purpose of ratifying the Constitution.

The country was divided over the issue of ratification. The small states that had initially opposed the establishment of a strong national government reversed their position and supported the Constitution. They felt that their demands had been well met by the Connecticut Compromise. In the large states—Virginia, Massachusetts, and New York, for example—opposition to the Constitution was especially strong.

There was division also within the states. The larger cities tended to support the Constitution, while in the rural areas, opposition was frequently fierce. Many farmers were suspicious of the band of lawyers and merchants that had conjured up this new Constitution. One Massachusetts farmer, Amos Singletary, told the state legislature, "These lawyers, and men of learning, and moneyed men, that talk so finely, and gloss over matters so smoothly, to make us poor illiterate people swallow down the pill, expect to get into Congress themselves; they expect to be the managers of this Constitution, and get all the power and all the money into their own hands, and then they will swallow up all of us little folks, like the great *Leviathan*, Mr. President; yes, just as the whale swallowed up *Jonah*.[12]

But the divisions were not always so clear-cut. Supporters and opponents of the Constitution came from every state, from cities and from towns, and from every social class. The greatest mark of division was age. As the well-known historian Samuel Eliot Morison has noted, "The warmest advocates were eager young men."[13]

The supporters of the Constitution were called *Federalists*. Those who opposed the Constitution were *Antifederalists*. The name Federalist by itself was an early and important advantage for the supporters of the Constitution —it pointed up the fact that their aims were positive, that they were presenting to the nation an important document for ratification. It meant support for the interests of the states. The Antifederalists could express only opposition and offer no constructive alternatives. Their arguments, sincere and valid as some of them were, tended to sound weak and obstructive as a result.

*Alexander Hamilton, James Madison, John Jay,* The Federalist Papers, *ed. by Clinton Rossiter (New York: The New American Library, 1961).*

The controversy over the adoption of the Constitution provoked fierce public debate, with the eminent debaters distributing literature, arguing from public platforms, and appealing to the public in eloquent and persuasive newspaper articles.

In New York, Federalists Alexander Hamilton, James Madison, and John Jay defended and explained the proposed Constitution in a series of such articles, written under the pseudonym of Publius. *The Federalist* pointed out the weakness of the national government under the Articles of Confederation, and, in paper Number 1, tried to convince the public of "the utility of the Union to [their] political prosperity." In *The Federalist* Number 85 Hamilton wrote:

I dread the more the consequences of new attempts because I *know* that *powerful individuals*, in this and in other States, are enemies to a general national government in every possible shape.

*Acelia Kenyon, ed., "Phildelphiensis Letter," in* The Anti-Federalist *(Indianapolis: Bobbs-Merrill, Co., Inc., 1966), pp. 87–88.*

During the debate over the ratification of the Constitution, the Anti-

[12] Jonathan Elliot, *The Debates in the Several State Conventions on the Adoption of the Federal Constitution* (Philadelphia: J. B. Lippincott Co., 1888), vol. 2, p. 102.

[13] Morison and Commager, *The American Republic,* p. 194.

federalists voiced strong objection to the vast power granted the President. One of their rank, Phildelphiensis, even believed that the President would hold more power than any absolute monarch:

> The writer of these essays [*The Federalist*] has clearly proven, that the president is a King to all intents and purposes, and at the same time one of the most dangerous kind too—*an elective King*, the commander-in-chief of a standing army, etc. and has a negative [veto] over the proceedings of both branches of the legislature: and to complete his uncontrolled sway, he is neither restrained nor assisted by a *privy council*, which is a novelty in government. I challenge the politicians of the whole continent to find in any period of history a monarch more absolute.

The Federalists hoped to get the Constitution ratified in as little time as possible. They had representatives traveling through the country championing their cause before the Antifederalists could organize. But both sides carried their arguments to the public as the debate progressed.

By the end of May 1788, eight states had ratified the Constitution. One more state was needed to make the Constitution legitimate. "A few short weeks will determine the political fate of America," wrote George Washington on May 28. But Washington was not certain of the direction America would choose. The Antifederalists had rallied by this time, and the debate had grown intense in the larger states, especially Virginia and New York.

The Antifederalists severely criticized the absence of a bill of rights in the Constitution. The Framers had not seriously considered a bill of rights in Philadelphia, and during most of the debate over ratification, they still believed that such a bill was unnecessary.

The Antifederalists declared that unless the fundamental rights of individuals were enumerated, such rights would be ignored by the national government. As a basis for their argument, the Antifederalists pointed out that a great majority of the states had already adopted bills of rights in their respective constitutions. The Antifederalists' argument for a bill of rights was so strong that, in New York and Massachusetts, the Federalists could secure ratification only by promising that the Constitution would soon be amended to include a bill of rights.

In June 1788, New Hampshire ratified the Constitution, bringing the total number of states to nine. This fulfilled the requirement for ratification, but the victory was not yet final. Virginia and New York were still debating the issues, and the Framers watched these ratifying conventions closely, for they realized that the union they had framed would be weak without these two important states. In Virginia, said George Washington, the Antifederalists employed "every art that could inflame the passions or touch the interest of men." Patrick Henry, dramatically supporting the Antifederalist cause

**Ratification of the Constitution, 1787–1790**

on the floor of the Virginia legislature, declared, "Four-fifths of our inhabitants are opposed to this new scheme of government." However, the persuasive powers of Randolph and Washington finally achieved a slim Federalist victory in Virginia (the final vote was 89–79).

The news of Virginia's ratification turned the tide. In July 1788, New York's convention adopted the Constitution by three votes. The remaining states, North Carolina (in November 1789) and Rhode Island (in May 1790), eventually followed suit, largely to avoid exclusion from the union.

The Constitution was now legitimate. The Framers had written and successfully obtained ratification for the new document. They then turned to the task of organizing and establishing the new government.

# Glossary

**Albany Plan**   A plan for intercolonial government, proposed by Benjamin Franklin in 1754, calling for a grand council of colonial delegates presided over by a royally appointed president general. The plan was designed to coordinate colonial defenses against Indian attack.

**Antifederalists**   Opponents of the Constitution who sought to preserve state control of government.

**Articles of Confederation**   First plan for national government, ratified in 1781. Congress, the only branch of government under the Articles, could not enforce taxation or commerce regulations and was unable to supply financial or military aid to its citizens.

**charter colonies**   The most democratic of the colonial political systems, in which the colonists were allowed to elect their own governor, and were not required to have their domestic laws approved by Parliament. The charter colonies, however, were under the laws of England, and their judicial decisions could be reversed by the Privy Council in London.

**council of revision**   A joint council of a national executive and national judiciary, as suggested in the Virginia Plan. The council could veto legislative laws, but the legislature could choose to overrule the veto.

**Connecticut (Great) Compromise (1787)**   A proposal, incorporated into the Constitution, that represented a compromise between the New Jersey and Virginia Plans. It specified that representation in a bicameral legislature would be based on population in the House of Representatives and would be equal for both large and small states in the Senate.

**Constitutional Convention (1787)**   A meeting of fifty-five prominent men, selected by the states, to revise the Articles of Confederation. The result of the Convention, however, was the writing of a new Constitution, finally ratified in 1788.

**English Bill of Rights (1689)**   Enumeration of the "rights of Englishmen," including the right of religious freedom, the right of petition, and the right to bear arms.

**Federalists**   Supporters of the Constitution who favored a strong national government.

**First Continental Congress (1774)**   A meeting of delegates from twelve colonies who sought to coordinate colonial opposition to the Intolerable Acts. The Congress was granted no authority to enforce any legislation it might pass.

**Intolerable Acts (1774)**   Series of regulatory laws passed by Parliament; for example, the Quartering Act, which required colonists to board British soldiers in their homes.

**Magna Charta (1215)**   English document claiming that a man's rights are determined by his peers and the rules of his government, rather than by his king.

**New England Confederation (1643)**   An organization, formed by the Massachusetts Bay, Connecticut, Plymouth, and New Haven colonies, for the purpose of suppressing Indian uprisings, returning runaway slaves, and settling boundary disputes.

**New Jersey Plan**  An alternative proposal to the Virginia Plan. Presented to the Constitutional Convention by William Paterson of New Jersey, the plan called for a unicameral legislature that would be empowered to tax and regulate interstate commerce, a national executive office presided over by two men, and a national judiciary.

**proprietary colonies**  One of the earliest colonial political systems. These colonies were founded by friends of the king who were allowed to sell land or charge fees for its use and who selected the colonial governor.

**ratification**  Legalization of a document by formal consent; for example, to be ratified, the Articles of Confederation had to be approved by all thirteen colonies, and the Constitution had to be approved by nine out of thirteen colonies.

**revolution**  A sudden, radical, or complete change of its government by the society.

**royal colonies**  Colonies governed directly by the laws of the king. The governors appointed as the king's spokesmen had veto power over all legislation passed by the colonists.

**Second Continental Congress (1775)**  The second session of colonial delegates, which, though granted no specific authority, nevertheless printed money, raised troops, and generally served to coordinate colonial activities in the fight against England.

**Shays's Rebellion**  Critical revolt led by ex-Revolutionary Captain David Shays in 1786, in protest against mortgage foreclosures and high taxes in Massachusetts.

**Stamp Act (1765)**  Law passed by Parliament requiring certain articles, such as newspapers, legal documents, almanacs, and playing cards, to be taxed and stamped. It was repealed in 1766.

**Suffolk Resolves**  A body of resolutions, suggested by Samuel Adams and accepted by the First Continental Congress, that recommended open resistance to the Intolerable Acts.

**Sugar Act (1764)**  Law passed by Parliament placing customs duties on certain colonial imports and requiring that all ships entering or leaving the colonies submit to checking procedures. Colonists who violated the Acts lost their right of trial of jury.

**supremacy clause**  A section of the New Jersey Plan, later incorporated into the new Constitution, claiming that any laws passed by the national government would govern all the states and take priority over any state laws.

**Virginia Plan**  The fifteen resolutions presented by Governor Edmund Randolph of Virginia to the Constitutional Convention. A major step in the decision to scrap the Articles of Confederation and write a new constitution, the plan called for a national government consisting of executive, legislative and judicial branches. The legislature was to be bicameral with representation based on population and taxes paid.

# Suggested readings

Bailyn, Bernard, *Ideological Origins of the American Revolution* (Cambridge, Mass.: Harvard University Press, 1967). Definitive work on major American ideological positions.

Bailyn, Bernard, *The Origins of American Politics* (New York: Alfred A. Knopf, Inc., 1970). Description of the politics of colonial America and the importance of politics on the origin of the Revolution.

Beard, Charles A., *An Economic Interpretation of the Constitution of the United States* (New York: The Macmillan Co., 1913). Classic work stating that the Framers of the Constitution were influenced primarily by economic considerations. The first critical analysis of the Convention, this book has been a great influence on historians and political scientists.

Becker, Carl L., *The Declaration of Independence: A Study in the History of Political Ideas* (New York: Alfred A. Knopf, Inc., 1942). Analysis of the Declaration and its author (Thomas Jefferson); emphasizes John Locke's defense of natural rights to restrain the political majority, a view accepted by most of the Framers of the Constitution.

Boorstin, Daniel J., *The Americans: A Colonial Experience* (New York: Random House, Inc., 1958). Excellent treatise on the formation of American character in politics, law, society, and religion.

Brown, Robert E., *Charles Beard and the Constitution* (Princeton, N. J.: Princeton University Press, 1956). Analysis and refutation of Beard's economic interpretation of the Constitution.

Bryce, James B., *The American Commonwealth*, ed. by Louis Hacker, 2 vols. (New York: G. P. Putnam's Sons, 1959). Descriptive observations of America, its people and institutions, originally published in 1888. This book is similar in content to Alexis de Tocqueville's *Democracy in America*, though less analytical.

Dumbauld, Edward, *The Declaration of Independence and What It Means Today* (Norman, Okla.: University of Oklahoma Press, 1968). Explanation of the document in relation to today's society.

Elliot, Jonathan, ed., *The Debates in the Several State Conventions on the Adoption of the Federal Constitution*, 5 vols. (Philadelphia: J. B. Lippincott Co., 1888). Thorough and detailed account of the debates in each state over the proposed ratification of the Constitution.

Farrand, Max, ed., *The Records of the Federal Convention of 1787*, 4 vols. (New Haven, Conn.: Yale University Press, 1966). Thorough and detailed study of the records of the Constitutional Convention.

Holcombe, Arthur, *Our More Perfect Union: From Eighteenth Century Principles to Twentieth Century Practice* (Cambridge, Mass.: Harvard University Press, 1950). The development of the Constitution, relating the principles of its Framers to the reality of contemporary politics. The author rejects the thesis that political ideas are the result of economic struggles.

Jensen, Merrill, *The Articles of Confederation: An Interpretation of the Social-Constitutional History of the Amercan Revolution, 1774–1781* (Madison, Wis.: University of Wisconsin Press, 1940). Analysis of the Articles viewed against the period after their conception and prior to their ratification.

Jensen, Merrill, *New Nation* (New York: Alfred A. Knopf, Inc., 1950). Overview of the United States under the Articles of Confederation, 1781–1789.

MacDonald, Forrest F., *We the People: The Economic Origins of the Constitution* (Chicago: University of Chicago Press, 1958). Critique of Beard's economic interpretation of the Constitution, with the conclusion that an economic interpretation alone is inadequate.

Main, Jackson T., *The Social Structure of Revolutionary America* (Princeton, N.J.: Princeton University Press, 1965). Description of society in the colonies at the time of the Revolution.

Main, Jackson T., *The Antifederalists: Critics of the Constitution, 1781–1788* (Chapel Hill, N.C.: University of North Carolina Press, 1970). Analysis of the philosophies and politics of the opponents of the Constitution.

Mason, Alpheus T., *The States Rights Debate: Anti-Federalism and the Constitution* (Englewood Cliffs, N.J.: Prentice-Hall, Inc., 1964). Antifederalist thought as seen through the debates that took place in the state conventions for ratification of the Constitution.

Minar, David, *Ideas and Politics: The American Experience* (Homewood, Ill.: Dorsey Press, Inc., 1964). Re-examination of traditional concepts in American political thought.

Rossiter, Clinton, *Political Thought of the American Revolution* (New York: Harcourt Brace Jovanovich, Inc., 1963). Revision of *Seedtime of the Republic: The Origin of the American Tradition of Political Liberty* (1953). Excellent analysis of colonial political ideas.

Rossiter, Clinton, *1787: The Great Convention* (New York: The Macmillan Co., 1966). History of the framing of the Constitution.

Smith, David G., *The Convention and the Constitution: Political Ideas of the Founding Fathers* (New York: St. Martin's Press, Inc., 1965). The philosophies of government underlying the formation of the Constitution.

Tocqueville, Alexis de, *Democracy in America*, ed. by Phillips Bradley, 2 vols. (New York: Vintage Books, 1945). Originally published in 1835. Classic study of American government by a Frenchman visiting the United States in the early nineteenth century.

Van Doren, Carl, *The Great Rehearsal* (New York: The Viking Press, Inc., 1961). Popular account of the history of the Constitutional Convention.

Ver Steeg, C. L., *The Formative Years: 1607–1763* (New York: Hill and Wang, Inc., 1964). Compact history of the colonial period.

# Topics of further study

Bailey, Jess, "John C. Fremont's Contribution to the Winning of California" (master's thesis, Oklahoma State University, 1948).

Dry, Murry, "Representation and Republican Government in the American Founding" (Ph.D. dissertation, University of Chicago, 1970).

Eggleston, Ronald, "The Meaning of the Mexican Revolution: A Study in Contemporary Political Ideology" (Ph.D. dissertation, Syracuse University, 1971).

Goodwin, Albert, *The French Revolution*, 4th ed. (New York: Harper and Row Publishers, Inc., 1966).

Graver, Lee, "The Parliamentary Support of Colonial Georgia" (master's thesis, University of Michigan, 1932).

Grogan, Francis J., "The Traditional Background of the Declaration of Independence" (Ph.D. dissertation, Fordham University, 1950).

# 4 the constitution

## stability and change

[1] D. W. Brogan,
*Politics in America*
(Garden City, N.Y.:
Doubleday and Co., Inc.,
1960), p. 1.

THE CONSTITUTION of the United States is the oldest written constitution in the world. "That it has survived so long," writes the Scottish political scientist D. W. Brogan, "is a tribute to the sagacity, moderation, and sense of the possible shown by its makers."[1]

Not all constitutional governments are so stable. France had constitutional forms of government dating from the French Revolution of 1789; but since that time, some fourteen constitutions have been adopted and subsequently discarded. France's constitutions failed to endure, partly because they were unresponsive to changing times and needs. In contrast, the Constitution drafted in Philadelphia in 1787 has provided an effective framework of government for an eighteenth-century agrarian nation of less than four million people, as well as for a twentieth-century industrial nation with a population of more than two hundred million.

The Constitution has remained viable because it was constructed to adapt to changing conditions. In 1787, Edmund Randolph of Virginia warned the national convention "to insert essential principles only lest the operations of government should be clogged by rendering those provisions permanent and unalterable, which ought to be accommodated to times and event." He called for "simple and precise language, and general propositions, according to the examples of the several constitutions of the several states; for the construction of a constitution necessarily differs from that of law."[2] The drafters of the Constitution followed Randolph's suggestions.

[2] Max Farrand, ed.,
*The Records of the
Federal Constitution
of 1787*, vol. 2
(New Haven: Yale
University Press, 1911,
1937), p. 137.

Thus, as an instrument of government, the Constitution has proved to be highly flexible. It has withstood civil war, severe economic depressions, and the upheavals of technological revolution. Moreover, as a document of human rights, it remains an expression of basic, irrevocable personal liberties.

# The Constitutional distribution of government power

Disenchanted with the virtually powerless national government established by the Articles of Confederation, the Framers gathered in Philadelphia to strengthen this central government. They knew, however, that the people, smarting from British oppression and fiercely loyal to their states, would not accept a national government of unlimited powers. As a result, the Framers reached a compromise; they established a system known as federalism.

*Federalism* is a system based on a written constitution which divides powers between a national government and the local governments. The national government exercises certain powers over the entire territory, while the constituent governments, be they states or provinces, have more-or-less independent jurisdiction over individuals within their geographical areas. Each level of government is assigned specific functions. In transportation, for example, only the national government can set safety standards for automobile manufacturers, and only the states can alter and enforce auto traffic codes.

*Daniel Webster*, Works, *Vol. 3 (Boston: Little, Brown and Co., 1853), pp. 317–324, 332–337.*

In the debate over the division of powers between the national and state governments, the industrialists of the Northeast and the grain producers of the West looked to the central government for more protective tariffs and more land. Daniel Webster, representing these interests, led the pre-Civil War nationalists in the Senate. In 1830, during a classic congressional debate, his legalistic interpretation of the Constitution served to refute the idea that states may nullify acts of Congress.

I must now beg to ask, Sir, Whence is this supposed right of the States derived? Where do they find the power to interfere with the laws of the Union? . . . We are here to administer a Constitution emanating immediately from the people. . . . It is not the creature of the State governments. . . . The people of the United States have declared that this Constitution shall be the supreme law. . . . So far as the people have restrained State sovereignty, by the expression of their will, in the Constitution of the United States, so far, it must be admitted, State sovereignty is effectively controlled.

Without this political order, Webster asked, "is not the whole Union a rope of sand?"

Sir, the people have wisely provided, in the Constitution itself, a . . . tribunal for settling questions of constitutional law. There are in the Constitution grants of powers to Congress, and restrictions on these powers. There are, also, prohibitions on the States.

The ultimate authority to "fix and ascertain" these provisions rests with the Supreme Court.

Could anything have been more preposterous, than to make a government for the whole Union, and yet leave its powers subject, not to one interpretation, but to thirteen or twenty-four interpretations? . . . shall constitutional questions be left to four-and-twenty popular bodies, each at liberty to give a new construction on every new election of its own members? . . . No, Sir. It should not be denominated a constitution. It should be called, rather, a collection of topics for everlasting controversy. . . . It would not be a government.

*John C. Calhoun.* Works of John C. Calhoun, *ed. by, R. K. Cralle, (New York: Appleton, 1851), I: 1–10, 13–17, 24–38.*

Conflicting interpretations of the Constitution often have roots in political controversy. In the early nineteenth century, with the population increases of the industrial Northeast and the expanding West, the South was doomed to a diminishing voice in Congress, particularly in the House of Representatives. Thus, southern leaders sought to minimize the powers of national government, while maximizing those of the states. John Calhoun, an exponent of states' rights, declared that states had a constitutional right to nullify national laws.

In his treatise, "A Disquisition on Government," he said that the right of states to veto laws and "the right of suffrage, constitutes, in fact, the elements of constitutional government."

Calhoun spoke of ensuring the rights of the minority through "suitable restrictions . . . to counter-act the tendency of the numerical majority to oppression and the abuse of power." (By the minority, he meant the southern states in the national government; by the "numerical majority," he meant the Northeast and West in the Congress.)

To protect the minority, he sought to integrate the power of veto into the constitutional machinery. He maintained that:

It is this negative power—the power of preventing or arresting the action of the government—be it called by what term it may—veto, interposition, nullification, check, or balance of power—which, in fact, forms the constitution.

This negative power safeguards the minority "against all measures calculated to advance the peculiar interests of others at its expense."

Calhoun declares, "It is, indeed, the negative power which makes the constitution—and the positive which makes the government. The one is the power of acting; and the other the power of preventing or arresting action. The two, combined, make constitutional government."

Calhoun felt that it was the states' prerogative to exercise the negative power of veto; thus, he is counted among the number of those who have supported decentralization, or "states' rights."

This distribution of powers varies with the particular system of federalism adopted by a nation. In Canada, for example, where the constituent units have substantial autonomy, more power is concentrated in the individual provinces than in the national government. By contrast, the American federal system concentrates power in the national government, rather than in the states. The implications of this division of power are many and complex, and will be discussed at length in Chapter 5.

## The separation of powers in the national government

Having divided the powers of government between the states and the national government by establishing a federal system, the Framers took further measures to protect the individual from governmental abuse. They distributed the operations of the national government among three distinct branches: the executive, the legislative, and the judicial.

The Framers' inclusion of this *separation of powers* doctrine in the Constitution was not surprising; long ago, the colonists had adopted such a system at the state and local levels. Basing their government on the ideas of John Locke and Baron de Montesquieu, they had sought to prevent the centralization of authority in a single institution by establishing three branches of national government, each with different powers.

*Alexander Hamilton, The Federalist Papers No. 67, ed. by Clinton Rossiter (New York: New American Library, Inc., 1961), pp. 407–411.*

Here, Alexander Hamilton analyzes the powers of the Chief Executive under the Constitution. He criticizes those who, in their zeal to define the authority of the President, have vested him with monarchal powers. One power, which Hamilton believes to be incorrectly allocated, is that of filling "casual" vacancies in the Senate. He claims that this prerogative is *expressly* given to the individual states by the Constitution.

In refuting those who have given this power to the President, Hamilton cites sections of the Constitution that apply to the Chief Executive's power of appointment, and calls attention to the exact point where interpretation has gone astray.

The second clause of the second section of the second article empowers the President of the United States "to nominate, and by and with the advice and consent of the Senate, to appoint ambassadors, other public ministers and consuls, judges of the Supreme Court, and all other *officers* of the United States whose appointments are *not* in the Constitution *otherwise provided for, and which shall be established by law.*" Immediately after this clause follows another in these words: "The President shall have power to fill up all *vacancies* that may happen *during the recess of the Senate*, by granting commissions which shall *expire at the end of their next session.*" It is from this last provision that the pretended power of the President to fill vacancies in the Senate has been deduced. A slight attention to the connection of the clauses and to the obvious meaning of the terms will satisfy us that the deduction is not even tolerable.

In interpreting the first clause, the individual must beware of the phrase "not otherwise provided for." The election of senators, for example, is provided for in the Constitution; therefore, the appointment of senators is not a presidential prerogative.

The second clause, writes Hamilton, must be understood not independently of the first, but as a "supplement" to the first, which it immediately follows. Thus, "vacancies," as stated, must logically apply to the appointments made by the President with approval of the Senate, not to the appointment of senators. This clause indicates only that there are times when the President must act *singly*, without Senate approval. Hamilton further notes that the Constitution, in the first clause of Article I, Section III, provides that state legislatures make permanent appointments to the Senate. The clause immediately following indicates that this same body or the executive of the state, acting while the legislature is in recess, shall be required to make temporary appointments to fill vacancies in the Senate.

Hamilton concludes that all attempts to interpret this power of casual senatorial appointment other than in his manner are "deliberate misrepresentations" offered with intent of deceiving the public.

This supposition destitute as it is even of the merit of plausibility, must have originated in an intention to deceive the people, too palpable to be obscured by sophistry, too atrocious to be palliated by hypocrisy.

Thus, in Article I of the Constitution, the Framers granted Congress "all legislative power"—that is, all power to enact the laws of the land. To the President, they gave the power to carry out and enforce the legislation passed by Congress. The judicial branch was intended by the Framers to safeguard and enforce constitutional law, thereby preserving and enhancing the constitutional character of government.

## Checks and balances in national government

The Framers did not stop at separating the powers of the national government, at dividing governmental powers among three distinct branches. Fearing that one of three branches (namely, the legislature) might dominate the government, the Framers established an intricate system of *checks and balances*.

The system of checks and balances prevents a concentration of powers in any one branch of government by allowing each division to exercise some authority over the other, and by requiring that members of the various branches be elected by separate constituencies to terms of differing lengths.

The Framers designed the legislature as two distinct bodies. The two chambers were elected by different constituencies, partly because the Framers wished to prevent domination of the government by an all-powerful and unified legislature. The Constitution prescribed that members of the House of Representatives be elected by popular vote in their local districts, and that senators be chosen by their state legislatures. The Senate was to be more representative of the elite and of vested land interests, whereas the House was to be more subject to the public will. Since the ratification of the Seventeenth Amendment in 1913, senators, too, have been chosen by popular vote. Nevertheless, the Senate is still the more elite of the two chambers. The two houses exercise absolute veto power over one another's bills, and so check and balance each other in the legislative process.

To safeguard against the takeover of the entire government by a single individual or group, the Framers made the terms of the various offices of different duration. Congressmen are elected for two-year terms, senators for six, the President for four, and the justices of the Supreme Court are appointed for life. Thus, a mass movement cannot seize control of the government in any single election.

The three branches of national government exercise power over each other in various ways. The Congress is authorized to pass laws, but the President can veto these laws, and the Supreme Court can declare them unconstitutional. The Constitution grants the President the power to enforce the law of the land, but the Congress controls the money requested by the President to execute his programs. The Congress also has the power to withhold its consent to treaties negotiated and appointments made by the President. The Supreme Court, by ruling on the constitutionality of the

Drawing by Carey Orr
© 1947 the Chicago *Tribune*.

*The Framers established a system of checks and balances in order to prevent any one governmental institution from assuming too much power. The original fear of domination by the legislature has been replaced for many today by a fear of the increased power of the President.*

President's actions, checks executive power. In turn, the Supreme Court is checked by the President and by Congress. The President appoints Supreme Court justices "with the advice and consent of the Senate." The Congress has the constitutional power to create the federal judiciary (with the exception of the Supreme Court), and to determine the number of judges and the jurisdiction of the lower courts. Although the Supreme Court is authorized by the Constitution to issue decisions on conflicts within the political system, it is the President who has the power to enforce the Court's ruling. He can block the Court's exercise of power by simply ignoring rulings.

# Constitutional change and development

The Constitution forms the framework of our system of government. The distribution of powers between the national government and the states, the separation of powers among the three branches of the national government, and the system of checks and balances to block the concentration of power within any single branch of government are as effective today as they were in 1790.

However, even a cursory inspection of our system of constitutional government reveals that it has changed and grown; the foundation has been built upon. In the original document, there is no mention of political parties or the President's Cabinet, and no provision for any form of local government. Yet, today, these institutions comprise an integral part of our political system. Similarly, the main text of the Constitution does not specifically grant the judiciary the power of judicial review; still, most Americans accept this power as a fundamental part of constitutional democracy.

In a genuine sense, the American Constitution is more than a written document. It includes "the whole body of custom, tradition, governmental practice, and statutory and judicial interpretation that functions at any one time as the fundamental law."[3] This fundamental law, which has been called "the living constitution," has evolved within the framework of the original document, a framework strong enough to provide the stability necessary for government and flexible enough to allow for growth and change. The instruments for change include both processes within the constitutional and legal system, and factors operating within the political culture, but outside the formal structure of government. Instruments entailing written law—constitutional amendment, congressional statutes, and judicial review—we categorize as *formal procedures*. Those involving unstated practices—custom and tradition, presidential practices, agency operations, and political coalitions—we categorize as *informal processes*. Together, these procedures and processes bring about constitutional change and development.

[3] Alfred H. Kelly and Winfred A. Harbison, *The American Constitution* (New York: W. W. Norton and Co., Inc., 1963), p. 2.

## Amending the Constitution

The Framers realized that, as the emerging nation faced new problems, the text of the Constitution itself would have to be changed or altered; and, in Article V, they authorized procedures by which the document could be amended. Because of the inherent flexibility of the Constitution, these formal procedures have seldom been utilized; in nearly two centuries, the text has been amended only twenty-six times.

The first ten amendments, the *Bill of Rights*, were proposed by the 1st Congress to meet widespread objections that the original text did not adequately protect the basic rights of citizens. The Framers, in fact, had been forced to promise that such an enumeration of rights would be forthcoming in order to secure ratification of the Constitution by some of the states (New York, for example). The fact that they did not incorporate the Bill of Rights into the original text of the Constitution is perhaps due to their perception of the Constitution as a blueprint for a political system, rather than a declaration of human rights. Alexander Hamilton expressed this attitude in *The Federalist* No. 84, when he said "a minute detail of particular rights is certainly far less applicable to a Constitution like that under consideration, which is merely intended to regulate the general political interests of the nation, than to a Constitution which has the regulation of every species of personal and private concerns."[4]

[4] Hamilton, et. al., *The Federalist Papers*, p. 513.

*Charles S. Hyneman and George W. Carey, eds.,* A Second Federalist: Congress Creates a Government *(New York: Appleton-Century-Crofts, 1967), pp. 47–49.*

On June 8, 1789, James Madison proposed to the House of Representatives that they accept ten amendments to the Constitution to protect citizens from abuses of the new government. These amendments were to be accepted by two-thirds of each house of Congress and three-fourths of the state legislatures; and, according to Madison, their inclusion into the Constitution would make the document acceptable to those who had originally opposed it. He considered this moderate revisal of the Constitution important, and the annals of Congress contain his argument:

It is possible the abuse of the powers of the General Government may be guarded against in a more secure manner than is now done, while no one advantage arising from the exercise of that power shall be damaged or endangered by it. We have in this way something to gain, and if we proceed with caution, nothing to lose. And in this case it is necessary to proceed with caution; for while we feel all these inducements to go into a revisal of the Constitution, we must feel for the Constitution itself, and make that revisal a moderate one. I should be unwilling to see a door opened for a reconsideration of the whole structure of the Government—for a reconsideration of the principles and the substance of the powers given; because I doubt, if such a door were opened, we should be very likely to stop at that point which would be safe to the Government itself. But I do wish to see a door opened to consider, so far as to incorporate those provisions for the security of rights, against which I believe no serious objection has been made by any class of our constituents.

Congressman Jackson of Georgia, however, was not in favor of this action. He believed that the Constitution should first be tested for adequacy and amended only after experience dictated a necessity for it:

Let the Constitution have a fair trial; let it be examined by experience, discover by that test what its errors are, and then talk of amending; but to attempt it now is doing it at a risk, which is certainly imprudent. I have the honor of coming from a State that ratified the Constitution by the unanimous vote of a numerous convention; the people of Georgia have manifested their attachment to it by adopting a State Constitution framed upon the same plan as this. But although they are thus satisfied, I shall not be against such amendments as will gratify the inhabitants of other states, provided they are judged of by experience and not merely on theory.

The Framers contended that there was no need for a bill of rights to protect citizens because the government would exercise only those powers delegated by the Constitution. They argued that the express provisions imposed sufficient restraints to prevent the government from subverting individual liberties. The Framers pointed out that to include a bill of rights that guaranteed some rights would presuppose that the rights *not* listed could be abridged or denied. However, there was strong sentiment for inclusion of a bill to safeguard basic freedoms. By 1791, the Bill of Rights had been ratified as the first ten amendments to the Constitution.

Most of the remaining sixteen amendments were drafted to make the political system more responsive to the popular will. Two of them, the Thirteenth and Fifteenth, dealt with the abolition of slavery and the rights of the freed slaves. Others provided for women's suffrage, direct election of senators, abolition of the poll tax as a prerequisite for voting in national elections, the franchisement of District of Columbia residents in presidential elections, equal protection for all citizens, and the lowering of the voting age to eighteen. The Twenty-first Amendment repealed the Eighteenth, which prohibited the sale of intoxicating beverages. See the Table on the Twenty-six Amendments to the Constitution.

**Proposing an amendment**

Article V of the Constitution provides two methods for proposing an amendment. "The Congress, whenever two-thirds of both houses shall deem it necessary, shall propose amendments to this Constitution," reads one provision. The other provision states that Congress, "on application of the legislatures of two-thirds of the several states, shall call a convention for proposing amendments, which, in either case, shall be valid to all intents and purposes, as part of this Constitution."

### The Twenty-six Amendments

#### The Bill of Rights (1791)

1. Freedom of religion, speech, press, assembly, and the right to petition the government.
2. Right of the people to keep and bear arms.
3. Right of home-owners or proprietors to refuse to quarter soldiers.

4. Right of the people to be secure in person and property against unwarranted searches and seizures.
5. Protection against self-incrimination, double jeopardy, and the taking of life, liberty, and property without due process of law.
6. Right to an undelayed, public, and impartial trial in criminal cases.
7. Right to a trial by jury in civil cases in which the value exceeds $20.
8. Prohibition against excessive bail, excessive fines, and cruel punishment.
9. Protection of rights not enumerated in the Constitution but "retained by the people."
10. Powers not delegated to the national government nor prohibited to the states are reserved to the states, or the people.

Later Amendments

11. Prohibition against the extension of federal judicial power initiated by an individual against a state, except with the consent of that state, or by foreign individuals or states (1798).
12. Prescriptions for separate election of a President and Vice-President (1804).
13. Abolition of slavery (1865).
14. Right of all citizens to "equal protection of the laws." Prohibition against a state's taking of life, liberty, or property without "due process of law." Prohibition against state laws which abridge the "privileges and immunities" of citizens. Provision to prohibit those who have "engaged in insurrection or rebellion" from holding public office. Provision to prohibit the questioning of the public debt (1868).
15. Guarantee of the right of citizens to vote by prohibiting the states from denying this right because of race, color, or "previous condition of servitude" (1870).
16. Power of Congress to levy the income tax (1913).
17. Election of senators by direct popular vote (1913).
18. Prohibition against the manufacture and sale of intoxicating liquors (1919).
19. Guarantee of women's suffrage by prohibiting the states from abridging the right to vote "on account of sex" (1920).
20. Rearrangement of the schedule of congressional and presidential terms so that congressmen begin their duties on January 3, and the President and Vice-President take office on January 20 (1933).
21. Repeal of the Eighteenth Amendment (1933).
22. Prohibition against any future presidents being elected to the office of President more than twice; stipulation that anyone succeeding to the presidency and serving more than two years may be elected to the office in his own right only once (1951).
23. Guarantee of the right of citizens residing in Washington, D.C., "the seat of government," to vote in presidential elections (1961).
24. Guarantee of the right of all citizens over the age of twenty-one to vote in national elections by prohibiting the states from denying this right because of failure to pay poll taxes or other taxes (1964).
25. Establishment of procedures for presidential succession and for determining presidential disability (1967).
26. Guarantee of right of citizens eighteen years of age or older to vote by prohibiting the United States or any state from denying this right "on account of age" (1971).

The first method, requiring a two-thirds vote of both Houses of Congress, is the only procedure for proposing an amendment that has been employed to date. However, Congress has received numerous petitions from various state legislatures requesting a national convention. In the first decade of this century, for example, thirty-one states—more than the necessary two-thirds at that time—petitioned for a convention to draft an amendment to elect senators by direct popular vote. But Congress eliminated the need for a convention by proposing and passing the Seventeenth Amendment. In 1970, the National Conference of State Legislative Leaders formulated a resolution calling for a constitutional convention in 1971 to draft an amendment which would make the sharing of federal revenues with state and local governments mandatory. However, this resolution was introduced to "spur Congressional action on several pending bills,"[5] rather than to petition Congress for a Constitutional convention of states.

[5] *The New York Times,* August 29, 1970.

Before a convention to propose amendments to the Constitution can convene, a number of procedural difficulties have to be surmounted. How will the delegates to the convention be chosen? What will be the convention's voting methods? The broad consensus is that it would be better not to call a national convention to amend the Constitution. However, were the necessity to arise, Congress probably would first pass a law prescribing these yet-undefined methods for convening and conducting a convention of states. In the meantime, Congress will continue to act as the institution for proposing an amendment.

## Ratifying an amendment

The Constitution grants the states the power to ratify an amendment. Neither the President, the Supreme Court, Congress, nor the governors of the various states can exercise this power. The exclusive role assigned to the states in the ratifying stage underlines their importance in the governmental process.

The Constitution provides two procedures for ratifying an amendment. An amendment can be ratified with the consent of the legislatures in three-fourths of the states, or it can be ratified by specially elected ratifying conventions. The Congress declares which procedure will be employed. Amendments to the Constitution must be ratified by the states within a "reasonable time." Congress can set the limit, and has usually done so, sometimes for as long as seven years.

The ratification of amendments by the state legislatures has been attacked on the grounds that it excludes the people in the states from direct participation. Regardless of this fact, all but one of the twenty-six amendments to the Constitution have been ratified in the state legislatures. The only amendment ratified by a specially elected convention was the Twenty-first, which put an end to prohibition. The supporters of the Twenty-first Amendment, realizing that the probabilities for ratification were much greater in a convention where urban, pro-liquor interests would be represented than in the rurally-controlled legislatures, pushed for the convention method.

The process of constitutional amendment is not crucial to the process of constitutional adaptation and change. Most modifications in the structure of government have been instituted by other methods, such as congressional statutes, presidential practices, judicial interpretation, and political custom.

## Congressional statutes

[6] Robert Hirschfield, *Constitution and the Court: The Development of the Basic Law Through Judicial Interpretation* (New York: Random House, Inc., 1962), p. 8.

Robert Hirschfield has commented that the Constitution "establishes institutions of government, but it virtually ignores the political processes which must breathe life into them; it lists the powers of the national government's three organs, but it does not define those powers; it creates a complex system of inter- and intra-governmental tension and conflict, but it does not attempt to resolve the power struggles which are thereby encouraged."[6] An important means of elaborating on the Constitution's prescriptions for government is congressional law. Article I, Section 8, simply states that Congress has the authority to make all laws "necessary and proper." It is the legislature's responsibility to determine what is needed to carry out this prescription. The 1st Congress broadly interpreted Article I and established an army and a navy, a national bank, and the federal judicial system.

Since the 1st Congress, congressional statutes have designated the number of judges in all federal courts, and have determined the right of appeal and the jurisdiction of all courts, with the exception of the original and appellate jurisdiction granted the Supreme Court in Article III, Section 2. In fact, the federal judicial system is primarily the creation of acts of Congress.

Statutes have also elaborated the original structure of the executive branch. For example, reorganization legislation granted President Franklin Roosevelt the authority to create, through executive order in 1939, the Executive Office of the President, which is comprised of staff agencies that cut across departmental lines. Included in this group, for example, is the Council of Economic Advisers, established under the Employment Act of 1946. Congressional statutes have established independent regulatory commissions and federal agencies, such as the Securities and Exchange Commission and the Interstate Commerce Commission. Pending before the 92nd Congress is a bill to establish a special agency to be called the Conquest of Cancer Agency, which would be part of the National Institutes of Health, and which would conduct and coordinate massive cancer research programs.

Statutes also specify rules for the operations and organization of the national legislature. For example, by an act of Congress, membership of the House is set at 435. Another legislative statute vested the House Rules Committee with the power of granting priorities and specifying the order of business in the House of Representatives. Generally, a bill cannot come up for action on the floor of the House without a special order or rule from the Rules Committee. By not granting a rule, the committee can kill a bill. Though not established in the Constitution, this committee is an exceptionally powerful institution.

"Design for Indigestion."

The institutions of the federal bureaucracy are products of congressional statutes. The twelve Cabinet-level departments and the bureaus within them were established by statutes. For example, an act of Congress created the National Highway Safety Bureau within the Department of Transportation.

In addition to detailing the operations of governmental institutions, congressional statutes expanded the powers of the national government. The enactment of bills for public welfare in the areas of unemployment compensation, aid to education, and economic assistance have broadened the activities of government to include areas previously under the jurisdiction of state and local governments. Thus, through congressional statutes, a document constructed for an agrarian nation extolling individual enterprise has been made to apply to and reflect an industrial society of collective responsibility.

## Judicial review

The power of judicial review—the power of the judges and, ultimately, the Supreme Court to declare null and void any legislative and executive actions which, in their judgement conflict with the Constitution—is based on Article VI of the Constitution and the Judiciary Act of 1789.

The principle of judicial review was firmly established in the case of *Marbury* v. *Madison*, when the Court, by invalidating an act of Congress, interpreted the Constitution as granting it this power. As Chief Justice John Marshall wrote in his decision,

> The powers of the legislature are defined and limited; and that those limits may not be mistaken, or forgotten, the Constitution is written. To what purpose are powers limited, and to what purpose is that limitation committed to writing, if these limits may, at any time, be passed by those intended to be restrained?[7]

[7] *Marbury* v. *Madison*, 1 Cranch 137 (1803).

Thus, the great precedent for judicial review of congressional law was set by the Supreme Court's decision in this case.

William Marbury was appointed justice of the peace for the District of Columbia by President John Adams at the close of his administration in 1801. The appointment was approved by the Senate, and the commission was signed and sealed on March 3, 1803. However, on March 4, President Thomas Jefferson took office and ordered his new Secretary of State, James Madison, to withhold Marbury's commission. (Jefferson, a Republican, viewed the appointment as part of Adams's strategy to pack the courts with Federalists.) Taking action, Marbury went directly to the Supreme Court for a *writ of mandamus* (a court order) to compel Madison to deliver the commission. Section 13 of the Federal Judiciary Act of 1789 authorized the Supreme Court "to issue writs of mandamus, in cases warranted by the principles and usages of law, to . . . persons holding office, under the authority of the United States."

Chief Justice Marshall, a staunch Federalist, pointed out that Marbury was entitled to his commission, and that Madison was subject to mandamus from the proper court; however, he held that the Supreme Court did not have original jurisdiction over cases such as Marbury's. Article III of the Constitution gives the Supreme Court original jurisdiction only in those cases involving an ambassador or other foreign minister, or a state. Thus, Section 13 of the Judiciary Act, which delegates additional original jurisdiction to the Court, is in conflict with Article III of the Constitution. Chief Justice Marshall, therefore, declared the Judiciary Act—an act of Congress—unconstitutional. Furthermore, he maintained, that since Marbury was not an ambassador, a foreign minister, or a state, the court was not authorized to try the case, and his claim must be dismissed.

The immediate legal issue in the case was the question of court jurisdiction. The long-range significance of the case is that it enacted the principle of judicial review by declaring, for the first time, that a provision of federal law was unconstitutional.

Periodically, the doctrine of judicial review has met with severe criticism, especially in the years before the Civil War, during the administration of Franklin Roosevelt, and in the last few decades. Critics maintain that the power of judicial review usurps legislative and executive authority and is a violation of separation of powers guaranteed by the Constitution. However, most criticism has been in response to specific decisions of the court, rather than to the power itself, which is now a universally accepted doctrine.

Drawing by Seibel
in the Richmond *Times-Dispatch*.

*Criticism of judicial review has been directed primarily at specific decisions, rather than at the practice itself.*

Partly because of these circumstances, the Court has been cautious in wielding this power. Following *Marbury* v. *Madison* in 1803, the Court did not declare another act of Congress unconstitutional until 1857, in the Dred Scott decision. And it was not until 1866, in the *Ex Parte Milligan* case discussed earlier, that an act of the President was invalidated by the Court.

In 1935, when the Supreme Court declared the National Recovery Act unconstitutional, many congressmen who supported the New Deal measure challenged the power of judicial review. Senator George Norris (D. Ohio) proposed that a constitutional amendment be drawn up to abolish judicial review. He further stated, "I think it is sad commentary on the democracy that when a law is passed by the House and Senate and signed by the Presi-

[8] "Norris Asks Ban on 5–4 Decisions," *The New York Times*, June 18, 1935, 2.

[9] "New Deal Hailed at Institute Talks," *The New York Times*, July 11, 1935, 16.

dent, it can be nullified by a majority of one on the Court. . . . **Millions of honest people** have shaped their business according to the law [that is, the NRA] and have spent vast sums on building them up under it. Then, finally, it is declared unconstitutional by a majority of one, which was never intended by the Framers of the Constitution."[8]

Representative Fred J. Sisson (D. New York) concluded, "The exercise or assumption of the veto power of the Supreme Court . . . is unconstitutional, unnecessary and positively harmful . . . and in these times constitutes a danger to our form of government and our economic system."[9]

# Custom and tradition

The form of our constitutional government has been further molded by custom and tradition. "Time and habit," remarked George Washington, "are at least as necessary to fix the true character of governments as of other human institutions." Government practices that are established, accepted, and continued have become part of the "living constitution," the nation's fundamental law. For example, after Washington retired from office at the close of his second term, it became established practice for a President to serve no more than two terms. Franklin Roosevelt broke with tradition by successfully seeking the office for a third and, then, a fourth term; however, some people felt that he had shaken democratic practice by attempting to entrench executive power. Largely because of Roosevelt's breach of custom, the Twenty-second Amendment was passed, prohibiting future Presidents from running for a third term.

Unstated traditions operate broadly within the governmental structure. In Congress, for example, committee chairmen are selected according to seniority, a procedure based entirely on tradition. Similarly, the President's Cabinet is a body established by custom. There is no constitutional provision for calling executive department heads together as an advisory institution. Yet, since the period when Washington met with the department heads for counsel on government matters, the Cabinet has enjoyed the status of a formal, legal institution of government.

Perhaps the most important sector of constitutional government to develop through custom and tradition has been the political party. There were no political parties in the nation when the Constitution was drafted, and the document makes no mention of them. In fact, the concept of organized formal interest groups was condemned by many of the Framers, including Washington and Madison; they held that such "factions" would endanger the future of the Republic. "Parties" stated James Madison in *The Federalist* No. 10 are "more disposed to vex and oppress each other than to cooperate for their common good." Still, by Washington's second term, two distinct parties, the Federalists and the Jeffersonian Republicans, had emerged as an integral part of the system.

The political parties filled a critical gap in The Constitution, which established the government's major institutions, but left no provisions for staffing them. The parties furnished the means to staff political offices, and to marshall national support for presidential candidates. Because of political organizations, the electoral college functions in ways not anticipated by the Framers. Originally conceived of as independent men free from popular biases, presidential electors in actuality are automatically pledged to cast their electoral vote for the candidate who receives the majority of popular votes in that state. Thus, the plan for an elite of independent electors who would temper the election of the Chief Executive was never realized. Although political parties are wholly an extraconstitutional development, their importance is such that the American system of government is frequently referred to as a "two-party" system. They provide a structure for broad popular par-

"Yes, You Remember Me"

Forgotten man—Drawing by Batchelor © 1936 the New York *Daily News*.

ticipation in government, and a means to answer responsively to aggregation of interests within a pluralist society.

## Presidential initiative

Through presidential initiative, executive power has increased more than was originally envisioned by the Framers of the Constitution. In the exercise of their constitutional powers, many Presidents have performed acts or given orders whose legal basis rests on a broad interpretation of executive authority. When these acts are accepted as precedents, presidential powers expand. The modern presidency has become the dominant force in national government, partly as a consequence of these acts.

Strong presidents have broadly interpreted their constitutional powers and thereby expanded the powers of the Chief Executive. Jackson, in his role as Chief of State, construed the President's duty to "take care that the laws be faithfully executed" as the basis for a vigorous use of his veto and removal powers. And for the first time, the *spoils system* began to function in the national government, adding one more weapon to the presidential armory.[10] As Commander-in-Chief, Lincoln's use of the war power implied that the President has the power to meet an emergency without awaiting action by Congress. As Chief Legislator, Woodrow Wilson enhanced the legis-

[10] The *spoils system* is a practice of awarding public office to supporters and members of the President's political party.

*Franklin Roosevelt's exercise of strong presidential power during the 1930s and 1940s brought both approval and criticism from the people. On the one hand, he was thought to be the people's protector as prescribed by the Constitution. On the other hand, his unilateral policies were considered to be destructive of the constitutional principle.*

New Deal tyranny—Drawing by Carey Orr
© 1935 the Chicago *Tribune*.

lative power of the President by overseeing the drafting of laws under his administration. Franklin Roosevelt, in order to deal with an economic crisis, claimed for the President powers that had been previously exercised only with the justification of war. During World War II, he further expanded the President's power as Commander-in-Chief. Today, with the enlarged role of the United States in international affairs, the Chief Executive has become the chief formulator of foreign policy.

Moreover, executive orders of the President have modified the system of government. In 1970, for example, the Commission on Population Growth and the American Future was established by executive order. The Pendleton Act (1883) empowered the President to extend the number of federal positions included under the civil service system through executive order. At that time, the number included only 10 percent of all offices. Today, as a result of successive presidential acts, over 90 percent of all federal positions are obtained through the civil service merit system. These executive orders have changed the character of government by basing the criteria for appointment on merit, rather than party affiliation or political clout. (The civil service system will be further explored in Chapter 16.)

## Commission operations

The operations of the federal independent regulatory commissions, such as the Federal Trade Commission, have modified the constitutional prescription for the "separation of powers." In fulfilling their administrative functions, these agencies also exercise legislative and judicial powers. Thus "quasi-judicial" powers include the authority to conduct investigations and hearings. Cases are dealt with in a formal, courtlike procedure; decisions are based on case and precedent. This procedure was instituted by the Interstate Commerce Commission to counteract court rulings in favor of vested interests who objected to standards prescribed by the Commission.

The "quasi-legislative" powers that the commissions also exercise involve the right to issue rules and regulations that have the effect of law. Thus, Congress enacts legislation that sets broad guidelines, leaving to the appropriate agency the formulation of the detailed rules that affect policy. It was within this framework that the Federal Trade Commission, on July 13, 1971, ordered seven automobile manufacturers to supply "all documentation and other substantiation" to back up such advertising claims as "over 700 percent quieter" and "the lowest-priced compact made in America."[11] The companies in question were given sixty days in which to submit sworn statements. Officials of the Commission said that in cases of inadequate documentation, the Commission will issue *cease-and-desist* orders. The data, when filed and indexed, will be open to public inspection. The basic aim, in the Commission's words, is to "assist consumers in making a rational choice among competing claims which purport to be based on objective evidence." The orders were issued as part of a program to reach and regulate all major advertisers on an industry-by-industry basis.

11 *The New York Times*, July 14, 1971, 1.

## Political coalitions

Interest groups have modified the constitutional system frequently by demanding an expansion of governmental responsibilities and participation in the private sector. The AFL–CIO, for example, has been influential in promoting the passage of social welfare legislation, such as increased social security benefits, and a 1970 industrial safety and health program that set work standards; and a commission was created to enforce them. The National Council of Senior Citizens' Clubs constitutes an effective lobby for medical care and other government aids for the aged. Agitation by environmental coalitions prompted the 91st Congress to complete action on the Resource Recovery Act, authorizing a three-year, $463-million extension of the federal solid waste disposal program. The demands of interest groups at the grass-roots level affect the decisions of local officials and representatives. This, in turn, affects the national administration. For example, on July 10, 1971, the Nixon administration, "yielding to pressure from city and state officials and a bipartisan group of Senators," announced that it would increase the budget of the summer free-lunch program by $15 million.[12] Pressure from the National League of Cities, a coalition of forty-five senators and various city officials, resulted in the Department of Agriculture's releasing more federal funds to schools, day-care centers, and day camps included in the original program.

[12] *The New York Times,* July 11, 1971, 46.

The manner in which the national government interprets the constitutional prescription "to provide for the general welfare" is influenced by the demands of interest groups.

# The contemporary constitution

The American system of constitutional government has undergone constant change since the 1st Congress convened in 1789. The characteristic pattern of development has been the increase of national power, and the subsequent decrease in state power. The technology of mass communications and swift transport has drawn the nation closer together. Geographic mobility of individuals is a factor that has weakened local and sectional loyalties. The man who is born in Massachusetts, goes to college in Pennsylvania, and then moves to California is likely to be concerned with national, rather than local or state politics. The formation of a mass market in which competing economic interests are interdependent, in which industry and labor are organized on a nationwide scale, has increased the opportunities for economic administration and business regulation by the national government; urbanization and industrialization created problems that seemingly cannot be solved by local government alone. Consequently, national government has broadened its powers to deal with contemporary problems on a large scale.

Within the national government itself, the balance of power among Congress, the President, and the Supreme Court has also shifted. The Congress, which the Framers envisioned as dominant, now exercises relatively few powers. Although the national legislature has enjoyed dominance during brief periods of history, particularly in the early years of the nineteenth century and the decades following the Civil War, it generally accedes to executive leadership. Today, the major effort to reassert congressional prerogative by challenging presidential policy in foreign affairs has been largely unsuccessful. As the national government has grown, Congress has greatly expanded its activities in the domestic field, moving in such areas as urban renewal, aid to education, job training, medical insurance, and promotion of business in poverty regions. Despite this development, however, it has not really increased its power as a national government institution.

The Supreme Court, on the other hand, has come to exercise more power. The Court, a body viewed by Hamilton in *The Federalist* No. 78, as having "neither *force* nor *will*, but merely judgment "[13] has increasingly manifested "force" and "will." In recent years, as it has assumed a leadership role in the struggle for extending civil liberties and civil rights, the Court has exercised final authority. On April 20, 1971, the Supreme Court unanimously upheld the compulsory use of school buses and other transportation modes to end segregation. The Court required that local officials not only be neutral in regard to race, but that they actually foster integration of school systems. The decision empowered federal courts to enforce bussing and other means to remove all vestiges of state-imposed segregation. "The Court said, in effect, that this is going to be an integrated country," commented one lawyer from the NAACP Legal Defense Fund.[14]

Even more significant than the growth of the power of the Supreme Court is the concentration of power in the office of the President. As the dominating and unifying force in national government, the President's constitutional position now is markedly different from that in 1789. The Framers had designed a presidential office with limited power; today, the President occupies the command position in American government. (The evolution of the modern presidency will be discussed in Chapters 12 and 13.)

# The course of constitutional change

The response of constitutional government to the contemporary challenge will determine its viability as a political system, and the direction of its development. The demand for increased mass participation in the electoral process, and the dilemma of executing broad-scale national programs without usurping the powers of local and state administrations, necessitate change and accommodation by the federal system.

In meeting the challenge of technological developments and urbanization, the national government has assumed major responsibility for formulating and implementing comprehensive programs in areas formerly under the jurisdiction of state and local governments. The centralization of control in the national government, as opposed to decentralization by reallocating responsibilities among regional administrations, is frequently debated. Federal

[13] Hamilton, et al., *The Federalist*, p. 465.

[14] John Herbers and Fred P. Graham, "Supreme Court, 9–0, Backs Bussing to Combat South's Dual Schools," *The New York Times*, April 21, 1971, 1.

projects such as the Model Cities Program have come under fire from local residents demanding grass-roots level participation and from the metropolitan administrations who demand city control over the distribution of federal resources. Revenue sharing is another bone of contention concerning national—state power. (In the upcoming chapters, we will further discuss these issues and the response of the federal system to the contemporary challenge.)

# Glossary

**amendment**   Addition to Constitution which either alters one of its articles, or specifies an item omitted from the Constitution.

**bill of attainder**   A legislative act which singles out either named individuals or easily ascertainable members of a group for punishment without trial.

**Bill of Rights**   First ten amendments to the Constitution, ratified in 1789, which guarantee the basic rights of citizens.

**checks and balances**   System whereby the executive, legislative, and judicial branches of government exercise some power over each other's activities, thus preventing a concentration of power in any one branch of government.

**concurrent powers**   Powers shared by state and national governments, the power to tax, for example.

**ex post facto law**   A law which makes criminal an act which was legal when performed or a law which increases the penalty for a crime *after* it has been committed.

**express powers**   powers of the national government listed in the Constitution.

**federalism**   Political system based on a constitution which divides powers between general or national government and regional or state government.

**internal procedures for changing the Constitution**   Congressional statute, presidential practices, custom and tradition, political parties.

**judicial review**   Power of the Supreme Court to rule on the constitutionality of executive and legislative acts.

**Judiciary Act of 1789**   Congressional Act that created a federal court system for appealing cases involving a conflict of national and state law.

**writ of mandamus**   Court order directing an official to perform a specific duty of office.

## Supreme Court decisions

*Marbury* v. *Madison*   1803 Supreme Court decision that a provision in the Judiciary Act of 1789 was unconstitutional, thereby setting the precedent for judicial review.

*Barron* v. *Baltimore*   1833 Supreme Court decision that the Bill of Rights applied to national government only and, therefore, was not binding on the states.

# Suggested readings

Andrews, William G., ed., *Constitutions and Constitutionalism* (New York: Van Nostrand-Reinhold Books, 1961). Comparison of different constitutional governments.

Corwin, Edward S., and Jack W. Peltason, *Understanding the Constitution*, 4th ed. (New York: Holt, Rinehart and Winston, Inc., 1964). Elementary, detailed explanation of the Constitution; brief and concise.

Crosskey, William Winslow, *Politics and the Constitution in the History of the United States*, 2 vols. (Chicago: University of Chicago Press, 1953). Interpretation of the Constitution based on the author's controversial and not generally accepted theory that the Framers intended to create a unitary government.

Dietze, Gottfried, ed., *Essays on the American Constitution: A Commemorative Volume in Honor of Alpheus T. Mason* (Englewood Cliffs, N.J.: Prentice-Hall, Inc., 1965). Eleven essays on the problems of the American Constitution.

Eidelberg, Paul, *The Philosophy of the American Constitution: A Reinterpretation of the Intentions of the Founding Fathers* (New York: The Free Press, 1968). Philosophical treatise that the Constitution was a mixture of both aristocratic and democratic intentions.

Friedrich, Carl J., *Constitutional Government and Democracy* (Boston: Ginn & Co., 1946). Comparative study of constitutional systems, specifically those of present-day democracies.

Gwyn, William B., *The Meaning of the Separation of Powers: An Analysis of the Doctrine from Its Origin to the Adoption of the United States Constitution* (New Orleans: Tulane University Press, 1965). Historical description and analysis, highlighting the development of the key doctrine of our political system.

Hamilton, Alexander, James Madison and John Jay, *The Federalist Papers*, ed. by Clinton Rossiter (New York: New American Library, Inc., 1961). Written in 1787–1788, the articles are an important source of American constitutional philosophy.

Hirschfield, Robert S., *The Constitution and the Court: The Development of the Basic Law Through Judicial Interpretation* (New York: Random House, Inc., 1962). Review of major court decisions, including the significance of each.

Kelly, Alfred H., and Winfred A. Harbinson, *The American Constitution*, 4th ed. (New York: W. W. Norton and Co., Inc., 1970). Excellent history of American constitutional development from its colonial beginnings to the present.

McIlwain, Charles H., *Constitutionalism: Ancient and Modern* (Ithaca, N.Y.: Cornell University Press, 1958). Brief historical overview of the struggle between arbitrary power and protection of fundamental rights (limits of power).

Pritchett, Charles H., *The American Constitution*, 2nd ed. (New York: McGraw-Hill Book Co., 1968). Analysis of the development of the major areas of American constitutional law.

Small, Norman J., ed., *The Constitution of the United States of America: Analysis and Interpretation*, revised and annotated, Senate Document 39, 88th Congress, first session (Government Printing Office, 1964). The most complete and authoritative interpretation of the Constitution.

Smith, James A., *Spirit of American Government: A Study of the Constitution: Its Origin, Influence, and Relation to Democracy*, ed. by S. C. Strout (Cambridge, Mass.: Harvard University Press, 1965). Originally published in 1907. Traces the influence of the Constitution on the political conditions of the early twentieth century; he points specifically to the fact that the Constitution opposed democracy and majority rule.

Strong, Charles F., *Modern Political Constitutions: An Introduction to The Comparative Study of Their History and Existing Form* (New York: G. P. Putnam's Sons, 1968). Originally published in 1930. Survey of the development of the constitutional state from its origins to the present.

Sutherland, Arthur, *Constitutionalism in America: Origin and Evolution of Its Fundamental Ideas* (Boston: Ginn and Co., 1965). Collection of essays tracing constitutional development from the Petition of Rights in 1628 to the present.

Vilt, M. J. C., *Constitutionalism and the Separation of Powers* (Oxford: Clarendon Press, 1967). The doctrine of constitutionalism from Aristotle to the present and the transformation of the theory of mixed government into the practice of separation of powers.

Wade, Emlyn C. S. (ed.), *Constitutional Law: An Outline of the Law and Practice of the Constitution, Including Central and Local Government, The Citizen and the State, The Administrative Law*, 7th ed. (Mystic, Conn.: Lawrence Verry, Inc., 1965). Monumental volume (over 700 pages) covering the laws that organize the powers of state government.

Warren, Charles, *Making of the Constitution* (New York: Barnes and Noble, Inc., 1967). Originally published in 1928. Compilation of material related to the formation of the Constitution, including a day-by-day account of the Convention and the state of public opinion in the country at that time.

Wormuth, Francis D., *The Origins of Modern Constitutionalism* (New York: Harper and Row Publishers, Inc., 1949). Discussion of the various sources that led to the doctrine of constitutionalism.

# Topics of further study

Henderson, Dan Fenno, ed., *The Constitution of Japan: Its First Years: 1947–1967* (Seattle, Wash.: University of Washington Press, 1968).

Lieberman, Jethro Koller, *Understanding Our Constitution* (New York: Walker and Co., 1967).

Warner, Earl, "De Gaulle's First Government, 1944–1946," *History Today*, July 1962, pp. 449–458.

# 5 the federal system

SINCE the dawn of history, when political communities were first created in the form of village settlements, man has been confronted with the problem of maintaining order within prescribed geographic boundaries. Today, in this age of nations, the design of government is necessarily more complex. Large countries, for example, require territorial subdivisions. Contemporary governments are confronted with the task of distributing authority among these geographic units, while retaining national cohesion. This problem has been resolved differently by the various systems of government. At one end of the scale is the centralized government, at the other end in the confederation; and in the middle stands the federal system, a system that dominates the American political experience.

## Centralized governments

In systems where a constitution delegates all decision-making powers and authority to the central government, the form of government is *centralized*. Centralized systems exist in France, England, and Israel. In most of these systems, the local governments are allowed and, in fact, do exercise considerable power, but this power is derived solely from the central government. As granted authority, the powers of the local government can be reclaimed by the central government.

## Confederations

A system in which the power of the central government is derived from the local units, and that power includes making laws for the local units but does not include regulating the actions of individuals within those units, is a *confederation*. In a confederation, the decision-making powers of the central government are granted by the local governments. In other words, the central government acts on the local governments, states, for example—but not on the citizens of the states. America, under the Articles of Confederation, was a *confederation*, since all political power resided in the states.

Governmental systems can be categorized according to how political power is divided between the national and local governments.

*Ivo D. Duchacek*, Comparative Federalism: The Territorial Dimension of Politics (*New York: Holt, Rinehart and Winston, Inc., 1970*), *pp. 201–207.*

Ivo Duchacek, in establishing criteria for measuring and comparing the success of different federal systems, begins by analyzing the American federal system, its advantages and disadvantages. He warns, however, that the birth and evolution of the American federal system is relatively unique to America and, thus, not entirely applicable to currently evolving systems.

The advantages of federalism for America are based on the reasons for the Framers' desire to form such a system. From the beginning, it was clear that the thirteen colonies had a collective identity and common interests. As Duchacek states: "They had indeed been a community before they became a federal nation." At the same time, each state also maintained its separate identity, a quality necessary for the effective operation of a federal system. Because of this separateness, there was little conflict between states for control of natural resources. In addition, the colonies were relatively isolated from the world and its tensions; war and its "corrosive or subversive domestic consequences" did not reach American shores.

In a word, it was a different century, a different physical, political, and international environment—an era marked by individual and local self-reliance and self-discipline in empty spaces rather than the present-day ferment of excessive expectations in the midst of our overcrowded world.

The same characteristics that promoted the adoption of a federal system also proved to have disadvantages. While the system could deal with the autonomy of thirteen colonies, it was unable to mediate conflicts between the two economically and socially different and unequal regional communities of the North and the South.

America's federal system is further complicated by the fact that its Constitution tends to recognize some territorial and ethnic communities, and not others. While Duchacek realizes that this cannot be avoided—that new communities were bound to emerge and assert themselves well after the federal pact had been formed—he fears that no proper provision has been made to deal with "potentially revolutionary or secessionist territorial communities that may either split some states or be regionally superimposed on several of them." Among these "interest coalitions" are the Northwest, the Eastern Seaboard, and individual communities, such as the Latin communities within large cities.

Duchacek concludes that the adoption of such a federal system in America, although perhaps untested to that date, was a necessity. Similarly, other countries find no other viable alternatives.

Whatever the relevance of the American federal experience for other nations, a final note should be added: the rejection of a unitary system and the adoption of some variant of a federal formula is rarely a matter of free choice on the part of a handful of constitutional lawyers gathered in an ivory-tower seminar on comparative constitutional law. There is often simply no practical alternative to the adoption of federalism—as we may assume, there really was no practical unitary alternative to the system as devised in Philadelphia in 1787.

# Federalism

*Federal* and *federalism* are familiar terms to almost all Americans. Daily, we read about "federal" funds, the "Federal" Reserve and the "federal" system. Yet, many conscientious newspaper readers do not know the precise meaning of the term. Although federalism is closely related to our conception of "government" (or perhaps "national government"), it is not a synonym for either term.

Strictly speaking, *federalism* denotes a system in which power is divided between a central or national government and smaller local units of government (such as states), and this division is usually defined in a written constitution. *Federal* signifies an activity, or institution, operated by the national or central government of a federal system. Federalism is a system that distributes the decisions and functions of government. In a federal system, the various units can make decisions independently. The rationale behind this division of power is that different units of government should have authority over different areas of life. For example, a national government should be able to make decisions concerning broad national issues, such as declaring war or making treaties without consulting state governments; on the other hand, local governments should have autonomy over local issues, such as building a local highway, without consulting the more distant national government. In actuality, however, the distribution of power within federal systems is often unclear and overlapping.[1]

[1] Many modern nations, including Canada, India, the Soviet Union, Switzerland, and West Germany, have federal systems of government. However, the decision-making authority is distributed differently in each of these systems.

# American Federalism

Although the American federal system was not formally established until 1787, its origins may be found in some of the colonial governments, which were independent units deriving power from a central authority, the king of England. The Albany plan, proposed by Benjamin Franklin in 1754, was the first attempt at a modified form of federal government. The initial purpose was to bring about intercolonial cooperation in dealing with the Indian uprisings and other related problems. The Albany plan included a Grand Council, which would have the power to control trade with the Indians, levy taxes on the member colonies, and collect them to provide for the common defense.

Early ideas about federalism can be found in the writings of some of the colonial thinkers. John Dickinson, in *Letters From a Farmer in Pennsylvania*, wrote that "Parliament unquestionably possesses the legal authority to regulate the trade of Great Britain and all her colonies. . . . [Since] we are but parts of a whole; and therefore there must exist a power somewhere to preside, and preserve the connexion in due order." But he also stipulated that these smaller units had the right to "complain to [their] parent," that is, to the central power.[2] As the celebrated American historian, Samuel Eliot Morison, has stated: "Dickinson was moving, somewhat fumbling, toward the principle of federalism which became implicit in the American Revolution and explicit in the Constitution of 1787."[3]

After the War of Independence of 1776 and the attempt to live under the Articles of Confederation, it was apparent that a relatively strong central authority was necessary in order to maintain security, promote economic growth, and raise needed revenues. For example, during the war, the national government had incurred great debts that it could not collect from the various states since it lacked the authority to levy taxes on its citizens; nor could it break up the pattern of state economic barriers that hindered the development of a national economy.

Although these and other factors made the colonists realize that some form of central authority was necessary, they did not want to establish a centralized government; they were afraid it would lead to tyranny and abuse.

When the Continental Congress drafted the Articles of Confederation, unitary governments were prevalent throughout Europe. Most European nations were ruled by monarchs (George III in England, Louis XVI in France, and Frederick II in Germany) who dictated policies without consulting the masses. The American colonists had fled Europe, particularly England, to escape the arbitrary, and often oppressive, policies of these governments. Emerging from a war of independence from British control they took care to set up a confederation of states in which power would be

[2] Quoted in Samuel Eliot Morison, *The Oxford History of the American People* (New York: Oxford University Press, Inc., 1965), p. 191.

[3] Morison, *Oxford History*, p. 191.

diffused among individual and independent geographic units. By 1787, however, they realized that the confederation was inadequate for dealing with the problems of the new nation. They were aware of the need for a stronger central government that would hold certain powers concurrently with the local colonial governments.

In the Contitution of 1787, the Founding Fathers established a system in which specific powers would be *delegated* to the national government, and remaining powers would be *reserved* for the individual states. They outlined the powers and limitations of the national government, and clarified the obligations of the national government to the states. They specified the powers to be denied the states, and the obligations of one state to another. By implication, they relegated undefined powers to the state governments. In addition, they established a Supreme Court, which could settle conflicts arising from the constitutional distribution of powers. Because of the many disputes over where one unit's power ends and the other begins, the Supreme Court has been a key agent in determining the evolution of our federal system of government.

## Powers of the national government

In establishing a federal system of government, the Constitution delegates certain powers to, and places certain restraints on, the central government. The two types of powers granted by the Constitution to the national legislature are delegated or *express powers*, and *implied powers*. The *express* powers are specifically listed in Article I, Section 8, of the Constitution. Among these are: the power to regulate interstate commerce, the power to levy and collect taxes, the power to borrow money on the credit of the United States, the power to raise and support armies, and the power to conduct military operations.

Equally important are the *implied* powers of the national legislature, provided in the necessary and proper, or elastic, clause of Article I, Section 8, of the Constitution. This clause gives Congress the right "To make all laws which shall be necessary and proper for carrying into Execution the foregoing Powers, and all other powers vested by this Constitution in the government of the United States, or in any Department or Officer thereof." On the basis of this clause, the national government can justify the use of an unstated power by showing that it is a means to implement a delegated power.

## Domestic affairs

The expansion of national government power in domestic affairs has been largely based on the constitutional grants to "collect taxes," "provide for the general welfare," and to "regulate commerce . . . among the several states." By the late 1930s, for example, Supreme Court interpretation of the interstate commerce clause served to support government regulation of business, labor, and agriculture. The Court upheld the constitutionality of the Fair Labor Standards Act of 1938 (which established working standards for

## Express Powers of Congress
### (Article I, Section 8 of the Constitution)

Congress shall have power:
1. To lay and collect taxes and duties.
2. To pay the debt of the United States.
3. To borrow money on the credit of the United States.
4. To regulate interstate and international commerce.
5. To establish standards for naturalization of foreign born.
6. To establish standards for the declaration of bankruptcy.
7. To punish counterfeiters of United States dollars and coins.
8. To establish post offices and post roads.
9. To provide for copyrights and patents for original materials.
10. To establish a system of federal courts.
11. To punish criminal offenses on the high seas, including those that violate international agreements.
12. To declare war (by a two-thirds vote).
13. To grant letters of marque and reprisal, that is, to license a private person to arm a ship against the enemy (a foreign nation with which the United States is at war).
14. To establish rules regarding prisoners of war held in the United States.
15. To establish, regulate, and finance the military, such appropriations to be valid for a maximum of two years at a time.
16. To establish, regulate, and finance the navy.
17. To establish, organize, arm, and regulate the militia and to call it forth in situations in which the national welfare is endangered. (The states are responsible for training the militia according to legislative standards.)
18. To legislate for the center of national government (Washington, D.C.) as well as for the forts, magazines, arsenals, dock-yards, and other military buildings erected in any of the various states.

[4] *United States* v. *Darby* 312 U.S. 100 (1941).

[5] *Katzenbach* v. *McClung* 379 U.S. 294 (1964).

## Foreign affairs

[6] *Missouri* v. *Holland,* 252 U.S. 416 (1920); *Holmes* v. *Jennison,* 14 Pet. 540 (1840).

those engaged in interstate commerce) on the basis that the commerce clause gave Congress the power to regulate related activities.[4] The commerce clause has also been used to outlaw discriminatory practices in restaurants, on the basis that because their customers may be from out of state, and some of the food they serve is also from other states, discriminatory practices restrict the flow of interstate commerce and are therefore unconstitutional.[5]

The national government possesses "inherent powers," unstated powers whose usage is vital to the conduct of foreign relations. The national government has the sole power to make treaties with other countries, appoint and receive ambassadors, regulate foreign commerce, raise and support an army and navy, and declare war. Moreover, Article I, Section 10, bars state involvement in many aspects of foreign affairs, for example, "no state shall . . . enter into any agreement . . . with a foreign power." In foreign affairs, national policies are superior to state laws and constitutions, as long as they do not violate any provision of the federal Constitution.[6]

## Implied powers and McCulloch v. Maryland (1819)

One of the most important, definitive, and far-reaching Supreme Court decisions was *McCulloch* v. *Maryland,* in which the Court gave a broad interpretation to the necessary and proper clause of the Constitution. This interpretation has greatly influenced the use of national power and the decisions of the Supreme Court.

McCulloch was a cashier in a federal bank in Maryland. He refused to pay a tax that the state of Maryland levied on his bank, arguing that since the bank was a branch of the Bank of the United States, the state of Maryland had no right to tax it.

McCulloch, convicted by the Maryland courts, appealed to the United States Supreme Court. When the case came before the Court, the counsel for the state of Maryland was Luther Martin, a vigorous proponent of states' rights. Daniel Webster of Massachusetts was the eloquent spokesman for the national government. Webster argued that the implied powers clause of the Constitution must be interpreted to mean that the establishment of a bank by Congress was a "necessary and proper" means of carrying out its powers to borrow money and collect taxes. Congress was not limited by the Constitution to only those powers that were expressly stated in the Constitution. He further argued that the states could not use their reserved powers (the right to tax, for example) in such a way that would hinder the national government's execution of its duties. Such action by the states would be a violation of the national supremacy clause of Article VI.

Martin argued that the implied powers clause in no way indicated that the creation of a federal banking system was "necessary and proper" for the execution of congressional powers. He narrowly interpreted the clause to mean that only those powers absolutely necessary for the enactment of the express powers could be established as congressional powers. Furthermore, he argued that the powers reserved to the states included the power to tax, the use of which was to be determined by the individual states.

In a momentous and significant victory for the national government, Chief Justice John Marshall upheld Webster's argument that the establishment of a bank was an appropriate use of the implied powers clause. Marshall stated: "Let the end be legitimate, let it be within the scope of the Constitution, and all means which are appropriate, which are plainly adapted to that end, which are not prohibited, but consist with the letter and spirit of the Constitution, are constitutional." The choice of means, as long as it did not violate the Constitution, could be selected at the discretion of the national Congress.

Marshall proceeded to declare that no state could use its reserved taxing powers to tax a federal institution. "The power to tax involves the power to destroy . . . If the right of the states to tax the means employed by the general government be conceded, the declaration that the Constitution, and the laws made in pursuance thereof, shall be the supreme law of the land, is an empty . . . declamation."

Marshall's decision was based on his belief that a narrow interpretation of the Constitution would unwisely restrict the operations of the national government, and make the problems of governing a growing nation even more difficult. He set the precedent for a liberal interpretation of federal authority.

**Limitations on the national government**

In Article I, Section 9, the Constitution *denies* the national government specific powers, among them the power to pass *bills of attainder* (a legislative act, which singles out either named individuals or easily ascertainable members of a group for punishment without a trial), or *ex post facto* laws (a law that makes criminal an act that was legal when performed, or a law that increases the penalty for a crime *after* it has been committed). It also denied the national government the power to suspend the privilege of the *writ of habeas corpus* (a legal right protecting the individual from arbitrary imprisonment, by requiring the government officers who hold him in custody to bring him to court, and there state the reasons for his arrest).

**Powers Prohibited to Congress**
**( Article I, Section 9 of the Constitution )**

1. Congress, until 1808, may not prohibit a state from importing slaves, but it can levy a tax of no more than $10 per person on such importations.
2. Congress may not suspend the writ of Habeas Corpus, except when the public safety may be endangered.
3. Congress may not pass a Bill of Attainder or ex post facto law.
4. Direct taxes levied by Congress must be in proportion to the census.
5. Congress may not levy taxes or duties on exports from any state.
6. Congress may not regulate commerce or revenue in such a way that it favors one state's ports over another's; nor may a ship, train, or other mode of transportation be required to pay duties in crossing from one state to another.
7. Congress may not make use of national funds except through appropriations legislation; all monies spent or received must be regularly recorded and periodically published.
8. The United States will not grant any title of nobility. If a foreign nation wishes to give a public official a present, office, or title, such grant must be approved by Congress.

The Constitution also restricts the national government from passing laws or engaging in activities that will deny individuals the rights guaranteed them in the various amendments to the Constitution, particularly the *Bill of Rights*. For example, the First Amendment declares that Congress "shall make no law respecting an establishment of religion." Because of this amendment, Congress may not enact legislation that will favor one religion over another or allocate government resources to religious activities in general.

Similarly, the federal government cannot curtail freedom of speech, the freedom of the press, the right of people to assemble peaceably, and the right of citizens to petition the government. These and other provisions of the Bill of Rights will be discussed in detail in Chapter 18.

## Powers and limitations on the states

The Constitution does not grant specific powers to the states, but the Tenth Amendment *reserves* to them or to the people all the powers not delegated to the national government and not denied to the states by the Constitution. The Constitution, however, specifically *denies* certain powers to the states, most of which are in the area of international relations and commerce. These *denied* powers, stated in Article I, Section 10, include the power to coin money, the power to negotiate with foreign government, the power to lay imposts or duties on imports and exports without the consent of Congress, and the power to raise and support a military force in times of peace.

## Interstate relations

### Full faith and credit

Federal systems require standards for determining the relationships between and among the various levels of government–national, state, and local. With regard to interstate relationships, the Constitution sets forth certain rules.

The *Full Faith and Credit* Clause in Article IV of the Constitution requires states to honor the civil rulings of other states, such as those concerning marriage laws, divorce decrees, and court rulings. (However, it excludes proceedings under criminal laws). The Constitution states that "Full Faith and Credit shall be given in each state to the public Acts, Records and judicial Proceedings of every other State." This clause was intended to protect the basic rights of each person whether in his home state or another and also to ensure that he does not escape legal responsibilities by moving to another state. For example, if Mr. Green is sued by Mr. Brown in a Michigan court for $10,000, and moves to Wyoming before paying the money, Mr. Brown may bring him to a court in Wyoming. The Wyoming court will respect the ruling of the Michigan court without another trial, and will order Mr. Green to pay.

Additionally, this clause has allowed people to gain civil judgments in states other than their own, where legal requirements are more lenient. For example, if two eighteen-year-olds from New York wish to marry without the consent of their parents, they may move temporarily to North Carolina, where the state permits eighteen-year-olds to marry without parental consent. Sometimes, however, legal problems arise from the disparity in state laws. This can occur when people go out-of-state (usually to Nevada) to gain a quick divorce, and then return to their state. Although the marriage may be effectively terminated, it does not settle issues of alimony or the custody of children. These incidental obligations usually are resolved in the state of residence.

## Privileges and immunities

Article IV declares, "The citizens of each State shall be entitled to all privileges and immunities of citizens in the several States." This "*privileges and*

*The truck, in crossing the line between New Hope, Pennsylvania, and Lambertsville, New Jersey, is subject to regulation by the national government, which has the constitutional right to regulate interstate commerce.*

*immunities*" provision was intended to eliminate any discriminatory practices by one state against citizens of another state, and to prohibit one state from denying fundamental rights to citizens of other states. A resident of New Jersey, for instance, is entitled to police protection in Vermont, or Washington, or South Dakota. He is also entitled to road privileges in other states and to negotiate business on an equal footing with the residents of other states. Under this clause, a citizen of one state cannot be denied access to the courts of another state.

In practice, however, states do make distinctions between out-of-staters and their own residents. Professional individuals qualified to practice in one state are seldom free to practice in other states without restriction. A lawyer from New Hampshire, for example, cannot practice law in South Carolina until he passes the state's bar examination. All states restrict such political privileges as voting to citizens who have resided in the state for a specified period of time.

**Extradition**

The *extradition* clause of Article IV, Section 2, of the Constitution, states that "A person charged in any State with Treason, Felony, or other Crime, who shall flee from Justice, and be found in another State, shall on Demand of the executive Authority of the State from which he fled, be delivered up, to be removed to the State having jurisdiction of the Crime."

This provision was meant to insure that persons accused of crimes did not escape legal action by fleeing from the place where the offense was committed to some other self-governing unit in the country.

The procedures for extradition are clearly defined. If a person is charged with a crime in one state, the governor of that state is entitled to demand his return from any other state. However, the governor of the state in which the fugitive is found is not bound to return the accused to the state in which the crime was committed; the Supreme Court has interpreted the wording of the extradition clause to mean that the governor has the discretionary power to decide whether or not he will return the prisoner.

**National obligations to the states**

Just as the various states have constitutional obligations to each other, the national government has obligations to protect the rights of people living in the various states. These obligations, guarantee of a republican form of government and protection against foreign invasion or domestic disturbance, are listed in Article IV of the Constitution.

The Constitution directs the national government to guarantee the states a *republican* form of government; but what constitutes a "republican" form of government is not specified. The Supreme Court has refused consistently to rule on cases related to this provision, claiming that such disputes are political, rather than judicial, and that "it rests with Congress to decide what government is the established one in a state . . . as well as its republican character."[7] Although it rarely has done so, Congress can enforce this provision of the Constitution by refusing to seat the congressional representatives of a state on the grounds that the state has a nonrepublican government.

The national government also is required to protect the states against invasion, and may, upon request by the legislature or governor of a specific state, protect that state against internal violence. The first part of this obliga-

[7] In re *Debs*, 158 U.S. 564 (1895).

tion is straightforward. When a state is invaded by a foreign power (as was the case when the British invaded Washington, D.C., Baltimore, and New Orleans in the War of 1812), the military force of the national government is committed to oppose the invaders.

The second provision, involving the control of domestic disturbances, is ambiguous. After Dorr's Rebellion—an 1842 uprising in Rhode Island spurred by the movement to broaden the state's very restrictive voting requirements—the issue came before the Supreme Court. In the case of *Luther* v. *Borden* (1849), the Supreme Court decided that Congress could determine the means of quelling violence. Congress, prior to this decision had empowered the President in 1795 to employ the militia to end domestic violence. The President was thus granted the power to decide "which is the government, and which party is unlawfully arrayed against it."[8]

The President also may intervene without the request of the governor or state legislature when federal law is violated in order to protect federal property, or to prevent interference with the federal mails and interstate commerce. In recent years, for example, Presidents Eisenhower, Kennedy, and Johnson have sent national troops into southern states, against the wishes of the state authorities, in order to enforce federal court orders requiring racial integration of schools.

Lastly, the Constitution directs the national government to refrain from altering the borders of a state without the state's consent. This provision was ignored in 1862, when West Virginia was admitted to the Union. Virginia's borders were altered substantially by the admission of West Virginia; but because Virginia had sided with the Confederacy against the Union, its protests were ignored. Instead, permission from the so-called "restored," or Unionist, government of Virginia was sued to justify the alteration.

[8] *Luther* v. *Borden*, 7 How. 1 (1849).

---

## Examples of Concurrent Powers of State and National Governments*

Public health and welfare
Taxes
Commerce (generally, states regulate intrastate commerce and the national government regulates interstate and international commerce)
Auto safety
Drug standards, sale, and use
Food standards, sale, and use

(* In many cases the national government relegates to the states the power to administer programs which it has constitutional power to enact and enforce.)

## Concurrent powers

Besides the separate powers of the state and national governments, there are concurrent powers—those powers exercised by both state and national governments within the federal system. For example, Congress has the constitutional right to regulate interstate and foreign commerce and to levy and collect taxes. In the first case, however, the states do regulate those aspects of interstate trade that do not affect the nation as a whole, but, instead, benefit the citizens of a particular state. In the second, the states may levy taxes on their citizens, as long as such taxes do not conflict with national taxes. Without this latter power, the states would not be able to function as governments, for they would be reduced to total dependence on the national government.

## Supremacy of the national government

When national and state laws conflict, which laws ultimately prevail? The Framers answered this question in favor of the national government, in Article VI, clause 2, of the Constitution. The doctrine of *national supremacy*

### U.S. Supreme Court Declarations of Unconstitutionality of Federal Laws, I (Arranged chronologically in accordance with tenure of the Chief Justices.)

| Time Span | Chief Justice(s) | Number of Declarations of Unconstitutionality | Commentary |
|---|---|---|---|
| 1789–1801 | Jay J. Rutledge Ellsworth | 0 | Weak, placid Court |
| 1801–1835 | Marshall | 1 | 1803: *Marbury v. Madison* |
| 1836–1857 | Taney | 0 | |
| 1857–1864 | Taney | 1 | 1857: *Dred Scott v. Sanford* |
| 1864–1873 | Chase | 10 | 1870: *Legal Tender Cases* |
| 1874–1888 | Waite Fuller | 8 | 1883: *Civil Rights Cases* |
| 1888–1910 | Fuller | 14 (15) | 1895: *Income Tax Cases* |
| 1910–1921 | White Taft | 13 | 1918: *Child Labor Case* |
| 1921–1930 | Taft | 13 | 1923: *Minimum Wage Case* |
| 1930–1936 | Hughes | 16 | Of these 13 came in 1934–1936! |
| 1936–1943 | Hughes Stone | 0 | |
| 1943–Present[a] | Stone Vinson Warren | 2 1 15 | See pp. 285ff., *supra*. |
| | | 94 (95) | |

[a] As of March 1968.
Source: Henry Abraham, *The Judicial Process*, 2nd ed. (New York: Oxford University Press, Inc., 1968), p. 288.

proclaims, "This Constitution, the laws of the United States which shall be made in pursuance thereof, and all treaties made or which shall be made, under the authority of the United States, shall be the supreme law of the land." Article VI also requires that state judges defer to the Constitution of the United States as the final source for judicial interpretation, thereby further subordinating state law to national law.

The Framers realized that to declare national supremacy was not enough; they had to establish a means to enforce it. Article III, Section 1, created the Supreme Court as a national court of final authority in cases of federal-state conflict. This provision authorized Congress to establish a system of inferior federal courts.

The 1st Congress in the *Judiciary Act of 1789* set up a federal court system and provided a procedure whereby cases involving a conflict of national and state laws could be appealed from the state to the federal courts. These cases can be appealed from the highest state court to the Supreme Court, which wields the ultimate power of review.

Thus, the Judiciary Act made national law supreme by giving to a national institution, the Supreme Court, the power of final decision in cases of state and national conflict.

# The changing character of American federalism

Because Constitutional provisions are subject to intrepretation, change, and revision, American federalism has evolved from a system in the eighteenth century, where much power remained with the states, to a system in the twentieth century in which the central government has come to wield vast powers while the states continue to carry out important governmental functions.

**Federalism amended**

Of the twenty-six amendments added to the Constitution, eleven directly affect the relationship between state and national governments within the federal system. Two amendments, the Eleventh and the Twenty-first, increase the power of the states. Eight amendments—the Thirteenth, Fourteenth, Fifteenth, Sixteenth, Seventeenth, Eighteenth, Twenty-fourth, and Twenty-sixth—limit the powers of the states; in so doing, they may increase the powers of the national government in some cases. One amendment, the Nineteenth, limits the powers of both the national and state governments.

**The Eleventh Amendment**

Adopted in 1798, the Eleventh Amendment declared that a state government cannot be sued by citizens of other states, or of any foreign country, in a federal court. This amendment was intended to guarantee that a sovereign state could not be summoned before the federal judiciary. It thereby nullified the 1793 Supreme Court decision in *Chisholm* v. *Georgia,* which held that states could be sued in federal courts. Chief Justice John Marshall, in 1821, declared that individuals could appeal decisions of state courts to the Supreme Court, however; thus, he gave the federal courts ultimate authority to settle controversies in state courts involving issues of federal law.

## The Thirteenth Amendment

The Thirteenth Amendment is one of the most important and historic amendments, for it dispossessed the states of what certain states considered to be an important state right—the right to decide whether or not its citizens might hold slaves. Ratified in 1865 at the conclusion of the Civil War, it states: "Neither slavery nor involuntary servitude, except as a punishment for crime whereof the party shall have been duly convicted, shall exist within the United States, or any place subject to their jurisdiction." The amendment also authorized Congress to pass legislation to enforce its provisions.

## The Fourteenth and Fifteenth Amendments

The Fourteenth and Fifteenth Amendments were also passed as a result of the Civil War; they further extended civil liberties to former slaves and thus deprived the states of the decision-making power on this important question. The Fourteenth Amendment, ratified in 1868, attempted to preserve the individual liberties of these new citizens by requiring that no state "deny to any citizen equal protection of the laws" nor "deprive any person of life, liberty, or property without *due process of law*." The Fifteenth Amendment, ratified in 1870, guaranteed the right to vote to all citizens by stating that the "vote shall not be denied or abridged by the United States or by any State on account of race, color, or previous condition of servitude." Both amendments gave Congress power to enforce their provisions—a power which only now is being exercised significantly.

## The Sixteenth Amendment

Adopted in 1913, the Sixteenth Amendment also gave more power to the national government—in this case, the power to levy a graduated income tax. Ratification of this amendment overturned a Supreme Court decision (*Pollock* v. *Farmers' Loan and Trust Co.*, 1895), which had denied this power to Congress.

## The Seventeenth Amendment

Also adopted in 1913, the Seventeenth Amendment decreed that United States senators be popularly elected, rather than chosen by the state legislatures. By making senators directly responsible to the people, this amendment weakened the influence of the state legislatures in Congress.

## The Eighteenth and the Twenty-first Amendments

Adopted in 1919, the Eighteenth Amendment gave the national government the power to prohibit "the manufacture, sale, and transportation of intoxicating liquors." Formerly, the regulation of the distribution and consumption of alcoholic beverages had been the province of the states. The Twenty-first Amendment, ratified in 1933, repealed the Eighteenth Amendment. The Twenty-first Amendment thereby returned the power to regulate liquor traffic to the states.

## The Nineteenth Amendment

Ratified in 1920, this amendment limited state power by denying the states the right to abridge the right to vote on account of sex. By depriving the state of a criterion for barring participation in the electoral process, the Nineteenth Amendment further enhanced national control over popular elections.

## The Twenty-fourth Amendment

Ratified in 1964, this amendment eliminated the requirement of paying a poll tax in order to vote in national elections. The poll tax was a discriminatory tax that had been used in a number of southern states to discourage voting by poor black residents. By prohibiting states from imposing this tax, the amendment further restricted their constitutional power to regulate elections.

## The Twenty-sixth Amendment

[9] *Oregon* v. *Mitchell* 91 S.C. 260 (1970) confirmed the constitutionality of congressional regulation of national elections.

This most recent amendment, ratified in 1971, extended suffrage to eighteen-year-olds in state and local elections, thus extending the Voting Rights Act of 1970, which had provided for the eighteen-year-old vote in national elections only.[9] The proposed amendment was rapidly adopted because it was popularly supported, and because it eliminated the inconvenience of a state's maintaining separate voting procedures for national and state elections (often held on the same day).

Although the constitutional guidelines remain the basis of our federal system, it is clear that the original conception has been greatly modified, as the states have had their powers reduced in some significant areas through the legal means of constitutional amendment.

## Toward a stronger national government

### Urbanization

Not all changes in the federal system have been the result of constitutional amendment. Some changes, as we have seen, have been the direct consequence of judicial interpretation. Other changes, particularly the more recent shift toward stronger national government, have come in response to political, social, and economic developments in the United States.

In the 1800s, America was a sparsely populated nation of widely separated rural communities. Travel and communications between communities were slow and inadequate. The few public problems of this small and rural society could be solved by local governments. However, as masses of people concentrated in cities during this century, local governments found themselves increasingly ill equipped to provide transportation, education, and health facilities for underskilled and often impoverished urban residents. Since state legislatures were often unresponsive to the needs of these urban areas, urban officials were forced to seek additional financial and administrative help from national authorities.

### A national economy

Broad-scale national involvement in local affairs began during the Great Depression of the 1930s, when the national government sponsored programs designed to give people food, clothing, shelter, and employment. Many social welfare programs (social security and unemployment compensation, for example) were initiated at this time. Since the Depression, national action in the economic sphere has steadily increased. During the 1960s, for example, national programs were extended to include health insurance and aid to education. In 1971, President Nixon imposed wage and price guidelines to protect the national economy.

The development of large interstate industries and corporations created a further need for more comprehensive regulation and control than had existed in agrarian America. In 1800, farms and businesses were as self-contained and self-sustaining as the communities they supported. Men rarely went beyond their immediate boundaries for goods, customers, or services; the price of corn in New Jersey did not affect the price in Pennsylvania. However, toward the end of the nineteenth century, as farms increased in size, as railroads facilitated the interstate transportation of goods, and as large corporations began to establish themselves in many states, a need developed for uniform regulations and controls. Extremely favorable or lenient business laws in one state might draw all business into that state, away from the states with stricter laws. For example, wage laws in one state might prompt businesses to relocate in another state to defray operating costs.

*Richard H. Leach, American Federalism (New York: W. W. Norton and Co., Inc., 1970), pp. 83–114.*

Richard Leach believes that the working of our federal system of government can be best observed in program areas, such as public education. Although education traditionally has been subject to regulation by state and local governments, the national government has promoted its existence by supplying land for public schools, by supporting agricultural and mechanical colleges, and later, by providing grants-in-aid for specified programs.

Today, educational institutions and programs are supervised concurrently by the local, state, and national governments. Although most elementary and high schools are under the jurisdiction of the local school district (which is free in administrative matters such as taxing and hiring certified teachers), the state can limit and proscribe their powers by certifying teachers, prescribing textbooks, maintaining buildings, and regulating employees under public employee labor laws. Most significantly, local school districts depend on state and national financial aid. In 1967–68, for example, local governments provided 52 percent of the total educational costs; state governments, 40 percent; and the national government, 8 percent; but the national government's share is increasing, while the local government's is decreasing. The state also exerts judicial review and the auditing of state funds to limit the freedom of the local school district.

The national government also restricts local influence. It administers extensive vocational education programs in home economics, industrial arts, and agriculture; gives technical aid; maintains school lunch programs, and teacher training programs; and allocates surplus federal property to schools.

The national government, noted Leach, became established as a "major participant" in the nation's educational system with the passage in 1965 of Johnson's "landmark education legislation."

[The Elementary and Secondary Education Act of 1965] was the first general aid-to-education law ever enacted by Congress. . . . Money appropriated under its terms must be spent on poor children, but it can be spent pretty much the way each individual school district decides. . . . Under its terms somewhere near one billion dollars has been handed over every year to school districts. . . . Perhaps no other act has had the impact on intergovernmental relationships that [the] ESEA already has. And since it represents a continuing commitment to the improvement of educational quality in the United States on the part of the national government, its effects will continue to be felt in intergovernmental relations for many years to come.

Civil rights legislation has also been pertinent to the educational system. The 1964 Civil Rights Act established the national government as a "guardian of the national conscience" in education; and in 1968, desegregation guidelines were made applicable to all areas of the country, with the imminent possibility that federal aid could be withdrawn if the guidelines were not maintained.

Statistics testify to the national government's increased attention to educational programs. In 1964, Congress provided $670 million in aid to elementary and high school education, and $1.5 billion for higher education; this amount was increased in 1968 to $3.3 billion and $3.8 billion, respectively. Also supported are adult, continuing, and vocational-technical education. Grants have risen in these areas from $200 million in 1964 to $1.1 billion in 1968. All these funds were allocated for specific programs initiated by local, state and private, or national agencies. Administration is usually conducted on the local, state, or private level, except in a few instances, such as the Headstart and Job Corps programs, which are administered by the national government.

This complicated federal system of education leads to several problems. Aside from those that exist in the local districts and on the state level, Leach focuses on two problems brought about by poor administration on the national level. He points out that the timing of funds is often poor and prevents good planning, as funds arrive at the schools a few months after school begins. Similarly, no good system of evaluating the effect of the funds has been instituted that would aid in long-range program planning. The problems in the system as a whole are difficult to contend with, because they exist on so many governmental levels and because improvements require staggering costs that affect our entire economic system.

Leach cites the recent Compact for Education signed in 1966, and supported by forty-two member states, as an indication of the positive direction we are taking in coordinating intergovernmental ventures. A commission formed by the Compact sets up a mechanism for dealing with problems, developing alternative policies, and gathering information. It serves as a forum for sharing experiences and ideas and debating performance and improvement and, most important, as a permanent political force for obtaining and administering funds.

The Compact for Education does put a new force at work in both American education and American federalism and points the way to at least a partial solution of some of the problems raised by the intergovernmental nature of American education. Indeed, its presence makes the program area of education unique in America today. It may well come to occupy the [necessary] role . . . as it develops and matures and may offer a model to areas outside of education where action in the American system is intergovernmental. As such, it bears a good deal of watching in the years ahead.

**War and national defense**

Because business activities in one state affect businesses in other states (a steel strike in Michigan, for example, will affect automobile sales in California, while a drought in Iowa will affect food markets in Rhode Island), it became necessary that the national government provide some uniform standards for regulating important aspects of the American economy. The Constitution gives the national government the power to declare and wage war; and during such times, the powers of the national government, particularly of the President, have increased greatly. Although this increase is only granted to the national government during wartime proper, almost every war has led to the increase of national powers during the period that followed. For example, after World War II, with the development of the cold war between the United States and the Soviet Union, the national government retained its control over atomic energy and many scientific projects that had been started in conjunction with the war. In fact, after World War II, it became apparent to almost all Americans that defense was a permanent peacetime occupation, demanding great sums of money, energy, and manpower. Because of this great increase in defense activities, ranging today from training a standing army to building long-range missiles, defense has become one of the greatest "industries" of our modern age, and it is largely supervised by the national government.

**Taxes and revenues**

An additional source of national power is that which accrues from its broad taxing powers, especially from the graduated income tax and corporate tax. This broad financial power directly affects the lives and budgets of most American citizens. It also has a major impact on state and local governments.

Federal monies help to finance a wide variety of programs, conducted by state and local governments—such as highway construction, education, housing, and aid to dependent children.

By imposing certain stipulations and conditions on federal money, Congress can control, in effect, the nature and scope of state and local governmental activities. On the one hand, Congress can halt local activities (such as the construction of a highway) by voting not to appropriate money for them. On the other hand, Congress can encourage needed housing projects in slum areas by offering large sums of money to state or city officials, who will use it for that express purpose. It can also enforce civil rights for minority groups by stipulating that grants of money will be awarded only on the condition that no discrimination be practiced in state programs which receive federal monies. The 1964 Civil Rights Act, for example, provided that "No person in the United States shall, on the grounds of race, color, or national origin, be excluded from participation in, be denied the benefits of, or be subjected to discrimination under, any program or activity receiving Federal financial assistance."

## Toward cooperative federalism

This increasing involvement of the national government in state and local affairs has not destroyed our federal system; however, it has created a new kind of federalism known as *cooperative* federalism. *Cooperative* federalism is distinguished from the *dual* federalism that characterized the American federal system in the first half of the nineteenth century.[10]

In *dual* federalism, the powers of the national and local governments remained separate and distinct. Instead of cooperating to solve common problems, the states and the central government functioned independently within their own spheres of influence. However, because of contemporary demands —industrialism, urbanization, war, and economic interdependence—a system of dual federalism became unworkable. States needed national assistance, and the national government could not function effectively without the cooperation of local authorities. As a result, state and local governments began to share responsibilities with the national government; and the national government relied more and more on state and local governments for the administration and operation of federally sponsored and financed programs.

The result was the emergence in the twentieth century of a system of cooperative federalism. In this new cooperative system, almost all governmental activities are carried out by a combination of national and local officials. The political scientist, Morton Grodzins, has compared this cooperative system to a "marblecake" in which all governmental levels run into each other like swirls of color; this is in contrast to *dual* federalism, where the layers of government are clearly separated, as in a layer cake.

While cooperative federalism has resulted in the growth of a stronger

[10] Morton Grodzins, *The American System: A New View of Government in the United States,* Daniel J. Eleazar, Ed. (Chicago: Rand McNally and Co., 1966), Chapter 2.

"I keep telling you, we don't have anything for you to see."

national government, it also has had many positive effects on states. Some critics argue that the states have lost power; but it is important to realize that some states have expanded their activities as a result of federal assistance. State financial resources come from small income taxes, sales taxes, property taxes, and a variety of other less lucrative taxes. Previous to the intervention of the national government in state and local affairs, a poor state, such as Arkansas, had scant funds to spend on education, while a rich state, such as California, had alloted a great deal of money to educational development. As a result, the children in Arkansas who could not afford private schools did not have educational facilities comparable to those provided to children from similar financial backgrounds in California. Under cooperative federalism, national government assistance has stimulated state activity in a wide range of programs to improve the quality of life.

*United States Senate Study by Subcommittee on Intergovernmental Relations of the Committee on Government Operations, "The Condition of American Federalism: An Historian's View," by Harry N. Scheiber (Washington, D.C., Government Printing Office, 1966), pp. 14–22.*

Harry Scheiber concludes a revisionist theory of federalism with an explanation of President Lyndon Johnson's "creative federalism," in which he notes how Johnson's theory differs from cooperative federalism, the predominant federalist theory in operation since 1933.

President Johnson generally saw his federalist theory as an extension of traditional American federalism, rather than as a totally new innovation. However, a close study of his speeches reveals that in theory it was, indeed, new and, as he named it, "creative." The President denied that he sought to further centralize federal power. Instead, he intended to create programs that called for "new federal partnerships" between national, state, and local governments, and to revitalize all three levels. Formalization of his concept began when he introduced the term "creative federalism" in an address on urban problems at the University of Michigan, May, 1964. The concept was clarified later that year in the course of his campaigning.

In speaking throughout the country, Johnson repeatedly stressed that he sought to broaden cooperative federalism to include not merely all levels of government, but also business, labor, private institutions, and individuals. Although Johnson held that working with private enterprise and local government was not new to the American government, Scheiber contends that the extensive manner in which Johnson included private enterprise did represent the first of several major departures from past practice. The President stressed the use of private and public means in the development of Appalachia and in the operation of the Poverty Program, for which he sought out business firms to operate job retraining centers and to train labor leaders and businessmen for participation in community action programs. In 1966, in both his messages on Transportation and Conservation, he urged private enterprise to aid in combating transportation problems and river pollution. The business world eagerly embraced President Johnson's new outlook, and hailed it as a positive break in the welfare-state trend.

Private interests have been quick to perceive that creative federalism promises to be operational consensus politics: it broadens the intergovernmental partnership to include elements of the private sector, even encouraging the involvement of rival private-interest groups eager to obtain a share of the influence and funds such programs offer.

The second significant departure from past federalist theories was the long-term objective of overall economic growth, as well as overall growth, of all levels of government "as a means of enlarging the problem-solving capacity of the society." The President, thus, was trying to speed up what he called the "tempo of effort" at all government levels with the net result of greater affluence.

In the manner of John Kenneth Galbraith, then, the Johnson administration is stressing the possibilities of affluence. It regards the revenue "pie" as one that is growing, and that must be helped to grow; and not as one that is static, so that slicing it in different proportions diminishes governmental power at one level while it enhances power at another.

President Johnson's final innovation was the implementation of a new administrative and planning method named the "Planning-Programming-Budgeting System." This system—derived from systems analysis, the Pentagon, and the program-budgeting of Secretary of Defense Robert McNamara—was aimed at finding the least costly alternative for meeting carefully defined and, preferably quantified, objectives.

Under PPBS, programs will be "project oriented"; and if the old political units or established administrative agencies are found irrelevant or obsolete, they will be disregarded. Program objectives, and budgeting of funds as well, will not be tied to the operations of specific Federal agencies or allocated to levels of government by formulae . . . solution[s] will be pursued pragmatically through whatever combination of public and private interests seems appropriate.

Scheiber hesitates in praising Johnson's new federalism. He foresees the possible clash of private interest groups, to the detriment of public programs, and an intensification of the "classic conflict" between policy-makers and the bureaucracy. In addition, observation of the "Planning-Programming-Budgeting System" in operation had already led to criticism of increased complexity, rather than smoother coordination, and a technocratic tone that Scheiber finds undesirable.

Scheiber concludes that if "creative federalism" is practiced as it exists in theory, the concept and practices of cooperative federalism may have to be totally discarded. We may see a destruction of the present balance of power between the various levels of government, and we must decide whether or not we want such change.

## Toward a more perfect Union

In the twentieth century, national–state cooperation has become a political issue, as well as a national concern. Legislators and bureaucrats at all levels have sought creative solutions to new problems. Traditionally, such solutions have included the federal grant-in-aid, which makes the resources of the national government available for financing programs administered by the state. Such federal grants are made for urban renewal, for land reclamation, vocational training, and countless other ventures. Nearly every grant program requires *the state* to match a proportion of the funds allocated. Although the state must comply with certain standards set by Congress or federal administrators, the actual operation of programs is decentralized, and local administrators make the decisions to enact policy. The federal role, then, is more financial and supervisory, and so serves to enhance the capabilities of state governments.

"You see, sir, my federal anti-poverty grant is now contingent on my ability to raise matching funds in the private sector . . ."

Drawing by Ed Fisher in the *Saturday Review*.

## Grants-in-aid

Grants-in-aid are the most traditional and significant forms of national–state cooperation. A *grant-in-aid* is a sum of money given by a higher level of government to a lower level of government for the development and/or expansion of specific programs in education, welfare, health, transportation, and other areas of public benefit. Examples of federal grants-in-aid can be found as early as 1785, when the national government gave land to states for the development of schools; but it is only since the 1930s that grants have become crucial to the financing of state and local programs. Today, state and local governments receive almost one-fifth of their annual budgets from the national government.

Although these grants have supplemented many needed programs, making it possible for poorer states to establish needed educational and welfare facilities, much controversy remains over the system of federal grants. Although the national government gives grants-in-aid to encourage the initiative of states and to minimize federal control, most grants-in-aid are given with certain stipulations and restrictions; for example, states are usually required to supplement federal funds with their own funds, establish agencies for the distribution of funds, and submit plans for national approval. If Washington does not approve the program's operation, the way money is spent, or the people doing the spending, the project may be abandoned.

These various controls have been instituted to insure that funds will be used honestly and effectively; however, the requirement that the money must be used for specific purposes, and that states must furnish matching grants, prevents states from spending money in those areas in which its needs may be greatest. For example, a state in need of more urban housing may not be able to receive enough federal funds to carry out a program. However, if federal funds for highway construction are available, it may be encouraged to spend money in this area, although the need for a new roadway is less pressing.

**Revenue sharing and block grants**

As an alternative to grants-in-aid, many observers in and out of government proposed *block grants* and *revenue sharing*. Far more flexible than grants-in-aid, block grants are blocks of money granted to states for programs in general areas, such as education, transportation, and health, without detailed prescriptions from the federal government. In addition, they do not require matching grants from the states. Several block-grant programs have already been established by the national government. In 1966, Congress gave numerous block grants for urban renewal under the *Demonstration Cities and Metropolitan Development Act*.

As another alternative to grants-in-aid, advocates of revenue sharing have proposed several programs. For example, President Nixon has proposed giving a certain portion of federal tax revenues to the states for state programs. Under this plan, each state would receive $16 million from the national government. Of this amount, $11 million would be redirected from current grants-in-aid. An additional $5 million would be provided for use by the state at its discretion; the plan would require that the money be used within five general program categories.

Although the grants-in-aid system continues to operate, debate still rages over the best way to help states to help themselves. Most debates over the relative merits of revenue sharing and block grants versus grants-in-aid reflect disagreements between men who maintain that Congress can best determine the use of money and those who believe that state and local governments are better equipped to do so. The first group contends that Congress best understands national needs, and that state and local governments are too inefficient and, occasionally, too corrupt to be given extensive freedom to use federal money without federal control. Supporters of local initiative argue that those governments closest to the problems are most effective in resolving them.

**Interstate compacts**

Since many problems are bistate or regional in nature rather than local or national, states have increasingly used *interstate compacts* to deal with them. Usually, a compact is negotiated between governors or their representatives, ratified by the legislatures of the states involved, and submitted to Congress for approval. Originally used to settle boundary disputes between states, interstate compacts are now used to handle many kinds of problems, including transportation, management of water resources, education, and the control of pollution; the best-known and most successful one is The Port of New York Authority, which was created in 1921 to administer interstate transportation between New York and New Jersey. Other compacts have created the Interstate Oil Compact Commission and the Interstate Great Lakes Commission. There are now over 150 interstate compacts.

Because these formal compacts do not cover all interstate problems or situations, more formal interstate agreements have been established to deal with particular problems—for example, residency and motor vehicle regulations. Often, these agreements have developed into political bodies, such as the Educational Commission of the States.

These compacts and commissions have been designed to facilitate interstate relations, but much difficulty still results from a lack of uniformity between the laws of the various states. Many states still have unique traffic signs, business laws, and court procedures. Despite the attempts that have been made to create uniform state laws in such crucial areas as narcotics and extradition, confusion still exists with individual states maintaining different laws for marriage, divorce, and abortion, for example. The real challenge for our federal system, therefore, is to create a system with enough uniformity to prevent confusion and hardship to individuals, and enough diversity to allow for experimentation and flexibility.

**City–state–national cooperation**

Cities have traditionally been considered both the prize and problem of state governments. Their increase in size and importance during this century is

"Tell us the part again about how we're going to live happily ever after . . ."

Drawing by Osrin;
© 1971 the Cleveland *Plain Dealer*.

enormous. Some cities today are larger than individual states; New York City, for example, has more people than the combined populations of Nevada, Colorado, and Rhode Island. Las Vegas accounts for almost one quarter of its state's inhabitants. Chicago has a population of three million, a total greater than New Mexico and Nebraska combined.

But most state legislatures, lacking the necessary financial resources, cannot appropriate large enough sums of money for their troubled urban areas. As a result, cities have been forced to turn to the national government for the funds and assistance that the states have been unwilling or unable to furnish. In March 1971, for example, the nation's mayors held a conference in Washington, D.C., to discuss the urban fiscal crisis. In fact, many city officials wield more influence in the national government than in their state capitols. Some large cities even have lobbyists in Washington. Urban mayors are likely to appeal to Washington, D.C., as well as to state governments for aid.

Many federal programs directly affect the activities of local government. Pollution control, urban renewal, sewage treatment, and welfare are examples of federal programs that have a strong impact on city government.

While states have also increased their efforts to help local governments to operate needed programs, there are strong indications—the current needs of the cities, the limited financial ability of state and local governments, and the growing cost of government services—that greater allocations of federal resources to local administrations will be necessary in the years to come.

*Morton Grodzins,* The American System (*Chicago: Rand McNally and Co., 1966*) *pp. 89–102.*

Morton Grodzins states that American police activity, although generally considered a typical example of a local function, in reality, reflects "the most intimate federal-state-local collaboration." For this reason, Grodzins refers to our present arrangement as a national police system.

Multilevel cooperation is necessary today because criminals are more mobile (many of them operating in and out of several states); syndicates also often operate in several states, providing illegal functions or transporting illegal goods in each, supplying artificial markets where natural ones do not exist, and communicating with workers and customers in scattered areas from central points.

In order to deal with this situation, law enforcement agencies have evolved on many levels in a piecemeal fashion. Local law enforcement units in counties, towns, and cities number approximately thirty-nine thousand. At the state level, every state, except Hawaii, maintains a police force. Although these state forces are generally concerned with highway patrol, the states of New York and Texas have criminal identification laboratories, assign state officers to a wide range of criminal problems, and hold training programs for local police forces.

At the national level, Grodzins outlines a "corresponding lack of neatness" in police forces. There are thirty-four independent enforcement or investigative agencies, organized under sixteen different commissions, departments, and agencies—the largest and most influential of which is the FBI—as well as police authorities under various other regulatory or service agencies.

These many components of the national police system have developed in an effort to enforce the new national legislation, and the even more rapidly expanding body of state laws and local ordinances. Grodzins writes that the aim of much of this legislation, which reached its height in the 1930s, is to aid states in their police enforcement, or to substitute federal penalties where state action is ineffective.

The greatest aid to state and local police from the national government lies in one particular body of law:

Perhaps the most significant federal laws in direct aid of state and local police work are those covering fugitive felons and witnesses, and persons attempting to avoid custody or confinement after conviction. . . . No initial federal offense need be involved. The federal offense is simply the act of attempting to avoid state prosecution. This legislation was passed at the request of state and local law enforcement officers. . . .

The robbery of a local bank with federally insured deposits illustrates the complete overlapping of state and federal laws, while stealing a car and transporting it over state lines illustrates breaking a state and then a federal law, respectively, or "the complementary quality of federal and state criminal legislation."

Collaboration, however, is by no means limited to those cases involving clear complementary or overlapping statutes. The mutual help relationship among federal, state, and local enforcement officers extends over the total area of their activity. There are in practice no "pure" federal or state or local fields of police work.

There have been attempts to overcome limited geographical jurisdictions of states by the formation of interstate compacts and uniform laws, such as those that aid in the capture and extradition of criminals. The chief formulators of these laws and compacts are the National Conference of Commissioners on Uniform State Law and the Drafting Committee of the Council of State Governments. Although the national government does not appear to have any part in such joint state undertakings, it stands in a prominent position when compacts are made, as it must approve them before they are effective.

In addition to complementary and overlapping legislation and enforcement agencies and interstate agreements, the Supreme Court plays an important role in the national police system by working toward uniformity of criminal law procedures.

The net effect of the Supreme Court's decisions on day-to-day police practices is difficult to gauge. A court decision invalidating a coerced confession does not end police brutality. Yet some direct impact of Supreme Court rulings can certainly be found at the local scene; and indirect effects follow state statutes which are at least partially the consequence of court decisions. The impact of the Court is by no means uniform with respect to states or to areas of police activity. And the major portion of criminal law administration remains relatively unaffected . . . . Nevertheless, the Supreme Court's decisions are clearly another nationalizing force in police work and criminal law administration.

# Federalism: How well does it work?

Throughout the nation's history, the growth of the powers of the national government has provoked controversy over the legitimacy, necessity, and effectiveness of a strong centralized authority. Although most people recognize the need for national supremacy in foreign affairs, they question the exercise of expanded authority over domestic affairs. Can American private enterprise be regulated by the national government? Does the national government have the right to alter relationships between labor and management in individual states?

[11] Thomas P. Ronan, "Buckley Calls His Two Rivals 'White Flag' Candidates on War," *The New York Times,* September 2, 1970, 29.

Some of these questions have been resolved; but many more are still vital political issues that have been debated in recent political campaigns. James Buckley, for instance, in his successful 1970 campaign for the United States Senate, advocated the return of *governmental* responsibility to state and local officials, and declared that competent local officials would do a better job than those in Washington.[11]

## The case for decentralization

Those men who favor reduced national power are sometimes *states' righters,* or advocates of stronger state control, or sometimes, simply advocates of "decentralization."

Today in general, members of the conservative wings of the two major political parties, as well as a few Republican liberals, favor decentralization. These men argue that the Constitution is a compact created *by* the states *for* the people. The compact delegates specified powers to the national government for the purpose of dealing with problems that are too large for individual states to handle on their own. However, in the case of conflicts over the exercise of power, advocates of decentralization contend that the states should receive preference. Practically speaking, they reason that since the states remain closer to the people than the more remote national government, they are more aware of what is beneficial for the people.

States' righters note that decentralization makes it possible for states to initiate new policies and programs on an experimental basis. If the programs are successful, other states can adopt them; if unsuccesful, then other states do not suffer from such a failure, a situation which might occur were the program first carried out on a national scale. Localized power makes it possible for individual states to develop programs geared to the particular needs of an area. A more theoretical argument advanced by some states' righters maintains that decentralization of power is essential for the prevention of arbitrary government. According to this argument, it is only through decentralizing power that America can prevent the creation of an unresponsive and perhaps even tyrannical government.

## The case for centralization

Those people who favor a strong central government are called *nationalists*, and advocates of "centralization." Nationalists argue that the powers delegated to the national government by the Constitution should be interpreted broadly. In cases of conflict between a state and the national government, the national government should be given priority, since it speaks for *all* of the people in the nation, rather than some of the people in the states.

Proponents of a strong centralized government point out that only the national government has the resources, talents, and political institutions to deal effectively with the problems of a continental, industrialized nation. Inasmuch as almost all commercial, educational, and social problems in the United States cross state borders, they must be dealt with on a national level. Furthermore, advocates of centralization argue that in times of crises, such as war and economic crisis, only the national government can promote effective action. Individual states lack the resources, manpower, and authority to deal with large-scale problems.

Advocates of centralization also demonstrate that states are often unwilling, or unable, to deal satisfactorily with their own problems. Many states simply do not have the financial resources to provide adequate educational and welfare benefits for their citizens. Wealthy states, on the other hand, may be ruled by conservative property-owners from suburban areas who refuse to give aid to the blighted and congested urban areas that need help the most. Advocates of centralization maintain that, in such cases, a strong national government is needed to provide funds and institute reform.

## Federalism and self-interest

It is important to realize that most groups and individuals evaluate the federal system—particularly, the expansion of the national government—in terms of their political needs, rather than in response to a political philosophy.

Thus, almost all political parties and interest groups—Democrats, Republicans, Socialists, businessmen, laborers, and farmers—have advocated, at one time, a strong central government. For example, during the late nineteenth century, businessmen favored the central government because that government was sympathetic to their interests. As labor agitation increased, however, and the government began to establish laws more favorable to labor than to management, the businessmen and the Republicans began to favor states' rights, since their influence was greater in the state legislature than in the national Congress. Similarly, segregationists have tended to favor states' rights because state support of the policies is far more easily obtained than national sanction. On the other hand, in the past few decades, federal policies have benefited such groups as labor, education, welfare recipients, and farmers. "Liberal" Democrats, labor leaders, civil rights leaders, and their like, who support national programs in these areas, inherently tend to support a strong central government. Were the national government to suddenly cease its activities in these areas, these same groups might look to the states for support.

Thus, people and groups may favor a stronger national government or stronger state governments, not out of any altruistic or theoretical consideration, but because they believe one or the other governing body will be more responsive to their policy goals.

## Federalism: Strengths and weaknesses

Federalism is even more difficult to assess than it is to describe. Certainly, federalism has been generally successful in America, and it retains the support of most Americans. The operation of the local units has made it possible for the national government to concentrate on problems of national dimensions. At the same time, the states have proved to be valuable testing grounds for experimental programs in fields such as highway safety, water pollution, and education. In addition, state and local politics have provided valuable "workshops" for the training of future congressmen, federal judges, and even Presidents. If federalism has worked in America, it is probably because it reflects our distrust of concentrated government power and our belief in individual initiative. For despite the growing centralization of power, state and local governments exercise more authority than ever before in our history.

It must also be realized, however, that this diffusion of power has been a source of weakness, as well as strength. Needed reforms often are slow to be instituted; thus, delay and a degree of inefficiency are built into a federal system of government. Some proponents of civil rights reforms contend that this system has hampered the reform. At times, the laws of the separate states may conflict and legal complications result. Overlapping powers may cause an unnecessary duplication of government functions.

Consequently, whatever the advantages and disadvantages of American federalism, it cannot be denied that federalism entails a mosaic of interactions among national, state, and local governments. Political scientist Richard Leach has summarized this characteristic of American federalism in the following way:

> Governmental power in the United States is, in sum, a matter for the joint exertion of the several units of government who among them share the responsibility for serving the people of the nation. There is no formula for the exact distribution of that responsibility; it is something that has to be determined in each case by the needs to be met, the pressures involved in bringing it to the attention of government, and the availability of resources to provide for it. Every time an exertion of power is called for, how it shall be made becomes a subject of debate and controversy, often protracted and sometimes bitter. Power is always in contest. That is the key to understanding the federal system.[12]

[12] Richard H. Leach, *American Federalism* (New York: W. W. Norton and Co., Inc., 1970), p. 45.

# Glossary

**bill of attainder** Legislative act which singles out either named persons or easily ascertainable members of a group for punishment without judicial trial.

**block grants** Blocks of money that are granted to states for programs in certain general areas and not for specific kinds of programs.

**centralized government** System in which almost all major decisions are made by national or central government without consulting local governments.

**concurrent powers** Powers shared by state and national government.

**confederation** System in which the decision-making powers are concentrated in the local government; the central government has only those powers given to it by local units of government.

**cooperative federalism** Type of federalism in which local, state, and national governments share the responsibility for providing services to the citizens.

**delegated powers** Powers given to the Congress by Article I, Section 8 of the Constitution. Also called express powers.

**dual federalism** Type of federalism in which the powers of the national and state governments are separate and distinct.

**due process of law** Clauses found in both the Fifth and Fourteenth Amendments which state that the federal and state governments, respectively, shall not deprive any individual of "life, liberty, or property, without due process of law."

**ex post facto laws** Retroactive laws that increase the punishment of a crime after it has been committed or make criminal an act which was legal when it was performed.

**express powers** Powers given to the Congress by Article I, Section 8, of the Constitution; also called delegated powers.

**extradition** Provision of Article IV, Section 2 of the Constitution, providing that an individual charged in any state with treason, felony, or other cirme who has fled from justice and is found in another state shall be returned to the state having jurisdiction over the crime.

**federalism** System of government in which power is divided between a central or national government and smaller geographic units of government, usually under the authority of a written constitution.

**full faith and credit** Provision of Article IV, Section 1 of the Constitution, requiring states to honor the civil rulings of other states (public acts, records, and judicial proceedings).

**grant-in-aid** A sum of money given by a higher level of government to a lower level of government to help finance specific governmental activities.

**implied powers** Powers given Congress in the necessary and proper clause of Article I, Section 8 of the Constitution, enabling the national government to carry out its express powers.

**interstate compact** Agreement between states for the solution of common problems which, according to Article I, Section 10 of the Constitution are forbidden without consent of Congress.

**Judiciary Act of 1789** Congressional act which established a basis for judicial review, that is, by creating a federal judicial system, its jurisdiction, organization, and procedure, and provided in Section 25 for a system of appeals from the state courts to the Supreme Court in cases concerned with the Constitution, federal laws, and treaties.

**national supremacy**   Doctrine in Article VI of the Constitution which declares that the Constitution and all national laws and treaties are the supreme law of the land.

**nationalists**   Those who advocate centralization of powers and thus a strong central government.

**privileges and immunities**   Provision of Article IV, Section 2 of the Constitution which prohibits a state from discriminating against citizens of another state in favor of its own. (A similar clause is found in the Fourteenth Amendment barring the states from denying freedoms inherent in citizenship to its citizens.)

**reserve powers**   Powers not already delegated to the national government, that are given to the states—by virtue of the Ninth Amendment to the Constitution.

**revenue sharing**   Alternative to grants-in-aid in which states are given a certain portion of federal tax revenues for use in financing state programs.

**states' righters**   Those who advocate "decentralization" of government and thus strong state powers.

**writ of habeas corpus**   A judicial writ provided for in Article I, Section 9 of the Constitution and applicable except in times of rebellion or invasion, which protects an individual from arbitrary arrest by requiring the government officers who hold him in custody to bring him to court, and there state the reasons for his arrest.

**Supreme Court decisions**

*Ex Parte Milligan* (1866)   Declared void President Lincoln's suspension of the writ of habeas corpus and the use of military tribunals, rather than the courts, to try persons accused of crime.

*In re Debs* (1895)   Upheld presidential action of obtaining an injunction to intervene in a railroad strike on the grounds that the strike would interfere with interstate commerce by disrupting the movement of mails.

*Katzenbach* v. *McClung* (1964)   Upheld a provision of the Civil Rights Act of 1964 outlawing discrimination in restaurants where "a substantial portion of the food" served comes from other states, and is therefore subject to federal regulation under the interstate commerce clause.

*Luther* v. *Borden* (1849)   Upheld congressional and executive power to quell domestic insurrection and to judge whether or not the government of a state is of a "republican character."

*McCulloch* v. *Maryland* (1819)   Major Supreme Court decision, in which the Court broadly interpreted the doctrine of implied powers and upheld the supremacy of the national government within its constitutional area of authority.

*Missouri* v. *Holland* (1920)   Upheld national government's power to make treaties, and to make laws to implement those treaties in areas which, in the absence of a treaty, would be reserved to the states.

*Pollock* v. *Farmers' Loan and Trust Co.* (1895)   Declared a federal income tax unconstitutional by maintaining that income taxes were "direct" taxes and therefore subject to the Constitution's specification of apportionment among the states according to population.

*United States* v. *Darby* (1941)   Declared the Fair Labor Standards Act of 1938 constitutional and thus upheld the power of Congress to regulate interstate commerce.

*Virginia* v. *Tennessee* (1893)   Ruled that only certain types of interstate compacts required the approval of Congress in order to protect national supremacy.

# Suggested readings

Anderson, William, *The Nation and the States: Rivals or Partners?* (Minneapolis: University of Minnesota Press, 1967). Originally published in 1955. Study of the historical relationship between nation and state, and exploration of the present relationship, by a well-known political scientist and member of the Commission on Intergovernmental Relations.

Clark, Jane P., *The Rise of a New Federalism: Federal-State Cooperation in the United States* (New York: Columbia University Press, 1938). Discussion of the several varieties of federal-state cooperation.

Earle, Valerie, ed., *Federalism: Infinite Variety in Theory and Practice* (Itasia, Ill.: F. E. Peacock Publishers, Inc., 1968). Collection of essays on the various forms of federalism.

Elazar, Daniel, *The American Partnership: Intergovernmental Cooperation in the Nineteenth Century United States* (Chicago: University of Chicago Press, 1962). Study of nineteenth-century federalism, pointing out that many domestic governmental activities were cooperative endeavors shared by both national and state agencies.

Elazar, Daniel, *American Federalism: A View from the States* (New York: Crowell, Collier and Macmillan, Inc., 1966). Study of American federalism, emphasizing the importance of the states in the American political system.

Fesler, James W., *Area and Administration* (University, Ala.: University of Alabama Press, 1964). Originally published in 1949. Series of lectures on the problems arising from functional and regional administrations.

Goldwin, Robert A., ed., *A Nation of States: Essays on the American Federal System* (Chicago: Rand McNally and Co., 1963). Five essays on the American federal system by noted political scientists and editors.

Graves, William B., *American Intergovernmental Relations: Their Origins, Historical Development, and Current Status* (New York: Charles Scribner's Sons, 1964). Comprehensive discussion of intergovernmental relations in America.

Grodzins, Morton, *The American System: A New View of Government in the United States*, ed. by D. J. Elazar (Chicago: Rand McNally and Co., 1966). Evaluation of the federal government's effectiveness; emphasizes the theory that the government is most effective when the traditional division of power is modified in favor of governmental cooperation and sharing of functions and responsibilities.

Kilpatrick, James J., *The Sovereign States: Notes on a Citizen of Virginia* (Chicago: Henry Regnery Co., 1957). Defense of the states' rights position, asserting the need for greater sovereignty of states and less consolidation by the federal government.

Maass, Arthur, ed., *Area and Power* (New York: The Free Press, 1959). Studies in the problems of operating within a governmental system where powers are divided.

MacMahon, Arthur W., ed., *Federalism: Mature and Emergent* (New York: Doubleday and Co., Inc., 1955). Selected essays analyzing the role of federalism in America and in the world.

Mason, Alpheus T., *The States Rights Debate: Anti-Federalism and the Constitution* (Englewood Cliffs, N.J.: Prentice-Hall, Inc., 1964). Anti-federalist thought viewed through the debates that took place in the state conventions for ratification of the Constitution.

Riker, William H., *Federalism: Origins, Operation, Significance* (Boston: Little, Brown and Co., 1964). Short excellent study of federalism.

Rockefeller, Nelson A., *The Future of Federalism* (Cambridge, Mass.: Harvard University Press, 1962). Defense of federalism by the Governor of New York.

Schmidhauser, John R., *The Supreme Court as Final Arbiter in Federal-State Relations, 1789–1957* (Chapel Hill: University of North Carolina Press, 1958). Discussion of the Supreme Court as an umpire of the American federal system.

Schwartz, Bernard, *A Commentary on the Constitution of the United States*, 2 vols. (New York: The Macmillan Co., 1968). In-depth discussion of federalism (vol. 1) and presidential powers (vol. 2).

Wheare, Kenneth C., *Federal Government*, 4th ed. (New York: Oxford University Press, Inc., 1964). Originally published in 1946. Standard comparative study of federalism.

Wildavsky, Aaron, ed., *American Federalism in Perspective* (Boston: Little, Brown and Co., 1967). Thirteen essays written between 1945 and 1966, containing general theory, analysis, comparative examples, and historical experience of American federalism.

# Topics of further study

Peterson, Wilfred H., "American Federal System and Church-State Relations," *Western Political Quarterly*, Spring 1963, pp. 598–609.

Watson, Richard, "Federalism vs. Individual Rights: The Legal Squeeze on Self-Incrimination," *American Political Science Review*, December 1960, pp. 887–898.

# 6 urban america

## challenge to the federal system

CONTEMPORARY AMERICA is almost exclusively a "city" civilization. Despite her pioneer ancestry and frontier destiny, most Americans live in cities, work in cities, and visit other cities on vacations. For many Americans the Wild West is a myth perpetrated by Metro-Goldwyn-Mayer; the range is a place to cook on, and an expensive stereo is a more meaningful success symbol than an expensive steer. Few Americans have seen the vast expanse of land that stretches from the Mississippi to the Rockies, and few plan to see it.

Yet, in spite of the predominance of urban living, the American city is virtually ignored as a political unit in the Constitution, which seeks to define the distribution of governmental power within the United States. In the Constitution, our most authoritative political document, cities and metropolitan areas are never mentioned. All local power springs from the power "reserved to the states"—and in most state constitutions the power of cities is severely restricted. This exclusion of the city as a significant political unit has created tremendous problems for modern government on all levels; yet it is not difficult to understand why it occurred.

The America of 1790 was radically different from the America of 1970. Cities, as we know them, did not exist. America was truly a frontier and rural civilization, a land dominated by farms, ranches, and plantations. Less than 3 percent of the 3,929,000 Americans who were counted in the first official census lived in towns of more than 10,000. Philadelphia led all the other cities with a population of 40,000 (the approximate

[1] U.S. Bureau of the Census, 1970.

size of the smallest town in Massachusetts). New York was second with a population of 25,000, and Boston third, with a population of 16,000. Today, greater Philadelphia has more than 2 million people; New York, 8 million; and Boston, 700,000.[1]

Not only were early American cities significantly smaller than even a moderate-sized modern city, but they lacked the sophistication we associate with a modern urban center. Carriages and wagons, chased by packs of yelping dogs, clattered noisily along cobblestone or gravel streets, often scattering flocks of chickens. Sheep and cattle were herded through the

*The difference between an eighteenth-century city and a twentieth-century city is clearly seen in these photographs of Detroit in 1794 and 1971.*

streets to the butchers, and pigs roamed untended, dining on garbage. Shops displayed merchandise seldom found in the country store—delicate fabrics, silver buckles, imported china, telescopes, and clocks—and rum flowed cheaply and plentifully in the city taverns. Prostitutes, dope peddlers, and gamblers walked the streets freely, while "respectable" young ladies sat quietly at home behind massive oak doors, sewing samplers and petticoats.

In the early 1800s, people began to move into the cities. "How Ya Gonna Keep Them Down on the Farm" became a theme song long before it was written, as the lights of New York and Philadelphia beckoned not only the dispossessed, but the ambitious and the adventuresome.

But although America was rapidly becoming a nation of cities and large towns, the nation's political system was still geared to a rural civilization. While droves of people moved into urban centers, the state remained the most powerful unit of subordinate government. Even though cities required special laws and special funds to provide services for the masses of people living in them, their state governments refused to give them the legal authority to pass the laws or collect the funds. And today we are grappling with the con-

sequences of this undeniable paradox and problem: four-fifths of our nation's taxable wealth is concentrated in urban areas, along with our major industries, television stations, newspapers, and intellectual institutions, yet the city is a poorly defined and still subservient political entity. John Lindsay, the mayor of New York City, is responsible for more people than the governors of Utah, Nevada, and Arizona together, yet on paper has less power and independence than any one of these men. It is for these reasons that cities are finally demanding the attention and concern that they merit. If America is to survive, it must come to terms with the city as a fundamental and significant unit of political life.

## The modern metropolis

[2] The U.S. Bureau of the Census in 1970 defines a standard metropolitan statistical area (SMSA) as a central city of at least 50,000 inhabitants and "adjacent counties that are . . . metropolitan in character and economically and socially integrated with the county of the central city." In 1968, 237 SMSAs were counted.

[3] This problem of overlapping boundaries is hardly a recent occurrence. See Robert C. Wood, *1400 Governments* (Cambridge, Mass.: Harvard University Press, 1961) for a description of the complex organization in New York Ctiy.

A major problem facing local and national governments is the diverse nature of modern cities. The simple straightforward cities of 1790 no longer exist. Today we have *central cities* surrounded by *suburbs*. These central cities and suburbs together form metropolitan areas.

Broadly speaking, a *metropolitan area* is an integrated social and economic unit containing a recognizable center of dense population, the *metropolis*.[2] This metropolis, or central city, is usually surrounded by a large fringe area of smaller cities, towns, villages, and communities—the suburbs of the metropolitan area. Some of these outlying communities are controlled by the metropolis; others are legally and financially independent. Almost all of them, however, have local governments with varying degrees of authority, overlapping boundaries, and overlapping functions. According to the 1970 Census, the metropolitan area of Portland included 374 distinct local governments; that of Pittsburgh, 806; and that of Chicago, more than 1,000.[3] This abundance of governmental authorities makes it almost impossible to govern a large metropolitan area efficiently and effectively.

In addition to the problems created by overlapping local governments, some metropolitan areas are so large that they sprawl over several states, creating conflicts on the state level as well. The residents of Trenton, New Jersey, for example, are affected by the affairs of both New York City and Philadelphia.

Daniel Elazar, "Are We a Nation of Cities?" The Public Interest, *no. 4,* (Summer 1966), *pp. 42–58.*

Daniel Elazar sees the reality of the city as quite different, and less foreboding, than what it has mythically been made out to be. He suggests that American cities are not unmanageable, for in fact, they are only semiurban in nature: large metropolitan areas are really clusters of small, essentially nonurban units.

What is developing in the United States is the spread of a relatively low-density population engaged in urban economic pursuits; many of these American-style city dwellers actually live on plots of land that would look large to a Chinese or Indian farmer.

This semiurban character reflects three major factors. Americans have historically praised *agrarianism* while being suspicious of city life—they moved to cities for economic gain while maintaining the old values of low-density development, family solidarity, individualism, and private ownership. An additional factor is *metropolitanism*. Elazar argues that, except for factory towns, most of our cities were formed to serve the hinterland around them. Though our country displays a high degree of *nomadism*, with one out of every five families moving each year, these moves generally occur between cities and suburbs. Thus, Americans remain in metropolitan areas, switching political involvement from one local community to another. The conclusion, writes Elazar, is that "in fact, the American urban place is a non-city because Americans wish it to be just that."

According to Elazar, if the city is in crisis, this crisis is merely a response to problems of the environment that do not call for drastic structural changes in our political system.

## Population Increase in a Metropolitan Area, San Jose, California

Source: "Populations of the Largest Metropolitan Areas: 1970, from *The World Almanac, 1971*; 466. © Hammond Incorporated #10379.

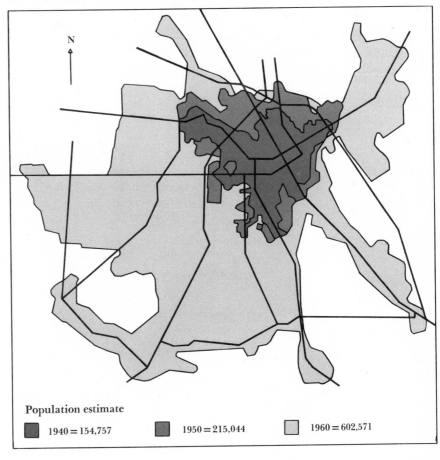

N

**Population estimate**

| | | |
|---|---|---|
| ■ 1940 = 154,757 | ■ 1950 = 215,044 | □ 1960 = 602,571 |

Students of urban affairs predict that if this pattern persists—and there is every indication that it will—the United States will soon be characterized by strips of densely populated areas, or *megalopoli*, which will stretch for hundreds of miles without a definable break. The so-called East Coast Megalopolis, a continuous belt of cities, towns, and suburbs that stretches from lower New Hampshire to upper Virginia, now contains 38 million people.[4] Urban specialists further predict that similar megalopoli will develop around the Great Lakes and down the length of the California coast and that 60 percent of our population will, by 1975, inhabit these strip cities. If so, the existing problems of maintaining authority and distributing services will become even more complex.

[4] Named by Jean Gottman in *Megalopolis: The Urbanized Eastern Seaboard of the United States* (New York: The Twentieth Century Fund, 1961).

# The shame of the central city

Diversity is only one of the problems that central cities now face. Even greater problems are those inherent in the very nature of such cities—congestion, crime, poverty, pollution, unemployment, unrest, and violence.

## Congestion and lack of planning

When people migrated to the cities from the rural areas of this country, or from the depressed nations abroad, they did so with the hope of finding new homes, new positions, and a new life. But their dreams were usually fuller than their pocketbooks. They found temporary and makeshift lodgings where they could—and instead of moving out they tended to make room for relatives and friends. While new buildings were constructed to accommodate growing families and businesses, they were generally built without planning or foresight. As a result, most central cities are today helter-skelter arrangements of apartment houses, stores, restaurants, and small businesses, all crowded together without rhyme or reason. Although many urban dwellers revel in the diversity of a large central city, it creates political problems for the men who try to govern.

The most tragic results of irrational growth are the troubled *ghettos* that exist in nearly every city in the United States. These areas today house large numbers of poor people, most of whom are black, Puerto Rican, or Mexican. The crowded and congested nature of these communities makes disease and crime common; such problems concern not only those people living in the ghettos, but those living in other areas of the city.

In order to remedy this situation, urban specialists are now studying ways of making central cities livable for those who want to live in them or must live in them. To implement these studies, the national government has allocated large sums of money to be used expressly for the purpose of renovating and rebuilding slum areas. In 1966, President Johnson signed the *Demonstration Cities and Metropolitan Development Act*, which authorized

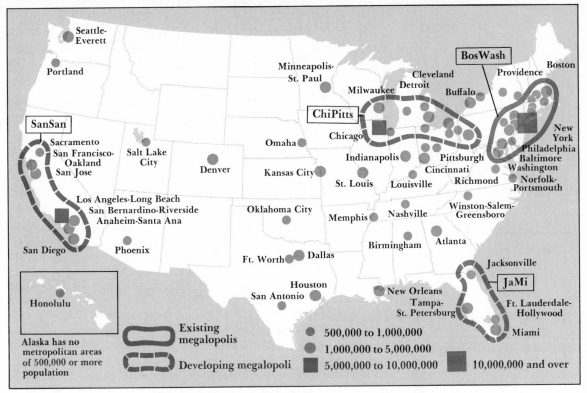

## Populations of the Largest Metropolitan Areas in 1970

Source: Reprinted with permission of the Macmillan Company from SICK CITIES by Mitchell Gordon. © by Mitchell Gordon, 1963; 21.

more than $900 million to be used over a period of two years for the building of new towns or "model cities" and the redevelopment of impoverished areas. More recently, President Nixon directed the funds used for the "Model Cities" plan into a branch of his own program of revenue sharing (which will be discussed later in this chapter).

*John F. Kain and John R. Meyer, "Transportation and Poverty," The Public Interest, no. 18 (Winter 1970), pp. 75–87.*

John Kain and John Meyer present the findings of a conference on transportation and poverty that they chaired on June 7, 1968.

After the 1965 Watts riots in Los Angeles, it was pointed out that better transportation for the poor would increase their job opportunities. Presently, transportation to central business districts from the centrally located residential districts, where most of the poor live, is adequate, but in the past twenty years, job opportunities have grown faster outside the central city. In order to get to the suburbs, more and more people use cars; yet a car is an expensive investment that demands a large initial cash layout, and consumes continual operating costs.

The urban poor, therefore, must rely on public transportation, which rarely provides a direct link between slum and suburb. The poor must travel first to the central business district, then transfer; the total trip usually involves two fares and long waits. As a result, many must refuse overtime employment. And to avoid the inconvenience, the poor who must work in the suburbs quickly seek car-pool service or purchase cars themselves.

The authors pinpoint the dilemma:

Increasingly, low-income workers are forced to choose between a higher-paying job that is inaccessible by public transit, and thereby pay more for transportation (e.g., by buying and operating an automobile), or a lower-paying job that is served by transit. To put it in somewhat different terms, low-income households now have at their disposal at most only a bit more, and oftentimes less, transit service than they once did for reaching what is, in effect, a much larger metropolitan region.

The suburban working situation is especially difficult for the low-income black, who finds it difficult to relocate outside the ghetto. He must stay where he is and pay more for his transportation.

To solve this problem, the authors state that city governments must improve "opportunities, employment and incomes" for the poor. Mere improvement of transportation may not be sufficient. In fact, transportation renovations in San Francisco and Boston have not benefited the ghettoized: the authors believe these cities' investments may actually be regressive.

Several suggestions for urban transit improvement emerged from the conference. One ambitious program is free public transportation, but the authors feel that such a program would cost a great deal, and even with the extra expense, service might not improve.

Another often-heard opinion is that the costs of public transit to the suburban area would far outweigh the costs of using private automobiles. Instead of improving mass transit, it is suggested that new or relatively new cars be leased, rented, or financed to the poor. However, the authors contend that, "Cheap used cars are seldom low-cost cars." And what of the nondriver? Increased automobile ownership may only deteriorate the quality of public transit by costing it additional revenue. Thus the authors propose a service similar to present taxi services, but better-run and capable of carrying more people in each vehicle. The cost of each ride in such a system would lie between the cost of a public bus and a private taxicab, and the service would be far more convenient. In addition, if it were not for present restrictions on franchises and group fares, taxi operations could simply be modified to produce full or part-time jobs for the poor. A family car could serve as a taxi on the side, thus defraying part of its high cost and providing more mobility for the owners. Kain and Meyer urge cities to adopt these plans in an effort to find low-investment solutions to the problem of urban transportation for the poor.

## Unemployment

Closely related to the problem of congestion, and even more basic according to some economists, are the problems of unemployment and underemployment. Most people who migrated or emigrated to the central cities lacked not only money, but the language proficiency, educational background, and skills needed to secure good positions. It was (and still is) difficult for them to find any but the most menial and low-paying jobs. As soon as they did move up the economic ladder, they also moved out. Their place, however, was soon taken by new blocs of unskilled and undereducated people.

In most American cities these new blocs of unskilled or undereducated Americans are black, Puerto Rican, or Mexican. Like the German, Irish,

### Percentage of Black Population in Cities and Suburbs

| | 1970 City | 1970 Suburb | 1960 City | 1960 Suburb |
|---|---|---|---|---|
| Washington | 71 | 26 | 54 | 24 |
| Newark | 54 | 19 | 34 | 13 |
| Gary, Ind. | 53 | 18 | 39 | 15 |
| Atlanta | 51 | 22 | 38 | 23 |
| Baltimore | 46 | 24 | 35 | 21 |
| New Orleans | 45 | 31 | 37 | 31 |
| Detroit | 44 | 18 | 29 | 15 |
| Wilmington, Del. | 44 | 12 | 26 | 12 |
| Birmingham, Ala. | 42 | 30 | 40 | 32 |
| Richmond | 42 | 25 | 42 | 26 |
| St. Louis | 41 | 16 | 29 | 14 |
| Memphis | 39 | 38 | 38 | 38 |
| National (67 largest metropolitan areas) | 23.3 | 4.5 | 17.7 | 4.2 |
| Actual numbers | 12,487,000 | 2,577,000 | 9,097,000 | 1,815,000 |

Source: "Data on Black Population," *The New York Times*, February 11, 1971, p. 24; © 1971 by The New York Times Company. Reprinted by permission.

From *The Herblock Gallery* (Simon & Schuster, 1968).

"Help!"

and Eastern European immigrants who came to America during the late nineteenth and early twentieth centuries, these Americans have moved to the central cities seeking opportunity, money, and freedom. For example, in 1910, 73 percent of all blacks lived in farm areas; by 1960, 73 percent had moved into central cities. Today, four central cities, as compared to one in 1960, have black majorities, and seven have a 40 percent black population. Most of the blacks who have made central cities their home cannot earn enough to properly support themselves or their families, and many are on welfare. According to Duane Lockard, these blacks are "a proletariat somewhat in the sense of which Marx meant the term: a dispossessed, jobless, alienated mass of people who are becoming increasingly rebellious."[5]

While the plight of the blacks is more pronounced than at any time in

[5] Duane Lockard, *The Politics of State and Local Government*, 2nd ed. (New York: The Macmillan Co., 1969), p. 483.

history, efforts to solve this problem are also more pronounced than at any time in history. Almost all cities have instituted special training programs designed to upgrade the skills of unskilled citizens. Many programs are sponsored by the national government (Head Start and Upward Bound, for example); others are sponsored by local governments and work in conjunction with local educational institutions and businesses. Most programs seek to provide the unskilled with the education, skills, and motivation that will enable them to secure steady and well-paying jobs. El Centro Junior College in Dallas and Cuyahoga Community College in Cleveland are current examples of systems, that have adopted a program of the "open enrollment" policy, which enables students with poor high school training to receive a college education. In addition to these training and educational programs, many cities are inaugurating day-care centers that will provide suitable environments for the children of mothers who want or need to work.

## Increasing taxes and decreasing services

Because of the large number of people that live, and work, in central cities, the costs of providing basic services, such as transportation, sanitation, pollution control, and education, are enormously high. In New York City, for example, 4,500,000 people ride the subways every day; 2,300,000 ride the buses; and 1,800,000 ride the Long Island Railroad. Although these facilities are used by millions of people who do not live in New York City, much of the revenue for operating them comes from city taxes. In addition to transportation services, most large cities must provide their populations with other essential and expensive services, such as education, medical care, housing, and welfare.

*Edward C. Banfield,* The Unheavenly City *(Boston: Little, Brown and Co., 1970), pp. 185–209.*

A major problem of city government is the control of disorders, or what has commonly come to be known as the issue of law and order. According to Edward Banfield, solving the problem lies in part in determining its cause, and he has turned to the black ghetto as a case in point.

The common assumptions that ghetto disorders are racially motivated and that they harm the black cause, are challenged by Banfield.

He argues first that black "riots" are emotional outbursts. They may simply be rampages sparked by an incident or they may be motivated by indignation or the desire to steal or further a political ideology. But the tenet that racial causes are primary is rejected.

The assumption that if Negroes riot it must be *because* they are Negroes is naive. If one rejects this as a starting place and looks at the facts instead, one sees that race (and, incidentally, poverty as well) was not *the* cause of any of the Negro riots and that it had very little to do with many of the lesser ones. Indeed, it is probably not too much to say that some of the riots would have occurred even if (other things being the same) the people in the riot areas had all been white and even if they had all had incomes above the poverty line. The implication of this view is, of course, that punishing police misconduct, providing decent housing, and so on will not significantly affect the amount of Negro rioting. The causes of rioting, it will be argued, will continue to operate for another twenty years or so no matter what is done.

In addition, Banfield believes that "although more and possibly worse riots are to be expected, rioting will not destroy the cities." Rather, he foresees positive results.

The immediate effects of the burning, looting, and killing are of little importance as compared to the enduring changes in attitudes, feelings, and opinions that have been brought about by the rioting. . . . The rioting may have given Negroes a new pride (that the facts do not justify it is of course beside the point), and this may do more for the lower-class Negro than all the compensatory education, public housing, job training, and community organization that could be provided with a dozen Freedom Budgets. It may also have impressed whites as nothing else would with the need for immediate and far-reaching reforms, and this may—although there is no reason for confidence—lead to much good and little or no harm.

Employed city residents, already overtaxed, resent the fact that they must pay more and more for less and less, and so they are moving out to the suburbs. Businesses and industries are following. As a result, central cities are losing not only essential and necessary revenue; they are losing skills and leadership. Not only do they lack the money to provide basic services for the poor and transient members of their central cities; they lack personnel who can perform these services. Many teachers, for example, are reluctant to teach in city schools dominated by racial tension and conflict. Similarly, many doctors and nurses are hesitant to practice in the over-burdened and ill-equipped city hospitals. Yet, good education and good medical services are desperately needed by the deprived populations of the city. In order to perform these seemingly impossible services, cities have had to offer attractive salaries, pension plans, and medical benefits to city employees. Since they cannot really afford these bonuses, they are now in serious financial trouble. For some of them the threat of bankruptcy is real; and for others it promises to become real unless measures are taken to refurbish city budgets.

It is for these reasons, argue politicians and urban experts, that central cities must be given increased attention and probably assistance. In 1968, the Advisory Commission on Intergovernmental Relations concluded that

6 Advisory Commission on Intergovernmental Relations, *Ninth Annual Report* (Washington, D.C.: Government Printing Office, 1968), p. 14.

the problems of central cities may well lead our federal system to the brink of destruction. According to the Commission, the way in which these problems are met "will largely determine the fate of the American political system; it will determine if we can maintain a form of government marked by partnership and wholesome competition among National, State, and local levels, or if instead—in the face of threatened anarchy—we must sacrifice political diversity as the price of the authoritative action required for the nation's survival."[6]

# The suburban solution

As a result of the central city's problems, each year more and more urban dwellers are turning to the suburbs—the Scarsdales, Shaker Heights', and Levittowns—for relief and restoration. These disenchanted urbanites hope to trade the problems and frustrations of city life—congestion, crime, pollution, racial conflict—for the quiet safety of the suburban community. Seldom, however, are their hopes fulfilled.

Drawing by H. Martin; © 1970
The New Yorker Magazine, Inc.

**Move to the suburbs**

Suburban communities developed in the nineteenth century when the introduction of trains made it possible to commute daily from outlying areas to the inner cities. Suburban communities sprang up along the railroad lines radiating out of central cities. However, not until 1920, and the introduction of the automobile, did suburbs as we know them develop. The improvement in automobile travel made it possible for scores of people to travel long distances easily and quickly, and the lure of the suburbs became as strong as the lure of the cities had been formerly. What began as a trend, soon turned into an exodus, as masses of people left the cities to find fresh air, green lawns, and quiet streets.

In 1950, 56.6 million Americans were living in central cities and 55 million were living in suburbs. Although the population in metropolitan areas continued to increase during the 1960s, this increase occurred mostly in the suburbs rather than in the central cities, where population generally declined. For example, the population of St. Louis dropped 18.9 percent, while the population of its suburbs grew more than 75 percent. Similarly, Milwaukee's population dropped 4.3 percent during this time, while its suburbs swelled by more than 40 percent.[7] Only a few new western and southern cities increased in size during this period.

[7] "Census," *Congressional Quarterly*, XXVIII, no. 3 (July 3, 1970): 1957.

## Suburban problems

Urban difficulties began to repeat themselves in suburbia. The move to the suburbs was so great and massive that many suburban communities turned into minor urban centers with major urban problems. In many suburban communities, for example, a teenager can purchase a bag of heroin almost as easily as he can on the crowded thoroughfares of downtown Chicago or Los Angeles. Similarly, his parents are burdened with the same high cost of living they sought to escape, this time in the form of high property taxes to compensate for the lack of industry in the suburbs.

The pastoral greenery that many urbanites sought in the suburbs has become increasingly remote as suburbs have become cluttered with industries, freeways, filling stations, and ugly tract developments. Humorist and film-maker Mike Nichols has described this urban sprawl as "creeping Los Angelism." Similarly, journalist Harrison Salisbury warns that urban America may soon become smothered by a universal suburb, "nestled under its blanket of smog, girdled by bands of freeways, its core eviscerated by concrete strips and asphalt fields, its circulatory arteries pumping away without focus . . . the prototype of Gasopolis, the rubber-wheeled living region of the future."[8]

[8] Quoted in Daniel P. Moynihan, "New Roads and Urban Chaos," *The Reporter*, April 14, 1960, pp. 13–20.

Many suburban problems are inherent in the special suburban structure and have created additional problems for both central cities and suburbs. The automobile, for example, which made suburban living possible, has become one of its greatest difficulties. The heavy flow of automobiles into the city not only contaminates the already polluted air of most central cities; it has forced both state and local governments to spend an unwarranted amount of time and money on the automobile instead of other badly needed services. Two-thirds of the central area in Los Angeles—where residents are badly in need of new housing, parks, and playgrounds—is devoted to garages, roads, and other necessities of the automobile.[9]

[9] Lockard, *State and Local Government*, p. 470.

In addition to these transportation problems, most suburbanites experi-

The trains, buses, and other methods of
intercity travel are rarely adequate to meet
the needs of the growing suburban
population. Thus, highway tie-ups such
as that pictured here, are frequent and
unavoidable occurrences for those who use
their own car.

ence a special kind of confusion that affects both their minds and their pocketbooks. Because they usually live in one community and work in another, suburbanites must pay taxes for their place of residence rather than for their place of working. A resident of Bucks County, for example, pays local taxes to the Bucks County government, yet he may work in Philadelphia. Similarly, he may vote for local representatives from Bucks County, but not Philadelphia. He may spend three-fourths of his time and one-fourth of his money in an area (Philadelphia) where he has no immediate political representation. (This means that he cannot vote on referendums—that is, express approval or disapproval of a legislative bill or amendment—that may affect his business; neither can he really complain about the service in this area.) On the other hand, he may have little interest in his local governing board, since he is only a nighttime and weekend boarder there. Even though his children go to school in his community, he often has a limited interest in the way it is governed, complains about the rising taxes that he left the central city to avoid, and, despite his "residence" in this community, is not part of it.

Partly as a result of this lack of commitment, many residents tend to move about metropolitan areas with increasing frequency. "Today," reports *Time* magazine, "one out of five families changes residence every year, and it is a common pattern for a married couple to start off in a small apartment, move to the suburbs when the children arrive, shift from suburb to suburb as income rises, and then move back into the city after the children are grown."[10]

[10] *Time*, February 9, 1968, p. 30.

*Scott Greer and David W. Minar, "The Political Side of Urban Development and Redevelopment,"* Annals of the American Academy of Political Science, *March 1964, pp. 63–67.*

Scott Greer and David Minar, in an assessment of current plans for urban development, discuss how questions of governmental jurisdiction create problems for urban renewal programs. There are two sets of conflicts involved: those caused by the dispersion of power in our federal system, and those resulting from vying bureaucracies at the local level, where the central city has sprawled to include a far-flung metropolitan area.

On the local level, the authors claim that the multitude of jurisdictions make overall planning a farce; instead of a holistic approach, planning ends up being limited to the central city or a few suburbs.

Tradition ties action programs to the legal structures of municipalities while problems overrun jurisdictional boundaries. Supplies of leadership and revenue are distributed differently from the stock of urban problems, such as standard housing, crime, and intergroup tensions. Most often, the problems of physical and social decay are seen as the central city's problems, and, even when their broader implications are understood, long-standing legal and ideological boundaries prohibit all but the most feeble of broadscale remedies. In many places the division of jurisdiction is not only spatial but also functional so that education and recreation and transit and sewage disposal and a host of other aspects of the urban development picture are charged to distinct units of government. Whatever the particular picture for a metropolitan area, its main blank spots are similar: no coordination, no power, no responsibility.

The urban renewal project in progress when this article was written was an ambitious one. However, it was finally stalled by the complicated political structure of the metropolitan area, the restrictions on land use, and the difficulty in coordinating local governments. In addition, there were conflicts with contradictory programs initiated by the national government, which has its own urban renewal bureaucracy.

Coordination among the federal agencies affecting a given city is almost nil; this may result from the use of the state as a middleman, as in the case of the federal highway program, or it may result from simple lack of concern, as in the planners of urban renewal. In any event, urban renewal may be at the mercy of powerful federal agencies over which it has no control. The federal highway program may site a cloverleaf in the middle of the urban-renewal area, may displace thousands of householders and completely disrupt the urban-renewal relocation operations, and may hold up the sale of urban-renewal land for months while officials decide where access ramps should go. Meanwhile FHA may cooperate with the highway program in stimulating dispersion to the suburbs while urban renewal struggles to revivify the central city.

Because of these problems of jurisdiction, the original conception may become buried in red tape; and the urban renewal project that emerges may be a distortion of what was first intended.

Because of this continuous movement from one area to another, suburbanites tend to feel little affiliation with their temporary local governments. As a result, the local authorities are often ineffective and unauthoritative; they lack the citizen cooperation and assistance that might facilitate their attempts at local improvements. In addition, many local governments may exist within a similar area, and the bewildered resident often does not know which government has jurisdiction over him for which governmental functions. "Political responsibility for government performance is divided to the point of obscurity," reports the Advisory Commission on Intergovernmental Relations. "Public control of government policies tends to break down when citizens have to deal with a network of independent governments, each responsible for highly specialized activities. Even where good channels are developed

11 Advisory Commission
on Intergovernmental
Relations, p. 7.

for registering public concern, each government is so restricted in its powers and in the area of its jurisdiction that important metropolitan action is virtually impossible for local governments to undertake."[11]

But even if the local governments were effectively organized—if they were capable of providing the services demanded of them—the cost of providing the necessary services would be prohibitive in most places. "One indication of the rising costs of local government," said President Nixon in his State of the Union message on January 22, 1971, "I discovered that my home town of Whittier, California—which has a population of 67,000—has a larger budget for 1971 than the entire Federal budget was in 1791." Many suburban communities do not yet have the substantial business or industrial interests that could pay for these services. Some must rely on the high taxation of private citizens. (Present zoning laws often restrict industries to relatively limited areas.) Suburbanites must be content with a minimum amount of services or a maximum load of taxes.

It is clear that the move to the suburbs has in many ways intensified the urban problems that we mentioned earlier. Because so many suburbs have become—or are becoming—self-sustaining communities, they are depleting the cities of money, services, and even people. Many suburbanites, fed up with the daily and arduous routine of commuting, have found jobs in adjacent or immediate communities. Many others have been brought to suburban communities as businesses and industries have moved out to get away from tiresome city problems and to accommodate the newly settled suburbanites. Not only have businesses and industries moved out to these areas, but stores, restaurants, and even cultural events have followed. Many suburbs have branch stores of Alexander's or Saks Fifth Avenue; almost all suburban centers have extensive shopping centers containing supermarkets, drug stores, restaurants, dress shops, movie houses, bank branches, indoor tennis courts, and bowling alleys. The result is that many suburbanites seldom leave their home area except for the night-life and cultural events offered by the city.

As a result of the changing nature of cities, the increasingly suburban character of American life, and the growing difficulties of America's metropolitan areas, it is imperative that government work out more effective methods for managing large and small metropolitan areas. Such methods have and will continue to involve changes in the structure of government within the metropolitan areas, greater financial support and cooperation from state and national governments, and new and imaginative programs for improving the quality of the services. As the Advisory Commission has declared: "Poor coordination and conflicts of interest among governments often block effective action to deal with metropolitan problems. Changes in the structure of government within metropolitan areas, and innovation in relations between the federal government, the States, and local communities are needed to overcome these obstacles. The complex federal system of the United States, however, is rich in possibilities for adaptation to meet the changing circumstances [of] metropolitan growth. With sufficient imagination and effort . . . the resources of the federal system can be brought effectively to bear on the urban problems that challenge our age, just as previous generations found ways of adapting the federal system to other national challenges."[12]

[12] Advisory Commission on Intergovernmental Relations, pp. 11, 168.

# The search for solutions

[13] The United States Government reports more than 20,000 units of local government in 1968.

Analysts of urban affairs generally agree that if the problems of the metropolitan areas are to be solved, changes must take place in two major areas. The first change involves the reduction of the number of and reorganization of local governments within the metropolitan areas.[13] The second involves increased financial support from state and national governments.

## Reorganizing local government

Two schools of thought exist concerning the reorganization of local governments. One school calls for *centralization*. Advocates of this school argue that the problems of the metropolitan area are too large to be managed by small, local governments. The other school calls for continued *decentralization* and argues that metropolitan areas are too diverse and complex to be ruled by a single government. The major question, however, is not whether or not to centralize. It is, rather, how and to what degree can or should one centralize a diverse and complex system of governments? How should the financial resources be distributed? How should power be distributed within the metropolitan area?

Several schemes for reorganizing local governments have been tried, among them annexation, federation, city-county consolidation, and the establishment of special districts and public authorities. None of these schemes has been totally successful, mainly because it is usually so difficult for varying local governments to agree on a solution—particularly when they must agree to which of them will be eliminated. In addition, local residents often refuse to be incorporated (and their consent is usually required before an agreement can be finalized). If and when such an agreement is made, the boundaries of the metropolitan area have usually changed, making the agreement meaningless.

## Annexation

*Annexation* is the most direct method for bringing many local governments under the control of one central urban government. When a city annexes an outlying area, it legally brings both the land and people of this area under its supervision and control. In 1898, New York City, by a single annexation (Brooklyn and Staten Island), increased its land area by 250 miles. Since 1910, Los Angeles has more than quadrupled its land area by annexation.

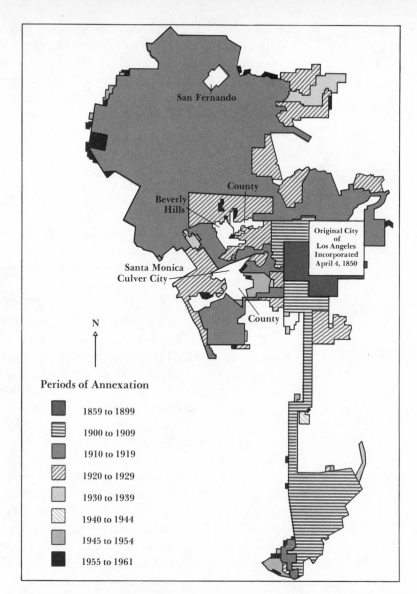

San Fernando

County

Beverly
Hills

Original City
of
Los Angeles
Incorporated
April 4, 1850

Santa Monica
Culver City

County

N

**Periods of Annexation**

1859 to 1899

1900 to 1909

1910 to 1919

1920 to 1929

1930 to 1939

1940 to 1944

1945 to 1954

1955 to 1961

## The Successive Annexations of Los Angeles, California

Source: From SOUTHERN CALIFORNIA METROPOLIS: A STUDY IN
DEVELOPMENT OF GOVERNMENT FOR A METROPOLITAN AREA by
Winston W. Crouch and Beatrice Dinerman, University of California Press, 1963:
161. Originally published by the University of California Press; reprinted by permission of The Regents of the University of California.

Oklahoma City. is today one of the largest American cities (in land area)
because of its annexations of smaller surrounding cities and towns (totalling
533 square miles).

Although, in the nineteenth century, annexation was widely used to increase the land and population of growing cities, it is not often used today. In Virginia, where annexation can be carried out through judicial proceedings, and in Texas, where it is accomplished by legislation, the practice still occurs frequently. In most other states, however, annexation requires the approval of the community to be annexed, usually obtained by referendum. Since most suburban communities do not want to be annexed by a larger city, approval is rare. Suburbanites, in fact, feel so strongly about not being incorporated into the central city that they band together in strong resistance at the mere mention of annexation. These suburbanites acknowledge the problems in their own communities, but they point out also the more serious problems found in the central cities. They want to hold on to their independence, and are willing to fight for it.

**Federation**

Another solution proposed for the problems of metropolitan areas is *federation*, a solution modelled after the national-state bargain struck in the Constitution. Proposals for metropolitan federation have taken many forms, but in all cases they involve an agreement among some or all of the local governments within a metropolitan area to the effect that they will share at least some of the responsibility for servicing community residents. In some metropolitan areas, for example, the central city provides such services as water supply, police protection, or mass transportation to the outlying areas, and the local suburban governments care for fire protection and building codes.

In practice, federation is not the form of government in most areas. Miami and Dade County have a dual-type federation, but this arrangement is a departure from the norm. The most striking example of urban federation is Toronto, Canada. In 1953, Toronto and its twelve suburbs agreed to form a federation. The separate municipalities retained authority over certain areas, although most of their functions were transferred to the new metropolitan governing unit. The Toronto system, however, has been difficult to duplicate in American metropolitan areas. Federation presents certain major difficulties: First, it is difficult to determine how services should be financed so that both urban dweller and suburbanite bear their fair share of the costs. Second, since participating governments often do not agree on an arrangement for legislative representation, the balance of government power is difficult to determine.

**City-county consolidation**

A solution similar to federation and employed in some metropolitan areas has been the *consolidation* of city and county governments into a single, central government; that is, all local units of government are virtually eliminated and the county assumes all or most of the tasks of government. This plan is not adaptable in some areas, however, because they are too large and too widespread. One could not consolidate the metropolitan area of Omaha, for example, because it sprawls over two states.

In some areas, however, city-county consolidation has been effective. An example of this is Los Angeles County's *Lakewood Plan*. Under the Lakewood Plan, local governments hire the county to perform specific functions, such as police protection, traffic signal maintenance, and tax and health services, on a contract basis. Services for the whole area are uniform, and the county performs only those functions specifically stated in the contract.

Another effective consolidation, the Miami *Metro*, has been enthusiastically endorsed by the residents of Dade County, since its inception in 1957. Dade County, Florida, which includes the metropolitan area of Miami, was given certain powers over the twenty-six local governments that made up the Miami metropolitan area—among them powers over zoning, traffic control, urban renewal, and highway construction. The Metro has consequently provided metropolitan Miami with many innovative services, including a uniform traffic code, a planning board, a metropolitan traffic court, and a bus system that services the entire area.

Although some people have criticized Miami's Metro government, the residents of greater Miami have voiced their approval of the Metro in several referenda called by opponents of the plan. Professor Edward Sofen, a careful student of the Miami Metro, suggests that the Metro has succeeded partly because it has no definable leadership and no well-organized, powerful interest groups.[14] As a result, it is relatively free from the conflicting views that plague most city governments.

Since World War I, two types of local government, the *special district* and a variation of the special district known as a *public authority*, have been increasingly employed to solve the problems of the metropolitan area. These agencies are generally single-purpose, autonomous, and independent in their revenue sources and borrowing powers, and have appointed memberships (although in school districts members are elected). Although many object to the independent functioning of public authorities, these local governments have several major advantages: citizens are not burdened with extra taxes to keep them running, their goals are usually achieved efficiently and quickly, and most importantly, they work.

Most Americans are familiar with at least one type of district or authority: school districts, park authorities, and fire districts are common in most metropolitan areas. The majority of these government agencies are set up to provide a specific service, such as pollution control, water supply, or education. One of the largest districts in the country, The Metropolitan Water District of Southern California, provides water to Southern California, primarily by tapping water supplies east of the Continental Divide (that is, the Rocky Mountains that separate east and west coast river systems.) In addition to service districts, school districts are also common within most metropolitan areas. Established to provide educational facilities for the area's

14 Edward Sofen, "Problems of Metropolitan Leadership: The Miami Experience," *Midwest Journal of Political Science*, 5 (1961): 18.

## Special districts and public authorities

"Now, don't make it *too* beautiful. I wouldn't want my successors someday to be confronted with a Landmark problem."

Drawing by Alan Dunn; © 1968
The New Yorker Magazine, Inc.

children, these districts are empowered to control all activities that affect the educational system. For example, all hiring, curricular, and extracurricular changes must be approved by the governing board of the school district before they can be put into effect.

Public authorities differ from most special districts in that they function, for the most part, independently of state and local governments. While special districts raise money by collecting taxes, public authorities collect individual fees or tolls, or borrow from private sources. Perhaps the best-known public authority in the nation is the Port of New York Authority, a governmental agency that controls airports, bridges, piers, tunnels, bus and freight terminals, and heliports. Recently, the Port Authority has begun construction on two buildings of the mammoth World Trade Center in lower Manhattan. The Authority's history, is perhaps the best example of how good management and organization contributes to greater independence.

The Authority which was established in 1921, is directed by a twelve-man board appointed for overlapping terms. The Authority services both New York and New Jersey, and half the governing board is selected by the governors of each state. Its holdings are valued at about $2 billion, and its outstanding bonds are thought to be worth another billion.

In spite of, and perhaps because of, their public orientation, special districts and public authorities have often been severely attacked by citizens and officials. Some critics have claimed that although the Port of New York Authority was set up to provide a public service, it avoids any nonprofit venture. These critics claim it "has been friendly to automobile travel and distinctly cold toward rail transportation,"[15] for tolls paid by automobiles on bridges and tunnels offer a sure profit, whereas railroads and subways are often deficit-ridden and offer little chance for profit.

Districts and authorities have been criticized also because they add still more government agencies to the tangle of local governments within the metropolitan areas. In addition, many districts and authorities are governed from outside urban centers, usually the state. Even though they perform local functions, the local community has little control over their operations.

There is, however, much to be said in support of these government agencies. They can be designed to attack specific problems within the area; they often appeal to the business-oriented citizen who distrusts politicians; and they usually are more efficient than other forms of local government.

15 Lockard, *State and Local Government*, p. 492. The Port Authority operates only one small commuter railroad but two interstate tunnels and several bridges.

# National and state assistance

## State aid

If the problems of central cities, and thus of metropolitan areas, are to be alleviated, much more financial assistance may have to come from both the national and state governments. At their best, national plans for local aid would provide a maximum of 2 percent of the federal taxes for local aid.

State involvement in the problems of central cities leaves a great deal to be desired. The states have traditionally ignored the problems of their urban centers, forcing urban leaders to turn to the national government for more and more support.

The difficulties of the state-local partnership arise from many sources. The state legislatures, often dominated by rural and suburban interests, are seldom sympathetic to urban problems. And state aid, when it is given, is frequently so tangled with restrictions and stipulations that it cannot be applied to the problems at hand. Effective paths of local action are often blocked because the states refuse to give the large cities the power to make important decisions—for example, the power to levy taxes.

According to many urban leaders, however, the main problem with state aid is that there is too little of it. They argue that their cities are not receiving their fair share of state revenues, that they pay out more than they take in.

In recent years, however, state aid to central cities has increased markedly. In 1968–1969, New York City produced 47 percent of the state's revenue and received 45 percent of the total state assistance to local government. In the last few decades, a significant portion of aid to urban areas has come from the national government through the state governments. "[From] the 1930's on," writes Richard Leach, "despairing mayor after despairing mayor

## National aid

## State Activities at the Local Level

| Mode of Activity | Examples |
|---|---|
| 1. State direct-to-people activities | Highways<br>Higher education<br>Health and hospitals<br>Welfare<br>Recreation<br>Courts and correctional institutions |
| 2. State aid to local units for specified activities | Education<br>Highways<br>Welfare<br>Safety<br>Health and hospitals |
| 3. Local activities made mandatory by state law | Local elections<br>School standards<br>Fire and police protection<br>Courts and jails<br>Tax assessment and collection standards<br>Health program<br>Sewage standards |

Note: This list does not indicate the overlap that frequently occurs between state and local activities.

Source: Duane Lockard, *Politics of State and Local Government*, 2nd ed. (New York: The Macmillan Co., 1969), p. 196.

journeyed to Washington to seek relief for specific urban problems. Washington's response was hearty. . . . at first Congress and later on presidents began to realize that votes followed action in behalf of the nation's large urban areas. Program after program was enacted, and grants-in-aid, subsidies, research activities, and direct federal relations with cities were all employed in the process."[16]

[16] Richard H. Leach, *American Federalism* (New York: W. W. Norton and Co., Inc., 1970), p. 150.

## State Aid to Representative New York Cities

| City | Total Revenue | | State Aid | | State Aid as a Percentage of Revenues | |
|---|---|---|---|---|---|---|
| | 1959 | 1970 | 1959 | 1970 | 1959 | 1970 |
| Buffalo | $ 76,569 | $ 143,724 | $ 14,822 | $ 54,066 | 19.4 | 37.6 |
| New York City | 2,057,345 | 6,579,486 | 383,161 | 1,960,807 | 18.6 | 29.8 |
| Rochester | 62,355 | 121,546 | 10,243 | 23,726 | 16.4 | 19.5 |
| Syracuse | 35,958 | 62,260 | 7,050 | 18,646 | 19.6 | 29.9 |

Note: Although the amount of monies given to the cities by the state has generally increased, it remains a relatively small percentage of the revenues collected by that city.

Source: New York State Department of Audit and Control.

Unfortunately, these programs have been poorly coordinated and have served, in many cases, to further complicate the already knotted process of government in the metropolitan areas. For example, the process of obtaining grants-in-aid involves an overwhelming amount of bureaucratic red tape. A neighborhood health center reported to the office of the Secretary of Health, Education and Welfare that its grant application expenses alone exceed $51,000, not to mention the loss of man-hours required to process the applications. Many agencies despair of ever receiving funds because of the antiquated system of disbursement, and because the plan for distributing the funds is set without regard for individual needs. In 1969, for example, educational grants-in-aid to St. Louis totalled $226 per student in the city's wealthier districts, but only $107 per student in those districts where poverty is rampant.

As discussed in Chapter 5, one proposed solution to the problem of national grants in revenue sharing, the distribution of federally collected

## National Activities on the Local Level

| Mode of Activity | Examples |
|---|---|
| 1. National direct-to-people activities | Old Age and Survivors Insurance<br>Veterans' benefits<br>Mail delivery<br>Taxation<br>Licensing |
| 2. Nationally engineered local governments, relatively independent of state or local governments | Soil Conservation<br>Agricultural Stabilization and Conservation<br>Grazing Service Advisory Board |
| 3. Nationally engineered local governments, relatively dependent on state or local governments | Selective Service<br>Civil Defense<br>Rationing during World War II<br>Public housing and urban redevelopment (in some states) |
| 4. National grants channeled through states | Welfare, highways, employment security, forestry, vocational education, public health, etc. |
| 5. National grants and other aid directly to local governments | Airports (in some states)<br>Public housing and urban redevelopment (in some states)<br>Flood control<br>School construction (in some states)<br>Disaster relief (in some cases)<br>Technical assistance in many fields<br>Services by contract |

Note: Overlapping functions are not indicated.

Source: Duane Lockard, *Politics of State and Local Government*, 2nd ed. (New York: The Macmillan Co., 1969), p. 191.

## Major Features of Five Revenue-Sharing Proposals

| Proposal | Basis for Revenue Sharing (permanent full-year effect) | Local Government Sharing | | Program or Project Restrictions |
| --- | --- | --- | --- | --- |
| | | Payment Mechanism | Local Units Participating | |
| Nixon administration | 1% of federal personal income tax base | Pass through from state government based on share of general revenues raised | All cities, counties, and townships | No discrimination |
| Advisory Commission on Intergovernmental Relations | 0.5% of federal personal income tax base plus 12½% of state personal income tax collections | Pass through from state government based on share of total taxes collected | Cities and counties of over 50,000 population, and independent school districts | None |
| Senator Javits | 2% of federal personal income tax base | Mandatory Local Sharing. Details to be Determined by State Government. | | Limited to Health, Education and Welfare, broadly defined |
| National League of Cities | 2% of federal personal income tax base | Direct from federal government | Cities and urban counties over 2,500 population | None |
| Douglas Commission | A legally authorized percentage of federal personal income tax base | Direct from federal government | Cities and urban counties over 50,000 population | None |

Source: "Major Features of Five Revenue-Sharing Proposals" from an article entitled "Alternative Approaches to Revenue Sharing: A Description and Framework for Evaluation" by Murray L. Weidenbaum and Robert L. Joss, *National Tax Journal*, vol. XXIII, no. 1, March 1970.

[17] Elliot Richardson, "We Are Embarked on a Great Mission of Reform," U.S. News and World Report, August 17, 1970, pp. 57–79; Murray L. Weidenbaum, and Robert L. Jess, "Alternative Approaches to Revenue Sharing: A Description and Framework for Evaluation," National Tax Journal, XXIII, no. 1 (March 1970): 2–23; and "Who'll Get What from Tax Sharing," U.S. News and World Report, August 17, 1970, p. 56.

revenues to state and local governments virtually without restrictions as to how the money will be spent.[17] Several revenue-sharing plans were introduced during the second session of the 91st Congress. Under each plan, a certain percentage (from 0.05 percent to a full 2 percent) of national revenues would be returned to the state and local governments to spend as they see fit.

These revenue-sharing plans, however, met formidable opposition in the 91st Congress. Many congressmen, especially liberal Democrats, opposed the new plan, because of their fear of losing control over federal funds and because of the history of corruption at the local level. Consequently, all the plans died in committee. They have, however, found strong support outside the Congress. At the National Governor's Conference in August of 1969, for example, the governors resolved to exert all possible pressure in support of revenue sharing. Similar resolutions have been adopted by the U.S. Conference of Mayors, the Urban Coalition, Urban America, the National League of Cities, and the National Association of Counties.

"Under this plan," said President Nixon, "the federal government will provide the states and localities with more money and less interference—and by cutting down the interference the same amount of money will go a lot further." The President argued that local governments, given sufficient financial aid, can best determine the solutions to the problems facing them. "The idea that a bureaucratic elite in Washington knows best what is best for people everywhere and that you cannot trust local government is really a contention that you cannot trust people to govern themselves," he said. "This notion is completely foreign to the American experience. Local government is the government closest to the people; it's most responsive to the individual person; it is people's government in a far more intimate way than the Government in Washington can ever be."

"Pecking order"

Drawing by C. H. Haynie; © 1971
L. A. *Times* Syndicate.

But even if a generous revenue-sharing plan is adopted by Congress, most cities will still be seriously short of funds. New York City, for example, faces a revenue deficit in 1971 of $800–900 million, yet the city would receive only $150 million under the best of revenue-sharing plans.

# Relieving the urban problems

In his 1965 message to Congress on cities, President Johnson stated: "In the remainder of this century—in less than forty years—urban population will double, city land will double, and we will have to build in our cities as much as all that we have built since the first colonist arrived on these shores. It is as if we had 40 years to rebuild the entire urban United States."

Redesigning the urban environment to accommodate this enormous increase of population will be a monumental task. It will require an enormous expenditure of resources and careful planning. Government at the national, state, and local level will have to devise and implement large-scale, farsighted programs, if the urban environment is to be successfully redesigned.

Some promising programs are already underway. New York State's Urban Development Corporation, for example, has begun construction of a new town on Welfare Island, a long, narrow strip of land that lies in the East River, which divides Manhattan and Queens in New York City. The first new government-sponsored town to be built in the United States since the administration of Franklin D. Roosevelt, Welfare Island will be a racially and economically mixed community housing 20,000 New Yorkers. The design for Welfare Island includes many plans for eliminating the problems of urban living. Pollution, for example, will be reduced by making the island off-limits to automobiles: Welfare Island will be the nation's first pedestrian town.

Redesigning the urban environment cannot be achieved by builders or architects or politicians alone. Specialists from every discipline will have to join together in a team effort to conquer the seemingly insurmountable problems of creating a livable, functioning urban environment. David Easton has accurately described the problem: "But here if we consider the matter [the nation's pressing problems] only as political scientists we create insurmountable difficulties for ourselves. Social problems do not come neatly packaged as economic, psychological, political and the like. Our crises arise out of troubles that involve all aspects of human behavior."[18]

[18] David Easton, "The New Revolution in Political Science," *The American Political Science Review*, LXIII, no. 4 (December 1969): 63.

# Glossary

**annexation**  Legal absorption of the territory of one government by another, especially of a small unit of government by a large city government.

**city-county consolidation**  A system of combining and coordinating local units of government, whereby they are entirely or largely eliminated, and almost all governmental powers are assumed by the county.

**Demonstration Cities and Metropolitan Development Act of 1966**  National grant-in-aid program designed to rehabilitate impoverished areas, help local governments plan their redevelopment, and promote the advance of an entire metropolitan area.

**federation**  Agreement between the central city government and the suburban local governments in a metropolitan area, whereby the responsibility for providing local services is divided according to plan. A new metropolitan government is granted certain powers over the entire area but the local governments continue to exist and perform other specified functions.

**ghetto**  Densely populated section of urban areas, comprised of low income workers and families of a specific racial or ethnic group, who, for economic and social reasons, are unable to find homes in other parts of the area.

**industrial suburb**  A suburb adjacent to a central city that is characterized by the presence of business and industry.

**megalopolis**  A densely populated area that is actually a continuous belt or strip of small and large cities, towns, and suburbs, which stretches over a large geographic area and crosses the boundaries of several states.

**metropolis (central city)**  A recognizable center of dense population within a metropolitan area.

**metropolitan area**  Integrated social and economic unit containing a recognizable center of dense population, the central city or metropolis, surrounded by smaller cities, towns, villages, and communities.

**public authority**  Type of special district that is a form of corporation created by government and assigned specific functions. Largely independent of state and local governments, authorities finance their activities by issuing bonds and charging fees and tolls for their services.

**special district**  An independent unit of local government devised to provide a specific service, such as pollution control, water supply, or education, through its power to tax and borrow.

# Suggested readings

Abrams, Charles, *The City Is the Frontier* (New York: Harper and Row Publishers, Inc., 1965). Critique of the city in colorful, controversial terms.

Agger, Robert E., Daniel Goldrich, and Bert E. Swanson, *The Rulers and the Ruled: Political Power and Impotence in American Communities* (New York: John Wiley and Sons, Inc., 1964). Comparative community-power study of four American cities.

Banfield, Edward C., *Big City Politics: A Comparative Guide to the Political Systems of Nine American Cities* (New York: Random House, Inc., 1965). Study of the politics, systems, and machines of nine large American cities.

Banfield, Edward C., and James Q. Wilson, *City Politics* (Cambridge, Mass.: Harvard University Press, 1963). Study of the day-to-day workings of city government viewed from the different interests and opinions of urban areas.

Bollens, John C., ed., *Exploring the Metropolitan Community* (Berkeley, Calif.: University of California Press, 1961). Detailed analysis of the government, economy, and politics of St. Louis.

Bollens, John C., and Henry J. Schmandt, *The Metropolis: Its People, Politics, and Economic Life* (New York: Harper and Row Publishers, Inc., 1965). Overview of the metropolis, including a particularly good description of the workings of its government.

Connery, Robert H., and Richard H. Leach, *The Federal Government and Metropolitan Areas* (Cambridge, Mass.: Harvard University Press, 1961). Analysis of the relationship between the national government and urban centers, with emphasis on the need for the national government to assume a larger role in solving urban problems.

Cook, Robert C., *Urban America: Dilemma and Opportunity* (New York: The Macmillan Co., 1965). Brief description of urban centers, highlighting various aspects of these areas.

Dahl, Robert A., *Who Governs? Democracy and Power in an American City* (New Haven, Conn.: Yale University Press, 1961). Study of how and by whom political decisions are made in an eastern city—New Haven, Connecticut.

Danielson, Michael N., *Federal-Metropolitan Politics and the Commuter Crisis* (New York: Columbia University Press, 1965). Study of urban transportation problems, emphasizing the working relationships among the several government agencies acting within the metropolitan area.

Danielson, Michael N., ed., *Metropolitan Politics: A Reader* (Boston: Little, Brown and Co., 1966). Collection of essays on urban government and politics.

Editors of *Fortune, Exploding Metropolis* (Garden City, N.Y.: Doubleday and Co., Inc., 1958). Six articles investigating the growth of cities and suburbs in the wake of World War II, and the resulting problems of these cities and their suburbs.

Gottman, Jean, *Megalopolis: The Urbanized Northeastern Seaboard of the United States* (New York: The Twentieth Century Fund, 1961). Historical sketch of how our northeastern area became "one giant city" and an analysis of the dynamics of this urbanization, by a French geographer.

Greer, Scott, *Governing the Metropolis* (New York: John Wiley and Sons, Inc., 1962). Collection of essays on the development, government, and future of the metropolis.

Greer, Scott, *Urban Renewal and American Cities: The Dilemma of Democratic Intervention* (Indianapolis, Ind.: Bobbs-Merrill Co., Inc., 1965). History of housing legislation (1937–1961), including the relationships between local, state, and national agencies for urban renewal.

Hunter, Floyd, *Community Power Structure* (Chapel Hill, N.C.: University of North Carolina Press, 1953). Analysis of city politics in Atlanta, Georgia, here viewed as dominated by an elite; a contrast to Dahl's book, *Who Governs?*

Jacobs, Jane, *The Death and Life of Great American Cities* (New York: Random House, Inc., 1961). Analysis of urban life, based on the theory that city neighborhoods thrive amidst diversity and that this attribute is often neglected or destroyed by city planners.

Lockard, Duane, *Politics of State and Local Government*, 2nd ed. (New York: The Macmillan Co., 1969). Analysis of state and local political processes, including the relationship between state and local governments and the national government.

Martin, Roscoe C., *The Cities and The Federal System* (New York: Atherton Press, 1965). Thorough analysis of the relationship between national government and cities in solving urban problems, indicating the capacity of the national government to be flexible in solving urban problems.

Mumford, Lewis, *The City in History: Its Origins, Its Transformations, and Its Prospects* (New York: Harcourt Brace Jovanovich, Inc., 1961). Important historical work presenting a philosophical and moral interpretation of the city.

Rossi, Peter A., and Robert A. Dentler, *The Politics of Urban Renewal* (New York: The Free Press, 1962). Study of urban renewal, emphasizing the process by which decisions are made.

Sanford, Terry, *Storm Over the States* (New York: McGraw-Hill Book Co., 1967). View that the growth of the national government is taking place at the expense of the state governments, inevitably leading to the destruction of the federal system. Solutions are offered by Sanford, the former governor of North Carolina.

Sayre, Wallace S., and Herbert Kaufman, *Governing New York City: Politics in the Metropolis* (New York: W. W. Norton and Co., Inc., 1965, paper). Description and analysis of the political organization and administration of America's largest city.

Weaver, Robert C., *Dilemmas of Urban America* (New York: Atheneum Publishers, 1965). Primarily an examination of the housing problem that has resulted from the metropolitan population explosion by the former Administrator of the United States Housing and Home Finance Agency.

Wood, Robert C., *1400 Governments: The Political Economy of the New York Metropolitan Region* (Cambridge, Mass.: Harvard University Press, 1961). Discussion of how the approximately 1400 local governments in the New York City area influence economic and social development.

Wood, Robert C., *Suburbia: Its People and Their Politics* (Boston: Houghton Mifflin Co., 1958). Analysis of the American suburb identifying it as an unsuccessful attempt to recreate in the twentieth century the small town of early America.

# Topics of further study

Abbott, David W., Louis H. Gold, and Edward T. Rokowsky, "The Civilian Review Board Referendum," Jule Bellush and Stephen David, eds., *Race and Politics in New York City: Several Case Studies in Decision Making* (New York: Praeger Publishers, 1971).

Adams, Robert W., "The Politics of Urban Renewal: Columbus, Ohio, 1952–1962" (Ph.D. dissertation, Ohio State University, 1969).

Barth, Norman, "William F. Buckley and Modern Urban Problems: A Critical Evaluation" (master's thesis, San Diego State College, 1967).

Bartley, Ernest R., and F. H. Bair, "The Text of a Model Zoning Ordinance with Commentary," *American Society of Planning Officials*, 3d ed. (1966).

Ericson, J. E., and J. H. McCrocklin, "From Religion to Commerce: The Evolution and Enforcement of Blue Laws in Texas," *Southwestern Social Science Quarterly*, June 1964, pp. 50–58.

Fuquay, R. F., and R. W. Maddox, *State and Local Government*, 2d rev. ed. (New York: Van Nostrand-Reinhold Books, 1966).

Goff, Charles D., "Appraisal of the City Manager Profession: Pitfalls City Managers Should Avoid," *Public Management*, January 1959, pp. 5–9.

Hunt, David W., "Oklahoma Management Study Commission: The Politics of State Government Reform" (master's thesis, University of Oklahoma, 1968).

Johnson, William, "The Power to Plan in American Metropolitan Areas," *International Journal of Comparative Sociology*, 1968.

Klein, Harold M., *Local Planning Process in New Jersey* (New Brunswick; N.J.: Rutgers University Bureau of Government Research, 1967).

Klein, Woody, *Lindsay's Promise: The Dream that Failed, a Personal Account* (New York: The Macmillan Co., 1970).

Maddox, R. W., *State and Local Government* (New York: Van Nostrand-Reinhold Books, 1962).

Monypenny, Phillip, "Intergovernmental Relations—Uniform State Laws," *Annals of the American Academy of Political and Social Science*, May 1965, pp. 53–60.

Nedweck, Brian, "The Ideological Basis of Metropolitan Growth: An Analysis of Public Policy Preferences in Milwaukee" (Ph.D. dissertation, University of Milwaukee, 1971).

Ross, Ernest F., "The Impact of State Administrative Supervision and Control on City Experimentation in Michigan" (Ph.D. dissertation, University of Michigan, n.d.).

Schultze, William, *Urban Politics and Policies: The Search for Community* (Belmont, Calif.: Wadsworth Publishing Co., Inc., 1971).

Westley, William M., "Consolidation of School Districts in Ramsey County, North Dakota" (master's thesis, University of Minnesota, 1935).

# portfolio
# campaigns
# then
# and now

The early attitude toward the election of the President was that the office should seek the man, not the man the office. At first, campaigns were staid, and largely directed at the legislature, but by 1828, popular selection of the presidential electors was the rule. A campaign to "Let the people rule" put Andrew Jackson, "Old Hickory," in the White House; it was the first in which handbills, leaflets, and ribbons were widely used. Competition deepened in 1832 when Jackson's supporters, reacting to heavy spending on leaflets by his opponents, raised hickory poles and held torchlight processions. However, it was not until 1836 that William Henry Harrison made the first campaign speech by a candidate for the presidency, drawing the comment from former President John Quincy Adams that "electioneering for the President has spread its contagion to the President himself." When Harrison ran again in the "Log Cabin and Hard Cider" campaign of 1840, the country was overrun with parades, log cabins on wheels, cider parties, song fests, and huge balls rolled from city to city. But this still was not a mass election; only 2.4 million men had voted in a population of 17 million. In reaction to these "excesses," James Polk's 1844 campaign was modest. Nevertheless he was known as the "Napoleon of the Stump."

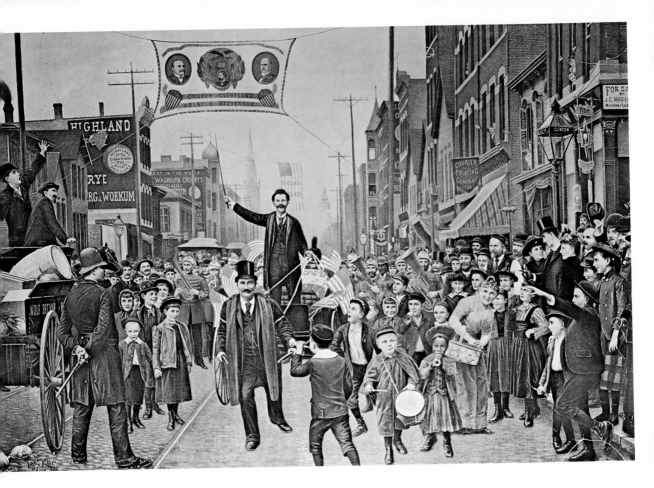

The introduction of a uniform national election day in 1848 set the campaign style for most of the rest of that century. Some candidates stumped, but others—notably, Abraham Lincoln—did not. Campaigns relied upon word of mouth, mail, processions, meetings, broadsides, leaflets, banners, and buttons. Toward the end of the nineteenth century, however, the growth in technology dramatically affected campaigning. By 1880, railroads had vastly expanded, enabling James Garfield to make seventy speeches throughout the country. During the 1884 campaign, which resulted in Grover Cleveland's election, advances in printing produced an unprecedented flood of printed materials with an accompanying increase in the readership of newspapers and in political advertisements. The press was the dominant medium when the popular Theodore Roosevelt ran in 1904. The next major change came with the advent of the radio in 1928, when Al Smith's New York accent shocked the rest of the nation. But the most effective use of this medium was made by Franklin Delano Roosevelt in 1932, to counter a hostile press and to promise the economically depressed nation a "New Deal." His familiar radio personality helped undermine the charge that he had royal ambitions when he ran for an unparalleled third term in 1940.

In 1964 bumper stickers and buttons urged voters to go "All the way with LBJ" (Lyndon Johnson, the incumbent Democratic President) and billboards told them that, "In your heart you know he's right," referring to Barry Goldwater, the conservative Republican from Arizona. Political observers noted that the contest between them was basically ideological, and that year saw extensive use of well-made television advertisements, modeled on commercial ones, for voters not attracted to the candidates' personalities. The next campaign, in 1968, was overshadowed by assassination, urban riots, student protests, and demonstrations against the war in Vietnam. Many Democrats were exhausted by the bitter intraparty fights in the primaries and at the convention and by the open conflict occasioned by their convention in Chicago and seen by most of the nation over television. Neither of the candidates, Richard Nixon nor Hubert Humphrey, attracted any great emotionalism, and there was little innovation in campaign techniques. Billboards and television spots told the voters that "Nixon's the one," and they favored him in a close contest that took all night to call. For the 1972 campaign, major changes have been made in the format of the conventions to make them even more into showpieces that kick off a presidential campaign, and to attract even more television viewers, including the eighteen to twenty-one year old voters who will vote for the first time in all states.

In the second half of the twentieth century, advances in technology again drastically affected campaigning. Harry Truman had "whistle-stopped" the nation in 1948, but only four years later, in 1952, Dwight Eisenhower and Adlai Stevenson relied more on planes than trains. That campaign also saw the first use of the new nationwide television networks, making the candidate and his personality visible in every section of the country. Speeches were scheduled more for prime viewing time than newspaper deadlines, and the conventions were seen "live" throughout the nation, in effect starting the campaign.

But traditional media continued to play a major role, and in 1952 and again in 1956, the slogan "I Like Ike" in newspaper advertisements and on buttons and banners was the simplest and most effective. The campaign in 1960 to succeed Eisenhower was one of the most strenuous in history. Using jets, John Kennedy and Richard Nixon were able to move quickly from coast to coast, and Nixon was able to keep his pledge to go to every state in the Union. But in a campaign centered almost entirely on personalities, television was a major factor. On election eve Nixon staged the first campaign telethon, but Kennedy's victory was due in great part to a series of four television debates between the two candidates. It has been estimated that these television debates reached more voters than previous candidates for President had been able to reach in their entire campaigns.

# part two

# the politics of participation

# 7 opinion
## and
## opinion
## making

THE FREEDOM of every adult citizen of the United States to participate fully in the American political system is the distinguishing characteristic of our constitutional democracy. Participation is not simply a matter of being able to vote, freely and secretly, for one's representatives in the government. The freedoms guaranteed by the First Amendment to the Constitution—free speech, the right to assemble, and the right to petition the government, in particular—keep open diverse means of political participation for all citizens.

All Americans can both have, and act on, political opinions. And, as will be shown, nearly everybody has political opinions. But few Americans choose to take the next step and vote regularly (much less become active in political matters). The number of Americans who participate in six or more political activities is 1 percent of the adult population, while the nonparticipants number 63 percent.[1]

We cannot be certain that the habitual apathy of the American citizenry really affects our political system adversely, or that it is even an unhealthy sign. "There are those who consider this [apathy] a serious malfunctioning of democracy," Morris Rosenberg has written. "If men are to maintain control over their political destinies, they must be aware of what is going on, and must take a hand in determining public policy. On the other hand, there are some political theorists who find such apathy a favorable, rather than an unfavorable sign. They interpret it to mean that society is fundamentally contented, is characterized by consensus rather than by broad cleavages, and is basically stable."[2] Those who feel that some degree of apathy is advantageous note that high participation may be an evidence of frustration—not the mark of a healthy political system—and that low participation connotes satisfaction and stability.

[1] John P. Robinson, Jerrold G. Rusk, Kendra B. Head, *Measures of Political Attitudes* (Ann Arbor, Mich.: Center for Political Studies, 1969), p. 594.

[2] Morris Rosenberg, "Some Determinants of Political Apathy," in Joseph R. Fizman, ed., *The American Political Arena: Selected Readings*, 2nd ed. (Boston: Little, Brown and Co., 1960), p. 560.

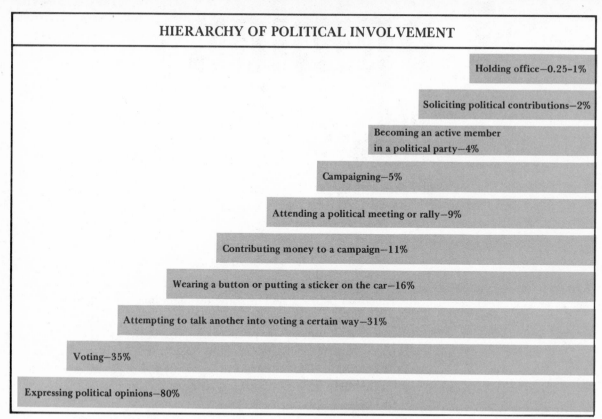

HIERARCHY OF POLITICAL INVOLVEMENT

Holding office—0.25–1%

Soliciting political contributions—2%

Becoming an active member
in a political party—4%

Campaigning—5%

Attending a political meeting or rally—9%

Contributing money to a campaign—11%

Wearing a button or putting a sticker on the car—16%

Attempting to talk another into voting a certain way—31%

Voting—35%

Expressing political opinions—80%

Source: Adapted from John P. Robinson, Jerrold G. Rusk, and Kendra B. Head, *Measures of Political Attitudes* (Ann Arbor, Mich.: Center for Political Studies, 1969), p. 591.

The character and extent of the American electorate's political activities is clearly delineated. For example, some 70 to 90 percent of all Americans are willing to express uninformed political opinions, but only 25 to 30 percent habitually vote.

In this and the next three chapters, we will examine the various ways that individuals can and do participate in the activities of the political system. Some of these ways are: voting; attempting to influence the political behavior of others; taking part in the political activities of interest groups, such as business associations, labor unions, professional associations, or conservation groups; and running for office.

# The nature of political opinion

As the individual matures, he accumulates various impressions about the political system in which he lives. At a very early point in his life he may begin to develop his own attitudes toward political activities—attitudes that have been shaped by, and are constantly being influenced by, the many types and groups of people with whom he comes into contact. Eventually, his attitudes lead him to form definite political opinions and perhaps to participate in political activities.

## Attitudes

[3] M. Brewster Smith, Jerome S. Bruner, and Robert W. White, *Opinions and Personality* (New York: John Wiley and Sons, Inc., 1956), p. 40.

*Attitudes* are unexpressed learned tendencies or predispositions that lead individuals to respond in a particular manner.[3] Because of a vague fear of nuclear destruction, an individual may adopt a favorable attitude toward national defense, for example. He may have no knowledge of the activities of the political system related to national defense and no interest in obtaining that knowledge. He does have a preference, however; he would prefer not to perish in a nuclear holocaust.

Attitudes are an important part of the political participation process. Although often vague and unstructured, they predispose the individual toward stronger kinds of preferences.

## Interests

When attitudes are associated with specific activities, they become *interests*. An individual with interests *cares* about the outcome of a certain activity, most commonly because the activity affects him. A person who favors a particular course of action within the political system—the election of a Democrat for President or the passage of legislation to restrict the sale of firearms—is said to have interests. As we will see in Chapter 9, *interest groups*, composed of individuals with similar interests, make up one of the most influential segments of the American political system.

## Opinions

[4] Robert E. Lane and David O. Sears, *Public Opinion* (Englewood Cliffs, N.J.: Prentice-Hall, Inc., 1964), p. 6, and Carl I. Hovland, Irving L. Janis, and Harold H. Kelley, *Communication and Persuasion* (New Haven, Conn.: Yale University Press, 1953), p. 6.

*Opinions* are individual preferences, stronger than impressions and weaker than facts. Opinions are usually expressions of general attitudes and specific interests "in response to a particular stimulus situation."[4] The manager who wishes an end to a railroad strike will almost certainly hold a strong opinion in favor of governmental intervention. The individual who has developed a negative attitude toward less fortunate and less educated persons may form an opinion against social welfare.

Opinions can be changed more easily than can attitudes or interests. The inflexibility of an opinion depends on its strength; on the influence exerted on the individual by groups to which he belongs; and on the amount of contrary evidence he receives. A Southerner who has always been a Democrat will probably be of the opinion that the "Solid South" should forever remain a Democratic fortress. If his local fraternal club begins to consider Republican candidates favorably, he may alter his opinion—depending on the degree of his identification with the group. That same person may be further convinced to change his opinion when he notes the numerous Republican gains in the South.

## Public opinion and political opinion

The terms public opinion and political opinion are often used interchangeably. Public opinion, however, covers a wider range of opinions or expressed

*These photographs depict levels of
political activity: expressing an opinion,
voting, and campaigning.*

preferences. Political opinion is but one form of public opinion (just as political behavior is only one form of social behavior).

*Public opinion* is the body of opinions expressed by the members of a community on any issue of interest to the community. Issues evoking public opinion can range from the length of women's skirts to the outcome of the Superbowl. Clearly, there is no single public opinion on any given issue. Instead, there are as many public opinions as there are views or sides to a specific issue.

*Political opinion*, on the other hand, is the body of opinions expressed by the members of a community on a political issue. (A political issue is here defined as an issue involving public policy and the resulting distribution of power in the political system.) The outcomes of elections, taxation, welfare, social security, and foreign policy are all issues that generate political opinions—and these opinions are just as varied as public opinions on nonpolitical matters.

## Variables affecting political opinion

Political opinions can be diametrically opposed, even in a group as small and close-knit as a single family. For example, members of a family may have opposing views on pollution control. As an employee of a manufacturing concern charged to be polluting the environment, the father is likely to defend

his company's efforts to control pollution. His son, however, who has no job interest to protect, may adamantly demand that the company be fined and active public surveillance of the company's manufacturing techniques be instituted.

Political opinion can also be qualified. An individual can support or oppose some action on a particular issue conditionally. "I will support the continued United States construction of nuclear weapons, only if there is clear evidence that the USSR is doing so," is an example of a qualified political opinion.

Some political opinions are held by large numbers of people, some by just a few people. In attempting to explain this variance, political scientists have identified four basic properties of political opinions: intensity; concentration; stability; and salience.

**Intensity**

The *intensity* of a political opinion refers to the fervor with which the opinion is held. Differences of intensity are due to many factors, one of which is personality. Some individuals are naturally intense about their opinions, clinging to them tenaciously, and refusing to acknowledge the possibility of error. Others are more open-minded. Some people, it appears, are naturally fickle—their opinions are as subject to change as the weather is.

The intensity of political opinion also varies according to the issue. Some

**Relationship between Intensity of Interest and Political Opinion in 1956**

| Selected Issues | Percentage of Total Sample with Strong Opinions |
|---|---|
| *High intensity issues:* | |
| Integration | 64 |
| Job guarantee | 60 |
| Acting tough toward Russia & China | 59 |
| Isolationism | 58 |
| Federal aid to education | 57 |
| Due process in firing communist suspects | 57 |
| *Low intensity issues:* | |
| Influence of big business | 46 |
| Public power and housing | 45 |
| Tax cuts | 44 |
| Economic aid to foreign nations | 37 |
| Aid to neutrals | 33 |

Source: Robert E. Lane and David O. Sears, *Public Opinion* (Englewood Cliffs, N.J.: Prentice-Hall, Inc., 1964), p. 97, based on V. O. Key, Jr., *Public Opinion and American Democracy* (New York: Alfred A. Knopf, Inc., 1961), pp. 213–218.

issues—civil rights and national defense, for example—provoke strong opinions of the majority of Americans. Others—farm subsidies and the antitrust laws, for example—produce strong opinions in much smaller segments of the society.

**Concentration**

The *concentration* of political opinion refers to the distribution of political opinion throughout the society. A political opinion is said to be concentrated if it is held uniformly by a specific segment of the society. For example, when we know that nearly all the corn and wheat farmers in the Midwest support farm subsidies, we can see that the political opinion in favor of farm subsidies tends to be concentrated in their particular segment of the society.

**Stability**

When the intensity and concentration of a particular political opinion are fairly constant over a substantial period of time, the opinion is said to be *stable*. The opinion that democracy is a satisfactory form of governing is clearly a stable opinion held by the majority of American citizens; if it were not, attempts to move the United States toward another form of government would have been successful long before now. It should be said, however, that there is no such thing as an absolutely stable opinion. Events and issues change; one generation supplants another, and, inevitably, ideas change.

**Salience**

The term *salience* simply denotes the importance of a particular issue given to an individual or group. To the majority of Americans, health, living standards, jobs, children, housing, schools, the war are salient issues; while United States policy toward Indonesia and the cost of grapes in Spain are not salient issues to most Americans. In recent public opinion surveys, environmental pollution has leaped to the top of the list of issues Americans consider most pressing.

# Political socialization: the source of political opinion

*Political socialization* is the process by which individuals acquire political attitudes and opinions. It is a complex process. An individual's political opinions are formed and shaped by all the groups to which he belongs. He is politically socialized by family, friends, work associates, labor union or professional association, church, political party. Moreover, all the factors by which men are grouped—race, religion, place of residence, education, social class, income level, and age—contribute to the individual's political opinions in one way or another.

## The family and peer groups

Immediate, personal associates—family, friends, and the like—and larger, less personal groups, such as political parties or national labor unions, all have an impact on an individual's political opinions.[5] However, there is some evidence to suggest that when the opinions of family and friends run counter to those of the larger organizations, the more intimate contacts may, more often than not, carry the day.[6]

The two most important groups in the socialization process are the *family* and the *peer group*. These primary groups are an individual's first contacts in the socialization process—the translators and modifiers of the opinions held by such groups as political parties and labor unions, which do not initially reach an individual.

[5] David Easton and Jack Dennis, *Children and the Political System: Origins of Political Legitimacy* (New York: McGraw-Hill Book Co., 1969).

[6] Norman Kaplan, "Reference Group Theory and Voting Behavior," in Angus Campbell, Philip E. Converse, Warren E. Miller, and Donald E. Stokes, *The American Voter* (New York: John Wiley and Sons, Inc., 1964), p. 162.

*Robert E. Lane* and *David O. Sears*, Public Opinion (*Englewood Cliffs, N.J.: Prentice-Hall, Inc., 1964*), *pp. 72–82.*

Robert Lane and David Sears have traced the lack of rationality—often characteristic of public opinion—to the manner in which opinions are formed. Holding rational opinions is difficult:

To be rational, a man must expose himself to congenial and uncongenial matters alike; he must be able to look at both and perceive them as they are, not merely as what he would like them to be, and he must be able to retain this information in undistorted form.

But most citizens are not, by these standards, rational; and their irrationality derives from the sources of their opinions.

The ways in which many opinions are formed violate these prescriptions for rationality. Most opinions seem to be formed from social referents; parents serve as referents for the child, and later on, group norms seem to guide many citizens toward the formulation of opinions on unfamiliar issues. These referents do not ordinarily reflect an adequate or unbiased sampling of the informational environment.

Opinions, then, are "handed down" or borrowed, rather than formed from individual knowledge and perception.

The group influence often discourages rationality; there have been instances, in fact, when seemingly entire nations have lost rationality. But, in general, argue Lane and Sears, group references may serve a positive function.

[They] may make the process of translating complex pieces of information into public opinion more "rational" than is the case when individuals are left to their own irrational thought processes. That is, opinions formed by this group reference may tend to reflect longer range, more salient individual interests than opinions formed in the absence of group reference.

## The family

[7] Richard E. Dawson and Kenneth Prewitt, *Political Socialization* (Boston: Little, Brown and Co., 1969), p. 133.

[8] Dawson, *Political Socialization*, p. 107.

The earliest and most powerful agent of political socialization is the family. "The orientations acquired in early childhood," write Richard Dawson and Kenneth Prewitt, "tend to be the most intensely and persistently held of all political views. They serve as the base on which later political learning is built."[7]

The enormous influence of the family on the development of political opinion is largely due to the family's almost exclusive access to the child as he develops and matures. The preschool years, the most important and emotionally intense portion of an individual's education, are spent almost entirely within the boundaries of the family—unless, however, "other important primary and secondary institutions take part in socialization."[8]

### Relationship between Parental Interest in Politics and Respondents' Political Involvement

| Respondents' Level of Involvement | Level of Parental Political Interest | | |
|---|---|---|---|
| | High | Medium | Low |
| High 1 | 36% | 19% | 14% |
| 2 | 25 | 27 | 12 |
| 3 | 19 | 29 | 19 |
| Low 4 | 20 | 25 | 55 |
| | 100% | 100% | 100% |
| Number of respondents | 658 | 422 | 274 |

Source: Center for Political Studies, University of Michigan, 1958.

"If you *don't mind,* Dr. Hervley, I do believe we could dispense with political opinion."

Drawing by W. Miller; © 1970
The New Yorker Magazine, Inc.

The family influences both the individual's interest in politics and the *positions* he holds on specific issues. In 1958, a research team from the University of Michigan asked a cross section of American voters whether they "personally cared a great deal about which party won the election to the Congress in Washington" or whether they "didn't care very much which party won?" Children of parents with high political interest expressed strong feelings about the outcome of the 1958 elections. Only 20 percent of this group expressed little or no concern. But less than half the children of low political interest parents showed any interest in the results of the election.[9]

Because families tend to conserve traditional political opinions and are slow to adopt new ones, the traditional family unit also functions as a *stabilizing* force in the political system. Political leaders have long been aware of the conservative character of the family unit, and for this reason, many a revolutionary regime has attempted to weaken the family structure.

[9] V. O. Key, Jr., *Public Opinion and American Democracy* (New York: Alfred A. Knopf, Inc., 1961), p. 302.

*Political opinions are frequently formed across peer group lines. Here we see three generations sharing their political opinions —in favor of peace in Vietnam.*

## The peer group

The start of formal schooling marks the first break in the lines of family influence. For the first time the child is involved in activities outside the family circle. The role of the family in the socializing process is slowly replaced by a second agent of political socialization—the peer group. In peer groups the status of the members is more or less equal. As in the family unit, ties between members within a peer group are fairly intimate and relationships are often highly emotional. As in the family, the peer group has frequent access to its members.

Certain peer groups exert greater influence on individuals than others. Moreover, the groups to which an individual belongs will change as an individual grows to adulthood. The child's peer group influences include neighborhood friends, school chums, school sports teams, and school social organizations. As an adult, the individual may belong to peer groups within his religious organization, political party, and ethnic group, as well as other more or less formal peer groups such as poker clubs, music societies, and educational groups.

[10] Dorwin Cartwright and Alvin Zander, "Group Pressures and Group Standards: Introduction," in Cartwright and Zander, eds., *Group Dynamics: Research and Theory* (New York: Harper, 1960), p. 169.

## Beyond the peer group

[11] Campbell, Converse, Miller, and Stokes, *The American Voter*, pp. 161–183.

## Social class

The results of peer group socialization are evident. Numerous studies have shown that peer group members tend to hold similar political opinions and exhibit similar political behavior. Dorwin Cartwright and Alvin Zander offer three explanations for the consistency of political opinion among peer groups:

1. "Membership in a group determines to a great extent many of the things a person will learn, see, experience, or think about."
2. "An individual may act like other members of a group because they are attractive to him and he wants to be like them."
3. "A person may act like other members of a group because he fears punishment, ridicule, or rejection by the rest of the group if he does not."[10]

Larger groupings, based on such distinctions as race, education, income, social standing, and place of residence, also influence the development of the individual's political opinions.[11] Within these secondary groups are both peer groups and family units. The group of Catholics in the United States, for example, is composed of Catholic families and various types of peer groups—childhood play groups and church organizations, to name two—in which all the members are Catholic. The political opinions of the leaders of larger groups—the political preferences of union officials, religious leaders, and interest-group leaders, for example—are refined and shaped within the family and peer groups.

The notion of social status or class has been employed throughout history to categorize each society into distinct units, each of which has an observable influence on its peoples' political opinions. Aristotle saw the plebians and patricians as distinct classes in the Greek political system. In the Middle Ages, Thomas Aquinas identified two classes—the lords and the serfs—as the basis of the feudal system of government. Karl Marx, one of the most influential political theorists of the nineteenth century, described all political, economic, and social activity as a conflict of class against class.

Contemporary societies continue to categorize their citizens in terms of class status. In Poland, for example, the individual's economic class—proletariat or elite—largely determines his political behavior and life style. In the United States, class distinctions are less constricting and are based on a broader spectrum of criteria: occupation, income, property holdings, education, and so on. Americans can and do improve their "social standing" by moving from one class to another.

Perhaps because social classes in the United States are neither definitely nor permanently defined, it is sometimes difficult for political scientists to obtain data on the political opinions of various classes. For example, researchers have had to deal with the fact that many individuals do not consider themselves to be part of the social class in which they are categorized by social

## Political Participation according to Socioeconomic Status and Level of Involvement in Groups

| Socioeconomic Status Level | Level of Involvement in Groups | Percentage of Group that Actively Participate |
|---|---|---|
| High | High | 75 |
| High | Low | 32 |
| Low | High | 67 |
| Low | Low | 10 |

Note: Political participation reflects strength of political opinion. Of the two categories, socioeconomic status and level of involvement in groups, the latter produces the greatest number of participants from both high and low socioeconomic groups.

Source: Adapted from Norman H. Nie, G. Bingham Powell, Jr., and Kenneth Prewitt, "Social Structure and Political Participation: Developmental Relations, Part I," *The American Political Science Review*, 63 (1969): 371.

[12] Richard Centers, *The Psychology of Social Classes,* reprint (New York: Russell and Russell Publishers, 1961). Originally published in 1949. Follow-up study in Campbell, *The American Voter,* pp. 189–190.

[13] Herbert McClosky, "Conservatism and Personality," *American Political Science Review,* LII (March 1958): 35.

scientists. As a matter of fact, one-third of the population does not identify with any social class at all. Categorization seems to depend on the individuals' attitudes toward each of the class distinctions. For example, when the term "working class" was added to the list of class distinctions, a sizable number of Americans who had previously identified with the lower and middle classes stated that they belonged to the working class. Working class is considered by many to be more respectable than lower class and less pretentious than middle class.[12] This identification with a particular class—an individual's class consciousness—has been found to be politically significant. Manual laborers who identify with the middle class tend to be more conservative than manual laborers who believe themselves members of the working class.[13]

## Relationship between Level of Education and Sense of Being Able to Affect Political Activities

| Sense of Political Efficacy | Educational Level | | |
|---|---|---|---|
| | Grade School | High School | College |
| High 4 | 3% | 8% | 27% |
| 3 | 14 | 28 | 37 |
| 2 | 29 | 38 | 26 |
| 1 | 23 | 15 | 6 |
| Low 0 | 31 | 11 | 4 |
| | 100% | 100% | 100% |
| Number of respondents | 897 | 1370 | 485 |

Source: Center for Political Studies, University of Michigan, 1952 and 1956 combined.

## Income, occupation, and education

[14] Additional information on these groups can be found in Seymour Martin Lipset, *Political Man: The Social Bases of Politics* (Garden City, N.Y.: Doubleday and Co., Inc., 1959).

[15] Key, *Public Opinion*, pp. 124–125.

Some studies have shown that upward mobility—movement from the lower class to the middle class, for example—leads to stronger political opinions, and that Americans moving up the social ladder tend to change their party affiliation from Democratic to Republican. Other studies further point out that people tend to change party affiliation with about the same frequency, whether they are moving up or down on the social ladder.

Each of these factors is closely related to the other two, and each has an impact on an individual's political opinions.[14] Traditionally, individuals with more education and higher income and occupational status have been more likely to identify with the Republican party and espouse more conservative political opinions. It is possible for a less educated individual to enter a high income bracket, but it is improbable that he will adopt the Republican views of his upper class counterparts. Most skilled blue-collar workers are part of unionized occupational groups, and the political attitudes of such groups often differ from the white-collar groups of the college graduate—even when salaries are roughly equivalent. Blue-collar political socialization will have run a different course than that of the college graduate. When asked to evaluate the statement "The government ought to help people get doctors and hospital care at low cost," about 50 percent of all professional people interviewed in one survey opposed it. More than 80 percent of the skilled and unskilled workers interviewed, on the other hand, supported the idea of government-supported medical insurance.[15] Although unskilled workers generally support government intervention in such domestic matters as medical insurance, they tend to take a more isolationist position on foreign policy than do professional or skilled workers.

V. O. Key, Jr., Public Opinion and American Democracy (*New York: Alfred A. Knopf, Inc., 1961*), *pp. 316–343.*

V. O. Key, Jr. examines the common assumption that the educational system shapes an individual's attitudes and opinions in a manner that will remain with him long after he has left school. Key claims that the average American education includes a large dose of ritualistic patriotism; moreover, he says that

ways and means are found to assure that the school system does not deviate markedly from the modal political values of the culture.

Throughout the nation, despite the decentralization of education, the schools work to instill the same basic premises in the student's mind. Thus, mass formal education may lead to mass inculcation of the official political values of a culture. These values, however, are not constant, inasmuch as they are subject to the changing mores of the society.

When other factors are constant, it has been determined that higher education does exert some lasting influence on the individual's opinions. Key argues, for example, that there is a relationship between level of education and level of information, as well as a relationship between level of education and the ability to understand and hold opinions on broad policies and philosophical problems.

According to Key, however, the educational system alone does not form political opinion.

While it is plain that education significantly shapes politically relevant attitudes, it must be conceded that isolation of the effects of the school system from other influences forming political man is not readily accomplished. Intensive studies of life histories of individuals would permit more confident assignment of weights to the factors of family, education, occupational interest, social status, and other such influences.

Investigating political socialization in terms of broad occupational categories—professional, managerial, white-collar, skilled, unskilled, and so on—can be misleading, however, because political opinions are often sharply divided *within* such groups. For example, in a population of college professors, sociology professors may as a group espouse political opinions that are significantly different from those of biologists. Similarly, among steel industry executives, those who control large firms may vote differently from those who operate smaller concerns.

## Race and religion

Race and religion, nearly impossible to isolate as factors in political socialization, do not appear to be so potent as an individual's social or economic level in their influence on his attitudes and opinions. But certain patterns of political opinion can be traced to religion and/or to race, for racial and religious groups have exhibited their socializing power in relation to specific contemporary issues. On civil rights issues, Vietnam, abortion laws, and aid to Israel, as well as several other issues, racial and religious groups have been highly opinionated, very active, and quite influential. Some studies show that Catholics hold very strong political opinions against Communist nations. Jews, on the other hand, are more concerned about social welfare. Along racial lines, blacks have been far more concerned about political activities in recent years than in the preceding decades. Finally, because of voting legislation and rulings of the Supreme Court, blacks have become increasingly interested in affecting the American political system.[16]

Most politicians, well aware of these facts, try to encompass as many groups as possible when choosing party candidates and political platforms. The major political parties in the nation's urban areas, where racial and religious groups are highly concentrated and often politically powerful, frequently offer "balanced tickets," made up of black, white, Jewish, and Catho-

[16] Key, *Public Opinion*, pp. 222, 514.

lic candidates (or whatever the "right" mix is) to satisfy the various groups within the politician's election district.

At least as often as not, the strategy of appealing to racial or religious segments of the population fails. Many other factors enter into the voting decisions of the electorate. For example, the Republican candidate for mayor of New York City in 1961 was a Jew, Louis Lefkowitz. Given a very large number of Jewish voters in New York City, he might have been expected to accumulate a certain number of votes cast on religious lines, since his opponent, the incumbent mayor, Robert Wagner, was a Catholic. But the vast majority of Jewish voters supported Wagner, because he was a Democrat, a liberal, and the son of a liberal United States senator.

### Relationship between Geographical Location and Political Opinion

| Opinion on Internationalism | Cities over 50,000 | Metro Fringe | Cities 10,000– 50,000 | Metro | Towns 2,500– 10,000 | Rural |
|---|---|---|---|---|---|---|
| High | 60% | 53% | 58% | 61% | 59% | 51% |
| Medium | 27 | 34 | 28 | 22 | 24 | 25 |
| Low | 13 | 13 | 14 | 17 | 17 | 24 |
| | 100% | 100% | 100% | 100% | 100% | 100% |
| Number of respondents | 217 | 159 | 148 | 223 | 260 | 408 |

Source: Center for Political Studies, University of Michigan, 1956.

## Place of residence

[17] V. O. Key, Jr., *Politics, Parties, and Pressure Groups*, 5th ed. (New York: Thomas Y. Cro well Co., 1967), p. 250.

[18] Norral D. Glenn and F. L. Summons, "Are Regional Differences Diminishing?" *Public Opinion Quarterly*, XXXI (Summer 1967): 176–193.

## Parties, candidates, and issues

Since 1928, most of the nation's large cities and urban centers have been predominantly Democratic. The majority of the suburbs surrounding these cities have tended to be Republican, the party of "rural interest " and . . . upperclass orientation."[17] Certain sections of the country—Maine, Vermont, Kansas, and North Dakota, for example—were traditionally Republican strongholds, but have recently elected Democratic governors. The South, by contrast, is still predominantly Democratic (at least at the state and local level). The traditional sectional or regional ties of Southerners to the Democratic party, ties that date back to the politics of the Civil War period, still frequently overpower the influence of educational, economic, and occupational groups that would tend to draw Southerners toward the Republican standard.

The South has been the most politically monolithic section of the nation since World War II, when isolationism (the policy of abstaining from direct involvement with foreign nations) died out in the then single-party Republican Midwest. But even in the South, the effect of regionalism is dying.[18]

The influence of parties, candidates, and issues on an individual's political opinions are much less personal, less direct, and less permanent than the influences of family, peer groups, and larger organizations are. In a very real sense, the latter associations are the principal backdrop against which both issues and candidates are measured and evaluated.

*Angus Campbell, Philip E. Converse, Warren E. Miller, and Donald E. Stokes, The American Voter (New York: John Wiley and Sons, Inc., 1964), pp. 16–26.*

In this study Campbell, Converse, Miller, and Stokes deal with the 1952 and 1956 presidential elections, in which Republican Dwight D. Eisenhower ran against Democrat Adlai E. Stevenson; their data illuminate the process by which public opinion is formed and changes.

In both contests, a few seemingly important issues did not significantly affect public opinion. The emotionally charged Senator Joseph McCarthy hearings, for example, were cited by the authors as having slight influence; domestic subversion of communism was not a salient partisan issue. And in 1956, Democratic corruption was not a major question:

Public concern about the corruption issue subsided rapidly with the Democratic Party out of power. However strong the sense of Democratic sin four years earlier, the party's loss of power seems to have accomplished its expiation by 1956. The swift decline of comment of this sort suggests that mismanagement and corruption are not issues that are easily kept alive after a change in control of the government.

Moreover, the party affiliation of the candidates did not have a great effect on voter evaluation.

Some predictable issues did work to shape opinion. For example, the impact of the depression was strong in the 1952 election; Democrats were regarded as having good domestic policies and as favoring the lower income groups. By 1956, however, the Republicans were able to show that "good times" could continue under their administration. The issues of war and peace, as reflected by World War II and the Korean crisis, also affected the campaign to an extent.

But the opinions formed about the presidential candidates themselves emerged as the most important factor in the elections.

It was the response to personal qualities—to his [Eisenhower's] sincerity, his integrity and sense of duty, his virtue as a family man, his religious devotion, and his sheer likeableness—that rose substantially in the second campaign. These frequencies leave the strong impression that in 1956 Eisenhower was honored not so much for his performance as President as for the quality of his person.

In Chapter 10, we will examine closely the role of political parties in the American political system. For now, let us note that 77 percent of all adult Americans identify themselves as Democrats or Republicans. Although many Americans identify so strongly with their party that they will support it no matter what the issue or who the candidate, a vast number of Americans do not consider that party membership binds them to invariable support of that party. Certain candidates, immensely popular for one reason or another, can cause wholesale party desertion—for example, Democratic Senator Edmund Muskie's amazing election record in once Republican Maine and President Eisenhower's landslide victories in a nation in which the majority of voters were Democrats.[19]

[19] Angus Campbell, Gerald Gurin, and Warren E. Miller, *The Voter Decides* (Evanston, Ill.: Row, Peterson, Inc., 1954), pp. 168–172.

## Party Identification Breakdown

| | 1970 Rep. | Dem. | Ind. | 1968 Rep. | Dem. | Ind. |
|---|---|---|---|---|---|---|
| Nationwide | 33% | 48% | 19% | 31% | 52% | 17% |
| *By region:* | | | | | | |
| East | 31 | 45 | 24 | 36 | 49 | 15 |
| Midwest | 36 | 43 | 21 | 33 | 45 | 22 |
| South | 22 | 64 | 14 | 20 | 68 | 12 |
| West | 38 | 44 | 18 | 36 | 53 | 11 |
| *By size of place:* | | | | | | |
| Cities | 24 | 52 | 24 | 20 | 64 | 16 |
| Suburbs | 34 | 43 | 23 | 36 | 44 | 20 |
| Towns | 39 | 47 | 14 | 39 | 46 | 15 |
| Rural | 37 | 47 | 16 | 34 | 49 | 17 |
| *By race:* | | | | | | |
| White | 36 | 43 | 21 | 34 | 48 | 18 |
| Black | 17 | 76 | 7 | 7 | 83 | 10 |
| *By age:* | | | | | | |
| 21–29 | 33 | 45 | 22 | 29 | 49 | 22 |
| 30–49 | 33 | 49 | 18 | 29 | 54 | 17 |
| 50 and over | 35 | 50 | 15 | 36 | 51 | 13 |
| *By income:* | | | | | | |
| Under $5,000 | 27 | 52 | 21 | 29 | 55 | 16 |
| $5,000–9,999 | 28 | 55 | 17 | 29 | 54 | 17 |
| $10,000+ | 40 | 39 | 21 | 36 | 44 | 20 |
| *By education:* | | | | | | |
| 8th grade or less | 30 | 60 | 10 | 27 | 61 | 12 |
| High school | 27 | 50 | 23 | 28 | 54 | 18 |
| College | 44 | 35 | 21 | 41 | 41 | 18 |
| *By religion:* | | | | | | |
| Protestant | 44 | 38 | 18 | 40 | 44 | 16 |
| Catholic | 22 | 53 | 25 | 24 | 57 | 19 |
| Jewish | 16 | 60 | 24 | 5 | 76 | 19 |

Source: Harris Survey; Chicago Tribune—N.Y. News Syndicate, Inc., 1970.

## Harris Surveys Showing the Distribution of Political Opinion on Two Major Issues

"The U.S. Supreme Court has ruled that public schools which are segregated must become integrated now without any further delay. In general, do you tend to approve or disapprove of this ruling for integration now by the U.S. Supreme Court?"

"Suppose the only way we could get peace in Vietnam were to agree to a coalition government which included the Communists in it. Would you favor or oppose such a coalition in Saigon?"

| | Approve | Disapprove | Unsure |
|---|---|---|---|
| Nationwide | 55% | 32% | 13% |
| *By region:* | | | |
| East | 64 | 24 | 12 |
| Midwest | 53 | 32 | 15 |
| South | 42 | 43 | 15 |
| West | 64 | 26 | 10 |
| *By race:* | | | |
| White | 53 | 34 | 13 |
| Negro | 69 | 16 | 15 |
| *By income:* | | | |
| Under $5,000 | 48 | 35 | 17 |
| $5,000–9,999 | 53 | 35 | 12 |
| $10,000–14,999 | 56 | 32 | 12 |
| $15,000+ | 69 | 24 | 7 |
| *By 1968 vote:* | | | |
| Nixon | 52 | 34 | 14 |
| Humphrey | 67 | 19 | 14 |
| Wallace | 32 | 58 | 10 |

| | Favor | Oppose | Not-Sure |
|---|---|---|---|
| Nationwide | 42% | 39% | 19% |
| *By region:* | | | |
| East | 50 | 28 | 22 |
| Midwest | 37 | 47 | 16 |
| South | 38 | 43 | 19 |
| West | 49 | 36 | 15 |
| *By age:* | | | |
| 18–29 | 47 | 39 | 14 |
| 30–49 | 46 | 38 | 16 |
| 50 and over | 37 | 37 | 26 |
| *By race:* | | | |
| Black | 41 | 30 | 29 |
| White | 43 | 40 | 17 |
| *By income:* | | | |
| Under $5,000 | 32 | 44 | 24 |
| $5,000–9,999 | 40 | 40 | 20 |
| $10,000–$14,999 | 45 | 39 | 16 |
| $15,000+ | 57 | 32 | 11 |

The influence of issues on an individual's political opinions and behavior depends very much on how directly the issue affects the individual, as noted earlier. Because most Southerners have strong opinions about the segregation issue, for example, many Democrats voted for presidential candidate Barry Goldwater, a Republican, whose vote against the Civil Rights Act of 1964 was interpreted by some Southerners as support for segregation.

# The influence of mass media upon political opinion

Some analysts of our political system see the *mass media*—radio, television, and newspapers—as socializing agents more powerful than the family, as molders of political opinion that grow more influential each year. In many American homes, the television set is on an average of seven hours each day. This electronic baby-sitter has extensive access to a preschool child and can evoke highly emotional responses in him. Its influence over children is undeniably great. Studies of children of different nations have shown, for instance, that children in developed nations cite television as their major source of information, while children in underdeveloped countries point to their parents as their primary source.

The various forms of the mass media are a major source of political information for adults and children. Citizens in Oregon learn of the activities of Congress in Washington, the protests of students in Wisconsin and California, and the movements of American troops in Southeast Asia through the mass media. The promises of politicians, the statements of public officials, and the opinions of political leaders are all transmitted to the public through the mass media.

These major sources of political information do not always form political opinion, however. Each person selectively perceives information that is consistent with his beliefs. In addition, much of the information he receives from the mass media is filtered through his group's *opinion leader*. Political socialization by the mass media is a two-step process, in which most individuals receive primarily interpreted information. "Ideas, often, seem to flow *from* radio and print *to* leaders and *from them* to the less active sections of the population."[20]

20 Elihu Katz and Paul Lazarsfeld, *Personal Influence* (New York: The Free Press, 1955).

21 See Joseph T. Klapper, *The Effects of Mass Communication* (New York: The Free Press, 1960), chap. 3.

## Comparison of Sources of Information Reported by Children of Different Nationalities

Nationality of Children

| | American | Bantu | Brazilian | English-Cana-dian | French | French-Cana-dian | German | Israeli | Japanese | Leba-nese | Turkish |
|---|---|---|---|---|---|---|---|---|---|---|---|
| 6-year-olds | TV-movies (parents) | parents | parents (contact) | TV contact | parents | TV | parents TV-movies (contact) | parents friends | parents TV-movies | contact parents | parents friends |
| 10- and 11-year-olds | TV-movies books courses texts maga-zines | parents (10 yrs. only) contact teachers | movies maga-zines contact | TV courses texts books | parents (10 yrs. only) texts books maga-zines (14 yrs. only) | TV texts books maga-zines (14 yrs. only) | TV-movies books maga-zines courses contact radio | books friends courses movies maga-zines | TV-movies courses texts teachers maga-zines | books maga-zines radio movies texts friends contact | books texts courses movies maga-zines |

Source: Wallace E. Lambert and Otto Klineberg, *Children's Views of Foreign Peoples, A Cross-National Study.* Copyright © 1967 by Meredith Publishing Company. Reprinted by permission of Appleton-Century-Crofts.

Nor is political information simply transmitted to the public *live*, as it happens; it is *interpreted* for the public by journalists.[21] For this reason, newspapers, television networks, and radio stations are often accused of propagandizing in their news presentations on behalf of one cause or another.

## Propaganda

22 *The New York Times*, May 17, 1952.

23 For information on the effect of politics on one form of the media, see Richard W. Lee, ed., *Politics and the Press* (Washington, D.C.: Acropolis Books, 1970).

## Trends in the mass media

24 Bryce W. Rucker, *The First Freedom* (Carbondale, Ill.: Southern Illinois University Press, 1968).

In its common usage, propaganda is a word much like massacre. Whether Custer's last stand was a glorious victory or a massacre depends on whether you side with General Custer or with Sitting Bull. A senator's impassioned defense of a tax bill will be labeled propaganda or wisdom, depending on an individual's feelings about the measure. "As generally understood," however, "propaganda is an expression of opinion or action by individuals or groups with reference to predetermined ends."[22] In other words, *propaganda* is an attempt to influence people's attitudes and opinions.

In this usage, it is hard to imagine any communication or form of reporting that is not propaganda. Consider a newspaper reporter, covering the proceedings of a school board meeting. Although he may claim he is "presenting only the facts" in his report, he is still dealing in propaganda. The question is *which facts shall he choose to report?* He cannot present *all* the information he receives, he must choose what to report, what to emphasize. Inevitably, in the selection process, the reporter propagandizes, because he wants others to see the meeting as he saw it, especially in terms of what he felt was accomplished at the meeting.

If some propaganda is unavoidable, perhaps we should be more concerned with the degree to which various factors influence the media's presentation of political information. A look at current trends in the news media will show some of the ways in which news is shaped and possibly modified before it reaches the nation.[23]

Certain trends in the mass media have been regarded with apprehension by some observers. One is the increasing *centralization* of media outlets. Just two wire services, the Associated Press (AP) and the United Press International (UPI), supply most national and world news to 83.6 percent of the American newspapers.[24] Large newspaper chains now account for more than half the nation's daily circulation. Various companies formerly involved in only one form of communications are moving into other media. Time, Incorporated, for example, has branched out from magazine publishing (*Time, Life, Fortune, Sports Illustrated*) into book publishing, television, films, radio, and education.

The *commercialism* of the mass media is another widely noted trend. Because most television and radio stations, newspapers, and magazines are businesses—that is, they seek to operate at a profit—they depend on income derived from circulation and/or advertising. To survive, most branches of the mass media must take into account the views of major advertisers, as well as the views of their readers or viewers. This process of "taking into account" has often led to charges of bias or sensationalism. One of America's most respected journalists, the late Edward R. Murrow, pointed out the problems of commercialism in the mass media: "One of the basic troubles with radio and television news," he said, "is that both instruments have grown up as an incompatible combination of show business, advertising, and news. Each of the three is a rather bizarre and demanding profession. And when you get all three under one roof, the dust never settles. The top management of the networks, with a few notable exceptions, has been trained in advertising, research, sales, or show business. But, by the nature of the corporate structure, they also make the final and crucial decisions having to do with news and public affairs."[25]

The owners of the mass media tend to support conservative policies—that is, they tend to support the established political and economic interests and activities—and vigorously resist any changes that could adversely affect profits. As V. O. Key notes, "the content . . . tends to reaffirm existing values, to buttress prevailing institutions, and to support ancient ways of doing things."[26]

However, these same businessmen know that it is also good business to take the sentiments of their viewers or readers seriously. If a large segment of the population holds liberal views, the mass media will reflect these attitudes. In addition, many employees of media companies—writers, reporters, photographers, editors, and newscasters—have traditionally been more liberal than their employers. In recent years, the dissemination of liberal ideas and opinions through the mass media has significantly increased. For example, in 1969, the New York *Daily News* supported United States' involvement in Vietnam. A group of *Daily News* employees who opposed the war ran a full-page advertisement stating their opposition in *The New York Times*.

## Newspapers

Since 1910, newspaper after newspaper has shut down or merged into one of the growing newspaper chains. Rising labor and printing costs, the increased use of radio and television, and intense competition from the chains has caused consolidations to the point that more than 49.3 percent of the nation's daily newspapers are chain-owned. In 1909, there were 2,600 dailies published in the United States. Today there are an estimated 1,750. In 1920, 42 percent of the cities with daily newspapers had competing dailies. By 1970, however, less than 3 percent of the nation's cities had more than one newspaper![27] The residents of most American cities must look to just one newspaper for their news.

Some publishers claim that lack of competition allows them to devote more time and money to accurate and thorough coverage of the news. Studies of single-newspaper versus competitive-newspaper cities, however, reveal no evidence of higher quality in single-newspaper cities.

The effect of the nation's newspapers on political opinion and participation is difficult to measure. Although five Democratic Presidents have been elected in this century, it was only in 1964 that a majority of the nation's newspapers endorsed the Democratic candidate for President. Nevertheless,

[25] Reprinted in Newton Minow, *Equal Time: The Private Broadcasters and the Public Interest* (New York: Atheneum Publishers, 1964). Also see Dan D. Nimmo, *Newsgathering in Washington* (New York: Atherton Press, 1964), p. 230, for a discussion of the importance of responsible leadership of the media.

[26] Key, *Public Opinion*, p. 396.

[27] Arthur E. Rowse, "The Press Dummies Up," *The Nation*, June 30, 1969, pp. 816–820.

newspaper influence can be much more subtle than direct editorial comments on political issues or candidates. Choices of what to report, and when, and how, all have direct bearing on the impressions of political life a newspaper brings its readers.

"You would be wasting your time with me. My mind is totally controlled by what the news media feed it."

Drawing by Alan Dunn; © 1970
The New Yorker Magazine, Inc.

## The electronic media

Television and radio reach more Americans than newspapers do, and probably have a greater impact. Almost every American has access to either a television set or a radio, and most Americans spend a very substantial portion of their waking hours watching or listening, as the case may be.

Almost all the radio and television stations and networks, are supported by advertising. In a very real sense, their overall programming output is dictated by the need to deliver the largest possible audiences to their advertisers—a need that appears to lead inevitably to "least common denominator" entertainment programming—programming that offends nobody. "I Love Lucy," "Petticoat Junction," "Bonanza," and dozens of similar programs play on and on, day in, day out, through endless reruns. In the words of V. O. Key, Jr., the stations and networks are in the business of providing programs that "arouse no controversy, irritate no sensitivity, disturb no gray cell."[28]

[28] Key, *Public Opinion*, p. 386.

**Television Ownership**

| City | No. of TV Stations | No. under Multiple Ownership |
|---|---|---|
| New York | 9 | 6 |
| Chicago | 10 | 6 |
| Los Angeles | 13 | 9 |
| Philadelphia | 8 | 5 |
| Detroit | 8 | 6 |
| Boston | 8 | 4 |
| San Francisco | 10 | 6 |
| Pittsburgh | 7 | 5 |
| St. Louis | 7 | 4 |
| Cleveland | 6 | 5 |

Source: *Broadcasting Yearbook 1969* (Washington, D.C.: Broadcasting Publications, Inc., 1969), pp. A102–A131.

Radio and television, especially the latter, have been criticized for the escapist quality of most of their entertainment programming. But radio and television news departments are criticized just as vigorously for *their* outputs, and for quite different reasons. It is charged, for instance, that all too often events are covered according to how pictorially "newsworthy" and dramatic they are. As a result, it is said, such emotionally charged activities as the war and the civil rights struggle receive close attention, while quieter (but scarcely less important) affairs such as congressional hearings or Supreme Court decisions receive little or no coverage.

In the last year or two, the television networks' news coverage has been attacked by Vice-President Spiro Agnew. Television news, according to Agnew, stresses the violent and exciting.[29] It exaggerates the importance of such people as H. Rap Brown, who, says Agnew, have no real following but know how to produce dramatic stories. The news media contend, in turn, that Agnew's criticism is unjustified. It is the newscaster's duty, they claim, to report everything he can, to the best of his ability. They argue that a news broadcaster should not be intimidated into the suppression of a news story, simply because it is controversial. (Perhaps it should be noted that almost all national administrations as far back as Jefferson's have criticized the news media.)

29 John Osborn, "The Nixon Watch: Agnew's Effect," *The New Republic*, February 28, 1970, pp. 13–15; M. L. Stein, "The Networks: The First Round to Agnew," *The Nation*, September 7, 1970, pp. 178–181; "The Threat from Spiro," *Commonweal*, XCI, no. 10 (December 5, 1969): 293–295; Spiro T. Agnew, *Speaking Frankly* (Washington, D.C.: Public Affairs Press, 1970).

# Participation and opinion

Political socialization implies more than a passive assimilation of the attitudes and opinions expressed by family, friends, groups, and the mass media. At an early age, the individual begins to formulate his own ideas and opinions and to exert his influence through one or more channels of political participation.

## Forms of expression

Voicing opinions on political issues—to family, friends, or business associates —is the simplest, easiest way to participate in the political system. Voicing an opinion requires little or no "hard" information, and the smallest expenditure of time, energy, and resources of any type of political participation. Thus, Americans rarely refuse to give an opinion on current political issues.

The fact that an individual voices an opinion about a specific political issue does not mean that the individual is *informed* about the issue. When asked *why* they held a particular political opinion, more than 10 percent of those interviewed in several public opinion surveys said they did not know. They just "felt that way." Survey after survey has shown that ignorance about political issues is widespread in the United States. In 1964, for example, only 58 percent knew that the United States is a member of NATO (The North Atlantic Treaty Organization); and only 37 percent could name the Chief Justice of the Supreme Court.[30]

For those who wish to do more than voice opinions, there are other means of participation in the American political system. Voting is the next most commonly exercised form. Studies of the 1968 presidential election have shown that more than 60 percent of the adult population of the United States voted. Of this number, however, a sizable portion are not habitual voters—only 25 to 30 percent of the adult population vote with any degree of regularity in state and local elections.[31]

Beyond voting, many Americans participate in politics by writing letters to public officials and the mass media, by working for political candidates, by contributing to political parties and candidates, and by joining groups formed to influence politicians in specific directions, for example, Common Cause, SANE, and other such organizations. A 1964 survey indicated that while 54 percent of Americans have tried to influence the political opinions of their friends, only 15 percent have ever written letters to public officials, and only 3 percent have written to newspapers and magazines. Less than 5 percent have ever done political volunteer work, and less than 10 percent have made monetary contributions to political organizations.[32]

Several political scientists have noted that political activity tends to be *interrelated*. The individual who supports a political party tends also to vote and to voice political opinions. Similarly, the individual who runs for public office tends to contribute both time and money to political organizations, to influence others through political discussions, to vote, and to express his political opinions openly.

## The functions of political opinions

Men may choose to participate in politics or to remain aloof; either way, they affect the nation's political system. V. O. Key has categorized the functions that political opinions may perform.[33]

Since most political opinions are not intensely felt, there is a *permissive con-*

[30] Lloyd A. Free and Hadley Cantril, *The Political Beliefs of Americans* (New Brunswick, N.J.: Rutgers University Press, 1968), pp. 190–191.

[31] Robert E. Lane, *Political Life* (New York: The Free Press, 1959), pp. 45–62.

[32] Philip E. Converse, Aage R. Clausen, and Warren E. Miller, "Electoral Myth and Reality: the 1964 Election," *The American Political Science Review,* LIX, no. 2 (June 1964): 333.

[33] Key, *Public Opinion,* pp. 29–37.

**Permissive consensus**

*sensus* in the political system. Public officials are *permitted* to select their own courses of action, so long as their actions do not meet intense and general opposition among their constituents. Countless examples exist, for instance, of congressional action (or inaction) on behalf of a particular interest group and against the majority-held opinion of the nation. If the interest group is strong and vocal, and if the general public is apathetic, the official selects the course of action most likely to please the more politically involved of his constituents.

> *Walter Lippmann*, The Phantom Public (*New York: The Macmillan Co., 1927*), *pp. 68, 69, 197.*
>
> Walter Lippmann, in one of his early books, *The Phantom Public*, offers his view of the role of public opinion.
>
> We say that the ideal of public opinion is to align men during the crisis of a problem in such a way as to favor the action of those individuals who may be able to compose a crisis. The power to discern those individuals is the end of the effort to educate public opinion.
>
> Public opinion, in this theory, is a reserve of force brought into action during a crisis in public affairs. Though it is itself an irrational force, under favorable institutions, sound leadership and decent training the power of public opinion, might be placed at the disposal of those who stood for workable law as against brute assertion. In this theory, public opinion does not make the law. But by canceling lawless power it may establish the condition under which law can be made. It does not reason, investigate, invent, persuade, bargain or settle. But, by holding the aggressive party in check, it may liberate intelligence.
>
> I have conceived public opinion to be, not the voice of God, nor the voice of society, but the voice of the interested spectators of action. I have, therefore, supposed that the opinions of the spectators must be essentially different from those of the actors, and that the kind of action they were capable of taking was essentially different too.

**Supportive consensus**

Once the government enacts a law or adopts a new policy, it is usually supported by the American public, even if the measure had met strong opposition prior to passage. In this sense, political opinion reflects a *supportive consensus*. Recent examples of such a supportive function can be found in the adoption of the Voting Rights Acts of 1964 and 1965. Although they were initially opposed by many Americans, these laws were generally accepted after adoption by Congress and support by the Supreme Court.

In some cases American political opinion is so strongly opposed to a specific policy or law that the supportive consensus does not apply. For example, public opposition to the Eighteenth Amendment, which made the sale and manufacture of alcoholic beverages illegal, was so strong that the amendment could not be enforced and was eventually repealed.

**Directive consensus**

As in the case of the Eighteenth Amendment, American political opinion is sometimes so intense on a particular issue that it directs or demands a specific response from the government. This function of political opinion does not often come into play in national political life, but when it happens it is usually dramatic. An interesting, though debatable, example of political opinion performing a *directive function* in recent years was capped by President Johnson's decision not to run for re-election in 1968. Outraged by the nation's growing involvement in Vietnam, a large number of Americans blamed Johnson directly and personally. Some analysts feel that the weight of adverse public opinion was so crushing that Johnson felt he had been directed to step down from the presidency—in effect, to resign.

# Measuring public opinion

[34] Niccolo Machiavelli, *The Prince*, ed. by Mark Musa (New York: St. Martin's Press, 1964), chap. 21.

Political leaders throughout history have been aware of the importance of political opinion. "And above all a prince must endeavor in every action to obtain fame for being great and excellent," wrote Machiavelli in the early sixteenth century.[34] But how do political leaders know what actions will bring them "fame for being great and excellent"?

**Direct communication**

Every elected official receives letters, telephone calls, and telegrams from concerned citizens stating their views on political matters. Many congressmen, especially during campaigns, spend a great deal of time talking directly with their constituents. In this way, political leaders can go directly to the sources of political opinion. It should be noted, however, that the Americans who write or speak to public officials are a small minority of the public. Their opinions are often intense, but not always representative of majority sentiment.

Direct communication occurs in another way, too. Both the interest groups and the political parties mentioned earlier provide politicians with much valuable information about political opinion in the nation, since the leaders of such groups are constantly presenting the views of their membership to public officials both informally, in private meetings, and formally, in committee hearings, for example.

**Polls and surveys**

Americans are the most "polled" nation in history. There are more than a thousand polling organizations in the United States, busily discovering the public's brand preferences, television preferences, political preferences, and ten thousand other things. Among politicians, polls are used to find the answers to two questions: What do my people want done? Who do they want to do it?

Politicians use polls often, possibly because the easiest thing (perhaps the *only* easy thing) about a poll is deciding to take one. Every poll is an attempt to measure the attitudes of a complete *population* on some particular subject or subjects. The population can consist of all the people in a town, a city, a state, a county, a religion, an age group, a race, or a nation. It is impossible to poll a complete population of any size—there are simply too many people to talk to. To speak for the population, a *representative sample* of the population is selected. The object is to obtain valid predictive evidence for the attitudes and/or future behavior of the population as a whole. Consequently, the range of attitudes inside the sample must faithfully reflect the range of attitudes in the population.[35]

[35] The major criticism of polls has been of the assumption that the sample—1600 in a national political poll—can be used to determine the behavior of millions.

Constructing a representative sample is not easy. Most poll-takers feel that it is by far the most difficult part of polling. If *As Maine goes, so goes the nation* were a demonstrably valid statement (it is demonstrably invalid, as a matter of fact), fleets of pollsters would be sailing down east on the next fresh wind. A representative sample must be small enough to be reachable and large enough to permit predictions about population attitude or behavior. It can be a *random,* or *probability* sampling, in which people are chosen at random for interview. Or it can be *quota* sampling, in which an attempt is made to represent the economic, religious, social, and other stratifications in the population of which it is a part, on an equal basis.

**Poll-taking**

Assuming a good representative sample has been constructed and will faithfully reflect the attitudes of the population it represents, it is still necessary to determine *what* the sample is to be asked, and *how* the question or questions are to be put. Two basic types of questions are used in polling. The first is the *fixed-alternative* type, in which the interviewee must choose between a group of answers provided by the interviewer. The second is the *open-ended* type, in which the interviewee is asked to formulate his own answers. Obviously, the second is much harder to "read" in a statistical way, since people seldom say what they mean or mean what they say. Open-ended questions are most often used in random sampling polls, which are frequently in-depth interviews of a relatively small number of people.

The way a question is answered frequently depends on how it is asked. Pollsters admit that there are serious problems in obtaining accurate data on American political opinions because of this. The American who answers "Yes" to the question "Ought America to honor its foreign commitment to China?" might answer "No!" to "Should we continue to prop up Chiang Kai-shek?" Wording is all-important, because it is extremely easy to introduce bias in the answers through sloppy expression of the questions. In a series of questions, even the sequence has been shown to be important. (As a matter of fact, everything relating to the conduct of the interview is important—the dress and personality of the interviewer are factors; sex is a factor; whether or not the interviewer wears a beard is a factor; and so on.)

On the whole, poll-taking techniques have advanced since the computer came into our lives, with its ability to assimilate and classify data within a complex population model. In 1968, both Gallup and Harris predicted the respective votes for Nixon, Humphrey, and Wallace within 3 percent of the actual count. Polls have become so accurate that politicians frequently accuse poll-takers of influencing election results by releasing information that particular candidates are likely winners, thereby persuading supporters of opposing candidates that they may as well stay home on Election Day. It does not usually work that way (if it ever has). The 1948 Gallup and Roper Polls, commencing in August, had Dewey such a certain winner that they stopped taking surveys more than a month before the election. The poll predictions along with Truman's "Give 'Em Hell" campaign produced public sentiment for Truman (since with little to lose, Truman could conduct a strong, partisan campaign), and a decisive Democratic victory on election day (and one unforgettable photograph: the tireless, nerveless Truman, a small man with a half-mile grin, holding up the Chicago *Sun-Times* with the big black headline "Dewey Defeats Truman"). The most definite expression of political opinion in the nation is the vote. Voting is the means by which Americans can state their preferences directly. Once the individual pulls the voting lever, his opinion is indelibly recorded. When the polls close in his district, his representatives in government have been elected, and when the polls close across the nation, the people's representatives have been chosen, long, long before David Brinkley or Walter Cronkite announces that winner.

In the next chapter we will examine the role of voting in the political system.

# Glossary

**attitudes**  Learned tendencies or predispositions that lead individuals to respond in a particular manner.

**concentration of political opinion**  The distribution of political opinions, specifically those held uniformly by specific segments of the society.

**consensus of decision**  Function of political opinion in which the citizens, because of intensity of opinion, direct or demand a specific response from government.

**intensity of political opinion**  The fervor with which an opinion is held, influenced by such factors as personality and specific issues.

**interests**  Attitudes that are associated with specific activities.

**opinions**  Individual preferences, stronger than first impressions and weaker than knowledge of facts.

**peer groups**  Small intimate groups in which the status of the members is fairly equal and the ties between members are fairly intimate.

**permissive consensus**  Function of political opinion in which public officials are allowed by public inaction to make their own, uninfluenced decisions.

**political opinion**  Body of opinions expressed by the members of a community on a political issue, involving the distribution of power in the political system.

**political participation**  Behavior aimed at influencing the political system.

**political socialization**  The process by which individuals acquire political attitudes and opinions.

**poll**  Survey of public opinion on various issues.

**propaganda**  Expression of opinion or action by individuals or groups with reference to predetermined ends.

**public opinion**  Body of opinions expressed by the members of a community on an issue concerning the entire community.

**salience**  The importance of a particular issue to a given individual or group.

**social class**  Categorization within society of a group of individuals that display certain patterns of social, economic, and political behavior, based on occupation, income, property holdings, and education.

**stability of political opinion**  The tendency of political opinion to remain constant in intensity and concentration over a period of time.

**supportive consensus**  Function of political opinions in which citizens tend to accept public policy as legitimate.

# Suggested readings

Almond, Gabriel, and Sidney Verba, *The Civic Culture: Political Attitudes and Democracy in Five Nations* (Boston: Little, Brown and Co., 1965). Theory of political development.

Berelson, Bernard, and Morris Janowitz, eds., *Reader in Public Opinion and Communication*, 2nd ed. (New York: The Free Press, 1966). Selected readings in public opinion and communication.

Cater, Douglas, *The Fourth Branch of Government* (New York: Random House, Inc., 1959). Critical analysis of the relationship between the press and national government.

Childs, Harwood L., *Public Opinion* (Princeton, N.J.: Van Nostrand-Reinhold Books, 1965). Introductory textbook in public opinion by a noted scholar in the field.

Choukas, Michael, *Propaganda Comes of Age* (Washington, D.C.: Public Affairs Press, 1965). Analysis of the important role of propaganda in twentieth century America.

Dawson, Richard E. and Kenneth Prewitt, *Political Socialization* (Boston: Little, Brown and Co., 1969). Analysis of the factors concerning political socialization, arranged in such categories as family, peer group, religion, and race.

Fagen, Richard R., *Politics and Communication: An Analysis* (Boston: Little, Brown and Co., 1966). Study of the communications media in relation to the political process.

Greenstein, Fred I., *Children and Politics* (New Haven, Conn.: Yale University Press, 1965). Study of the political socialization of American elementary school children.

Hennessy, Bernard L., *Public Opinion*, 2nd ed. (Belmont, Calif.: Wadsworth Publishing Co., Inc., 1970). Introduction to the study of public opinion.

Hoffer, Eric, *The True Believer* (New York: Harper and Row Publishers, Inc., 1958). Dramatic analysis of the psychology of mass movements and the behavior of the fanatic who is personally compelled to sacrifice everything for his political beliefs.

Hyman, Herbert H., *Political Socialization: A Study in the Psychology of Political Behavior* (New York: The Free Press, 1969). Study of the process by which a child becomes an adult political participant.

Kelley, Stanley, Jr., *Professional Public Relations and Political Power* (Baltimore: Johns Hopkins University Press, 1956). Analysis of the important role of advertising techniques in political campaigns.

Key, V. O., Jr., *Public Opinion and American Democracy* (New York: Alfred A. Knopf, Inc., 1961). Classic study of major concepts in public opinion, including descriptions of all the factors that influence political socialization.

Lacy, Dan, *Freedom and Communications*, 2nd ed. (Urbana, Ill.: University of Illinois Press, 1965). Series of lectures describing the communications systems in America today and their importance in our political process.

Lane, Robert E., *Political Life: Why People Get Involved in Politics*, rev. ed. (New York: The Free Press, 1959). Studies of the American voter's political behavior, including the degrees of his involvement in politics.

Lane, Robert E., *Political Ideology: Why the American Man Believes What He Does* (New York: The Free Press, 1962). Description of the American voter, based on in-depth interviews, with the conclusion that voters have no consistent political ideology or firm traditional belief.

Lane, Robert E., *Political Thinking and Consciousness: The Private Life of the Political Mind* (Garden City, N.Y.: Doubleday and Co., Inc., 1969). Study of the development of political ideas among college students, based on twenty-four essays by college undergraduates. Lane concludes that minimum satisfaction of basic personal needs (love, safety, and so on) fosters political thinking and consciousness.

Lane, Robert E., and David O. Sears, *Public Opinion* (Englewood Cliffs, N.J.: Prentice-Hall, Inc., 1964). Brief, but well-done analysis of the dynamics of opinion formation.

Lasswell, Harold D., *Psychopathology and Politics* (New York: The Viking Press, 1960). Application of psychoanalysis to the study of political personality and behavior.

Lippmann, Walter, *Public Opinion* (New York: The Free Press, 1965). Analysis of the social and psychological forces underlying the formation of public opinion.

Lipset, Seymour Martin, *Political Man: The Social Bases of Politics* (Garden City, N.Y.: Doubleday and Co., Inc., 1959). Analysis by a leading political sociologist of politics and participation in a democracy.

Luttbeg, Norman R., *Public Opinion and Public Policy: Models of Political Linkage* (Homewood, Ill.: Dorsey Press, Inc., 1968). Analysis of the mechanics by which public opinion is transmitted to policy-makers.

McConnell, Grant, *Private Power and American Democracy* (New York: Alfred A. Knopf, Inc., 1966). Analysis of the influence of private power groups on public opinion.

Milbrath, Lester W., *Political Participation: How and Why People Get Involved in Politics* (Chicago: Rand-McNally and Co., 1965). An attempt to develop a general theory of participation in the political process.

Rivers, William L., *Opinion Makers* (Boston: Beacon Press, Inc., 1965). Analysis of the relationship between reporters and government officials, including a critical evaluation of the effect of the press on public opinion.

Rubin, Bernard, *Political Television* (Belmont, Calif.: Wadsworth Publishing Co., Inc., 1967). Discussion of the influence of television on elections and the presidency.

Smith, Mortimer B., Jerome S. Bruner, and Robert W. White, *Opinions and Personality* (New York: John Wiley and Sons, Inc., 1956). Analysis of what opinion is, how it shapes our behavior, and how opinions are studied.

# Topics of further study

Alexander, Rudolph P., "Grouping Factors in the Central Valley Elementary Schools" (master's thesis, Gonzaga University, 1963).

Derrig, James Raymond, "The Political Thought of the Catholic Press, 1880–1920" (Ph.D. dissertation, St. Louis University, 1961).

Feierabend, Ivo K., and Rosalind L. Feierabend, "Aggressive Behavior within Politics, 1948–1952: A Cross-National Study," *The Journal of Conflict Resolution*, X (1966): 249–269.

Greenstein, Fred I., "Benevolent Leader: Children's Images of Political Authority," *American Political Science Review*, December 1960, pp. 934–943.

Hutter, Mark, "Transformation of Identity, Social Mobility and Kinship Solidarity," *Journal of Marriage and the Family*, Fall 1970, pp. 133–137.

Katz, Alan N., "The Political Socialization of Indian Students in the United States" (Ph.D. dissertation in progress, New York University, 1972).

Paris, Phillip, "The Political Socialization of Mexican-American Students: A Case Study in Ventura County, California" (Ph.D. dissertation, University of Southern California, 1971).

Patterson, Samuel C., and R. S. Walker, "Political Attitudes of Oklahoma Newspaper Editors: The Prohibition Issue," *Southwestern Social Science Quarterly*, December 1961, pp. 271–279.

Poppel, Norman, "The Importance of Social Groups," *Proceedings of the Vocational-Educational Rutgers University Workshop*, July 3, 1970.

Prentiss, William, "Learning through Participation," *Junior College Journal*, 40 (May 1970): 22–23.

Ryles, Tim, "The Partisan Basis of Political Attitudes: A Study of Issue Orientations and Ideology among Rank and File Democrats and Republicans" (Ph.D. dissertation, University of Georgia, 1970).

Willie, Charles, "Age, Status and Residential Stratification," *American Sociological Review*, April 1960, pp. 260–264.

Don't Buy Where
You Can't Eat!
Register to Vote

# 8 voters

[1] Joseph A. Schlesinger,
*Ambition and Politics:
Political Careers in the
United States* (Chicago:
Rand McNally and Co.,
1966), p. vii.

"THE CLASSICAL definitions of government, of monarchy, oligarchy, and democracy," writes Joseph Schlesinger, "hinge upon the manner in which the political leaders are chosen."[1] In some countries, heredity determines who occupies the positions of power in the government. In others, the usual route to political power is through the military coup. In the American political system, elections are the means by which most political leaders are selected. Voting is, therefore, a vital part of the political system and the simplest means by which Americans can actively participate in politics. It is both the instrument and symbol of the citizen's power to affect the course of government.

As such, voting is one of the most studied and analyzed activities in the political system. Every election spawns countless polls, surveys, and studies, and generates an overwhelming mass of voting statistics. In a sense, elections themselves are a kind of mass opinion poll, carefully studied by political scientists, sociologists, psychologists, anthropologists, and interested citizens.

For the political scientist, voting statistics provide a valuable tool with which to analyze and predict political behavior. When the votes are counted, they are found to display definite patterns or trends. These voting patterns are translated by researchers into trends of political behavior—trends that provide insights into future behavior. To understand and interpret these trends or patterns, the political scientist must attempt to answer three basic questions:

1. Who is qualified or allowed to vote?
2. Of those qualified, who actually takes the time and trouble to cast his ballot?
3. Why do those who vote cast their votes the way they do?

## Who is qualified or allowed to vote

In 1792, less than 10 percent of the population was qualified to vote in national elections. Today, more than 60 percent of the population has the right to vote for national officials. In 1792, only white, male property-holders could vote. Today, adults without property, blacks, females, and eighteen-year-olds can also vote. Clearly, the trend in voting requirements has been toward *universal suffrage*, the right of all men and women of a specified age to cast their vote.

> *Seymour Martin Lipset*, Political Man: The Social Bases of Politics (*Garden City, N.Y.: Doubleday and Co., Inc., 1960*), *pp. 207–211.*
>
> Seymour Lipset explains how both voting and nonvoting can be acts of nonconformism, depending on what the group norm is. The radical who abstains from voting as a protest against "bourgeois democracy" is a familiar phenomenon; in this case, voting is the norm and nonvoting the protest.
>
> Nonvoting as a means of protest has often been used in "semi-free" elections by the opposition. Similarly in plebiscites in which none of the alternatives was considered acceptable, massive nonvoting has sometimes appeared as a way of expressing political opinions.
>
> On the other hand, Lipset notes that
>
> within groups where the norms oppose voting, the usual situation is reversed: the conformists become the nonvoters, and the nonconformists—the "non-class-conscious worker" . . . —the voters.

In his State of the Union message of January 4, 1965, President Johnson called for the elimination of "every remaining obstacle to the right and the opportunity to vote." In recent years many of these obstacles have been removed, among them literacy tests and lengthy residency requirements that have kept millions of Americans from the polls. Most recently, the Twenty-sixth Amendment lowered the voting age in state, local, and national elections to eighteen, bringing 25 million new participants into the political system.

Many Americans assume that the right to participate through voting is granted in the Constitution. The Constitution, however, does not guarantee the right to vote. *Suffrage qualifications*—the determination of who is allowed to vote—are left to the states. In Article I, Section 2, the Constitution states that those allowed to vote for members of the House of Representatives "shall have the qualifications requisite for electors of the most numerous branch of the State legislature." In other words, the standards applied to state elections establish the qualifications for voting at the national level.

Since the Constitution was ratified, five amendments have been passed that directly affect suffrage qualifications.

1. The *Fifteenth Amendment*, ratified in 1870, states, "The right of

citizens of the United States to vote shall not be denied or abridged by the United States or by any State on account of race, color, or previous condition of servitude." With the Fifteenth Amendment, the states were denied the right to use race or color as standards for determining the right to vote.

2. The *Nineteenth Amendment*, ratified in 1920, prohibited the states from using sex as a voting qualification. According to this amendment, "The right of citizens of the United States to vote shall not be denied or abridged by the United States or by any State on account of sex."

3. The *Twenty-third Amendment* empowered the residents of the District of Columbia to appoint in a manner to be prescribed by Congress "a number of electors of President and Vice President equal to the whole number of Senators and Representatives in Congress to which the District would be entitled if it were a State." Before this amendment was ratified in 1961, residents of Washington, D.C. had no voice in the selection of a President and Vice-President.

4. The *Twenty-fourth Amendment*, ratified in 1964, outlawed the state poll tax as a prerequisite for voting in national elections.

5. The *Twenty-sixth Amendment*, ratified in 1971, prohibited states from denying the vote to anyone eighteen years old or over.

Although the net effect of the five amendments has been to extend the vote to a large portion of the American public, they do not affirm the right of Americans to vote in any positive sense. Rather, they prohibit the state from using certain standards—race, sex, or economic status—as voting qualifications.

The move toward universal suffrage in the United States can be examined in four stages. First, the vote was extended to all white, male adults, regardless of their property holdings. Then it was extended to blacks, to women, and finally to eighteen-year-olds.

## White male suffrage

Before the ratification of the Constitution, all the states required voters to be either taxpayers or property owners. The Constitution, as we have noted, left the states the power to retain these requirements. In the early nineteenth century, however, the states slowly abandoned property holding and tax paying as requirements for voting. The common man—the man without money or property—went to the polls. Recognizing that this was not the intention of the Founding Fathers, Massachusetts's George Cabot stated in 1801, "The spirit of our country is doubtless more democratic than the form of our government."

Vermont was the first state to abolish property-holding and tax-paying requirements for voting. The Vermont Constitution, drafted in 1777, gave the vote to all white, adult males, and when Vermont entered the Union in 1791, its original constitution remained unchanged. Kentucky followed suit in

1799, New Jersey in 1807, Maryland in 1810, and Connecticut in 1818. Also, between 1816 and 1821, six new states—Maine, Indiana, Mississippi, Illinois, Alabama, and Missouri—were admitted to the Union. These states, perhaps realizing that the additional voters would increase their representation in Congress, granted the vote to all their white, male, adult citizens. With the exception of Maine, all were west of the Appalachians, where the ability to survive the perils of the wilderness carried more weight than property holding, tax paying, or eastern notions of economic superiority.

*A 1905 depiction of the common man.*

Drawing by F. Opper in *The Arena*, 1905.

The extension of the vote to the "common man" had a marked effect on the evolution of the political system. Presidential elections drew larger and larger percentages of the population to the polls. Americans began to realize that they not only could but should take an active part in their government.

By the time of Jackson's administration (1828–1836), the vote had been extended to the majority of the nation's adult, white males. Even the electoral college was beginning to be selected by popular vote; only Delaware and South Carolina still left the selection of presidential electors to the legislature. Throughout the nation more and more state and local offices were filled by election rather than appointment.

The southern states were the last to extend the vote to all white, adult males. Louisiana kept a rigorous tax-paying qualification until the late 1840s, and Virginia abolished her property restrictions only in 1852. Southern states, however, did not abolish voting restrictions solely out of a trust in the common man, but rather because of the increasing fear of slave revolts. As Senator Morgan of Virginia stated in 1829, "We ought to spread wide the foundation of our government, that all *white* men have a direct interest in its protection."

# The black voter

The extension of the vote to black Americans by individual states has been the most difficult and dramatic phase of the move toward universal suffrage. In the first two decades of the nineteenth century, free Negroes—blacks who were not indentured as slaves—had the legal right to vote in many New England states, in New York and Pennsylvania, and even in Tennessee and North Carolina. This right, however, was based on loopholes in the law rather than on any positive statement guaranteeing the black man the right to vote. By 1840, most of these loopholes were eliminated and black suffrage suffered severe setbacks. In 1818, for example, Connecticut passed legislation that allowed already freed Negroes to continue to vote, but denied the franchise to blacks freed after that date. In 1837, Pennsylvania amended its constitution to block free Negroes from the vote. As one delegate to the Pennsylvania Constitutional Convention of 1837 stated, "The people of this state are for continuing this commonwealth, what it always has been, a political community of white persons." Between 1819 and the Civil War, no new state admitted to the Union granted the vote to free blacks.

After the Civil War, the cause of black suffrage received some help from three new amendments to the Constitution, each one further restricting the states' original constitutional right to deny voting privileges to black Americans. The *Thirteenth Amendment*, ratified in 1865, outlawed slavery. The *Fourteenth Amendment*, ratified in 1868, granted blacks national and state citizenship and stated that "no state shall make or enforce any laws which shall abridge the privileges and immunities of citizens of the United States; nor shall any state deprive any person of life, liberty or property without due process of law; nor deny to any person within its jurisdiction the equal protection of the laws." The Fifteenth Amendment, ratified in 1870, provided that the right to vote could not be restricted by the United States or any state "on account of race, color or previous condition of servitude."

## Black Vote in the South

| Year | Number of Blacks Registered | Percentage of Eligible Blacks |
|------|-----------------------------|-------------------------------|
| 1940 | 250,000 | 5 |
| 1947 | 595,000 | 12 |
| 1952 | 1,008,614 | 20 |
| 1956 | 1,238,038 | 25 |
| 1958 | 1,266,488 | 25 |
| 1960 | 1,414,052 | 28 |
| 1964 | 1,907,279 | 38 |
| 1966 | 2,306,434 | 46 |

Source: Donald R. Matthews and James W. Prothro, *Negroes and the New Southern Politics* (New York: Harcourt Brace Jovanovich, Inc., 1966), p. 18.

[2] The *Supreme Court in South Carolina* v. *Katzenbach*, 383 U.S. 301 (1966) declared the 1965 Voting Rights Act constitutional.

[3] Donald R. Mathews and James W. Prothro, *Negroes and the New Southern Politics* (Harcourt Brace Jovanovich, Inc., 1966), pp. 18, 19, 46, 49.

The *Voting Rights Act of 1965* was the most significant step in ending activities, legal or extralegal, that curtailed the voting rights of black citizens.[2] In 1940, only about 5 percent of voting-age blacks in the South were registered. By 1966, the number had risen to more than 45 percent—a sure sign that the Voting Rights Act was beginning to take effect.[3] The 1970 Voting Rights Act furthered the cause of disfranchised blacks by eliminating all literacy tests. The latest figure of 50 percent black registration is expected to rise to 70 percent in 1975.

Legal barriers to voting have been eliminated and black voting has increased, but the problem of extending black suffrage has not yet been satisfactorily resolved. Blacks continue to be turned away from some of the nation's polling places, and certain state legislatures and political party units continue to try to minimize the effect of black votes.

The Fifteenth Amendment to the Constitution prohibited states from denying the right to vote because of race, color, or previous condition of servitude. But it was not until 1965, with the passage of the Voting Rights Act, that black suffrage was shown to increase substantially.

The increase in black voting that has occurred, however, is largely responsible for the increase in black political power. Black mayors have been elected in Cleveland, Ohio; Gary, Indiana; and Newark, New Jersey. Of even greater significance is the fact that Democratic governors were elected in Arkansas, Florida, and South Carolina on platforms pledging equal treatment of all citizens and an end to racial disfranchisement. Naturally, as the number of black voters increases, the degree to which political candidates espouse their views will also increase.

## The female voter

In 1869, Wyoming, then still a territory, granted the vote to women. By 1900, Colorado, Idaho, and Utah also extended suffrage to women, and by 1915, Washington, California, Arizona, Kansas, Oregon, Montana, Nevada, and Illinois discarded sex as a voting qualification. Sex had of necessity been discarded as a qualification for sawing wood, building fences, skinning deer, and raising a large family. The men could not justifiably use sex as a qualification for voting, especially when the additional voters could add to their representation in Congress.

During the first two decades of the twentieth century a large and colorful movement developed demanding the extension of voting rights to women on a nationwide scale. Women mounted soapboxes and even picketed the White House to demand their rights. In answer to these demands, Congress proposed the Nineteenth Amendment in 1919, declaring, "The right of citizens of the United States to vote shall not be denied or abridged by the United States or by any State on account of sex." Called the "Susan B. Anthony Amendment" after one of the leading advocates of women's rights, the Nineteenth Amendment was ratified by the states in 1920. With its ratification, the right to vote was extended, at least constitutionally, to all adult citizens.

## The eighteen-year-old voter

Countless young Americans drafted into the armed services have stated that, if they are old enough to fight for their country, they are old enough to vote. Supporters of a change in voting-age requirements further noted that today's young people are better educated and are more actively concerned with political activities than many of their parents were at the age of eighteen. The original Constitution makes no mention of voting age, but the Fourteenth Amendment does refer to "male citizens twenty-one years of age." Traditionally, twenty-one has been considered the minimum age at which citizens are qualified to vote in national elections.

The *Voting Rights Act of 1970* was the first national legislation to deal with voting-age requirements. In addition to abolishing literacy tests and residency requirements of more than thirty days, the law lowered the voting age to eighteen in all national, state, and local elections. Problems arose, however, when the constitutionality of the legislation was tested. In the case of *Oregon v. Mitchell* (1970), the Supreme Court upheld the change in residency re-

*The campaign for women's suffrage in 1919
was as energetic and determined as the
women's liberation movement is today.*

quirements for voting and the prohibiting of literacy tests. But the Court
declared that Congress had the power to regulate only national elections and
was overstepping its powers by lowering the voting age to eighteen in state
and local elections.

In declaring Congress's right to lower the voting age in national elections, the Supreme Court created several procedural problems for the states.
In 1970, Georgia and Kentucky permitted eighteen-year-olds to vote; Alaska
allowed nineteen-year-olds, while Hawaii set the age at twenty. The remaining

states set the voting age for local elections at twenty-one; thus, they were virtually forced by the Supreme Court ruling to take one of two steps: either to amend their state constitutions to lower the voting age to eighteen for local elections or, during a national election, to provide separate registration books, separate ballots, and perhaps separate voting machines and booths in order to administer the vote according to age. State constitutions usually take several years to be amended; and the latter alternative would, of course, be an expensive and time-consuming proposition. In December 1970, Senator Edward Kennedy of Massachusetts introduced in the Senate the most workable solution: a twenty-sixth amendment to the Constitution, which prohibited the states from denying the right to vote on account of age. The amendment, passed by Congress, has now been ratified by two-thirds of the state assemblies in time for the 1972 elections.

Most analysts of voting behavior predict that, although the extension of the vote to eighteen-year-olds will add approximately 25 million new voters to the rolls, the effect on the political system will be minimal. Young people register and vote less frequently than people between thirty-five and sixty.[4] And, as we shall see, of the young people who do vote, 75 percent initially vote for the same party their parents do. The independent voters, the voters who opt for the candidate and not the party, are distributed between the major parties in the same proportion as the rest of the voting population.

[4] Angus Campbell, Philip E. Converse, Warren E. Miller, Donald E. Stokes, *The American Voter* (New York: John Wiley and Sons, Inc., 1961), p. 262.

# To vote or not to vote

"The act of voting," writes Angus Campbell, "requires the citizen to make not a single choice but two: he must choose between rival parties or candidates. He must decide also whether to vote at all."[5] Faced with the decision to vote or not to vote, in recent years about 40 percent of all voting-age Americans have chosen not to vote.

[5] Campbell, Converse, Miller, Stokes, *The American Voter*, p. 49.

According to several studies, voter participation in the United States is markedly lower than in many other democracies. In Italy and Austria, for example, about 90 percent of the adult population voted in recent elections. Figures for voting participation are also higher in France, Britain, West Germany, Canada, and the Scandinavian countries. However, the situations are not comparable: voting requirements—residency qualifications, for example—are more stringent in the United States than in most democracies, and for that reason voting is likely to be lighter.[6] Also, the American voter must take two positive steps in order to participate at the polls. He must register on one day in order to vote on another, whereas in most European countries and Canada, the government automatically registers voters when they come of age, thereby greatly reducing the time and energy necessary for voter participation. The effect of required registration on voter turnout in the United

[6] Seymour Martin Lipset, *Political Man: The Social Bases of Politics* (Garden City, N.Y.: Doubleday and Co., Inc., 1959), Part II.

[7] Stanley Kelley, Jr., Richard E. Ayres, and William G. Bowen, "Registration and Voting: Putting First Things First," *The American Political Science Review*, 61, no. 2 (June 1967): 359–380.

States is considerable. Studies have shown that about 10 million Americans who would otherwise cast their ballots cannot do so because they neglected to register.[7]

## State-by-State Compliance to Each of the Major Provisions of the Voting Rights Act of 1970

| State | 18-year-old Vote | Literacy Test Suspension | Residency Abolition |
|---|---|---|---|
| Alabama[a] | | | |
| Alaska | ✓ | ✓ | ✓ |
| Arizona | x | x | ✓ |
| Arkansas | ? | | ? |
| California | ? | ✓ | ? |
| Colorado | ? | | ✓ |
| Connecticut | ✓ | ✓ | ? |
| Delaware | ✓ | ✓ | ✓ |
| Florida | ✓ | | ✓ |
| Georgia | ✓ | | ✓ |
| Hawaii | ✓ | | ✓ |
| Idaho | x | x | x |
| Illinois | ✓ | | ✓ |
| Indiana | x | | x |
| Iowa | ✓ | | ? |
| Kansas | ✓ | | ✓ |
| Kentucky[a] | | | |
| Louisiana | ? | | ? |
| Maine | ✓ | ✓ | ✓ |
| Maryland | ✓ | | ✓ |
| Massachusetts | ✓ | ✓ | ✓ |
| Michigan | ✓ | | ✓ |
| Minnesota | ✓ | | ? |
| Mississippi | ? | | ? |
| Missouri | ? | | ? |
| Montana | ✓ | | ✓ |
| Nebraska | x | | ✓ |
| Nevada | ? | | ? |
| New Hampshire | ? | ? | ? |
| New Jersey | ✓ | | ✓ |
| New Mexico | ✓ | | ? |
| New York | ✓ | ✓ | ✓ |
| North Carolina | x | x | ✓ |
| North Dakota | ✓ | | ✓ |
| Ohio | ✓ | | ? |
| Oklahoma | ? | | ? |
| Oregon | x | ✓ | ✓ |
| Pennsylvania | ✓ | | ✓ |
| Rhode Island | ✓ | | ✓ |

| | | | |
|---|---|---|---|
| South Carolina | ? | | ? |
| South Dakota | ? | | ? |
| Tennessee | ✓ | | ✓ |
| Texas | x | | ✓ |
| Utah | ? | | ✓ |
| Vermont | ✓ | | ? |
| Virginia | ? | | ? |
| Washington | ? | ✓ | ✓ |
| West Virginia | ✓ | | ? |
| Wisconsin | ✓ | | ✓ |
| Wyoming | ✓ | ✓ | ✓ |

x—refusal to comply
✓—agree to comply
?—doubtful response
a Alabama and Kentucky (where the voting age is already 18) did not reply by the date that this information was compiled.

Source: Department of Justice.

The fact remains, however, that a sizable proportion of the American population, for one reason or another, simply chooses not to participate by voting. The widespread apathy of the American voter has been well documented.[8] Voter participation was at its peak in 1876 when 86 percent of the nation's qualified voters cast their ballots. In 1920 and 1924, less than 50 percent of the eligible population participated at the polls. Suffering under a severe economic depression, many Americans returned to the ballot box during the era of Franklin D. Roosevelt—52 percent voted in 1932—but, with the end of the New Deal, voting again declined. In recent presidential elections, voter participation has risen and then stabilized at about 60 percent.[9]

# Why some people vote and others do not

Most Americans are taught in school, and reminded again and again by civic organizations, public officials, and the media, that it is their civic duty to vote. Many (121 million Americans in 1970) learn this lesson well, and faithfully cast their vote in every election. Others, however, do not.

In a classic study, C. E. Merriam and H. F. Gosnell suggested that simple lack of interest in politics is a major cause of nonvoting.[10] Edgar Litt, on the other hand, attributes nonvoting to improper civic indoctrination.[11] But while lack of interest or knowledge may be primary causes of nonvoting, some Americans make a rational decision not to vote. Disgusted with politics, or disenchanted with the electoral process, they purposefully withhold their vote. Still others would vote if the polls were open on Sunday rather than Tuesday, or for several days, as in many nations. Interestingly enough, some people do not vote because to do so, they must reveal their age.

Clearly, the factors influencing an individual's decision to vote or not

[8] Robert E. Lane, *Political Life: Why People Get Involved in Politics*, rev. ed. (New York: The Free Press, 1959), pp. 47–52.

[9] *Statistical Abstracts of the U.S., 1970* (Washington, D.C.: Department of Commerce, 1970), p. 369.

[10] C. E. Merriam and H. F. Gosnell, *Non-Voting* (Chicago: University of Chicago Press, 1924).

[11] Edgar Litt, "Civic Education, Community Norms, and Political Indoctrination," *American Sociological Review*, 28, no. 1 (February 1963): 69–75.

to vote are many and complex. Voting, like any form of participation, is an expression of political opinion—opinion that has been formed by an intricate process of political socialization. All the factors that influence an individual's political socialization—all the political stimuli he receives from his environment—affect his decision to vote or not to vote.

## Political stimuli

12 Angus Campbell, Gerald Gurin, and Warren E. Miller, *The Voter Decides* (White Plains, N.Y.: Row, Peterson and Co., 1954), p. 87.

Political scientists suggest that political participation in general and voting in particular can best be considered as a function of political stimuli (the various influences of peer, family, and interest groups as well as the political information derived from mass media sources). "The greater the number of positive forces activating an individual in an election situation the more likely he will be to respond."[12] The more stimuli he receives, the more likely he is to participate. And as the number of stimuli continues to increase, the degree of his participation also increases.

### Characteristic of High- and Low-Turnout Voters

| Higher Turnout | Lower Turnout |
|---|---|
| High income | Low income |
| High education | Low education |
| Occupational groups: | Occupational groups: |
| Businessmen | Unskilled workers |
| White-collar employees | Servants |
| Government employees | Service workers |
| Commercial-crop farmers | Peasants, subsistence farmers |
| Miners | |
| Whites | Negroes |
| Men | Women |
| Middle-aged people (35–55) | Young people (under 35) |
| Older people (over 55) | |
| Old residents in community | Newcomers in community |
| Workers in western Europe | Workers in United States |
| Crisis situations | Normal situations |
| Married people | Single |
| Members of organizations | Isolated individuals |

Source: From *Political Man* by Seymour Martin Lipset. Copyright © 1959, 1960 by Seymour Martin Lipset. Reprinted by permission of Doubleday & Company, Inc.

Some people, because of the environment they move in, are exposed to more political stimuli than others. Men are exposed to more political stimuli than women; for example, they may use the time spent in commuting for a thorough reading of daily newspapers. Men at a higher income level have more frequent contact, through business and occupational groups, with individuals having strong political opinions. Similarly, middle-class and white citizens are exposed to more political stimuli than lower-class and black citizens respectively, because they are usually better educated, hold higher-income jobs, and have more free leisure time to devote to political activities.

Since television provides political stimuli to virtually all segments of the population, it would seem that the difference in voter participation among various groups within the political system would tend to level out or even disappear. (An estimated 80 million Americans, for example, more than 85 percent of the nation's qualified voters, watched the celebrated Kennedy-Nixon debate on television in 1960.) As Joseph Klapper has pointed out, however, this has not been the case; television is one influence, "working amid other influences, in a total situation."[13]

Individuals who are exposed to equal amounts of political stimuli do not necessarily *accept* equal amounts. Some individuals tend to pick up political stimuli; others tend to shut them out. Political stimuli, observes Lester Milbrath, are filtered through the individual's perceptual screen: "The perceptual screen operates to protect the organism from an overload of stimuli. Overload can occur in two ways: the total amount can be so excessive that all messages are garbled (like a radio tuned to several stations at once); or the stimuli hammer so incessantly that the senses are dulled (like the villagers' reaction to the boy who cried wolf too often)."[14]

Certain groups of people display discernible patterns of perception. Less educated and politically unsophisticated individuals tend to be more susceptible to reinforcing stimuli, that is, to stimuli that agree with their views and events that prove out those views. Similarly, people who identify strongly with political parties or candidates tend to pick up more stimuli about politics than those who do not.

Where do these political stimuli come from? What are the sources of stimuli that affect the decision to vote or not to vote? Broadly speaking, there are two major sources of political stimuli: candidates and issues, and the various groups to which the individual belongs.

## Candidates and issues

In general, presidential elections elicit greater voter participation than off-year congressional or state and local elections. However, it is not only the type or excitement of the election that determines voter turnout; certain political candidates tend to draw people to the polls. Eisenhower, for example, had no actual experience in public office. Yet his image as a war hero and as a strong "fatherly" type inspired the confidence and trust of the majority of Americans and resulted in a large voter turnout in his behalf. Similarly, Franklin D. Roosevelt possessed a charismatic quality that persuaded otherwise apathetic citizens to cast their ballots.

In addition, voter turnout increases during times of national crisis, when the issues at stake are crucial. When the issue is war—as evidenced in 1916 (World War I), 1940 (World War II), and 1952 (the Korean War)—voter

[13] Joseph T. Klapper, *Effects of Mass Communication* (New York: The Free Press, 1961), p. 5.

[14] Lester W. Milbrath, *Political Participation* (Chicago: Rand McNally and Co., 1965), p. 44.

participation tends to be unusually high. Similarly, in periods of serious economic crisis—1896 and 1932, for example—a larger percentage of Americans are drawn to the polls than in periods of prosperity.

Political issues also influence the election turnout of various groups. Countless studies have shown that Americans who otherwise stay away from the polls tend to vote when the issue at stake either affects them directly or is of high interest to them. For example, when local elections raise such issues as abortion or federal aid to parochial schools, the turnout of Catholic voters displays a marked increase. Seemingly moral issues, such as prohibition and gambling, tend to draw women to the polls.

*V. O. Key, Jr., Politics, Parties, and Pressure Groups, 5th ed. (New York: Thomas Y. Crowell Co., 1964), pp. 579–585.*

In the United States, not all potential voters faithfully exercise their "civic duty." V. O. Key, Jr. suggests that the level of participation in elections is largely based on the type of election and the degree of interest it can generate.

State elections attract fewer voters than national elections. Moreover, when state officials run on the same ballot with presidential candidates, percentage of voting is higher; the figures from New York's 1962 gubernatorial election show a drop of 1.6 million voters from the 1960 gubernatorial election, which coincided with a presidential election.

In city and county elections, turnouts are low. For example, in Kansas cities of 5,000 to 50,000 in population, no more than 30 percent of eligible voters turned out for municipal elections. Key argues that this poor showing is due in part to unchallenged tickets, lack of local power to deal with issues, and general satisfaction of the citizenry.

Primary elections, in which party candidates are chosen, have traditionally attracted large turnouts in the South, historically a one-party area. In other areas, primaries rouse even fewer voters than regular elections, especially for the weaker party in the state. In a sample of gubernatorial primaries and elections, 35 percent participated in the primaries, while 50 percent voted in the general elections.

Behind these statistics of varying levels of participation lies the fact that close races with intense campaigns attract more voters than those in which the conclusion is obvious. Similarly, elections which barrage the citizen with intense stimuli, as national elections do, make him more likely to vote.

The significance of this study is discussed by Key:

It is a nice question whether the higher turnout in presidential voting tends to make the national government more responsive than state governments

> to the great surges of sentiment that sweep the country. Or, to put the question in another way, whether a different constituency, a different shade of opinion, may not tend to be dominant in state and local affairs from that which moves the national government. If this should be true, variations in levels of voting may be among the factors conducive to federal centralization on the assumption that a smaller and generally more conservative voting constituency tends to form around state and local governments.

Since issues play such an important part in voter participation, it might be expected that the poor and the uneducated—Americans who are most affected by welfare, housing, guaranteed minimum income, and other major issues of the day—would display high voter participation. Study after study has shown that, in fact, the opposite is true. Although such issues may affect them directly, the poor and the uneducated are frequently disinterested in or even unaware of the issues at stake. Political stimuli have either not reached them or have been blocked out by the immediate concern of hunger, child care, and financial tribulation. The poor and uneducated tend to stay away from the polls.

# Who votes most

Because certain groups are exposed to more political stimuli than others, those groups naturally vote more regularly than other groups. Even among those exposed to political stimuli, there are some who are more likely than others to respond repeatedly to the political stimuli. For example, men are exposed to more stimuli than women, but some men vote more than other men. Although there are innumerable factors that affect an individual's political behavior, political scientists have discerned certain patterns of frequency in voting.

**Education**

In general, the greater an individual's education, the more likely he is to hold strong political opinions and thus to vote. The converse is true: those with meager education more often lack the political motivation to vote. Education appears to develop a man's confidence in his ability to affect the political process. And the college-educated vote more than the high-school-educated. The high-school-educated person, in turn, votes more than those who attended only grade school.

**Occupation and income**

Since professionals have more education than nonprofessionals, it follows that professionals vote more frequently than the rest of the population. Generally professionals have higher incomes than nonprofessionals. This factor—income—becomes important in analyzing the relationship between voting behavior and occupation. The further down the occupational ladder one moves, the fewer regular voters one is able to find. The unskilled vote less than the skilled, and the unemployed vote less than the unskilled employed. Blacks tend to vote less than whites, since blacks more often than whites are unable to find employment and satisfactory education.

**Sex**

Given the right to vote, approximately 50 percent of all women have chosen not to do so. Of those women who do vote, a large percentage vote for the same candidates as their husbands. According to observers, sex has less to do with determining a vote than does place of residence, income, occupation, race, religion, or nationality.

**Age**

Middle-aged people—those between thirty-five and fifty-five—vote more than the young or the old. According to the June 1968 Gallup Opinion Index, only 34 percent of those between twenty-one and twenty-four years old registered to vote. And the number who vote is less than the number who register.

## Group Voting Trends in Presidential Elections, 1948–1968
### (Percentage Voting for the Democratic Party in a Two-Party Vote)

|  | 1948 | 1952 | 1956 | 1960 | 1964 | 1968[d] |
|---|---|---|---|---|---|---|
| Female | 49 | 40 | 37 | 46 | 68 | 42 |
| Negro | 68[a] | 76[a] | 63[a] | 66[a] | 98 | 94 |
| Under 34 | 57 | 45 | 41 | 52 | 71 | 40 |
| 35–44 | 57 | 45 | 41 | 50 | 67 | 44 |
| 45–54 | 44 | 42 | 39 | 54 | 68 | 36 |
| 55–64 | 40[a] | 34 | 32 | 43 | 68 | 37 |
| 65 or over | 46[a] | 36 | 43 | 37 | 53 | 40 |
| Metropolitan areas | 56 | 42 | 44 | 57 | 71 | 45 |
| Cities over 50,000 | [c] | 51 | 33 | 50 | 66 | 50 |
| Towns, 2,500–50,000 | [c] | 37 | 36[b] | 40 | 60 | 40 |
| Rural | 61 | 39 | 42 | 47 | 67 | 29 |
| Protestant | 43 | 36 | 35 | 36 | 61 | 32 |
| Catholic | 62 | 51 | 45 | 82 | 79 | 54 |
| Jewish | [b] | 71[a] | 77[a] | 89[a] | 89[a] | 85 |
| Business and professional | 19[a] | 31 | 31 | 44 | 57 | 34 |
| White-collar | 47[a] | 35 | 39 | 48 | 63 | 38 |
| Skilled and semiskilled | 72 | 51 | 44 | 57 | 76 | 43 |
| Unskilled | 67 | 67 | 47 | 59 | 80 | 53 |
| Farm operator | 59[a] | 37 | 46 | 33 | 63 | 34 |
| Union member | 76[a] | 55 | 51 | 62 | 83 | 46 |
| Grade school | 63 | 48 | 41 | 54 | 78 | 48 |
| High school | 51 | 43 | 43 | 52 | 68 | 40 |
| College | 22[a] | 26 | 31 | 35 | 53 | 33 |

[a] Fewer than 100 cases; sampling error may be sizable.
[b] Too few cases to compute a stable proportion.
[c] Data not available.
[d] Takes into account a three-party spilt.

Source: Center for Political Studies, University of Michigan.

Westerners vote more than Easterners, and Easterners vote more than Southerners (perhaps because most southern states are one-party states where the most important voting occurs in the primaries); most Southerners, assuming that the candidate chosen in the primary will automatically win in the actual election, do not bother to cast their ballots.

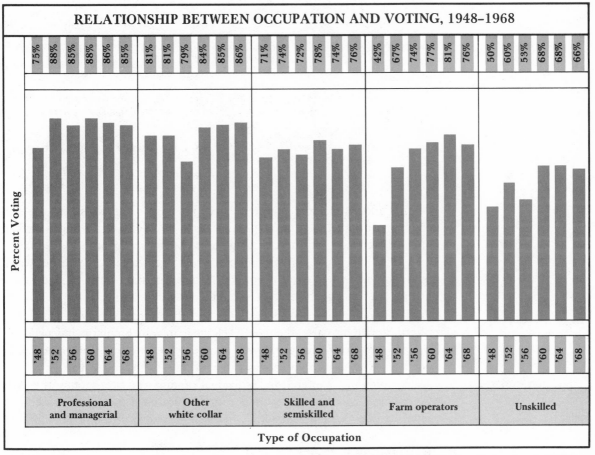

**RELATIONSHIP BETWEEN OCCUPATION AND VOTING, 1948–1968**

| | Professional and managerial | Other white collar | Skilled and semiskilled | Farm operators | Unskilled |
|---|---|---|---|---|---|
| '48 | 75% | 81% | 71% | 42% | 50% |
| '52 | 88% | 81% | 74% | 67% | 60% |
| '56 | 85% | 79% | 72% | 74% | 53% |
| '60 | 88% | 84% | 78% | 77% | 68% |
| '64 | 86% | 85% | 74% | 81% | 68% |
| '68 | 85% | 86% | 76% | 76% | 66% |

Type of Occupation

Source: Center for Political Studies, University of Michigan.

Currently a more important distinction has been revealed between central cities and their outlying suburbs and between metropolitan areas and the truly rural regions of America. Urban residents as a rule vote more than rural Americans. They are exposed to more political stimuli, and, because of their personal concerns, are more likely to respond to those stimuli.

**Religion**

Religion has never been a major factor in determining whether or not a person will vote. The more influential factors have been, in fact, occupation and income. A Catholic, for example, who has a low income is less likely to vote than a Catholic with a high income. In general, however, Jews vote more than Catholics, and Catholics vote more than Protestants. In fact, a Jew with a low income is more likely to vote than the Catholic with a high income.

## Percentage of Religious Groups Voting for the Democratic Party, 1948–1968

|  | 1948 | 1952 | 1956 | 1960 | 1964[b] | 1968 |
|---|---|---|---|---|---|---|
| Protestant | 43% | 36% | 35% | 36% | 61% | 35% |
| Catholic | 62 | 51 | 45 | 82 | 79 | 56 |
| Jewish | [a] | 71 | 77 | 89 | 89 | 85 |

Note: Jews have the strongest affiliation with the Democratic party (85% in 1968), while Protestants most often are affiliated with the Republican party (65% in 1968).
[a] Too few cases to compute.
[b] In 1964, the plurality of President Johnson is reflected in a majority vote from all three religious groups.
Source: Center for Political Studies, University of Michigan.

Clearly, all these factors are interrelated. For example, professionals tend to be highly educated and have high incomes and middle-aged people have had more of a chance to raise their income level than young people. Whether a man votes as a Protestant, a Southerner, an educated man, a rich man, or a physician depends on the degree of his identification with each of these groups, the issues at stake, and the candidates in question.

**Party Affiliation**

Partisans vote more than independents, and the stronger the individual's identification with his party, the more likely he is to vote. Similarly, independents who do not favor one party over another vote less frequently than independents who relate to a certain extent to one of the major parties.

**Cross pressures**

As we noted in Chapter 7, the individual's family and peer groups as well as his social, religious, racial, economic, and educational groups all combine to influence the development of his political opinions, including his opinions

## Relationship between Age and Peer-group Influence on Voting

| Age | Percentage of Respondents Whose Vote Concurred with That of Three Best Friends |
|---|---|
| 21–25 | 53 |
| 26–34 | 69 |
| 35–44 | 75 |
| 45 and over | 77 |

Source: Bernard R. Berelson, Paul F. Lazarsfeld, and William N. McPhee, Voting (© 1954 by the University of Chicago Press. All rights reserved), p. 97.

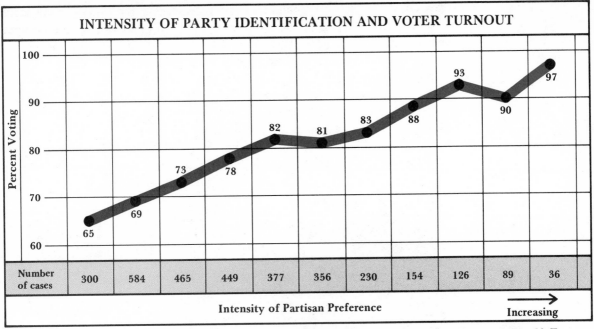

## INTENSITY OF PARTY IDENTIFICATION AND VOTER TURNOUT

| Number of cases | 300 | 584 | 465 | 449 | 377 | 356 | 230 | 154 | 126 | 89 | 36 | |

Intensity of Partisan Preference → Increasing

Source: Angus Campbell, Philip E. Converse, Warren E. Miller, and Donald E. Stokes, *The American Voter* (New York: John Wiley and Sons, Inc., 1964), p. 53. Copyright © 1964. Reprinted by permission of John Wiley & Sons, Inc.

about voting. Each attempts, consciously or unconsciously, to direct his political behavior. A man may be pressured to vote one way by his religious group and in another way by his social group. If he identifies with both groups and if he psychologically feels the pressure of conflicting interests, he is said to be *cross pressured*. According to several studies, voters who are caught in cross pressures tend to resolve the conflict by not voting.[15]

# How people vote

The Democrats have traditionally been supported by the lower classes while the Republican party and its predecessors the Federalists and the Whigs, have won the favor of the upper classes. Obviously, it would not be difficult to find scores of Democrats at the top of the social ladder, and host of Republicans on the lower rungs.[16] Nor would it be difficult to find Republicans who vote for an occasional Democrat and vice versa. To complicate matters, the independents—as much as one-third of the voting population—identify with no political party. Still, political scientists have clearly identified factors that influence the voting behavior of individuals. Briefly, these factors are:

1. *Education.* Statistically, the more education an individual receives, the more likely he is to vote Republican. Education tends to lead people into

the higher social and economic strata of the society—the realm of the Republican party. Much depends, however, on the kind of education the individual receives. Political scientists and psychologists, for example, tend to vote strongly Democratic, whereas engineers, doctors, and mathematicians tend to vote Republican.

2. *Occupation, Income, and Class.* These three determinants are closely related. A person's occupation usually determines his income and his income, in part, determines his class. The higher the individual's occupational status, the greater his income, and the higher his class, the more likely he is to vote Republican. Conversely, the lower his occupational status, and thus his income and class, the more likely he is to vote Democratic.

"This year I'm not getting involved in any complicated issues. I'm just voting my straight ethnic prejudices."

Drawing by Whitney Darrow, Jr; © 1970 The New Yorker Magazine, Inc.

3. *Religion.* Statistically speaking, Catholics and Jews tend to vote Democratic. As poor immigrants, they came first to the large cities, where the Democrats helped them socially and economically. Protestants, who were already well-established with relatively higher educations and incomes, tended to vote Republican and continue to do so.

4. *Race*. From the Civil War until the New Deal, blacks in America—or at least those who voted—were strongly Republican. Understandably they supported the party of Lincoln, the man who had given them privilege to vote. In 1932, Roosevelt's welfare policies swung the black vote into the Democratic party, where it has solidly remained.

5. *Age*. Many young people tend to label themselves independent voters. Yet the voting behavior of the young varies significantly and depends on such factors as education, location, and political socialization. Surveys have shown that about 75 percent of first voters support the same political party as their parents. Urban youth, especially the better educated, tend to favor social and economic reform and government centralization, while rural and high-school-educated youth lean toward policies that support the status quo and favor local independence. And as the voter grows older—and his income and social position presumably grow higher—he is more likely to switch from Democrat to Republican than he is to switch from Republican to Democrat.

6. *Location*. Citizens in some states vote monolithically. The South has been and remains predominantly Democratic. Recent trends—the election of a Republican governor in Virginia—have indicated a trend toward bipartisanship. Other traditionally one-party states support the Republican party. Vermont, for example, has supported a Democratic presidential candidate only once in its history (in 1964, by a margin of two to one). In most states, however, voting is competitive.

Perhaps a more important distinction can be made between voters in urban areas and rural areas, between the cities and the suburbs. Before 1928, many large cities tended to support the Republicans. However, since that time, America's rural and suburban areas have tended to vote Republican, while its urban centers, especially in older parts of the United States, have become strongly Democratic.

## Partisans and independents

17 V. O. Key, Jr., *The Responsible Electorate* (Cambridge, Mass.: Harvard University Press, 1966).

One of the most powerful influences on the individual's voting behavior is his party affiliation. V. O. Key has divided the American voting population into three categories: the standpatters, the switchers, and the new voters.[17] *Standpatters*, who make up about 60 percent of the voting population, are those Americans who support the same party in every election. *Switchers*, who make up about 20 percent of the electorate, are those who change their vote from one party to another. *New voters*, who make up from 15 to 20 percent of the voting population, are those who have just come of voting age or, for one reason or another, did not vote in previous elections.

Many of the new voters and switchers fall under the category of *independents*, the roughly 30 percent of the voting population that do not register affiliation with either political party. Many political scientists also categorize as independents those who split their tickets and those who psychologically do not identify with a party. Many an independent has proclaimed himself to be the only kind of rational voter—the man who "votes for the man rather than the party." And indeed there is some evidence to support the image of the cautious and critical independent voter. However, some self-styled independents, in "voting for the man" end up voting for the same party year after year. Their "man" always turns out to be a Democrat or a Republican.

*Donald E. Stokes and Warren E. Miller, "Party Government and the Saliency of Congress," Public Opinion Quarterly, 26 (Winter 1962): 531–546.*

In a study conducted immediately after the 1958 midterm congressional election, Donald Stokes and Warren Miller found confirmation of the political cliché that off-year elections are "triumphs of party government." Most voters do indeed choose their party's candidate; however, the triumphs may not be qualitative ones, since the voters do not seem to make their choices on an informed basis.

The study reveals that 84 percent of the voters supported their parties in the 1958 election, while very few independents even bothered to vote. However, the authors do not see this strong party identification as indicative of an acceptance of a party's legislative record. In fact, of six thousand recorded comments about parties, less than 12 percent related to current legislative topics. Moreover, the reasons given for voting Republican or Democratic related to legislative issues only 7 percent of the time. Not more than half of the voters even knew which party controlled the 85th Congress (1956–1958). Whether the voters were loyal to their party or deviated from it, familiarity with issues and knowledge of who controls Congress did not significantly affect their votes. Clearly, neither one of these factors is a key to understanding the congressional vote.

Voters are not only ill-informed about the national party; they are also uninformed about their local candidates for Congress. A study during the last election, conducted at the district level, showed that 59 percent had read or heard nothing of either candidate for Congress, while less than 20 percent felt they knew something about both; 46 percent of those who actually voted claimed they did so knowing nothing about either candidate. However, incumbents are better known than their rivals. Thirty-nine percent of the respondents claimed they knew something of their present congressman, while only 20 percent knew anything about the opposing candidate. Interestingly, any awareness of a rival candidate may lead to vote switching.

The condition of no information leads to fairly unrelieved party-line voting, and so to an even greater degree does the condition of information only about the candidate of the voter's own party. But if partisan voters know something about the opposition's man, substantial deviations from party appear. In fact, if such voters know *only* the opposition candidate, almost half can be induced to cast a vote contrary to their party identification.

Despite these facts, 80 percent of successful incumbents interviewed believe they were re-elected because of their record and their personal standing with their constituency.

In view of the way the saliency of candidates can move the electorate across party lines, great stress should be laid on the fact that *the public sees individual candidates for Congress in terms of party programs scarcely at all.* Our constituent interviews indicate that the popular image of the Congressman is almost barren of policy content . . . . *By the most reasonable count, references to current legislative issues comprised not more than a thirtieth part of what the constituents had to say about their Congressmen.*

Electoral strength, write Stokes and Miller, may come not from positions on issues or heeding the party line, but from clever campaigning and servicing over the years, factors "almost totally disassociated" from what a congressman's party may want of him.

Studies have attempted to ascertain whether the independent is a more informed, interested, or rational voter than the partisan. Campbell has stated that "far from being more attentive, interested, and informed, Independents tend as a group to be somewhat less involved in politics. They have somewhat poorer knowledge of the issues, their image of the candidate is fainter, their interest in the campaign is less, their concern over the outcome is relatively slight, and their choice between competing candidates, although it is indeed made later in the campaign, seems much less to spring from discoverable evaluations of the elements of national politics."[18]

[18] Campbell, Converse, Miller, and Stokes, *The American Voter*, p. 143.

*Paul F. Lazarsfeld, Bernard Berelson, and Hazel Gaudet,* The People's Choice, *2nd ed. (New York: Columbia University Press, 1948), pp. 52–64.*

Paul Lazarsfeld, Bernard Berelson, and Hazel Gaudet have used the time of a voter's final decision to categorize three types of voters: the "May Voters," who, because of traditional party affiliation or an evaluation of the incumbent, pick their man before the preliminary campaign for nomination; the "June-to-August Voters," who decide during the convention period, and the "September-to-November Voters," who make their choice in the last few months or even in the voting booth.

The time a final choice is made depends on two major factors: interest and cross pressures. The authors found that by May, nearly two-thirds (63 percent) of those with great interest had made a decision, while less than half (41 percent) of the voters with little interest had made up their minds. Only 12 percent of the very interested voters waited until late in the campaign. The authors suggest that this professed lack of interest among September-to-November voters arises from the voter's feeling that the election will not affect him; thus, a candidate who could convince him otherwise would be likely to gain his support.

The people who make up their minds last are those who think the election will affect them least. It may be, then, that explicit attempts by the candidates and their managers to prove to them that the election will make a difference to them would be more effective than any amount of continued argumentation of the issues as such. One hypothesis is that the person or the party that convinces the hesitant voter of the importance of the election to him personally—in terms of what he concretely wants—can have his vote.

Another cause of late voting is cross pressures. They cause voter delay for two reasons. First, the voter may have good reasons for voting for both candidates. Second, the voter may be waiting for events to resolve the conflict.

Cross pressures thwart a decision most when they are evenly balanced; lack of agreement within the family seems to be the cross pressure most influential in delaying voter decision. Except in a few instances where interest is high enough to override cross pressures, the cross-pressured voter loses interest in the election because in doing so he can conveniently escape from his dilemma. "As the number of cross-pressures increases, the degree of interest shows a steady decline," according to the study. If cross pressures are negligible, interest determines the time of a voter's decision.

Clearly, great interest and the absence of cross pressures lead to an early decision, while many cross pressures and little interest lead to a late one.

But what of the people with one of the factors favorable to an early decision and the other unfavorable, i.e., those with several cross-pressures and great interest and those with no or one cross-pressure and less interest? These middle-of-the-roaders do not differ from each other in the time at which they made their final decision. In other words, when the two factors—interest and cross-pressures—work in opposing directions, they are about equal in strength.

Of course, many partisans (single-party supporters) are no better informed about party platforms or issues; their support of party candidates has become merely a ritual. Some partisans, however, feel obliged to understand the issues involved and are more concerned than many independents with the speeches of candidates and expressed opinions of their party. Others are well-versed in the political philosophy that determines many of their party's policies and, therefore, tend to be more interested in expressing and debating political issues.

Studies of voting behavior can give the political scientist valuable insights into the many factors that influence and affect participation at the polls. These analyses cannot, however, guarantee that they know exactly how a particular man will vote when he steps inside the polling booth. When an individual participates in the political system by voting, he participates as a totally unique creature; party membership, age, economic background, race, and religion—all these factors may affect different voters in different ways, some exerting greater influence than others at the particular time the individual casts his ballot.

# Glossary

**Fifteenth Amendment ( 1870 )** Constitutional amendment that prohibits state or national governments from denying the vote to citizens because of "race, color, or previous condition of servitude."

**independents** The approximately 30 percent of the American electorate who have no affiliation with any political party, including new voters, switchers, ticket-splitters, and those who do not formally identify with a party.

**new voters** The 15–20 percent of the American electorate who are voting for the first time.

**Nineteenth Amendment ( 1920 )** Constitutional amendment that prohibits the states from denying the vote to citizens on account of sex.

**political cross pressure** Situation in which an individual is simultaneously confronted by two opposing political influences, the psychological effect of which determines his political behavior.

**standpatters ( habitual party voters )** The 60 percent of the American voting population who support the same party in every election.

**suffrage** Voting.

**switchers** The 20 percent of the American electorate who do not consistently vote for one party or another, usually ticket–splitters or swing voters.

**ticket-splitting** Voting for individual candidates from different parties during a single election.

**Twenty-sixth Amendment ( 1971 )** Constitutional amendment that prohibits states from denying the vote in local and state elections to citizens eighteen years old or older.

**Voting Rights Act of 1965** Legislation that suspended all literacy tests and other devices used to deny black suffrage in all states and counties where less than 50 percent of the population had been registered to vote in the 1964 presidential election, and provided for federal examiners to register voters and monitor election procedures in states covered by the Act.

**Voting Rights Act of 1970** Legislation that lowered the voting age to eighteen in local, state, and national elections, abolished state residency requirements in presidential elections, and finally eliminated all literacy tests.

# Suggested readings

Bell, Daniel, ed., *The Radical Right* (Garden City, N.Y.: Doubleday and Co., Inc., 1963). Ideas and activities of the American political right as viewed by eight noted social scientists.

Berelson, Bernard, Paul F. Lazarsfeld, and William N. McPhee, *Voting: A Study of Opinion Formation in a Presidential Campaign* (Chicago: University of Chicago Press, 1954). Analysis of the 1948 election in a New York community.

Burdick, Eugene, and Arthur J. Brodbeck, eds., *American Voting Behavior* (New York: The Free Press, 1959). Collection of critical essays on voting behavior and voting patterns.

Campbell, Angus, Philip E. Converse, Warren E. Miller, and Donald E. Stokes, *The American Voter* (New York: John Wiley and Sons, Inc., 1964). Analysis of voting behavior, in presidential elections, based on data from 1948 to 1956, and concentrating on the elections of 1952 and 1956.

Campbell, Angus, Philip E. Converse, Warren E. Miller, and Donald E. Stokes, *Elections and the Political Order* (New York: John Wiley and Sons, Inc., 1966). Examination of the function of elections in the American political system, with emphasis on the effect of voting on the party system.

Campbell, Angus, Gerald Gurin, and Warren Miller, *The Voter Decides* (New York: Harper and Row Publishers, Inc., 1954). Study of voting behavior during the 1948 and 1952 presidential elections.

David, Paul T., Ralph M. Goldman, and Richard C. Bain, eds., *Presidential Nominating Politics in 1952*, 5 vols. (Baltimore: Johns Hopkins University Press, 1954). Monumental report on the 1952 election by 150 political scientists; each volume covers a major geographical section.

Davis, James W., *Presidential Primaries: The Road to the White House* (New York: Thomas Y. Crowell, 1967). Study of the evolution of the presidential primary system, including examples of strategies employed by presidential candidates.

Flanigan, William H., *Political Behavior of the American Electorate* (Boston: Allyn and Bacon, Inc., 1968). Study of voting behavior based on findings in four major national elections from 1952–1964.

Key, V. O., Jr., with the assistance of Milton C. Cummings, Jr., *The Responsible Electorate: Rationality in Presidential Voting, 1936–1960* (New York: Random House, Inc., 1968). Defense of voters against the charge of irrational behavior during elections.

Lazarsfeld, Paul, Bernard Berelson, and Hazel Gaudet, *The People's Choice*, 2nd ed. (New York: Columbia University Press, 1948). Study of the effect of the campaign on the decision in a presidential election, based on panel interviews.

Lipset, Seymour M., and Stein Rokkan, eds., *Party Systems and Voter Alignments: Crossnational Perspectives* (New York: The Free Press, 1967). Essays on voting behavior and the social basis for voter support of different political parties.

Matthews, Donald R., and James W. Prothro, *Negroes and the New Southern Politics* (New York: Harcourt Brace Jovanovich, Inc., 1966). Comprehensive description and analysis of Negro participation in the political process of the contemporary South.

Phillips, Kevin, *The Emerging Republican Majority* (New York: Anchor Books, 1964). Theory that the 1968 national election was the beginning of a political shift to the right and the creation of a new Republican majority, which would dominate American parties in the near future.

Scammon, Richard M., and Ben J. Wattenberg, *The Real Majority* (New York: Coward McCann, Inc., 1970). Provocative analysis of the contemporary American voter and an assessment of strategies to be used in the future by presidential candidates.

Wolfinger, Raymond E., ed., *Readings in American Political Behavior* (Englewood Cliffs, N.J.: Prentice-Hall, Inc., 1966). Collection of recent research and case studies illustrating behavioral patterns of political man.

# Topics of further study

Blair, Harry W., "Akron Forum's Reach Voters," *National Civic Review,* April 1963, pp. 226–228.

Clem, Alan L., "A Presentation and Analysis of Election Statistics, 1889–1960," Report no. 4, *South Dakota Political Almanac* (Brookings, S.Dak.: South Dakota State University Government Research Bureau, 1962).

Kingdon, John W., "Politicians' Beliefs about Voters," *American Political Science Review,* March 1967, pp. 137–145.

Opferkuch, Paul R., "The Voting Patterns of Southern Ontario, 1945–1957" (master's thesis, University of Wisconsin, 1963).

# 9 interest groups in action

In a televised newscast from a union hall in San Francisco, an official from the AFL-CIO argues in support of a bill to establish national health and safety standards for workers. In a Boston restaurant, a member of the National Association of Theatre Owners debates the merits of pay television with a state official. In Boise, Idaho, a group of housewives runs an ad in the local newspaper advocating government withdrawal from Vietnam. In Alaska, a member of the Alaskan legislature is besieged with demands for fair settlement of Eskimo-land claims from members of the Alaskan Federation of Natives. The AFL-CIO official, the theater-owner, the Idaho housewives, and the members of the Alaskan Federation of Natives are all trying to influence public officials to take political actions favorable to the groups to which they belong—to their interest groups.

About 64 percent of the American population belongs to interest groups of one kind or another, and almost all Americans are in some way represented by at least one of the many interest groups: whether or not they are members, pet-owners are represented by the Society for Prevention of Cruelty to Animals, and gun-owners by the National Rifle Association. Like expressing political opinions and voting, belonging to an interest group is a form of political participation. And it can be a powerful form: "In conjunction with political parties, interest groups constitute the principal avenue outside of official public government through which political power is marshaled and applied."[1]

[1] Abraham Holtzman, *Interest Groups and Lobbying* (New York: The Macmillan Co., 1966), p. 1.

# What are interest groups?

2 David L. Sills, *The Volunteers: Means and Ends in a National Organization* (New York: The Free Press, 1957) projected the future of the March of Dimes organization, upon discovery of a cure for infantile paralysis. Similarly, Abraham Holtzman, *The Townsend Movement: A Political Study* (New York: Bookman Associates, Inc., 1963) describes the institutionalization of old-age groups with the development of new issues.

An *interest group* is an organization of people who share common attitudes and interests and who attempt to influence the decisions made within the political system. There are many kinds of interest groups. Some are large and boast a national constituency: the AFL-CIO, for example, represents about 14 million workers, the American Legion has a membership of about 2.5 million veterans, and the American Farm Bureau includes about 2 million farm families. Others, like a city-block association working for tenants' rights, may involve only a handful of individuals attempting to influence policy decisions at the local level.

Most interest groups are formal organizations, complete with governing councils, boards of directors, and formal rules and regulations; the highly structured National Association of Manufacturers is a prominent example. On the other hand, a group of neighborhood women who jointly write a letter to their mayor protesting the poor quality of the city's education system are an equally valid, if more informal, interest group. They share common attitudes and interests and are seeking to influence political decision making. But such informally organized interest groups tend to dissolve when the issue that sparks them is resolved. If the issue is long-term or replaced by a more current question, the group is institutionalized—that is, it becomes a formal organization.[2]

*David Truman,* The Governmental Process *(New York: Alfred A. Knopf, Inc., 1952), pp. 33–34, 47–52, 505–508.*

David Truman, defining an interest group as a group having shared attitudes toward what is needed or wanted in a given situation, seeks to give an adequate account of the role of such groups in the American political process. Although political scientists have recently focused on interest-group roles, they have traditionally been neglected by theorists. Two arguments have usually been offered to refute any interpretation of government in terms of group patterns.

The first argument suggests that the "individual" is left out of such interpretations. But Truman argues:

We do not, in fact, find individuals otherwise than in groups; complete isolation in space and time is so rare as to be an almost hypothetical situation. . . . "The individual" and "the group" are at most convenient ways of classifying behavior, two ways of approaching the same phenomena, not different things.

The persistent idea of a conflict between the individual and the group is understandable, notes Truman, because for three centuries we have embraced "doctrines of individualism." We have insisted that individuals are the cause of complicated human events because multiple causes and group affiliations are difficult to interpret.

The second argument against group interpretation of the political process is that it ignores a greater unity, namely the society or the state.

Many of those who place particular emphasis upon this difficulty assume explicitly or implicitly that there is an interest of the nation as a whole, universally and invariably held and standing apart from and superior to those of the various groups included within it. This assumption is close to the popular dogmas of democratic government based on the familiar notion that if only people are free and have access to "the facts," they will all want the same thing in any political situation.

But, according to the author, "such an assertion flies in the face of all we know of the behavior of men in a complex society." The political party itself would have no substantial base in our government if we accepted this concept. Truman adds that the notion of such a national interest is appealing in times of national crisis, when it works as a promotional device to unify the country.

Moreover, he admits that the American political system cannot be viewed simply as a conglomeration of battling interests: the extent to which they find areas of agreement and compromise points out that something like a "national interest" exists.

Denying the existence of an interest of the nation as a whole does not completely dispose of the difficulty raised by those who insist that a group interpretation must omit "the state." We cannot deny the obvious fact that we are examining a going political system that is supported or at least accepted by a large proportion of the society. We cannot account for such a system by adding up in some fashion the National Association of Manufacturers, the Congress of Industrial Organizations, the American Farm Bureau Federation, the American Legion, and other groups that come to mind when "lobbies" and "pressure groups" are mentioned. . . .

If these various organized interest groups more or less consistently reconcile their differences, adjust, and accept compromises, we must acknowledge that we are dealing with a system that is not accounted for by the "sum" of the organized interest groups in the society.

In addition to organized groups, thus, there are various "potential" groups, having no formal office or organization, but always in the "becoming" stage of activity.

[3] David B. Truman, *The Governmental Process: Political Interests and Public Opinion* (New York: Alfred A. Knopf, Inc., 1951), pp. 157–159.

Interest groups often share members, for individuals may belong to a number of groups—sometimes even to groups that take opposing stands on political issues.[3] A man may be a member of a taxpayers' association and also belong to the local roadbuilders' union. If these groups take conflicting positions on the issue of highway construction, the direction the man will take depends on a number of factors, among them how strongly he identifies with each of the groups to which he belongs and how strongly the group is concerned with the issue in question.[4]

[4] See Angus Campbell, Philip E. Converse, Warren E. Miller, and Donald E. Stokes, *The American Voter* (New York: John Wiley and Sons, Inc., 1960) on group identification; and Dorwin Cartwright and A. Zander, eds., *Group Dynamics: Research and Theory*, 3rd ed. (New York: Harper and Row Publishers, Inc., 1968) on group concern.

Some interest groups are formed in response to a single political issue or candidate. These groups are often active only while that issue is in question or the candidate is running for office. A group formed specifically to elect a particular political candidate, for example, is usually dissolved on election day.[5] Whether the candidate is elected or defeated, the issue is settled and the group has no reason to continue its activities.

[5] Some campaign groups, however, continue in operation after the election. The Movement for a New Congress has been in existence for several years and several campaigns.

Most interest groups, however, are established to represent the *continuing interests* of their members. The United Automobile Workers and the Congress of Railway Unions were established to represent the interests in all political issues of auto workers and railroad workers, respectively.

Some interest groups claim to support "the public interest," rather than that of any particular group. One such group, called Common Cause, was established in 1970 to "uphold the public interest against all comers, particularly the special interests that dominate our lives today."[6] Headed by former Secretary of Health, Education and Welfare John Gardner, Common Cause has begun a campaign to revise the seniority system in Congress (whereby the heads of congressional committees are selected according to the number of years they have held office). It also announced plans to oppose the (now-defeated) bill for financing supersonic transport (SST) planes, to push for reform of campaign-spending practices, and to fight for total withdrawal from Vietnam.

[6] Richard Halloran, "New Lobby Fights Special Interests," *The New York Times*, February 3, 1971.

Clearly, such groups as Common Cause do not represent *the* "public interest." There is no *single* public interest. For any political issue, no matter how widely supported, there is at least one group or interest in the nation that opposes it. There are numerous groups, for example, that *support* the supersonic transport, *oppose* reforms of campaign-spending practices, *support* the seniority system in the Congress, and *support* the war in Vietnam.[7]

[7] See for examples, Glendon A. Schubert, *Public Interest* (New York: The Free Press, 1961); and Walter Lippmann, *The Public Philosophy* (Boston: The Atlantic Monthly Press, 1955).

# The growth of interest groups

[8] Alexis de Tocqueville, *Democracy in America*, ed. by Phillips Bradley (New York: Random House, Inc., 1945), vol. II, p. 123.

"There is only one country on the face of the earth where the citizens enjoy unlimited freedom of association for political purposes," wrote Tocqueville in reference to the United States in the nineteenth century.[8] This freedom of association—the right to join interest groups—has been exercised by Americans throughout the nation's history. In 1867, the Grange was formed to protect the interests of farmers. And, in the early part of the twentieth century, as manufacturing became more important and as the number of skilled and unskilled laborers increased, a few small, unorganized labor unions were formed. As labor increased in importance, the number and size of labor unions also increased. When the skilled and unskilled laborers of the late nineteenth century gained government assistance and cooperation, they did so by organizing—that is, by forming interest groups (unions) established to protect their rights. When unions today seek political action, they often get it, because they are a large, organized, and accepted political force.

"To that great melting pot of silent Americans and effete snobs, of unconscious racists and bleeding hearts, of reactionaries and liberals, hawks and doves! To the good old U.S.A.!"

Drawing by Dana Farber; © 1970 The New Yorker Magazine, Inc.

The history of American interest groups, especially in the twentieth century, has been one of growth. Political scientists, depending on their orientation, suggest different reasons for this growth. For example, some note that party systems are so fragmented that they are not responsible to the public; thus, interest groups become a necessary alternative. Others believe interest groups have proliferated because of separation of occupational and kinship roles.[9] Here, we will concentrate on three basic reasons for the growth of organized interest groups in the United States:

*The Pluralistic Nature of America.* The United States is a nation of widely diverse political attitudes and interests. The interests of Jews on the exportation of arms to Israel may differ from those of Protestants; the interests of labor, in the short run, may differ from those of management; the interests of eighteen-year-olds appear to differ from those of elder citizens.

[9] Bernard Barber, "Participation and Mass Apathy in Association," in Alvin W. Gouldner, ed., *Studies in Leadership: Leadership and Democratic Action* (New York: Harper and Brothers, 1950), p. 504.

To protect each of these varying interests, various interest groups are formed. As individual or group needs and interests change, as existing interest groups fail to meet their members' needs, or when one group's interests are being met at the expense of another, new interest groups emerge.

Increased specialization has increased the number of categories by which individuals can be classified and, as a result, has led to the proliferation of interest groups. Such specializations as computer programming, commercial airline piloting, and nuclear engineering, for example, are only a few decades old. Americans employed in these new specialized occupations tend to have similar interests and have formed groups to promote them. And with each new interest group established, other groups tend to be organized in self-defense.

## National Associations—Number, by Type, 1969

| Type | 1969 |
|---|---|
| Trade, business, commercial | 2,914 |
| Agricultural | 515 |
| Governmental, public administrative, military, legal | 334 |
| Scientific, engineering, technical | 541 |
| Educational, cultural | 1,413 |
| Social welfare | 424 |
| Health, medical | 838 |
| Public affairs | 518 |
| Fraternal, foreign interest, nationality, ethnic | 670 |
| Religious | 811 |
| Horticultural | 97 |
| Veterans, hereditary, patriotic | 211 |
| Hobby, avocational | 458 |
| Athletic, sports | 340 |
| Labor unions | 241 |
| Chambers of commerce | 129 |
| Greek letter societies | 369 |
| General[a] | 110 |
| Total | 10,933 |

[a] Not elsewhere classified.

Source: *Statistical Abstracts of the United States*, 1970.

*The Regional Diversity of America.* A host of interest groups were formed in the past to protect the interests of people in specific sections of the country, for the interests of Americans in Waco, Texas were once considered to be markedly different from the interests of Americans in Bangor, Maine; Portland, Oregon; or Little Rock, Arkansas. Although regionalism is less significant today, such groups as the *Southern* Pine Industry Committee, the *Southwestern* Peanut Shellers' Association, the Association of *Western* Rail-

[10] V. O. Key, Jr., *Public Opinion and American Democracy* (New York: Alfred A. Knopf, Inc., 1961), chap. 5.

ways, and the Labor Bureau of the *Middle West*, actively work to influence the policies of the national government.[10]

*The Dispersion of Power in America.* The structure of American government, the division of responsibility among national, state, and local governments, has fostered the growth of interest groups. Our federal system allows the decision-making process to be approached from many points of access; interest groups, therefore, can compensate for lack of success at one source of governmental power by concentrating their involvement at another level. But to utilize all these channels of political influence in an effective and timely manner, a large and organized group is necessary: an interest group like the Chamber of Commerce, for example, has the numbers to maintain group units at local, state, and national levels of government. If a state legislature should wish to increase the tax on radio and television parts, the state Chamber of Commerce is ready and on the scene to protest the new tax to the appropriate legislators. And if the national government is considering a raise in the minimum wage, the chamber has a fully organized group in Washington to counter the proposal.

A second factor in determining interest-group structures is the separation of powers among the legislative, executive, and judicial branches of government. Interest groups with sufficient power and prestige can try to influence political decisions through each branch. For example, the NAACP at first tried acting against segregation through the legislature, but the number of southern representatives hindered the group's success. Because of separation of powers, the NAACP was able instead to accomplish its goals through the Supreme Court.

# The power of interest groups

Political power is not evenly distributed among the various interest groups within the political system: some interest groups inspire trepidation, others only laughter. What, then, are the factors that determine the strength of an interest group? How do interest groups acquire political power?

The *size* of an interest group has much to do with its political power—bigness means voting strength, prestige, and ability to raise funds. The 14 million-member AFL-CIO can exert more political power than a few dozen urban mothers banded together to oppose cuts in state educational spending.

But as a power determinant, size may hold second place to solidarity. If the group is unified, if its members are able to agree upon and work together toward specific goals, then the group will be politically powerful. If, on the other hand, the group members have overlapping loyalties, if they differ over the goals of the group and how they are to be obtained, then the group will be politically weak. A unified group of draft board officials will be better able to achieve its goals than a group of selective service reformers who have not agreed upon a single course of action.

Thus, an important problem faced by all interest groups is *loyalty*, primarily the loyalty of their most active participants. Their members often belong to a number of other interest groups, each desiring their attention. It is not unusual for an American to find that his labor union, his rifle association, his veterans' organization, and his neighborhood league are all holding meetings on the same night or that the political attitudes and policies of two or more of these groups differ from one another. Which meeting he attends and which doctrine he adheres to depend on how strongly he identifies with each of the groups, how persuasive the leadership of each group is, and whether or not he already has an opinion about the issue at hand.[11]

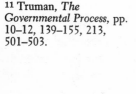

11 Truman, *The Governmental Process*, pp. 10–12, 139–155, 213, 501–503.

An interest group's ability to influence public policy is further determined by society's opinion of the group, the type of issues of concern to the group, the group's leadership, the group's wealth, and the political power of the interest groups that oppose it. An interest group (such as the Clock Makers Union) confronted by a powerful organization like the National Association of Manufacturers or the American Bar Association may find its

"All right, break it up!"

Drawing by Modell; © 1971
The New Yorker Magazine, Inc.

political power drastically diminished. It is unlikely that the Clock Makers, with 1,500 members and a treasury of $10,000, will be able to overpower the National Association of Manufacturers, with 215,000 members and $1 million in the treasury.

# The structure of interest groups

The structure of most interest groups is remarkably similar to the structure of our constitutional democracy. Most interest groups have constitutions or charters, conduct regular elections, and tax their members. And many of the largest interest groups employ a federal system of government. Their charters divide power between the national organization and the local branches, much in the manner that the Constitution divides power between the national government and the states.

In addition, the levels of participation within most interest groups are similar to those of the political system. In interest groups, as in the political system, there are three types of participants: nominal participants, active participants, and leaders. The number in each category may vary according to the size of the group, for the larger the group grows, the larger the list of in-active members, because of a feeling of individual ineffectiveness in a large group. *Nominal participants* are those individuals who are members in name only. They do not attend meetings, or work to promote the goals of the group. Some may even be directly opposed to the policies of their interest groups. In some industries, for example, membership in a labor union is a requirement of continued employment. A man who joins a union only in order to keep his job is likely to become a nominal participant in that union's activities.

*Active participants* are those who identify strongly with an interest group and work to secure its goals. They may be regular members with a strong interest in group affairs or, in the case of the larger interest groups, profes-sionals hired on a part-time or full-time basis to promote group aims. Active participants are the legmen of an interest group. They are vital to group power, but, as in the political system, much of the power lies with the leaders.

The *leaders*, the men who direct the active participants of an interest group, have direct access to an interest group's political machinery and use that machinery to promote the group's objectives. They sometimes have almost total control over the group's professional staff and over the dissemina-tion of information within the group. By controlling the group's newspaper or magazine, for example, the leaders can effectively localize opposing fac-tions and promote their own cause.

Since the group's leaders represent the group in negotiation and bargaining, the more politically effective the leader, the more powerful the group. A leader who is popular and politically visible can greatly unify an interest group, thereby increasing its political power. For example, the International Brotherhood of Teamsters was, under the leadership of Dave Beck (during the late 1950s), much less well-known nationally than it has been under the forceful, often criticized leadership of Jimmy Hoffa, who helped the union to prosper and flourish as an important national element of the American political system.

# The types of interest groups

The variety of American interest groups is as great as that of American interests. Some groups are based on relatively *noneconomic* interests, such groups ranging from the Italian-American Civil Rights League to the Millard P. Fillmore Society formed to improve the reputation of our thirteenth President. Many noneconomic interest groups are based on interests common to a race, religion, age, or sex group. But traditionally the bond joining most interest groups has been *economic*. The common economic interest of farmers, businessmen, workers, professionals, and consumers has led to the establishment of interest groups within these categories. No single economic group or category has enjoyed a monopoly of power, but each has exerted at least some power within the political system.

## Agriculture groups

Jefferson called the farmer "the most noble and independent man in society." Because of his independence, the farmer, until the Civil War, had little reason to form interest groups; the group that he belonged to was the small and self-sufficient family unit. The farmer fed and clothed his family from the products of his land. He was, in effect, largely insulated from outside pressures.

After the Civil War, however, the economics of agriculture changed markedly. In 1820, the average farm worker produced enough for himself and 3 others. Gradually, the farmer began to raise crops to sell, rather than to supply the needs of his family—that is, subsistence farming gave way to commercial farming. The farmer was now involved in the national economy; price fluctuations, whether in nearby urban areas or in states far removed from his own, affected the farmer's income and way of life. In 1920, he produced enough for himself and 9 others; in 1945, for 14 others; and in 1970, for 132 others.

This increased productivity, however, has several drawbacks. For example, the trucks and tractors that aided the farmer in increasing his output seriously affected the market for animal feed, because draft animals (horses and mules) were no longer needed. It has been estimated that between 1918

## 25 Top Spenders

| Organization | 1969 | 1968 |
|---|---|---|
| National Association of Letter Carriers (AFL-CIO) | $295,970 | $ 63,797 |
| United Federation of Postal Clerks (AFL-CIO) | 250,827 | 170,784 |
| Realty Committee on Taxation | 229,223 | — |
| AFL-CIO (headquarters) | 184,938 | 154,466 |
| American Farm Bureau Federation | 146,337 | 147,379 |
| National Committee for the Recording Arts | 139,726 | 25,949 |
| National Association of Home Builders of the United States | 138,472 | 70,095 |
| United States Savings and Loan League | 126,421 | 119,784 |
| Record Industry Association of America, Inc. | 115,334 | 111,394 |
| American Legion | 114,609 | 141,134 |
| Council for a Livable World | 112,603 | 154,022 |
| National Education Association, Office of Government Relations and Citizenship | 97,537 | 84,146 |
| National Housing Conference, Inc. | 95,562 | 96,935 |
| American Medical Association | 91,355 | 56,374 |
| Railway Labor Executives Association | 86,286 | — |
| National Association of Theater Owners | 84,049 | — |
| Citizens Committee for Postal Reform | 83,951 | — |
| Brotherhood of Railway, Airline and Steamship Clerks, Freight Handlers, Express and Station Employees (AFL-CIO) | 80,985 | 93,456 |
| American Trucking Associations, Inc. | 80,896 | 121,399 |
| Liberty Lobby, Inc. | 79,927 | 75,807 |
| National Federation of Independent Business, Inc. | 75,528 | 102,455 |
| National Farmers Union | 73,264 | 95,639 |
| National Association of Postal Supervisors | 68,365 | 35,694 |
| National Council of Farmer Cooperatives | 62,496 | 57,832 |
| National Federation of Federal Employees | 61,269 | 57,148 |

Note: Listed are the 25 top spenders of the 269 organizations that filed lobby spending reports for 1969, with the amounts they reported spending in 1969 and 1968.

Source: "Lobby Report 4," *Congressional Quarterly*, July 31, 1970, p. 1967.

and 1953 about 70 million acres formerly used to grow food for draft animals were turned to other purposes. Furthermore, although the decline in export markets after 1900 was compensated for by an increase in the general population, after 1910 the supply of farm products outweighed the demand for them. During periods of inflation, the problem grew worse: the demand for farm produce fell far below the ever-rising cost of farm production. Consequently, many farmers were forced to move to the cities to find work. From 1948 to 1970, for example, the farm population dropped by 14.4 million, from 24.4 million to 10 million.[12]

[12] *Congressional Quarterly,* June 12, 1970, p. 1550.

*Theodore Lowi, "How the Farmers Get What They Want,"* The Reporter, *May 21, 1964, pp. 34–37.*

Theodore Lowi observes that the farmers are a unique interest group. Traditionally, agricultural policies have been shaped exclusively by the farm community, and no serious challenge to this separatism has emerged in our age of governmental centralization. A complicated system of ten highly decentralized, highly autonomous subgovernments has evolved, allowing the agricultural community to be self-regulating. Under this system, locally elected committees hold an inordinate amount of power, and these committees stand as a bulwark between the farmer and Washington.

The self-governing local units become one important force in a system that administers a program and maintains the autonomy of that program against political forces emanating from other agricultural programs, from antagonistic farm and nonfarm interests, from Congress, from the Secretary of Agriculture, and from the President. To many a farmer, the local outpost of one or another of these systems *is* the government.

A few examples point out the effectiveness of the farm lobby. In 1947, Secretary of Agriculture Clinton P. Anderson proposed the consolidation of several farm programs; he was met with opposing bills by farm organizations, resulting in a stalemate. President Eisenhower, in his turn, repeatedly was blocked by the farm lobby in his attempts to eliminate farm-housing and improvement loans. Later, President Kennedy attempted to replace the policy of controlling surplus by limiting the number of acres a farmer could cultivate, with a policy limiting the amount of bushels, tons, or other units he could produce. But the farmers objected, since the acreage system enabled them to produce a greater quantity by cultivating more per acre. Secretary of Agriculture Orville L. Freeman tried to make a more attractive offer of $2.00 wheat supports instead of $1.79 supports, but the farmers rejected it. Finally, when the administration persisted, the wheat farmers in 1963 rejected any reforms. Even if they would be paid more, they refused greater regulation.

According to Lowi:

It is not so odd that wheat farmers would reject a proposal that aims to regulate them more strictly than before. What is odd is that only wheat farmers are allowed to decide the matter. It seems that in agriculture, as in many other fields, the regulators are powerless without the consent of the regulated.

He adds that the strength of the agricultural self-governing systems has thus been repeatedly reinforced.

Secretaries of Agriculture have tried and failed to consolidate or even to coordinate related programs. Within Congress, they are sufficiently powerful to be able to exercise an effective veto or create a stalemate. And they are almost totally removed from the view, not to mention the control, of the general public.

All these changes have made the farmer more and more vulnerable to outside pressures and have led him to seek the protection of membership in organized interest groups. Because of the specialized nature of modern farming (Americans involved in agriculture today think of themselves as potato growers, dairymen, tobacco growers, or poultrymen, rather than simply as farmers), the nation's agricultural population holds widely diverse and often conflicting interests. As a result, a number of groups has been formed to represent the interests of farmers growing a specific crop. Typical are such organizations as the American Livestock Association, the National Wool Growers Federation, the American Pork Producers Association, and the National Apple Institute.

There are, however, several organizations that claim to represent farmers in general. The largest and most active of these are the National Grange, the American Farm Bureau Federation, and the National Farmer's Union. More recently, these groups (with the exception of the American Farm Bureau Federation) have organized to form the *Coalition of Farm Organizations,* for the purpose of strengthening their position against the President's attempts to "change the direction of farm policy."[13]

Organized in 1867, the *National Grange*—first known as the *Patrons of Husbandry*—was originally a fraternal and educational organization. "It places emphasis, according to its literature, 'on moral and spiritual idealism. It is a fraternity with a beautiful ritual.' "[14] As farm prices fell in the decade after the Civil War, however, the Grange's activities became political. Blaming the railroads for the economic problems brought on by the high cost of shipping

[13] *Congressional Quarterly,* June 12, 1970, p. 1550.

[14] V. O. Key, Jr., *Politics, Parties, and Pressure Groups,* 5th ed. (New York: Thomas Y. Crowell Co., 1964), p. 32.

## The National Grange

crops, the Grangers lobbied in Congress and successfully secured the passage of railroad regulation laws.

The Grange reached the height of its popularity and political power in 1875, when its membership consisted of more than 750,000 farmers across the nation. Although today its membership remains fairly large (600,000 members), the Grange has declined in size relative to other farm organizations. What remains of the Grange membership is concentrated in the rural Northeast, in Ohio, New York, Pennsylvania, and the New England states, although some branches have been maintained in Oregon and Washington.

In recent years, the Grange has adopted a political program that is basically middle-of-the-road, although leaning somewhat on the conservative side. The Grange supported legislation favoring passage of "right-to-work" laws by the states and opposed the establishment of smaller, independent labor unions for farmers or farm workers.

## American Farm Bureau Federation

The *American Farm Bureau Federation*, like the Grange, claims to represent the nation's farmers. And, like the Grange, it primarily represents regional interests and is closely linked to the agricultural services offered by the state university land-grant colleges. About 50 percent of the almost 2,000,000 farm families who belong to the Farm Bureau are located in the Midwest and more than 30 percent in the South.

Emerging as the most powerful of the general agricultural interest groups, the Farm Bureau opposes most governmental controls over agricultural production, preferring instead to concentrate on helping the farmer to help himself—with loans at low interest rates, low premium insurance, and so on.

On issues outside the sphere of agriculture, the Farm Bureau tends to side with the major business groups and, in return, these groups usually support the Farm Bureau on farm issues.

## The National Farmer's Union

Founded in Texas in 1902, the *National Farmer's Union* "carries on the tradition of old-fashioned, militant agrarian radicalism"[15]—radicalism not in the sense of revolutionary changes, but rather in a return to the "roots," to the original concept of farming as a way of life, rather than a way to make money.

[15] Key, *Politics, Parties, and Pressure Groups*, p. 37.

In upholding this tradition, however, the Farmer's Union has proposed measures that some (especially the other major farm organizations) find rather extreme and contrary to the "American way." For example, the Union has called for the establishment of cooperative terminals, insurance agencies, and other centralized groups, so that "the potential abundance of this Nation may be made available to all its people." In Oklahoma, Nebraska, the Dakotas, Wisconsin, Minnesota, Montana, and Colorado, where the Union is strongest, its collective bargaining orientation and its friendships with labor officials and their empathizers in government have caused it to be the only one of the three major agricultural interest groups to support the labor movement and generally to support Democratic candidates and policies.[16]

# Business groups

[16] Stephen K. Bailey, *Congress Makes a Law* (New York: Columbia University Press, 1950), p. 2.

[17] Harmon Zeigler, *Interest Groups in American Society* (Englewood Cliffs, N.J.: Prentice-Hall, Inc., 1964), p. 93.

The owner of a soda shop, the chairman of the board of IBM, the manager of a chain of supermarkets, and the local undertaker would seem to have few common interests, yet they frequently band together in pursuit of common goals. They are all businessmen: they are directly concerned with making a profit. "Since businessmen [want] to make money," writes Harmon Zeigler, "it is reasonable that the achievement and maintenance of a satisfactory margin of profit is a major purpose behind the formation of associations of businessmen."[17]

Business interest groups date back to the guilds of the late Middle Ages. They have been active in American politics throughout the nation's history. In 1741, for example, the Baker's Guild of New York City publicly opposed a city ordinance fixing the price of bread. Until the Civil War, however, business interest groups were local, rather than national. After the Civil War, as industry grew rapidly, business associations began to expand their activities to a national scale.

As business groups proliferated, their success in influencing legislation favorable to their interests increased because of unity, acceptability, and political skills. Though some differences in political attitudes may exist between the small businessman and the president of a corporation, basically their interests coincide; if nothing else, both seek to protect their profits. And though some individuals have been highly critical of business practices and the whole idea of profit-motivation, "the small businessman has always been identified with all of the homely virtues of Main Street America and thus is in something of a charmed if not sacred category along with Motherhood and the American Flag."[18] Those who view businessmen favorably can usually be counted upon to support business programs.

[18] John H. Bunzel, *The American Small Businessman* (New York: Alfred A. Knopf, Inc., 1962), p. vi.

In addition to unity and acceptability, business interest groups enjoy the advantages of considerable political resources, such as money, prestige, and political skill. The bargaining, organizing, and public relations skills that lead to business success can be helpful also in exerting effective pressure on the political decision-making process.

There are about 2,000 national business interest groups, as well as about 12,000 local and state groups. The majority of these groups—about 1,800 of the national business interest groups, for example—are *trade associations*. They represent a single type of industry, and are concerned primarily with exchanging information, obtaining mutual benefits, encouraging specialized tax legislation, stabilizing import-export regulations, and licensing. Illustrative of this type of business interest group are the Synthetic Organic Chemical

Manufacturers Association, the American Bankers Association, the Automobile Manufacturers Association, and the American Federation of Retail Kosher Butchers.

Some groups, on the other hand, claim to represent business in general. The most important of these associations are the National Association of Manufacturers, the Chamber of Commerce of the United States, and the Committee for Economic Development.

## The National Association of Manufacturers

Established in 1895, the *National Association of Manufacturers* (NAM) represents about 16,000 individuals, companies, and corporations engaged in manufacturing. Although its members make up only about 8 percent of the nation's manufacturers, these same members produce about 75 percent of the nation's manufactured goods.

Throughout its history, the NAM has strongly opposed organized labor and has argued against "federal centralization, and, indeed, the expansion of governmental authority generally."[19] A conservative organization, the NAM views the growth of the national government and increased governmental intervention in business activities as undesirable.

[19] Key, *Politics, Parties, and Pressure Groups,* p. 88.

*The earliest labor unions met with open resistance. Compare this photograph of laborers confronted by armed soldiers to some recent campus scenes.*

## The Chamber of Commerce of the United States

20 *Our First Fifty Years* (Washington, D.C.: Chamber of Commerce of the United States, 1962), p. 26.

## The Committee for Economic Development

21 *Forum for Leadership in a Changing Society* (New York: Information Committee of the Committee for Economic Development, 1970).

## Labor unions

22 See Harwood L. Childs, *Labor and Capital in National Politics* (Columbus, Ohio: Ohio State University Press, 1930); and John R. Commons et al., *History of Labor in the United States*, 4 vols. (New York: Augustus M. Kelley, Publishers, 1918–1935) for the history of labor movements.

The *National Chamber*, as it is known to its membership, is a federation of more than 3,000 local and state business interest groups and claims "to bring the leadership and wisdom of the business and professional community to bear on the solution of national economic problems for the long-range good of the country—and for the greater good of all."[20] Like most business groups, the Chamber of Commerce urges the reduction of existing government controls on business, and opposes any new controls. It prefers state action to national action on most social issues, arguing that the states should be responsible for such things as the financing of public schools and the regulation of insurance.

Organized in 1942 primarily as a research organization, the *Committee for Economic Development* (CED) is an organization of 200 trustees (leading businessmen and educators). "Nonprofit, nonpartisan and nonpolitical," CED concentrates on research and education "designed to contribute to the preservation and strengthening of our free society, and to the maintenance of high employment, increasing productivity and living standards, greater economic stability and greater opportunity for all our people."[21]

CED's leaders believe that big business is here to stay, and thus have sought to promote a state of "peaceful coexistence" between big government and big business. They prefer the offensive to the defensive and concentrate on preparing new legislation, rather than obstructing government policies that they find disadvantageous to business. Unlike the NAM and the Chamber of Commerce, the CED does not actively try to initiate legislation based on its recommendations.

The earliest labor unions in the United States were established during Washington's administration. But up until the Civil War, since industry employed only a small, scattered work force, labor-union activity was confined to the local level. Then, in the last half of the nineteenth century, the rise of manufacturing and supporting industries, such as mining and transportation, created a rapidly expanding labor force, a force with common attitudes and interests. The workers' national interests (in higher wages and shorter work hours, regardless of industry) led to the formation of several national labor organizations in the years after the Civil War.[22] The most important of these was the *Knights of Labor*. Originally a secret organization, the Knights of Labor was operating quite openly by the 1880s, claiming membership of over 700,000; but it rapidly declined in size, when most of its membership were absorbed into the *American Federation of Labor* (AFL), which was formed in the late 1800s.

The American Federation of Labor was established and grew in size because it could succeed where the Knights of Labor had failed—namely, in meeting the increasing need for strong national representation for craftworkers (the glasscutters, for example). The Knights of Labor was a single national union; its interests were too narrow and its membership too small. The AFL, on the other hand, was a union of national unions, a confederation of all the skilled workers brought to light by the growth of the nation's industrial power.

In the 1930s, when the Great Depression struck the most severe blow against labor, the increasingly larger numbers of unskilled workers demanded stronger and more independent representation. Many—including the United Mine Workers, under the fiery guidance of John L. Lewis—broke away from the AFL and banded together to form the *Congress of Industrial Organization* (CIO). The two major rivals, the AFL and the CIO, were working toward the same goals, but were using different methods.

## The AFL-CIO

By 1955, the AFL-CIO rivalry had eased enough for the two major unions to merge. The nation's largest labor organization, the AFL-CIO, is a federation of 121 national and international labor unions. Only about fifty national unions are not represented. The majority of the national unions in the AFL-CIO are small, with 40 percent having fewer than 25,000 members. Such AFL-CIO affiliates as the Electrical Workers, the Carpenters, and the Steelworkers, however, have memberships of over 700,000.

The merger created an organization claiming 15 million members, the bulk of the nation's organized labor. The size of this organization, however, does not define its power. Rather it is the structure of the AFL-CIO, the skill and personality of its leaders, the size of its treasury, and the strength of its belief that "every citizen has the right and responsibility to take part in the political affairs of his city, his state and the nation"[23] that determines its political effectiveness. For instance, in 1969, the AFL-CIO reported spending $184,938 for lobbying purposes—the fourth largest amount spent by interest groups in that year. The AFL-CIO's successful opposition to President Nixon's appointment of both Clement Haynsworth and G. Harrold Carswell as associate justices of the Supreme Court in that same year is another example of the power of labor interest groups. Although labor was not the only powerful group to express opposition, its influence was considerable in effecting the defeat of the appointments.

[23] *This Is the AFL-CIO*, Publication no. 20, rev. ed. (Washington, D.C.: American Federation of Labor and Congress of Industrial Organizations, 1969), p. 9. Note that most AFL-CIO political achievements are accomplished by COPE, their Committee on Political Education.

[24] For a description of a specific professional interest group, see Oliver Garceau, *The Political Life of the American Medical Association* (Cambridge, Mass.: Harvard University Press, 1941).

## Professional groups

Professional people, such as doctors, lawyers, teachers, and architects, hold common interests; to protect those interests they have banded together in a host of professional organizations.[24] For the most part, these organizations are small, but the respect and wealth that professional people command in our society lend considerable power to their meager membership.

A primary concern of most professional interest groups is licensing, the control of entrance into the profession. Since licensing is usually a state matter, professional interest groups are highly active at the state level. Most professional associations have continually fought for stricter licensing qualifications, in most cases calling for more rigid educational requirements. The associations argue that they are protecting the public interest by keeping quacks and incompetents from their ranks. Another factor, to be sure, is an economic one: by making qualifications for entrance into professions more rigid, the associations can effectively restrict competition in their area and, thus, drive up the prices of their services.

"I'll have to check the safe, Senator Thurmond . . . there's been a run on the bank . . ."

Drawing by Conrad in the Los Angeles *Times.*

## The American Medical Association

The two largest professional interest groups in the nation are the *American Medical Association* (AMA) and the *American Bar Association* (ABA). In recent years, the AMA has been more actively involved in politics than any other professional interest group. In 1948, after President Truman proposed a system of compulsory health insurance, the AMA initiated a massive campaign to educate the American public about the supposed dangers of "socialized medicine." This campaign, which cost the AMA more than $4.5 million in less than four years, succeeded in burying the plan until the 1960s, when a new movement for a government health plan began. Despite its vigorous campaign against the Medicare Plan, the AMA was overpowered and Medicare was finally enacted in 1965.

In areas of interest to the AMA, its membership has traditionally placed its strength behind conservative and Republican programs, and has opposed the proposals of the Democratic Party and the liberal wing of the Republican party. In 1969, for example, the AMA effectively blocked the appointment of Dr. John Knowles, a liberal Republican, as the assistant secretary of the Department of Health, Education and Welfare. Knowles supported increased community services (especially for the poor) and backed Medicare and Medicaid programs, areas then under fire from the AMA. Knowles had been suggested to the President by HEW Secretary Robert Finch and had even received the unofficial support of the President. When opposition developed, however, Finch withdrew Knowles's name. The AMA—with its $26 million fund—played an important role in Knowles's defeat.[25]

25 "Just What the Doctor Ordered?" *Newsweek*, July 7, 1969, pp. 15–16; "The Curious Case of Dr. Knowles," *Time*, July 4, 1969, pp. 12–13; and "Caught in a Crunch: Secretary Finch," *U.S. News and World Report*, July 7, 1969, p. 11.

## The American Bar Association

In contrast to the AMA, the major professional organization for lawyers, the American Bar Association, involves itself with a different section of the political arena—the judiciary. Although some of its members serve as legislative counsels to the interest groups working through Congress, most of its membership concentrate on the legal proceedings that they are trained to handle.

Within the political arena, the ABA generally attempts to preserve the American form of representative government, improve the administration of justice, and promote peace by establishing an international system of law consistent with American ideals of equality and liberty.[26] More specifically, the ABA is involved in such activities as legal aid, defendants' rights, and lawyers' conduct.

26 *Constitution and By-Laws: Rules of Procedure, House of Delegates 1970–1971* (Chicago: American Bar Association, 1971).

The scope of the ABA membership provides it with strong potential for political power. More than half the Congress of the United States and almost all the justices of the Supreme Court have been lawyers and members of the ABA. Depending on their degree of identification with the organization in relation to the issue at hand, these men may exert strong pressure in the direction of the ABA's interests. For example, local bar organizations are currently lobbying within state legislatures to have the right to nominate local judges.

## Consumer groups

Traditionally, interest groups have been formed around the producer—the businessman, the farmer, the professional, and the laborer. In recent years, however, a number of groups has been established to protect the hapless consumer.

To work with these groups, the President has appointed a special assistant for consumer affairs, Mrs. Virginia Knauer. Several cities and states have appointed officials—such as Mrs. Bess Myerson Grant, New York City's Commissioner of Consumer Affairs, and Betty Furness, chairman and executive director of the New York State Consumer Protection Board—to lend assistance to the consumer. In Minnesota and Illinois, the Attorney General —Warren Spinnaus and William Scott, respectively, has inherited the function of consumer protection. These public officials are generally expected to mediate disputes between the consumer and business and between the consumer and government; more specifically, they investigate and set standards for product quality, and they educate the public on what standards to look for.

Simon Lazarus, "Advocates for the Consumer: Who's the Boss?" The New Republic, May 1971, pp. 22–23.

Simon Lazarus stresses the need for new programs to defend the consumer. The present setup suffers from the President's need to protect his agencies; charges by zealous consumer advocates that the agencies function ineffectively would be embarrassing politically. Mrs. Virginia Knauer, President Nixon's Special Assistant for Consumer Affairs, stressed this problem when she appeared before the Committee on Government Operations in April of 1971. She reported on

the President's determination to keep tight control over any machinery Congress might set up to give the consumer advocates greater status before federal regulatory agencies. The President, after all, is responsible for the performance of the bureaucracy and for the integrity of its programs. It would hardly suit his political convenience were gadfly lawyers to reveal that one agency after another has been faithless to its mandate.

However, some government-controlled agencies have been found to be less than effective. For example, the consolidation into the government's bureaucracy of agencies providing legal services for the poor would not, according to many authorities, benefit those intended. Lazarus has concluded:

Justice for the intended beneficiaries of welfare and regulatory programs will never be satisfactorily achieved, unless new governmental or quasi-governmental arrangements are devised; these arrangements must channel adequate resources to advocates for public interests, without at the same time subordinating advocacy programs to the political imperatives of the Executive Branch.

One proposal, introduced by Congressman Benjamin Rosenthal in the House and Senator Abraham Ribicoff in the Senate, would create an "Independent Consumer Protection Agency Act." Lazarus contends that such an agency would wind up as a "paper tiger," since the President appoints its administrator. Ideally, the administrator should not be obligated to the President, because

the more vigorously the administrator performs his job, the more political trouble he will create for his boss.

Lazarus cites three alternatives. One is Senator Edward Kennedy's "Public Counsel Corporation," which would have as first objective to arrange for private organizations to represent specific public interest groups and individuals wishing to appear before the administrative agencies. The second proposal is Senator Philip Hart's "Independent Consumer Council," which would be managed by a board of directors elected from local chapters open to anyone. The third alternative, proposed by the Center for Law and Social Policy, recommends that the government pay the cost for *private attorneys* to represent consumer groups on a case-by-case basis. Though some find this suggestion far-fetched, it is in current practice; for example, the Federal Trade Commission is paying the legal fees for public interest groups charging Firestone Tire and Rubber with advertising deception. Similarly, the Security and Exchange Commission pays lawyers' fees. But this policy is not a standard one for government agencies.

Lazarus advocates that consumer, environmental, minority and taxpayer interest-group expenses be funded by the government under one of these plans.

One of the most important and influential consumer interest groups, unaffiliated with any formal public office, is popularly referred to as "Nader's Raiders." Led by attorney Ralph Nader, this group—comprised of lawyers, students, and concerned private citizens—has been the gadfly of big business as well as big government. Working out of the Center for the Study of Responsive Law in Washington, D.C., Nader's group has supported the consumer in such matters as automobile safety, nursing care for the elderly, industrial pollution, and the quality and price of consumer products. In addition to affecting legislation, the Raiders have influenced the political socialization of the consumer by making him more aware of his role in the economy and more suspicious of business and industry.

## Noneconomic groups

Interest groups can be found under virtually every category by which people can be classified. Whether or not a person joins or participates in an interest group depends on the issues of the day and the claims made upon him by other groups.

"*That* ought to satisfy Ralph Nader!"

Drawing by Ed Fisher; © 1970
The New Yorker Magazine, Inc.

27 Key, *Politics, Parties, and Pressure Groups*, p. 106.

Veterans' associations, for example, have tended to be politically active after every war, mainly in attempts to acquire pensions for newly returned soldiers. "The American idea of war," said Thomas B. Reed, Speaker of the House of Representatives in 1897, "is to take the farmer from his plow, and return him to his plow—with a pension!"[27] The first veterans' association was the Grand Army of the Republic, established after the close of the Civil War. Since then, a number of veterans' organizations have been formed, among them the American Legion, the Veterans of Foreign Wars, the American Veterans of World War II, and the American Veterans Committee.

The American Legion has traditionally been the nation's largest and most influential veterans' association. Formed after World War I, the Legion's membership reached almost 3 million in 1962. Today, however, such groups as the Legion are politically less effective and numerically much smaller; the passage of extensive legislation in favor of the homecoming veteran has reduced the need for their participation in government.[28] The Legion is a nonpartisan group in that it does not directly support political candidates; it does, however, take stands on a wide range of public policies, for the most part siding with conservative causes. Although splinter organizations composed mainly of Vietnam veterans have expressed opposition to the present war in Asia, the American Legion has been fairly constant in its support of the Vietnam policies of Presidents Johnson and Nixon; when it has dissented, it has been in favor of a more hawkish point of view.

28 Arnold Bortz, "Washington Pressures: American Legion's Influence wanes on Capitol Hill," *National Journal*, 2, no. 25 (June 20, 1970): 1308–1314.

Religious groups also frequently seek to influence the political system—particularly when the issue is a seemingly moral one, such as abortion, aid to parochial schools, and birth control. The major Protestant organization is the National Council of Churches. Catholics are represented by the National Catholic Welfare Council, for one; and Jews are represented through such organizations as the American Jewish Congress.

The list of noneconomic interest groups is virtually endless. Women, traditionally represented by such groups as the League of Women Voters, have in recent years been championed by a number of new interest groups springing out of the Women's Liberation Movement—ranging from the more moderate National Organization of Women (NOW) to various radical groups, such as the Women's International Terrorist Conspiracy From Hell (WITCH). These groups have been formed to secure equal pay for equal work, child day-care centers, and revision of the abortion laws; some advocate a complete re-examination of the role of women in American society.

Perhaps most striking in the last decade has been the proliferation of groups opposed to the war in Vietnam. Antiwar groups are not new in American politics, but never in the nation's history have so many groups been formed to oppose national military policy. In July 1970, for example, more than one-third of the registered lobbyists were antiwar groups. SANE, MOBE, Continuing Presence in Washington Inc., and Congress of Young Professionals for Political Action were among those registered.[29]

[29] "Antiwar Lobbyists Prominent in New Lobby Fillings," *Congressional Quarterly*, August 21, 1970, p. 2108.

## Black interest groups

[30] Michael Parenti, "Ethnic Politics and the Persistence of Ethnic Identification," *The American Political Science Review*, September 1967, 717–726. Also see chap. 1 of Everett C. Ladd, *Negro Political Leadership in the South* (Ithaca, N.Y.: Cornell University Press, 1966).

[31] See James Q. Wilson, *Negro Politics: The Search for Leadership* (Illinois: The Free Press of Glencoe, 1960) for a description of black political structures and civic systems.

Race, religion, or national origin has often been the basis for the formation of interest groups; however, members of these groups have, in time, usually been assimilated into the general population.[30] At present, numerous black interest groups are functioning independently. Whether or not they too will be absorbed into other organizations is a matter of conjecture.

Until recent times, the major interest group representing nonwhites was the *National Association for the Advancement of Colored People* (NAACP).[31] Established in 1910, the NAACP has fought to extend the vote to black Americans and has used its influence to combat all forms of racial discrimination. Since 1910, a number of other black interest groups have been formed. The Urban League, for example, was established to provide economic opportunities for blacks. Also notable among black interest groups are the Southern Christian Leadership Conference, organized by the late Dr. Martin Luther King, Jr., and the Congress of Racial Equality (CORE).

Disenchanted by the slow progress achieved by such groups as the NAACP, the Urban League, and CORE, a number of more militant black leaders have emerged—men such as Malcolm X, Huey Newton, Eldridge Cleaver, and Ron Karenga. Though they have differed in their attitudes and policies for achieving social change, they basically agree that the present political system serves only to perpetuate unjust conditions for blacks and the poor. These leaders have proposed controversial alternatives ranging from the "back to Africa" movement, and the foundation of a separate country for blacks, to a total restructuring—by violent revolution, if necessary—of the present political system.[32]

[32] Herbert Storing, ed., *What Country Have I: Political Writings by Black Americans* (New York: St. Martin's Press, Inc., 1970).

How much of the black population is represented by these groups is open to question. Some say they represent only a tiny minority; others claim they speak for the bulk of the black community. Louis Harris Associates, in a 1970 survey for *Time* magazine, noted that one in four blacks identified with the Black Panthers and 64 percent felt that the Panthers gave them a sense of pride. It seems that if they can resolve their internal conflicts, such groups have a considerable number behind them.

# The techniques of interest groups

We have noted that in recent years some interest groups, despairing of traditional courses of political action, have resorted to violence. The use of violence by interest groups is not new in the American political system. The Boston Tea Party, the Whisky Rebellion of 1794, and the Zootsuit Riots in the 1920s are examples of group violence. Student rebellion, especially in the late 1960s, was often accompanied by open violence.

[33] Michael Lipsky, "Protest as a Political Resource," *The American Political Science Review*, 62, no. 4 (December 1968): 1144–1158.

Most interest groups, however, employ peaceful means. In recent years, sit-ins, marches, and mass demonstrations have been widely employed by various groups.[33] Although these techniques have met with some success, most interest groups still favor four formal channels of political influence—elections, propaganda, lobbying, and the courtroom.

## Electioneering

The election of a political candidate favorable to the interests of a particular group may be accomplished by *electioneering*—the mobilization of voters to support their chosen candidate and to make financial contributions to candidates or parties.

Most interest groups claim to be nonpartisan; but that generally means that they publicly support a candidate based on his personal views, rather than supporting him merely because he is affiliated with a particular party. The AFL-CIO's Committee on Political Education, for example, ranks candidates according to their voting records on specific issues and then supports or opposes them accordingly. Naturally, over a period of time, one party does find more favor in the eyes of a particular interest group. Business and professional associations usually back Republican candidates, whereas labor has traditionally supported the Democrats.

The actual effectiveness of electioneering is still open to question. Clearly, the size, unity, and leadership of a particular interest group, as well as its

34 Nicholas A. Masters, "The Organized Labor Bureaucracy as a Base of Support for the Democratic Party," *Law and Contemporary Problems,* 27 (Spring 1962): 252–265.

financial resources and concern over specific issues, greatly affect the group's strength in electioneering. Labor unions, for example, did not attain national influence over elections until they had attained the resources of power: votes and money.[34] At the national level, a group represented in many states reaches more people than a group limited to a particular region. But at the local level, the more decentralized or localized the group is, the more effective it is in getting its candidate in front of the people. In either case, though, the group must be unified in purpose. It does not help the Teamsters in Illinois if the Teamsters in Idaho support a Republican, while they support a Democrat. A combination of all these factors add up to determine whether or not the group's candidate gets elected.

## Propaganda

All interest groups propagandize. They actively try to influence the opinions of individuals and groups so that their goals will be realized. They try to create a favorable image of themselves in the public eye so that their recommendations will be turned into public policy and their interests protected.

Interest groups disseminate propaganda in a number of ways. They distribute literature. They initiate letter-writing campaigns. They defend their positions in newspapers and magazines and in the electronic media of radio and television. When they can, they take to the streets and present their views to the public.[35]

35 Zeigler, *Interest Groups,* chap. VII.

*A group of citizens in St. Cloud, Minnesota wanted to make their position perfectly clear to all passing motorists.*

36 Stanley Kelley, Jr., *Professional Public Relations and Political Power* (Baltimore: The Johns Hopkins Press, 1956).

In recent years, a large number of interest groups have enlisted professional help to aid them in presenting their story to the public. Public relations firms now direct the propaganda campaigns of hundreds of interest groups.[36] Such services are expensive and, therefore, available only to the wealthier groups, whose number is growing daily. A group like the American Dairy Association, for example, will pour money into reminding the public that it is healthy to drink milk.

Propaganda campaigns by interest groups fall into two categories: intense, short-range campaigns directed toward a specific political issue, and generalized, long-range efforts designed to create a positive image of the group without reference to specific issues. One short-range effort began in 1970, when the individual local insurance companies organized a massive campaign against the states' proposed "no fault" insurance legislation (compulsory insurance in which both parties receive settlements and the cause of the accident is irrelevant). In Massachusetts, where the "no fault" insurance bill was passed, claims were settled at a generally faster rate. In New York, however, the legislation is pending and the insurance companies continue their war against "no fault" insurance—on the radio, on TV, and in the newspapers. The effectiveness of this propaganda cannot yet be evaluated. A long-range effort at positive propaganda is clearly seen in the AFL-CIO brochure entitled "The All Union Family": the labor family is described as "Mr. and Mrs. John Q. America and their two wonderful kids." They live, of course, at "99 Shady Lane, Anytown, U.S.A."[37]

37 See AFL-CIO, Industrial Union Department, "Mr. and Mrs. America: The All Union Family," p. 3 and Gerald Pomper, "The Public Relations of Organized Labor," *Public Opinion Quarterly* XXIII (Winter 1960): 488 as noted in Ziegler, *Interest Groups*, p. 236.

Interest groups also conceive of public relations as a means of mobilizing *membership*. The AFL-CIO, for example, directs much of its propaganda toward its 14 million members in efforts to have its members respond to a particular issue as a unified bloc. Smaller groups, on the other hand, like minor political parties, are more unified and have little need to direct their propaganda campaigns toward their membership. Rather, they seek to expand the base of their support by influencing groups and individuals outside their boundaries.

The content of much interest-group propaganda attempts to present opponents of group interests as selfish and thoughtless, perhaps even un-American, while group members are pictured as righteous, thoughtful Americans. For example, several newly formed ecology associations have emphasized in their advertising the potential destruction of mankind if the air sound waves are polluted by powerful, noisy supersonic transport jets.

38 Zeigler, *Interest Groups*, p. 235.

39 Joe McGinniss, *The Selling of the President: 1968* (New York: Trident Press, 1968).

It is difficult to measure the effects of interest-group propaganda; some critics believe that it is negligible. "It is one thing to sell a particular brand of soap through advertising," writes Zeigler; "it is quite another matter to sell a candidate or a legislative proposal by the same techniques."[38] Others, for example, claim that the President can indeed be sold like soap.[39] In some cases, propaganda proves detrimental to group interests. Public relations campaigns tend to spawn opposing public relations campaigns, and often the original group comes out with its image badly soiled. Some groups have realized the value of remaining silent. In other cases, propaganda works to the group's advantage. The propaganda of ecology and other interest groups against the supersonic transport helped to defeat pending appropriations legislation.

## Lobbying

Along with electioneering and disseminating propaganda, most interest groups employ representatives who establish direct contact with public officials and try to influence political activities related to their group's interest. The technique is called *lobbying*, and it is widely employed by interest groups at the national, state, and local levels.

"It's awful the way they're trying to influence Congress. Why don't they serve cocktails and make campaign contributions like we do?"

From *The Herblock Gallery* (Simon & Schuster, 1968).

The term "lobbying" has a decidedly unfavorable connotation to many Americans, who envision the lobbyist as wheeler-dealer continually wining and dining public officials in order to secure political favors at the expense of the general public. The wining and dining does occur, as evidenced, for example, by the 1963 case of then Senate Majority Leader Lyndon Johnson's closest aide, Bobby Baker. Representing himself as the collector for the Democratic Senatorial Campaign Committee, Baker was convicted of accumulating more than $2 million in eight years from bankers with specific political interests.[40]

This romanticized view of the lobbyist, while perhaps true in some cases, describes the exception, rather than the rule. Most lobbyists are hard-working men representing such specialized interests as The National Limestone Institute, American Soybean Association, or Hometown Free Television Association. Their interests are narrowly defined, and for the most part, they are concerned with a few pieces of legislation and deal with only a few public officials (sometimes working through their "constituents," rather than directly with the particular official).[41] Perhaps their major function is to supply information—facts and figures, rather than champagne and caviar—about their specialized interests to a few select public officials, committee members, and others who are concerned with their problems.

Some lobbyists represent the larger and more powerful interest groups, such as the oil interests or the tobacco industry, and operate on a wider scale. They are skilled professionals, experts in the art of influence, trying to promote and protect the broad interests of their group. Samuel Patterson has described this breed of lobbyist:

> He is the legislative representative who conceives his job to be that of making crucial contacts with the members of the legislative group. He devotes his time and energies to walking legislative halls, visiting legislators, collaring them in the halls, establishing relationships with administrative assistants and others of the congressman's staff, cultivating key legislators on a friendship basis, and developing contacts on the staffs of critical legislative committees.[42]

## Lobbying the legislators

The legislative branch of government is the traditional arena of the lobbyist. Several thousand lobbyists are currently at work in Washington today, most of them directing their activities toward the Senate and the House of Representatives. Appropriately enough, lobbyists have been called "The Third House of Congress." The first two houses—the Senate and the House of Representatives—represent groups of Americans on the basis of geographic boundaries, while lobbyists represent Americans according to their interest groups, thus contributing to the pluralist interpretation of American democracy (see Chapter 2).

The job of the lobbyist in the legislature is by no means an easy one. He informs, argues, cajoles, and even testifies before congressional committees to convince legislators to act on behalf of his group's interests. Public officials are subject to pressure from numerous interest groups and are not likely to be swayed by a charismatic personality or a skillful argument. The effect of

[40] "New Light on How Bobby Baker Rose to Riches," *U.S. News and World Report,* July 28, 1969, p. 8.

[41] Lester W. Milbrath, *The Washington Lobbyists* (Chicago: Rand McNally and Co., 1963).

[42] Samuel C. Patterson, "The Role of the Labor Lobbyist" (Paper presented to the 1962 annual meeting of the American Political Science Association), p. 11, as quoted in Zeigler, *Interest Groups,* p. 267.

## Lobbying the administrators

lobbying depends on a legislator, to a great degree—on whether or not the legislator agrees with the ideals and goals of the group represented by the lobbyist and on the influence of the lobby on the voters at home.

Historically speaking, the lobbying of legislators has been the dominant technique employed by interest groups. In the twentieth century, however, as the legislators have created more and more administrative agencies and given them more power, the lobbyist has directed an increasing amount of attention toward the administrator.

It is understandable that interest groups should be seriously concerned with administrative agencies, especially those established to regulate them.

*A common interest-group technique is to testify before congressional committee hearings. In 1971, antiwar demonstrators sought a hearing before the Senate Foreign Relations Committee.*

Corporations and business interest groups have a strong interest in the activities of the Federal Trade Commission and the Department of Commerce, for example. Similarly, labor unions are vitally concerned with the activities of the National Labor Relations Board and the Department of Labor, and agricultural interest groups closely observe the activities of the Soil Conservation Service of the Department of Agriculture. It is not unusual, in fact, for a particular interest group to work in harmony with the agency established to regulate it.[43] The close relationship between the airlines and the Federal Aviation Commission is a notable example. Such harmonious relationships are due in part to the interest group's success in getting its friends appointed to the governmental agencies that most directly affect them. Beyond the help of their friends, interest groups rely on their representatives' power of persuasion—on a one-to-one basis or before an agency hearing—to oppose or support changes in the rules that govern the group's activities.

[43] Charles M. Hardin, *Politics of Agriculture* (New York: The Free Press, 1952).

*"The Effects of Lobbying on the Natural Gas Pipeline Safety Act,"* Congressional Quarterly, Weekly Report, *August 16, 1968, pp. 2221–2224.*

The record of the formulation of the 1968 Natural Gas Pipeline Safety Act is illustrative of how lobbies work to influence the legislative process. The Act was introduced in Congress in March of 1965, after an explosion in Natchitoches, Louisiana—killing seventeen people and burning everything combustible in a thirteen-acre area—brought the issue to public attention. At the onset of congressional consideration, there was no federal legislation on gas-line safety, and twenty-two states lacked legislation. Over the three-year period, legislative lobbyists, representing all levels of the industry as well as those determined to regulate it, warred to protect their particular interests.

As federal legislation appeared imminent, the number of states with varying pipeline regulations increased to forty-seven. The industry, which felt its safety record was good when compared to other American industries dealing with dangerous products, wanted to keep control at the state level only and avoid all safety legislation by the national government. However, the administration noted that the state regulatory agencies were ineffective.

The lobbying occurred on each level of the congressional process. The industry attempted to have its standards adopted: it did not want criminal penalties or large civil penalties included in the bill, and hoped for a grace period to bring equipment up to par. Distribution companies, frequently privately owned, fought to prevent bad publicity for gas as a form of fuel. The lobbyists in Washington were so numerous that they were grouped into seven groups.

The end result of the flurry of arm twisting and ear bending was a compromise bill, stronger than the representatives of the gas industry would have liked and weaker than supporters of strong safety regulators had hoped for. When the battle had ended in a manner typical of the American legislative process, both sides conceded that the settlement was workable.

## Lobbying within the interest group

The lobbyist serves as a middleman between public official and interest group. He not only presents the case for his interest group before public officials; he also transmits facts and recommendations back to the interest group.

*An important part of the lobbyist's activity involves his work within the interest group. He must mediate between the interests of government officials and his employers at home. Here a labor union's district council evaluates the information and opinions obtained by its representative in Washington, D.C.*

Some lobbyists find that dealing with public officials is often a great deal easier than dealing with the home organization. The lobbyist working in Washington becomes aware of the problems of the legislators and is often persuaded of the necessity for compromise between his interest group and the policy-makers. However, some organizations—far removed from Washington— are not so aware of the legislator's problems, and sometimes disregard the advice of their lobbyists, adamantly refusing to compromise.

## Court action

The courts are usually protected from the influence of interest groups. Open lobbying of courts is a criminal offense. Interest groups, however, realizing the importance of judicial decisions to their interests, have found ways to make their influence felt in the courts.

Many interest-group leaders exert their influence on the legislative and executive branches, especially at the state and local levels of government, in order to secure the selection of judges favorable to their interests. The American Bar Association is especially powerful in this respect, since its members rate each of the men nominated by the President for a judicial position. Other groups, especially minority groups and the smaller interest groups, have instituted lawsuits themselves or helped others to start court actions in order to protect their interests. Blacks have been particularly successful with this type of action: The NAACP/Legal Defense of Education Fund, for example, has for years brought the question of black civil rights to the courts.[44] Since 1930, they have found that it is easier to reach their goals through the courts than through campaigns to influence Congress, especially considering the power of the southern representatives. The NAACP has won many notable victories in the courts, among them the critical case of *Brown* v. *Board of Education of Topeka* (1954), in which school segregation was declared unconstitutional; *Alexander et al.* v. *Holmes County* (Miss.) *Board of Education* (1969), in which immediate school integration was ordered, and four additional 1971 cases in North Carolina, Georgia, and Alabama, in which busing was approved as a legal means of integration.

Some interest groups have tried to influence the decisions of the courts by entering legal disputes—usually with the permission of the court—as an *amicus curiae*, friend of the court. Utilizing this device, the interest group can file briefs in a case in which they are not a party.

## Government control of interest-group activity

Criticism of lobbying tactics has led to a number of efforts to control lobbying, which in large part have been ineffectual. Most states have taken measures requiring lobbyists to register and file expense records, while the state of Georgia as early as the late 1800s actually made lobbying a crime. A few categories of interest groups were required to register with the national government in the 1920s, but not until 1946 did Congress pass the *Federal Regulation of Lobbying Act*, requiring that anyone employed to influence

[44] Clement E. Vose, *Caucasians Only: The Supreme Court, the NAACP, and the Restrictive Covenant Cases* (Berkeley, Calif.: University of California Press, 1959).

45 William Keefe and
Morris Ogul, *The
American Legislative
Process: Congress and
the States* (Englewood
Cliffs, N.J.: Prentice-Hall,
Inc., 1964), chap. 10.

legislation in Congress must register, listing his employer and stating his salary. Also, he must file a statement every three months listing publications in which he has obtained publicity and the particular bills he supports or opposes.[45] Nevertheless, many interest groups have bypassed registration and continue to lobby. In 1969, only 269 interest groups registered with Congress.

### Number of Registered Lobbies, 1947–1969

| Year | Registrations | Year | Registrations |
|---|---|---|---|
| 1947 | 731 | 1961 | 365 |
| 1948 | 447 | 1962 | 375 |
| 1949 | 599 | 1963 | 384 |
| 1950 | 430 | Jan. 1, 1964– | |
| 1951 | 342 | Oct. 3, 1964 | 255 |
| 1952 | 204 | Oct. 4, 1964– | |
| 1953 | 296 | Oct. 23, 1965 | 450 |
| 1954 | 413 | Oct. 24, 1965– | |
| 1955 | 383 | Oct. 22, 1966 | 332 |
| 1956 | 347 | Oct. 23, 1966– | |
| 1957 | 392 | Dec. 15, 1967 | 449 |
| 1958 | 337 | Dec. 16, 1967– | |
| 1959 | 393 | Oct. 14, 1968 | 259 |
| 1960 | 236 | Oct. 15, 1968– | |
| | | Dec. 23, 1969 | 656 |
| Total | | | 9,297 |

Note: Although there has been an increase in the number of registrations annually, the total number registered is far below the number of existing lobbies.

Source: *Congressional Quarterly Almanac 1969*, vol. 25 (Washington, D.C.: Congressional Quarterly, Inc., 1970), p. 1097.

Many critics say that this legislation is obviously insufficient, but it is doubtful that Congress will pass more stringent rules governing lobbyists.

# Interest groups: pro and con

Throughout their existence, interest groups have been slandered and condemned—most often by members of opposing interest groups who feel they themselves belong to the only justifiable organizations. To many individuals, all groups who oppose their interests are "pressure groups," employing political pressure tactics to protect their interests against the "common good." These competing organizations, on the other hand, term themselves as "interest groups" or "civic organizations," working to achieve goals that coincide with the interests of the "American public."

The major argument against interest groups revolves around their relative strength. Interest groups are indeed becoming increasingly powerful and

*In order to make themselves heard, farmers seeking higher prices drove into Washington, D.C. with truckloads of pigs from their farms.*

are only minimally restricted by lobbying regulations. Some public officials have viewed their growth as a definite danger to the political system. The larger a group becomes, the more power it exercises and the more people its leadership controls. What these officials fear is a return to minority control—rule by a few with very specific, narrow interests.

Instead of threatening us with minority control, some interest groups tend to benefit society by representing more than their membership. The labor union that obtains higher wages for its members simultaneously obtains higher wages for all laborers performing that same job. Interest groups further serve as agencies of public opinion-makers; they help the individual to make his opinions heard. While they serve definite political interests, these groups also provide the more sociological and psychological function of interest aggregation—the chance for people to get together.

Thus, political scientists contend that most attacks against interest groups tend to be exaggerated. There is little danger that any single interest group will become so powerful that its leaders can totally control the decision-making process. The real defense against group tyranny, according to David Truman, lies in the groups themselves.[46] As one group becomes powerful, others spring up to oppose it.

[46] Truman, *The Governmental Process*, chap. 8.

James Madison, writing in *The Federalist* Number 10, cogently described the nature of interest groups in American politics. Though he probably did not imagine the power and influence these groups would one day wield, he did realize that these "factions," as he called them, were necessary in any society. Attempts to eliminate interest groups from American politics, he noted, would be far more dangerous than the interest groups themselves.

[47] Alexander Hamilton, James Madison, John Jay, *The Federalist Papers*, ed. by Clinton Rossiter (New York: The New American Library, 1961), p. 78.

> It could never be more truly said than of the first remedy that it was worse than the disease. Liberty is to faction what air is to fire, an aliment without which it instantly expires. But it could not be a less folly to abolish liberty, which is essential to political life, because it nourished faction than it would be to wish the annihilation of air, which is essential to animal life, because it imparts to fire its destructive agency.[47]

# Glossary

**amicus curiae**   Literally "friend of the court," actually a party (a person or group) that, in an attempt to influence a decision of the court, files a brief in a legal dispute to which it is not a party.

**electioneering**   Technique used by interest groups for mobilizing voter support and contributions to the campaign treasury of the candidate and party it seeks to get elected.

**Federal Regulation of Lobbying Act (1946)**   A largely unsuccessful attempt by Congress to control lobbying through required registration of all congressional lobbyists.

**interest group**   Organization of people who share common attitudes and interests and who attempt to influence certain decisions made within the political system.

**litigation**   The use of representation by interest groups, for example, to indirectly influence court decisions in favor of particular organizations.

**lobbying**   Technique used by interest groups to influence directly the actions of public officials.

**lobbyist (Washington representative)**   Interest-group representative who conveys the desires and concerns of the interest group to legislators and administrators, and conversely, the concerns of legislators and administrators to his interest group; middleman between public officials and interest groups.

**pressure group**   Term used in reference to an interest group, usually to express criticism of so-called tactics used in influencing legislators.

**Third House of Congress**   Term given to lobbies, because of their powerful role in the legislative branch of the national government.

**trade associations**   National business interest groups that are based on a single industry.

# Suggested readings

Baker, Roscoe, *The American Legion and American Foreign Policy* (New York: Twayne Publishers, 1955). General description of the American Legion, one of the country's leading interest groups.

Bauer, Raymond A., Ithiel de Sola Pool, and Lewis A. Dexter, *American Business and Public Policy: The Politics of Foreign Trade* (New York: Atherton Press, 1963). Study of the methods used by American business organizations to influence foreign trade policy.

Bentley, Arthur F., *Process of Government* (Chicago: University of Chicago Press, 1908). Theoretical study of the governing process as a reflection of intergroup pressures.

Blaisdell, Donald C., *American Democracy Under Pressure* (New York: The Ronald Press Co., 1957). Analysis of the American political system in terms of pressure politics.

Bone, Hugh A., and Austin Ranney, *Politics and Voters* (New York: McGraw-Hill Book Co., 1963). Study of American parties, with particular emphasis on interest groups and opinion measurement.

Deakin, James, *The Lobbyists* (Washington, D.C.: Public Affairs Press, 1966). Historical view of lobbying, the major technique used by pressure groups to influence the legislative process; includes many examples.

Ebersole, Luke Eugene, *Church Lobbying in the Nation's Capital* (New York: The Macmillan Co., 1951). Study of the history, organization, and functioning of church lobbies.

Ehrmann, Henry W., ed., *Interest Groups on Four Continents* (Pittsburgh: University of Pittsburgh Press, 1958). Comparative essays on interest groups as a global phenomenon of politics. Of particular interest is Samuel Elderswild's chapter on the state of interest group research in the United States.

Garceau, Oliver, *The Political Life of the American Medical Association* (Cambridge, Mass.: Harvard University Press, 1941). Classic study of the organization and functioning of the AMA, with particular emphasis on its activities as an interest group.

Holtzman, Abraham, *Interest Groups and Lobbying* (New York: The Macmillan Co., 1966). Clear and concise description of interest groups and their relationship to Congress and administrative agencies.

Kelman, Steven, *Push Comes to Shove: The Escalation of Student Protest* (Boston: Houghton Mifflin Co., 1970). Study of student radicalism at Harvard, a more violent form of interest group activity.

Key, V. O., Jr., *Politics, Parties, and Pressure Groups*, 5th ed. (New York: Thomas Y. Crowell Co., 1964). Authoritative study of American political parties and interest groups.

Lane, Edgar, *Lobbying and the Law: State Regulation of Lobbying* (Berkeley, Calif.: University of California Press, 1964). Study of state laws designed to control lobbying, their origins and suggestions for improvement.

Latham, Earl, *Group Basis of Politics: A Study in Basing-Point Legislation* (Ithaca, N.Y.: Cornell University Press, 1952). Case study of interest-group politics.

Mahood, H. R., ed., *Pressure Groups in American Politics* (New York: Charles Scribner's Sons, 1967). Collection of articles on the role of interest groups in the development of public policy with emphasis on the group theory of politics that all public policy is a result of group behavior.

McKean, Dayton David, *Party and Pressure Politics* (Boston: Houghton Mifflin Co., 1949). Text on interest groups, public opinion polls, and other matters related to interest group activities.

Milbrath, Lester W., *The Washington Lobbyists* (Chicago: Rand McNally and Co., 1963). Social and political analysis of lobbyists at the national level and their functions.

Mills, Charles Wright, *The Power Elite* (New York: Oxford University Press, Inc., 1956). Analysis of the American political system as one governed by a political and economic elite composed of several groups, making all significant decisions, and, thus, the most significant and powerful of interest groups.

Salisbury, Robert H., ed., *Interest Group Politics in America* (New York: Harper and Row Publishers, Inc., 1970). Selected readings on the organization, activities, and theory of interest groups in American politics.

Schattschneider, E. E., *Politics, Pressures and the Tariff: A Study of Free Private Enterprise in Pressure Politics, as Shown in the 1929–1930 Revision of the Tariff* (Englewood Cliffs, N.J.: Prentice-Hall, Inc., 1935). Study of pressure groups and their impact on tariff legislation.

Schattschneider, E. E., *The Semisovereign People: A Realist's View of Democracy in America* (New York: Holt, Rinehart and Winston, Inc., 1960). Analysis of American democracy, emphasizing the importance of interest groups.

Schriftgiesser, Karl, *The Lobbyists: The Art and Business of Influencing Lawmakers* (Boston: Little, Brown and Co., 1951). Study of lobbying in Congress from the 1820s until 1950.

Scott, Andrew M., and Margaret A. Hunt, *Congress and Lobbies: Image and Reality* (Chapel Hill, N.C.: University of North Carolina Press, 1966). Study of the actual impact of interest groups on members of Congress.

Taft, Philip, *Organized Labor in American History* (New York: Harper and Row Publishers, Inc., 1964). History of American labor from colonial times to the 1960s, including their lobbying activities.

Truman, David, *The Governmental Process: Political Interests and Public Opinion* (New York: Alfred A. Knopf, Inc., 1951). Theoretical analysis of the formation and activities of interest groups, with emphasis on groups as the "raw materials" of politics.

Wildavsky, Aaron, *Dixon-Yates: A Study in Power Politics* (New Haven, Conn.: Yale University Press, 1961). Study of pressure politics in the Dixon-Yates controversy during the Eisenhower administration.

Zeigler, Harmon, *Interest Groups in American Society* (Englewood Cliffs, N.J.: Prentice-Hall, Inc., 1964). Study of the role of organized interest groups in the American political system, including criteria for their successful interaction with society.

Zeigler, Harmon, *The Political Life of American Teachers* (Englewood Cliffs, N.J.: Prentice-Hall, Inc., 1967). Discussion and analysis of the functioning of one particular interest group: teachers.

Zeller, Belle, *Pressure Politics in New York: A Study of Group Representation before the Legislature* (Englewood Cliffs, N.J.: Prentice-Hall, Inc., 1937). Analysis of interest group activity in the New York state legislature.

Zisk, Betty, ed., *American Political Interest Groups: Readings in Theory and Research* (Belmont, Calif.: Wadsworth Publishing Co., Inc., 1969). Collection of readings on the most recent analyses of interest group activities.

**Supreme Court decisions**

*Alexander et al.* v. *Holmes County* (Miss.) *Board of Education* (1969)   Supreme Court decision that ordered immediate integration of schools in Mississippi.

*Brown* v. *Board of Education of Topeka* (1954)   Supreme Court decision brought by the NAACP Legal Defense and Education Fund, that declared the segregation of schools in the South to be unconstitutional.

# Topics of further study

Aronfreed, Eva, "Public Relations in the Field of Organized Labor" (master's thesis, University of Pennsylvania, 1947).

Hazel, David W., "The National Association for the Advancement of Colored People and the National Legislative Process, 1940–1954" (Ph.D. dissertation, University of Michigan, 1957).

Klein, Malcom W., "Some Consideration in the Use of Qualitative Judgments as Measure of Organizational Performance," *Sociology and Social Research*, October 1961, pp. 26–35.

Longley, Charles H., "Interest Group Interaction in a Legislative System," *Journal of Politics*, August 1967, pp. 637–658.

Watson, Richard, "Defeat of Judge Parker: A Study in Pressure-Group Politics," *Mississippi Valley Historical Review*, Spring 1963, pp. 213–234.

# 10 politics of parties

THE AMERICAN two-party system has evolved entirely outside the original framework of the Constitution. It is, nonetheless, one of the most enduring and stable institutions within the political system. The Framers in 1789 could not envision the formation of political parties to capture the offices they established. Yet, as Clinton Rossiter has stated, "parties and democracy arose together; they have lived and prospered in a closely symbiotic relationship; and if one of them should ever weaken and die, the other would die with it."[1] In fact, as the Scottish political scientist D. W. Brogan has noted, "The greatest breakdown of the American constitutional system, the Civil War, came only when the party system collapsed. The last bond holding the sections together was the last remaining national party, 'the Democrats,' and when that broke in two at the Charleston Convention of 1860, war was at hand."[2]

Broadly defined, *political parties* are organizations that attempt to influence the political system by placing their members in government offices. They are much like interest groups in that they work to influence the decision-making process, but they differ from interest groups in a number of important ways. Interest groups, for example, usually work to influence the decision-making process from *outside*. Political parties, by placing their members in government offices, influence the decision-making process from the *inside*. Interest groups are made up of individuals sharing common goals, whereas political parties in the United States are made up of individuals and groups often holding widely diverse interests. Finally,

[1] Clinton Rossiter, *Parties and Politics in America* (Ithaca, N.Y.: Cornell University Press, 1960), p. 67.

[2] D. W. Brogan, *Politics in America* (Garden City, N.Y.: Doubleday and Co., Inc., 1960), p. 38.

interest groups tend to represent relatively small segments of the society—blacks, laborers, Catholics, or women—whereas the major political parties represent an aggregate of all these segments of society.

# The functions of political parties

Political parties are justified by their functions, according to Clinton Rossiter, "functions that are performed as services to the entire nation." Rossiter contends that "we tolerate and even celebrate their existence because they do things for us in the public realm that would otherwise be done poorly or not done at all."[3] The parties function as personnel agencies for government positions, educators of the public, simplifiers of election choices, national unifiers, organizers of the policy-making machinery of government, and providers of opposition to the political majority, as expressed in the Congress and the White House.

[3] Rossiter, *Parties and Politics in America,* p. 39.

## The party as personnel agency

The major function of a political party is the election or appointment of its members to public office. In performing this function, the political party acts much like a personnel agency employed by the nation to fill the official positions of power in the political system. Like personnel agencies, political parties recruit candidates to fill available jobs, display the candidates' records and credentials, and work to get them elected or hired.

The importance of this function of political parties cannot be overstated. By supplying personnel for government offices, political parties provide a peaceful means by which power can be transferred within the political system. "The party system sublimates that ancient conflict (between those who wish to overthrow a government and those who wish to protect it) into behaviors no more bellicose than the oratory of an election campaign."[4]

[4] V. O. Key, Jr., *Politics, Parties, and Pressure Groups,* 5th ed. (New York: Thomas Y. Crowell Co., 1964), p. 9.

## Educator of the public

In addition to filling the official positions of power in the political system, political parties, along with interest groups and the mass media, also perform an important role in the political socialization process. Through speeches, congressional debates, television broadcasts, and press conferences, partisan leaders keep the public abreast of the crucial political issues of the day and exercise considerable influence over the political opinions of individuals in the society, especially those identifying with their party. This influence is often subtly communicated, through undetectable cues that gradually result in the public's education as the party wishes.

## Election simplifier

Without political parties, the voter would be faced with a long list of candidates representing a host of different and possibly conflicting interests. Party systems serve to categorize and define political issues and help to clarify the choices open to the voter. Instead of offering a dozen or more political candidates, each with a divergent view, the nation with a two-party, and sometimes a multiparty, system limits the number of candidates and issues. This is particularly evident in the American two-party system, though the multiparty systems of several countries also serve to classify and define the voter's options.

In the United States, the choices tend to promote unity between segments of the populace. No matter what their "official" ideological stance, both political parties tend to support broad programs that will appeal to economically and politically diverse segments of the population—farmers, industrialists, blue-collar workers, professionals, and so on. On the issue of civil rights, for example, a party platform will often be constructed so as to gain black support, without offending or alienating those who are prejudiced against blacks.

*Seymour Martin Lipset*, Political Man: The Social Bases of Politics (*Garden City, N.Y.: Doubleday and Co., Inc., 1960*), *pp. 303–331.*

In a discussion of classes and party affiliation in American politics, Seymour Lipset disputes what he sees as the European notion that American political ideology is basically "classless." He notes that, in fact, studies have consistently revealed that workers tend to be Democratic, while those in professional and business-managerial positions tend to be Republican. Correspondingly, voters of low-income status favor the Democrats; the well-to-do vote for Republicans. And Anglo-Saxons, a high-status group, are more likely to be Republican than are Americans of comparable income who are of recent immigrant background. A certain stripe of upper-class liberals, however, does not fit into this class interpretation.

Contemporary studies of political attitudes indicate that it is necessary to distinguish between so-called economic liberalism (issues concerned with the distribution of wealth and power) and noneconomic liberalism (issues concerned with civil liberties, race relations and foreign affairs).

Those of "established, old family background," as opposed to the newly rich, have led the way in noneconomic liberalism. Lipset calls this group the American Tory radicals, "men of upper-class background and values, who as conservatives helped to democratize the society as part of their struggle against the vulgar *nouveau riche* businessman."

The Tory radical, according to his analysis, has reappeared at crucial points in American history:

Though linked to the Whig and Republican parties, these upper-class liberals have been ready to help organize "third" parties whenever their issues have become salient. They played a major role in creating the demand for a new antislavery party before the Civil War; they played a dominant role in the effort to create a new Liberal Republican party in the 1870's designed to eliminate governmental corruption and enact civil service reform; they fostered the Progressive party of Theodore Roosevelt; and in the 1940's some of them, including their leader Wendell Willkie, seriously considered forming a new party.

Recently the Tory, of a venerable family background, has been joined by the college-educated, wealthy corporate executive. The two elements stand together against the predominant, conservative strain in the Republican party that draws support from small towns.

Lipset believes that the Tory radical has contributed to political stability in America:

From the standpoint of political stability, Tory radicalism has served to retain the loyalties of both the underprivileged out-groups who gain from needed reforms and the conservative strata who are outraged by the same measures. The participation of upper-class persons in liberal politics may also be seen as enlightened self-interest, since they are able to achieve needed reforms, exercise restraint, and exert their influence. At the same time, their presence serves to blur the class lines separating the parties.

## Government organizer

[5] Frank J. Sorauf, *Political Parties in the American System* (Boston: Little, Brown and Co., 1964), p.3.

Political parties serve also to organize the policy-making machinery of the government. "In the United States Congress and in state legislatures the basic unit of organization is the party caucus," writes Frank Sorauf. "From it flows the appointment of powerful presiding officers, committee chairmen, floor leaders, and steering committees."[5] Political parties, by organizing the legislature, are thus able to influence national policy making.[6]

## Countercheck

[6] William J. Keefe and Morris S. Ogul, *The American Legislative Process: Congress and the the States*, 2nd ed. (Englewood Cliffs, N.J.: Prentice-Hall, Inc., 1968), pp. 281–327.

Finally, a political party, when its members are out of office, often operates as a check on the party in power. The minority party performs the function of examining and criticizing the programs of the majority party, frequently suggesting alternative programs. Many congressional Democrats, for example, have openly criticized President Nixon's economic program. Much of their criticism is constructive and, as such, may lead to more workable policies and effective programs. Invariably some of the criticism from the "out party," however, is aimed at discrediting the party in power.

# The history of the American party system

In the first nine elections (from 1789–1820), the President and Vice-President were both nominated and elected by the electoral college, and candidates for other offices either announced their own candidacy, were asked to serve by the President, or were nominated by groups of local leaders. The Constitution, in fact, was designed to prevent the monopolization of power by parties or factions. The division of powers—between the states and the national government, among the executive, legislative, and judicial branches, and between the Senate and the House of Representatives, for example—was intended to inhibit the dominance of any single faction or party.

Drawing by Costello in *The Knickerbocker News*, November 13, 1938.

[7] From a poem entitled "Retaliation," originally published in London, April 1774.

[8] Alexander Hamilton, James Madison, John Jay, *The Federalist Papers*, ed. by Clinton Rossiter (New York: The New American Library, 1961), pp. 77–84.

[9] Joseph Charles, *The Origins of the American Party System* (New York: Harper and Row Publishers, Inc., 1956).

Political parties were not popular organizations in the closing years of the eighteenth century. In England, Oliver Goldsmith spoke regretfully of his friend Edmund Burke whom he said gave up to party "what was meant for mankind."[7] In America, James Madison, writing in *The Federalist* Number 10, warned that party or faction might well destroy the new nation much as it had destroyed the popular republics of ancient Greece and medieval Italy.[8]

Nevertheless, shortly after the start of Washington's second term in office, there emerged two distinct political parties, the Federalists and the Antifederalists (or Jeffersonian Republicans). By John Adams's term as President, both were operating on a national scale. Since that time, parties have played a major role in every election held in the nation.[9]

From its inception, the American party system has displayed two observable characteristics. First, it has been a *two-party system*—almost every election held in the nation has been primarily a contest between two political parties. Only in 1912, when Theodore Roosevelt deserted the Republican party to run on the Progressive party ticket, did a third party pose a serious threat to the two major parties in a twentieth-century presidential election.

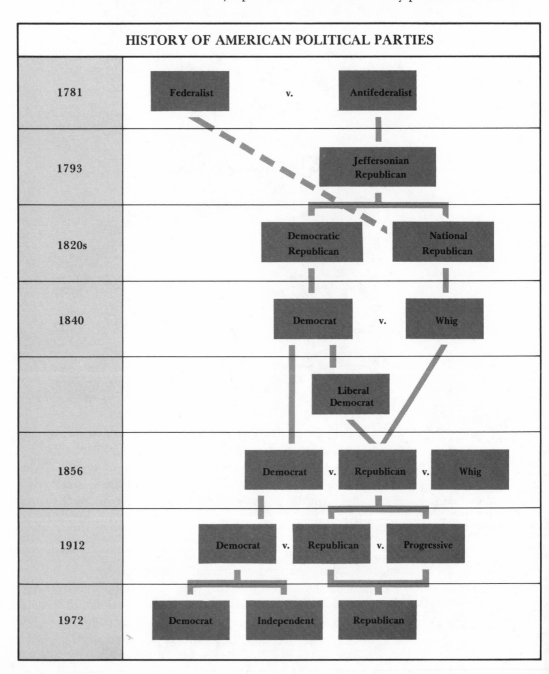

### HISTORY OF AMERICAN POLITICAL PARTIES

| | |
|---|---|
| 1781 | Federalist v. Antifederalist |
| 1793 | Jeffersonian Republican |
| 1820s | Democratic Republican / National Republican |
| 1840 | Democrat v. Whig |
| | Liberal Democrat |
| 1856 | Democrat v. Republican v. Whig |
| 1912 | Democrat v. Republican v. Progressive |
| 1972 | Democrat / Independent / Republican |

Second, the party system at the presidential level has been marked by long stretches of *single-party dominance*. For long periods of time, one or the other of the two major parties has controlled the office of the President. From 1800 to 1860, the Democrats won twelve out of fifteen elections, and from 1860 to 1932, the Republicans were defeated only in the elections of 1884, 1892, and 1912. The Democrats returned to power in 1932 with the election of Franklin D. Roosevelt, and, except for Dwight D. Eisenhower's elections in 1952 and 1956, won every national election until 1968, when Richard Nixon, a Republican, was elected to office.

There are several factors accounting for one party dominance over considerable spans of time. The first and most apparent is the party's popularity, which generally springs from an ability to see that "loaves and fishes are divided in a manner to command popular approbation."[10] Secondly, the party in power is better able to comprehend shifting political, social, and economic trends and to adapt its programs accordingly. Republicans in 1971 are aware of a national mood in favor of ending the Vietnam War, and, as the party in control, they have the power to influence policy toward that end. The dominant party is in the position to recommend legislation, leaving the other party in the less desirable position of having to support the dominant party's proposals, criticize them, or offer alternative and sometimes less favored programs. Finally, it is common to reelect *incumbents* (those who already hold political office), and, of course, this means the party in power tends to remain so.

[10] Key, *Politics, Parties, and Pressure Groups*, p. 196.

## The Federalists

As mentioned, during Washington's second administration, two distinct political parties began to develop national followings. One party, the *Federalists*, advocated a centralized national government led by a strong Chief Executive. Headed by Washington's Secretary of the Treasury, Alexander Hamilton, the Federalists drew much of their support from eastern bankers, manufacturers, and traders; they were the party of the well-heeled and well-bred.

The opposing party, the *Antifederalists*, or *Jeffersonian Republicans*, as they were later called, was primarily an agrarian group, made up of small farmers, workers, small businessmen, southern slaveholders, and frontiersmen. Headed by Thomas Jefferson (John Adams's former Vice-President) and James Madison, the Antifederalists drew most of their support from the southern and middle-Atlantic states. The Jeffersonian Republicans were the forerunner of the modern Democratic party.

In the beginning, Washington vowed to remain nonpartisan, but more and more, he sided with Hamilton's Federalists. Washington's Federalist leanings caused Jefferson to resign as Secretary of State in 1793 and made the first President the target of a hostile Antifederalist press, a press that openly rejoiced when he retired from office in 1796.

11 In the earliest
presidential elections, the
two candidates receiving
the highest electoral-college
vote, regardless of party
affiliation, were named
President and Vice-
President, respectively.

The two parties clashed in the election of 1796 with Jefferson running against the Federalist candidate, John Adams. Adams defeated Jefferson, and Jefferson became Vice-President.[11] During Adams's administration, the Jeffersonians, led by Madison, worked tirelessly to organize their party at the grassroots level. This organization captured the loyalties of much of the rapidly expanding electorate, and in the election of 1800, Jefferson won a landslide victory. Jefferson's election—and concurrent economic and political events—fatally threatened the Federalist party. By 1816, the party had completely vanished from the political arena.

## The era of the Democrats (Jeffersonian Republicans)

The election of Jefferson in 1800 marked the beginning of a period of Democratic dominance that was to run until 1860. For a time, the Jeffersonian Republicans were virtually unopposed in their control of the government, but by Andrew Jackson's administration (1829–1837), the party had begun to split into two factions, the *Democratic Republicans* (the *Democrats*) and the *National Republicans* (the *Whigs*). Jackson hoped to work toward forging party unity, but the issues at hand—the equitable division among bordering states of millions of acres of government-held land, a new and controversial national bank, a debate over high protective tariff, and disputes between abolitionists and southern slaveowners—resulted inevitably in party division.

The Democrats, led by Jackson, styled themselves as the party of the common man. Their support lay mainly in the South and West, and in the poorer segments of the eastern population. The Whigs, on the other hand, advocating a high tariff, were strongest in the northern, industrial states, the states that needed the tariff to protect themselves against loss of business to other nations. Although the Whigs were supported by "the most respectable sections of society,"[12] and were led by the glamorous Henry Clay and the nation's greatest orator, Daniel Webster, their victories were few and they remained the minority party.

By the 1850s, the issue of slavery caused serious splits in both the Democratic and Whig parties. The split in the Whig party over slavery reached a head when some conservative Whigs, favoring slavery, defected to the Democratic camp. This split effectively destroyed the Whig party, almost causing such local Whig leaders as Lincoln to denounce politics entirely.

The question of slavery caused an even more severe split in the Democratic party. Originally based on an alliance between the West and South and the poorer portions of the eastern population, the Democrats were split into two sectional parties, southern Democrats and northern Democrats. As the Civil War approached, both the Whigs and Democrats were caught in a state of internal confusion.

# Republican supremacy

13 Brogan, *Politics in America*, p. 45.

14 The election of 1896 was particularly crucial, because it was then that the Republicans achieved a permanent and broad base of socioeconomic support.

The party that was to dominate the political arena from 1860 to 1932, the new *Republican party*, was formed in 1854 in Wisconsin by a group of Whigs, liberal Democrats, and splinter third-party supporters. The Republican party, based to a great extent on Lincoln's maxim that "if slavery is not wrong, nothing is wrong,"[13] was dedicated to preserving the nation's morality. Putting their forces behind this single "moral idea," the Republicans nominated John Fremont for President in 1856, but the declining Democratic party mustered enough support to carry James Buchanan into the White House. The Republicans learned a valuable lesson in this first defeat: that it requires more than a single issue, especially a moral issue, to capture the presidency.

In their next election, the Republicans advanced Abraham Lincoln, who ran on a platform advocating agrarian land reform, increased industrial wages, and the restriction of slavery. Lincoln, although he won less than 40 percent of the popular vote, carried the electoral votes of every state outside the South, and in 1860, brought the Republicans to power. Once in control of the government, they were to prove exceedingly difficult to unseat.

After the Civil War, the Republicans widened their base of support considerably. They had little or no support in the solidly Democratic South, but almost everywhere else the Republicans were firmly entrenched.[14] Capitalizing on their image as the party of Lincoln, the party that freed the slaves and saved the Union, the Republicans won the loyalties of the newly franchised blacks. Catering to commercial and industrial interests through such policies as the protective tariff, they captured the support of bankers, manufacturers, traders, and many workers who believed these policies meant jobs and prosperity. Aside from generous land policies, the Republicans had little to offer the farmer, but they rallied farm support by recalling the crimes of the South —"waving the Bloody Shirt," as it was called.

The Democrats suffered badly from the war but, supported by the "Solid South," the party survived the crisis and slowly rebuilt its electoral base. For half a century after the war, the Democrats leveled attack after attack against the entrenched Republicans, capturing the presidency in 1884 and again in 1892. But these were only interim victories. Riding on the crest of acceptance and unprecedented prosperity, the Republicans remained the dominant party well into the twentieth century.

The Republicans suffered their most serious setback in 1912 when they nominated President Taft for a second term in office. Theodore Roosevelt, who had hoped for the nomination himself, deserted the Republicans to organize the Progressive party. In the election of 1912, with the Republicans split between Taft and Roosevelt, the Democratic candidate, Woodrow Wilson, was elected President. Wilson stole some of the Republican "progressive" thunder by championing several reform measures—notably antitrust laws and reduced tariffs—and hoped to broaden his party's electoral base by appealing to average citizens. But Wilson's administration was only a brief interlude during a period of Republican supremacy. After his re-election in 1916, the Republicans returned their people to office with the elections of Warren G. Harding, Calvin Coolidge, and Herbert Hoover.

## The return of the Democrats

The Great Depression ended the reign of the Republican party. After "Black Tuesday," the day the stock market crashed in October 1929, the memory of Republican prosperity faded quickly as Americans stood in breadlines, searched for jobs that did not exist, and sold apples on street corners. Franklin Roosevelt, offering Americans a "New Deal," returned the Democrats to power in the election of 1932.

The Democrats held on to enough disenchanted Republicans to re-elect Roosevelt three times and to place Harry Truman in the White House in 1948. (Truman, who had been Vice-President under Roosevelt, took office after Roosevelt's death in 1945, and was elected on his own in 1948.) Then, in 1952, the Democrats suffered a temporary setback as General Dwight Eisenhower, running on the Republican ticket, was elected President. But Eisenhower's victory did not, as many political analysts had declared, mark the return to Republican dominance. It was simply Eisenhower's image as a war hero and his noninvolvement in "corrupt" party politics that temporarily overshadowed Democratic partisan loyalties. Although Eisenhower's appeal won him re-election in 1956, his party lost both the House and the Senate —the first time in over a century that "a President elected with a popular majority failed to carry along a Congress of his own party."[15] The Democrats regained executive power in 1960 when their presidential candidate, John

15 Wilfred A. Binkley, *American Political Parties*, 4th ed. (New York: Alfred A. Knopf, Inc., 1962), p. 455.

Kennedy, narrowly defeated Richard Nixon, former Vice-President under Eisenhower. And in 1964, Democratic control was reasserted with the overwhelming presidential victory of Lyndon Johnson.

In 1968, Nixon narrowly defeated Democratic candidate Hubert Humphrey, returning the office of Chief Executive to the Republicans. Whether his election marks the beginning of a new Republican era or only a temporary break in Democratic supremacy remains to be seen.

# The American two-party system

16 See Austin Ranney and Willmoore Kendall, *Democracy and the American Party System* (New York: Harcourt Brace Jovanovich, Inc., 1956) for a full description of the different systems.

17 Douglas W. Rae, *The Political Consequences of Electoral Laws* (New Haven, Conn.: Yale University Press, 1967), p. 47.

Political party systems are usually categorized by the number of parties actively competing in the political arena for dominance in the government. There are three basic classifications for party systems—one-party systems, two-party systems, and multiparty systems.[16]

The American party system is clearly a *two-party system*, a "democratic competition for the right to rule."[17] Although more than two parties nominate candidates for most elections, for the most part only the two major parties—since 1854, the Democrats and the Republicans—have a real chance of winning. Two-party systems, however, are not common. The majority of the nations in the world today have either one-party or multiparty systems.

*John Harvey Wheeler, "American Notebook: Portraits and Problems," in "Danger Signals in the Political System," Dissent, IV, no. 3 (Summer 1957): 298–310.*

Harvey Wheeler postulates that a political system in which competition is between two large organizations, such as the Republican and Democratic parties, produces similarity, just as competition between two large economic powers—Ford and Chevrolet, for example—fosters similarity. In both fields "violent partisanship" rages, but the end products—be they candidates for office or new model automobiles—differ little from each other. Wheeler takes the economic term *duopoly* (rule of two major competitors) and forms the word *duocracy* (rule of two political systems) as a label for the American two-party system.

From this premise, Wheeler reasons that voter disaffection from the parties may exist, but is never given public expression, partly because the parties' similarity leaves little room to register electoral opposition.

If it were possible to pose the question of an alternative political culture with a changed public morality to support it . . . an astonishing amount of latent political disaffection with the existing American political system might be revealed. We are not justified in assuming positive affection for present political ideas and institutional forms merely because voters continue to vote traditionally, and to answer polls traditionally.

In fact, claims Wheeler, three times in our history "new systems of political morality" have been adopted, but always suddenly and belatedly; the changes were made not in response to public demand, but rather because a crisis situation created a need for transition. In the first case, the business culture of the twenties was abruptly replaced by the liberal welfare institutions of the New Deal. Secondly, this liberalism gave way to the conservatism of the fifties, whose "security sensitive doctrines, suffused with religiosity" served cold war needs. The technological revolution in progress since the late fifties appears to be the third and most powerful change.

*One-party systems* are best illustrated by dictatorships. In these systems, the party is virtually identical to the government. Criticism is usually directed at the obvious point that with only one party operating in the political arena there is little choice between members of the party. Some of these critics suggest, however, that in one-party states such as Egypt, Burma, and Guinea, the existing one-party systems may develop into two-party or multiparty systems as the nations develop. The change may occur because differences of opinion develop from within the party and dissenters form their own parties.

*Multiparty systems* are common in most western European nations as well as in such countries as Israel, India, and Japan. In these countries as many as ten or twelve parties actively participate in the electoral process, offering the voter a choice of candidates running the length of the political spectrum. It is difficult to discuss the relative value of multiparty and two-party systems: both offer advantages and disadvantages. The major advantage cited for multiparty systems is, of course, the wide range of alternatives offered the voter. On the other hand, multiparty systems are often unstable and incapable of providing effective government. Even if a single party can gain a majority of political offices in one election, it is unlikely that the same party will stay in power long enough to implement its program of government. When no party consistently wins a majority, consensus among the partisan public officials is often impossible and governmental powers become fragmented and ineffectual.

## Why a two-party system?

The majority of the democracies in the western world employ multiparty systems—only about one-quarter operate under two-party systems. Why then does the United States have a two-party system?

Several theories have been offered to explain the origins and determinants of the American two-party system.

1. *Theories of national character.* According to these theories, the character, culture, and emotional climate of a nation determine the type of party system it will adopt. For example, highly emotional, politically volatile peoples such as the French and the Italian supposedly develop multiparty systems, while the more somber and moderate English and Americans supposedly adopt two-party systems, the assumption being that two-party systems lend themselves to moderation and stability. Emotional people, according to these theories, find it hard to agree on an absolute policy and are more fickle in their opinions; while the moderates maintain their party affiliation and, as a whole, agree on major principles. The national character theories have fallen out of favor in recent years for fairly obvious reasons. It could be argued, for example, that multiparty systems create, rather than result from, an excitable, emotion-charged population, while two-party systems spawn a more sober, docile electorate.

2. *Theories of natural dualism.* "The 'natural dualism' theories of the two-party systems," writes Frank Sorauf, "attribute them to the natural tendency for political options to fall into alternatives: 'ins' and 'outs,' left and right, government and opposition, status quo and change, for and against, and presumably, yes and no."[18] Such theories argue that the divisions between North and South, urban interests and rural interests, and rich and poor naturally spawn a two-party system. Critics, however, claim that the dualistic nature of a society and the existence of a two-party system within that society are not necessarily related; that is, the existence of one does not invariably produce the other. There is "room" within the Democratic party, for example, for both a high-income urbanite opposed to welfare payments and a low-income urbanite in favor of such payments.

[18] Sorauf, *Political Parties,* p. 28.

3. *Institutional theories.* According to the institutional theories, the structure of government and the electoral system is responsible for the type of party system employed. The most influential of the institutional theorists, Maurice Duverger, has argued that electoral systems based on proportional representation (systems in which seats in the legislative body are awarded according to the percentage of the popular vote won by each party) tend to create multiparty systems.[19] With a system based on proportional representation, a minor party winning only a small percentage of the vote can still have a voice in the legislature. In the United States, however, members of both houses of Congress are elected from *single-member districts.* Candidates who receive the most votes in their particular districts are awarded positions of power. Thus, there is no political reward for third and fourth parties; their only alternative is to merge with one of the two national parties and hopefully influence the party platform.

[19] Sorauf, *Political Parties,* p. 29.

4. *Consensus and diversity theories.* Societies that display consensus or widespread agreement on basic social issues, according to consensus and

diversity theories, tend to develop two-party systems. In the United States, for example, the majority of the population is basically agreed upon the value of constitutional democracy. Parties calling for another basic form of government are seldom of any real influence in the political arena. Societies that are irreconcilably divided on basic social issues, on the other hand, supposedly tend to adopt multiparty systems. In recent elections in France, parties that opposed the French Constitution itself received much of the popular vote (as much as 40 percent).

## Characteristics of the American two-party system

Major parties in the United States have always been coalitions of different groups and interests. An American party, to be successful, must adopt a program that is broad enough to attract almost anyone, from the midwest farmer to the northern industrialist, the urban Easterner and the rural Californian, the executive and the laborer. Because a plurality wins a position in the American electoral system, a party must build as large an electoral base as it possibly can.

### Pragmatism

To develop this wide electoral base, American political parties have constantly avoided taking firm ideological stands on political issues. A political party must be pragmatic and flexible in its approach to contemporary issues if it is to capture a majority at the national level and enlist the support of widely diverse interest groups—groups that often hold conflicting opinions.

### Moderate platforms

To protect its electoral base, the political parties in the United States tend to weed out those candidates who deviate too far from middle-of-the-road policies. Evidence of the dangers of running a candidate who differs from the mainstream of party thought can be seen in Barry Goldwater's campaign for the presidency in 1964. Goldwater, representing the conservative wing of the Republican party, lost the support of moderate and liberal Republicans and was badly beaten at the polls.

### Stability of affiliations

Another characteristic of the American two-party system has been the stability of voter preference over long periods of time. As we noted in earlier chapters, first voters tend to support the same party as their parents, labor has tended to support Democratic candidates, and business has tended to support Republicans. The socialization process is largely responsible for this stability. Individuals are socialized by the groups to which they belong and tend to favor the parties supported by these groups. The parties themselves also lend stability to the system. Once a party has captured the loyalties of a specific group, it will work hard to maintain those loyalties.

### Multiplicity of smaller party systems

Finally, the American two-party system has been marked by smaller one-party and multiparty systems operating within it. As noted earlier, many southern communities are dominated by the Democratic party and the results of their primary elections usually determine the winners of the regular elections. In the Midwest, on the other hand, splinter groups, such as the Progressive party, are still powerful enough to maintain their independence from the two major parties and to affect elections, at least at state and local levels.

## One-party systems in the United States

Thus far, we have discussed American politics in terms of a two-party system. In some regions, states, and localities, however, one party or another enjoys such widespread support that the area can be said to operate under a one-party system. By 1970 true two-party systems were operating in thirty-four states. Moreover, less than half the members of the House of Representatives have been elected in districts where there is genuine two-party competition.

Certain regions have traditionally been the stronghold of one of the major parties. Republicans, for example, have usually drawn almost total support from northern New England and much of the Midwest. The most obvious one-party region, however, has been the so-called Solid South.

The Democratic majority in the South, although it has diminished in recent elections, historically has been the result of several factors, the major one being the issue of race. "In its grand outlines," writes Key, "the politics of the South revolves around the position of the Negro."[20] Southerners have traditionally flocked to the sympathetic Democratic party. The Republicans, blamed for the horrors of the Civil War and the turmoil of the Reconstruction period, have been little more than a shadow in the southern political arena.

Race has not been the only factor, however, to unify Southerners under the Democratic banner. Other factors include "a one-crop (mostly cotton) agrarianism, a dearth of industry and metropolitanism, low per capita income, ethnic and religious homogeneity, and an intense nativism."[21]

The one-party system in the South has displayed two distinct characteristics, multifactionalism and bifactionalism.[22]

*Multifactionalism*, the existence of three or more groups supporting separate candidates in the Democratic primary, is common in many southern states. In Florida, for example, in four gubernatorial Democratic primaries held between 1936 and 1948, more than eight candidates made serious efforts to grasp the party nomination and, therefore, the election. Thus it may be said that multifactionalism occurs in all southern states, except when they experience temporary periods of bifactionalism.

*Bifactionalism*, the existence of two distinct groups supporting two separate candidates within the Democratic party, has occurred in a number of southern states. In Louisiana, for example, a bifactional one-party system grew up around the Louisiana "Kingfish," Huey Long, in the 1920s. Long, who was elected governor in 1928 and senator in 1930, died from an assassin's bullet in 1935, but the two factions founded during his prime, the Longites and the anti-Longs, continue to shape the course of Louisiana politics.

Evident in the past few years has been the steady decline of the one-party

[20] V. O. Key, Jr., *Southern Politics* (New York: Alfred A. Knopf, Inc., 1949), p. 5.

[21] Allen P. Sindler, *Political Parties in the United States* (New York: Alfred A. Knopf, Inc., 1962), p. 26.

[22] The following discussion is based on Sindler, *Political Parties*, pp. 31–42.

system in various parts of the country, particularly the South. "[The] national pattern of Democratic-Republican competition has spread to the states and localities of the country," writes Frank Sorauf, "gradually eliminating the pockets of one-party dominance."[23] As evidenced in recent elections, the Democrats can no longer depend on the support of a "Solid South." For example, Republicans received more than the usual amount of southern support in the 1956 and 1968 presidential elections. At the state level, Republicans have captured the governors' offices in Virginia, Tennessee, Kentucky, and West Virginia.

[23] Sorauf, *Political Parties*, p. 32.

"Dangerous Erosion"

Drawing by Doyle in the Philadelphia *Daily News*, November 3, 1968.

## Minor parties

Characteristic of the American two-party system is the lack of powerful third, fourth, or fifth parties. In virtually every national and state election, however, minor parties sporting names like Greenbackers, Free-Soilers, Silver Republicans, Bull Moosers, Socialist-Laborers, and Communists have nominated candidates. Although these parties seldom marshal wide support, they nevertheless play an important role in the American party system. Minor parties have presented the American public with a number of strong and controversial leaders—such men as Norman Thomas of the Socialist Party and George Wallace of the American Independent Party—who have taken stances opposed by the major parties. In some states and localities, in fact, third parties once wielded considerable political power. For example, the Progressives in Wisconsin and the Liberals in New York were active for decades and elected numerous candidates. As recently as 1970, James Buckley was the successful Conservative Party candidate from New York for the United States Senate.

Broadly speaking, there are two types of minor parties in the American party system, doctrinal parties and transient parties.[24]

[24] Key, *Politics, Parties, and Pressure Groups,* pp. 254–281.

## Doctrinal parties

*Doctrinal parties* are not truly political parties in that they serve primarily to propagandize their particular ideologies rather than to have their members occupy positions of power. Since they do not depend on their performance at the polls, doctrinal parties tend to have long histories. The Socialist Labor party, founded in the late nineteenth century, has never won an election, yet its candidates still appear on many ballots.

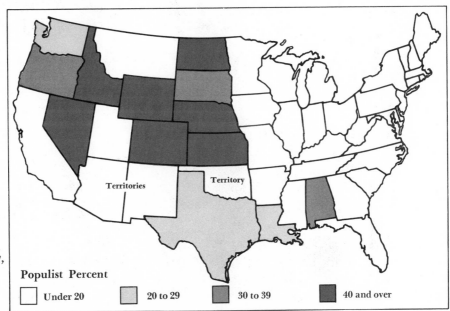

*Rarely does a minor party gain substantial national power. The Populist Party, in 1892, however, did make large inroads in one section of the country.*

Populist Percent

☐ Under 20    ☐ 20 to 29    ◼ 30 to 39    ◼ 40 and over

Source: POLITICS, PARTIES, AND PRESSURE GROUPS, 5th Ed. by V. O. Key, Jr. Copyright © 1942, 1947, 1952, 1958, 1964 by Thomas Y. Crowell Company. Reprinted with permission of the publisher.

## Transient parties

*Transient parties* are short-term organizations formed to oppose the policies of the major parties. Some transient parties are *splinter* or *secessionist parties* —they have broken with one of the major parties because of ideological differences. Outstanding examples of splinter or secessionist parties are the Progressive party formed by Theodore Roosevelt in 1912 and the States' Rights, or Dixiecrat party founded in 1948. When neither party won an election, each was dissolved, and those who had joined them returned to their original parties. One of the strongest secessionist parties has been the American Independent party founded in 1968 by Alabama Governor George Wallace. In the 1968 presidential election, Wallace's party won 13 percent of the vote, the largest turnout for a minor party in nearly fifty years.

Since World War II, however, minor parties have been slowly disappearing. A number of factors have led to this decline. Paramount has been the spread of major-party competition to the state and local levels. The states themselves, in fact, have made it increasingly more difficult and expensive for third parties to place candidates on the ballot.

"It's a little hazy. I can't quite tell whether he's joining the Democratic Party or starting a third party."

Drawing by Dana Fradon; © 1970
The New Yorker Magazine, Inc.

The decline of the minor parties has paralleled the growing concern for national politics and the subsequent decline of localism. An exception is exemplified by the party politics of New York's Mayor John Lindsay. Lindsay, a nominal Republican, re-elected as a Liberal Independent, maintained the support of the New Democratic Coalition, a major party affiliate. (In 1971, he switched to the Democratic party.) Coalition parties, especially in major urban areas, have somewhat diffused party loyalties and have offered new alternatives to the voter. The present mayors of Minneapolis and Philadelphia were elected by a coalition of party affiliates.

# The structure of political parties

In 1911, the German-Italian political scientist Robert Michels set down his *iron law of oligarchy*. According to Michels's iron law, "It is organization which gives birth to the domination of the elected over the electors, of the mandatories over the mandators, of the delegates over the delegators. Who says organization says oligarchy."[25] Thus, the power of organization is usually granted to a small, active minority. The iron law holds true for nonpolitical as well as political organizations. In political organizations, however, the ruling minority is responsible to the electorate; that is, in order to maintain party strength, they must consider the demands of the electorate when making or influencing policy decisions.

25 Robert Michels, *Political Parties*, trans. by Eden and Cedar Paul (New York: The Free Press, 1962), p. 15.

To better understand how the small groups that run political parties operate within the American two-party system, it is important to study the fundamental structure of political parties. Organization exists on two levels, which correspond to the two major functions of political parties—running the government and electing officials.

## Electing officials

To perform their major function, the placing of their members in the official positions of power in the political system, our major parties are organized similarly to our federal system of government. Both the Democrats and Republicans are organized on a national, state, and local basis. In both organizations the state and local units operate independently of the national unit.

## State and local organization

At the top of party organization at the state and local levels is the *state committee*. Made up of locally selected committeemen and headed by the *state chairman*, the state committee is usually organized according to state law. All conduct state campaigns, but some exercise considerably more political power than others. Most, however, are weak organizations, often the tool of the governor, one of the state's senators, or a group of local leaders.

Below the state committee are numerous *city* and *county committees*. Like the state committees, these city and county organizations vary in the amount of political power they exercise. The chairmen of many city and county committees are, however, token appointees in the party hierarchy. Others, like Chicago's Mayor Richard Daley, have turned their committees into powerful organizations that influence the decision-making process from the local to the state and even to the national congressional levels.

Below the city and county committees, at the grass-roots level, the parties are organized into precincts and wards. Party leaders working at this level— the *ward leaders*, *precinct captains*, and *local bosses*—are the enlisted men of the party system. Today, for the most part, party organization at this level is active only in the weeks before an election. In the recent past, however, party activity in some precincts and wards has been constant, often providing the only unifying force within the community. In their prime, local-party organizations have been involved in everything from providing welfare to holding social events.

Samuel C. Patterson, "Characteristics of Party Leaders," Western Political Quarterly (University of Utah), 16 (1963): 332–352.

Samuel Patterson has conducted a study to determine "the nature and functions of party leadership at the county level." The state of Oklahoma was chosen for the study since its voters adhere to two viewpoints, Midwestern Republican and Southern Democrat; in addition, recent Republican gains in the state, which has predominantly Democratic officials, have led to revitalized party organization in both camps.

Patterson's data indicate that county party leaders in Oklahoma tend to rank high in social status, education, and income. His study did not support the generalization that "the Republican party in Oklahoma is the party of business, managerial, and professional groups, and the Democratic party the vehicle of the common man." In fact, "Oklahoma Democratic chairmen tend more than Republicans to come from high-status occupations, to have more education, to have higher incomes, to be older"; a party in power over a length of time attracts men of such standing.

County party leaders were shown to be long-term county residents, though there were some exceptions in the Republican party, where newcomers with out-of-state political experience were in office. More than half the Democrats were found to have served in their positions three or more years, whereas more than half the Republicans served less than three years.

Patterson discovered that Democratic county leaders played a larger role in their national organization than Republicans. However, Republican county leaders acknowledged a greater part in selecting local candidates; they indicated that it was difficult to persuade candidates to run for office and expressed a desire for more two-party competition.

Patterson discusses the twin functions of county leaders, who must maintain viable political organizations *and* wage campaigns.

In general, Democratic leaders have a clearer conception of their role than Republican leaders. To some degree Democratic leaders are more campaign-oriented than Republicans. The slightly greater organizational emphasis given by Republican leaders may be the result of temporary organizational demands in a party just beginning to build party machinery. In addition, it seems likely that the most effective county leader will be both organization and campaign-oriented.

## National organization

The basic unit of party organization at the national level is the *national convention*. Consisting of thousands of delegates from the various states, the national convention meets every four years to nominate the party's candidates for President and Vice-President, to formulate a platform on which the candidates will run, to establish party procedure, and to formalize the selection of national committee members. Despite its impressive numbers and its often dramatic proceedings, the national convention has surprisingly little power. It has no say about who the party supports for Congress or for local and state offices, and it has little power to enlist support for the party platform.

Between conventions, the party is run at the national level by the *national committee*. The members of the national committee are formally elected by the national convention but, in reality, this is merely a token gesture. The convention simply appoints the nominees presented by the delegation from each state—nominees often selected according to the size of their financial contribution to the party.

In the Democratic national committee there are 108 members, one man and one woman representing every state and territory in the Union. Since 1952 the Republicans have included, in addition to one man and one woman, the chairman of the state's committee, if that state has elected a Republican governor or a Republican majority in Congress, or has voted for the Republican presidential nominee in the last election. Like the national convention, the national committee has little real power. Mainly its function is to decide where and when to hold the next national convention, to appease warring factions within the party whenever it can, and to raise campaign funds. What power it has is exercised by the committee's leader, the *national chairman*.

The national chairman directs the party's presidential campaign and acts as the official spokesman for the party. Although he is formally elected by the national committee, the chairman is usually the choice of the party's presidential candidate. As the closest aid to the presidential nominee the chairman is in line for substantial patronage prizes if his party is victorious, and, therefore, may exert considerable political power. This is not often the case, however, for the turnover in national chairmen is so great that there is little time to establish a base of support—from 1940 to 1970, for example, the Republicans had fifteen national chairmen, while the Democrats had thirty. If the party loses the presidential election, the national chairman, with no patronage to distribute and no President to rely on, is usually relatively powerless.

Party organization at the national level is primarily the concern of the presidential wing of a political party. The congressional wings of the major parties, however, also organize along national lines.

The units of organization for the congressional wings are the *Congressional Campaign Committee* and the *Senatorial Campaign Committee*, whose members are selected by Democratic and Republican representatives in the House and Senate.[26] These committees basically serve to aid and support party members seeking election without regard for the candidate's position on matters of national policy.

## Decentralization of party power

[26] Charles O. Jones, *The Republican Party in American Politics* (New York: The Macmillan Co., 1967), p. 30, describes "the principal activities of the House [Republican] committee [as] research, field service, finance, and public relations." Similarly, Cornelius P. Cotter and Bernard C. Hennessy, *Politics without Power: The National Party Committees* (New York: Atherton Press, Inc., 1964), p. 9, notes these functions in both houses and for both parties.

## Bosses and machines

In most countries the distribution of power within the party system corresponds to the distribution of power within the government. In Switzerland, for example, where power of government is highly centralized, the party system also tends to be centralized. In the United States, however, the increasing trend toward governmental centralization has not radically affected the structure of political parties; and local groups—especially the congressional wings of the various parties—continue to block attempts to strengthen the national party.

With nearly 100,000 decentralized units of government within the United States and elective positions numbering over 750,000, it is understandable that the major political parties have concentrated their sources of power at the state and local levels, most often at the level where the city *boss* operates to provide for and control his constituency. Only two offices of political power are contested at the national level—the presidency and the vice-presidency—and even the men who fill these offices are nominated by a convention representing the states and elected by a state-organized electoral college. This decentralization provides power for local officials.

In the late nineteenth century and in the opening decades of this century the local boss and his machine flourished in one of the most colorful eras of American politics. The political boss of this period found much of his power in the newly arrived immigrant groups. The boss and his party took these new immigrants under wing, providing food for the hungry, jobs for the unemployed, citizenship papers, entertainment, and often a sense of connection with the homeland. In return, the political boss asked only for votes.

The Great Depression, strongly felt by the political bosses and their machines, was one of the major causes of their loss of power. During periods of growth and prosperity, the political machine could easily provide jobs and welfare for new immigrants; but when, in the wake of the depression, unemployment and poverty became a reality to large sections of the society, the machines found that the demands for assistance were more than they could meet.

Other factors also drained power from the local bosses. As the immigrant groups were assimilated into the society, they no longer turned to the local machine for aid. Political patronage controlled by the local bosses was substantially reduced by extending the Civil Service. And social welfare became a standard function of government rather than the arbitrarily distributed "handouts" of local bosses.

*In 1890, politicians were beginning to sense the decline in power of bosses.*

Times have changed.

Drawing by Dalrymple in *Puck*, 1890.

The Great Depression and the growth of the national government unquestionably crippled the political boss and his machine, but by no means drove him from the political arena. Although the machines are now referred to as "organizations" and the local bosses as "local leaders," they still wield considerable power in the party system. Such machines as the Daley organization in Chicago are powerful political forces, exercising almost total control over their party in the community.

## The American party system: reform or status quo

The American two-party system has been the subject of much political controversy. Supporters of the system argue that the loosely structured, decentralized, nonideological parties in the United States allow for peaceful change and popular control of the government.

Critics of the two-party system argue that the major political parties do not offer the voter a clear choice—that the two major parties are more easily distinguished by their similarities than their differences. They claim also that the lack of discipline of American parties, with their power based at the state and local levels, and their absence of national leadership, leads to irresponsible government. Once the partisan candidate is safely in national office he is not forced *by his party* to fulfill campaign commitments made to his constituency "back home." Furthermore, claim some critics, the division of responsibility and the differences in policy within the same party are so pronounced as to categorize both Republicans and Democrats into congressional and presidential parties—a four-party instead of a two-party system. Because each congressman concentrates on only a relatively small segment of the political system, his interests differ from those of Presidents and presidential candidates. In addition, Democrats have different views from their counterpart Republicans. Finally, the critics of the two-party system have consistently pointed out that the major parties are ruled by a privileged minority and are, therefore, undemocratic.

*Daryl R. Fair, "Party Strength and Political Patronage,"* Southwestern Social Science Quarterly, *45 (December 1964): 264–271.*

Daryl Fair has tested the empirical basis for the politician's maxim that "strong political parties are essential to responsible party government; patronage is essential to strong political parties; therefore, patronage is essential to responsible party government."

In his research, Fair identified twenty-four competitive state party systems. Defining party strength in terms of the degree of control exerted over candidate nomination, he determined that strong competitive party systems existed in the four states that relied on conventions (Connecticut, Delaware, Indiana, and New York) and in the seven states in which both parties had a high percentage of uncontested primary races for statewide offices during the years 1950–1960 (Arizona, Colorado, Idaho, Illinois, Massachusetts, Michigan, Rhode Island).

Having thus established which states had strong parties, Fair examined state patronage. In order to measure patronage, he looked at the percentage of state administrative employees not under a merit system—states with a high percentage of such employees were classed as having strong patronage systems. In this group were Delaware (94 percent), Montana (92 percent), New Mexico (91 percent), West Virginia (91 percent), Utah (89 percent), and Arizona (88 percent). Those with a low percentage of positions assigned outside the merit system were Connecticut (11 percent), Ohio (16 percent), New Jersey (17 percent), Rhode Island (19 percent), and New York (20 percent). Fair summarizes:

The hypothesis to be tested . . . is the following: states in which both political parties are strong will have a high percentage of state administrative employees not covered by merit systems.

A chart shows his findings:

### Strong and Weak Party States in Relation to High and Low Incidence of Patronage

|  | High Incidence of Patronage | Low Incidence of Patronage | Totals |
|---|---|---|---|
| Strong party states | 4 | 7 | 11 |
| Weak party states | 8 | 5 | 13 |
| Totals | 12 | 12 | 24 |

On the basis of the data presented in this study however, it seems reasonable to venture the hypothesis that no one-to-one relationship exists between patronage and party strength; that is, a high incidence of patronage in a given jurisdiction is not indicative of strong parties in that jurisdiction. Rather party strength would seem to de dependent upon a complex of factors, a high level of patronage *not* being a necessary factor, though it may be helpful in certain specific cases.

In 1950, the Committee on Political Parties of the American Political Science Association, in a report titled "Toward a More Responsible Two-Party System," made a number of proposals for reform of the party system. These proposals called for more centralized and democratic political parties, the formulation of more issue-oriented programs, and a greater effort by officeholders to carry out the programs established by their parties. Today, more than twenty years after "Toward a More Responsible Two-Party System" was published, the parties remain almost exactly as they were in 1950. "The reforms of the reformers do not endure, and the prescriptions of the American Political Science Association committee have not even pitted the stony resistance of the parties. Indeed, a good share of the cynicism with which so many men of good will view the parties may be a result of these unreal hopes and illusions. The parties are, as are all social institutions, deeply

[27] Sorauf, *Political Parties*, p. 168.

conservative organizations, rooted in political cultures, conventions, and other institutions. They will not and cannot be easily displaced or easily altered without altering some or all of their envrionment."[27]

The major question relative to the effectiveness of political parties, however, is not whether or not they will change quickly. It is whether or not they are serving their stated purpose: to represent the salient needs of the people.

# Glossary

**Antifederalists (Jeffersonian Republicans)** Forerunners of the modern Democratic party, this party was primarily an agrarian group comprised of small farmers, workers, small businessmen, shareholders, and frontiersmen.

**bifactionalism** Existence of two distinct groups supporting two separate candidates, characteristic of the one-party system in the South.

**Congressional Campaign Committee** Congressional unit of party organization formed by in-office congressmen to aid all party members seeking election.

**consensus and diversity theories** Theories that two-party systems tend to develop in societies displaying consensus or widespread agreement on basic social issues, while multiparty systems tend to develop in societies divided on basic issues.

**Democratic Republican (Democratic Party)** Party originating from the old Jeffersonian Republicans that styled itself as the party of the common man.

**Doctrinal party** Minor political party that exists primarily to propagandize its particular ideologies rather than to have its members elected to positions of power.

**Federalists** Early major American political party that advocated a centralized national government led by a strong Chief Executive.

**incumbent** Person who holds political office.

**institutional theories** Theories that the structure of government and the electoral system is responsible for type of two-party system employed.

**iron law of oligarchy** Robert Michels's theory that power is granted to a small, active minority within a political organization.

**multifactionalism** A characteristic of the one-party system in the South in which three or more groups support separate candidates in a Democratic primary.

**multiparty systems** Political system in which exist more than two major political parties representing the interests of large segments of the population.

**national chairman** Political party official who primarily manages the party's presidential campaign and acts as official spokesman for the party. Although elected by the national committees, in practice he is the choice of the presidential candidate.

**national convention** Basic unit of party organization at the national level, consisting of state delegates who nominate the party's candidates for President and Vice-President, determine party platforms and rules, and elect members to the national committee.

**one-party system** Political system in which only one major party exists to nominate candidates during an election.

**political party** Organization that attempts to influence the political system by placing its members in government offices.

**reform party** Transient third party dissatisfied with programs and policies of the major parties and interested in promoting social and economic reform.

**Republican party** Party founded in 1854, by a group of Whigs, dissident Democrats, and former third-party members who shared a desire to end slavery.

**Senatorial Campaign Committee** Congressional unit of party organization formed by in-office senators to aid and support all party members seeking election.

**splinter (secessionist) party**   Transient third party that has broken with one of the major parties because of ideological differences.

**state chairman**   Leader of the state committee of a major political party.

**state committee**   The top of the political-party organization at the state and local levels. The committee is composed of locally selected committeemen and is usually organized according to state law.

**theories of national character**   Theories claiming, for example, that the type of party system is determined by the character, culture, and emotional climate of a nation.

**theories of natural dualism**   Theories attributing two-party systems to natural, polar oppositions between regions, political attitudes, and other variables.

**transient party**   Short-term organization (third party) formed to oppose the policies of the major parties.

**two-party system**   Political system in which candidates from only the two major political parties have any real chance of being elected to office.

**ward leaders, precinct captains, local bosses**   Low-ranking party leaders who organize and control their party's activities below the city and county levels.

**Whigs**   In American history, a splinter party that included those Jeffersonian Republicans who advocated a high tariff, and was supported mostly by the northern and industrial states.

# Suggested readings

Agar, Herbert, *The Price of Union* (Boston: Houghton Mifflin Co., 1950). History of American political parties designed to prove that the decentralized party system promotes compromise.

Banfield, Edward C., and James Q. Wilson, *City Politics* (Cambridge, Mass.: Harvard University Press, 1963). Study of the political processes, as opposed to the administrative form and structure of city government.

Binkley, Wilfred E., *American Political Parties: Their Natural History*, 4th rev. ed. (New York: Alfred A. Knopf, Inc., 1964). Description of political parties since their conception, emphasizing the theory that parties are coalitions of many interests.

Bone, Hugh A., *American Politics and The Party System*, 3rd ed. (New York: McGraw-Hill Book Co., 1965). Standard text on political parties and party organizations.

Burns, James MacGregor, *The Deadlock of Democracy: Four-Party Politics in America* (Englewood Cliffs, N.J.: Prentice-Hall, Inc., 1962). Critical analysis of the national political system, with emphasis on the fact that the present system leads to delay and an inability to respond to pressing national needs.

Chambers, William, *Political Parties in a New Nation: The American Experience, 1776–1809* (New York: Oxford University Press, Inc., 1963). History of early American political parties (post-1776) compared with those in new nations today.

Costikyan, Edward N., *Behind Closed Doors: Politics in the Public Interest* (New York: Harcourt Brace Jovanovich, Inc., 1966). Reflections on New York City politics by the former head of Tammany Hall.

Cotter, Cornelius P., and Bernard Hennessy, *Politics Without Power: The National Party Committees* (New York: Atherton Press, 1964). Analysis of the national committees of the Republican and Democratic parties.

Duverger, Maurice, *Political Parties: Their Organization and Activity in the Modern State*, 2nd ed. (New York: John Wiley and Sons, Inc., 1964). Major comparative study of the party systems in several western countries.

Eldersveld, Samuel, *Political Parties: A Behavioral Analysis* (Chicago: Rand McNally and Co., 1964). Analysis of local party leaders' political orientations and their influence on the public.

Fenton, John H., *Midwest Politics* (New York: Holt, Rinehart and Winston, Inc., 1966). Historical analysis of party politics in six midwestern states.

Goldman, Ralph M., *The Democratic Party in American Politics* (New York: The Macmillan Co., 1966). Short history of the Democratic Party with particular emphasis on recent developments and trends.

Goldwin, Robert A., ed., *Political Parties, U.S.A.* (Chicago: Rand McNally and Co., 1964). Seven essays designed to explain and analyze the functioning of the American political party system.

Greenstein, Fred I., *The American Party System and the American People* (Englewood Cliffs, N.J.: Prentice-Hall, Inc., 1963). Condensed survey of recent research on party affiliations and individual attitudes toward the American two-party system.

Herring, Pendleton, *The Politics of Democracy: American Parties in Action* (New York: W. W. Norton and Co., Inc., 1965). Classic defense of the American party system, stressing its importance in shaping American democracy.

Jacob, Herbert, and Kenneth N. Wines, eds., *Politics in the American States: A Comparative Analysis* (Boston: Little, Brown and Co., 1965). Essays on the operation of the parties at the state level.

Jones, Charles O., *The Republican Party in American Politics* (New York: The Macmillan Co., 1965). Short history of the Republican party with particular emphasis on recent developments and trends.

Key, V. O., Jr., *American State Politics* (New York: Alfred A. Knopf, Inc., 1956). Scholarly study of party politics at the state level.

Key, V. O., Jr., *Politics, Parties, and Pressure Groups*, 5th ed. (New York: Thomas Y. Crowell Co., 1964). Standard text, including a detailed history and analysis of American political parties.

Key, V. O., Jr., and Alexander Heard, *Southern Politics* (New York: Alfred A. Knopf, Inc., 1949). Survey of politics in the South, including ethnic, social, and economic factors.

Lockard, Duane, *New England State Politics* (Princeton, N.J.: Princeton University Press, 1959). Comparative analysis of politics in the New England states, with emphasis on the influence of ethnic groups.

Riordan, William L., *Plunkitt of Tammany Hall* (New York: E. P. Dutton and Co., Inc.,). Intriguing dialogues on inner workings of a big city (New York) political machine.

Schattschneider, E. E., *Party Government* (New York: Holt, Rinehart and Winston, Inc., 1942). Critical analysis of the American party system, and a defense of the thesis advocating increased centralization and discipline in American political parties.

Sindler, Allan P., *Political Parties in the United States* (New York: St. Martin's Press, Inc., 1966). Brief analysis of the American party system.

Sorauf, Frank J., *Political Parties in the American System* (Boston: Little, Brown and Co., 1964). Major survey of the role, function, and behavior of American parties and their members, including some comparisons with political parties abroad.

# Topics of further study

Abbott, David W., and Edward T. Rogowsky, eds., *Political Parties: Leadership, Organization, Linkage* (Chicago: Rand McNally and Co., 1971).

Amaru, Augustine, "*Transformismo* and the Italian Communist Party" (master's thesis, Michigan State University, 1966).

Barber, Kathleen L., "Legal Status of the American Communist Party" (master's thesis, Case Western Reserve University, 1965).

Blank, Blanche, "Bossism and the Complexity of Power," *The Nation*, August 11, 1962, pp. 57–58.

Fair, Daryl, "Party Strength and Political Patronage," *Southwestern Social Science Quarterly*, December 1964, pp. 264–271.

Feigert, Frank, "Motivation, Incentive Systems and the Political Party Organization," *American Political Science Review*, December 1968, pp. 1159–1173.

Johnson, William, "The Volunteer Republicans" (Ph. D. dissertation, Claremont Graduate School, 1965).

Joyner, Conrad, "Political Party Affiliation of University Administrative and Teaching Personnel," *Southwestern Social Science Quarterly*, March 1963, pp. 353–356.

Karsch, Robert, *Political Parties, Elections and the General Assembly in Missouri* (Columbia, Mo.: University of Missouri Research Center, 1964).

Owen, Mary Alice, "Interest and Articulation and the Party System in Sweden," (master's thesis, University of Florida, 1963).

Patterson, Samuel C., "Characteristics of Party Leaders," *Western Political Quarterly*, June 1963, pp. 332–352.

Patterson, Thomas, "Failure of Party Realignment in the South, 1937–1939," *Journal of Politics*, August 1965, pp. 602–617.

Rakove, Milton, "Democrat Looks at the Republican Party," *Virginia Quarterly Review*, Summer 1965, pp. 342–357.

# 11 campaign dynamics

## the electoral process

THE EXTENT to which people take part in the process that elects their representatives is a measure of their active concern for the governing of the country. In the decade of the 1950s, although the number of voters was larger than in past elections, the "weak ideological focus" of the two major parties directly related to lack of involvement with political issues and leaders. In sharp contrast to the Eisenhower era, the years following the election of John Kennedy were filled with a turbulent activity; the political atmosphere was crowded with political issues: civil rights, uprisings in urban ghettoes, campus unrest, protest against the Vietnam-Southeast Asian conflict, open violence at the Chicago Democratic convention, emergence of a voluble third-party movement, and the pervasive theme of a new need for "law and order," were part of a trend in American politics that changed the political character of the nation during the 1960s.[1] The percentage of people (60 percent) interested enough to vote has grown in the 1950s and 1960s, and may continue to grow, because of the supposed increase in political awareness.

In this chapter, we will describe the procedures through which individuals gain the power to make policy decisions. Our discussion will involve the role of the voter, and the nomination and campaign that leads to the election of a chosen candidate. The campaign strategies employed to help individuals achieve political power at both the congressional and presidential levels will also be examined and evaluated.

## Registration

Before an individual can participate in the electoral process, he must meet certain requirements. Under Article I of the Constitution, each state has the

[1] Herbert F. Weisberg and Jerrold G. Rusk, "Dimensions of Candidate Evaluation," *The American Political Science Review*, 64 (1970): 1183–1185.

right to set its own standards for allowing a person to vote. Certain of these requirements are common to most states, either because of constitutional amendment or national legislation. Although some states, in order to increase their voting population, originally allowed certain noncitizens to vote, the Fourteenth Amendment requires that all voters must be citizens of the United States. Although residency requirements are also restricted to an extent by national legislation, the states vary considerably on the length of residency required (from three months to two years) before a voter is qualified.

"Billy Graham as a Presidential candidate—now that's what I call giving voters a clear choice!"

Drawing by Interlandi; © 1964 the Los Angeles *Times*.

Once all the basic legal requirements are met, a person is required by most states to register with the state in which he resides. *Registration* is the formal procedure whereby a prospective voter appears before an appointed election official to establish that he meets the legal requirements for voting in the next election. Within only two states are areas that are exempt from this requirement: certain towns and municipalities in North Dakota and Texas cities with a population under 10,000 have an optional registration in local elections.

There are two types of registration systems—*periodic* and *permanent*. Most states have a permanent list of registered voters, and the person who has recorded his name once does not have to reappear at the election board unless he changes name or address, switches party affiliation, or has not voted in a given number of elections. Fourteen states, on the other hand, require a voter to register periodically, usually every two or four years. Of the two methods, permanent registration encourages a larger voter turnout because it demands less of the potential voter.

# Nomination procedures

How are candidates nominated for public office in the United States? The *caucus* was the earliest means of choosing state, local, or national candidates for election; the men who were in control of the party met privately to put forward their favorite choice. This nominating procedure was, however, discontinued after the victory in 1828 of Andrew Jackson, who wished to democratize the electoral system. When the caucus was outlawed as a nominating procedure, many state party organizations were determined to find some system whereby candidates would be selected by the party elite. The state convention system, which would ensure continued control by party leaders, was adopted. Under the convention system, candidates were selected by delegates chosen from among the party faithful. The delegates met privately and chose men favorable to their own interests rather than members of the general electorate; however, the two interests were not always mutually exclusive.

**General primaries**

Early in the twentieth century, Progressive reformers urged the adoption of the *primary* system, an electoral procedure by which the voter could select the man or woman he wished to represent his party in the final election of a public official. In this way, the voter could select his party's nominee. Three general types of primaries exist today: closed, open, and blanket primaries; nonpartisan primaries; and runoff primaries. The primary system spread so rapidly that today only Delaware retains the use of the convention system to nominate its public officials.

**Closed and open primaries**

The most popular method of primary election is the *closed primary*, in which participation is restricted to those who have formally declared their affiliation with a particular political party. Forty-two states choose their candidates in this manner.

The standard *open primary* system is conducted in six states; here, the voter is allowed to choose his candidates from the party of his choice, without having to publicly affiliate with a particular political party. He marks only the ballot of the party in whose primary he participates. The states of Washington and Alaska use the *blanket primary*, a special type of open primary: the individual may vote for a candidate of either party. He may decide, for example, that he prefers the Democratic candidate for governor and the Republican candidate for congressman.

**Nonpartisan primaries**

Many smaller cities and villages (except in the South) use *nonpartisan primaries* to nominate candidates, especially local officials. There are no party distinctions listed on the ballots in these primaries. Qualified candidates just file their names, and those two who receive the highest number of votes are the candidates who will run against each other in the general election.

**Runoff primaries**

Winning the Democratic nomination for local and state offices, in some southern states, is practically equivalent to winning the general election: this is why the Democratic primary is so significant in such "one-party" states. Sometimes, however, no candidate receives a majority of the votes. When this occurs in any one of ten southern states and Oklahoma, the *runoff primary*, which is a contest between the two highest vote-getters in the first primary, is used.[2] The runoff primary may become less important in the future, because of the gradual increase in Republican party influence in the South (exemplified by the 1970 elections of Republican governors in Kentucky, Tennessee, Virginia, and West Virginia), which has threatened the Democratic party domination that has characterized most of the southern states since the Civil War.

[2] *Book of the States* (Lexington, Ky.: Council of State Governments, 1970), pp. 34–35.

# Nominating a congressman

[3] C. Ewing, "Primaries as Real Elections," *Southwestern Social Science Quarterly*, 29 (March 1949): 293–298.

Success in the primary for a congressional candidate may well mean success in the general election.[3] The choices made by the voters of the dominant party in the primary election are the ones that make headlines on election day. These results are not confined to the basically one-party states of the South, but are obtained from all over the country.

Thus, the major competition occurs prior to the nominating primaries. How the candidate wages the battle may depend on whether or not it is a year in which a presidential election will be held. If it is, then a congressional candidate may be able to and may want to "ride the coattails" of a popular presidential candidate in his party, or plan his strategy to buck the strong opposition candidate. In "safe" districts (that is, in the camp of one party), however, a congressman is not especially concerned with the presidential election; his election is relatively secure and he does not need or want to inject an unknown factor into the campaign (if he runs a campaign at all). In an off-year, when there is no presidential election, the prospective congressional nominee has to use local party machinery in a different way: he may have to stand on a recognizable platform, develop tactics and strategies that will make him a winner.

# Nominating a President

Presidential nominating procedures differ from congressional ones in their emphasis on the national convention instead of the state primary; primaries are utilized, but they are separate and involve a special set of procedures.

## Selecting the delegates

[4] For a comprehensive discussion of nominations in states, see V. O. Key, Jr., *Politics, Parties, and Pressure Groups*, 5th ed. (New York: Thomas Y. Crowell Co., 1964), Chap. 14, pp. 370–395.

[5] Richard D. Hupman and Robert L. Tienken, *Nomination and Election of the President and Vice President of the United States* (Washington, D.C.: Government Printing Office, 1968), p. 46.

Because presidential nominations are made by national conventions, the emphasis prior to the convention is on the selection of delegates. The manner in which a delegate is chosen is established by state law, and each state has its own method.[4] Two-thirds of the states employ party conventions, and approximately one-third select their delegates through direct election in a presidential primary. Three states use a combination of the two methods.

Despite the fact that the majority of states use the convention system to elect their delegates, some critics object to it on the grounds that it is undemocratic and subject to the control of the state's party leaders. Although use of the primary has increased slightly in the twentieth century, most states maintain the convention system for the selection of delegates to the national convention. If delegates are elected from the congressional district, they are called *district delegates*, and if they compete on a statewide basis, they are called *"at-large" delegates*.[5]

The presidential primary may not be the most commonly employed method of selecting delegates to the national convention. It is, however, the method most widely publicized and thus of most interest to the greatest number of Americans. First adopted by the state of Wisconsin in 1905, this type of primary serves not only to elect the delegates, but also in some primaries to demonstrate the potential candidate's ability to obtain popular support.

State presidential primaries take two forms. First, there is the Presidential Preference Poll, in which the ballot lists the candidates for the nomination, and the voter indicates his preference. Whether the state's convention delegates are bound by the outcome of the poll varies with the laws and party system of that state. Second, there is Delegate Election, in which delegates to the national convention are chosen by the voter. Here again, the system varies with the state. Delegates may run on a "no preference" basis; that is, they are not pledged to any candidate. They may indicate a preference toward a particular candidate, or they may run as supporters of a presidential candidate. Some states utilize both forms of presidential primaries, holding them either separately or at the same time. Other states employ only one type of primary. In all cases, the election laws of the state determine the type of election system employed.

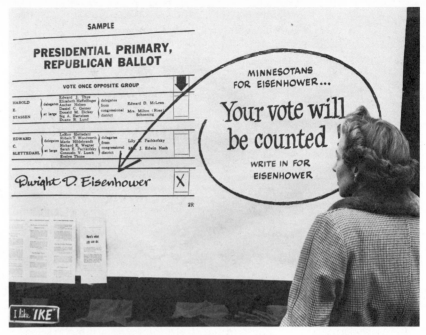

Two types of presidential primary ballots: in
one case, the candidates alone are listed,
and in the other, the delegates pledged to
the candidate are shown on the ballot with
the candidate. In neither instance does the
voter indicate a preference for individual
delegates to the national convention.

## Preconvention campaign

The preconvention campaign, the fight for delegate support, is the first step toward presidential nomination. There are many strategies and organizational techniques used by a contender for his party's nomination.

The presidential hopeful usually concentrates on state primaries in which he has a good chance of winning; a good showing in a major state may win him delegate support from that state, influence delegates from other states, and earn him free publicity with the voting public. In addition, victories in the primary, combined with growing popularity in the public opinion polls, may produce a bandwagon effect among the delegates. State delegations switch to support a candidate when they sense he is a winning candidate.

The candidate also sends scouts to all the nonprimary states to sound out the possible support of party leaders, as well as the maneuverability of particular delegates who may reverse their opinions and decide to support the candidate. In nonprimary states he can be open or secret about his desire to win the attention of delegates and their delegations. The entire preconvention campaign is thus geared to the winning of delegate support, whether through primaries or direct contact with the delegates themselves.

A good example of preconvention planning was that which led to John Kennedy's landslide victory at the Democratic national convention in 1960. His preconvention campaign was controlled by a dedicated staff that followed him as he actively stumped throughout the country from 1957 until the convention date of 1960. He toured, gathered information, and entered the right primary contests to record victories in Wisconsin, West Virginia, Maryland, and Oregon. He pursued, with exhausting intensity, the votes of each state delegation to the convention. He had, for example, up-to-the-minute resumes on each delegate, including his likes, dislikes, probable vote, listed in files that were constantly revised by his staff. Kennedy's ship was so well run that he knew, within one vote, how each of the state delegations were going to vote on the convention ballot.[6] The first balloting verified the value of his preplanning: those delegates who had favored Senator Stuart Symington (who had avoided primaries as well as much open campaigning), or who had backed Adlai Stevenson or Lyndon Johnson, joined the bandwagon of state delegations that gave Kennedy an exciting and impressive victory on the first roll call of the convention delegates.

The presidential primary is an integral part of the preconvention campaign strategy of most candidates, although only fourteen states and the District of Columbia hold presidential primaries. The results of these primary contests influence state delegations and the voting public, because they are given widespread media coverage.

Several important criticisms have been leveled at these primaries. For one thing, favorite sons, usually the state governors, often place their names on the primary ballot, although their limited following gives them little chance

[6] Nelson W. Polsby and Aaron B. Wildavsky, *Presidential Elections*, 2nd ed. (New York: Charles Scribner's Sons, 1968), pp. 89–92, provides a succinct discussion of the Kennedy organization as it plotted the road to the White House from 1957 to 1960.

*Campaigning requires all the candidate's time and energy. He is constantly on-the-go, traveling throughout the country, meeting the people, answering questions, and attending special party dinners.*

of a final national victory in the campaign for their party's nomination; this technique prevents a contest in the primary. Secondly, the primary campaign is very expensive, therefore discriminating against those candidates who do not have great financial backing. Third, leading contenders for the office of President, since they already have wide support, do not want to expend time, energy, and money on every primary race. Thus, primaries frequently do not reflect all the major aspirants in a party. Fourth, a presidential primary, run on local rather than national issues, may result in the defeat of a national figure, who then finds it impossible to muster money or support to run in other primaries or the general election.

Despite objections, the presidential primary is often important as an indication of a future victory. For example, in 1952, the victories of General Dwight Eisenhower over Senator Robert Taft in several primary contests ended with the nomination of General Eisenhower at the Republican convention, despite some earlier opposition from some delegates. In 1960, Senator John Kennedy demonstrated that a moderate Democrat and a Catholic

[7] Theodore H. White, *The Making of the President, 1960* (New York: Atheneum Publishers, 1960).

could sweep a state like West Virginia, solidly Protestant and plagued by a constantly high rate of unemployment, although it was expected that his challenger, Senator Hubert Humphrey, both Protestant and liberal, would be the victor.[7] The primary elections of the preconvention campaign have eliminated many candidates as contenders for their party's nominee. Some potential contenders have, in fact, withdrawn because of primary defeats, as did Wendell Willkie, while others have refrained from entering primaries because of lack of popular support, as did Governor George Romney of Michigan in 1968.

Although presidential primaries can destroy a candidate who loses or shows little strength in several contests, they cannot nominate a candidate. Only one-third of the convention delegates are chosen in primaries. But a candidate who proves his voter appeal will tend to capture the support of delegates from nonprimary states who want a winner. It is, however, possible to be nominated without running in a single primary—Humphrey, for example, accomplished this in 1968.

## The national convention

The national organizations of the major political parties concentrate heavily on the *national convention*. Each convention is potentially the scene of tremendous struggles for power and control. The purpose of all activity, up to and including the convention, is for a candidate to win a majority of the convention delegates on one of the ballots.

The number of delegates to the national convention may amount to nearly 3,000. The different formulas used by the Democrats and the Republicans to assign seats to each state have resulted in different numbers of delegates at their respective conventions. Each party allots a different weight to the votes of individual delegates. Because Democrats tend to assign half-votes to certain delegates, the number of delegates to their convention is much larger than those to the Republicans'. The Democrats had 2,622 delegates at the 1968 Democratic Presidential Convention, and the Republicans had 1,333 at their convention in that same year. In order to obtain a majority of these votes, only the most expertly run campaigns can be successful.

The convention hall is frequently a vibrant world (except during those years when an incumbent President is to be renominated); big wheels and novices gather round their state's delegation sign and talk excitedly of the latest events, rumors, possibilities. The stereotyped cigar-chomping politician mixes with the college graduate and newcomer to the scene; some delegates sit serenely confident that their sure choice (if the delegation is committed to a candidate) is going to win on the first roll call of the states; others favor dark horses (surprise entries), and still others are determined to set a precedent with a new resolution on the convention floor, something that will stir up the delegations. Flags, banners, pins, leaflets, placards of a popular nominee, noisemakers, streamers, fancy hats, wooden chairs, cluttered aisles, blaring music, bright lights, demonstration plans for the "spontaneous outbursts" of support later on during the convention—all this is part of the panorama that may give witness to the rise of a new hero.

## Adopting a platform

Republicans and Democrats follow similar procedures in conducting their conventions. The main business of the convention, the nomination of candidates for the President and Vice-President, takes place a few days after the opening with the keynote speech. After this speech an election is conducted to choose convention officials, hearings of committee reports are held, and the party platform is adopted.

The platform tends to consist of statements of policy rather than specific opinions on issues: the art of the platform is the art of compromise, and it is by this means that a diverse party can successfully unite its many constituents, even though it answers very few questions in a direct, forthright manner. If the party is renominating an incumbent President, the platform is written by him to suit his policies, as with Franklin Roosevelt in 1944, Lyndon Johnson in 1964, and Dwight Eisenhower in 1956. The incumbent's platform is

*The goal of each candidate before and during his party's national convention is to amass as much delegate support as he can. The delegates, very much aware of their importance, may take advantage of the situation.*

**Nomination of a presidential candidate**

offset, in such cases, by the opposing party's platform, which often includes criticism of the men who hold office.

Both parties use basically the same system of nominating a presidential and vice-presidential candidate: roll call of the states, whereby delegates from certain states are called upon to give their nominating speeches, followed by balloting. One of the most dramatic moments is the oral vote; as each state is polled and one candidate is named again and again, the tension and excitement mount to fever pitch. An incumbent President seeking re-election is usually nominated by acclaim. For the last fifty years, the results of the presidential primaries, and the increased use of the media and opinion polls, have helped the party delegates in their choice: more than two-thirds of both parties' nominees have been given their party's pledge of support through nomination on the first ballot.

**Similarity and Conflict in Platform Pledges: Pledges of Designated Year or Topic** (in percentages)

| Year or Topic | (Number of Pledges) | One-Party Pledge Only | Bipartisan Pledges | Conflicting Pledges |
|---|---|---|---|---|
| *Election year* | | | | |
| 1944 | (102) | 70 | 28 | 2 |
| 1948 | (124) | 51 | 42 | 7 |
| 1952 | (205) | 52 | 29 | 19 |
| 1956 | (302) | 61 | 34 | 5 |
| 1960 | (464) | 51 | 39 | 10 |
| 1964 | (202) | 70 | 19 | 11 |
| *Policy topic* | | | | |
| Foreign | (216) | 47 | 47 | 6 |
| Defense | ( 84) | 65 | 33 | 2 |
| Economic | (177) | 62 | 22 | 16 |
| Labor | ( 84) | 42 | 33 | 25 |
| Agriculture | (150) | 56 | 33 | 11 |
| Resources | (185) | 63 | 26 | 11 |
| Welfare | (255) | 60 | 27 | 13 |
| Government | (136) | 76 | 24 | 0 |
| Civil rights | (113) | 40 | 60 | 0 |
| *All pledges* | (1,399) | 57 | 33 | 10 |
| No. Total | 1,399 | 799 | 464 | 136 |

Note: Rows add horizontally to 100% for the three columns.

Source: Gerald M. Pomper, *Elections in America* (New York: Dodd, Mead and Co., 1968), p. 193.

The man nominated for the President must have qualities to endear him to most of his party's members, as well as to inspire confidence in the electorate. The man most likely to be chosen to lead his party to victory is usually a nationally recognized politician—frequently he comes from a two-party state with a large electoral vote. He is even more attractive if he is known to have popular appeal and comes from a strategic geographic location. The timing of candidates' remarks and public appearances is an uncharted, but crucial, element; experiences in his life as a private citizen and as a politician also influence the way voters react to particular candidates.

Since early in the 1960s many United States senators have begun to aspire to the presidency (for example, John Kennedy, Lyndon Johnson, Barry Goldwater, Hubert Humphrey, and Richard Nixon were senators). Prior to that, most candidates had political careers as governors.[8] Senators have been increasingly successful in securing presidential nominations because they are thought to possess greater knowledge of foreign affairs than do governors, and because they tend to receive more attention from the national media.

[8] For example, both Theodore and Franklin Roosevelt were governors of New York in 1898 and 1928 respectively.

## Nomination of the vice-presidential candidate

The man picked to join the presidential nominee is usually from an area of the country different from that of the party's presidential choice. His views either balance, or modify, the positions taken by the candidate for Chief Executive. Sometimes this balance counteracts the candidate's religious background, especially if the presidential nominee's religion is thought to incur a negative reaction from certain voters.

The vice-presidential candidate is chosen by the presidential nominee, and although the position lacks both constitutional and political authority, the illnesses of Eisenhower and the assassination of Kennedy have dramatized the potential importance of the vice-presidential nominee. Most recent presidential candidates have, in fact, been concerned with nominating a Vice-President who has the qualifications to serve as President.

## The national convention: criticism and reform

[9] Barry Goldwater represents an important exception to the theory that conventions tend to choose middle-of-the-roaders. His strongly defined stands on important issues made him the choice of the Republican convention against the advice of political experts. Goldwater's conservative views alienated many liberal and moderate Republicans, and the Republicans suffered a disastrous loss at the polls in 1964.

Despite the uproar and confusion of events that lead to the final election of a President, there is an undercurrent of aim and purpose that inevitably and inexorably directs all the events to the choosing of a new Chief of State. The winning candidate at a nominating convention usually represents the broad middle of the party, someone who can unite the disparate wings of the party: he is not too liberal, not too conservative; liberal enough on civil rights to win the support of black voters, but not so liberal as to lose nonliberal sections of the population.[9]

Because the convention system has worked, it has been kept. Yet the years since the election of John F. Kennedy have been years of an increasing awareness of the fallacy inherent in assuming that a structure will work simply because it has for many years. Frustration arising from the seeming inflexibility of the "system" has given way to a heightened political activity and reform. The publicity of the battle on the streets of Chicago and on the convention floor defined, in a clearer fashion, the interests of the status quo, as they were countered by a rising tide of dissent within the Democratic party itself. Before the convention was concluded, the Democrats had made two important resolutions toward reform. The unit rule, whereby a delegation must vote as a unit rather than as individuals, was abolished. Further, a rule was passed that required that the delegates to the convention be selected during the convention year.

## Suggested reforms

President Woodrow Wilson, as early as 1913, proposed to allow for the direct nomination of presidential candidates by national primaries, which would let each voter choose from a field of candidates. This voting would eliminate the need for national conventions, and would open the nominations to direct control by the people.

The weaknesses in this type of reform, however, have prevented it from gaining much support. For one thing, the cost of a national primary would be exorbitant. Wealthy candidates would thus have an advantage over their less affluent colleagues. Second, the time allotted to the preprimary campaign would not be sufficient for an unknown—like McCarthy in 1968—to cultivate adequate support. Finally, it might require runoffs that would result in greater confusion for the voters, most of whom do not participate in primaries anyhow.

Although no reform suggested thus far has proven to be workable, it is important that we keep an open mind toward ideas that might improve on the current nominating procedures. The following standards may serve as criteria that can be used to consider the utility of a method used to nominate a man for office: the method of nomination should 1. aid in the continuance and preservation of the two-party system; 2. help engage vigorous competition between parties; 3. maintain a degree of unity within the parties; 4. result in the choice of a candidate who will be likely to win voter support; 5. produce intelligent, capable men as potential Presidents; and 6. lead to the acceptance by the public of the legitimacy of the chosen candidates.[10]

[10] Based on Polsby and Wildavsky, *Presidential Elections*, p. 229.

# Campaigning

The *campaign* for President and Vice-President, the process by which candidates seek popular support in open elections, is one of the world's most closely watched political events. With the aid of campaign managers, public relations experts, speech writers, devoted party members, endless energy, tireless smiles, and an insurmountable will, the party's nominees seek the right to govern the nation for a four-year term. The nominating convention occurs during the summer; the campaign trail and trial begins in September after Labor Day. Printers are busy manufacturing buttons, stickers, pamphlets, banners, posters, and meeting announcements; newspapers are receiving advertising copy from public relations men; campaign headquarters are preparing spot commercials to air on television, and so on. In short, the machine is slowly warming up for the first gear of speech making and banner waving.

The United States has the world's longest campaign trail; other countries limit theirs to six weeks (as in Italy) or three weeks (as in England and France in 1969).

[11] Costs from the 1950s are drawn from figures of the 1950s and early 1960s found in *Financing the 1964 Election* (Princeton, N.J.: Citizens' Research Herbert E. Alexander, Foundation, 1966), pp. 7 and 13.

## Campaign funding

The strategy of campaigning depends, to a great extent, on the amount of money the candidate has or can raise for his campaigning. The increased use of television—a medium much more expensive than newspapers, leaflets, or magazines—has made campaigning a costly affair. The national-level committees of the two major parties spent $17.2 million in 1956; by 1968, the cost had rocketed to almost $50 million. The campaign expenditures for the candidates at *all* levels of government during presidential election years have gone from $140 million in 1952, to $300 million in 1968.[11]

## Campaign Financing—1954, 1958, 1962, 1966 and 1970

### Committee Spending Reported Nationally

| | 1954 | 1958 | 1962 | 1966 | 1970 |
|---|---|---|---|---|---|
| *Republican committees* | 27 | 14 | 11 | 21 | 17 |
| Receipts | $ 5,380,994 | $4,686,423 | $ 4,674,570 | $ 7,640,760 | $11,754,305 |
| Expenditures | 5,509,649 | 4,657,652 | 4,637,586 | 7,863,092 | 12,702,215 |
| Percentage of total spending | 53.5% | 53.7% | 39.4% | 41.5% | 45.3% |
| *Democratic committees* | 13 | 7 | 8 | 8 | 19 |
| Receipts | 2,168,404 | 1,733,626 | 3,699,827 | 4,055,310 | 3,809,883 |
| Expenditures | 2,224,211 | 1,702,605 | 3,569,357 | 4,282,007 | 4,263,722 |
| Percentage of total spending | 21.6% | 19.6% | 30.3% | 22.5% | 15.2% |
| *Labor committees* | 41 | 32 | 33 | 42 | 54 |
| Receipts | 1,882,157 | 1,854,635 | 2,112,677 | 4,262,077 | 5,290,822 |
| Expenditures | 2,057,613 | 1,828,778 | 2,305,331 | 4,289,055 | 5,235,173 |
| Percentage of total spending | 20.0% | 21.1% | 19.6% | 22.7% | 18.7% |
| *Miscellaneous committees* | 15 | 11 | 26 | 44 | 98 |
| Receipts | 517,804 | 492,710 | 1,313,959 | 2,123,868 | 5,603,790 |
| Expenditures | 514,094 | 486,430 | 1,271,214 | 2,545,080 | 5,817,494 |
| Percentage of total spending | 5.0% | 5.6% | 10.8% | 13.3% | 20.8% |
| Totals | | | | | |
| Receipts | $ 9,949,359 | $8,767,394 | $11,801,033 | $18,082,015 | $26,458,800 |
| Expenditures | $10,305,567 | $8,675,465 | $11,783,488 | $18,979,234 | $28,018,604 |

Note: This table shows reported campaign spending included in reports to the Clerk of the House for the midterm campaigns since 1954. Numbers on the committee line indicate the number of groups reporting.

Source: "Political Spending," *Congressional Quarterly*, XXIX, no. 3 (July 23, 1971): 1572.

## Regulations governing party finance

The conflicting ideals of American life present themselves in full force when the problems of campaign-fund regulation are considered. The ideal is that people should have the opportunity to run for office regardless of their personal wealth and that wealth is wrongly used when it allows one person to obtain a wider audience than another. The desire to give everyone an equal chance at the prize, however, conflicts with the belief that a man should be allowed to spend as much money as he wishes to help himself get elected; it conflicts, too, with the notion that an individual should have complete freedom to support the candidate of his choice with as much money and help as he wishes.

Despite these objections to limiting individual funding, the government has seen fit to set legal limits on campaign funding. The first of these laws was passed in 1907, and was specifically intended to restrict federally-chartered corporations (for example, national banks) from donating money to any political campaign. By 1943, all labor unions and corporations were forbidden to contribute to national campaigns. Means did exist, however, for circumventing the law. Finally, in 1947, with the passage of the Taft-Hartley Act, all forms of corporation and union expenditures were forbidden.

In addition to setting limitations on campaign funding by large organizations, Congress has also attempted to regulate individual contributions. The *Hatch Act* of 1940 prohibits an individual from contributing more than $5,000 a year to a candidate or a nationally affiliated party committee. This limitation, however, becomes meaningless when one considers that there are unlimited numbers of private individuals who can spend money on behalf of a candidate. The ceiling on individual contributions may be $5,000, but a benefactor may contribute money in excess of that figure in the name of members of his family, or he may give $5,000 to any number of party and candidate committees.

The control of campaign funding is, therefore, an extremely complex issue because while national law prohibits contributions from certain large organizations, individuals and political organizations created by these organizations can contribute to a candidate's campaign. This practice has resulted in labor unions contributing hundreds of thousands of dollars to support their favored presidential candidate.

"Rockefeller must be pouring money into his campaign. I'm beginning to feel an urge to vote for him."

Drawing by Dana Fradon; © 1970
The New Yorker Magazine, Inc.

Campaign spending is also subject to regulation. The *Corrupt Practices Act* of 1925 limited a candidate for Congress to spending $2,500 for his campaign; a potential senator could spend no more than $10,000. Candidates who complained that they had a large electorate to reach and, therefore, had to spend more money in their campaigns could choose an alternative plan of spending three cents per vote cast for their seat in the last general election, but under no circumstances could a candidate for the House exceed spending more than $5,000. This plan allowed a candidate for the Senate to have a spending ceiling of $25,000. The 1940 *Hatch Act* limits a political committee to spending no more than $3 million.

There have been other efforts to keep track of expenditures and receipts of congressional and presidential candidates. Candidates for Congress and certain political committees have been required since 1910 to provide the clerk of the House of Representatives with statements of total expenditures and receipts. Listed must be all individuals who have contributed more than $100, and candidates who have received contributions of more than $10. These records become public information.

The reporting of such statements in the press is one method by which the public may be informed of the financial affairs of political aspirants; publication of campaign funding also lessens the possibility of fraud and deceptive practices. But public officials have felt that the Corrupt Practices Act is almost totally ineffective in accomplishing its goal. For example, although the reports are supposed to be filed prior to the election, candidates often wait until after the election, explaining their delayed report as the result of a clerical backlog.

The Corrupt Practices Act further invites glaring omissions in the required filing statement, because it states that only those expenses of which a candidate has personal knowledge must be itemized. (Seven senators announced that it cost them nothing to get elected in the 1968 campaign race.)[12]

[12] *The New York Times,* December 10, 1969.

The inadequacy of the Corrupt Practices Act is evidenced most in its lack of enforcement powers. Candidates who do not file a report or file incorrect information cannot be punished or fined for their "oversight."

States have similar laws to regulate campaign spending, laws that also are inadequate. In New York, for example, the law provides that no candidate spend more than the equivalent of ten cents of his personal money for every registered voter in his party. In 1970, this sum came to about $350,000 for the Democrats, an amount that their candidates were able to evade through borrowing or by establishing numerous campaign committees that individually contributed no more than $350,000 each. A New Yorker who ran unsuccessfully for the Senate, for example, filed reports stating that his campaign costs were $1.8 million, with more than $1.7 million borrowed from his mother.[13]

[13] "Money Talks for Well-Heeled Office-Seekers in 1970," *Congressional Quarterly,* August 14, 1970, pp. 2059–2060.

## Sources of money

Where money comes from is always a problem; presidential campaigns require large sums of money, but the number of people able and willing to contribute to political activities is relatively small. In 1964, only 10 percent of the population contributed, and in 1968, the number rose only slightly to 11 percent.

Wealthy individuals who make large contributions have generally favored the Republican party more than the Democratic. A 1968 study of the political contributions of executives in the top twenty-five defense, space, and nuclear industries revealed that they contributed at least $1,235,402 to political campaigns during the 1968 presidential election, and that the contractors' officers favored the Republicans over the Democrats by an almost six-to-one margin. These contractors have maintained their allegiance to the Republicans, despite eight consecutive years of Democratic rule.[14]

[14] "Contractors' Officers Favor GOP 6–1 in Contributions," *Congressional Quarterly*, September 18, 1970, pp. 2290–2294.

The Democratic party, however, has traditionally received large contributions from labor organizations. In 1964, close to $4 million was spent by these groups. The Political Action Committee of the AFL-CIO circumvented laws by spending vast sums to increase voter registration. In 1968, labor contributions increased to almost $6 million, with the money used in preconvention campaigning first for Lyndon Johnson, and then for Hubert Humphrey, who opposed Senators Robert Kennedy and Eugene McCarthy for the Democratic nomination.

A significant source of funds comes from the annual Jackson Day dinner of the Democratic party and the Lincoln Day dinner of the Republican party, and from a steady stream of cocktail parties—functions designed to help the candidates build up the party treasury. Wealthy candidates are an obvious advantage to a political party, because they are able to handle a significant amount of the campaign expenses.

## Reforms in campaign spending

Congress attempted to provide fair means of financing campaigns through legislation passed in 1966. The intention was to raise large sums of money through voluntary provisions in income taxes, the total of which would be equitably distributed to each party. The law, however, was repealed a year later, and the controversial nature of the problem continues to make a solution acceptable to all political parties and congressmen impossible. Although public officials have expended a great deal of time and energy discussing the issue recently, campaign-spending practices have not changed significantly. Other reforms are, however, currently under consideration. Democratic Senator George McGovern, a candidate for the 1972 presidential nomination of his party, proposed reshaping the 1972 national campaign by shifting the major burden of financial support from private contributors to the United States Treasury (in the presidential and congressional elections). McGovern's suggestion is to limit private contributions to $50 in any one contest, with federal funds paying $18 million for presidential candidates' expenses, $3.5 million for Senate candidates, and $125,000 for House candidates.[15]

[15] *The New York Times*, December 10, 1969.

Another reform was suggested in 1970, when Congress voted to limit television and radio spending by presidential and congressional candidates.

[16] Senate Votes to Limit TV-Radio Campaign Spending," *Congressional Quarterly*, April 17, 1970, pp. 999–1000.

[17] "Radio-TV Spending," *Congressional Quarterly*, October 2, 1970, p. 2406.

This legislation, vetoed by President Nixon,[16] was designed to reduce the candidate's dependence on a relatively few wealthy contributors, because, as Senator John Pastore remarked during Senate debate: "The idea of the magic of television and radio and newspapers and all the other paraphernalia that money can buy in an election, I am afraid, is going to destroy the very roots of the democratic process."[17]

"They say to get elected to public office in America one must be rich. Well, my friends, *I'm* rich. I'm *very* rich."

Drawing by Dana Fradon; © 1970 The New Yorker Magazine, Inc.

Despite the long history of proposals and commissions—from President Theodore Roosevelt's suggestion, in 1907, that the national government subsidize political campaigns, through President John Kennedy's appointment of a bipartisan commission to make recommendations concerning the financial affairs of presidential elections—the tax check-off plan that passed, and was then repealed by Congress in 1967, has been the only concrete effort made to reform campaign funding and spending. Regulations are important, not because of the great expense of a campaign, but because of the unbalanced influence of wealthy candidates and contributors. Only with the regulation of campaign spending will men of moderate means be able to run for office and compete effectively.

# Campaign strategy

[18] "Campaign Management: Expertise Brings Dollars," *Congressional Quarterly*, May 1, 1970, p. 2406.

[19] Robert MacNeil, *The People Machine* (New York: Harper and Row Publishers, Inc., 1968), p. 327.

In the early days of American politics, it was not uncommon for local candidates to know their constituents personally. Politics is much less personal today, even at the local level. The candidate today makes plans, much as a general maps out his battleground, months before the actual battle begins. One study notes that a wealthy candidate might enlist the services of a professional consultant (at $500 a day), a computer firm, a pollster, an advertising agency, a film-maker, a speech-writer, a television and radio time-buyer, a direct mail organization, and even an accounting firm.[18] The traditional campaign manager and advance man of the past (who planned the entire campaign and gathered voters to listen to a candidate's speech) are now assisted by the contemporary political consultant, who provides public opinion surveys, electronic data processing, fund-raising, budgeting, media research, public relations and press services, advertising, and volunteer recruitment. The practice of image making that these consulting firms engage in has provoked both humorous comment and serious complaint. According to television commentator Robert MacNeil, "Sooner or later a major office is going to be filled by some computer-primed and wealthy nonentity put over by (television) commercials as a national savior."[19]

*Dan Nimmo*, The Political Persuaders: The Techniques of Modern Election Campaigns (*Englewood Cliffs, N.J.: Prentice-Hall, Inc., 1970*), *pp. 52–56.*

Dan Nimmo, in discussing how the campaign manager plots his strategies, begins with the most fundamental decision made by the manager and client: how much authority will the professionals exercise in running the campaign? In recent years, as public image has become an increasingly important factor in elections, managers have come to hold increasingly prominent roles as policy-makers and chiefs of staff. The candidate may be the "star," writes Nimmo, but the manager "runs the show."

The manager must make three big preliminary decisions: the attack, the theme, and the pace of the campaign.

In the attack, the candidate seizes the initiative to avoid being on the defensive. A classic example—the Republican attack of 1952 designed by Robert Humphreys and an advertising firm—aimed first at keeping for Eisenhower the votes of the twenty million conservative Republicans who had favored the nomination of Senator Robert Taft, and secondly, at acquiring the "normal stay-at-home vote." The stay-at-home vote could be roused only if people thought there was something to vote against. Thus the managers drummed up the theme "Crime, Communism and Korea"; the stay-at-homes unequivocally opposed all three and came out to vote against them. Hubert Humphrey's 1968 campaign, on the other hand, suffered from having no attack at all until the eve of his nomination.

As the Eisenhower campaign shows, the campaign theme is directly related to the attack.

The purpose of the campaign theme is to simplify complex public issues into brief, clear, recognizable statements to the advantage of the candidate. The theme should run through all rallies, television performances, brochures, billboard ads, publicity releases, and other forms of communicating with the electorate.

John Kennedy's theme, "Get America Moving Again," was geared to Americans' dissatisfaction with the complacency of the Eisenhower years; Kennedy "spontaneously" injected it into informal speeches. The theme's success contrasts with the effect of Barry Goldwater's theme "In Your Heart You Know He's Right." Critics seized upon the word "Right" and stressed Goldwater's extremism. Again, Humphrey's poor management hurt him in the case of a theme: he waited until a month before the 1968 election to choose "Trust," demanding whether the voters wanted to trust their futures to Nixon or Wallace.

The last major decision is campaign pace. Planning, organizing, researching, fund raising, and buying of media time should all begin early. The manager must consider "when to schedule rallies, when to appear on television, when to devote the maximum money and effort (peaking) and so forth." In addition, the candidate's announcement, or his "surfacing," must be paced along with these other phases, but since a candidate "surfaces" to acquire additional support that he cannot muster when operating covertly, his manager's hands become somewhat tied after the announcement:

The timing of the announcement of candidacy, the accumulation of momentum, and the closing blitz frequently depend on the personnel and finances available.

[20] Warren E. Miller, "The Political Behavior of the Electorate," in E. Latham, ed., *American Government Annual, 1960–1961* (New York: Holt, Rinehart and Winston, Inc., 1960), pp. 40–61.

[21] Polsby and Wildavsky, *Presidential Elections*, chap. 3, presents a detailed description of the campaign strategies of both parties in the 1960 national elections.

Because the two major parties face different problems with the electorate, their respective candidates are likely to adopt different strategies. Seventy percent of the adults in America feel that they belong to a party; although the Democrats enjoy a three-to-two advantage in registration, they have less financial strength and do not get the vote out as well as Republicans.[20] The strategy that the Democrats have had to adopt is that of stressing party unity and voter turnout. The Republicans, on the other hand, are the minority party and, therefore, must rally voters behind a specific personality; they have to attract the uncommitted voter by soft-pedalling partisan association and asking the voters to look at the man rather than at the party.[21] During the 1952 campaign, for example, Eisenhower was represented as the war hero, the man above party; Stevenson, on the other hand, attempted to use his standing as a Democrat to appeal to the voters.

*John W. Kingdon, "Politicians' Beliefs About Voters,"* American Political Science Review, *61 (1967): 137–145.*

Political scientists have frequently examined the factors that shape the voters' image of a candidate; in his study, John Kingdon takes the opposite approach, delving into the politician's view of the voters. Beginning with political scientist Lewis Dexter's assumption that an elected official does not actually represent his district, but rather his *image* of the district and its constituents, Kingdon considers the degree of voter interest office-seekers perceive and how informed they feel their electorate is. The candidate's beliefs on these matters could affect, among other things, his policy stands, roll call votes, and, most significantly, his campaign strategies and their eventual success or failure.

The data in the case of voter interest is clouded by the candidates' subjectivity. Winners tend to believe that voters are somewhat interested in their campaigns, while losers either feel that voters are apathetic or that they are very concerned. Moreover, most of those losers who attest to strong voter interest have never held any public elective office.

On the question of whether voters are informed, Kingdon found that while 26 percent of the winners classed their electorate as "very informed," only 3 percent of the losers did so—70 percent, in fact, considered the voters poorly informed. Beyond the politicians' rationalizations for victory or defeat, Kingdon suggests that traditional wisdom holds that voters are informed and vote on issues—therefore, winners may feel obliged to espouse this "correct" opinion while losers are free to challenge it. In addition, incumbent winners may have greater contact with people who are informed and involved with government; thus, they may generalize about voters on the basis of this biased sample. The winner chooses his reality, the loser may admit to a different one.

Kingdon's study was conducted after an election; he stresses that results would probably be different if the data had been collected beforehand.

One might perhaps expect that the potential winners' and losers' beliefs about voters would be similar with the congratulation and especially the rationalization occurring after election day. Or one might expect that the potential winners would have a higher estimate of voter political involvement than potential losers because both are anticipating the outcome to some extent.

But the idea that winners succeed in elections because they have a more accurate conception of voter beliefs than losers is tenuous. It may be that campaigns rely on other factors entirely, such as timing, the media, and party activists. The findings do imply, however, that an official's successful election may lead him to believe that his constituents watch his actions closely, that issues are important to them and that they are well-informed. Thus, the incumbent may be attentive to his constituents and subject to their influence. He may come to anticipate their reactions, and, because of his positive image of their interest and issue-orientation, he may be a more responsive legislator.

## Appeal

The candidate has to master his own personal shortcomings, or invent images to change his public impression. The Yankee seriousness of Calvin Coolidge was capitalized upon by his campaign managers, who emphasized the slogan, "Keep Cool with Coolidge" in the 1924 campaign. Franklin Roosevelt was presented to the voters as a benevolent father in the 1936 campaign, to counter his opposition's picture of him as a tyrant. The Eisenhower campaign of 1952 was victorious because "Ike" was a hero-father who promised to be as capable a President as he was a general. John F. Kennedy's problem was age. Only forty-three, he had to answer to the charge that he was too immature to serve as President; his campaign showed him to be an inspiration to youth and a challenge to inertia. Richard Nixon's 1968 strategy combated a different yet serious problem. Using a tone of moderation in his speeches, he sought to offset his former negative image of a skilled and partisan politician.[22]

Despite their slogans and images, presidential campaigners do not attempt to woo the entire voting population. Instead, they do most of their campaign-stumping in a selected few states that have large populations and thus many electoral votes. The object of the candidate is to win the states that will give him 270 or more electoral votes. If all or most of the large states are carried by the nominee, he is well on his way toward winning the election.

The issues that the candidate discusses in his personal appearances vary with the group he is speaking to. A speech usually professes attitudes that appeal to the specific group addressed. The voters of Maine are interested in different topics from those in Nebraska, and city dwellers have different problems from those in rural areas—the candidate must prepare a speech for each major group, being careful not to please any one group at the expense of another.

The increasing number of speeches that is published or aired nationally, however, requires a different approach from the candidate. He cannot alter or reverse his views from one television appearance to another. The

[22] See Joe McGinniss, *The Selling of the President* (New York: Trident Press, 1968).

issues are usually national in scope and of concern to most Americans; and his opinions must not offend any potential voter.

How does a candidate approach the opposition? Does he take the offensive, as did Truman in 1948, Kennedy in 1960, and Johnson in 1964, or does he play it safe, and project the image of a unifier and statesman, as did Eisenhower in 1952 and 1956, and Nixon in 1968?

## Relating to the opposition

*Alan L. Clem*, Spirit Mound Township in 1960 Election, *Government Research Bureau Report no. 44* (*Vermillion, S. Dak.: State University of South Dakota, 1961*).

Alan Clem, in his study of rural reactions to campaigns, used a sample of 135 registered voters from Spirit Mound Township, located in the southeast section of South Dakota. The area was selected because it is distinctly rural (most of the residents are farmers), yet accessible to communications media. In addition, the voting records of its inhabitants are considered typical of the nation, since they supported six Democratic presidential candidates between 1932 and 1960; between 1930 and 1960, they supported Democratic and Republican gubernatorial candidates an equal number of times.

In the part of his study concerned with the media, Clem asked the question, "Toward which campaign media are the voters most favorably disposed?" He found that the percentage of respondents noticing various campaign media was as follows:

| Media | Percentage Noticing Media |
|---|---|
| Newspaper articles | 73 |
| Television news | 70 |
| Radio news | 66 |
| Television advertising | 64 |
| Direct mail | 58 |
| Radio advertising | 53 |
| Newspaper advertising | 51 |
| Bumper stickers | 51 |
| Billboards, posters | 44 |
| Personal contacts by workers | 30 |

The data reveal that newspapers, television and radio were noticed most often—and significantly, in each case, the news reports receive more attention than political advertising. Direct mail, highway billboards and bumper stickers were noticed less often and personal contact by campaign workers was noted only by 30 percent of those questioned. The study found that Republicans are more likely to be aware of printed material, while Democrats notice radio news and television advertising. Generally, women were found to pay more attention to campaign appeals than men, but men have more contact with campaign workers.

When respondents were asked whether they reacted favorably or unfavorably to the media, the highest praise went to news reports in newspapers, and on radio and television. Republicans, however, were "unfavorably disposed" toward radio and television. Personal contact, when it occurred, frequently met with approval. Advertising in all media received a lukewarm reception, and direct mail, bumper stickers and highway billboards and posters inspired even less enthusiasm.

Clem contends that these data are significant to campaign strategy, since they show that the media that voters most respond to are those that candidates can least control.

The difficulty that the practical politician will find with these facts is that he can do little about the media that seem to be most important. The candidate, assuming he has plenty of money at his disposal, can order virtually all the newspaper space and radio and television time and bumper stickers and billboards and pamphlets that he wants, and he can hire workers to personally canvass his constituency. But few, if any, candidates can order the newspapers or radio or television stations to insert plugs for him in their news reports. The candidate can control the advertising, but he cannot control the news.

Some old-guard politicians advise the candidate to emphasize the difference, if one exists, between the opponent's views and those held by the majority of his party. Johnson in 1964 tried to show that there was a difference between the good, liberal Republican and the bad, conservative Goldwater. Others attempt to attribute elitism and other evils to the opposition, while claiming that they represent the people's choice. The 1968 campaign conducted by both major parties tried to suggest that evil factions were at work behind the scenes in the opposition: Nixon hinted at subversive elements in the Democratic party; Humphrey claimed business monopolies controlled the Republicans and brought repeated attention to the lack of concern for labor, minorities, and other special interest groups that the Republicans are reputed to ignore. Nixon appealed to middle America, and raised the specter of the "welfare state" that supposedly encourages people to loaf and have no incentive to progress, while Humphrey concentrated on the liberality of the Civil Rights Acts, emphasizing urban problems and the successful resolutions of racial, social, and economic inequality, the standard banner of the Democratic spokesmen.

## Timing

Armed with the consultant's public opinion survey, along with the latest Gallup, Roper, and Harris polls, accompanied by the advice of managers who have primed areas for a candidate's arrival, the presidential hopeful embarks on a physically exhausting campaign trail that may lead him to the White House.

Where should he visit? How long should he stay in each area? If he is an incumbent, when and what should he do to impress the people? Timing is still a mysterious variable, and is crucial in the general swing of the campaign. Eisenhower's visit to Korea in 1952 was an example of perfect timing in a political campaign. His arrival in a war zone demonstrated his concern for the national welfare and our commitment to "contain communism" in Asia, and strategically reinforced his image of father-general-protector. The energy of the campaign comes from skilled maneuvers like this one, and slowly builds in momentum until it reaches a peak in the final weeks and days before election. The party that concludes its campaign with a dynamic message or gesture may swing the undecided voters into its camp and win the election.

## Campaign organizations

Many organizations participate in the procedures of the presidential campaign, and most of their activities are coordinated by professional consultants. Each candidate has a full-time party organization, a cadre of personal attendants, and at the local level, temporary subsidiary organizations. Occasionally, there may be disaffection in the ranks of an organization, and a local group may give its support to the opposite candidate.

## Congressional strategy

The techniques of the congressional campaign are usually very similar to that of the campaign for the President: major decisions concerning organization, advertising, timing, polls, consultants, and interest groups are as characteristic of the campaigns run by congressmen, and especially senators, as they are of a presidential campaign. The major difference is that the congressional issues are more likely to be state and local interests, rather than those of general concern to the nation. The candidates' appeals are made to a much smaller segment of the nation's population, and often (especially in the case of representatives) the candidates face an audience of people whose socioeconomic grouping is more unified than the widely divergent groups that a presidential candidate has to face.

The 435 seats in the House of Representatives, as well as a third of the Senate seats, are up for election every two years. Campaigns for these seats are more or less directed by the past political affiliation of the specific district: if a district is so strongly one-party in sentiment that re-election is certain, an exhaustive and expensive campaign need not be waged. Furthermore, a campaign for a Senate seat, in particular, if held during a presidential election year, needs a set of strategies that are clearly different from those of a nonelection year. Depending on the position of the nominee for Congress, and his relationship to the presidential nominee's stance on key issues, the senatorial hopeful must decide whether or not to attach himself to

The campaign of a candidate for Congress usually parallels that of a presidential candidate.

the presidential candidate's coat tails—that is, he must determine whether the presidential candidate will be an asset or a liability in his state. If the presidential candidate is an incumbent, the senatorial candidate usually swings with him. If the presidential candidate is a nonincumbent, the senatorial candidate must decide how strong the candidate is and determine how he must run his own campaign.

## What do campaigns achieve?

23 Paul F. Lazarsfeld, Bernard Berelson, and Hazel Gaudet, *The People's Choice: How The Voter Makes Up His Mind in a Presidential Campaign* (New York: Columbia University Press, 1968), p. 53.

Most studies show that up to two-thirds of the voters during a presidential contest make up their minds in the early part of the campaign. Moreover, opinion surveys indicate that approximately one-tenth of the people decide on their candidate in the final two weeks before the elections.[23] It seems that all the campaign strategies and tactics, the entire network from personal consultant and cadre of devotees, down to the volunteer housewife stuffing envelopes at the hometown headquarters, accomplishes very little in the way of changing voters' minds. The campaign is, however, a successful means of maintaining political involvement and bringing out the vote in November.

"I was packaged by Candidates Limited. Who packaged you?"

Drawing by Hendelsman; © 1970
The New Yorker Magazine, Inc.

"Spread out, pound on every door, yell 'Smith for Congress! Power to the people!' Then barge in, tell 'em Smith is groovy, ask for a handout, and leave."

Drawing by Stevenson; © 1970
The New Yorker Magazine, Inc.

People will continue to debate about the efficacy of campaigns, but they are a solidly entrenched part of American political tradition. As long as elections are fought, political hopefuls will present their platforms, avoid certain issues, shake countless hands, attack the opposition, appeal to reason, stump and barnstorm across the country, exhaust their physical and mental energies meeting "the people." A new professionalism, as we have noted earlier, has changed the nature of the campaign; it has become more mechanized and more streamlined, and perhaps because of this, a bit less frustrating, but also just a bit less fun.

# Elections

The election of the President, Vice-President, and most other state and local officials occurs on one legally designated day—the first Tuesday after the first Monday in November. In this section we will consider the events of that day, including the types of ballots used, and the electoral college, which is constitutionally empowered to select the President and Vice-President of the United States.

## Balloting

The basic model for the American election system since the end of the nineteenth century has been the "secret" ballot developed in Australia in 1857. Under this system, the government is responsible for printing the ballots that list all the candidates' names, and for providing officials to distribute them at specified polling stations on election day. A policeman is usually on duty at the polls to guard against tampering with the election procedures. Traditionally, paper ballots were employed; the voter marked the ballot and folded and placed it in a ballot box. Today, however, in most urban areas voting machines record the voter's choice, which is made by the turn of a lever.

*The Massachusetts block ballot lists candidates according to the office for which they are running.*

*The Indiana party-column ballot lists the candidates by party.*

There are two main methods of organizing the ballot, and the method selected may have a direct effect on the outcome of the elections. The *office-block,* or *Massachusetts-type ballot* lists all prospective candidates, according to the governmental office for which they are running. For example, one block lists all candidates for the United States Senate, a second all candidates for governor, and so on until the least important local office is reached. This ballot encourages split-ticket and independent voting. One of the negative factors in this ballot is that the voter gets tired and often ignores the blocks of candidates appearing toward the bottom of the list.

The *party-column,* or *Indiana-type ballot* places prospective candidates for all offices together in a column according to their party. The voter can vote a straight ticket by marking the circle or box next to the party's name and

## The long ballot and the short ballot

24 See D. S. Hecock and H. M. Bain, Jr., *The Arrangement of Names on the Ballot and It's Effect on the Voter's Choice* (Detroit: Wayne State University Press, 1956).

25 *Current*, 104 (February 1969): pp. 33–40.

insignia or by pulling the lever at the top of the column. Or he can move across or down the columns, selecting candidates from different parties for their respective offices. This ballot encourages straight party voting and tends to discourage consideration of individual merits for each office.[24]

The *long ballot*, which is used in most states, is one in which the voter is required to choose the best candidates for President, Vice-President, United States senator and congressman, and local officials, including judges, commissioners, and executive department heads. A study by the nonpartisan Committee of Economic Development has suggested that elections be confined to a much smaller number of individuals at the state and local levels, running for office in a policy-making body, and having a single Chief Executive in each governmental unit—for long ballots are likely to baffle even the intelligent and seasoned voter.[25]

Most experts are urging the creation of a *short ballot*, which would limit the list to candidates for offices concerned with broad policy decisions. State and local office elections, such as those for state attorney general, would be eliminated. Most state and local election officials, however, have resisted this modification of the full slate of candidates. They fear the too strong dependence on the popularity of their party's national candidates.

The presidential short ballot, which has also been suggested in several states, would carry only the names of the presidential and vice-presidential candidates. By voting for a particular candidate, the voter would also be selecting the electors pledged to him.

## The electoral college

Article II of the Constitution, as modified by the Twelfth Amendment, provides for the final selection of the President and Vice-President by an electoral college that is theoretically controlled by the state legislatures. Thus, presidential elections are won by obtaining a majority of the electoral votes cast by the electoral college. The winning candidate must receive a majority or 270 votes; he can get this number by capturing the majority vote of any combination of states that produces this total. Because of the winner-take-all rule, obtaining the largest number of popular votes in a state captures the entire electoral vote from that state.

The electoral college system, established by the Founding Fathers in 1787, was a compromise between those who desired direct popular elections and those who feared the decision-making abilities of the "uninformed masses." The direct vote for electors would allow for popular expression of opinion, but the college—composed of educated legislatures—was supposed to correct any mistaken judgments.

The size of each state's electoral delegation is determined by the number of senators and congressmen the state has in Congress. The members of the college are chosen every four years, as determined in the state legislatures;

they vote separately for President and Vice-President. The electors actually meet in each state capitol on the first Monday after the second Wednesday in December following the election, to formally cast their states' electoral vote for the new President. The results are forwarded to the president of the Senate, and at a joint session of the two houses of Congress the votes are officially counted and the President and Vice-President actually chosen. According to the Twelfth Amendment, the person with the most votes on the presidential ballot (if that number is a majority of electors) becomes President, and the person with the most votes on a separate ballot becomes the Vice-President. (Originally, only one ballot was used: the person with the most votes became President, and the person in second place was named Vice-President.)

*Each state's electors meet within their state to vote for the President of the United States.*

If no person receives a majority for President, the decision is forwarded to the House of Representatives, which chooses from one of the three highest men on the list of electoral college votes. The vote is by state, each having one vote. In this deadlock situation, a majority of all the states is necessary for election of the President. Similarly, in case of tie for Vice-President, the Senate, by a majority vote, selects one of the two candidates having the most electoral votes.

## Defects of the electoral college

There are many people who would like to revise the present system of electoral voting, and others who would even like to abolish it.

"See, doctor! . . . even *you* hate me!"

Drawing by Darcy; © 1968 *Newsday*.

The electoral college can potentially produce results that seem to many to be out of character with a democratic society. The elections of 1876 (Hayes versus Tilden) and 1888 (Harrison versus Cleveland) have shown that it is possible for the victor to receive more electoral votes even though he has received fewer popular votes than his opponent. Both Tilden and Cleveland received a higher popular vote, but lost the election: Tilden by only one electoral vote, and Cleveland by a more substantial 65 electoral votes.

Another major weakness is the original problem first seen in the Jefferson-Burr election of 1800: the necessity of using the House of Representatives to decide on the winner of the election, in case the candidates fall short of the required 270 majority of electoral votes. This is of special concern during years when a third party has gained national prominence, for a House vote would give the third-party candidate the power to influence the outcome of the vote. He could bargain with each of the major party candidates, since both would be seeking to swing the election with the votes of states originally committed to the third party. Nevertheless, since the adoption of the Twelfth Amendment in 1804, the House has only once decided on the election of a President—in the election of 1824.

Congress's current emphasis on change extends to the reformation of the electoral college; proposals range from modification (Senator Bayh of Indiana) to fundamental change of the college (Senator Curtis of Nebraska).[26]

[26] "Senate Faces Early Decision on Electoral Reform," *Congressional Quarterly*, April 17, 1970, pp. 1025–1031.

## Proposed reforms

*President Richard Nixon, Special Message to Congress, February 20, 1969.*

On February 20, 1969, President Nixon addressed Congress on the topic of electoral college reform. Previously, he had suggested that the President be chosen directly by popular majority; he reaffirmed his support of this plan, but at the same time noted the likelihood that some form of the electoral college system would be kept as it is "deeply rooted in American history and federalism." Taking a pragmatic point of view, he suggested reforms that he believed could be accepted by Congress and the states.

The President stated:

I will support any plan that moves toward the following objectives: First, the abolition of individual electors; second, allocation to Presidential candidates of the electoral vote of each state and the District of Columbia in a manner that may more closely approximate the popular vote than does the present system; third, making a 40 per cent electoral vote plurality sufficient to choose a President.

The proportional plan, whereby a state's electoral votes would be divided in proportion to the popular vote, would meet these stipulations, but the President stressed that he was not bound exclusively to any one proposal.

Several specific points of reform were brought out in the address. Nixon called for a runoff election between the top two candidates in the event that no presidential slate received 40 percent or more of the electoral vote. Under this system, proposed by the American Bar Association, the runoff would select the President by popular majority.

Nixon proposed also that if the President-elect dies before the electoral votes are counted, the Vice-President-elect should become President. If the Vice-President-elect dies before taking office, the President must appoint a Vice-President upon taking office, according to the provisions stated in the Twenty-fifth Amendment. Should both the President and Vice-President die or become disabled during their term of office, Congress must fill the vacancies by "a new election or some other means."

Finally, President Nixon appealed to Congress to "clarify the situation" presented by the death of a presidential or vice-presidential candidate before the November election.

There are six basic plans for altering the system of electing the President and Vice-President:

1. The *District Plan* retains the elector and gives his vote to the candidate with a plurality in each congressional district. An additional two electoral votes are given to the candidate with statewide plurality, and whoever receives the majority of electoral votes becomes President.

2. The *Proportional Method* abolishes the electoral college but retains the electoral vote. Candidates receive shares of the state's electoral vote based upon how well they did in the state (for example, 60 percent of the popular vote would yield 60 percent of the electoral vote).

3. The *Federal System Plan* makes a candidate the President if he receives a majority of the popular vote. However, according to this plan, the candidate's popular vote must include either (a) pluralities in more than half the states, including the District of Columbia, or (b) pluralities in states with 50 percent of the voters in the election. The electoral college—which would be retained, with the number of electors equal to the number of senators and congressmen from each state—would only be called upon to decide the issue if no such plurality was achieved. If no candidate received a majority of the electoral vote, the third-party candidate's electoral votes would be divided between the two leading national candidates proportionate to their share of the popular votes in those states.

4. The *Ervin Proposal* (Senator Samuel Ervin, Jr.'s plan) eliminates the elector, but keeps the electoral votes. The winner of a state's popular vote automatically receives all its electoral vote, and both houses of Congress choose the next President, each member having one vote in the process.

5. The *American Bar Association Plan* allows for the direct election of the President and Vice-President. Proposed in the form of a constitutional amendment, it requires a runoff election between the two leading candidates, if neither receives at least 40 percent of the popular vote.

6. *Direct election* abolishes the electoral college, and provides that the President be the candidate with the popular vote plurality.

Change in the electoral college system has so far been blocked, because public officials and the nation cannot agree on what should replace it. Each of the major plans has its supporters and opponents. Any change would alter political power in the presidential elections.

The electoral college, however, is useful, because it maintains a balance between the rural areas and small states, which tend to be overrepresented

## Interpreting elections

27 Angus Campbell, Philip E. Converse, Warren E. Miller, and Donald E. Stokes, *The American Voter* (New York: John Wiley and Sons, Inc., 1964), pp. 274–279 and Pomper, *Elections in America*, p. 104.

## Why do we have elections?

in Congress and the highly populated and urban-centered two-party states, which have a greater voice in presidential elections.

Political scientists are, of course, eager to interpret elections. Depending on the control of power, the election can be classified in one of five ways: 1. *maintaining*, in which the victory occurs when the majority party (Democratic) is re-elected, as occurred in 1944 and 1964; 2. *deviating*, when the majority party loses, as in the election of 1968; 3. *realigning*, in which a significant internal change in the majority party causes it to lose control, as in 1952; 4. *converting*, when the majority party suffers internal change and a shifting of support, yet still manages to maintain its dominating position, as in 1896.[27]

Elections are, in part, devices to safeguard against the wanton use of power by public officials. They are an effort to give the ordinary man a share in the government that exists to act in his name. The vote does not always keep unscrupulous people from reaching positions of authority, nor always check the unwise use of power, nor does it always arouse much enthusiasm in the population itself. Elections, however, remain as a means of changing officials peacefully and keeping government responsible to the people.

### Pre-election Poll of Voter Preference in 1968

|  | Humphrey | Nixon | Wallace | Not Sure |
|---|---|---|---|---|
| Nation-wide | 35% | 40% | 18% | 7% |
| *By region* | | | | |
| East | 38 | 40 | 12 | 10 |
| Midwest | 35 | 43 | 16 | 6 |
| South | 29 | 30 | 35 | 6 |
| West | 37 | 47 | 10 | 6 |
| *By education* | | | | |
| 8th grade or less | 44 | 26 | 19 | 11 |
| High school | 36 | 37 | 20 | 7 |
| College | 29 | 53 | 14 | 4 |
| *By age* | | | | |
| Under 35 | 35 | 41 | 20 | 4 |
| 35–49 | 34 | 42 | 18 | 6 |
| 50 and over | 37 | 37 | 16 | 10 |
| *By size of place* | | | | |
| Cities | 46 | 33 | 14 | 7 |
| Suburbs | 35 | 43 | 13 | 9 |
| Towns | 28 | 45 | 21 | 6 |
| Rural | 31 | 37 | 26 | 6 |

Note the similarity of this data to the final results of the election.

Source: Louis Harris Associates, 1968.

Our election system encourages debate and division, and provides a guard against extremism, while giving the nation a maximum of stability. It is the reason that democracy, despite its tolerance for error and corruption, has survived.

■

# Glossary

**"at-large" delegates**   Delegates to the national convention who are chosen on a statewide basis.

**blanket primary**   Election in which a voter may vote for either party's candidates for local, state, and national offices.

**campaign**   Process whereby political candidates seek election to specific government office.

**caucus**   Closed session held by a few party members to choose party candidates or determine party policy; originally the method of selecting the party's presidential candidate.

**closed primary**   Election in which only registered party affiliates may vote for the party's candidates for local, state, and national offices.

**convention system**   Method of nominating a party's candidates for state or national office, where appointed or elected delegates to the convention, rather than the voters as a whole, choose the candidates.

**converting election**   Election in which majority party undergoes internal change, and a shifting of support, but maintains its dominating position.

**Corrupt Practices Act (1925)**   Legislation limiting the amount congressional candidates can spend in election campaigns.

**deviating election**   Election in which the party previously out of office is returned to power.

**district delegates**   Delegates to the national convention who are chosen from a congressional district rather than from the state at large.

**electoral college**   The constitutional system of indirect presidential election whereby the voters of a state vote for electors, who in turn vote for President, normally casting their ballots as a unit for the candidate who received the majority of the state's popular votes.

**Hatch Act (1940)**   Legislation limiting the amount individuals and political committees can contribute to their candidate's campaign for election.

**Indiana-type or party-column ballot**   Type of ballot used in general elections in which candidates are grouped according to party affiliation.

**long ballot**   Usual type of ballot, which lists all candidates, including, in a presidential election, all electors.

**maintaining election**   Election in which the party in power is returned to power.

**Massachusetts-type or office-block ballot**   Type of ballot used in general elections in which candidates are grouped according to the offices for which they are running.

**national convention**   National party meeting held every four years at which elected or appointed delegates nominate candidates for President and Vice-President and draw up a platform to convey their party's views.

**nonpartisan primary**   Election in which the candidates for nominations to local or state office are not listed as being affiliated with any particular party.

**open primary**   Election in which a voter may choose a party's candidates for local, state, and national offices without having publicly stated an affiliation with a party.

**party platform**   Political party's statement of general principles, adopted at the party's national convention.

**periodic registration**   System of voter certification that requires a voter to appear before election officials, after a specified period of time has elapsed, to maintain his status of voter eligibility.

**permanent registration**   System in which a voter appears before election officials only once, and is listed as eligible for as long as he continues to vote and does not change his party or address.

**presidential preferential primary**   State election in which voters choose delegates to a party's national convention to nominate the President.

**presidential short ballot**   Ballot sometimes used in presidential elections, carrying names of candidates only, not electors.

**primary**   Election in which qualified voters nominate or express a preference for a candidate for local, state, or national office, or select delegates who will nominate such a candidate.

**realigning election**   Election in which the party in power falls out of power because a significant number of voters change their party affiliation.

**registration**   The procedure whereby a prospective voter appears before election officials who certify him as an eligible voter.

**runoff primary**   A second election in which the two top candidates for a party's nomination for local, state, or national office face each other, after having both failed to win a majority of votes in the first election.

**short ballot**   Type of ballot, proposed by some states, which would limit the list to candidates for offices concerned with broad policy decisions.

# Suggested readings

David, Ralph T., Ralph M. Goldman, and Richard C. Bain, *Politics of National Party Conventions*, rev. ed. (Washington, D.C.: The Brookings Institution, 1960). Analysis of the presidential-nominating process, including state primaries, party conventions, and candidates.

Felknor, Bruce L., *Dirty Politics* (New York: W. W. Norton and Co., Inc., 1966). Analysis of campaign techniques, the state of modern campaigning, and the growing political role of public relations men.

Heard, Alexander, *The Costs of Democracy* (Chapel Hill, N.C.: University of North Carolina Press, 1960). Authoritative and revealing analysis of campaign costs and financing.

Kelley, Stanley, Jr., *Political Campaigning: Problems in Creating an Informed Electorate* (Washington, D.C.: The Brookings Institution, 1960). Study of campaign strategies and techniques.

Lubell, Samuel, *The Future of American Politics*, rev. ed. (New York: Harper and Row Publishers, Inc., 1956). Classic study of major forces that shape the direction of American politics.

Moos, Malcolm C., *Politics, Presidents, and Coat Tails* (Westport, Conn.: Greenwood Press, Inc., 1952). Study of the interaction of presidential and congressional elections.

Nimmo, Dan D., *The Political Persuaders: The Techniques of Modern Political Campaigns* (Englewood Cliffs, N.J.: Prentice-Hall, Inc., 1970). Analysis of election campaigns and a demonstration of how modern campaign technology may be a serious threat to our democratic system.

Ogden, Daniel M., and Arthur L. Peterson, *Electing the President*, rev. ed. (San Francisco: Chandler Publishing Co., 1968). Analysis of presidential nominations and campaigns.

Petkov, Steven M., "A Study of the Candidates in the 1965 Philadelphia Anti-Poverty Election" (Unpublished Ph.D. dissertation, University of Pennsylvania, 1972).

Pettingill, D. B., "Campaign Finance in Maryland" (Unpublished Ph.D. dissertation, Johns Hopkins University, 1960).

Polsby, Nelson W., and Aaron Wildavsky, *Presidential Elections: Strategies of American Electoral Politics*, 2nd ed. (New York: Charles Scribner's Sons, 1968). Description of presidential campaigns and the strategies used by candidates for election.

Pomper, Gerald, *Nominating the President: The Politics of Convention Choice* (New York: W. W. Norton and Co., Inc., 1966). Analysis of the presidential-nominating conventions, including a historical description of conventions between 1831 and 1960.

Pomper, Gerald, *Elections in America: Control and Influence in Democratic Politics* (New York: Dodd, Mead and Co., 1968). Analysis of elections, their effect on public policy, and the real value of the voting system.

Sayre, Wallace S., and Judith H. Parris, *Voting for President: The Electoral College and the American Political System* (Washington, D.C.: The Brookings Institution, 1970). Analysis of the electoral college and of the major reform plans that have been proposed.

Shadegg, Stephen C., *How to Win An Election: The Art of Political Victory* (New York: Crestwood Publishers, 1968). Controversial account of Senator Barry M. Goldwater's 1964 presidential campaign, by one of his aides.

Tillet, Paul, ed., *Inside Politics: The National Conventions, 1960* (Dobbs Ferry, N.Y.: Oceana Publications, Inc., 1962). Study of the 1960 convention, with emphasis on the delegates rather than the national leaders, and the process rather than the issues.

White, Theodore H., *The Making of the President, 1960* (New York: Atheneum Publishers, 1967). The first in a series of in-depth accounts of a presidential campaign and election.

White, Theodore H., *The Making of the President, 1964* (New York: Atheneum Publishers, 1966). The second in-depth, behind-the-scenes account of a presidential election.

White, Theodore H., *The Making of the President, 1968* (New York: Atheneum Publishers, 1969). The third volume in this excellent series of books describing the 1968 presidential nomination, campaign, and election.

Wilmerding, Lucius, Jr., *The Electoral College* (New Brunswick, N.J.: Rutgers University Press, 1958). Critical analysis of the electoral college system, with suggestions for change.

# Topics of further study

Barber, Kathleen L., and Louis Masoti, "Better Men Running?" *National Civic Review*, 1968.

Beals, William, "The Democratic Publicity Campaign, 1932" (master's thesis, University of California, 1955).

Chapman, Shirley, and Richard Claude, "Deviant Election in a One Party Country," *Public Opinion Quarterly*, 29 (1965): 247–258.

Culver, William Lowell, "Land Elections in West German Politics," *Western Political Quarterly*, June 1966, pp. 304–336.

Eyre, John R., *The Colorado Preprimary System* (Boulder, Colo.: University of Colorado Press, 1968).

Hinckley, Barbara, "Interpreting House Midterm Elections: Toward a Measurement of the In-Party's Expected Loss of Seats," *American Political Science Review*, September 1967, pp. 694–697.

Joyner, Conrad, and Ronald Pedderson, "Electoral College Revisited," *Southwestern Social Science Quarterly*, June 1964, pp. 26–36.

Smith, Paul A., and K. A. Lamb, *Campaign Decision-Making: The Presidential Election, 1964* (Belmont, Calif.: Wadsworth Publishing Co., Inc., 1968).

# part three

# the institutions of national government

# 12 the presidency

## power
## and
## restraint

A man elected to the office of President is inaugurated with austere ceremony. In accordance with tradition, he rises, places his right hand on the Bible—symbolically held by the Chief Justice of the Supreme Court —and recites the oath:

> I do solemnly swear that I will faithfully execute the office of President of the United States and will to the best of my ability preserve, protect and defend the Constitution of the United States, so help me God.

George Washington, first President of the United States, contributed the phrase "so help me God," perhaps in deference to the awesome scope of his new duties.

The Founding Fathers had decreed, "The Executive Power shall be vested in a President of the United States." The Constitution they designed remains basic to an understanding of presidential power. Yet, the extent to which a President wields that power is determined by political restraints and demands outside the Constitution, and the relation between the character of the President and historical circumstance.

## Presidential qualifications and succession

Under Article II of the Constitution, "no person except a natural born Citizen, . . . shall be eligible to the office of President." "Natural born" includes not only those born in this country, but also those born abroad of parents who are United States citizens.[1]

[1] When George Romney, a former governor of Michigan, put himself forward as a candidate for the presidency, some question arose about his qualifications, as he was born in Mexico. The problem has not yet been resolved, but most officials accept his citizenship, because his parents, Mormon missionaries at the time, were both United States citizens.

The Constitution also stipulates that the candidate must have lived in this country for a minimum of fourteen years and must be at least thirty-five years old. Only two United States Presidents, Theodore Roosevelt and John F. Kennedy, were younger than fifty when they assumed office. Roosevelt took office at the age of forty-two, after the assassination of McKinley in 1901. Kennedy, who became President at age forty-three, was the youngest Chief Executive to be elected.

## Presidents, 1900–1968

| Name | Party | Age | Native State | Religion | Education |
|------|-------|-----|--------------|----------|-----------|
| Theodore Roosevelt | Rep. | 42 | New York | Reformed Dutch | Harvard |
| William Taft | Rep. | 51 | Ohio | Unitarian | Yale |
| Woodrow Wilson | Dem. | 56 | Virginia | Presbyterian | Princeton |
| Warren Harding | Rep. | 55 | Ohio | Baptist | Ohio Central College |
| Calvin Coolidge | Rep. | 51 | Vermont | Congregationalist | Amherst |
| Herbert Hoover | Rep. | 54 | Iowa | Quaker | Stanford |
| Franklin Roosevelt | Dem. | 51 | New York | Episcopalian | Harvard |
| Harry Truman | Dem. | 60 | Missouri | Baptist | Kansas City School of Law |
| Dwight Eisenhower | Rep. | 62 | Texas | Presbyterian | West Point |
| John Kennedy | Dem. | 43 | Massachusetts | Roman Catholic | Harvard |
| Lyndon Johnson | Dem. | 55 | Texas | Christian Church | Southwest Texas State Teachers College |
| Richard Nixon | Rep. | 56 | California | Quaker | Whittier College |

In practice, a man is nominated by his party for the presidency if, in addition to fulfilling constitutional qualifications, he has demonstrated a sound knowledge of foreign affairs and policy, an understanding of and ability to cope with domestic conflicts, and—probably the most important qualification—if he has received considerable national media exposure through his prior work in public office. Primarily because of the increased importance of media exposure and first-hand knowledge of foreign affairs, more and more senators have recently been named for presidential candidacy (Kennedy, Johnson, Goldwater, and so on). In the past, governors of large states were most likely to be presidential candidates.

Recognizing the unique and important role of the President, the Framers of the Constitution included in Article II a provision for execution of presidential duties should the elected official be unable to carry them out himself. The Constitution reads "In case of the removal of the President from office, or of his death, resignation or inability to discharge the powers and duties of said office, the same shall devolve on the Vice-President." This wording indicates, but does not clearly define, the apparatus for *presidential succession*. In the event of a President's death, does the Vice-President only assume the powers and responsibilities of that office or does he actually become President? John Tyler, the first Vice-President to inherit the office on the death of a President (William Henry Harrison in 1841), set a precedent by taking office and assuming both the powers and duties of the President. When John Kennedy was assassinated in 1963, Vice-President Lyndon Johnson immediately took the title of President. This orderly succession was credited with keeping the nation stable during the transitional crisis.

However, difficulties have arisen in those instances in which a President has become incapacitated to the extent that he is unable to fully perform his duties. President Woodrow Wilson suffered a stroke after a draining cross-country tour and was disabled close to a year; serving minimally at times; he remained in office because the Constitution had no provision for declaring a President unable to govern. Having been ill in office, Dwight D. Eisenhower recognized this problem and made a secret agreement with Vice-President Richard Nixon empowering his "successor" to assume office in case of complete incapacitation.

The Twenty-fifth Amendment, ratified in 1967, seeks to resolve the problem of presidential succession by providing detailed provisions for the transference of office. "The Vice-President shall become President" in the event of the "removal of the President from office or of his death or resignation." The Amendment further provides for the appointment of a Vice-President by the newly appointed President, if such appointment is confirmed by a majority vote of both houses of Congress.

The main provision of the Twenty-fifth Amendment relates to presidential disability. In the event the President becomes incapacitated, he submits a written declaration to the Speaker of the House and to the President *pro tempore* of the Senate that he can no longer discharge the duties of office. The Vice-President then becomes *Acting President*, performing the functions of the Chief Executive. The problem of enforcing this provision depends on the President's desire or ability to recognize his incapacitation; if a President is truly incapacitated, he may also be incapable of sending a message to the Speaker.

Such a transfer of power can also occur without presidential consent. Although it is highly improbable that a Vice-President will exercise this power, he, along with a majority of Cabinet members, can submit to Congress a written statement declaring that the President is incapacitated.

If both houses of the legislature concur by a two-thirds vote arrived at within twenty-one days, then the Vice-President may take on the responsibilities of the Chief Executive.

2 Clinton Rossiter, *The American Presidency*, rev. ed. (New York: Harcourt Brace Jovanovich, Inc., 1960), p. 81.

# The growth of the presidency

"The Presidency today has much the same general outlines as it had in 1789, but the whole picture is a hundred times magnified," writes Clinton Rossiter.[2] The Framers of the Constitution deliberately worded Article II so that the powers of the Chief Executive would expand in relation to the growing needs of the nation. But the Founding Fathers could not have envisioned how dominant the presidency was to become in response to the demands of a modern, industrialized, and closely interrelated twentieth-century society.

In 1789, the Republic was comprised of thirteen states situated in a single band along the Atlantic Seaboard. The population numbered 4.2 million, and many were farmers. Committed to a policy of isolationism, the country avoided all foreign entanglements. Congressional debate and deliberation—rather than executive initiative—was the prime force in the political process.

[3] Edward S. Corwin, *The President: Office and Powers* (New York: New York University Press, 1957), p. 307.

"Taken by and large, the history of the presidency has been a history of aggrandizement."[3] As an institution responsive to the times, the office of the President has become more powerful as it has assumed governing an industrial society. Technology has created an economy that produces a gross national product (the total market value of all goods and services over a given period of time) of a trillion dollars and an interdependent network of management, labor, and consumers that requires unified national leadership.

Drawing by Don Hesse; © 1962 the St. Louis *Post-Dispatch*.

Strong leadership is necessitated not only by national but also by international conditions. As a world power, the United States is enmeshed in an intricate web of foreign alliances and commitments, the management of which demands the concerted action that many believe to be achieved best by the Chief Executive. One man can act more swiftly than a body of legislators of differing interests and temperaments.

# Roles of the President

The presidency demands extraordinary flexibility from the man who occupies the office. He must be Chief of State, Chief Legislator, Chief Administrator, party leader, Commander-in-Chief, foreign policy-maker, and leader of the nation. "From outside or below, a President is 'many men' or one man wearing many 'hats,' or playing many 'roles' . . . the President himself plays every 'role,' wears every 'hat' at once," writes Richard Neustadt. "Whatever he may do in one role is by definition done in all, and has effects in all. When he attempts to make his wishes manifest, his own will felt, he is one man, not many."[4]

Whichever role the President assumes, whether he is drumming up support among the citizens of the Midwest for his legislative program, campaigning for a favored party candidate, discussing economic policy with members of his Cabinet, or entertaining foreign dignitaries at the White House, constant bargaining is entailed. In fact, the President's power frequently boils down to the politics of persuasion.[5]

We will examine the President's various roles separately; but one should bear in mind that these roles are interrelated, and their effectiveness is contingent on successful interplay.

[4] Richard E. Neustadt, *Presidential Power* (New York: The New American Library, 1964), p. viii.

[5] President Lyndon Johnson's legislative efficiency and reputation as Chief Executive was based largely on his effective powers of persuasion. For his own account of his years as President, see Lyndon Baines Johnson, *The Vantage Point: Perspectives of the Presidency 1963– 1969* (New York: Holt, Rinehart and Winston, 1971).

## Party leader

The presidential candidate who emerges from the national nominating convention is initially called upon to act as *party leader*. Through the period of his election campaign and presidency, he will be the major national spokesman for the party. Although this role is not assigned by the Constitution, it is one that affords him real political leverage.

The moment a man accepts the party nomination for presidential office, he is the focus of party policy and power. Despite dissidence within the party, he can, through skillful manipulation of patronage, influence, and favors, forge strong bonds of loyalty and discipline.

The President is expected to render favors in exchange for support. As party leader he is expected to help elect state and local candidates, appear at party gatherings to raise campaign funds, confer appointments on members of his own party, attend and address party meetings and rallies, and strive to maintain party unity.

### Promoter of local candidates

The President is expected to endorse the local party officials who helped elect him. He can often swing an election for the party candidate. The appearance on the ballot of a popular President is particularly effective in getting votes for local candidates. In the election of 1964, Lyndon Johnson's overwhelming victory in the presidential election carried many of his party's local, state, and national candidates into office; the President's endorsement, however, is no guarantee of victory. Local elections are often fought on local issues that have little to do with strict party affiliation. In the midterm elections of 1970, the Republican President, Nixon, campaigned heavily for state Republican candidates, but twenty-eight governorships were won by Democrats, a loss of eleven by the Republicans.

**Campaign-fund raiser**

The President is expected to appear at local gatherings, where his support has a strong positive effect on the number and size of the contributions made. Johnson and Kennedy were both adept at raising campaign funds, garnering millions of dollars by appearing throughout the country at one-hundred- and one-thousand-dollar-a-plate dinners. One device that has been used for party fund raising is the "President's Club," by which a wealthy contributor could be more closely allied to the President through a check donation of $500 or more. And when he is elected to office, the President is expected to reward many of his supporters with executive appointments or other favors.

**Appointment delegator**

Woodrow Wilson, who was particularly successful in controlling the Democratic party, took special interest in the thousands of presidential appointments, including the placement of postmasters across the country. It is assumed that most of the President's major appointments will be from the ranks of his own party, although Democrats sometimes select Republicans for positions in the Departments of State and Defense. President Kennedy appointed Republican candidates to high level posts within his Democratic administration—Robert McNamara as Secretary of Defense, Douglas Dillon as Secretary of the Treasury, and McGeorge Bundy as special adviser to the President.

**Head promoter in the legislature**

Any real control the President exercises over his party is due to the fact that the party needs him—to publicize their platform, to raise funds, to have their members elected or appointed, to push their bills through Congress.

The President's role as party leader considerably enhances his efforts in the legislature. "The President has traditionally employed the techniques of

6 David E. Haight and Larry D. Johnston, *The President: Roles and Powers* (Chicago: Rand McNally and Co., 1965), p. 248.

persuasion, patronage and 'dealing' to build a congressional majority. Since Franklin D. Roosevelt, the White House staff and informal advisors have worked on Capitol Hill to guide legislation. When necessary, the President could tap his alliances with state and local party organizations to apply pressure to recalcitrant congressmen and senators."[6] One should keep in mind,

Drawing by Oliphant; © 1968 the Denver *Post.*

*An artist's view of the President's many roles.*

however, that members of the party often hold conflicting viewpoints whose expression cannot always be quelled by the Chief Executive. One of President Johnson's severest critics concerning his Southeast Asian policy was Senator Fulbright, a fellow Democrat. Clearly, the President also needs the party—for legislative support and as a political machine for renomination.

# National opinion leader

As both leader of the nation and party leader, the President must mobilize popular support for his programs and party. Today his effectiveness in molding public opinion depends to a great extent on his skill in utilizing the resources of mass media. His unlimited access to radio, television, and the press provides him with great leverage in the American system of power. But he must use it with discretion. Overexposure can tarnish the presidential image and diminish his influence. If the Chief Executive projects the attributes of fine leadership, he can work wonders. "Let him once win the admiration and confidence of the country, and no other single force can withstand him, no combination of forces will easily overpower him. His position takes the imagination of the country. . . . If he rightly interpret the national thought and boldly insist upon it, he is irresistible; and the country never feels the zest so much as when its President is of such insight and calibre," stated President Woodrow Wilson.[7]

7 Quoted in Erwin C. Hargrove, *Presidential Leadership* (New York: The Macmillan Co., 1966), p. 40.

One of the earliest channels for direct communication with the public was the White House Press Conference, which was instituted in about 1920.

Since that time, the number of Washington correspondents has increased from 200 to 1,500. "The White House Press Conference," writes columnist Roscoe Drummond, "helps to hold any Administration accountable to the people. . . . In our Government of divided powers, where the President does not sit with Congress, it is the Washington press correspondents who question the President."[8]

[8] Roscoe Drummond, "Mr. Kennedy's Calculated Risk," *Saturday Review*, February 11, 1961, p. 83.

The use of mass media to marshal public support first rallied the nation in the days of the Great Depression and during World War II. In a series of radio broadcasts called "fireside chats," President Franklin D. Roosevelt carried on a dramatic monologue designed to instill hope and confidence in the listener. With the advent of television, the press conference became a nationwide broadcast. Today close to 20 million Americans are able to view television's on-the-spot coverage. In gearing his message to a mass audience, the President must be a keen judge of public sentiment. If he speaks on potentially explosive issues, such as the war in Vietnam, and if he wants to influence public opinion, he must set the tone of his statements according to his perception of the national mood. The President's tone greatly affects the public's reaction to his words.

Whether on television or in person, the President must combine all the attributes of a statesman and politician: he must be both careful and decisive —both diplomatic and bold. Effective use of image and influence is essential to strong leadership.

# Chief Legislator

The President's role as *Chief Legislator* has grown out of the Constitution, which prescribes his power to advise Congress on the State of the Union, to propose and sign legislation, and to call special sessions of Congress. The President, as the only government official elected by a national constituency, is the natural leader of Congress. The 535 congressmen represent geographical areas, some no larger than two or three square miles. The President, on the other hand, has access to all the resources necessary to formulate a balanced national perspective. All material, including highly classified information, is available for his evaluation.

For these reasons, it has become the President's *responsibility* to devise a detailed legislative program. This function was not delegated by the Constitution, which stated that the President could suggest to Congress, "such measures" as "he shall judge necessary and expedient"; it evolved through presidential practice.

The extent to which a President might assume leadership of Congress is a question to be considered in the next chapter. It is sufficient here to note that the public has come to expect presidential initiative in legislation. Thus, when Franklin D. Roosevelt in 1933 led Congress in developing a recovery program for the depression, he was considered by most to be performing the duties of his office. In 1955, when President Eisenhower did not come forth with a legislative program, there was a hue and cry that he had abandoned his executive duty.

## Legislative messages

The President issues legislative directives through public addresses and written communiques. Today, there are three major messages conveyed annually before Congress: State of the Union, State of the National Budget, and State of the World. In addition, the President sends numerous dispatches to the legislature, defining the administration's position on policy matters.

The *State of the Union message* is the first, and most publicized, message to Congress. It consists of a general statement of domestic policy, delivered in person by the President to a joint session of the two houses. It establishes priorities for a legislative agenda.

In the *National Budget message,* the President states the condition of the economy, domestic-policy objectives, and prime expenditures for the forthcoming year. He outlines the plans detailed in the Bureau of the Budget compilation, a volume thicker than the standard telephone directory. This publication contains the information for carrying out the priorities declared in his State of the Union message.

In the *State of the World address* (first prepared and delivered in 1971 by President Nixon), the President deals with foreign policy. For example, when President Nixon delivered this message to Congress on February 25, 1971, he pledged continuing support for the North American Treaty Organization (NATO). He rebuffed Soviet proposals for limitations on strategic missile defenses, and said the United States would continue a "minimum" ABM program. He indicated his desire to improve relations with the Chinese People's Republic by declaring that the United States was prepared to see Peking play a constructive role in the "family of nations."[9] Generally, in the State of the World address, the President explains the rationale behind policies carried out by his administration and clarifies the country's international goals.

Executive influence is most effectively exercised through countless written communiques dispatched from the White House to Congress. These important messages state presidential priorities and are often followed by detailed legislative proposals drafted by the legal experts of the President's staff.

[9] *The New York Times,* February 26, 1971.

## The veto power

The Constitution decrees a "separation of powers" between the legislative and executive branches of government. The President may formulate the bill, but it is up to Congress to enact it. Executive directives provide a catalyzing influence but the legislature does have the option of accepting, modifying, or rejecting specific policy proposals.

The President generally signs those bills he initiates, after they are approved by both houses, unless they have been altered to his dissatisfaction. The Constitution delegates him three other alternatives in dealing with proposed legislation.

The President may keep a bill ten days and not act upon it. Following this grace period, the unsigned bill automatically becomes law. A President might follow this course with a bill that has strong public and congressional support, but not his personal approval. However, this form of passive disapproval has rarely been used by contemporary Presidents.

Active disapproval is registered by the power of *veto*. When the President vetoes a bill, he sends it back to Congress without his signature; accompanying the unsigned bill is a statement of his objections to it. This *regular veto* can be *overridden* (or negated) by a two-thirds vote of both houses in Congress. But such a majority is rarely obtained, and for all intents and purposes, a bill vetoed by the President is dead. President Roosevelt, during his terms of office, exercised the regular veto 631 times. Only on nine occasions was he overridden.

The *pocket veto* may be utilized in the last ten days of a congressional session. During this period if the President does not sign a bill, and Congress adjourns, that bill automatically dies. Exerting presidential influence in this manner is common, for Congress often passes much legislation in its final days of session. Eisenhower exercised the pocket veto 107 times.

The veto power is limited by the fact that the President must accept or reject a bill in its entirety. Unlike most state governors, he cannot exercise an *item veto*, rejecting specific provisions while approving the bill as a whole. This restriction allows congressmen to attach *riders* to a bill. Riders are legislative additions that often cater to localized interests and may be irrelevant to the main purpose of the bill. For example, a bill to appropriate essential funds for a national mental health program may include a provision to erect a number of modern apartment buildings in downtown Tuskegee. When riders are part of a bill the President wants enacted, he cannot veto them. "[The] manifest fact remains that this practice robs the executive of legitimate and essential freedom of action in dealing with legislation," stated President Roosevelt in 1938.[10]

All Presidents have had informal relations with individual members of the Congress. President Kennedy, however, was the first to assign a member of the White House Staff, with excellent connections in Congress, to full time liaison with Congress. While such a lieutenant lines up support for the key administration measures, the President himself may approach individual senators and representatives. Meetings between the President and various congressmen—as in the "congressional breakfast," in which potential and actual supporters of a proposal are invited to an early breakfast at the White

[10] *The New York Times,* January 6, 1938, cited in Corwin, *The President: Office and Powers,* p. 475.

**President's influence on Congress**

# portfolio
# the
# presidency

The presidency is many things to many people. One's concept of the office varies with his political beliefs, region, economic and social condition, and interest in national and international affairs. This can be seen in the following quotations by people actively engaged in government. Some of these people stress the nature of the office and the qualities needed for that office. Others are more concerned with its problems.

# NATURE OF THE PRESIDENCY

More than any other office, whether elective, appointive, inherited, or obtained through force, the office of the President of the United States will stand the test of history as the one position in world and human affairs that most beneficially affected the course of mankind.

> *Governor J. James Exon (D. Nebraska)*
> *April 20, 1971*

Of the many qualities that Presidential leadership requires I believe three are absolutely indispensable. They are vision, candor and courage.... Vision of what America is and can become ... candor to level with the people and treat them with respect ... courage to make ... hard decisions that can help shape a new America....

> *Secretary of Housing and Urban Development*
> *George Romney (R.), January 17, 1968*

It has become virtually a matter of historical necessity that the President ... evaluate, articulate, and effectively espouse public needs and the policies to meet those needs....

> *Governor Daniel J. Evans (R. Washington)*
> *April 22, 1971*

... the job of the President must be as much to chart the national purpose as it is to execute the country's laws.

> *Senator Birch Bayh (D. Indiana)*
> *April 21, 1971*

A President is as much an emblem in a symbolic sense of our country as is the American eagle. Yet he is a living symbol and ... he sets a moral tone for the nation.

> *Governor Kenneth M. Curtis (D. Maine)*
> *October 22, 1971*

... the years ahead ... demand the concept of the open Presidency. Not decisions made at the top of a vast pyramid, but the exposure of ideas ... to a maximum number of people....

> *Senator Hubert H. Humphrey (D. Minnesota)*
> *June 1968*

In these days of enormous and always expanding government, I cannot see that the President can do much more than give leadership and formulate policy and rely on staff and administrative heads of agencies to carry it out.

*Governor Bruce King (D. New Mexico)*
*April 14, 1971*

The President's power to direct foreign affairs is greater than is his power to direct domestic affairs. . . . No other person has so much knowledge, from so many sources. . . .

*Representative Barry Goldwater, Jr. (R. California)*
*April 22, 1971*

The President should appeal to the best in Americans. He should have the capacity to rally the people around the rock of principle when the going is hard and treacherous.

*Senator Edmund S. Muskie (D. Maine)*
*June 4, 1971*

Richard Nixon meeting with his Cabinet (President as chief administrator).

Richard Nixon delivering the 1971 State of the Union message before a joint session of Congress (President as chief legislator).

. . . the most important responsibility of the President is moral leadership. . . . A President has a duty to exert such leadership, for if he does not, the people feel a lack of direction and a relaxation of moral standards throughout the country.

*Governor Frank Licht (D. Rhode Island)*
*April 30, 1971*

The Presidency means leadership, a willingness to offer a new direction to the Nation. The President must be more than a manager . . . , he must be creative and courageous.

*Senator George McGovern (D. South Dakota)*
*April 16, 1971*

The most important single quality a President should have is that of courageous leadership . . . the truly great Presidents were those who not only had dreams and worthy goals but were able to inspire the vast majority of Americans to seek those goals.

*Governor Russell W. Peterson (R. Delaware)*
*May 17, 1971*

Richard Nixon attending a weekly press conference (President as public opinion leader).

The President must provide strong, open leadership for the people of this nation. He is their ultimate spokesman, and he must make it clear where he stands on all the issues. . . . The President must also be a statesman, not a politician. . . . He must base his actions on what he honestly believes to be in the interest of the nation as a whole.

> *Senator William Proxmire (D. Wisconsin)*
> *April 14, 1971*

Successful politics is always a team effort. . . . But . . . there is only one quarterback—one man who calls the plays.

> *Governor Richard B. Ogilvie (R. Illinois)*
> *January 9, 1971*

The President may well be the most powerful and influential leader on the globe, but his responsibilities are even more awesome than his power.

> *Governor Preston Smith (D. Texas)*
> *April 1971*

# PROBLEMS OF THE PRESIDENCY

In the history of our country the power relationship between the President and the Congress has had many ups and downs, reflecting generally the strength of the personalities involved.
*Senator Strom Thurmond (R. South Carolina)*
*From* The Faith We Have Not Kept   1968

No human being can be entrusted with such enormous powers. . . . Even the wisest and most competent of Presidents is still a human being, susceptible to human flaws and human failures. . . .
*Senator Frank Church (D. Idaho)*
*April 30, 1970*

For a very long time . . . the "strong President" was much admired. This had a good deal to recommend it. . . . But a by-product was to blind the nation to the potential danger of the power center it was creating in the White House.
*Senator Clifford P. Case (R. New Jersey)*
*February 4, 1971*

Some rather fundamental defects seem to be inherent in the office itself. . . . The most important appears to be the unique capacity of the office to isolate and deceive its occupant.
*Senator J. William Fulbright (D. Arkansas)*
*April 3, 1971*

Too many Chief Executives had been so concerned with threats from abroad . . . that they have ignored the threat from within that neglected social problems invariably create.
*Mayor Kenneth A. Gibson (D. New Jersey)*
*May 17, 1971*

In the field of foreign affairs, the President's power obviously has increased, because he is the only man who has the power to push the button to incinerate the earth. And, of course, that is the ultimate power. . . .
*Representative Hale Boggs (D. Louisiana)*
*March 22, 1971*

Lyndon Johnson socializ
(President as chief of sta

The public officials quoted on the nature of the presidency who stressed the importance of leadership were expressing an ideal—what the president should be. Some were running for that office. But the men quoted on the problems of the presidency who were concerned with the abuse of that leadership were mostly congressmen who felt that recent presidents have seriously infringed upon the war-making, purse-control, and "advice and consent" powers of Congress.* Views on the strength of the President relative to Congress change with the times, but in this century the growth of technological warfare and rapid communications has forced both to reassess the powers of one another.

*The opinions expressed on the preceding pages do not necessarily reflect those of the author. Those that are presented represent the answers received in response to letters to every major political official at the state and national level of government.

[11] For a discussion of various presidential styles in influencing Congress, see Louis W. Koenig, *The Chief Executive* (New York: Harcourt, Brace and World, 1968), pp. 140–149.

[12] Grant McConnell, *The Modern Presidency* (New York: St. Martin's Press, Inc., 1967), p. 35.

[13] James T. Patterson, *Congressional Conservatism and the New Deal* (Lexington, Ky.: University of Kentucky Press, 1967), p. 281.

House—have become an institution in Washington. Lyndon B. Johnson often called forth his "100 loyal Democrats" on the mornings when a bill he wanted backed was scheduled for House debate. Johnson was a master at political bargaining after twenty-three years in Congress, including seven years as Senate Majority Leader under President Eisenhower. He utilized the telephone as an important legislative instrument, calling key congressmen at almost any hour to discuss a vote.[11]

Because of the very fact that the President and Congress have different constituencies, "a president is often sharply at odds with the views and purposes of many of the men of Capitol Hill."[12] During the 1950s, for example, Eisenhower proposed numerous bills providing aid to education, but these were repeatedly defeated by the 88th Congress.

Sometimes, however, the President effects a kind of supremacy. During a period of crisis such as war or economic depression, a President tends to become dominant; historically, Congress has either supported or deferred to the President during periods of national emergency.

Lincoln, for example, assumed near-dictatorial powers during the Civil War, casting Congress into shadow. The Emancipation Proclamation was an executive order, conceived and signed by the President without his consulting Congress. Similarly, Franklin D. Roosevelt assumed almost total responsibility for lifting the country out of the Great Depression. His Congress resented being required to rubber-stamp the legislation needed. "Roosevelt," Senator Tydings complained, "wants a Senator with a detachable head which he must leave with his hat in the cloakroom before going on the floor."[13]

Today, the complexity and pace of modern affairs has forced more responsibility on the President, who must act quickly on information not available to Congress. The exercise of this power is frequently a subject of debate and controversy. Does the President have the right, without consulting Congress, to wage an undeclared war? The Constitution gives Congress the power to declare wars, but what of "undeclared wars"? Who indeed has the war-making power? What is Congress's role in foreign policy? How much access should congressmen be given to highly classified information? How much authority should Congress assert in limiting a President's activities? How accountable is the President to Congress?

These and other questions grow more insistent, especially during times of difficult controversy. The questions act as a check on the executive and a caution to the legislative branches of the government. In analyzing the history of presidential-congressional relations, one can see that the system of checks and balances, designed by the Founding Fathers to keep any single branch of our government from assuming too much power, does in fact work. At different times in our history one or the other of the branches has been most influential, but no one branch has consistently dominated the government of the United States.

# Chief Administrator

14 Herman Miles Somers, "The President as Administrator," *The Annals*, CCLXXXIII (September 1952): 104.

In an article entitled "The President as Administrator," Herman Miles Somers begins: "It may be that full performance of the duties derived from the Constitution which have accrued to the President is impossible."[14]

In fact, every President has complained about the unwieldy and burdensome job of *Administrator*. Franklin Delano Roosevelt said:

> They say, what has been common knowledge for twenty years, that the President cannot adequately handle his responsibilities, that he is overworked; that it is humanly impossible under the system which we have, for him to fully carry out his Constitutional duty as Chief Executive, because he is overwhelmed with minor details and needless contacts arising directly from the bad organization and equipment of the Government. I can testify to this. With my predecessors, who have said the same thing over and over, I plead guilty.[15]

15 Quoted in Somers, "The President as Administrator," p. 104.

The basic administrative problem lies in numbers—the size of the bureaucracy. The executive branch has 2,830,000 employees, 57 percent civilian and 43 percent military, and an estimated payroll of more than $29 billion; the White House Staff alone numbered 340 in 1970. Obviously the President cannot know or fully control 3 million people; yet, he is responsible for them and for what they do.

## Staffing the executive offices

The President can solve some of his administrative problems by appointing men whose abilities he knows and trusts. A new President will want to staff the upper levels of the government with his own choices; he has the power to do this with the "advice and consent of the Senate." He also "shall appoint Ambassadors, and other public Ministers, and Consuls, Judges of the Supreme Court, and all other officers of the United States," whose appointments "are not . . . otherwise provided for" by the Constitution. In addition, Congress can delegate to the President or department heads the power to appoint lower-level officers so classified by Congress. The Senate rarely interferes with presidential hiring and firing of upper-level administrative personnel, recognizing the necessity for having men who have the trust and confidence of the President serving in policy-making positions within the executive branch of the government.

The power of the President to appoint men to federal posts within the states is limited by *senatorial courtesy*. The President must clear his nominations with the Senator of the state, if he is of the same party. If a senator declares a nominee "personally obnoxious" (that is, if the senator opposes his nomination), his fellow senators will close ranks and join him in rejecting the President's nomination. Such reciprocity between senators restricts executive power over federal appointments of federal district judges, marshals, and other officials with localized jurisdiction.

*Edwin S. Corwin,* The President: Office and Powers (*New York: New York University Press, 1957*), *pp. 69–79.*

Edwin Corwin, in discussing presidential appointments, notes that all federal offices are directly or indirectly provided for in the Constitution: some are specifically named, others are created by Congress on the authority of the necessary and proper clause. The President then fills the positions with the advice and consent of the Senate; only lower-level offices need not be approved.

In some cases, however, the normal appointment procedures have been disregarded. Since President Washington's time, Chief Executives have disregarded senatorial consent in appointing secret agents on diplomatic or semidiplomatic missions. They have also appointed congressmen to serve on international commissions and at diplomatic conferences despite the constitutional stipulation that "No senator or representative shall, during the time for which he was elected, be appointed to any civil office."

Theodore Roosevelt instituted the practice of forming voluntary, unpaid, fact-finding commissions. Congress, declaring the practice unconstitutional, finally outlawed it. "Mr. Roosevelt signed the measure but proclaimed his intention of ignoring the restriction. 'Congress,' he argued, 'cannot prevent the President from seeking advice,' nor disinterested men from giving their service to the people."

Succeeding Presidents also maintained and carried out their right to appoint certain offices and commissions without senatorial consent. President Hoover, for example, "appointed literally dozens of fact-finding commissions, most of them without statutory basis."

Corwin suggests that Presidents usually justify these appointments by not considering them "offices" in the constitutional sense, since they are often short-term and unpaid.

Although Congress generally frowns on presidential appointments made without their consent, it has at times given the President the sole power to create and fill offices. Franklin Roosevelt, by authority of Title II of the National Recovery Act of 1933 (passed in Congress and later declared unconstitutional by the Supreme Court), set up the office of Federal Administrator of Public Works and was permitted to fill all the offices in the new agency without regard to civil service laws. The author notes the basis for past expansions of authority:

> President Wilson's creation during the First World War of the War Industries Board, the Committee on Public Information, and the first War Labor Board, all bodies that exercised vast powers in the President's name, must be credited to the general expansion that presidential authority always undergoes in wartime; and the second Roosevelt's enlargement on his predecessor's practice in this matter, not only during but before the Second World War, can be explained in more or less the same way.

## Removal powers

16 *Humphrey's Executor* v. *United States,* 295 U.S. 602 (1935)

Control can be exercised also by the President's *removal powers,* which were first upheld by the Supreme Court in 1926 (*Meyers* v. *United States*). The Court stated that the President has the power to remove any executive official, including members of the independent agencies commissions, such as the Federal Aviation Commission. The Court contended that the removal power was a part of the President's power as Chief Executive, and any attempt by Congress to restrict the removal right violates the Constitution.[16]

In a later decision, the Supreme Court stated that presidential removal extends only to executive officers, and not to members of independent agencies who perform legislative and judicial, as well as executive, functions. Such agencies as the Interstate Commerce Commission and the Federal Communications Commission (whose members hold fixed terms of office) must remain free of political control by the Chief Executive.[16]

Like the head of a large corporation, the Chief Executive must deal gracefully and in a politic manner with administrators. When the President and a Cabinet officer have irreconcilable views, the officer will usually resign to avoid the adverse publicity of outright dismissal. The firing of Interior Secretary Walter Hickel by President Richard Nixon in 1970, prompted by differences over national conservation policy, was the exception, rather than the rule.

Because there are so many agencies and no clearly defined lines of authority, enforcement of presidential orders is often near impossible. There are over thirteen major agencies in the Executive Office of the President, and each has a detailed and fairly complex reporting system. By the time an executive order reaches the lower echelons, where it must be acted upon, the order has lost its immediacy and the executive his control over its enactment.

## Interpreting legislation

As Chief Administrator, the President must unify and mobilize diverse departments and agencies for his own purposes. He must also assist Congress in filling in the details of official legislation. In appropriations acts, for example, Congress may allot a lump sum, and leave the specifics of distribution to executive discretion. In 1921, the Budget and Accounting Act specified the executive function of planning expenditure and the legislative practice of grant and consent. More recently, the 1962 Trade Expansion Act authorized the President to construct trade agreements raising or lowering tariff rates by as much as 50 percent. Through "contingent legislation," he could subsequently abolish tariffs on some items if warranted by fluctuating costs of production at home and abroad.[17]

[17] On August 14, 1971, President Nixon announced that all imports shipped after August 15 would be subject to a 10 percent duty.

*"If we knew what conclusions the President wants our commission to come to, we could come to them, and that would be that."*

Drawing by Handelsman; © 1971
The New Yorker Magazine, Inc.

Such delegation of authority is tempered by the Constitution and by Congress's power of *concurrent resolution*, in which both houses can vote to repeal presidential action.

# Commander-in-Chief

"The President," according to Article II, Section 2, of the Constitution, "shall be Commander in Chief of the Army and Navy of the United States, and of the Militia of the several States, when called into the actual service of the United States." Because of this constitutional provision, the President has final authority for all military policy. He appoints military officials and plans strategy with his Secretary of Defense and National Security Council. In consultation with his advisers, the President determines the deployment of forces and the functions of the three branches of the military: army, navy, and air force.

The organization of the defense establishment, with the President and Secretary of Defense having final authority over the generals, guarantees civilian control of the military. This authority has been exercised time and again. For example, during the Korean War, President Truman fired General MacArthur. The General enjoyed great popularity on the home front, but his conduct of the war defied presidential strategy.

In practice, the day-to-day operations of the military establishment are left to the Joint Chiefs of Staff of the three services, under the Secretary of Defense.

In wartime, the President is constitutionally empowered to direct the course of the war, but Congress officially declares the war and appropriates the funds to maintain it. The President, however, has sometimes taken military action without an official declaration of war by Congress. President Jefferson, a strict constitutionalist, sent ships after the Barbary pirates without consultation with Congress; Lincoln responded to the firing on Fort Sumter, which occurred while Congress was in recess, by sending troops into action against the southern rebels. President Truman sent troops into Korea without Congressional authorization. He incurred the wrath of Senate Majority Leader Robert Taft, who said "The President simply usurped authority, in violation of the laws and the Constitution."[18]

[18] Quoted in Haight and Johnston, *The President*, p. 350.

With the need for emergency decisions in war, however, the Congress often gives the President a free hand to prosecute major wars. It stands to reason that one man, as a single authority, can act more swiftly than 535 men holding conflicting views.

We have noted that during the Civil War, Lincoln commanded with an absoluteness that often incurred harsh criticism from the Senate. In World War II, Roosevelt too assumed sweeping powers both at home and abroad; he used the full powers of the Presidency in pursuit of victory. He took over strike-threatened industries and war plants; he rationed consumer goods and foods, he requisitioned property for defense purposes. And with Winston Churchill, he planned the strategy of the United States and her Allies abroad.

The wartime powers of the President are especially awesome in the age of nuclear capabilities. At the end of World War II, President Truman made the decision to drop the atomic bomb on Hiroshima, an act that changed the tone of history and expanded the President's war-making powers to apocalyptic dimensions.

An enormous growth of power has occurred in the time that has elapsed between Jefferson's dispatching of ships in order to curtail piracy and the President's deployment of nuclear missiles. For today, every decision of international concern could imply the release of nuclear energy. For example, during the Cuban Missile Crisis of 1962, when the Russians moved missiles into Cuba and President Kennedy demanded their removal, a slip by either side could have provoked nuclear war. When the crisis was resolved peacefully, the community of nations learned a stark new lesson about the role of the President as Commander-in-Chief: although nuclear weapons provide him with immense new power, his actions are constricted by those very powers because of the incredible and irreversible damage they can do to the world.

**In domestic affairs**

The recent turmoil in our streets has brought into play the President's role as keeper of the domestic peace. When several twentieth century presidents used National Guard troops, they did so through national legislative authorization. In 1957, Eisenhower sent troops to Little Rock, Arkansas, to enforce a federal court order requiring integration; and in 1962, President Kennedy sent troops into Mississippi to enforce the integration of the University of Mississippi. In domestic circumstances such as these, when the military is used in conjunction with the National Guard, forces are under civilian command aiding the authorities to keep the peace.

# Foreign policy maker

The single authority for relations with other countries rests in the person and office of the President. In the *United States* v. *Curtiss-Wright Export Corporation* (1936), however, the constitutionality of presidential authority over international relations was challenged. This case, reputed to be the most complete Supreme Court discussion of foreign affairs, affirmed executive prerogative in two major points: the national government holds all power in foreign affairs, and the President is the prime agent and Congress must cede to his wishes. The Constitution specifically authorizes the President to make all appointments of our representatives abroad, to "make treaties" (both with the "advice and consent" of the Senate), and to receive "ambassadors and other public ministers." Only the President or his appointees can serve as the official channel of communication between the United States and foreign powers.

> *Wilfred E. Binkley*, President and Congress (*New York: Random House, Inc., 1962*), *pp. 348–350.*
>
> The Economic Recovery Program, better known as the Marshall Plan, stands as a testament to President Harry Truman's expertise in formulating foreign policy with the aid of Congress. Wilfred E. Binkley examines the "masterpiece of management" that enabled the plan to pass Congress with unusual ease.
>
> To initiate the process, Secretary of State George Marshall, speaking at Harvard University, proposed economic aid to the war-ravaged nations of Europe. England, who had announced her withdrawal from

Greece and Turkey, expressed open opposition to Marshall's suggestions, but Truman counteracted this criticism by publicly supporting his Secretary of State, thus giving the plan impetus. Then, aware of the need for bipartisan approval of the controversial proposal, the President obtained the support of Republican Senator Vandenberg. The senator established a functioning liaison between Congress and the administrative agencies concerned, and asked, in turn, that a Republican, Paul Hoffman, be appointed head of the European Recovery Authority. Truman agreed, although he preferred another candidate. In addition to this give-and-take attitude, the President appealed often to the nation, reminding it of the required congressional action.

Thus, in the true spirit of wheeling-and-dealing, Truman did pay a price for Vandenberg's help: a Republican became head of the program. But his handling of the affair, as the author writes, "is an example of Truman at his best in dealing with Congress": the President made certain that his own low prestige did not prevent the implementation of an important foreign-policy program.

As the official channel of foreign relations, the President is empowered to select the most suitable men he can to represent the United States abroad as "ambassadors, other public ministers and consuls." The talent for selecting the right person for the right place is not given equally to all men, nor is it always exercised. Quite often ambassadorial appointments—especially to smaller nations like Ceylon or Monaco—are given in return for important political favors.

In larger or more powerful nations, the ambassador is in a critical position, and the President must rely on criteria other than patronage to determine the appointment. It is essential that these ambassadors show tact, diplomacy, and administrative skill. The United States spends enormous sums of money in foreign countries; such programs as the Marshall Plan, Lend-Lease (during World War II), and Food For Peace demand constant administrative attention by the ambassadorial offices. With troops stationed in 34 countries of the world, the United States government faces constant problems in housing, conduct, and maintenance of staffs abroad—problems that become the responsibilities of the President's representatives abroad.

In sending an ambassador to a foreign nation or in receiving representatives from other nations, the President is exercising constitutional power of *diplomatic recognition*. The United States has frequently been first to recognize new nations, such as Panama in 1902, Algeria in 1965, and several recently formed African nations. The most continuing example of United States refusal to recognize another country has been its United Nations rejection of Red China a position refuted in 1971 by a majority in the United Nations General Assembly.

## Treaties and executive agreements

The United States has agreements with most of the nations of the world. These international agreements take the form of treaties or executive agreements.

A *treaty* can be negotiated by any representative of the President, but only the President can sign it. Before final executive ratification, however, treaties must receive the advice and consent of two-thirds of the Senate. Successful international negotiation on the President's part does not always guarantee Senate consent. For example, after World War I, President Wilson negotiated a far-reaching peace at Versailles, which included a provision for a League of Nations. The Versailles Treaty failed to get a two-thirds vote of the majority of the Senate. (Wilson had not included any senator in the delegation to the Peace Conference at Versailles in 1919, and had refused to compromise with Senate critics over the provisions of the treaty. Since his disappointment, Presidents have tried to place influential senators on negotiating teams, to insure or at least help achieve advice and consent.)

*Executive agreements* have been widely used for international agreements, though the Constitution does not mention them. Expanded use of them in this century has resulted in their reevaluation and in 1937, *United States* v. *Belmont* gave executive agreements the same legal status as treaties. Whether an executive agreement or a treaty is used is a decision only the President can make, a decision usually based on the relative importance of the agreement. If financial appropriations are needed or if the agreement would conflict with existing domestic legislation, then approval by a simple majority of both houses is needed.

**Executive Agreements**
**(The Countries with Which the United States Has Defense Agreements by Executive Agreement)**

| | | | |
|---|---|---|---|
| Denmark | 1951 | Iran | 1959 |
| Iceland | 1951 | Turkey | 1959 |
| Spain | 1953 | Pakistan | 1959 |
| Canada | 1958 | Philippines | 1959, 1965 |
| Liberia | 1959 | | |

A commitment as massive as membership in the United Nations or the settling of a war demands a treaty with Senate approval. However, a transaction involving trade with Indonesia usually results in the signing of an executive agreement. There are exceptions, however: the 1940 executive agreement between Franklin D. Roosevelt and the British and the 1945 agreements at Yalta and Potsdam represented major decisions. In Roosevelt's 1940 Lend-Lease Agreement, the President signed over fifty destroyers in exchange for ninety-nine-year leases on certain British naval bases.

## The conduct of foreign affairs

[19] Alexis de Tocqueville, *Democracy in America,* ed. by Phillips Bradley (New York: Alfred A. Knopf, Inc., 1945), vol. I, p. 243.

[20] Hans J. Morgenthau, "Conduct of American Foreign Policy," *Parliamentary Affairs,* III (Winter 1949): 147–161.

Alexis de Tocqueville wrote, "Foreign politics demand scarcely any of those qualities which are peculiar to a democracy; they require, on the contrary, the perfect use of almost all those in which it is deficient . . . a democracy can only with great difficulty regulate the details of an important undertaking, persevere in a fixed design, and work out its execution in spite of serious obstacles. It cannot combine its measures with secrecy or await their consequences with patience."[19] Tocqueville's analysis correctly defines a problem that confronts all Chief Executives. The conditions of an open society and free press seldom aid the President managing the delicate issues of foreign affairs; withholding crucial information is at times necessary. This clash of cross-purposes forces the President and his advisers to face a dilemma where, writes Hans Morgenthau, "they must sacrifice what they consider good policy upon the altar of public opinion, or they must by devious means gain popular support for policies whose true nature is concealed from the public."[20]

*Joseph E. Kallenbach,* The American Chief Executive (*New York: Harper and Row Publishers, Inc., 1966), pp. 497–501.*

Joseph Kallenbach notes that in addition to a reliance on formal diplomatic communications between the Department of State and foreign governments, a President has recourse to less official means of communication, both direct and indirect.

For example, realizing that foreign governments scrutinize all his public actions and statements, a President may announce important policy in speeches to particular groups or over the national media. President Monroe used this tactic when he outlined his Monroe Doctrine in messages to Congress. And President Truman revealed the "Point Four" Program of technical and economic aid to underdeveloped countries in his Inaugural Address of 1949.

At other times policies have emerged from radio and television interviews, or White House and Department of State press releases. President Johnson, for example, frequently used the televised press conference to appeal to North Vietnam, The People's Republic of China, and the Soviet Union to enter into Vietnam peace negotiations.

A more subtle but equally effective method of announcing policy is the public statement of a high executive official known to have the President's clearance. This device was employed by President Truman in 1947, when his Secretary of State, George Marshall, initiated the Marshall Plan in a speech at Harvard. Finally, the executive branch often favors planned "leaks" and rumors, which they know will be eagerly snatched up by the press. Whichever indirect method is used, it requires a skillful foreign observer to grasp the relative importance of the information conveyed.

It therefore becomes a necessary part of the job of a foreign diplomatic representative to keep in touch with these sources of information, to try to separate the wheat from the chaff, and to make an intelligent report on the drift of presidential thinking on matters of concern to his home government.

Direct presidential negotiations have become increasingly more popular since President Wilson's years in office. Before that time, most communications between heads of states were done by exchange of notes, conversations, or ceremonial visits; but Wilson, while he did conduct voluminous correspondences, moved beyond this limited method by attending the Paris Peace Conference in 1918. President Franklin Roosevelt carried this "personal diplomacy" to its height in numerous World War II meetings.

Kallenbach cites President Kennedy's "hot line" as representative of modern trends in direct negotiations. The innovation was undertaken in the hope that this "instantaneous contact" between the two Chief Executives would prevent disastrous misunderstandings in times of world crisis.

Today, it is expected that the President will engage in personal diplomacy. Congress, in providing for United States participation in the United Nations, recognized this by specifying that the President himself may serve as head of the United States delegation to the United Nations at any time he deems fit.

The scope of foreign relations ranges from the diplomatic recognition of governments to the commencement of hostilities verging on war. For formulating and carrying out these policies, the President has immense facilities: American embassies and consulates, the State Department, the Central Intelligence Agency, and those agencies in the Executive Office charged with foreign affairs. The President has full command of civilian and military agencies to help him with the planning and fulfilling of foreign policy.

Although the Secretary of State is the man technically charged by the President with the conduct of foreign affairs, not every President makes the same use of this Cabinet officer. Dwight D. Eisenhower, at one extreme, increased John Foster Dulles's powers to the extent that he assumed almost total control over foreign affairs. Woodrow Wilson, at the other extreme, went so far as to type his own diplomatic messages. Recent presidents—John Kennedy, Lyndon Johnson, and Richard Nixon—have retained this complete autonomy, but have sought and often followed the advice of their closest aides. Kennedy relied a great deal on his brother, the Attorney General; Richard Nixon, although very explicit in setting forth his belief that he is the chief spokesman for the United States on matters of foreign policy, has made extensive use of advice from Henry Kissinger, his special assistant for national security affairs.

The concentration of power into the President's hands evolved in response to the demands of world politics. In an age of rapid communications, the effects of international crises are immediate and far reaching. Swift decisions arrived at and executed by a central authority are essential. Because the President alone has the power to unleash the destructive potential of atomic weaponry, his responsibility in maintaining peace is awesome. He is always accompanied by a member of the military who carries an attaché case containing the day's atomic code for emergency deployment; this military presence shadows each of the Chief Executive's diplomatic decisions.

# Chief of State

Soon after President Nixon assumed office, he arranged to establish a home for himself in San Clemente, California as a retreat from the hurly-burly of Washington; President Johnson vacationed at his ranch in Texas; all Presidents have established some place away from Washington to take working vacations. Whether known as the "Western White House" or the "Texas White House," the government is always considered to be where the President is. This attitude reflects the President's role as *Chief of State*, the center of the entire national government. The President, as the spokesman for 200 million Americans, represents the nation as a whole.

He is expected to stand "above politics," to disdain factions, to unite the country by and through his person. His very being commands attention and respect. When a man assumes office, even his most personal and oldest friends call him "Mr. President."

The President governs the nation, protects it as best as he can from domestic and foreign crises, tries to keep his party united, and administers the government. In performing these functions, he provides the nation with a sense of unity or stability. This sense of stability is upset if the country feels itself to be without a leader.

When President Kennedy was assassinated, the nation suffered terrible moments of disorientation. People rushed home to their families for a sense of community; during the three days of the mourning and funeral, television knit the nation into a single, grieved union. In that moment of loss the nation saw what the person of the President symbolized to the country *as a whole*.

## Ceremonial head

The image of the President at the head of a long table, wine glass raised, toasting several hundred guests is a familiar one, and also representative of his role as ceremonial head. Whether greeting Girl Scouts on the White House lawn, meeting the President of France in the shadow of a jet liner, laying a wreath on the Tomb of the Unknown Soldier—he is the ceremonial presence of the United States, the symbol of American government.

Because ceremonial duties are numerous and draining and sometimes superficial, it has been suggested that the Vice-President wear this ceremonial mantle instead of the President. But the President, although he does delegate some duties to his Vice-President, continues to perform most of the rituals required of him.

## The pardoning power

As Chief of State, the President serves individuals and groups within the larger national population. The Constitution authorizes the President to appoint judges and "to grant reprieves and pardons for offenses against the United States except in cases of impeachment." This is the *pardoning power*, which authorizes him to commute (or lessen) sentences, to grant a delay in execution, or even to give full pardon. Every year the President briefly reviews the Attorney General's recommendations for thousands of reprieve requests and pardons, and in most cases simply approves the recommendations. The President's decision cannot be overruled. The best-known cases involving this rarely exercised power, although rare, are those of convicted foreign spies. In the course of trading the Russian spy Rudolf Abels for the American U-2 pilot Francis Gary Powers in 1962, the President pardoned the convicted Russian, and his action could not be overruled by Congress or the courts.

The President may also grant *amnesty*—that is, he may pardon a specific group of people, usually for the purpose of reintegrating them within the political and social system. For example, after the Civil War, President Lincoln granted amnesty to many secessionists. In so doing he protected not only the group breaking the law, but the entire nation, which stood to lose more from further conflict than a peace induced by amnesty.

# Limitations on the presidency

A complex interplay of politics and protocol defines the American political system. To insure against any usurpation of power by the Chief Executive, the Founding Fathers built restraints into the Constitution so that nearly all presidential powers are checked by other agencies of government. For example, the President's war power is checked by Congress's power over all appropriations.

In addition, there are extraconstitutional restraints on executive action. Existing laws, which the President cannot unilaterally nullify or circumvent, constitute one such restraint. Congressional legislation, however, is much less restricting internationally than domestically. Except for the Cooper-Church Amendment in 1969 to restrict the use of troops in Laos and Thailand, most congressional action has dealt primarily with domestic issues, such as labor-management relations (for example, the Taft-Hartley Act).

Also limiting the President's authority is the force of judicial interpretation. In *Youngstown Sheet and Tube Co.* v. *Sawyer* (1952) for example, the Supreme Court ruled against President Truman's seizure of the steel mills. Truman's action was declared unconstitutional, and he was ordered to relinquish possession.

*Public opinion*, though it can be the President's greatest ally, is also potentially a restraint and limitation. When public opinion is on his side, his reach is extended. When it is not—or when he suspects it is not—his reach is greatly limited. To accomplish national goals, he must consider all the publics. He cannot lower the quota on imports without considering the impact on our commitments to other countries; he cannot conclude a treaty with Japan on trade and textiles without considering congressional reaction. He must remain constantly aware of all his responsibilities, and he must be certain that his actions in one role do not constrain him in another.

# Staff apparatus

The President needs a great deal of help in running the government. The executive branch has a budget of over $25 billion and employs nearly 3 million civilians. In appointing the President to be Chief Administrator, the Constitution empowers him to appoint administrators for this vast and burgeoning bureaucracy.

For the formulation of government policies, the President relies on the Executive Office of the President, and other executive agencies designed as specialized institutions for initiating and carrying out specific programs. In addition to the Executive Office of the President, aid in administering the government is given by the Vice-President and, more importantly, by the Cabinet. But for all the advice the President receives from any number of experts, he remains the final arbiter of decisions.

## Executive Office of the President

21 Rossiter, *The American Presidency*, p. 128.

The *Executive Office of the President* was the creation of Franklin Delano Roosevelt's administration. In 1936, Roosevelt established a President's Committee on Administrative Management. Clinton Rossiter states, "The Committee reported to Mr. Roosevelt in January 1937, and in the shortest scholarly sentence on record told him what he had known ever since his first day in the White House: 'The President needs help.' "[21]

To give him the help he needed, the committee recommended the addition of six presidential administrative assistants and an Executive Office of the President, with separate offices for personnel management, budgeting and finance, and planning for the executive branch of government.

In 1939, the Executive Office of the President was established by an act of Congress. It should be noted that the term *Executive Office* does not signify a single organization, but, rather, the several agencies that provide staff assistance to the President.

The effect of the 1939 establishment of the Executive Office was to convert "the Presidency into an instrument of twentieth-century government; it gives the incumbent a sporting chance to stand the strain and fulfill his constitutional mandate as a one-man branch of our three-part government."[22]

[22] Clinton Rossiter, "The Constitutional Significance of the Executive Office of the President," *American Political Science Review*, XLIII (December 1949): 1206–1217.

In the initial organization of 1939, The Office of Management and Budget (formerly the Bureau of the Budget) was transferred from the Department of the Treasury to the Executive Office. The rest of the agencies now operating as part of the Executive Office have been added since World War II. These offices include the White House Staff, the Council of Economic Advisers, and the National Security Council.

The *White House Staff*, although part of the Executive Office of the President, is distinct from the other administrative divisions. It currently includes the President's *personal staff* of twenty special assistants. This staff is the most immediate extension of the President's personality. Members confer with the President almost daily. They are appointed by the President without Senate confirmation and he relies heavily on their judgment.

The importance of personal advisers has increased with the growing complexity of contemporary government. Members of the President's personal staff provide vital information and analysis of domestic and international conditions. Two of the most influential members function as the principal liaisons between the President and the public. These are the *Press Secretary*, who is the President's voice to the mass media on a day-to-day basis, and the *Appointments Secretary*, who screens the people requesting to see the President. Other presidential aides serve to define and propose solutions for a wide range of government problems. Because the issues involved are so complex, President Nixon has assigned staff members to specific areas of responsibility. These include international affairs, presidential speech writing, economic problems, congressional liaison, coordination of administrative agencies, and specialized affairs, a category determined by current domestic conditions. For example, in the early part of the Nixon administration, Daniel Moynihan was named the President's assistant for Urban Affairs, a position then created to give specialized attention to the urgent problems of urban areas.

But in addition to the twenty special assistants, there are three hundred other persons comprising the White House Staff. Their functions are clerical and custodial. This sector of the White House Staff has expanded to meet the demands of the modern presidency. In the nineteenth century, Presidents were able to handle White House correspondence with the aid of a few clerks. By the mid-twentieth century, fifty were needed to perform this task adequately.

The President's personal staff, as the least formalized sector of the Executive Office, is subject to modification and has been utilized differently by each

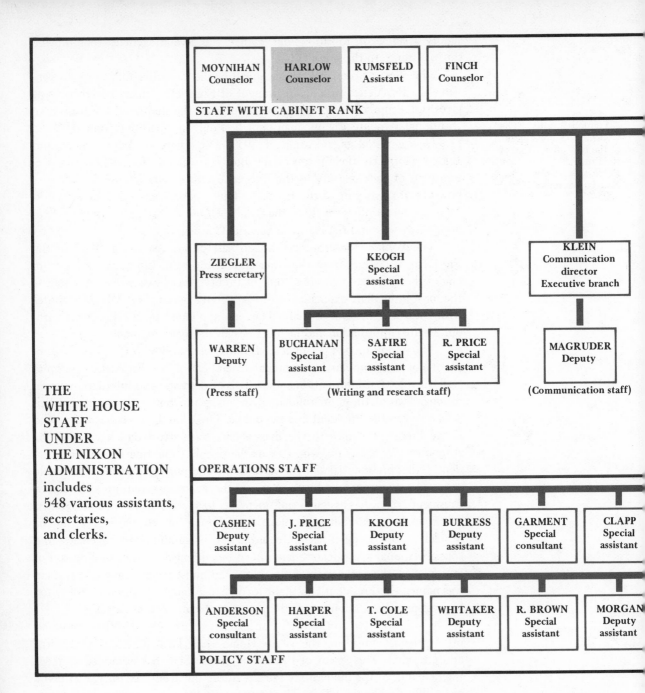

THE
WHITE HOUSE
STAFF
UNDER
THE NIXON
ADMINISTRATION
includes
548 various assistants,
secretaries,
and clerks.

**STAFF WITH CABINET RANK**

| MOYNIHAN Counselor | HARLOW Counselor | RUMSFELD Assistant | FINCH Counselor |

**OPERATIONS STAFF**

ZIEGLER Press secretary — WARREN Deputy (Press staff)

KEOGH Special assistant — BUCHANAN Special assistant, SAFIRE Special assistant, R. PRICE Special assistant (Writing and research staff)

KLEIN Communication director Executive branch — MAGRUDER Deputy (Communication staff)

**POLICY STAFF**

| CASHEN Deputy assistant | J. PRICE Special assistant | KROGH Deputy assistant | BURRESS Deputy assistant | GARMENT Special consultant | CLAPP Special assistant |

| ANDERSON Special consultant | HARPER Special assistant | T. COLE Special assistant | WHITAKER Deputy assistant | R. BROWN Special assistant | MORGAN Deputy assistant |

President. Franklin Roosevelt did not employ any staff to formulate legislation. His assignments were for a specific task, and when it was completed, he
assigned those who worked on it to duties outside the White House. In contrast, the Eisenhower staff received fixed assignments that kept them perma-

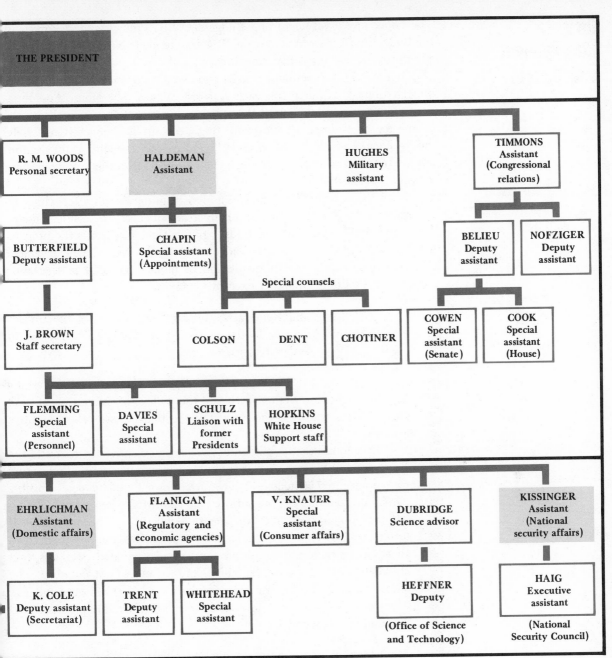

**THE PRESIDENT**

**R. M. WOODS**
Personal secretary

**HALDEMAN**
Assistant

**HUGHES**
Military
assistant

**TIMMONS**
Assistant
(Congressional
relations)

**BUTTERFIELD**
Deputy assistant

**CHAPIN**
Special assistant
(Appointments)

**BELIEU**
Deputy
assistant

**NOFZIGER**
Deputy
assistant

Special counsels

**J. BROWN**
Staff secretary

**COLSON**

**DENT**

**CHOTINER**

**COWEN**
Special
assistant
(Senate)

**COOK**
Special
assistant
(House)

**FLEMMING**
Special
assistant
(Personnel)

**DAVIES**
Special
assistant

**SCHULZ**
Liaison with
former
Presidents

**HOPKINS**
White House
Support staff

**EHRLICHMAN**
Assistant
(Domestic affairs)

**FLANIGAN**
Assistant
(Regulatory and
economic agencies)

**V. KNAUER**
Special
assistant
(Consumer affairs)

**DUBRIDGE**
Science advisor

**KISSINGER**
Assistant
(National
security affairs)

**K. COLE**
Deputy assistant
(Secretariat)

**TRENT**
Deputy
assistant

**WHITEHEAD**
Special
assistant

**HEFFNER**
Deputy

**HAIG**
Executive
assistant

(Office of Science
and Technology)

(National
Security Council)

m Cardamone for Fortune Magazine, *Fortune* (July 1970); 59.

nently and firmly stationed within White House confines. In requiring fewer executive directives for its operations, the Eisenhower staff had greater autonomy than Franklin Roosevelt's and was, therefore, less responsive to executive control.

# Office of Management and Budget

The *Office of Management and Budget* (OMB), known as the Bureau of the Budget until it was renamed in 1970 by President Nixon, performs both administrative and legislative functions.

Before 1921, cabinet departments and executive agencies submitted their projected budget requirements each year to Congress. The House Appropriations Committee assembled all the requests, but it was very difficult for the committee to evaluate all the competing demands for money. Conversely, the President had no way of formulating an executive budget or of examining the spending of monies, although the Constitution formally charged him with that responsibility.

With the passage of the Budget and Accounting Act of 1921 which established the OMB, it became possible to create an effective executive budget. The Office of Management and Budget fulfills three functions: the preparation and execution of the federal budget, the coordination and management of executive agencies, and the regulation of monies provided in legislation initiated by the President and enacted by Congress.

*James W. Davis and Randall B. Ripley,* "The Bureau of the Budget and Executive Agencies: Notes on their Interaction," *The Journal of Politics, 29 (November 1967): 749–769.*

In 1965, James W. Davis and Randall B. Ripley conducted a study to clarify the interaction between the Office of Management and Budget, then known as the Bureau of the Budget, and other executive agencies.

They found that a few contacts between executive agencies and the Bureau of the Budget, such as the submittal of a new yearly budget, are formal and prescheduled, but most are informal and frequent, possibly daily. For example, the bureau must be contacted when proposed legislation to Congress is under consideration, when a new agency budget is formed, and when subsequent supplementary appropriations are needed. In addition, there are many questions of management, statistics, and automatic data processing for which contacts must be maintained. The bureau must gather information regularly for the President, and the agencies find it necessary to consult the bureau on interpretation and clarification of executive orders.

When branch chiefs and division chiefs of the bureau contact agencies, they generally contact high-level management, and their concerns are usually major program changes or negotiations.

Several considerations affect bureau-agency relations. First of all, what interests the President must take priority in the bureau. Secondly, budgetary decisions of the bureau affect its relationship with agencies

—if an agency does not receive a large enough allocation, "strained relations" may result. Thirdly, the need the agency feels for bureau support is another factor affecting relations. A fourth factor is the organization within each agency: decentralized bureaus within a department may result in inefficient coordination with the Bureau of the Budget. The last and most important consideration is the factor of personality.

One abrasive or difficult person on either side can affect how the organizations get along and view each other. Conversely, a sympathetic or supportive person can also affect the relationship.

Davis and Ripley come to four broad conclusions:

First, the relationship between the Bureau of the Budget and any given operating agency is not predictably hostile.

Second, access to and control over information appear to be the most important internal factors affecting the bargaining process between the Bureau and the operating agencies.

Third, resolution of conflict between the Bureau and an agency, when necessary, can come at a variety of levels. Disagreements may be settled at the lowest level, that is, by the examiner. But some conflicts escalate. Each higher level in the Bureau may try its hand at conflict resolution. Conflicts, of course, are also escalated in the agencies.

Fourth, delay and the avoidance of decision on the part of the Bureau may be a tactic in conflict resolution.

The OMB receives requests from all executive agencies. The proposed budgets are reviewed, necessary hearings are conducted, and finally the requests are altered so that all agency proposals conform to the overall budget policy established by the President. The OMB director, in fact, frequently confers with the President on budget plans in order to formulate a comprehensive policy reflecting executive economic priorities.

In seeing that agency appropriations follow executive guidelines, the OMB often prunes allocations accordingly. After months of analysis, a consolidated set of findings and recommendations on revenue and expenditures is completed and sent to the President for review and approval. In January, the President submits the final estimates to Congress in the *National Budget message*.

Following congressional review, modification, and approval or rejection of individual items in the budget, the office is responsible for administration of the government's programs. The OMB maintains a watchful eye on expenditures by specific agencies, as every allocation requires OMB approval.

In order to exercise increased control, the Office conducts organizational research and, based on findings, makes recommendations to agencies to improve the functioning of executive agencies. This keeps agencies sensitive to opportunities for improvement and helps them curtail waste and inefficiency in spending.

The *Legislative Reference Office* of OMB studies all legislative proposals originating with executive agencies and keeps the President informed about bills pending in Congress. With this help from the OMB, the President can inform members of Congress of what expenditures he deems wise or wasteful. The Office also advises the President on the consequences of bills that have been passed by Congress and, after a survey of all affected agencies, suggests to him that the new bill be signed or vetoed. If the OMB advises a veto, a veto message is written and submitted to the President.

## Council of Economic Advisers

In 1946 Congress passed the Employment Act, creating the *Council of Economic Advisers*. The council is made up of three economic analysts appointed by the President and approved by the Senate. These three counselors review the state of the economy, and the chairman passes their advice on to the President. The council recommends actions to be taken by the President in the management of the economy, that is, in employment, production, and government expenditure. The council also prepares the annual *Economic Report* to Congress, based on their analysis of current economic trends and programs.

Today when government spending and taxes can directly affect the economy, it is the council that recommends to the President when more government spending is needed to stimulate the economy, or when money should be taken from the economy to slow down the pace of expansion.

## National Security Council

The 1947 National Security Act created the *National Security Council* to advise the President on the maintenance of the nation's security through the coordination of domestic, foreign, and military policies. During World War II, the absence of such a coordinating body prompted President Roosevelt to improvise an informal "War Cabinet." After the war, the political aspects of action abroad became even more important, and a body was needed to harmonize foreign and defense policy.

The National Security Act of 1947 provides that the council shall "assess and appraise the objectives, commitments, and risks of the United States in relation to our actual and potential military power, in the interest of national security." Drawing on experts from the military and civilian bureaucracy, the council considers political and military aspects of security, thus assisting the President in the making of foreign policy decisions.

The council has a director, who serves on the White House Staff, and includes the President, in the position of chairman, the Vice-President, the Secretaries of State and Defense, and the director of the Office of Emergency Planning. The meetings are often expanded to include the chairman of the Joint Chiefs of Staff, the Ambassador to the United Nations, the director of the Central Intelligence Agency, other Cabinet members, or members of the White House Staff—all of whom might have specialized knowledge of particular issues.

## Other executive agencies

A number of other agencies is contained within the Executive Office of the President. These agencies are the National Aeronautics and Space Council, the Office of Emergency Planning, the Office of Science and Technology, the Urban Affairs Council, the Domestic Council, the Environmental Quality Council, the Office of Economic Opportunity, the National Council on Marine Resources and Engineering Development, and the Office of the Special Representative for Trade Negotiations.

The *National Aeronautics and Space Council* was established by the National Aeronautics and Space Act of 1958 to advise the President on all aspects of our space program. With the Vice-President serving as chairman, members include the Secretary of State, the Secretary of Defense, the chairman of the Atomic Energy Commission and the administrator of NASA.

The *Office of Emergency Planning*, established in 1950, is charged with the planning and mobilizing of the nation's resources to meet a wide variety of domestic and international emergencies, especially major wars. The director of the Office of Emergency Planning sits on the National Security Council.

In June 1962, the *Office of Science and Technology* was established with aims of assisting the President in the use of science for national security purposes, coordinating federal policies in scientific research, and evaluating such programs conducted by national agencies. The creation of this agency reflects the emphasis placed on scientific development after the Soviet Union launched its first space satellite in 1957. Since then, billions of dollars have been spent to attain United States primacy in scientific and technological advancement.

The *Urban Affairs Council* was established in 1969 by President Nixon to coordinate the government's urban policies, in much the same way as the National Security Council coordinates foreign policy. Its members are the President, Vice-President, Attorney General, and the Secretaries of Agriculture; Commerce; Labor; Health, Education and Welfare; Housing and Urban Development; and Transportation. Formed by executive order, the council develops programs for improving the nation's sick cities and saving others from decay. It works to coordinate federal expenditures and efforts in areas such as civil rights, transportation, housing and health services.

The *Domestic Council*, organized by President Nixon in 1970, is the newest of executive agencies. Its purpose is to clarify objectives for domestic policy, evaluate current government programs, and compile alternate plans for achieving the necessary goals. It is a major source of advice to the President on domestic issues. The staff is under the jurisdiction of a director, who also serves as a special assistant to the President. Its formal chairman is the President, and members include the Vice-President and most department heads. The council utilizes task forces and other planning groups and has the cooperation of the Office of Management and Budget, as well as the President's personal staff.

*The White House and some of its rooms:*
*The East Room, the Blue Room, the*
*family dining room, the Diplomatic*
*Reception Room, and the Lincoln*
*Bedroom.*

President Nixon, in response to the growing concern over industrial pollution, formed the *Environmental Quality Council* in 1969 to advise him on air and water pollution and to devise policies to protect the nation's natural resources. Members of the Environmental Quality Council include the President, the Vice-President, the President's science adviser, and the Secretaries most involved with environmental matters—those of Agriculture;

Commerce; Interior; Transportation; Housing and Urban Development; and Health, Education and Welfare.

Three more agencies complete the Executive Office:

The *Office of Economic Opportunity* (OEO) was formed by Congress to maintain programs to combat poverty. A detailed discussion of the OEO is contained in Chapter 23.

The *National Council on Marine Resources and Engineering Development* advises the President on the use and development of marine resources.

The *Office of the Special Representative for Trade Negotiations* assists

the President in formulating and administering trade agreements with other countries.

**The Cabinet**

Though Washington met with his cabinet, the *Cabinet* itself was not even mentioned in the original Constitution.

Unlike the British Cabinet, which is made up of elected officials who share government responsibility with the prime minister, our Cabinet is made up of presidential appointees, approved by the Senate, who administer major governmental departments but are called together as a presidential advisory *group* only by the choice of the President. The Cabinet is not a policy-making body. Though the President may poll his Cabinet for a decision on a certain subject, he is not duty-bound to accept their opinion. For example, before Lincoln delivered the Emancipation Proclamation, he appeared before the Cabinet to read them the address. He introduced it by saying: "I have got you together to hear what I have written down. I do not wish your advice about the main matter, for that I have determined for myself."[23]

[23] Quoted in Corwin, *The President*, p. 302.

Today there are eleven Cabinet-level departments: the Departments of State; Treasury; Defense; Justice; Interior; Agriculture; Commerce; Labor; Health, Education and Welfare; Housing and Urban Development; and Transportation. Cabinet-level posts, such as Ambassador to the United Nations, are considered part of the structure, and officials appointed to them may take part in Cabinet meetings. Other high-level officials, such as the Director of the Office of Management and Budget, may be invited to attend as well.

The President consults with the Cabinet only if he wishes to do so; thus Cabinet power derives from usage according to executive choice rather than constitutional specification. During the Civil War, for example, Lincoln seldom summoned the Cabinet. During World War II, Roosevelt tried to institute procedural innovations, but then did not rely on Cabinet members for much advice or policy. Eisenhower, in an attempt to make weekly cabinet meetings more effective, appointed a *Cabinet Secretariat*—an official to organize an agenda and summarize major problems prior to each meeting. In contrast, President Kennedy considered cabinet meetings totally unnecessary, preferring to work individually with each Cabinet-level official.

Essentially, Cabinet members as agency heads are executives in their own right, serving the constituency of their separate departments and responsible to the President. "In the day-to-day work of the Cabinet member, each man fends for himself without much consideration for Cabinet unity."[24] In appointing Cabinet members, the President tries to distribute the positions to party leaders from various parts of the country, to influential members of his party of various ethnic, business, and professional backgrounds, and occasionally to members of the opposition party. A Cabinet position may be given to a prime supporter as a repayment for services rendered. But executive experience and a record of past service and opinions acceptable to the large constituencies of the separate departments are also necessary qualifications. Charles Wilson and Robert S. McNamara were appointed Secretaries of Defense under Eisenhower and Kennedy respectively because, as presidents of

[24] Richard G. Fenno, Jr., *The President's Cabinet* (Cambridge, Mass.: Harvard University Press, 1959), p. 247.

large automobile companies (GM and Ford), both were accustomed to dealing with large sums of money and complex corporate problems. Stuart Udall, Kennedy's Secretary of the Interior, was chosen as a known and respected conservationist.

## The Vice-President

John Adams, the first to fill the office of Vice-President, stated, "I am Vice-President of the United States. In this I am nothing, but I may be everything."

The *Vice-President* is closest to the President in line of succession, but he may be the furthest in real political influence or power. The Constitution merely states that a Vice-President shall be chosen by the electors; that he shall take over the office and duties of the President upon death, illness, disability, resignation, or removal; and that he shall be President of the Senate, voting only when the Senate is deadlocked.

In this century the vice-presidential office has received more serious attention than at any other time in American history. Four times in the last four decades Presidents have died in office, and two—Presidents Wilson and Eisenhower—were incapacitated during their terms in office. Clearly the extent to which the Vice-President is in the President's confidence is critical in such instances. Franklin D. Roosevelt, who died in office, never informed his Vice-President, Harry Truman that the atomic bomb was being developed. Upon Roosevelt's death, he said: "When they told me yesterday what had happened, I felt like the moon, the stars, and all the planets had fallen on me." Consequently Truman was mindful of keeping his Vice-President informed.

But it was Dwight Eisenhower, more than any previous President, who encouraged his Vice-President, Richard Nixon, to take a more active part in the functions of the government. Nixon chaired meetings in the President's absence and became a member of the National Security Council. Subsequently, President Kennedy tried to involve Lyndon Johnson in as many executive procedures as possible, adding the chairmanship of the Space and Aeronautics Commission to his other posts. Vice-President Spiro Agnew is a member of six other councils and committees, and is in charge of the Office of Intergovernmental Activities, where he serves as principal liaison between the national government and state and local administrations. Yet, despite this recent proliferation of political assignments, the Vice-President still has no assured resources for political power other than what the President wills, nor is he politically responsible for any executive decision. In any capacity, his function is to act for the President according to executive instructions.

Thus, any talk of making the Vice-President an "assistant president" has never gone beyond the discussion stage. The President often prefers as his closest advisers men chosen for their views and temperament rather than for political expediency. Unfortunately, the Vice-President is often selected to balance the ticket for philosophical or geographic reasons and is not personally close to the President. Nevertheless, the Vice-President is a permanent constitutional fixture who serves well as a traveling emissary and as someone who can relieve the President of some minor burdens of office. These slight indications of status for the Vice-President have become apparent only within the last fifteen years and are still largely undeveloped.

# Glossary

**Acting President**   Government official, usually the Vice-President, who assumes the powers and functions of the Chief Executive, in accordance with the constitutional provisions on presidential succession.

**amnesty**   Act whereby a group of people is pardoned, usually for the purpose of reintegrating them within the political and social system.

**Cabinet**   Executive institution composed of presidential appointees, who administer the eleven major governmental departments—the Departments of State; Treasury; Defense; Justice; Interior; Agriculture; Commerce; Labor; Health, Education and Welfare; Housing and Urban Development; and Transportation.

**Ceremonial Head**   Aspect of the President's role as Chief of State in which, as a symbol of the American government, he performs ritual acts such as laying a wreath on the Tomb of the Unknown Soldier, conferring awards, or greeting dignitaries.

**Chief Administrator**   Role of the President as prime manager of government operations, specifically those in the executive branch.

**Chief Diplomat**   Role of the President as the prime representative and policy-maker in international affairs.

**Chief Legislator**   Role of the President in which, according to the Constitution, he recommends to Congress "such measures as he shall judge necessary and expedient," and which in practice entails giving the State of the Union message, the National Budget message, and the State of the World address, exercising the power to veto legislation, and proposing and drafting bills.

**Chief of State**   Role of the President as the spokesman for the nation, voicing national aspirations.

**Commander-in-Chief**   Role of the President as the ultimate authority on military operations, strategy, war, and the maintenance of domestic peace and tranquility.

**concurrent resolution**   Resolution on the same matter by both Houses of Congress but not including the President's signature, and lacking the force of law. Usually deals with either congressional procedures, or the sentiment of Congress toward a certain issue or country.

**Council of Economic Advisers**   Three economic advisers, appointed by the President and approved by the Senate, who review the state of the economy and, through their chairman, pass their advice on to the President.

**Domestic Council**   Agency of the Executive Office of the President that advises the President on pressing domestic issues, recommends policies, and evaluates current government programs.

**Economic Report**   Annual study prepared by the Council of Economic Advisers for the Congress as an appraisal of current economic programs and a description of trends in employment and production.

**Environmental Quality Council**   Agency of the Executive Office of the President that advises the President and recommends policies to control air, water, and land pollution.

**executive agreement**  International agreement between the United States and a foreign nation, made by the President without the advice and consent of the Senate.

**Executive Office of the President**  A complex of administrative agencies including the Office of Management and Budget, the White House Staff, the Council of Economic Advisers, the National Security Council, the National Aeronautics and Space Council, the Office of Emergency Planning, the Office of Science and Technology, the Urban Affairs Council, the Domestic Council, the Environmental Quality Council, the Office of Economic Opportunity, the National Council on Marine Resources and Engineering Development, and the Office of the Special Representative for Trade Negotiations.

**filling in the details**  Process of specifying the exact terms of a legislative proposal, a task usually performed by the Executive Office of the President.

**item veto**  rejection of specific provisions or items in a bill; a power not exercized by the President.

**National Aeronautics and Space Council**  Agency of the Executive Office of the President that advises the President on space programs, policies, and plans.

**National Budget message**  The President's annual speech to Congress and the nation on priorities for government spending.

**National Council on Marine Resources and Engineering Development**  Agency of the Executive Office of the President that advises the President on the use and development of marine resources.

**National Security Council**  Agency of the Executive Office of the President that coordinates foreign policy and military strategy for the purpose of national defense.

**Office of Economic Opportunity**  Agency of the Executive Office of the President that maintains programs to combat poverty.

**Office of Emergency Planning**  Agency of the Executive Office of the President that plans and mobilizes the nation's resources to meet domestic and international crises.

**Office of Management and Budget (OMB)**  Agency of the Executive Office of the President that formulates national economic policy and regulates government expenditures in accordance with executive priorities.

**Office of Science and Technology**  Agency of the Executive Office of the President that advises the President on federal policy concerning scientific research for national security purposes.

**Office of the Special Representative for Trade Negotiations**  Agency of the Executive Office of the President that assists the President in executing trade agreements with other countries.

**pardoning power**  Absolute power of the President as Chief Magistrate to commute (or lessen) sentences, to grant a delay in execution, to grant full pardon, or to give a partial pardon according to certain stipulations.

**party leader**  Role of the President as national spokesman for his political party, and as focus of party power and unity.

**pocket veto**  Veto used during the last ten days of a congressional session, whereby the President leaves the bill unsigned within the ten-day grace period always allotted to him to decide on a bill and thus kills the bill for that session of Congress.

**presidential succession**   The provision in Article II, Section 1, of the Constitution, and later in the Twenty-fifth Amendment, whereby, in the case of the President's death or disability, the Vice-President (or in the event of his absence, the Speaker of the House, the President pro-tempore of the Senate, and then through the seniority ranks of the Cabinet—Secretary of State, Defense, Treasury, and so on) becomes Acting President.

**removal powers**   Power of the President to remove from office any appointed official who performs strictly executive functions.

**reprieve**   Type of pardon that temporarily delays the execution of a sentence.

**riders**   Provisions attached to a bill, which may be irrelevant to the main purpose of the bill and which often favor local interests.

**senatorial courtesy**   Informal presidential practice in which the President must clear his nominees for local and state appointments with the senators of his party, or risk Senate rejection of his candidates.

**State of the Union message**   The President's annual address to Congress declaring domestic policy and legislative priorities.

**State of the World address**   The President's annual address to Congress on United States foreign policy.

**treaty**   International agreement, established by the Constitution and signed by the President with the advice and consent of the Senate.

**Twenty-fifth Amendment**   Constitutional amendment ratified in 1967 for the purpose of clarifying the line to presidential succession and creating an apparatus for carrying out the transference of office.

**Twenty-second Amendment**   Constitutional amendment, ratified in 1951, limiting the President's stay in office to two elected terms, or in the case of a Chief Executive who completes the term of his predecessor, to no more than ten years in office.

**Urban Affairs Council**   Agency of the Executive Office of the President that develops and coordinates federal programs in urban areas.

**veto**   Refusal of the President to sign a bill passed by Congress, which can be overridden by a two-thirds vote in Congress.

**Vice-President**   Selected as politically advantageous running mate to the President, the government official nearest to the President in line of succession, and serving as President of the Senate.

## Supreme Court decisions

*Humphrey's Executor* v. *United States*   1935 ruling, also based on upholding the principle of separation of powers, that the President's removal power was limited to executive officers and did not extend to those administering the independent regulatory agencies.

*Myers* v. *United States*   1926 ruling that upheld the President's power to remove his appointees from office on the grounds that the demand for senatorial confirmation here violates the principle of separation of powers and therefore, is unconstitutional.

*United States* v. *Belmont*   1937 ruling that gave executive agreements the same legal status as treaties.

*United States* v. *Curtiss-Wright Export Corporation*   1936 ruling that the national government holds all power in foreign affairs and the President is the prime agent, with Congress ceding to his wishes.

*Youngstown Sheet and Tube Co.* v. *Sawyer* 1952 ruling in which the Court checked executive power by declaring President Truman's seizure of the steel mills unconstitutional.

# Suggested readings

Binkley, Wilfred E., *The Man in the White House: His Powers and Duties* (Baltimore: Johns Hopkins Press, 1959). History of the presidency, emphasizing the President's constitutional and extra-constitutional powers.

Binkley, Wilfred E., *President and Congress*, 3rd ed. (New York: Random House, Inc., 1962). Account of what presidential-congressional relations have been and what they should be.

Burns, James MacGregor, *Presidential Government: Crucible of Leadership* (Boston: Houghton Mifflin Co., 1966). Evaluation of the presidency, citing the concentration of power in the White House as the distinctive American contribution to democracy in the twentieth century.

Cornwell, Elmer E., Jr., *Presidential Leadership of Public Opinion* (Bloomington, Ind.: Indiana University Press, 1965). Study of the presidential methods and techniques in dealing with the communications media.

Corwin, Edward S., *The President: Office and Powers*, 4th ed. (New York: New York University Press, 1957). Classical discussion of the historical and constitutional development of the office of the President.

Fenno, Richard N., Jr., *The President's Cabinet: An Analysis in the Period from Wilson to Eisenhower* (Cambridge, Mass.: Harvard University Press, 1959). Thorough study of the Cabinet and explanation of why it cannot be an effective governing device in the American form of government.

Harris, Joseph P., *The Advice and Consent of the Senate* (Westport, Conn.: Greenwood Press, Inc., 1968). Description of the Senate's constitutional power to approve all presidential appointments.

Hilsman, Roger, *To Move a Nation* (Garden City, N.Y.: Doubleday and Co., Inc., 1967). Excellent study of the President's role in foreign policy-making.

Hirschfield, Robert S., ed., *The Power of the Presidency: Concepts and Controversy* (New York: Atherton Press, 1968). Collection of essays, judicial opinions, and writings by Presidents and their advisers on presidential powers.

Jackson, Carlton, *Presidential Vetoes, 1792–1945* (Athens, Ga.: University of Georgia Press, 1967). History of presidential veto power and an evaluation of its significance.

Jackson, Henry M., *The National Security Council: Jackson Sub-committee Papers on Policy Making at the Presidential Level* (New York: Frederick A. Praeger, Inc., 1965). Discussion of problems of presidential policy-making in foreign policy and national defense, including a description and evaluation of the National Security Council and its relationship to the President.

Koenig, Louis W., *The Invisible Presidency* (New York: Holt, Rinehart and Winston, Inc., 1960). Acount of persons who have held considerable "behind-the-scenes" power in the White House, including Alexander Hamilton, Martin Van Buren, Colonel Edward House, Harry Hopkins, and Sherman Adams.

Koenig, Louis W., *The Chief Executive*, rev. ed. (New York: Harcourt Brace Jovanovich, Inc., 1968). Good general introduction to the presidency, including descriptions of all the major roles of the office.

Laski, Harold J., *The American Presidency: An Interpretation* (New York: Grosset and Dunlap, Inc., 1958). Discussion of the presidency, emphasizing the value of expanding presidential powers, by a noted British political scientist.

McConnell, Grant, *The Modern Presidency* (New York: St. Martin's Press, Inc., 1967). Brief study of the Presidency and the changes it has undergone and is undergoing.

Neustadt, Richard E., *Presidential Power* (New York: John Wiley and Sons, Inc., 1960). Major work on the President's problem of winning power for himself while holding office (politics of administration), with three case studies.

Rossiter, Clinton, *The American Presidency*, rev. ed. (New York: Harcourt Brace Jovanovich, Inc., 1960). Analysis of the various roles of the presidency in a historical context.

Rossiter, Clinton, *The Supreme Court and the Commander-in-Chief* (New York: Plenum Publishing Corporation, 1970). Detailed study of the development of the President's powers as Commander-in-Chief and the Supreme Court's role in interpreting this constitutional power.

Schubert, Glendon A., Jr., *The Presidency in the Courts* (Minneapolis, Minn.: University of Minnesota Press, 1967). Examination of the relationship between the President and the judiciary.

Sorensen, Theodore C., *Decision-Making in the White House: The Olive Branch or Arrows* (New York: Columbia University Press, 1963). Analysis of how Presidents steer a course between war and peace by an adviser to the late President John F. Kennedy.

Tourtellot, Arthur B., *The Presidents on the Presidency*. (Garden City, N.Y.: Doubleday and Co., Inc., 1964). Presentation of the views of former presidents on their constitutional and political powers.

Warren, Sidney, *The President As World Leader* (New York: McGraw-Hill Book Co., 1964). Study of twentieth century Presidents from Theodore Roosevelt to John F. Kennedy, in their role as world leaders.

Wildavsky, Aaron, *The Presidency* (Boston: Little, Brown and Co., 1969). Essays on the various views of the office.

Williams, Irving, *The Rise of the Vice-Presidency* (Washington, D.C.: Public Affairs Press, 1956). Good account of the function of the Vice-President, although slightly outdated by recent developments in that office.

# Topics of further study

Davis, J. W., and R. B. Ripley, "The Bureau of the Budget and Executive Branch Agencies: Notes on their Interaction," *The Journal of Politics*, November 1967, pp. 749–769.

Travis, Thomas, ed., *Congress and the President: Readings in Executive-Legislative Relations* (New York: Teachers College Press, Columbia University, 1967).

# 13 the president

In the previous chapter we discussed the constitutional and political powers and limitations of the presidency. We saw that the office of the President has changed in response to the immediate social, economic, and international needs of the nation—and how legislation, judicial interpretation, and tradition have defined the responsibilities and powers of the presidency over the years.

The presidency, however, is more than the sum total of legal powers. Since Washington's inauguration in 1789, thirty-seven men have won title to the office. Each of these men imprinted on the office his manner of using presidential powers, his character, his interests, and his perception of the office of the presidency.

Thus, the office of the President changes according to how its holder interprets and uses the powers and duties given to him.

## Two opposing interpretations of presidential authority

Generally, critics assess a President by analyzing the use he makes of his powers and the effect that his character has on the image of the presidency.

The argument for *limited* executive power was best stated by William Howard Taft, a President who refused to exercise any authorities except those that were strictly delegated to his office. When he retired from office, he wrote:

> The true view of the Executive function is, as I conceive it, that the President can exercise no power which cannot be fairly and reasonably traced to some specific grant of power or justly implied and included within such express grant as proper and necessary to its exercise. . . . There is no undefined residuum of power which he can exercise because it seems to him in the public interest.[1]

In other words, Taft felt that the President could exercise only those powers specifically granted to him by the Constitution or by Congress. He

[1] William Howard Taft, *Our Chief Magistrate and His Powers* (New York: Columbia University Press, 1925), p. 138.

[2] See Stuart Gerry Brown, *The American Presidency* (New York: The Macmillan Co., 1966), pp. 146–157 for an application of Roosevelt's concept of the strong presidency.

[3] David E. Haight and Larry D. Johnston, *The President: Roles and Powers* (Chicago: Rand McNally and Co., 1965), p. 33.

[4] Arthur Larsen, *Eisenhower: The President Nobody Knew* (New York: Charles Scribner's Sons, 1968), p. 12.

disapproved of Teddy Roosevelt's concept of the President as the strong central executive exercising sweeping powers in the national interest.[2]

James Buchanan, a nineteenth-century President who also rejected the notion of the President as the political leader of the nation, viewed himself as an administrative officer carrying out the will of the Congress and the people. In January 1860, on the eve of the Civil War, he "offered the legal opinion that he had no power to use force against the seceding Southerners."[3] All he or anyone else in the government could do was "conciliate them." This opinion, based on his literal interpretation of the Constitution, encouraged rebel states to loosen ties with the Union. Both Buchanan and Taft might be called *weak Presidents* because they believed in a relatively weak executive.

Popular appeal often has nothing to do with a President's strength. The attitude and accomplishments of the President, rather than the opinion of the people, determines whether political scientists will evaluate a President as "weak" or "strong." President Eisenhower was admired by the majority. Yet he is not classified as a strong President because he too believed in limited executive power. "He approached that office" with "a conviction that the principle of separation of powers required the President actually to impose restraints on himself because of the overwhelming power that the Presidency had acquired; and . . . a belief that the incidental influence flowing from the Presidency itself should not be exploited to promote causes beyond those assigned to the President by the Constitution."[4] Conversely, Wilson was not very popular during his term of office, and Franklin Delano Roosevelt was hated by a large proportion of the population—yet both these men are considered strong Presidents, because they extended the range of the office.

Presidents categorized here as weak generally are those who do not use their extra-constitutional powers to lead public opinion or influence Congress. They view themselves as limited in power. Thus Eisenhower spoke of the need to end "Executive usurpations of power" and "to restore the Congress to its rightful place in the Government." Eisenhower retired from office satisfied that he had brought a kind of peace to the country after the difficult years of the Truman regime.

A *strong President* gives broad meaning to his constitutional powers in order to deal with current conditions. This involves reinterpreting and expanding the delegated powers.

The earliest defense for a strong Chief Executive was advanced in 1787 by Alexander Hamilton in *The Federalist*:

> Energy in the executive is a leading character in the definition of good government. It is essential to the protection of the community against foreign attacks; it is not less essential to the steady administration of the laws; to the protection of property against those irregular and high-handed combinations which sometimes interrupt the ordinary course of justice; to the secu-

rity of liberty against the enterprises and assaults of ambition, of faction and of anarchy. . . . A feeble executive implies a feeble execution of the government. A feeble execution is but another phrase for a bad execution; and a government ill executed, whatever it may be in theory, must be, in practice, a bad government.[5]

[5] Alexander Hamilton, "Federalist No. 70," *The Federalist Papers*, ed. by Clinton Rossiter (New York: New American Library, Inc. 1961), p. 423.

Years later Lincoln espoused a similar view—regarding his office as the most politically effective position in the land. He conceived of himself as the primary legislator and as originator as well as the executor of policy. He felt the President was "the source as well as the summation of the nation's political consciousness."

Theodore Roosevelt, generally acknowledged to be the first strong modern President, gave the following interpretation of the presidency:

> My view was that every executive officer, and above all every executive officer in high positions, was a *steward* of the people bound actively and affirmatively to do all he could for the people, and not to content himself with the negative merit of keeping his talents undamaged in a napkin.[6]

[6] *Theodore Roosevelt, An Autobiography* (New York: Charles Scribner's Sons, 1913), p. 357.

In rebuttal to critics who considered his authority too extensive, Roosevelt said:

> I did not usurp power, but I did greatly broaden the use of executive power. In other words, I acted for the public welfare, I acted for the common well-being of all our people, whenever and in whatever manner was necessary, unless prevented by direct constitutional or legislative prohibition. I did not care a rap for the mere form and show of power; I cared immensely for the use that could be made of the substance.[6]

From the beginning, our Presidents have been faced with situations in which they had to define the scope of their power. Washington expanded his delegated powers through the executive decisions he was called upon to make in establishing the new government. Jefferson, although theoretically a strict constructionist, was a "strong" President when he authorized the Louisiana Purchase without consulting Congress. Jackson was bold enough to tell the Supreme Court he would not enforce one of their decisions. Lincoln is often cited for his power in assuming complete authority during the Civil War, and Woodrow Wilson showed no hesitation in taking his ideas to the people when Congress thwarted him.

In this chapter, we will study six Presidents—Herbert C. Hoover, Franklin D. Roosevelt, Dwight D. Eisenhower, John F. Kennedy, Lyndon B. Johnson, and Richard M. Nixon. We will view each in his respective political context and broadly evaluate each in terms of his accomplishments and failings as President.

# Herbert Clark Hoover

[7] Richard Neustadt, *Presidential Power* (New York: John Wiley and Sons, Inc., 1964), p. 172.

Richard Neustadt writes that "Hoover had a sense of purpose so precise as to be stultifying."[7] In the years before he became the thirty-first President, Herbert Clark Hoover employed that enormous sense of purpose to achieve immense success.

Hoover was born in West Branch, Iowa, in 1874, the son of Quaker parents. Orphaned by the age of eight, he was raised by relatives in the far West. In 1891, he entered the first class of Stanford University, where he displayed ability for hard work and concern for administrative detail.

Shortly after graduation, Hoover earned his fortune and reputation as a highly capable international mining engineer. During World War I, he set aside business interests to become chairman of the American Relief Commission. In this post, Hoover was assigned the task of alleviating the suffering of people displaced by the war. His success made him a highly respected public figure and earned him such titles as the "great engineer" and the "great humanitarian."

In 1921, President Harding appointed Hoover Secretary of Commerce, a post he continued to hold with great competence under President Calvin Coolidge. This reputation for social concern and administrative efficiency won him the Republican presidential nomination in 1928. Hoover easily defeated his opponent, candidate Alfred E. Smith of New York, winning majorities in forty-one of the forty-eight states and 444 electoral votes to Smith's 87.

In his inaugural address Hoover, at the peak of his popularity, sounded an optimistic note. "In no nation," he said, "are the fruits of accomplishment more secure." Seven months later, in October 1929, the stock market crashed, and Herbert Hoover presided over a nation suffering the most disastrous depression of its history.

## Hoover as legislator

Hoover felt that the Great Depression was somehow related to a loss of public confidence in government, and that if public confidence could be restored through such measures as the loosening of bankruptcy laws, loans to railroads, banks, and industry, then the depression would end. But Hoover's personality did not foster the confidence that was needed. By nature a shy man, he delivered totally uninspiring speeches. He felt the public wanted the exact facts. He distrusted emotional language.

Hoover's disdain for bargaining hampered his dealings with Congress. He could not play the political game of manipulation and maneuver, and simply presented his proposals to Congress assuming that his detailed logic alone would prompt legislative action. During his term of office, Hoover appointed sixty-two fact-finding commissions to advise him on critical issues.

*Herbert Hoover, who typically disliked extended interaction with the press, usually delayed questioning until shortly before he had to leave for another appointment.*

But he personally prepared all his legislation. Seldom did he consult with Congress. This approach kept him from actively seeking support for his proposals; without a champion in the legislative branch many of his programs failed. Walter Lippmann wrote of Hoover as

> undecisive at the point when the battle can be won or lost . . . this weakness appears at the point where in order to win he would have to intervene in the hurly-burly of conflicting wills which are the living tissue of popular government; he is baffled and worried and his action paralyzed by his own inexperience in the very special business of democracy.[8]

Hoover never gained any real support from Congress or the people. His unpopularity is reflected by the name given the shanty towns established on the outskirts of big cities to house the refugees of the Great Depression; they were called "Hoovervilles."

## Hoover as administrator

Herbert Hoover made his reputation as an administrator if not as a legislator. He had a capacity for absorbing details and he personally attended to even the smallest matter. "A repairman behind a dyke," he described himself: "No sooner is one leak plugged up than it is necessary to dash over and stop another that has broken out. There is no end to it."

[8] Quoted in Erwin C. Hargrove, *Presidential Leadership* (New York: The Macmillan Co., 1966), p. 110.

Thus, Hoover sought to combat the Great Depression as he would an administrative problem. He drew up plans and proposals. He studied statistics and tried to derive from them solutions to the crisis.

> Few, if any, Presidents have worked as hard on the job as Hoover. Up at six and at his desk by eight-thirty, he drove his staff ragged by relentless application.[9]

[9] Louis Koenig, *Chief Executive* (New York: Harcourt Brace Jovanovich, Inc., 1968), p. 368.

"To Hoover's brain facts are water to a sponge," said Bernard Baruch, a noted American businessman and statesman. "They are absorbed into every tiny interstice." "He has the greatest capacity for assimilating and organizing information of any man I ever knew," said his Secretary of State, Henry L. Stimson.[9] Yet Hoover's marshalling of facts was not enough to meet the crisis effectively. Secretary Stimson lamented the President's habit of "seeing the dark side first."

Hoover saw the Great Depression as a condition that could be managed —through hard work and earnest application. But ironically, the harder he worked, the worse the depression became—and the more desperate the national mood.

## Evaluation

Certainly Herbert Hoover was not a weak man. However he was a weak President in that he refused to extend his constitutional powers to meet the demands of crisis. The times called for an inspirational leader, a consummate politician who could weld Congress and the people together into a union to wage war against a depressed economy.

> *Erwin C. Hargrove*, Presidential Leadership: Personality and Political Style (*New York: The Macmillan Co., 1966*), *pp. 103–107.*
>
> Erwin Hargrove views the successes and failures of Herbert Hoover's presidency primarily from the vantage point of Hoover's role as a leader and molder of public opinion. Hoover's lack of adeptness at public relations first showed itself during his campaign for the presidency. He was never skillful at manipulating the press; believing reporters to be prying, he displayed his resentment publicly. He did not seek to improve his relations with the press while in office, and frequently substituted press releases for press conferences while delegating press relations to incapable secretaries who often sought to censor reporters. Most significantly, he refrained from using the press to enhance his political image. Rarely did Hoover outline policy during a press conference; he withheld information or misstated facts and was usually general and vague.
>
> In addition, Hargrove contends, that Hoover was unable to "conceive stories and slogans" for the press. He held back on releasing in-

formation until he had consensus on policy, and felt reporters were only making everyone's job harder by searching out discord within the government, publicizing it, and, in the process, perhaps revealing misinformation.

Erwin Hargrove elaborates,

> In short, he wanted to structure decision-making and inform the public in terms of his habitual style of influence, the dominance of leaders and publics by his superior knowledge. The press, on the other hand, finds free-for-all political process more congenial.

Hoover's retreat from the press may also have resulted, according to Hargrove, from his sensitivity to criticism. He collected clippings from newspapers and was visibly hurt by his critics. There were times when he tried to have reporters fired, though he did have favorites among the White House correspondents.

The Great Depression aggravated all of Hoover's inadequacies. He insisted that policies had to remain secret for the good of the public, and at times he was right. But the overall result was certainly detrimental to the President's image. As time passed and conditions worsened, his optimism made him look foolish, and his refusal to speak out gave the impression that he was doing little to alleviate the country's economic plight. He avoided dramatizing his policy solutions when such dramatization would have helped the public morale. Hargrove explains,

> It seems likely that Hoover's policy of quiet was a rationalization of his distaste for drama and the limelight and his fear of discord.

All of Hargrove's observations contribute to his portrait of Hoover as administratively capable but lacking in public leadership ability. He was a great engineer, but "the great engineer could not inspire."

Hoover was an able administrator, but he lacked all the other requirements of a strong President. He could not persuade, trade, bargain, or play politics. He could not use the power and prestige of the presidency to lead the Congress and the people during the crisis of the early 1930s. He had little sense of power—either of how much power his position commanded, or how he might use it.

# Franklin Delano Roosevelt

Hoover reluctantly ran for a second term. His opponent, Franklin Delano Roosevelt, waged a vigorous campaign—promising the depression-weary people a "New Deal." Hoover hardly campaigned, and Roosevelt won 472 electoral votes in forty-two states. Herbert Clark Hoover retired from office, his ordeal over.

Roosevelt's energy and enthusiasm for office was refreshing after the gloomy years between 1929 and 1933. Born in 1882, Roosevelt was the only son of a wealthy family from Hyde Park, New York. At Groton and Harvard, where he attended prep school and college, he was a popular student leader. After graduation he went into politics. By the age of twenty-eight he had been elected to the New York State Senate. By age thirty-one he was Assistant Secretary of the Navy under President Woodrow Wilson. He was nominated to run for Vice-President with James M. Cox in 1920.

Struck by polio in 1922, Roosevelt worked manfully (but unsuccessfully) to regain the use of his legs. Waging this personal battle further intensified his powerful capabilities of concentration and perception. He thrilled the 1924 Democratic Convention by mounting the podium without assistance and nominating Al Smith for the presidency. He became Governor of New York in 1929 and was re-elected to a second term in 1931.

When Roosevelt gave his inaugural address as thirty-second President on March 4, 1933, the country was probably at the lowest point of the Great Depression. Long breadlines of the unemployed were a familiar sight; banks foreclosed on unpaid mortgages; other banks were shut down. Despair gripped the nation. The new President immediately set the tone for his administration: "This nation asks for action, and action now," he declared. "This great nation will endure as it has endured, will revive and will prosper. The only thing we have to fear," he said, "is fear itself."[10]

[10] Quoted in Koenig, *Chief Executive*, p. 368.

## Roosevelt as legislator

Roosevelt's first act in office was to close all banks for three days, from March 6 to March 9. The decisiveness of this act convinced the people that the government was taking command. When Roosevelt called Congress to convene on March 9, he presented legislation to aid the recovery of the banks by controlling bank activity. Thus began the famous "100 days" in which more major legislation was passed than ever before in American history.

Between March and June of 1933, Roosevelt introduced and shepherded fifteen major bills through Congress, including the Emergency Banking Act, Economy Act, Truth-in-Securities Act, Emergency Farm Mortgage Act, Home Owners Loan Act, the National Industrial Recovery Act, the Tennessee Valley Authority (TVA), and the Agricultural Adjustment Act. He further established a number of new agencies to help those hit hardest by the depression.

The extraordinary times diminished the usual legislative in-fighting. Moreover, the combination of a large Democratic majority with effective White House leadership helped speed the legislation through. The image of an energetic administration setting up machinery to solve the complex problems of the depression began to restore confidence in the government.

### F.D.R.: The Congressional Record of his First One Hundred Days

| | |
|---|---|
| March: | Emergency Banking Act |
| | Economy Act |
| | Civilian Conservation Corps established |
| April: | Gold Standard abandoned |
| May: | Federal Emergency Relief Act |
| | Agricultural Adjustment Act |
| | Emergency Farm Mortgage Act |
| | Tennessee Valley Authority Act |
| | Truth-in-Securities Act |
| June: | Gold Clause abrogated in contracts |
| | Home Owners' Loan Act |
| | National Industrial Recovery Act |
| | Glass-Steagall Banking Act |
| | Farm Credit Act |
| | Railroad Coordination Act |

11 Clinton Rossiter, *The American Presidency*, 2nd ed. (New York: Harcourt Brace Jovanovitch, Inc. 1960), pp. 68–69.

12 Quoted in Wilfred E. Binkley, *President and Congress*, 3rd rev. ed. (New York: Alfred A. Knopf, Inc., 1962), pp. 302–303.

"No President . . . wielded more power . . . than did Franklin Roosevelt in 1933 . . . to rescue a stricken Nation in the midst of a stricken world."[11]

"For a hundred days," wrote Bernard Fay, "he kept Congress at work. . . . He had innumerable conferences with congressional leaders"[12]

This remarkable record of legislative accomplishments was due in large part to a sense of emergency; Congress sought to work together with the Chief Executive to pull the nation out of the Great Depression. Roosevelt was a superb bargainer, always willing to listen to the other point of view. He was charming and could often coax an opponent over to his side. He had an excellent sense of timing, introducing measures at just the right moment and then preparing public opinion to support him. For example, on March 9, 1933, he sent an "economy message" to Congress recommending extreme reductions in the salaries of government officials. Congress opposed the measure. In a dramatic radio appeal to the nation, Roosevelt marshaled public support for his bill.

13 Binkley, *President and Congress*, p. 305. 3rd rev. ed. (New York: Alfred A. Knopf, Inc., 1962), p. 305.

> It has been said that during the hundred days he had only to glance toward a microphone or suggest that he might go on the air again and a congressional delegation would surrender. . . . But Roosevelt realized that there were limits to the use of this device and he did not overwork it.[13]

But his influence in the legislature did not extend to the judiciary. In 1935 and 1936, the Supreme Court declared such key measures as the National Industrial Recovery Act and the Agricultural Adjustment Act unconstitutional. Roosevelt, after an overwhelming re-election victory in 1936, tried to change the structure of the court. He proposed a bill to Congress that would allow him to appoint a new justice for every presiding judge over seventy. His attempt to *pack the Court* with loyal supporters was perpetrated under the guise of increasing the "efficiency" of the Supreme Court.

14 Hargrove, *Presidential Leadership,* p. 68. (New York: The Macmillan Co., 1966), p. 68.

> This way of proceeding showed his delight in the secret strategem, the indirect ploy rather than the frontal attack. But in choosing indirectness he badly miscalculated. The devious method of the reform became more a cause célèbre than the substance of his criticism of the Court. He seemed too clever by half.[14]

By 1937, Congress was no longer willing to accept presidential programs without critical examination. In fact, congressmen were openly rebellious throughout his second term. The many legislative defeats Roosevelt suffered were thought to be the result of a Congress bucking against the success of his first term. His skill as a leader caused people to fear him as a threat to the principle of separation of powers—and Congress reflected those fears.

## Roosevelt as administrator

Roosevelt believed in competition within his administration. In order to gather all the information he could and to keep the power of decision in his own hands, he encouraged differing points of view, appointed several people to study the same problem, and duplicated activities. With such a dispersion of duties, Roosevelt remained the central and unifying authority.

For example, Roosevelt appointed Harry Hopkins and Harold Ickes to administer different aspects of the works relief programs. The Secretary of the

Treasury, Henry Morgenthau, Jr., was given authority over money spent by the Works Progress Administration. The tension among the three men with similar responsibilities grew so great that Hopkins threatened to resign. "There is something to be said," Roosevelt observed, "for having a little conflict between the agencies. A little rivalry is stimulating, you know. It keeps everybody going to prove that he is a better fellow than the next man. It keeps him honest too."[15]

[15] Koenig, *Chief Executive*, p. 164.

Roosevelt first allowed all the people and forces around him to contend and compete for the resolution of issues. Then, letting the information sift and filter through his mind, he made his decisions.

Thus, Roosevelt, unlike Hoover, preferred a little chaos and controversy to neatness and strict organization. He wanted his advisers to grapple with an idea or plan until all possible routes to a solution had been exhausted. Then, after letting a question sift and filter through his mind, waiting until his acute sensitivity told him when to act, he would make his decision. Although Roosevelt's somewhat unusual and disorganized advisory system may have been less efficient than a straightforward chain of command, it promoted all the ingenuity and inventiveness needed in a time of national crisis.

## Roosevelt and public opinion

[16] See Hargrove, *Presidential Leadership*, p. 62 for a concise description of Roosevelt's use of the media.

Roosevelt enhanced his leadership through deft, clever use of the press and radio. He held two private news briefings a week, keeping the reporters informed about his plans and progress. The reporters were flattered by this privilege and were usually sympathetic to presidential policies, although the management of most papers was critical of the President and his methods.[16]

His most famous and successful technique for leading and educating the people was the "fireside chat," which captured the attention of millions of Americans. These "fireside chats" were filled with direct, homey analogies; for example, Roosevelt described the Lend-Lease to Britain in terms of loaning the garden hose to a neighbor whose house was on fire.

Roosevelt viewed himself as a molder of public opinion. During the congressional debate over social security, he carefully lectured the public on the soundness of the bill, the facts of salary deductions, the limited involvement of the government, the benefits to all. He spent two "fireside chats" on the subject and then went on tour to speak on it. In this manner he prepared a public suspicious of government participation in the insurance business to accept social security.

## Evaluation

[17] Rossiter, *The American Presidency*, p. 151.

Roosevelt transformed the presidency, enhancing its powers and modernizing its structure. "The press conference, the Executive Office, the right to reorganize the administration, and the powers to protect industrial and financial peace are all parts of Roosevelt's legacy to the modern President."[17] Roosevelt exercised full personal control of the machinery of government. He

*The "fireside chats" of Franklin D.
Roosevelt were nationally awaited events.*

was flexible, yet strong. He was, in short, *willing* to lead and unwilling to rely on traditional solutions. Unlike Hoover, he did not think of himself as president of a large corporation, but rather as leader of all the American people.

> Roosevelt's leadership talents lay in his ability to shift quickly and gracefully from persuasion to cajolery to flattery to intrigue to diplomacy to promises to horsetrading—or to concoct just that formula which his superb instincts for personal relations told him would bring around the most reluctant congressmen.[18]

It would be a mistake to interpret the fact that he was a strong leader to mean that he was a wise or beloved leader. At times he was. But there are still people today who refer to Roosevelt in the harshest, most derogatory terms.

In terms of his place in history, Charles Beard has said, "President Roosevelt has made a more profound impression upon the political, social, and economic life of America than any or all of his predecessors."[19]

[18] Quoted in Hargrove, *Presidential Leadership,* p. 66.

[19] Charles A. Beard, "Roosevelt's Place in History," *Events,* February 1938, p. 86.

# Dwight David Eisenhower

Like Hoover, Eisenhower believed in administration and organization as the focus of the executive function—a conviction arrived at during a long and successful career in the army, in which he coordinated Allied efforts in World War II and acted as Supreme Commander of Allied forces in Europe after the war. Eisenhower was a skilled practitioner of the art of organization. This talent, combined with his amiable manner, were twin factors in winning the allegiance of those he commanded.

Like Hoover, Eisenhower considered himself nonpolitical. Both the Democrats and Republicans were interested in him as a presidential candidate in 1948. Not until shortly before the 1952 campaign began did he declare himself a Republican, defeating Robert A. Taft, Senate majority leader, for the nomination.

Eisenhower ran as a conciliator. After the scandals and unpopular war of the Truman years he pledged himself to "clean up the mess in Washington." He said "I shall go to Korea" to end the Korean War. Immediately after taking office he did go to Korea and worked out a settlement within a few months.

He felt the country needed someone to calm and pacify it after so much turmoil. His views on the exercise of presidential authority were shaped by his abiding belief in the basic goodness of human nature.

[20] Hargrove, *Presidential Leadership*, p. 120.

"Power as a fact of life was not part of this vision."[20]

## Eisenhower as legislator

Dwight D. Eisenhower viewed the legislature as embodying the popular will, and he was reluctant to interfere with that "will." Unfortunately, he found that because he did not intrude, most of his legislation often was not passed. He was opposed by both Democrats and members of his own party, specifically by such highly conservative Republicans as Joseph McCarthy, William Knowland, and Robert Taft. But Eisenhower refused to quell dissent. He felt he could lead Congress through quiet persuasion. "I am not one of the desk-pounding types that likes to stick out his jaw and look like he is bossing the show," he declared.[21]

[21] Binkley, *President and Congress*, p. 354.

Because of his unwillingness to take a strong stand, Eisenhower nearly relinquished a major Presidential power—that of treaty making. Ohio's Senator John Bricker, a Republican, proposed to amend the Constitution, making congressional approval of all treaties mandatory. Eisenhower gave Bricker a friendly hearing at the White House, which the senator interpreted as willingness on Eisenhower's part to compromise. In reaction, Bricker became more inflexible. Finally, immediately before the vote on the bill, Eisenhower sent a letter of opposition to the Senate Majority Leader. Perhaps because of this modest attempt at influence by Eisenhower, Congress defeated the bill by three votes.

Eisenhower's limited use of presidential powers more often worked to his disadvantage. He would not bring the influence of his office to bear on censuring Senator Joseph McCarthy of Wisconsin. McCarthy was a "demagogue" who initiated a purge of so-called Communists from the executive branch of government. Eisenhower refused to intervene in this escalating inquisition, even when McCarthy's investigations became a televised national scandal in character defamation. "I will not get in the gutter with the guy," Eisenhower responded. Ultimately, McCarthy was censured by the Senate, but the President had given no moral leadership in this attack on basic American liberties.

*Stuart Gerry Brown*, The American Presidency: Leadership, Partisanship and Popularity (*New York: The Macmillan Co., 1966*), *pp. 99–111.*

Stuart Gerry Brown examines Dwight Eisenhower's record on desegregation to show that sometimes a President must opt for partisanship, even if conflict and division will result.

Eisenhower sought repeatedly to avoid partisanship on the issue of civil rights. Thus the Supreme Court decision that schools must be integrated with all deliberate speed posed a problem to the President. To support and enforce the decision would alienate many segregationists; to refuse to endorse it would disturb a large number of civil rights supporters. Attempting to placate both sides, Eisenhower stated several times that he stood for equality of all Americans, but said nothing specifically about civil rights.

> In the North and West the general assumption was that the President's statement of his belief in 'equality' meant his endorsement of the civil rights claims of Negroes; the South assumed that his failure to stress civil rights meant that he was not eager to break down segregation customs and institutions.

Eisenhower remained noncommittal for almost two years. When four southern states enacted legislation to defy integration, the President refused to intervene. Desiring the support of the southern Democrats for his re-election in 1956, Eisenhower did not push the states to speed up the integration process, nor did he refuse the support of those impeding it. Adlai E. Stevenson, the Democratic candidate for President, suggested that Eisenhower exert his moral leadership and call a conference of black and white southern leaders to ease racial tensions. Eisenhower postponed action and later formed the bipartisan Civil Rights Commission in 1957. He was not on the commission himself, and refused to take "positive action," writes Brown, as he was afraid of "inflaming racial feelings." In 1957, there was a desegregation crisis in Arkansas, one of the states that had rejected the Court decisions. United States army troops finally had to be summoned by the President to Little Rock, Arkansas, in the fall of 1957, to suppress violence and to escort high school students to their newly desegregated schools.

Eisenhower did retain his popularity, but certainly his disassociation from civil rights issues did not discourage the actions of Governor Faubus of Arkansas and other Southerners who defied the Supreme Court. The President affirmed verbally that "the Constitution, as interpreted by the Supreme Court is our basic law." But Brown believes that Eisenhower was obliged to uphold the "basic law" in a forceful, partisan manner.

For Brown, a principle emerges from an examination of Eisenhower's handling of this major constitutional problem. Nonpartisanship, or unpartisanship, may help a President to retain his popularity even among groups and factions who are violently opposed to each other. But if the issue involves a matter so fundamental as the meaning of the Constitution, nonpartisanship may constitute an abdication of responsibility; and repeated assertions that the President will do his duty in accordance with his oath of office cannot eradicate that abdication. "Doing one's duty" is not always an adequate substitute for taking a position on a controversial question.

Eisenhower's limited use of moral and political persuasion was such that even moderate Republican congressmen felt deserted. He seldom assumed the legislative leadership necessary to persuade Congress to act on his bills.

## Eisenhower as administrator

22 The army staff system involves the establishment of an intermediary between the highest ranking official and his assistants. In Eisenhower's presidential staff system, his assistant was extremely powerful, with the authority to decide who and what gets to the President.

Most political scientists agree that "Eisenhower's most important innovation was his organization of the White House staff," an organization that disencumbered him from the petty details of watching over a large bureaucracy. Eisenhower disliked informality in the executive, an attitude that was perhaps a product of his long years in the army, where the staff system prevails.[22] These same critics, however, considered the system a weak innovation, a barrier that blocked people, ideas, and problems from the President.

The President maintained the system because he trusted his Cabinet members and authorized them to act on their own initiative. He increased the responsibilities of the Vice-President, Richard Nixon, including him in Cabinet meetings and assigning him to preside over sessions of the Cabinet and the National Security Council when the President could not attend.

His staff was so successful in carrying out the work of the presidency that, when Eisenhower suffered a heart attack in 1955, the administration continued to function smoothly. The staff was run by his administrative assistant,

Sherman Adams, who served as a kind of "assistant President." Criticism was leveled against Eisenhower and Adams, criticism that reflected not only an uneasiness over Adams's power, but also a general discontent with the Eisenhower presidency, rather than dissatisfaction with staff organization.

Eisenhower's conscientious staff acted as a channel to the President. A channel is narrow and direct: the information that Eisenhower received was carefully reviewed by his staff. Eisenhower received only what his staff had already chewed over, and he did not see what others had deemed irrelevant. The President, said speech writer Emmett John Hughes, was often the last man in the chain of command to know of things. "One reason for Eisenhower's tardiness in learning the art of presidential politics was the extraordinary protection provided him by the White House Office."[23]

[23] Binkley, *President and Congress*, p. 358.

## Evaluation

Eisenhower, the war hero who had led the Allied armies of Europe and the United States to victory in World War II, was probably one of the most popular American Presidents. Although he was severely criticized by some during his term of office, his personal popularity never really declined, in part because "Ike" seemed to be above the mudslinging of politics. Many attribute his success to his ability to relax, to remain calm in the midst of a crisis. For example, one of Eisenhower's speech writers, hard at work on a major address, looked out the window of his office and saw the President putting golf balls on the White House lawn. The speechwriter at first felt resentful. But then, he thought, that is the President's strength; he never loses his sense of composure.

*Dwight D. Eisenhower was welcomed and honored as a national war hero who, having cleaned up Europe, would bring prosperity to the nation.*

Eisenhower's 1956 election victory was as decisive as his first. In this second election, however, he did not help elect a Republican Congress. His personal popularity earned him an electoral triumph, but did not extend to popularity for his party. The public identified with the President, not with his programs. In 1955, he exerted little direct effort in persuading a Democratic Congress to enact his programs. On vital issues such as federal aid to education he had the support of only a minority of his own party in the Congress. And he did not fully utilize the personal confidence of a great majority of the people to influence Congress.

As popular as he was, Eisenhower was a weak President, a strict interpreter of the powers of the office. He did not expand or even use the powers at hand. He refused personally to resolve congressional or public issues, refraining in most cases from intervention. A fine organizer, he gave his appointees freedom of action.[24] But, Clinton Rossiter has written:

24 Instead of exerting his presidential authority, Eisenhower relied heavily on the advice of Sherman Adams and John Foster Dulles, two of the most powerful men in Washington during the 1950s.

> This President, I fear, may be dealt with much more harshly by posterity. . . . It was not so much that he failed to catch the right vision of the future, but that he was unwilling to draw steadily on his overflowing reservoir of popularity to get us moving in the direction of the vision. Historians will be reluctant to accord the judgment of greatness to a President who kept so much of his immense influence in reserve. To put the matter another way, no President in history was ever more powerfully armed to persuade the minds of men to face up to the inevitable—and then failed more poignantly to use his power.[25]

25 Rossiter, *The American Presidency*, p. 163.

# John Fitzgerald Kennedy

Kennedy entered office on a wave of hope and promise. His inauguration day glittered in magnificent winter sunshine. Eighty-year-old Robert Frost, one of America's leading poets, read a poem commemorating the occasion. In an eloquent inaugural address, the young President proclaimed: "The torch has been passed to a new generation of Americans." And with vigor, he set out to shape his administration and its program.

**Kennedy as legislator**

Kennedy rarely employed pressure tactics or the power of his personal prestige to marshal congressional support for his legislative program. In the House, he was confronted by a hostile coalition of conservative Republicans and Democrats. In the Senate, he failed to give liberals the strong backing necessary to curtail the filibuster; as a consequence, he had to withhold civil rights proposals, which had little chance of passage as long as the filibuster could be practiced.

As heir to Franklin Roosevelt's philosophy of a personal and vigorous administration, Kennedy might have exercised more direct and personal influence in getting his legislation enacted. Instead, he issued congressional directives via legislative drafts, public addresses, and press conferences. He exercised the power of logic more than outright bargaining. The result of his approach was the defeat of his farm bill, a proposal for a Cabinet Department of Urban Affairs, a health care plan for the aged, his education bills, and finally the failure of Kennedy himself as a strong legislative leader.

Drawing © 1962 Mauldin in the St. Louis *Post-Dispatch*. Reproduced by courtesy of Bill Mauldin.

## Kennedy as administrator

As President, Kennedy reached down the line of command for the information he sought. He did not wait to hear from Cabinet secretaries or department heads. Like Franklin Roosevelt, Kennedy called upon the man in charge no matter how far down his position in the bureaucracy. Moreover, Kennedy was interested in administrative efficiency. He appreciated Eisenhower's attempt at management, but rather than receive decisions for approval, he received information for decisions. This tended to place him at the hub of a wheel with spokes radiating from his office, rather than at the tip of a pyramid where all action culminated. Kennedy, like Johnson after him, enjoyed being "in the thick of things." His presidency was energetic and personal.

*Arthur M. Schlesinger, Jr., A Thousand Days: John F. Kennedy in the White House (Boston: Houghton Mifflin Co., 1965), pp. 604–609.*

In his account of the Kennedy presidency, Arthur Schlesinger asserts that "the part of the aid effort which best expressed the distinctive spirit of the New Frontier was the Peace Corps." The germination of the Corps came when General James Gavin urged Kennedy to adopt a plan similar to the one proposed by Senator Hubert Humphrey in 1960. Kennedy had tentatively advanced such a plan while campaigning on college campuses in Michigan and had been presented with a list of prospective volunteers. Finally, in California he called for its establishment, widening Humphrey's concept to include women and older volunteers.

The plan met with a positive response, especially from the young, which affected Kennedy: "He was sure there was a . . . fund of idealism among the youth of America; and the Peace Corps seemed a means of demonstrating the reality of this idealism to the world."

After Kennedy was elected, Sargent Shriver was chosen chairman of the Peace Corps National Advisory Committee. In March 1961, he submitted a report recommending its establishment.

> The objectives of the Peace Corps, according to the report, were three-fold:
>     It can contribute to the development of critical countries and regions.
>     It can promote international cooperation and good will toward this country.
>     It can also contribute to the education of America and to more intelligent participation in the world.

The reorganization of foreign aid in the Kennedy administration had originally called for the absorption of the Peace Corps into the Agency for International Development. But, as Arthur Schlesinger writes in his memoirs of the Kennedy years, "nothing could take the heart out of new ideas more speedily than an old bureaucracy." It was therefore proposed that the program retain its own "identity and élan." According to Schlesinger, President Kennedy supported this proposal, since he "held the Rooseveltian view that there were things in life more important than the symmetry of organization charts."

Thus, the same day the report was submitted by the task force, Kennedy set up the Peace Corps by executive order and sent a message to Congress asking for legislation. Shriver's staff included Bill Moyers and Richard Goodwin, who were to be well-known as presidential aides and speechwriters. Recruitment and training were under way by Spring 1961:

> Having defended the autonomy of the Corps in Washington, Shriver was determined not to let his men become involved in diplomatic or intelligence activities overseas. Their only job, he told them, was to help people help themselves; and in personal visits around the world Shriver convinced mistrustful governments that he meant exactly what he said . . . neutral states began to ask for volunteers to aid village development and public health, to improve farming methods and, most important of all, to teach their own coming generations of national leaders. The original authorization of 500 grew to 5000 by March 1963 and to 10,000 in another year, and volunteers were soon working in forty-six countries. Congressional doubt turned into enthusiasm: even Barry Goldwater applauded the Corps.

Much of this energy came from the bright young "idea men" Kennedy surrounded himself with. The Peace Corps was an innovative approach to foreign policy that was the brain child of his staff advisers. His men also developed for him a proposal for aid to education, a supply program of medical care for the aged under social security, tax reduction and reform, freer foreign trade, urban renewal, new civil rights legislation, and other laws that Johnson was able to push through Congress after his landslide election in 1964.

# Lyndon Baines Johnson

Lyndon B. Johnson became thirty-sixth President when John F. Kennedy was assassinated in Dallas, Texas, on November 22, 1963. Johnson immediately set a tone of confidence and strength during the days of public mourning that followed Kennedy's death.

This sense of strength marked Lyndon Johnson's presidency as it had characterized his terms as a Democratic congressman during the Roosevelt years and then as Majority Leader of the Senate. From his recitation of the oath of office to his final decision not to run for a second term, Johnson was a strong President in a period of turbulent change.

## Johnson as legislator

Johnson was a child of Congress. Most of his adult life was spent in the House of Representatives and the Senate. He reached his peak of influence between 1954 and 1960, when he served as Democratic Majority Leader of the Senate.

An excellent persuader, Johnson the President believed in finding and using points of power. "In every town," he once said, "there's some guy on

26 Koenig, *Chief Executive*, p. 204.

27 Johnson not only carried a Democratic majority in Congress, but also maintained Republican as well as Democratic support for his programs; Senator Everett Dirksen, a powerful Republican leader, was a main force in passing Johnson legislation.

top of the hill in a big white house who can get things done. I want to get that man on my side."[26]

His talent for backstage manipulation and his deep knowledge of the workings of Congress helped him as President to pass one of the most sweeping sets of domestic laws ever legislated by a President. His "Great Society" program included medical care for aged under social security, the first comprehensive aid-to-education law, several major civil rights laws, a broad housing program, immigration reform, programs for highway beautification, programs for combating heart disease and cancer, and programs to alleviate water and air pollution.[27] Johnson looked for the *consensus*—the broad coalition of agreement—that would support and enact each proposal. But Johnson's political adroitness did not inspire public confidence. Manipulative skills remain suspect. His popularity in 1964, polled at 70 percent of all voters, fell to less than 30 percent in 1968.

*John Bibby and Roger Davidson*, On Capitol Hill: Studies in Legislative Process (*New York: Holt, Rinehart and Winston, Inc., 1967*), *pp. 219–251.*

Lyndon Johnson's extensive role in formulating the Economic Opportunity Act of 1964 illustrates the increasing trend toward executive legislation, according to a study by John Bibby and Roger Davidson.

The bill itself generated much publicity, because it openly acknowledged the reality of American poverty and promised basic changes in community structure and social services. But it did not germinate from the people's representatives in Congress. It was first considered by President Kennedy, then immediately and enthusiastically expanded by President Johnson the day after the late President's death. The President's Council of Economic Advisers, headed by Walter Heller, began to confer with the Bureau of the Budget; by mid-December President Johnson had allocated $500 million to begin the eradication of poverty in the 1965 draft budget.

The Bureau of the Budget approved the concept of a "Community Action Program." A decentralized system, wherein grants would be administered by the local community, became the keystone of the program; emphasis would be placed on grass-roots initiative and new coordination of federal funds.

Some administrators, however, opposed the measure out of fear of losing control of the funds. Others, for example, Secretary of Labor Willard Wirtz, opposed the plan on the grounds that it did not emphasize minimum wage, job training, and employment.

President Johnson called on Peace Corps Director Sargent Shriver to serve as the "poverty czar." He immediately began preparation of the final legislation with the aid of an unusual task force consisting of agency and other governmental representatives, as well as personal friends and associates who were professors, authors, businessmen, mayors, and welfare officials. It became quickly apparent to them that the situation called for a "package" of legislative proposals; the administration went to work on their ideas with dispatch and political expertise.

> In less than a year's time, the executive branch had . . . combined a number of specific-purpose programs into a legislative package designed to draw support from most of the groups currently engaged in social welfare activities. Finally, the Administration had endeavored to sell the program as responsible and consistent with the American traditions of local initiative, voluntarism, and self-help. The public had appeared to be enthusiastic. It remained to see how Congress would react to such an initiative.

Johnson was skillful in collecting support. In announcing a billion dollar cut in defense expenditure in 1963, he added that the saved funds would pay for the war on poverty, that the money would go from the "haves" to the "have-nots." He visited depressed areas, dangling future funds before the eyes of mayors and local officials. Finally, on March 16, he submitted the package to Congress, replete with military metaphors urging victory in the War on Poverty.

Congressional opposition came primarily from states' rights supporters and Republicans who felt unprecedented pressure and coercion.

> More broadly, the Republicans charged that the bill was not needed, that inflation, and not welfare, was the prime problem, and that in any event more research into the question was needed.

The House and Senate hearings were, however, heavily weighted for the bill (seventy pro speakers and nine con speakers appeared in the House), and several Republican amendments were defeated. Both sides courted southern votes; the administration made concessions to this end. The bill was finally passed in the Senate 61 to 34. To avoid a conference with the Senate, the House bill was an amended version of the Senate's instead of a committee bill, and it passed 226 to 185. President Johnson signed it into law on August 20, 1964.

Bibby and Davidson contend that "in retrospect, the congressional contributions can hardly be viewed as of major importance to the Economic Opportunity Act." Rather, the act represents a triumph of executive legislation:

> The case of the war on poverty demonstrates the full potentialities of the "executive" pattern in domestic as well as foreign and military

policy-making. And it must be observed that this pattern is becoming more the rule than the exception.

## Johnson as administrator

We have seen that Eisenhower's strength and weakness lay in his image of being above the "tumult of the times." In contrast, Johnson remained in the thick of the tumult. He was a large-spirited "take-charge" Texan, who, like Roosevelt, acted decisively. He enjoyed being at the center of power.

*Although Lyndon Johnson extended presidential authority over international affairs, he consulted with and listened to the advice of congressional leaders and other government officials. Here Johnson and key public officials attempt to determine which course of action to take during the 1968 Czechoslovakia crisis.*

Like Eisenhower, Johnson held Cabinet meetings frequently, and even called upon members to offer opinions on issues beyond the direct concerns of their departments. But Johnson also counted heavily on the advice of his old-time political colleagues in Congress. In addition, he sought counsel from, and utilized the talents of, people who were outside the structure of government. Clark Clifford, for example, a lawyer in Washington and long-time friend of the President, was often asked to give advice on pressing domestic and foreign issues. Moreover, Clifford was frequently Johnson's *legislative liaison*, conferring with influential congressmen whose votes could determine the passage of crucial bills.

## Evaluation

Lyndon Johnson was a strong President because he made full use of the powers of the presidency. He combined many of the strengths of previous modern Presidents. He was skillful in working with Congress. He believed in (but was eventually unsuccessful in) mobilizing public support. Once committed to a course of action, he followed it through to completion. His strength as a legislator, however, was overshadowed by his continuation of an unpopular war in Vietnam.

"Man can fly—can't he?"                    Drawing © Oliphant in the Denver *Post*.

By 1968, as his first term neared an end, the President was suffering from a damaging "credibility gap" that affected not only the war but all his actions in office. In March of that year he stopped the bombing of North Vietnam and announced that he would not run for re-election, pledging to devote the rest of his term to achieving peace in Vietnam. He failed in this attempt, although he did manage to get peace talks started.

Even more significantly, Johnson failed in projecting himself effectively to the people. His presidency became a study in the decline of popular support. He dealt effectively with the personalities of individual congressmen, but his ability to reach the people was curiously limited:

> He felt that he had incontestably established his right to the national leadership by his landslide victory in the election of 1964. Millions felt that he had incontestably established that he was ready to double-talk about anything, including taking the country into a major war, in order to protect votes. He believed that the great success of his legislative program after the election earned him the confidence and admiration of the nation. The great success of that drive was, among other things, his great undoing. It brought to full development that central irony of his career. The conspicuousness of his political skills, combined with the general impression left by the man, made more people more sure that he did everything only by political legerdemain and only for personal political advantage.[28]

[28] Eric Goldman, *The Tragedy of Lyndon Johnson* (New York: Alfred A. Knopf, Inc., 1969), p. 523.

Clearly, in pursuing controversial policies, Johnson exercised a masterful politics of action. As one news reporter stated, "He is, above everything, a politician and it is as such that he is running the Presidency. . . . There are various kinds of politicians: . . . the pompous, the placid, . . . and the very aggressive who tries, often behind the scenes, to anticipate and shape events. Johnson is the aggressive kind."[29]

[29] James Marlow, Associated Press News Analysis (April 27, 1964).

# Richard Milhous Nixon

Richard Nixon came to office in 1968—a year infamous for the assassinations of Martin Luther King and Robert Kennedy, the disruption of the Democratic National Convention in Chicago, and the volatile division of the public over the war in Vietnam.

[30] *Newsweek*, January 25, 1971, p. 21.

The new President pledged to "get people off the welfare rolls and onto the payrolls."[30] He sought action to achieve national goals. In spite of his strong view of the presidency, Nixon has as yet not been able to execute all of his plans. A Democratic Congress and the maintenance of fighting men in Vietnam have in different ways hindered his free exercise of presidential power.

**Nixon as legislator**

Nixon was the first President since Zachary Taylor (in 1848) who in his first term of office did not bring his party a majority in either house of Congress. The Democratic majority in Congress partly accounts for the fact that Nixon, a Republican, has often been unsuccessful in persuading Congress to enact programs. For example, Nixon and many Republicans advocate revenue sharing, a form of *federal* financing of state and local governments. In 1969, Nixon proposed that revenue sharing with the states begin on a small scale in 1971. His urban affairs adviser, Daniel Patrick Moynihan, suggested that the national government contribute one third of all state and local expenditures. The concept of federal revenue sharing has brought the President into sharp conflict with many congressmen—Wilbur Mills, for example—who favor centralized control of federal funds.

In dealing with a Democratic Congress, Nixon practices the standard presidential tactic of coalition politics, concentrating primarily on a compromise between conservative Democrats and Republicans. His techniques for political bargaining are less effective than Johnson's direct arm-twisting style; yet he does make use of legislative liaisons and other intermediaries to reach congressmen. He sends frequent messages to the Congress stating executive guidelines for legislation.

As a President with a minority in Congress, Nixon has been forced to rely on his office for executive authority. In dealing with the Vietnamese War, which he has pledged to bring to a close, he has used his constitutional powers as Chief Executive and Commander-in-Chief, rather than his influence with the legislative branches. He has ordered troop reductions and, in a highly debated move, has sanctioned attacks on the neighboring countries of Cambodia and Laos. His slowness in achieving a settlement of the war, in combination with actions that seem to cause escalation, has brought Nixon into conflict with a Congress seeking to reassert its power. But to date, the office of the President has had the last word in the conduct of the war.

## Nixon as administrator

Nixon firmly controls the Executive Office of the President and the rest of the bureaucracy. In this sense, he is a strong and effective President. He relies to some extent on Henry Kissinger, his closest personal adviser, and makes limited use of the Secretary of State, William P. Rogers. Nixon's control extends to full exercise of his constitutional power of removal: the executive branch of government should be of a common mind and should work in unison. Thus, when Walter Hickel publicly disagreed on policy, he was removed from office. The efficiency of the organization is his prime concern as Chief Administrator. In 1971, he proposed a reorganization of the Cabinet which would cut its then existing eleven departments to eight. This overhaul would consolidate the Cabinet and expand its powers.

Nixon has taken command of the economy by enacting a "New Economic Policy" to halt the rising trend of inflation and unemployment. On August 15, 1971, he ordered a ninety day freeze on prices and wages, and later declared, "We will continue wage and price restraints until inflationary pressures are brought under control."[31] To supervise this complex program, the President established a Cost of Living Council and subsidiary agencies including a Price Commission to determine and enforce price and rent guidelines, and a Pay Board to set fair wage levels. Nixon has also initiated a new

[31] *Newsweek*, October 18, 1971, p. 26.

*Richard Nixon uses the press conference to announce major decisions and events to the nation.*

32 *The New York Times,* August 11, 1971, p. 37.

33 The following passage is derived from Grant McConnell, *The Modern Presidency* (New York: St. Martin's Press, Inc., 1967), pp. 82–84.

China policy by recognizing the legitimacy of the government of China, a nation containing one quarter of the world's population. In July, 1971, he said, ". . . there can be no stable peace and enduring peace without the participation of the People's Republic of China . . . that is why I have undertaken initiatives in several areas to open the door for more normal relations . . ."[32] Among these "initiatives" will be a Presidential trip to China, called a "hopeful and creative move," by China scholar John Fairbank. Nixon, however, like Kennedy, has been in office for too brief a time for political scientists to fully assess his strengths and weaknesses.

# The presidency: traits and trends

One cannot paint the portrait of the ideal Chief Executive. Different qualities of leadership are required at various periods in history. One can, however, state the general characteristics of an effective President:[33]

*Charisma* is the quality to inspire by personal magnetism. Teddy Roosevelt had it; so did Franklin D. Roosevelt. John F. Kennedy also inspired the nation by his charisma, but he was not in office long enough to make effective use of it.

*Intuition*, at least in the political sense, is the ability to perceive what people are thinking and how they can be led. President Franklin Roosevelt in 1937 exercised his intuition in order to ensure public approval of American aid to the Allies. In his famed "Quarantine Speech," Roosevelt requested that European Allies line up against Germany and Japan. The public reaction was adamantly negative, forcing Roosevelt to delay his plans until public opinion could be improved. Roosevelt had intuitively seen that he was ahead of the public and was able to retreat in time.

A *sense of power* is probably the most important quality a president can possess. One should not confuse a sense of power with a drive for power. A sense of power is the ability to employ power skillfully. The restrained use of power at the appropriate time will curtail the necessity to use massive power later. For example, in 1962 President Kennedy used a combination of verbal denunciation and loss of government contracts when the steel companies, reneging on a presidential agreement raised their prices. Kennedy feared this violation of executive contract not only because it would contribute to inflationary tendencies, but also because it might discredit future agreements. His counterattack was successful, and the steel manufacturers rolled back their prices.

We have discussed the President's *ability to negotiate and bargain*. This too is an essential component of executive leadership. The politics of persuasion are more effective in reaching policy goals than are attempts at coercion or meager proposals to Congress. Much of the legislation in the Great Society Program of Lyndon Johnson resulted from this bargaining and persuasion. No President can function effectively without the ability to negotiate with congressmen, interest groups, and other officials of the government.

Every President possesses some of the above-mentioned qualifications. The kind of administration a man will run, the kind of President he will be is determined by a combination of talents. Hoover's administrative skill alone was not enough to halt the Great Depression; on the other hand, Roosevelt's lesser capacity as an administrator did not hamper him from taking decisive action to stop that same depression. Through an intangible system of weaknesses and strengths, we assess the effectiveness of Presidents.

The complexity of contemporary civilization demands that the men who lead the nation make swift and informed decisions.

Thus conditions seem to demand that future Presidents be strong. But legislation and judicial review, as well as national trends, will shape the presidency in ways that cannot be forseen. There is a rule stating that every action inspires a reaction: years of strong presidential leadership may foster an era of congressional assertiveness. Thus Congress reasserted itself after the strong administration of Lincoln and again after Cleveland. But in this century, Wilson, Roosevelt, Johnson, Kennedy, and Nixon have all been strong executives. Although Congress is beginning to assert its long-dormant authority to restrain executive power, the presidency remains the only office structured to act in a period of international crisis.

The essence of our free government is "leave to live by no man's leave, underneath the law—to be governed by those impersonal forces which we call law. Our government is fashioned to fulfill this concept so far as humanly possible. . . . With all its defects, delays and inconveniences, men have discovered no technique for long preserving free government except that the Executive be under the law, and that law be made by parliamentary deliberations."[34]

[34] J. Robert Jackson in *Youngstown Sheet and Tube Co.* v. *Sawyer.* 343. U.S. 579 (1952).

# Glossary

**bi-partisan politics**   Politics based on agreement between members of different political parties.

**coalition**   Joining of differing political forces to effect policy.

**consensus**   General agreement.

**court packing**   Specific reference to a few attempts by a President to alter the political makeup of the Supreme Court by appointing justices who he believes will support his policies.

**legislative liaison**   Person who serves as the President's personal voice to various members of Congress; he speaks with influential legislators to marshal support for executive programs.

**qualities of presidential leadership:**

**ability to negotiate and bargain**   The capacity to manipulate events and opinions for the purpose of gaining political support.

**administrative ability**   The capacity to control the bureaucracy so that it functions efficiently and effectively to carry out one's political objectives.

**charisma**   The quality of personal magnetism that inspires support.

**intuition**   The ability to sense public sentiment, to perceive what policies will be acceptable, and to know when to initiate or postpone action.

**sense of power**   Inner knowledge of how and when to use political power to gain one's objectives.

**steward of the people**   Term coined by President Theodore Roosevelt to describe the duty of the President to do all he actively can for the welfare of the people.

**strong President**   One who extends the range of office by the full use of his constitutional, political, and moral or personal powers.

**weak President**   One who does not choose to exercise fully the constitutional, political, and personal powers of the office.


# Suggested readings

Bailey, Thomas A., *Presidential Greatness: The Image and the Man from George Washington to the Present.* (New York: Appleton-Century-Crofts, Inc., 1966). Evaluations of United States Presidents and their administrations.

Bernstein, Barton J., and Allen J. Matusow, eds., *The Truman Administration: A Documentary History* (New York: Harper and Row Publishers, Inc., 1968). Presentation of selected documents that represent the trends in policy-making during the administration of former President Harry S Truman.

Blum, John M., *Woodrow Wilson and the Politics of Morality* (Boston: Little, Brown and Co., 1956). Brief study of the clash between ideals and political realities during President Wilson's administration.

Blum, John M., *The Republican Roosevelt* (New York: Atheneum Publishers, 1962). Excellent study of Theodore Roosevelt as President.

Burns, James M., *Roosevelt: The Lion and the Fox* (New York: Harcourt Brace Jovanovich, Inc., 1956). Excellent study of Franklin Delano Roosevelt's technique of governing during the Great Depression, revealing important changes in the roles of the Presidency.

Burns, James M., *Roosevelt: The Soldier of Freedom: 1940–1945* (New York: Harcourt Brace Jovanovich, Inc., 1970). Award-winning sequel to *Roosevelt: The Lion and the Fox* that analyzes Franklin D. Roosevelt's conduct of diplomacy and war from 1940 to 1945.

Donovan, Robert J., *Eisenhower: The Inside Story* (New York: Harper and Row Publishers, Inc., 1956). Analysis of the Eisenhower administration during his first few months in office, and on notes taken during Cabinet meetings.

Eisenhower, Dwight D., *White House Years*, 2 vols. (vol. 1, *Mandate for Change, 1953–56*; vol. 2. *Waging Peace, 1956–61*) (Garden City, N.Y.: Doubleday and Co., Inc., 1965). Personal account of White House affairs during the 1950s.

Evans, Rowland, and Robert Novak, *Lyndon B. Johnson: The Exercise of Power* (New York: The New American Library, 1968). Critical analysis of Lyndon Johnson, the congressional politician and the President, by two noted journalists.

Gross, Bertram M., ed., *A Great Society* (New York: Basic Books, Inc., 1968). Study of the aims and achievements of Lyndon·Johnson's administration.

Hargrove, Erwin C., *Presidential Leadership: Personality and Political Style* (New York: The Macmillan Co., 1966). Examination and evaluation of the personalities and styles of six Presidents—Theodore Roosevelt, Franklin D. Roosevelt, Woodrow Wilson, William Taft, Herbert Hoover, and Dwight Eisenhower.

Johnson, Donald B., and Jack L. Walker, *Dynamics of the American Presidency*. (New York: John Wiley and Sons, Inc., 1964). Collection of essays on the men who held the office.

Leuchtenberg, William E., *Franklin D. Roosevelt and the New Deal, 1932–1940* (New York: Harper and Row Publishers, Inc., 1963). Complete study of Franklin Delano Roosevelt's first two administrations.

Schlesinger, Arthur M., Jr., *A Thousand Days: John F. Kennedy in the White House* (Boston: Houghton-Mifflin Co., 1965). History of the Kennedy administration by a noted historian and presidential adviser.

Sherwood, Robert, *Roosevelt and Hopkins*, rev. ed. (New York: Harper and Row Publishers, Inc., 1950). Excellent study of the Franklin D. Roosevelt administration and the presidential adviser Harry Hopkins during the depression and New Deal era.

Sorensen, Theodore C., *Kennedy* (New York: Harper and Row Publishers, Inc., 1965). Account of John F. Kennedy's political career, emphasizing the organization and procedures utilized during his years as President, by Kennedy's friend and political adviser.

Taft, William H., *The President and His Powers* (New York: Columbia University Press, 1967). Originally published in 1913. Theory of a limited presidency as seen by a former President.

Tugwell, Rexford G., *The Democratic Roosevelt* (Garden City, N.Y.: Doubleday and Co., Inc., 1957). Interesting, factual account of Franklin D. Roosevelt's presidency by one of his early advisers.

Tugwell, Rexford G., *How They Became President* (New York: Simon and Schuster, Inc., 1968). Brief analysis of every presidential election in the United States.

Wicker, Tom, *JFK and LBJ: The Influence of Personality upon Politics* (New York: Penguin Books, Inc., 1969). Evaluation of the administration of John F. Kennedy and Lyndon B. Johnson, emphasizing the importance of each man's personality in the political successes and failures of his term in office.

# Topics of further study

Pease, Alan G., "Senator Robert A. Taft, Concept of the Presidential Powers," (master's thesis, Iowa State University, 1952).

# 14 congress
## makers of the law

In an age when parliamentary action shook the foundations of Europe, the delegates to the Constitutional Convention of 1787 long debated the question of how to structure the national legislature. Their objective was twofold: first, they wished to create a lawmaking body that would reflect the aspirations of the general populace as well as the reasoned judgment of the propertied class; second, they wished to appeal to the political interests of both the large and small states, for the state legislatures would ultimately ratify or reject the resulting Constitution.

The first of these objectives was satisfied by the decision to establish two different legislative bodies: the Senate, which was to reflect the abilities of the educated and propertied class, and the House of Representatives, which was to protect the interests of the average citizen. In order to ensure that the two houses represented their respective constituencies, the Constitution originally prescribed that senators be elected by the state legislatures, while congressmen were to be elected by a direct vote of the people. (Subsequently, the *Seventeenth Amendment*, passed in 1913, has provided for the popular election of senators.)

The second objective—the conciliation of the large and small states—was the more difficult to achieve. Understandably, the small states demanded a legislative representation equal to that of most of the larger states. Large states supported proportional representation—that is, representation based on population—in the hope that they might exercise more power than their smaller neighbors. On July 16, 1787, the Convention resolved this conflict with a plan proposed by Roger Sherman of Connecticut. This plan, which became known as the Connecticut or Great Compromise, provided for equal representation in the Senate, to be offset by proportional representation in the House of Representatives. Every state was to send two members to the Senate; but in the House, the larger states enjoyed an advantage, with one member representing every thirty thousand people in the 1st Congress.

On March 4, 1789, the 1st Congress convened with twenty-six senators and sixty-five congressmen. Today there are 100 senators and 435 congressmen. As a representational institution, the national legislature is comprised of 535 persons, whose personalities, aspirations, and local interests are brought to bear on the process of government.

# Election of congressmen

[1] Alexander Hamilton, James Madison, John Jay, *The Federalist Papers*, ed. by Clinton Rossiter, (New York: The New American Library, 1961), p. 327.

[2] "Characteristics of Members of the 92nd Congress," *Congressional Quarterly*, XXIX, no. 3 (January 15, 1971): 126–133.

Every two years, the entire House and one-third of the Senate must stand for re-election. The authors of *The Federalist* maintained that "frequent elections are unquestionably the only policy by which . . . dependence and sympathy can be effectually secured."[1] Congressional elections do not, however, result in a high turnover of representatives. In 1969, 57 percent of the House and 54 percent of the Senate had served for ten years or more. People tend to vote for the candidates who have already served in the legislature. In the 92nd Congress, for example, there were only 67 newly elected members, a turnover of only 12.5 percent.[2] Many of the re-elected congressmen are from so-called *safe districts*, congressional districts with a predominantly one-party constituency that consistently votes for the candidate of that particular party.

### The Electoral Risks of Incumbents, by State Party Systems

| Number of Re-election Bid | Percentage of Time Incumbent Won | | | | |
|---|---|---|---|---|---|
| | One-Party, | Modified One-Party, Senator in Stronger Party | Two-Party | Modified One-Party, Senator in Weaker Party | All Senators |
| 1st | 100%(23) | 77%(35) | 75%(77) | 33%(6) | 80%(141) |
| 2nd | 100%(19) | 78%(14) | 81%(30) | 50%(2) | 84%( 65) |
| 3rd | 86%( 7) | 83%( 6) | 92%(12) | 0%(0) | 88%( 25) |
| 4th plus | 67%( 6) | 50%( 4) | 60%( 5) | 0%(0) | 57%( 15) |

Source: Donald R. Matthews, *U.S. Senators and Their World* (New York: Vintage Books, 1960), p. 241.

As a consequence of the low turnover in congressional membership, the length of stay in office has increased. There are many who view the tendency toward longer terms as detrimental to the legislative process. They argue that long-term members become isolated in Washington and lose touch with the rapid and demanding changes in American society. On the other hand, proponents of long service contend that long-term members lend an expertise and a continuity and stability to government that would be lacking were there a high turnover of representatives. Moreover, as senior members of Congress, they wield more power; consequently, they may be more effective in representing their constituents.

# The congressional district

A congressman's primary allegiance is to his district. Its residents vote him in or out of office. His actions in the national legislature must take into account the reactions of the voters back home.

The number of people represented by a congressman is specified by the Constitution, which states that "the number of representatives shall not exceed one for every thirty thousand, but each state shall have at least one representative." In the 1st Congress, the sparsely populated state of Delaware was represented by only one member, while New York had six representatives. With the expansion of the population, it became necessary to limit the total number of House members. A 1929 congressional statute set the membership of the House of Representatives at 435.

Every ten years, the population of the United States is counted in a national census. The census shows the population shifts of the decade, revealing the whereabouts of the people and the votes. The Constitution has prescribed that Congress after each census, is to apportion seats among the states according to population; but the redrawing of district lines is left to the state legislatures.

Congressional districts are supposed to be redrawn to reflect population shifts and achieve fair and equal representation. State legislatures, however, with a bias in favor of rural and small town areas, have not adhered generally to this policy. Thus, malapportionment in the House of Representatives, in time, became more prevalent. It was particularly apparent after World War II, when the bulk of the population came to be concentrated in urban and suburban, rather than in rural, areas; and these massive population shifts were not reflected in Congress.

The disproportionate representational weight given to the less populous rural areas eventually resulted in grave inequalities. For example, in 1960, the sixteenth congressional district in Michigan had a population of 802,994. The twelfth district had 177,431 people. Each district sent one representative to Congress. The people in the twelfth district had a vote equal to 4½ times the vote of the people in the sixteenth.

This malapportionment has been due in part to the fact that the state legislatures, which were responsible for drawing congressional districts, were themselves often grossly malapportioned. In many cases, their representation was according to area or county, and not the number of people residing in the state. As a consequence, the majority of state legislators came from rural and small-town areas, and rural interests continued to determine congressional district lines.

Those most adversely affected by malapportionment were residents of the large cities and the new suburbanites of the late fifties. Residing in newly developed areas containing vastly expanded populations, they still sent to Congress the number of representatives that would have been sent from the

# Senate Membership in 92nd Congress

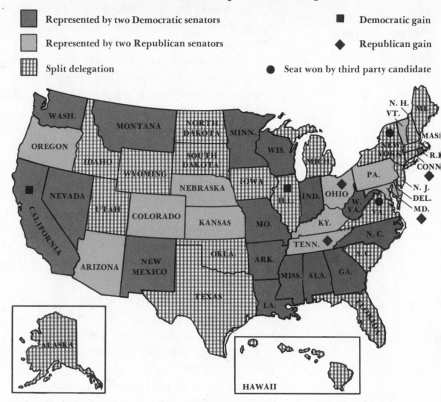

Source: *Current American Government* (Washington, D.C.: Congressional Quarterly, 1970), p. 5.

same district were it still a sparsely populated rural community. The state legislatures, with a stake in retaining the old boundaries, were not inclined to correct this condition. To make the political system responsive to contemporary demands, the issue of malapportionment had to be taken to the federal courts.

In 1962, the Supreme Court, in *Baker* v. *Carr*, affirmed that the right of citizens to sue on the grounds of malapportionment was a "dilution" of the constitutional privilege to vote and a violation of the equal protection clause of the Fourteenth Amendment.

Another factor that fostered unequal representation was the use of the *gerrymander*, which, unlike malapportionment (referring to numbers of people), refers to shapes of districts. Gerrymandering was named for Eldridge Gerry, governor of Massachusetts in 1812, who mapped out a congressional district with a voter population that he knew would re-elect him. The irregular shape of the district, as drawn on the map, resembled a salamander. Gerry's critics immediately dubbed it a "gerrymander" and, since then, the term has been used to describe the division of a state, county, or city into

## Gains and Losses in U.S. House Seats by State

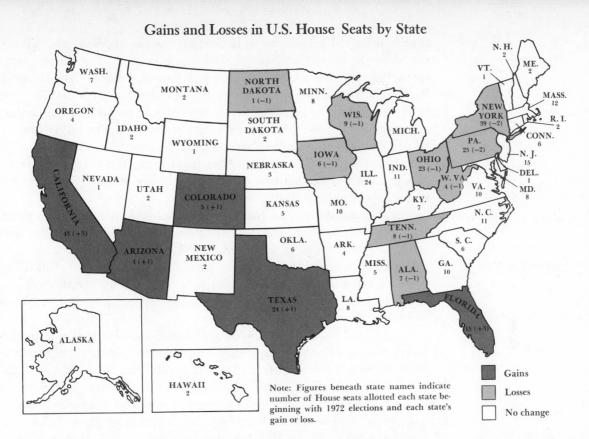

Note: Figures beneath state names indicate number of House seats allotted each state beginning with 1972 elections and each state's gain or loss.

Gains
Losses
No change

Source: "House Districts: Changes for at least 41 States," *Congressional Quarterly*, XXIX, No. 13 (March 26, 1971); 646.

voting districts in such a way as to give unfair advantage to one party or faction in elections. In practice, gerrymandering has merged some far flung areas into one district to assure political support for the party in control of redistricting—that is, the majority party in the state legislature.

The legal protest to gerrymandering congressional districts came in 1964, in *Wesberry* v. *Sanders*. At issue were the boundaries of congressional districts in the state of Georgia. Georgia's fifth congressional district, numbering 823,680 citizens (including the city of Atlanta and the surrounding rural counties), was the second largest district in the nation. Prior to the decision, Atlanta, which had been the most politically liberal area in the state, was gerrymandered into a district that gave undue power to the conservative rural counties that surrounded her. However, in *Wesberry* v. *Sanders*, the Supreme Court ruled that congressional representation must be based on population "as nearly as practicable," and declared that congressional districts must meet the standard of "one man, one vote."

The Court maintained that it would "defeat the principle solemnly embodied in the Great Compromise—equal representation in the House for equal numbers of people—for us to hold that, within the States, legislatures may draw the lines of congressional districts in such a way as to give some voters a greater voice in choosing a Congressman than others." The House of Representatives, according to the Constitutional Convention of 1787, was to be elected "by the people of the several states." Inasmuch as the Georgia apportionment "grossly discriminates against voters in the Fifth Congressional District," the Supreme Court declared the system a violation of Article I, Section 2, of the Constitution. After redistricting, the conservative representative lost the election to a moderate who more accurately reflected the views of the popular majority.

In subsequent decisions, the Supreme Court made it clear that its ruling in *Wesberry* v. *Sanders* (and the constitutional principle of "one man, one vote") would be enforced, and, thus, state legislatures would be required to redraw congressional districts to accurately reflect population distribution.[3] In 1969, for example, the Supreme Court rejected a Missouri redistricting law, in which some districts were overrepresented, while others were markedly underrepresented.[4]

[3] *Reynolds* v. *Sims* (1964).

[4] *Kirkpatrick* v. *Preisler* (1969).

Before the *Wesberry* v. *Sanders* ruling, rural areas exercised a disproportionate amount of power because of malapportionment in the Congress. Congressmen from "safe" districts in rural communities had been returned to the House in election after election. The result was that Congress was dominated by men from rural communities, who were bound to serve agrarian interests, while the United States was becoming predominantly a nation of cities. Reapportionment made the House of Representatives a body that more accurately reflected the views of the local majorities.

## Who can be elected?

The Constitution specifies the requirements for national legislative office. A senator must be thirty years of age and a citizen of the United States for at least nine years before he is eligible for office; a congressman must be twenty-five years of age and a citizen for seven years. Candidates for each office must establish legal residency in the state they represent (and by traditional practice, congressmen must live in their districts).

Clarence D. Long, "Observations of a Freshman in Congress," *The New York Times, December 1, 1963, section 6, pp. 34, 70–78.*

After twenty-five years as a professor of economics, Clarence Long (D. Maryland) left the academic life to serve in the House of Representatives. Being well-versed in the workings of Congress, and having testified before congressional committees during three administrations, Congressman Long was surprised that there is seemingly quite a distance between the "Hill" and the rest of Washington; in short, he was impressed by how much he had to learn.

Long, who ultimately found much to admire and to criticize in Congress, explains here what he considers to be the sources of the legislature's problems. Although he cites outmoded procedures, he contends that these are not so harmful to Congress as are:

The *two-year term* of House members, which forces them to campaign continually for re-election;

The vast amount of time Congressmen and their staffs must spend on *service for their districts*;

The modest net *salary* of Congressmen, which forces many of them to practice law or run businesses on the side, in order to support dual residences and educate their children.

The two-year term, Long notes, was established by the Constitutional Convention at a time when constituencies were much smaller than they are today, when sessions lasted only a few months, and when the national government was concerned only with defense, the excise tax, and a few internal improvements. Today's congressman, on the other hand, works seven days and five nights a week.

Furthermore, because the congressman is judged by the personal service and contracts he brings, half of his time and two-thirds of his staff are consumed in efforts to please the voters back home. Thus, Long has spent time working through the bureaucracy to help elderly ladies with income tax problems and young men who were unhappy with their draft classifications; his "good will" actions have even included obtaining a scoop of dirt from the White House lawn for a seven-year-old girl.

On a less personal level, the congressman must be attentive to business needs in his district; Long, for example, set up a business desk to help firms to contact government agencies, especially for defense business. Inasmuch as these increased duties leave little time to campaign for re-election, the lengthening of the two-year term would provide more adequate time for successful accomplishment of both obligations. Understandably, Long wonders if the legislator somehow can reduce his work load. He notes that other countries have begun using ombudsmen—administrators assigned by the legislature to deal with constituent problems relating to the bureaucracy or executive branch. However, Long argues that this system would never work in the United States because the congressman's re-election depends upon his personal handling of constituent inquiries, and the power of his vote enables him to get things done in the executive branch. In addition, Long feels that the ombudsman system would not work in a large country such as ours.

Long concludes that the naive view that a congressman simply proposes and votes on laws is equally as unsound as the cynical view that he should placate constituents and otherwise "stay out of trouble."

Here seems to be the ideal role of the Congressman: To represent his constituency, by knowing its needs and aspirations—at the same time inspiring it to something better. Both functions—to represent and to lead—are indispensable if a democracy of ordinary humans is to survive scientific revolutions every decade.

The one requires the Congressman to keep close to his constituency. The other requires him to know what goes on, in economics, in science, and in law. No Congressman is capable of all this, but a surprising number attempt it and a few come amazingly close.

This small band could be enlarged if the public would support better working conditions for Congressmen. Since it is not likely to do this very soon or very materially, Congress will continue to be less than fully effective as a purely legislative body.

Congressmen receive from the government a salary of $22,500, a year; senators receive an annual salary of $42,500. Expenses, however, range from $100,000 a year for congressmen, and from $190,000 to $325,000 for senators. These additional funds are provided by congressional appropriations, supplemented in some cases by personal funds or contributions from supporters.

The money appropriated to congressmen and senators is used for staff assistance and stationery, telephones, telegrams, travel, and office rental in the official's home state or district. Congressmen usually support a staff of seven; and senators generally employ twenty assistants, secretaries, and clerks. Robert Kennedy (1964–1968), as senator from New York and possessor of extensive personal funds, had a staff of eighty, the largest on Capitol Hill.

Both congressmen and senators receive additional staff assistance. They can utilize, for example, the services of committee staffs and many of the 24,000 people employed directly by Congress. Free mailing, or *franking* privileges, accounts for about 200 million pieces of mail a year.

5 Quoted in Committee on House Administration, *History of the United States House of Representatives* (Washington, D.C.: Government Printing Office, 1962), p. 35.

# The legislators

Cabell Phillips (formerly of *The New York Times*), casting an eye over the quality of the men serving in Congress, concluded that:

Congress is neither as doltish as the cartoonists portray it nor as noble as it portrays itself. While it has its quota of knaves and fools, it has its fair share of knights. And sandwiched between these upper and nether crusts is a broad and representative slice of upper-middle-class America [5]

## The Backgrounds of Senators and Congressmen in the 92nd Congress

| | |
|---|---|
| *Age* (average is 52.7): | |
| Senators | 56.4 |
| Congressmen | 51.9 |
| New senators | 45 |
| New congressmen | 45.4 |
| *Occupation*[a]: | |
| Lawyers | 301 |
| Businessmen or bankers | 172 |
| Professors | 72 |
| Farmers | 49 |
| Journalists | 37 |
| Clergymen | 2 |
| *Religion:* | |
| Roman Catholic | 113 |
| Methodist | 85 |
| Presbyterian | 83 |
| Episcopalian | 66 |
| Baptist | 50 |
| Jewish | 14 |
| Other | 24 |
| *Sex:* | |
| Male | 422 |
| Female | 13 |
| *Race:* | |
| White | 422 |
| Black | 13 |

[a] Several listed more than one occupation.

Source: *Congressional Quarterly*, January 15, 1971.

The men who serve in Congress have many similarities in their occupational and social backgrounds. Most arrive on Capitol Hill from some previous political office. New House members tend to have had prior service in their state legislatures or as local officials; newly elected senators usually have served a few terms in the House or as a state governor. The legislator's average age is 52.7 years. Most have had college educations; the majority—56 percent—are lawyers; 32 percent are businessmen; 75 percent have served in the armed forces.

Despite the fact that ours is a pluralistic society containing countless minority groups, members of Congress tend to represent the upper middle class, white Protestant, male Anglo-Saxon, middle-aged stratum of the population. In the 92nd Congress, there are only thirteen women and thirteen black legislators.

Although the United States is predominantly urban, many congressmen are originally from rural areas. Sixty-four percent of the senators in 1959 were raised in rural areas or small towns, while only 19 percent came from metropolitan areas.

## Leadership posts in Congress

### Presiding officer of the House: the Speaker

The leadership posts in the two houses of Congress retain a host of powers, traditions, and prerogatives. Those who fill them can influence and possibly even determine whether legislative proposals will become law. Those who wield authority are generally skilled political strategists who are elected to their positions by colleagues in Congress.

In the lower chamber, the Speaker is the most powerful elected officer. The Constitution designates the *Speaker of the House* as the presiding officer of the House of Representatives and prescribes that he be elected by its members. In practice, he is chosen by the majority party caucus and, as a prerequisite, must have served in the House for a considerable period of time. His power is great. Sam Rayburn, who served in the House for fifty years and was Speaker for sixteen, said, "I haven't served *under* anybody. I have served *with* eight Presidents."[6]

The Speaker's power springs from two sources: his political base (he is elected by the representatives of *all* the people, so that in a sense, he is a national officer like the President) and his administrative authority, accruing from the exercise of his official duties. He has the authority to recognize members on the floor and interpret the rules of the House during debate; he can cast the tie-breaking vote on legislation; in consultation with the majority leader, he schedules the order in which legislation comes to the floor. He organizes and sets in motion select and conference committees, when they are needed.

William S. White has noted,

> Officially, his job is in many respects comparable to the job of heading any great corporation or enterprise. He is the ultimate chief of everything in the House, from the nature of its legislative program to the conduct of its dining room, and the direction of its personnel—hired and elected—is his endless concern.[7]

Perhaps more important than the Speaker's formal authority is his political influence. As "the elect of the elect" (and, in particular, of the majority party), he is a political officer. As a party leader, he is expected to marshal forces for the passage of the party's legislative program. He can exercise tremendous personal influence over his party members, and his support can be decisive in the outcome of major House debates and the enaction of key legislation.

Some Speakers have exerted more influence than others. Personality is as much a determinant of strong leadership as are the formal powers of office. Sam Rayburn had the confidence and loyalty of his colleagues after

[6] Neil MacNeil, *Forge of Democracy: The House of Representatives* (New York: David McKay Co., Inc., 1963), p. 67.

[7] *History of the House*, p. 96.

serving in the House for half a century. When he became Speaker, he commanded great influence as much through his personal ties as his formal powers. However, a less commanding figure can effectively wield power as House Speaker by efficient bestowal of favors, rational administration, and the exercise of diplomatic force to break informal deadlocks between House members.

## Speakers of the House of Representatives

*Party:*

| | |
|---|---|
| Federalist | 4 |
| Democratic Republican | 6 |
| Whig | 2 |
| American | 1 |
| Democrat | 21 |
| Republican | 12 |

*State:*

| | |
|---|---|
| Massachusetts | 7 |
| Kentucky | 4 |
| Virginia | 4 |
| Tennessee | 3 |
| Pennsylvania | 3 |
| Miscellaneous states | 23 |

*Term of Office:*

| | |
|---|---|
| 1 year | 7 |
| 2 years | 17 |
| 4 years | 7 |
| Between 6 and 9 years | 12 |
| 10 years | 1 |
| 11 years | 1 |

The office of Speaker used to be much more powerful than it is today. Speaker Joseph Cannon, who served in that office from 1903 to 1911, had such a reputation for being a "czar" that one congressman, when asked by a constituent to send a copy of the rules and procedures of the House, sent instead a picture of Speaker Cannon. In Cannon's era, the Speaker served as chairman of the powerful House Rules Committee, appointed all standing committees and their chairmen, and had almost unlimited powers to recognize members on the floor of the House. Between the years 1903 and 1910, he increasingly used these powers to the detriment of the progressive Republicans and their legislative programs. In 1910, Senator George Norris led a coalition of progressive Republicans and Democrats to curb the powers of the Speaker's office.

The 1910 "revolt" removed the Speaker from chairmanship of the Rules Committee, restricted his power to make committee appointments and his powers to recognize speakers from the House floor by providing that the House, by vote, carry out these functions.

Still, the House of Representatives, as a large unwieldly body of competing interests, requires a moderating and unifying force. Consequently, the speakership has retained much of its old influence. It remains the locus of power in the House.

Carl Albert (D. Oklahoma) *is sworn in as Speaker of the House of Representatives.*

## Presiding officers of the Senate: the President, and the President *pro tempore*

[8] Dale Vinyard, *Congress* (New York: Charles Scribner's Sons, 1968), p. 77.

The formal presiding officer of the Senate is the Vice-President of the United States. As *President of the Senate,* he has the authority to vote in order to break a tie; but aside from this function, there are no significant duties attached to his legislative office.

> Individual vice presidents have exercised influence on a personal basis and have occasionally used their rulings to advance partisan concerns. . . . But the split nature of their position—part executive, part legislative—has posed serious problems for a vice president trying to exert influence in the Senate.[8]

The Vice-President does not attend Senate sessions regularly. The Constitution specifies that, in his absence, the President *pro tempore* preside. He is nominated by the majority party in the Senate and formally elected by the entire membership. However, unlike the functions of the Speaker of the House, his are largely ceremonial and entail few powers. The position of President *pro tempore* is prestigious; but if the senator who holds the post wields any power at all, it is derived from some other office he occupies.

The *majority leader of the Senate*, as the chief political officer of the Senate, is the equivalent of the House Speaker. He does not, however, wield authority as far-reaching as that of the House Speaker. One reason is that the Senate has neither the organizational nor hierarchical structure of the House. In the House, power tends to filter down from the Speaker, at the top, through the committee chairmen; in the Senate, power is dispersed among the elected leaders and the longer-serving, more influential senators. Nevertheless, the majority leader can be a significant force in determining when legislative proposals will come before the Senate.

The leader of the majority party becomes the center of negotiations of the Senate by combining his formal powers as majority leader with his informal powers of political persuasion. The Democrats give their majority leader control of three key organizations: the Democratic caucus, which nominates and appoints the Steering Committee; the Steering Committee itself, which makes committee assignments; and the Policy Committee, which controls the scheduling of bills on the floor.

Lyndon Johnson, who served as majority leader from 1954 to 1960, utilized these organizations so adroitly that he became one of the most powerful and respected majority leaders in history. For example, he won the support of newly elected senators by assigning them to at least one major committee, in preference to the usual practice of appointing them to serve on the minor committees. The exceptional influence he eventually had was also based on personal politics. "Johnson would strive to identify as early as possible those senators who held the balance of power on the given legislation. His subsequent efforts could be focused on devising and executing the tactics which would capture these crucial votes."[9]

Lyndon Johnson was the consummate bargainer who gave the Senate strong centralized leadership. The current majority leader, Mike Mansfield (D. Montana), is often said to be more of an organizer than a wheeler-dealer and power-broker. One political scientist stated that as majority leader, "His principal duty was to maintain a system which permitted individual, co-equal senators the opportunity to conduct their affairs in whatever ways they deemed appropriate."[10]

The *majority leader of the House* is second in importance to the Speaker. Chosen by the majority party caucus, he, in contrast to the Speaker, is responsible only to his party and not to the entire House. His formal duty is to determine the schedule for House debates. "Scheduling legislation to ob-

## The majority leaders

[9] John G. Stewart "Two Strategies of Leadership: Johnson and Mansfield," in *Congressional Behavior*, ed. by Nelson W. Polsby (New York: Random House, Inc., 1971), p. 67.

[10] Stewart, "Two Strategies of Leadership . . . ," p. 69.

11 Charles Clapp, *The Congressman: His Work as He Sees It* (Garden City, N.Y.: Doubleday and Co., Inc., 1964), p. 318.

## The minority leaders and floor whips

tain maximum results is a tricky matter, and the effective majority leader possesses a canny sense of timing."[11] The majority leader plans party strategy, confers with the Speaker and other party leaders and fosters party unity. He attempts to reconcile committees' disputes on legislative policies. Although he generally does not serve on any committee, the impact of his opinion can determine who receives committee assignments.

*Minority leaders* are elected by their party caucus. (In the House, the minority leader is usually the potential candidate for the speakership.) In both chambers, the minority leaders direct the floor strategy of their party and are expected to detect and criticize the inconsistencies in the majority's arguments.

The leaders on both sides of the aisles, majority and minority, are aided by the party whips, an office borrowed from the British Parliament, in which the whip enforces party unity. (The British system derived the term from fox hunting, in which the "whipper-in" keeps the hounds from straying away from the pack while in pursuit of the fox.) The function of the whips in Congress is to assist the party leaders in rounding up votes by conveying information for or against a bill. The whip serves as the principal means of communication between the leader and his party members. On some issues, when a single vote may be decisive, the skill of the party whip can directly affect the final vote.

*Senator Mike Mansfield of Montana is currently serving as the Democratic leader.*

*The sometimes controversial and always outspoken Everett M. Dirksen served for many years as the Senate GOP leader.*

In the House, the Democratic whip is chosen by the floor leader—either majority or minority, depending on the position of his party—in consultation with the Speaker, and he is then formally approved by the party caucus. The Republican whip in the House is appointed by the Republican Committee on Committees. Generally, the House whips and their assistants inform the party members of pending legislation and urge their attendance at crucial votes. They take *whip checks* which are surveys on how the representatives in their party will vote on particular legislative proposals.

*Randall B. Ripley,* "The Party Whip Organizations in the United States House of Representatives," *Americana Political Science Review* 58 (1954): 561–576.

As deputy Democratic whip in the House from April to September, 1963, Randall Ripley gathered the data for this study of the whip's role during the second session of the 87th Congress (1962) and the first session of the 88th (1963). These years were particularly active for the Democratic whip organization. John McCormack, the Speaker of the House at that time, had served earlier as party whip and was aware, therefore, of the position's potential value. The new majority leader, Carl Albert, had also served as whip.

During the years in which Ripley interned, Hale Boggs of Louisiana was whip; both he and his deputy, John Moss of California, were loyal administration supporters. The assistant whips, however, varied in the extent of their loyalty. While the Democratic delegation has the power to replace anyone who strays from the party line, Ripley notes that disloyalty is not generally the determining factor in removal.

Loyalty is less important than accuracy and thoroughness. The Democratic assistant whips are expected to perform the functions involving attendance, information, and polling, but they have a great deal of discretion in deciding whether they also wish to pressure their zone members to vote the Administration position.

The author evaluates the performance of the Democratic whip organizations in terms of four major functions. The first function analyzed is that of insuring maximum Democratic attendance in the House for important votes. The whips try to determine who will be in the House on specific days and, occasionally, schedule votes on the basis of this information. On the day of the vote, a check is conducted to see who must be contacted or paired. The whip's office is especially eager to set up live pairs, whereby an antiadministration vote actually on the House floor is invalidated by an absent proadministration vote. Ripley also observes that "the whip's office goes to great lengths to guarantee the presence of members on crucial votes." All their effort has some effect:

On the 17 bills in these two sessions on which the whip organization was fully active total Democratic voting attendance was 94 percent. This can be compared with the Democratic attendance on all roll calls: 83 percent in 1962 and 84 percent in 1963. This higher attendance was partially a function of the importance of the bills. Yet the specific instances [studied] suggest that the whip organization had some marginal effect in producing a high voting turnout.

The second function analyzed is that of providing information related to the schedule of floor action and the contents of legislation. Depending on how important the legislation is to the administration and House leadership, the whip may circulate a neutral letter of information or a highly partisan one.

The whip's third function consists of ascertaining how his party will vote on bills crucial to administration programs. Polls are used to determine congressmen's inclinations; the interpretation of them is very tricky. If the whip belongs to the same party as the President (as in Ripley's study), the results of his poll will be received by officials in the White House.

Finally, the whip is an arm-twister; the direction of pressure is, according to Ripley, the whip's most important function, although it is difficult to gauge its effect:

This fourth function of the whip's office—that of directing pressure—is, in some ways, the most important of the four. There is no precise systematic or statistical way of charting the effectiveness of this whip-guided pressure, since the ultimate test would compare what happened with what might otherwise have happened.

An example of this direction of pressure can be seen in the passage of the 1962 tax bill. To pressure the southern delegates, the whip called a caucus of the North Carolina delegation; this caucus, along with effective work by the assistant whip from Texas, helped maintain lost southern votes at fifteen. When the support of a midwestern state became dubious at the last minute, the whip (Boggs) took a representative to his office to confer with both the Speaker and (by telephone) the President. Ripley concludes:

The weight of evidence is that the efforts to insure a maximum attendance, to inform the Democratic membership of undesirable effects on the country if a Democratic Administration proposal is defeated, to ascertain voting expectations with great accuracy in advance, and to direct pressure to the precise spots where it will do the most good, result in some small, yet definite, net gains for the Democratic majority in the House.

# Committees

"Congressional government is committee government," wrote Woodrow Wilson in his 1885 study on American government. Most legislative systems, in order to formulate bills, need to organize themselves into small functional units that can focus effectively on single issues. Floor debates, though useful for recording opinions and votes, are generally carried on to score political points and to garner publicity. They tend to make headlines rather than statutes. Much of the actual work of Congress is done in committees and subcommittees.

Committee assignments are controlled by the senior members of Congress. In the House, Republicans receive their appointments from the *Committee on Committees*. This committee was established in 1910 to choose members of the permanent committees. It is composed of one congressman from each of the numerous states having Republican members in the House. The representative to the Committee on Committees is elected by his state delegation and is likely to be its most senior member. He has as many votes as there are Republicans in his delegation. For this reason, the committee is controlled by the longest serving Republicans in the House. Since 1910, Democratic assignments are made by the Democrats serving on the House Ways and Means Committee. (However, before making an assignment, these members confer with the senior Democrats of their respective state delegations.) Appointments are automatically approved by the House.

Committee assignments for both parties in the Senate are made by small *steering committees*, which may have from eight to over fifteen members, according to political representation in the party. The members with seniority control the selections. Their appointments are confirmed by the Senate as a whole. Committee assignments are of great importance to the party leadership as well as to the individual congressman. For example, if a congressman from rural South Dakota serves on the Agriculture Committee, he is more likely to aid his constituents than if he is a member of the Labor and Public Welfare Committee. In 1971, Congressman Herman Badillo, whose New York City district is plagued with the social and economic ills that confront many urban areas, found himself assigned to the House Agriculture Committee as a freshman representative. He petitioned for a change and was assigned ultimately to the Education and Labor Committee.

There are four kinds of congressional committees: the standing (permanent) committees, special and select committees, joint committees, and conference committees.

# Standing committees

The most important committees in the Congress are the *standing committees*, which do most of the work in formulating and evaluating legislative proposals. Each of the standing committees in the House and the Senate specializes in a particular field and deals only with bills related to its area of specialization. The House has twenty-one standing committees and the Senate has seventeen. A congressman generally serves on one such committee, whereas a senator usually serves on three standing committees.

Standing committees have a bipartisan character. The parties are represented roughly according to the number of seats that each holds in the House or the Senate. The majority party always holds the majority of seats on the committee, and the chairmanship goes to one of its senior members.

Standing committees are established by the rules of each chamber as permanent committees (unless modified or eliminated by future legislation), possess stated jurisdiction in a specific field (such as agriculture or foreign relations), and are responsible for examining and reporting all legislation referred to them.

The standing committees are subdivided into subcommittees that possess a greater degree of specialization. There are nearly two hundred and fifty subcommittees of Congress. One hundred and twenty-five are subdivisions of standing committees. A powerful committee, the Senate Committee on Foreign Relations, for example, has ten subcommittees: African Affairs, Western Hemisphere Affairs, Arms Control and International Law and Organization, Economic and Social Policy Affairs, European Affairs, Far Eastern Affairs, Genocide Convention, Near Eastern and South Asian Affairs, Ocean Space, and U.S. Security Agreements and Commitments Abroad.

The standing committees and their subcommittees are the arms and hands of Congress, digging in and getting the work done. It is they who analyze the thousands of bills proposed each year and assess their worth. They are responsible for drawing up and wording the legislation that goes before the floor. Finally, it is the committees who determine whether or not a bill is to be voted on, and if the decision is affirmative, it is the committee members who shepherd the bill through the intricate voting procedures of the legislature.

## Select and special committees

*Select and special committees* are created by congressional resolution to do specific jobs: to pursue a single investigation or to conduct hearings on an individual bill. Usually, a select committee studies a particular area for a definite period. As soon as it has submitted its report to Congress, the select committee is disbanded. For example, the Committee on War Contracts, established during World War II, was disbanded as soon as its function had been completed and the war was over. The select committee is usually an investigating committee with the power to call forth witnesses and records and to administer oaths. However, in recent years, the investigating function has been performed primarily by the subcommittees of the standing committees.

## Joint committees

*Joint committees* are permanent committees composed of House and Senate members. They are created in order to deal with issues and problems requiring consideration by both houses of Congress. Joint procedure provides the advantage of integrated discussion and decision. (The Joint Committee on Atomic Energy and the Joint Economic Committee are current examples of the use of this type of committee.) However, the joint committee is the exception, rather than the rule, in the committee system. Many House members fear Senate domination in joint committees, and the creation of them has been discouraged.

## Conference committee

The most common type of joint committee is the *conference committee*. These are temporary committees, formed when different versions of a bill have been passed in the House and Senate, and one chamber will not accept the other's version. The committee's members, chosen by the leaders of their separate houses, convene to rewrite the bill so that it will include the terms of both houses. The new version of the bill is then resubmitted to each house and put to a vote. Of the legislation proposed, approximately 10 percent goes to a conference committee.

## Committee chairmen

The individual committee chairman wields great authority. He determines when his committee will meet, selects the professional staff, establishes each subcommittee, designates the order in which bills will be considered, and decides whether or not to have hearings on a bill. He has the power to decide whether or not a bill will be considered by the committee. By ignoring a bill or never reporting it out, he can, in effect, kill a legislative proposal in committee. Although, theoretically, his decisions can be overruled by a majority of the committee members, in practice, the chairman's decisions are rarely challenged or overruled.

When a bill is brought to the floor for a vote, the committee chairman manages the debate, a responsibility entailing the selection of members who will share in the debate. If and when that bill is passed, he serves as chief representative of his chamber on the conference committee, if it becomes necessary to reconcile the differences between the bills passed by the two chambers. A freshman member of Congress once stated, in amazement:

> I knew committee chairmen were powerful, but I didn't realize the extent of the power or its arbitrary nature. Recently, when my chairman announced he planned to proceed in a particular way, I challenged him to indicate under what rules he was operating. "My rules," he said. That was it, even though there were no regularly authorized rules permitting him to function in that manner. There is great reluctance to challenge committee chairmen even though you don't agree with them. Everyone seems fearful; all members have pet projects and legislation they want passed. No one wants to tangle too much because they realize what the results would be.[12]

12 Clapp, *Congressman*, p. 252.

The committees and their chairmen carry out the constitutional mandate of the legislature to make laws. In studying their mode of operations, it becomes apparent that lawmaking is a slow, grinding process of careful thought and definition, of investigation and testing.

# The legislative process

The legislative process entails a complex interplay of formal power structures and informal political strategies. The way the system operates presents obstacles to the enaction of legislative proposals. This design was intended to insure that the laws would be a product of careful and reasoned deliberation. As it now functions, sponsors of a bill must marshal broad support in order to achieve passage.

| Record of 91st Congress | | |
| --- | --- | --- |
| | First Session | Second Session |
| Bills and resolutions introduced | 21,553[a] | 7,487 |
| Bills that became public law | 150[b] | 505 |
| Vetoes | 0 | 9 |
| Vetoes overridden | 0 | 2 |

The first session ran from January 3, 1969 to December 23, 1969; the second session ran from January 19, 1970 to January 2, 1971, the longest session since the 1950 session of the 81st Congress.

[a] Highest number in the history of Congress.
[b] Lowest number in 36 years.

More than 22,000 bills are introduced every year. Between January and June of 1970, some 9,000-odd bills were introduced in the House and 3,000 in the Senate. There are several reasons for the fact that many more bills are introduced in the House than in the Senate. The first, and most obvious, is the numerical difference: there are 335 more congressmen than senators introducing bills. Second is the procedural differences. In the Senate, members can join forces and sponsor the same bill. In the House, members generally submit their individual versions of a similar legislative proposal. Third is the constituency difference. Congressmen, in legislating for their districts, have more specific demands to meet, and thus more measures to propose, than senators with statewide interests requiring broader legislation. Fourth, all bills concerning money must originate in the House.

Only a fraction of all legislative proposals are reported out of committee, and the number of bills eventually passed by Congress is far lower.

The fate of a major bill depends to a great extent on who supports it. (Noncontroversial private bills that few oppose are more readily enacted.) A major bill that is sponsored by one congressman will probably not be passed unless he can gain backing from members in the two chambers and from powerful lobbies. If he can obtain presidential backing for his proposal, then the chances for adoption may be greatly increased if the congressional majority is of the President's party. This applies particularly to controversial legislation. A number of reform measures, such as social security, had been proposed and tabled for years until President Franklin Roosevelt included them in the New Deal program he presented to Congress.

## The introductory stage

The idea for a bill may originate in one of two places. It may be the creation of one or more senators or congressmen, or it may originate in the executive branch of government and have the support of the President (who proposes a bill through a brief note to a party member or a detailed draft of a measure to the appropriate committee). Only a senator or congressman can actually introduce the bill, yet approximately 80 percent of the legislation passed by Congress is originated by the President.

Regardless of its origins, every bill follows certain standard procedures in order to become law. Stage one is the drafting and introduction of the bill. An individual congressman will use his staff and the services of the Office of Legislative Counsel to write the bill in the right legal terms and format. Sometimes, a proposed law goes simultaneously to the House and Senate. But in the case of legislation about which some controversy is anticipated, the bill is usually first introduced in the chamber where passage is most likely. With the exception of appropriations legislation, which always must be introduced in the House first, the chamber in which a bill is first presented is chosen according to the criteria of legislative strategy. Acceptance by the first chamber may facilitate passage in the next, whereas heated debate and publicized controversy could wreck its chances for adoption.

*Lewis A. Froman, Jr.,* The Congressional Process: Strategies, Rules and Procedures (*Boston: Little, Brown and Co., 1967*), *pp. 155–158.*

The present legislative system requires that both houses of Congress must either pass identical bills or reconcile their differences before a bill can become law. Because of the differences in the membership and structure of the two houses, the question of where the bill should originate is a key factor in the ultimate fate of the bill.

Lewis Froman notes that the most common, most effective strategy is to present the bill first to the house where it is most likely to be passed in its strongest version.

If the more favorable house should go first this opens up the possibility of either skipping the committee stage in the other house, or forcing the other house to deal with a bill already passed. The house which is less likely to act, or to act more weakly, is then confronted with a different problem. The question is no longer whether there will be a bill or no bill; the probability of there being a strong bill versus a weaker bill becomes one of the alternatives. If committees in the house which acts second do not act at all, a stronger bill might pass the floor of that house than if the committees in that house had an opportunity to work out a weaker bill.

Naturally, once a bill has passed in one house, it is more likely that it will pass in the other house, for its original supporters will exert pressures on behalf of its passage.

In some cases, however, a bill is first introduced in the house in which passage is questionable. Legislation takes time and energy, and if it is very likely that a bill will be defeated by one house, the bill may be presented to that house first. In such cases, it is felt that the house in which passage is assured should not waste the little time it has on a bill that is unlikely to become law.

How does a legislator determine which house is likely to be most favorable to his bill? Generally, legislative strategy is based on each house's prior record on bills in a given area, and, in particular, on the strength of the bills passed previously. For example, if, today, an aid-to-education bill were being proposed, Froman suggests that the bill first be submitted to the Senate, the house that has passed four education-aid bills (as compared to the House's one), and which, in every case, has presented the strong versions of these bills.

## Committee review

Once a bill is formally introduced, it is then assigned to the appropriate standing committee for investigation, debate, and analysis. However, the committee may choose not to consider a bill. Many proposals are *tabled*—put aside—until they are no longer pertinent, or until they are considered "dead" by their sponsors. More than 10 percent of all bills proposed die in committee. The bills that do move from the committee to the floor undergo the rigorous process of committee review. This process is essentially the same in both House and Senate.

The committee—or, more commonly, the subcommittee—may first conduct a staff investigation of the measure. The organization of subcommittees according to highly specialized areas gives Congress the capability to assess specialized subject matter. A congressman assigned to a subcommittee may develop an expertise over the years that is equal to that of any expert sent by the administration to argue for or against the bill. Consequently, Congress often has the capacity to criticize, challenge, and investigate most measures in depth.

On important bills, the committee will conduct *public hearings* at which proponents and opponents of the measure can testify as to its merits and demerits. Committee members question the witnesses: technical experts, executive officials, fellow congressmen, lobbyists, and private citizens. In the case of a controversial bill, hearings may last for weeks or months. The hearings provide important information on the bill, while simultaneously assessing support for its passage.

After this stage, the bill then is intensively reviewed by the full committee's *executive session*; generally, committee members only are permitted to attend. Witnesses and congressmen may be called upon, but the public and the press are never admitted to observe proceedings. The measure is analyzed item-by-item, revised (or "marked up") accordingly, and then submitted to the full committee for a vote by its members. For the bill to be reported out, majority approval is necessary. The executive session prepares a formal report on its findings. Often, there will be two reports on a bill, the majority's and the dissenting minority's, which are then published for the consideration of Congress. In general, however, when a majority of the committee's members vote against reporting the bill to the floor, the bill dies in committee.

After a bill is reported out of committee, it is then placed on the appropriate "calendar" of the chamber. These calendars are business agendas listing the order in which bills are to be considered on the floor.

## Floor procedure

The House and the Senate employ different procedures in bringing a bill before the entire chamber. In the Senate, routine measures may be considered by the order in which they are listed on the calendar. This works, despite the fact that unanimous consent is required for consideration by the Senate. However, the scheduling of bills that will be debated, rather than routinely considered, is more complex. Their scheduling is subject to the influence of the policy committee, the majority and minority leaders, and key senators.

In the House, the Rules Committee controls the order in which bills come to the floor. It may or may not operate in conjunction with the Speaker and the majority leader. If a bill is not granted a rule from the committee, it cannot come up for action on the floor. The rule specifies the time and duration of debate and may stipulate the type of revisions that can be made.

Current American Government (*Washington, D.C.: Congressional Quarterly, Inc., Spring 1971*), *pp. 83–84*

In 1964, Congress established a joint committee to study congressional operations and suggest improvements. Although many of its suggestions were not accepted, several were, and these were incorporated into the Legislative Reorganization Act of 1970. For example, the bill provided for:
1. committee roll-call votes to be made public
2. hearings of the House committee to be televised or broadcast, if a majority of the committee agree to it

3. teller votes of the (House) Committee of the Whole to be recorded, and

4. revision of several rules, so as to limit the committee chairman's power and safeguard the rights of minority members.

Whether or not the new bill will be effective depends primarily on the willingness of congressmen to forego traditional practice and adhere to the new rules—rules that were resisted earlier, especially in the House. Experience has shown that retention of power in the hands of a few senior members of the House tends to inhibit the impact of a change of rules. Reorganization of power is far more difficult to legislate than reform of rules.

The Legislative Reorganization Act of 1970, however useful it has been, will not satisfy all the critics of Congress. Many of the traditional rules and practices of Congress remain intact, even though many political scientists see these traditions as deterrents to the development of an efficient legislative process. The *seniority system*, for example, continues, untouched by time and regulation, despite protests from younger members whose contributions to Congress are limited by their seniors. Similarly, the *Congressional Record* continues to be published *after* it has been amended, revised, and supplemented.

The procedures for floor debate also differ greatly in the two chambers. In the House, the duration is set in advance. In the Senate, the length of debate is seldom restricted. (These differences in floor procedures are discussed further in Chapter 15.) Debate is not usually the crucial phase of the legislative process, for it changes few votes. What has happened before in the committees and in back-stage politics will most likely decide the final outcome of a bill. After floor debate, a vote is taken. If the bill passes both houses, it is then signed by the Speaker of the House and the President of the Senate and is sent to the President of the United States for his consideration.

**Presidential decision**

The final step in lawmaking is the President's signature. As was said in Chapter 12, the President has several alternatives—to sign the bill, to veto it either by regular or pocket veto, or to permit it to be enacted by not signing it. A presidential veto can be overridden by a two-thirds majority in each house; however, this is most difficult and it is relatively rare that a bill becomes law over a presidential veto. In the 91st Congress, President Nixon vetoed nine bills, only two of which were overridden.

**Evaluating the legislative process**

The legislative process inherently facilitates delay and inaction. In some urgent matters, such as a national railroad strike, Congress can meet and enact restraining legislation in a matter of hours. But, generally, Congress moves slowly, because of power politics and power structure. The dispersion of authority among party leaders, committees, and committee chairmen in particular, and the intricate factors of political negotiation, curtail the swift enactment of legislation.

Separate consideration of bills in the two houses was originally intended by the Framers to prevent hasty and rash action by the Congress. However, the legislative process that has evolved over the past 180 years on the constitutional principle of deliberated action often involves cumbersome and inefficient procedures. Congressman Richard Bolling of Missouri has written:

13 Richard Bolling, *House Out of Order* (New York: E. P. Dutton and Co., Inc., 1966), p. 221.

> In the many years that I have been a Member of Congress, the House has revealed itself to me as ineffective in its role as a coordinate branch of the federal government, negative in its approach to national tasks, generally unresponsive to any but parochial economic interests. Its procedures, time-consuming and unwieldly, mask anonymous centers of irresponsible power. Its legislation is often a travesty of what the national welfare requires.[13]

## HOW A BILL BECOMES LAW

This graphic shows the most typical way in which proposed legislation is enacted into law. There are more complicated, as well as simpler, routes, and most bills fall by the wayside and never become law.

| Introduction | Committee Action | Floor Action | Enactment into Law |
| --- | --- | --- | --- |

Introduced in House → Referred to House committee → House debates and passes

Committee holds hearings, recommends passage

Most legislation begins as similar proposals in both houses

House and Senate members confer, reach compromise

House and Senate approve compromise

All bills must go through both House and Senate before reaching President

President signs into law

Introduced in Senate → Referred to Senate committee → Senate debates and passes

Committee holds hearings, recommends passage

*Current American Government*, Congressional Quarterly Inc., 1970; 89.

As head of the Democratic Study Group in 1968, he put forth plans to increase the efficiency of House operations by consolidating and centralizing power. He proposed that the Speaker be given the authority to appoint the chairmen and the Democratic members on the Ways and Means Committee and the Rules Committee, and to select chairmen of the other standing committees to exercise such powers as would represent, in effect, a return to the system before the 1910 "reform."

Thus far, Congress has resisted adopting these and other plans for reforming the internal structure, in part because of the nature of the reforms themselves, and in part because vested power interests have a stake in maintaining the old mode of operations.

### Tips for Writing to Congressmen

The following hints on how to write a member of Congress were suggested by congressional sources and the League of Women Voters.

- Write to your own senators or representatives. . . .
- Write at the proper time, when a bill is being discussed in committee or on the floor.
- . . . Avoid signing and sending a form or mimeographed letter.
- . . . Don't try to instruct the representative or senator on every issue that comes up.
- Don't demand a commitment before all the facts are in. Bills rarely become law in the same form as introduced.
- Whenever possible, identify all bills by their number.
- If possible, include pertinent editorials from local papers.
- Be constructive. If a bill deals with a problem you admit exists but you believe the bill is the wrong approach, tell what you think the right approach is.
- If you have expert knowledge or wide experience in particular areas, share it with the member. But don't pretend to wield vast political influence.
- Write to the member when he does something you approve of. A note of appreciation will make him remember you more favorably the next time.
- Feel free to write when you have a question or problem dealing with procedures of government departments.
- Be brief, write legibly and be sure to use the proper form of address.

A 15-word telegram called a Public Opinion Message (P.O.M.) can be sent to the President, Vice-President or a member of Congress from anywhere in the United States for $1. Name and address are not counted as part of the message unless there are additional signers.

Source: *Current American Government* (Washington, D.C.: The Congressional Quarterly, Inc., 1970), p. 99.

In a pluralist democracy, the formulation of public policy reflects conflicts between competing interest groups. It is a process of accommodation in which laws are made through slow bargaining, rather than decree. The legislators must be responsive to the will of their constituents in order to retain their right to legislate; but demands in a pluralist society are often in conflict.

Because of these factors, and the nature of the legislative process, congressional action entails lengthy deliberations. Nevertheless, Congress, for all its intricate power relations, is an effective legislative body. It fulfills the constitutional mandate to make the laws that govern society. It stands as an essential political institution in the democratic system of government.

Yet, Congressional responsibility is insured by the fact that congressmen are held accountable for their actions by their constituents at election time. Stephen K. Bailey has written:

> For all its weaknesses and inadequacies, Congress is a major bastion of human freedom. . . . Of what does freedom consist, unless it is the atmosphere of human dignity made possible by the existence of representative restraints upon rulers? The Founding Fathers fully understood that although you could have government without a representative assembly, you could not have *free* government without a representative assembly.[14]

[14] Stephen K. Bailey, *Congress Makes a Law* (New York: Random House, Inc., 1950), pp. 109–110.

# Glossary

**committee on committees**   In the House of Representatives, a committee of Republican leaders established in 1910 to appoint members of their party to the standing committees.

**conference committee**   Type of joint committee formed to reconcile different versions of the same bill passed by both houses of Congress.

**congressional district**   Area of land that a congressman represents, theoretically determined on the basis of population.

**executive session**   Committee meeting, closed to the public, to discuss and revise a bill after public hearing.

**franking privilege**   Privilege of congressmen to send mail postage-free.

**gerrymander**   Division of a state, county, or city into voting districts in such a way as to give unfair advantage to one party or faction in elections.

**joint committee**   Committee created to deal with issues necessitating consideration by both chambers of Congress, and comprised of senators and congressmen.

**majority leader of the House**   Congressman selected by majority party caucus, second in command to the Speaker, and serving as chief strategist and floor spokesman.

**majority leader of the Senate**   Senator elected by the party in control as Senate program director and chief strategist and spokesman for that party.

**minority leader of the House**   Congressman elected by party colleagues, serving to unify opposition to majority party policies and programs.

**minority leader of the Senate**   Senator elected by party caucus, serving to criticize the policies of the majority party and marshal opposition to their bills.

**President of the Senate**   President officer of the Senate, usually the Vice-President of the United States.

**president *pro tempore***   (president for the time being). Senator, elected by the majority party, to preside over the session in the absence of the President of the Senate.

**public hearing**   Hearing conducted by a committee or subcommittee on a proposed bill, and open to the public.

**quorum**   Number of legislators required to be present for the transaction of business. In the Senate, when there are no vacancies, a quorum of 51 is required, and in the House of Representatives, 218.

**safe district**   Congressional district with a predominantly one-party constituency that consistently votes for the candidate of that particular party.

**select (special) committees**   Committees created to do a specific job, pursue a single investigation, and disband upon completion of the assignment.

**seniority system**   System of appointment to congressional posts on the basis of length of service in Congress.

**Seventeenth Amendment**   Constitutional amendment ratified in 1913, providing for the popular election of senators.

**Speaker of the House**   Presiding officer of the House of Representatives, theoretically elected by all members of the House and, in practice, elected by the majority party.

**standing committee**   Permanent congressional committee with jurisdiction over a specific field, serving to assess and revise legislative proposals referred to them.

**whip**   Congressman or senator appointed by his party to inform party members on legislative proposals for the purpose of obtaining votes.

**whip checks**   Polls on the voting intentions of party members, taken by the party whips.

## Supreme Court decisions

*Baker* v. *Carr*   1962 Supreme Court decision that effectively outlawed the gerrymander by directing the state of Tennessee to redraw its state legislative districts.

*Reynolds* v. *Sims*   1964 Supreme Court decision that representation in both houses of state legislatures must be based on population.

*Wesberry* v. *Sanders*   1964 Supreme Court decision requiring that congressional redistricting follow each national census.

# Suggested readings

Bailey, Stephen K., *Congress Makes a Law: The Story Behind the Employment Act of 1946* (New York: Columbia University Press, 1950). Case study of how a law is made, with emphasis on the pressures of conflicting interests in the legislative process.

Bailey, Stephen K., *The New Congress* (New York: St. Martin's Press, Inc., 1966). Brief study of congressional responsibilities and activities, with emphasis on the changes that have altered the character of Congress.

Baker, Gordon T., *The Reapportionment Revolution: Representation, Political Power and the Supreme Court* (New York: Random House, Inc., 1965). History of legislative apportionment in the United States, including excerpts from major judicial decisions and analyses of the issues raised by the cases that led to the decisions.

Barber, James D., *The Lawmakers: Recruitment and Adaptation to Legislative Life* (New Haven, Conn.: Yale University Press, 1965). Analysis of the backgrounds and personal adjustment of congressmen during their first terms in office.

Berman, Daniel M., *In Congress Assembled* (New York: The Macmillan Co., 1964). Commendable introduction to the national legislative process.

Berman, Daniel M., *A Bill Becomes a Law: Congress Enacts Civil Rights Legislation*, 2nd ed. (New York: The Macmillan Co., 1966). Case studies of the enforcement of the Civil Rights Acts of 1960 and 1964.

Bibby, John, and Roger Davidson, *On Capitol Hill: Case Studies in the Legislative Process* (New York: Holt, Rinehart and Winston, Inc., 1967). Case studies of the lawmaking process in the United States Congress.

Bryen, Stephen D., and Frank Colon, *The Congress of Government* (Philadelphia: Pennsylvania Department of Community Affairs, 1970).

Clapp, Charles L., *The Congressman: His Work as He Sees It* (Washington, D.C.: Brookings Institution, 1963). Study of the responsibilities and performance of United States congressmen—based on interviews iwth thirty-six congressmen—particularly good on committee system and leadership in the House of Representatives.

Clark, Joseph S., *Congressional Reform: Problems and Prospects* (New York: Thomas Y. Crowell Co., 1965). Essays on the need for congressional reform by a former liberal senator from Pennsylvania.

Cornelius, William G., *South Eastern State Legislatures* (Atlanta: Emory University imprint, 1968).

Crouch, Carroll W., "Reapportionment of the Legislature in North Dakota" (Unpublished Master's thesis, University of North Dakota, 1960).

Froman, Lewis A., Jr., *Congressional Process: Strategies, Rules, and Procedures* (Boston: Little, Brown and Co., 1967). Examination of the rules, procedures, and bargaining involved in lawmaking in the Senate and in the House of Representatives, and their effects on national policy.

Galloway, George B., *The Legislative Process in Congress* (New York: Thomas Y. Crowell Co., 1953). Standard text on the organization and operation of the Congress by a man who participated in the 1946 reorganization of Congress.

Griffith, Ernest S., *Congress: Its Contemporary Role*, 4th ed. (New York: New York University Press, 1967). Analysis of congressional pluralism and a defense of loose party discipline by a sympathetic and experienced observer of our national legislature.

Gross, Bertram, *The Legislative Struggle: A Study in Social Combat* (New York: McGraw-Hill Book Co., 1953). Excellent study of the legislative process emphasizing the various conflicts of interest.

Harris, J. P., *Congressional Control of Administration* (Washington, D.C.: Brookings Institution, 1964). Study of the means by which Congress oversees the functioning of the executive branch of government.

Jewell, Malcolm E., and Samuel Patterson, *Legislative Process in the United States* (New York: Random House, Inc., 1966). Comparative analysis of the American legislative process at the national and state levels.

Jones, Charles O., *Minority Party Leadership in Congress* (Boston: Little, Brown and Co., 1970). Historical analysis of the positions of and strategies employed by minority parties in Congress during the twentieth century.

Keefe, William J., and Morris Ogul, *American Legislative Process: Congress and the States*, 2nd ed. (Englewood Cliffs, N.J.: Prentice-Hall, Inc., 1968). Analysis of Congress, the political parties, interest groups, courts, and bureaucratic agencies that influence its behavior, combining historical, legal, behavioral, and normative materials.

Mayhew, David R., *Party Loyalty Among Congressmen: The Difference between Democrats and Republicans, 1947–1962* (Cambridge, Mass.: Harvard University Press, 1966). Analysis of congressional voting between 1947 and 1962, with particular emphasis on the influence of constituency pressures on party voting.

Truman, David B., *The Congressional Party: A Case Study* (New York: John Wiley and Sons, Inc., 1959). Analysis of voting behavior in the 81st Congress, showing the influence of party leadership on the voting of congressmen.

Truman, David B., ed., *The Congress and America's Future* (Englewood Cliffs, N.J.: Prentice-Hall, Inc., 1965). Essays on the reform and reorganization of Congress by eight recognized writers on American politics.

Turner, Julius, *Party Constituency: Pressures on Congress*, rev. ed., ed. by Edward V. Schneider, Jr., (Baltimore: Johns Hopkins University Press, 1967). Statistical analysis of the relative influence of party and constituency on congressional voting over a twenty-five-year period (1920s–1940s).

Vinyard, Dale, *Congress* (New York: Charles Scribner's Sons, 1965). Brief analysis of congressional activities, including some suggestions for reform.

Wahlke, John C., and Heinz Eulau, eds., *Legislative Behavior: A Reader in Theory and Research* (New York: The Free Press, 1959). Essays on the four basic factors of legislative behavior: institutional, social, psychological, and political.

Wilson, Woodrow, *Congressional Government: A Study in American Politics* (New York: World Publishing Co., 1956). (Originally published in 1885.) Classic analysis of congressional dominance in the nineteenth century.

Wolfinger, Raymond T., ed., *Readings on Congress* (Englewood Cliffs, N.J.: Prentice-Hall, Inc., 1971). Up-to-date collection of essays on Congress and pressure groups, public opinion, and elections, as well as presidential-congressional relations.

# Topics of further study

Aurand, Art R., "The Impact of Reapportionment on the California Senate" (master's thesis, San Jose State College, 1969).

Boyd, Richard, "Apportionment Facts," *National Civic Review*, April 1963, pp. 530–534.

Dionosopoulos, P. Allan, *Rebellion, Racism and Representation: The Adam Clayton Powell Case and its Antecedents* (De Kalb, Ill.: Northern Illinois University Press, 1970).

Goodwin, George, *Congress: Anvil of American Democracy* (Glenview, Ill.: Scott, Foresman & Co., 1967).

Jewell, Malcom Edwin, "State Legislators in Southern Politics," *Journal of Politics*, February 1964, pp. 177–196.

Patterson, Samuel C., and M. E. Jewell, *The Legislative Process in the United States* (New York: Random House, Inc., 1966).

Ripley, R. B., *Majority Party Leadership in Congress* (Boston: Little, Brown and Co., 1962).

# portfolio
# committees
# in
# action

Congressional committees are not only
concerned with promoting legislation.
With their great independence, they
often use their powers to investigate
and hold public hearings, to publicize
issues and build up public pressure
on the President and the rest of
Congress. In an area such as foreign
affairs, where Congress is relatively
weak, this power serves to limit the
power of the Executive. In the late
1960s, the Senate Foreign Relations
Committee held hearings on the war in
Vietnam that were embarrassing to
the Administration. Cabinet members
and other high government officials
were made to appear; in addition, the
committee also called members of the
general public not ordinarily heard in
the law-making process, including
veterans who had served in Vietnam.

Even though the seniority system protects committees from fluctuations in popular opinions, grass-roots interest in an issue can affect the most insular of committees. The recent nationwide concern for protecting the environment, which cut across political and generational lines, has resulted in much committee—and as a result, congressional—action. Laws to limit the exhaust emission of automobiles, to control oil spills from offshore drilling, to conserve public lands, to expand national seashores, and to protect near-extinct species were given priority by committees and passed by Congress.

Another law set up the Environmental Protection Agency in the Executive branch, but in Congress responsibility for legislation and investigation in this area is still spread throughout many committees. Some committees have created specialized subcommittees, but most have relied on the full committee or subcommittees handling areas that are more traditionally the concern of Congress. Which committee an environmental measure is sent to is crucial, as it is for bills in many other areas, and such legislation is usually carefully written so that it will go to a committee with a sympathetic chairman.

Committee compromise is evident in
most laws passed by Congress. It is
even more so in a controversial area
such as gun control, where there are
powerful and popular lobbies, strong
regional differences, and emotional
issues. Even when the chairman favors
strong legislation, he will prevent
committee action unless an acceptable
compromise can be worked out. The
Gun Control Act of 1968 was a
compromise limiting interstate traffic
in guns and also cutting foreign
imports to aid U.S. gun manufacturers.
In 1971, committee hearings were
again held on compromise gun control
legislation—this time to outlaw
cheap handguns.

The work of committees is not limited to dramatic hearings or to the major issues of our times; and the committees that stage such hearings and deal with these issues are not the only committees of consequence in Congress. Other committees, which do not get or seek as much public exposure, regularly process legislation—often routinely passed by Congress—that affects the daily lives of nearly all Americans. Many bills carefully worked out between government specialists and the "specialist" congressmen in the committees with their large staffs are too technical to be understood by the rest of Congress, much less the general public. Other committee actions involving rules and procedure may seem insignificant but they preordain the passage or defeat of many bills. Little of the important work of Congress is done on the floor of either house; it is delegated to the committees which have become in effect "little congresses."

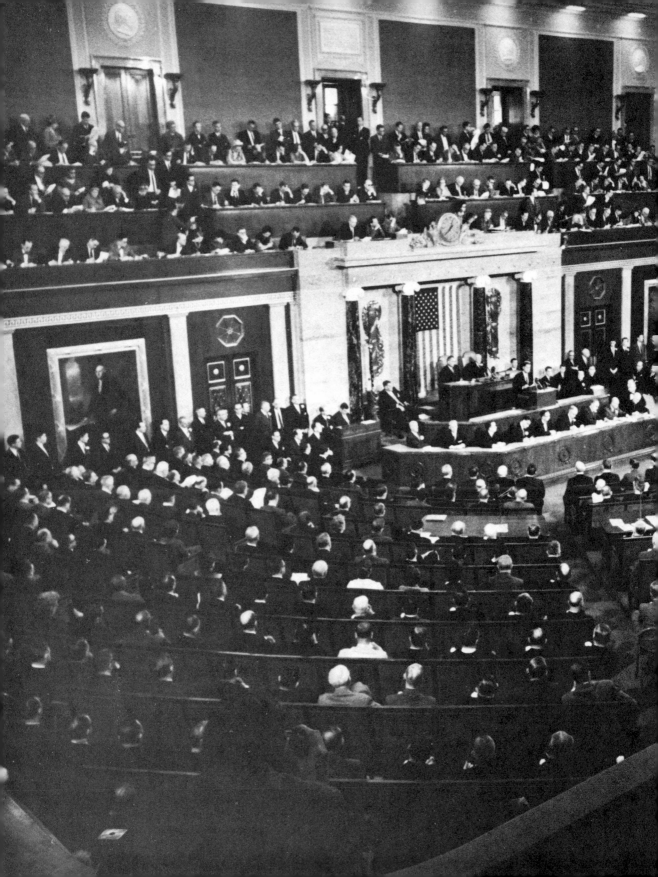

# 15 the senate and the house

## separate and distinct

A MEMBER of Congress once stated, "Occasionally, perhaps just once or twice a session, you sit there on the floor and are able to think of yourself as one tiny particle in the whole stream of history. The hard work falls away, and the tension is relaxed, and you have a sense of purpose . . ."[1] It is this sense of purpose that underlies the activities of the upper and lower chambers of Congress. As government institutions, the two Houses share the responsibility of lawmaking; but as unique legislative bodies, they are separate and distinct in traditions and procedures.

The Senate in size and mode of operation can be viewed as a "club" of one hundred individuals and individualists, each wielding a degree of personal power. There is an informality of procedure not present in the House. The House is a larger, more unwieldy body of 435 men. In contrast to the Senate, the House can be viewed as a hierarchical power structure, parallel in some respects to the bureaucratic organization of a large corporation. This setup necessitates numerous rules of procedure that make personal influence only one of many factors that determines passage on a bill. "Perhaps the most striking difference noticed by most visitors to the Capitol is the apparent formality and impersonality in the House chamber as contrasted with the relatively informal and friendly atmosphere in the Senate."[2]

Another major difference between the two houses is the political outlook of its members. Senators, unlike congressmen, have state-wide constituencies. Hence, they must consider a diversity of interests—rural,

[1] Charles L. Clapp, *The Congressman* (Garden City, N.Y.: Doubleday and Co., Inc., 1964), p. 487.

[2] Lewis A. Froman, Jr., *The Congressional Process: Strategies, Rules and Procedures* (Boston: Little, Brown and Co., 1967), p. 7.

big city, suburban, ethnic, economic, and so on. The constituencies of congressmen are far narrower than those of senators. The districts to which they are responsible may be in rural areas, and their constituents may reflect relatively few differences of interest. Thus, representatives are often bound to parochial interests, and their concern may be rooted in local issues. Those congressmen able to retain office for a long period of time and, hence, able to accrue power in the House, are often those re-elected from "safe" districts, usually in rural areas. The constituencies they serve favor the status quo. Primarily because of this political base, the House, with influential members serving geographically smaller, more rural constituencies, generally adheres to a more conservative stance than does the Senate.

These differences between the two chambers sometimes lead each house to consider the same legislation from alternate points of view. Yet Senate and House are equal partners in lawmaking, for each can veto the acts of the other. The two institutions must perform a common function—that of legislating for the nation.

The process by which a bill is considered is similar in the two chambers at the committee stage. The committee system constitutes the most important phase in the evolution of a bill into law and is, therefore, of major consequence to the legislative process. Our discussion will highlight the activities and functions of the specific committees in both Houses.

# The committee system

"The committees," writes Donald Matthews, "are highly autonomous organizations; the spirit of reciprocity suggests that it is best to allow other committees to go their own way if one's own committees are to enjoy a similar freedom. Thus a Senator's committee work is of paramount importance to him. It is here that he makes his reputation with his colleagues and leaves his mark on the legislation."[3] Although Matthews is referring specifically to the Senate, his observation applies equally to the House. Committee assignments can determine congressional careers. A senator from a rural state may seek membership on the Agriculture Committee in order to have a hand in legislation beneficial to his constituents. If the citizens of his state see he is effective in furthering their interests he is likely to be re-elected and have the opportunity to remain on that committee, thus building up his seniority, so that he may wield more power within the legislature.

Although a congressman will try to serve on a committee whose area of specialization relates to his constituency, he will also vie for an appointment on one of the powerful committees that deals with broad legislation, related to national and international policies (for example, the Senate Foreign Relations Committee). Appointments to these prestigious committees are controlled in part by the most senior members in Congress.

[3] Donald Matthews, *U.S. Senators and Their World* (New York: Random House, Inc., 1960), p. 146.

The appointment of the powerful committee chairmen is based solely on seniority. Under this system, the chairmanship automatically goes to the majority party member who has served longest on the committee. "Seniority looms large as a factor in congressional behavior, and establishes autonomous centers of power that can be powerful determinants of the fate of policies and of subordinate congressional careers."[4]

The seniority system has come under increasing criticism, particularly from the younger members of Congress, whose political leverage is limited by its operation. Critics contend that the system, by holding seniority as the prime criterion, fails to distinguish between highly capable and less capable members. Moreover, as a consequence of this process of selection, the majority of committee chairmen, say critics, are not truly representative of Congress as a whole: they tend to over-represent "safe" districts, and under-represent liberal, urban districts in which there are hard fought elections.

[4] Stephen K. Bailey, *The New Congress* (New York: St. Martin's Press, Inc., 1966), p. 59.

"He considers just getting to and from Congress a productive day."

Editorial cartoon by John Fischetti. © 1970 Chicago *Daily News*. Reprinted by permission.

When the Democrats have the majority in Congress, the chairmanships tend to go to the South. When the Republicans control the legislature, the chairmen are generally from the Midwest. In both cases, the beneficiaries of the seniority system are usually from rural areas. A member of Congress once described the committees as "bastions of conservatism, obstructive units subject to control by special interests, and dictatorships ruled by misfits."[5]

[5] Quoted in Bailey, *New Congress*, p. 57.

Defenders of the seniority system argue that it provides a nonpolitical and stable method for the transferring of positions of leadership. They maintain that alternative methods such as reward by merit and achievement, would lead to constant argument, counter productive bargaining, acquiescing, and jealous vying for positions within Congress, and thereby obstruct the legislative process. As one House Democrat wrote, "It is not that Congress loves seniority more but alternatives less."[6] Proponents of the system contend that by emphasizing experience, the seniority rule generally places in positions of power those who, through experience, have become experts in a particular area and in the process by which committees work.

[6] Clapp, *The Congressman*, p. 257.

The seniority system, however, is not all-encompassing. For example, the proliferation of subcommittees provides an opportunity for junior members of Congress to rise to positions of authority.

Membership on the ranking committees is coveted; once a congressman is assigned a seat on a powerful committee he rarely forsakes it. In each chamber, there are specific prestigious committees that exercise the most extensive authority over major legislation and policies. These committees will be discussed in the following section.

# Major Senate committees

In the Senate the major committees have sweeping legislative authority. The Appropriations Committee, chaired by Allen J. Ellender (D. Louisiana), wields great power, for it considers government expenditures for all programs and administrative operations. The Foreign Relations Committee, chaired by J. William Fulbright (D. Arkansas), is a key force in influencing foreign policy. To the committee is referred legislation dealing with protection of American citizens abroad, interventions and declarations of war, diplomatic service, American business interests abroad, the American National Red Cross, the United Nations, and international monetary organizations and foreign loans.

The constitutional basis of the Senate's foreign affairs power is its right to give its advice and consent to treaties. The Senate's advice and consent on a treaty, however, can be contingent on the opinion of the Foreign Relations Committee. For this reason, Presidents have found it wise to consult with key committee members during the actual negotiation process in order to eventually obtain Senate consent, and the Secretary of State and other executive officials concerned with foreign policy normally treat members of the committee with particular respect. In 1967, for example, the Senate was virtually uninformed about American arms sales to the Middle East. Because they had been shut out from this important program, they abolished Pentagon loan programs and put restrictions on arms sales.[7]

[7] "Nixon Doctrine May Boost U.S. Arms Sales Abroad," in *National Diplomacy 1965–1970* (Washington, D.C.: Congressional Quarterly, Inc., 1970), p. 29.

The *Senate Finance Committee*, under Russell Long (D. Louisiana), reviews proposals for revenue, taxes, deposit of public monies, customs, transportation of dutiable items, reciprocal trade agreements, tariff quotas, social security, veterans pensions, life insurance, and compensation. Its power is illustrated by its handling of President Nixon's welfare reform bill, which he sent to Congress in 1969. The Finance Committee blocked action on this welfare reform bill, the Family Assistance Plan, by not reporting it to the floor.

## Major committees in the House of Representatives

In the House, the three major committees are the House Rules Committee headed by William Colmer (D. Mississippi), the Ways and Means Committee chaired by Wilbur Mills (D. Arkansas), and the Appropriations Committee chaired by George H. Mahon (D. Texas).

The *House Rules Committee* is one of the most powerful committees in Congress because it designates the order in which legislation will be considered by the House as a whole. (Note that it has no control over money bills.) Through special orders, or rules, the committee determines when a bill will be debated on the House floor.

> *Resolved*, that upon the adoption of this resolution it shall be in order to move that the House resolve itself into the Committee of the Whole House on the State of the Union for the Consideration of the bill (H.R. _____ ), entitled etc. After general debate, which shall be confined to the bill and continue not to exceed _____ hours, to be equally divided and controlled by the chairman and the ranking minority member of the Committee on _____, the bill shall be read for amendment under the five minute rule. At the conclusion of the consideration of the bill for amendment, the Committee shall raise and report the bill to the House with such amendments as may have been adopted and the previous question shall be considered as ordered on the bill and amendments thereto to final passage without intervening motion except one motion to recommit with or without final instructions.[8]

8 Froman, *The Congressional Process*, p. 67.

By not granting a rule, the committee can prevent floor action on legislation. The Rules Committee has been described as

> a separate force in the House. Arrogating to itself without challenge the right not only to schedule floor debates and amendments for pending bills, but to amend bills in committee, to block them entirely, and even to report out legislation *de novo*, the Rules Committee became a House within a House.[9]

9 Bailey, *The New Congress*, p. 47.

The power of the committee has evolved over time. It was House Speaker Thomas Reed (R. Maine) who in 1889 saw the opportunities of turning the then obscure Rules Committee into a powerful instrument of leadership. Because at that time the Speaker was also chairman of the Rules Committee, Reed was able to alter the rules to broaden the committee's responsibilities.

He did this by initiating the *special rule*, a rule issued by the committee stating the conditions for floor debate—which include time limits on debate, and may include restrictions on the number and kind of revisions to be made on a particular bill. The rule could be adopted by majority committee vote; since the Speaker automatically controlled the majority, he could ensure action or avoid consideration on most legislative proposals.

In 1910, however, the arbitrary exercise of power by House Speaker Joseph Cannon so outraged his colleagues in the House that they changed the rules of the House to prevent the Speaker from chairing the Rules Committee, thus diminishing his authority.

At the same time, the discharge rule was adopted to curb Rules Committee power. A *discharge petition* can be used to force the Rules Committee to report a legislative proposal. The process involves circulating a petition among House members. The majority, 218, must sign in order for the committee to report the bill to the floor. However, this number has seldom been obtained because congressmen generally regard committee decision as final. There is an unstated premise that the power of the Rules Committee is not to be flouted. Challenging the committee's power might incur blocking future legislative deliberations.

From 1937 to 1961, a conservative coalition of four Republicans and twenty-five Southern Democrats blocked liberal legislation and defied the will of the House Democratic majority. President Kennedy, with the support of Speaker Sam Rayburn, pushed through a bill that changed the membership of the Rules Committee from twelve to fifteen. The newly created seats were assigned to liberal congressmen, and the committee came to better reflect majority will in the House.

In defense of the Rules Committee it must be said that it is most often an effective institution for controlling the order of legislative business in the House. It contributes to the efficiency of its procedures. In 1824, for example, the House spent almost ten weeks debating and voting on that year's tariff bill. In 1894, seventy years later, the time allowed for debating a similar tariff bill had been cut to three weeks. In 1962, the House again adopted a tariff bill this time allowing only two days for floor debate and voting. In processing the 1962 bill, the House made full use of the Rules Committee's power to limit debate and even to forbid almost all amendments. Without the special rules proposed by the Rules Committee, and adopted by the House, debate on controversial bills could run on indefinitely. In so doing, the committee performs a valuable function in the lawmaking process.

The *House Ways and Means Committee* is a major force in formulating and enacting tax programs and policies. To the committee are referred all revenue and tax measures; for example, bills providing for the addition and later elimination of the 10 percent tax surcharge. The committee also wields considerable power within the internal political structure of the House. Since 1910, the Democrats on the committee have nominated members of their party to the standing committees. Also, Ways and Means is one of the few committees of the House whose chairman can report a bill to the floor without going through the Rules Committee.

The *House Appropriations Committee* is particularly powerful because all appropriation bills originate in the House. Operating through a system of highly specialized subcommittees, the committee recommends specific monetary allocations for particular programs, agencies, bureaus, and government operations. In so doing, it has the power to determine the fate of countless programs and operations provided for in the national budget. The Appropriations Committee decides on money for programs (for example, the amount of money for a welfare program); its jurisdiction is distinct from the Ways and Means Committee, which reviews all bills to obtain money by levying taxes.

# Floor procedures

After a bill passes through the committee stage it enters an intermediary stage before floor debate. Each house employs different procedures in order to bring the bill before the entire chamber.

## The House of Representatives: the order of debate

### Calendar

### Committee of the Whole

In general, when a bill is reported out of committee, it is placed on one of three major calendars: the *Union Calendar* for appropriations, revenue, and tax legislation; the *House Calendar* for public bills not appropriating money or raising revenue; the *Private Calendar* for bills dealing with individual concerns such as immigration rulings, land titles, and the settlement of claims against the government. There are two minor calendars that also serve to order legislation. The *Consent Calendar* lists noncontroversial measures that will entail little or no debate, and the *Discharge Calendar* lists motions to discharge a committee from further consideration of a bill.

Generally, when a bill comes up for floor debate, the House converts itself into the *Committee of the Whole*. In so doing, the House designates itself a committee at work, and is not subject to the cumbersome procedures that control full House debate. In the Committee of the Whole, the time allotted for each speech on the measure is five minutes. Instead of the requirement that 218 members be present, the necessary number is scaled down to 100 Representatives. There are no time-consuming roll call votes. The committee's rejection of a proposed amendment is final; however, any amendment it adopts is subject to consideration by the entire House. When the committee completes its action on the measure, it dissolves itself. The House then reconstitutes itself as a legislative body to consider the committee report. A roll call can be requested by any congressman on any legislative revision accepted in the Committee of the Whole. In this way, the House as a body can nullify the revisions of the House as a committee. In practice, however, the House approves the decisions of the Committee of the Whole.

"Congressional calendar"

A 1949 copyright cartoon by Herblock.

## The Senate: the norms of deliberation

The Senate prides itself on its statesmanship and elegant, civilized ways. In this so-called upper house of Congress, one does not find the same extensive procedural rules that characterize the House of Representatives.

The Senate operates more through the informal rules derived from its own set of norms, traditions, and manners. These manners have been termed "folkways" by Donald Matthews; they form a system of behavior that guides the business of the chamber.

In many ways the informal rules or folkways of the Senate allow it to function efficiently. Through consultations among members and elected Senate leaders, for example, a specific time for voting is agreed upon. In other instances, however, Senate folkways inhibit inventiveness and aggressiveness. Newly elected senators are discouraged from participation in the floor debate if they wish to ultimately wield influence within the chamber, and not arouse the animosity of senior members. They are termed "mavericks" if they violate these informal rules by speaking frequently, and as a consequence their influence in the Senate can be retarded or prevented by the older members.

In scheduling bills, measures released by the committee are placed on the calendar, and are called in the order in which they were released. Any senator can veto the measure, since unanimous consent is required for discussion. The majority leader, negotiating with other key senators, seeks to obtain unified agreement on the order of debate.

**The filibuster**

In the Senate, debate tends to be more active and dramatic. Many a floor speech has been significant in American history. The contests on the floor of the Senate before the Civil War when such men as Daniel Webster, Henry Clay, and John C. Calhoun raised their voices to define the issues of union and slavery are classic examples of eloquent debate. But since the Civil War this tradition and the importance of floor debate has declined.

Once a senator has the floor, he may continue speaking. This custom makes possible the use of the *filibuster*, a tactic to prevent passage of a bill by drawing out proceedings (usually by speaking continuously), and thus curtail voting on the proposal under discussion. Filibusters occasionally require great physical prowess. In 1953, Senator Wayne Morse (D. Oregon) spoke non-stop for twenty-two hours to curtail voting on a measure that would have given the states certain rights to offshore oil. The filibuster, however, is most destructive when it involves a coalition of senators; the possibility of a filibuster by an organized minority may dissuade Senate leadership from bringing the measure to the floor. As long as several senators cooperate, a filibuster can tie up proceedings for days and weeks, and prevent Senate action on any legislation. The filibuster is particularly effective toward the close of a session, when major bills are pending. However, only on the most controversial measures are filibusters threatened or actually attempted.

*The 1960 filibuster was the longest one in the history of Congress.*

In theory, the filibuster can be stopped by invoking *cloture:* a process to end debate. But the procedures for obtaining cloture are so involved that it is not usually a viable means to restrict debate. First, sixteen senators must sign a petition for the cloture motion. Two days after that, it comes before the Senate for a roll-call vote. For the motion to be enacted, two-thirds of the senators must agree. If passed, a senator may speak no longer than one hour. Since 1917, when the cloture rule was instituted, Rule 22 has been successfully invoked only eight times, for example, during debate over the 1964 Civil Rights Act. Senators view cloture as a violation of their right to unlimited debate; this is why a two-thirds vote in the chamber is difficult to obtain.

### The 53 Cloture Votes since Rule 22 was Adopted in 1917

| Issue | Date | Successful |
|---|---|---|
| Versailles Treaty | Nov. 15, 1919 | ✓ |
| Emergency tariff | Feb. 2, 1921 | |
| Tariff bill | July 7, 1922 | |
| World Court | Jan. 25, 1926 | ✓ |
| Migratory birds | June 1, 1926 | |
| Branch banking | Feb. 15, 1927 | ✓ |
| Disabled officers | Feb. 26, 1927 | |
| Colorado river | Feb. 26, 1927 | |
| D.C. buildings | Feb. 28, 1927 | |
| Prohibition bureau | Feb. 28, 1927 | ✓ |
| Banking Act | Jan. 19, 1933 | |
| Antilynching | Jan. 27, 1938 | |
| Antilynching | Feb. 16, 1938 | |
| Antipoll tax | Nov. 23, 1942 | |
| Antipoll tax | May 15, 1944 | |
| Fair Employment Practices Commission | Feb. 9, 1946 | |
| British loan | May 7, 1946 | |
| Labor disputes | May 25, 1946 | |
| Antipoll tax | July 31, 1946 | |
| FEPC | May 19, 1950 | |
| FEPC | July 12, 1950 | |
| Atomic Energy Act | July 26, 1954 | |
| Civil Rights Act | March 10, 1960 | |
| Amend rule 22 | Sept. 19, 1961 | |
| Literacy tests | May 9, 1962 | |
| Literacy tests | May 14, 1962 | |
| Comsat Act | Aug. 14, 1962 | ✓ |
| Amend rule 22 | Feb. 7, 1963 | |
| Civil Rights Act | June 10, 1964 | ✓ |
| Legislative reapportionment | Sept. 10, 1964 | |
| Voting Rights Act | May 25, 1965 | ✓ |

| | |
|---|---|
| Right-to-work repeal | Oct. 11, 1965 |
| Right-to-work repeal | Feb. 8, 1966 |
| Right-to-work repeal | Feb. 10, 1966 |
| Civil Rights Act | Sept. 14, 1966 |
| Civil Rights Act | Sept. 19, 1966 |
| D.C. Home Rule | Oct. 10, 1966 |
| Amend Rule 22 | Jan. 24, 1967 |
| Open Housing | Feb. 20, 1968 |
| Open Housing | Feb. 26, 1968 |
| Open Housing | March 1, 1968 |
| Open Housing | March 4, 1968     √ |
| Fortas Nomination | Oct. 1, 1968 |
| Amend Rule 22 | Jan. 16, 1969 |
| Amend Rule 22 | Jan. 28, 1969 |
| Electoral College | Sept. 17, 1970 |
| Electoral College | Sept. 29, 1970 |
| Supersonic transport | Dec. 19, 1970 |
| Supersonic transport | Dec. 22, 1970 |
| Amend Rule 22 | Feb. 18, 1971 |
| Amend Rule 22 | Feb. 23, 1971· |
| Amend Rule 22 | March 2, 1971 |
| Amend Rule 22 | March 9, 1971 |

Source: *Congressional Quarterly*, March 12, 1971, p. 549.

Under ordinary circumstances, however, debate on a measure in the Senate is closed by the majority leader's request for the chamber's unanimous consent. Since almost everyone has had his say by the time the request is made, most senators will agree to conclude debate.

*Jacob K. Javits "The Public Business Must Go Forward,"* Proposed Amendments to Rule XXII of the Standing Rules of the Senate, *Senate Report No. 1509, 85th Congress 2nd Session, pp. 9–19.*

Senator Jacob Javits was one of several Republican and Democratic senators who in 1959 fought for a change in Senate Rule 22, the infamous filibuster. These reformers sought to limit the use of the filibuster by allowing cloture to be invoked by a simple majority rather than the two-thirds vote now required.

I do not believe that the present rule XXII serves the purpose of deliberation within the Senate or of education of the public generally. No one questions those two objectives. What I do question is a delegation of the power and responsibility of the majority to a determined minority, which has been and can be again and again an arbitrary block to action, contrary to the will of the majority of this body and of the people to whom they are responsible.

Javits charges that Rule 22 is archaic, and contends that a study of the Articles of Confederation and the Constitution reveal that such a powerful tactic would have been opposed by the Founding Fathers.

The premise of rule XXII violates fundamental parliamentary law. It is at odds with early Senate procedures, British Parliamentary practice, and almost without exception, is contrary to all our State legislative rules of procedure.

The senator notes that even the threat of a filibuster may influence the course of legislation, if those involved are capable of carrying it out:

The *ability* to carry on a filibuster can affect the kind of legislation passed by the Senate even though no actual filibuster is undertaken. The incidence of a filibuster or the certain knowledge that a filibuster would be organized has made the majority come to terms before. The mere threat that a filibuster of great length would be undertaken against some proposal or unless amendment to a bill was accepted has in effect resulted in the majority of the Senate acquiescing in changes in legislation which otherwise they would probably not have considered wise or desirable.

The "persuasive" and "subtle" effect of Rule 22 is illustrated in the passage of the Civil Rights Act of 1957. Part III of the bill provided for the Attorney General to enforce the Fourteenth Amendment through civil action. One group of senators was anxious to retain this provision; however, aware that their insistence would lead to a filibuster that could kill the bill, and would at any rate stop all Senate business for an interminable length of time, they agreed to delete Part III from the bill.

Javits draws his argument from the Constitution itself, noting that that document calls for a majority vote of both houses to pass a bill. Clearly a filibuster represents a minority imposing its view on the majority, and a simple majority vote cannot prevent it.

Legislation of the most profound national effect requires the assent of fewer than half of those required to bring a filibuster to a reasonable close so that that very legislation may be acted upon. I fail to see what balance is maintained by continuance of the present rule.

Most supporters of the filibuster believe that it adds to the deliberative character of the chamber and to the protection of minority rights. On the contrary, Javits asserts that the Senate has maintained its status as a great forum in spite of the filibuster. To indulge in sheer rhetoric, to read recipes, Aesop's Fables, and sections of Victor Hugo from the Senate podium (as some Senators have done)—and for as long as seventeen hours, to a total of seventy-five days—damages the character and delays the business of the Senate, and belies the true spirit of the Constitution.

## Voting: methods and patterns

Both the House and the Senate generally employ a *voice vote* in which each member calls out his "yea" or "nay" when he is called upon to vote on a measure. Because these votes are not recorded separately, this gives more leverage to members subject to conflicting interests. Any member doubting the count may request a *standing vote* in which the proponents and opponents of the measure stand and are counted in place. In the House the standing vote totals are announced; in the Senate they are not. In the House a request by one-fifth of the members can produce a *teller vote*. In this instance, individual votes are checked off by tellers as each member files past the Speaker's desk. The teller vote is not used in the Senate.

The two chambers, upon demand by one-fifth of the members present, may require a *record vote*, whereby each vote is recorded next to the congressman's name. The final vote is then a matter of public record that can be examined by voters and political supporters. This fact may influence a senator's final position on the measure. Occasionally, conflicting interests may lead to absence during a record vote, so that a member can avoid taking a stand on a particular bill.

### Party Unity Scoreboard

|  | Total Roll Calls | Party Unity Roll Calls | Percentage of Total |
|---|---|---|---|
| **1970** |  |  |  |
| Both Chambers | 684 | 219 | 32 |
| Senate | 418 | 147 | 35 |
| House of Representatives | 266 | 72 | 27 |
| **1969** |  |  |  |
| Both Chambers | 422 | 144 | 34 |
| Senate | 245 | 89 | 36 |
| House of Representatives | 177 | 55 | 31 |
| **1968** |  |  |  |
| Both Chambers | 514 | 172 | 33 |
| Senate | 281 | 90 | 32 |
| House of Representatives | 233 | 82 | 35 |
| **1967** |  |  |  |
| Both Chambers | 560 | 198 | 35 |
| Senate | 315 | 109 | 35 |
| House of Representatives | 245 | 89 | 36 |

Source: *Congressional Quarterly Almanac* (Washington, D.C.: Congressional Quarterly, Inc., 1971), p. 1140.

Although individual congressmen are not bound strictly to the party leadership, they rarely vote against a measure supported by the majority of their party members. According to the roll call votes in the 1970 session of

[10] *Congressional Quarterly Almanac* (Washington, D.C.: Congressional Quarterly, Inc., 1971), p. 1140.

the 91st Congress, for example, the average Democrat voted with the majority of his party 59 percent of the time, and the average Republican voted with his party 60 percent of the time.[10] This may be due to ideological similarities among party members and the fact that the favors bestowed by party leaders may be withheld from a member who dissents from the leadership's position too often, and every congressman realizes that he can benefit from the support of his party's leaders, for with their help he can be more effective in the legislature.

*Gerald M. Pomper,* Elections in America (*New York: Dodd, Mead and Co., 1970*), *pp. 195–200.*

Gerald Pomper, in a study of party unity in Congress, evaluated seventy roll call votes that were related to "issues presented by platform conflicts."

If the platforms have any significance in Congress, we would expect the parties to differ on these "conflict roll calls." They would then constitute party-unity votes, in which a majority of Democrats take a position in opposition to a majority of Republicans.

Of the votes he reviewed during the Truman, Eisenhower, and Kennedy-Johnson administrations, Pomper found that approximately 88 percent of the "platform conflict" votes taken during those periods displayed party unity. In contrast, unity was less evident on roll call votes that did not involve platform issues: the parties split on half the votes. Thus, the party platform is not only a significant aspect of congressional party voting, "but the most obvious and dramatic instances of larger differences between parties."

After determining that party unity does exist in Congress, Pomper further notes the degree of unity within each party on platform pledges.

The degree of cohesion on the controversial platform pledges is similar to that which exists in Congress generally. The most relevant comparison is that between "conflict roll calls" and all party-unity votes. Both are cases of partisan conflict, and the degree of party cohesion is similar. Unity of the parties does tend to be somewhat higher on the platform votes, and this finding is significant. Given the visibility, pressures, and importance which attach to these votes, relatively high party solidarity indicates that a large proportion of the party does stand behind its pledges. Party unity does not melt in the heat of controversy. It is maintained, and even some increased fusion of the party can be observed. . . .

The typical platform vote would find the two parties opposed, with somewhat less than a fifth of each faction joining the opposition. In all congressional votes, however, the parties would be relatively similar to one another, and actually in agreement on half or more of the roll calls.

# The functions of Congress

In addition to legislating for the nation, Congress has additional constitutional and political functions.

**Appointments**

Under Article II, Section 2, of the Constitution, the Senate must give its advice and consent to treaties and presidential appointments, thereby providing a check on the power of the Chief Executive.

The President nominates, with the advice and consent of the Senate, candidates as "ambassadors, other public ministers and consuls, judges of the Supreme Court, and all other officers of the United States, whose appointments are not herein otherwise provided for, and which shall be established by law." This includes Cabinet members and ranking officers of the army and navy. Although the Senate can reject an appointment, it rarely does so. Presidents tend to take into account Senate reaction to nominations.

There are occasions, however, when the Senate does reject a presidential appointee. In 1958, President Eisenhower nominated Admiral Lewis Strauss to be his Secretary of Commerce. Senate Democrats had been antagonized by the Admiral's policies as the chairman of the Atomic Energy Commission (1953–1958) and the upper chamber rejected the nomination.

**Treaties**

All treaties negotiated by the President must receive the Senate's advice and consent, accomplished by a two-thirds vote of its members. For example, Senate consent was needed for the Nuclear Nonproliferation Treaty to become official in 1969. Senate advice and consent to treaties is one aspect of the constitutional checks and balances system, in which each branch of government oversees the other; just as the President can use his veto power to prevent the passage of a legislative measure, so the Senate can use its power of "advice and consent" to control treaty commitments (for example, the Treaty of Versailles in 1919 was rejected by the Senate).

The Constitution has also delegated the Congress electoral and judicial functions.

**Presidential elections**

Article II specifies that in the event that no presidential candidate receives a majority of the electoral votes, the House of Representatives shall choose the President. The House votes as a gathering of 50 delegations from the various states, rather than as a group of 435 members. Each state has one vote; the candidate who receives the majority of votes from the representatives of a state becomes that state's choice. Only once in the nation's history (1824) did the House select the President when none of the three candidates —John Quincy Adams, Andrew Jackson, and William Crawford—received a majority of the electoral vote. Voting by states, the House of Representatives selected Adams as President. But this has been the only occasion where the choice of the President has been left to the House.

The Senate, in the event of such electoral circumstances, is charged with the responsibility of choosing the Vice-President. Finally, the President of the Senate (who is also the Vice-President of the United States) has the ceremonial function of counting the total of electoral votes received by the presidential candidates. In 1960, Richard Nixon, as President of the Senate and the Republican candidate for President of the United States, had the duty of announcing the election returns in which his Democratic opponent, John F. Kennedy, was victorious.

## Vice-presidential nomination and presidential disability

The Twenty-fifth Amendment (ratified in 1967) gives Congress a role in selecting a Vice-President when the Vice-President has become President because of presidential death, removal, or resignation. "Whenever there is a vacancy in the office of the Vice-President, the President shall nominate a Vice-President who shall take office upon confirmation by a majority vote of both Houses of Congress."

The amendment, as discussed in detail in Chapter 12, also invests Congress with the responsibility to act when a President is disabled. Congress can designate, by a two-thirds vote in both chambers, that the "President is unable to discharge the powers and duties of his office." The vote is initiated by a written declaration by "the Vice-President and a majority of either the principal officers of the executive departments or of such other body as Congress may by law provide" that the President is unable to carry out the duties of office.

## Impeachment

The Constitution gives Congress the power to remove from office "the President, Vice-President and all Civil Officers of the United States" (which includes judges as well as executive officials) for "Treason, Bribery, or other high Crimes and Misdemeanors." The constitutional process for removing officials (*impeachment*) involves several steps. The House of Representatives hears evidence and, if its members determine that there is sufficient evidence to warrant a trial, it can vote to impeach the official. If a motion to impeach is adopted by the majority of the House, the Senate sits as a court and tries the case. Conviction requires a two-thirds vote of the Senate. Thus, the House has the power to bring impeachment charges, and the Senate the authority to make the final ruling. Only one President, Andrew Johnson in 1867, has ever been impeached by the House, and he escaped conviction by a single vote. Since 1789, only eleven other impeachment cases have come before Congress; nine involved judges (only four of whom were convicted).

> *Henry J. Abraham,* The Judicial Process *(New York: Oxford University Press, Inc., 1968), pp. 43–44.*
>
> Henry Abraham describes the Senate's action in acquitting Supreme Court Justice Samuel Chase after the House impeached him in 1804 as "not only a single victory for the narrow interpretation of the impeachment process but also for an independent judiciary." The case stands

today as a most important impeachment precedent and the only one involving a Supreme Court Justice.

Samuel Chase was appointed to the high court by President Washington. A convert to the Federalist cause, he became one of its ardent supporters. While he did not commit the crimes that the constitution stipulates as grounds for impeachment—that is, treason, bribery or other high crimes, and misdemeanors—Abraham acknowledges that:

He had made himself obnoxious to the Jeffersonians and others by a long series of injudicious and partisan attacks against them, both on and off the bench; by his "tyrannical trials (of opponents) under the Alien and Sedition Law (of 1798)," and by his obvious general favoritism toward Federalists.

In November, 1804, he was impeached by the House. In the Senate, however, with Vice-President Aaron Burr presiding and Chief Justice Marshall serving as the distinguished defender, he was narrowly acquitted in March, 1805, by a four-vote margin. Because of Chase's acquittal, judges no longer fear impeachment as a punishment for decisions offensive to Congress or the President.

## Constitutional amendments

Congress has remained the chief institution for proposing amendments to the Constitution. Although that document prescribed two procedures for this purpose, to date, only one has been used. (A national convention agreed upon by two-thirds of the states has never been held). The procedure employed calls for a two-thirds vote in each chamber of Congress on the proposed amendment. Congress also designates whether the proposed amendment will go before state legislatures or state conventions for ratification, and has usually assigned the role to the state legislatures. (Amendments are ratified when they are approved in 75 percent of the state legislatures or conventions.)

## Watchdog function

The National Aeronautics and Space Administration (NASA), an executive agency that administers the nation's space exploration program, was created by an act of Congress. By holding hearings on the new appropriations and the progress and priorities of space programs, Congress oversees the functioning of the new department. Steven K. Bailey has referred to this as the surveillance or watchdog function of Congress. The power of appropriating funds allows Congress a degree of control over the direction and implementation of agency programs and policies. To find out whether the agencies are performing their delegated functions, and whether the funds allocated are properly spent, congressional investigations are conducted by the committees concerned. Some public hearings—for instance, when a cabinet member, such as the Secretary of Defense, is asked to appear before a committee in order to justify an administrative action or policy—are aimed at probing administration policies. A current example of this function is the Senate Foreign Relations Committee's hearings on the war in Vietnam. Executive officers, such as Secretary of Defense Melvin Laird, were called before the committee to explain their expenses and activities.

*Neil MacNeil,* Forge of Democracy: The House of Representatives *(New York: David McKay Co., Inc., 1963), pp. 179–180, 204.*

In 1791, Justice Wilson predicted that the House would be the branch of government to "inquire into grievances arising both from men and things." But this prerogative, not specified in the Constitution, was to be established by precedent.

On March 27, 1792, the House of Representatives opened discussion of a resolution proposing that President Washington investigate General St. Clair's embarrassing defeat by the Delaware, Shawnee, and Miami Indians in the Northwest Territory. Many House members protested, however, that such an investigation came properly under their jurisdiction. As a result, the resolution permitting executive investigation was defeated 35 to 21 and, in its place, the House passed 44 to 10 a resolution to "create a select committee" to investigate General St. Clair's defeat. The committee was authorized by the House itself and given the right to subpoena necessary records and witnesses.

Seriously concerned about establishing the proper precedent, Washington conferred with his Cabinet, which, after lengthy deliberation, agreed that Congress had the investigative right. Thus the President sent the needed documents to the House and the precedent for the congressional investigation, so widely practiced today, came to be.

These extra-legislative functions of Congress may result in friction between it and other branches of government. This is particularly apparent in relations between Congress and the chief executive, and sometimes between Congress and the Supreme Court.

Friction between the two chambers of Congress is also built into our constitutional system. In addition to differences in constituencies and collective political bias, there is the sentiment of pride in prerogatives. The House is particularly sensitive to references to the Senate as "the upper body." Members of the House designate it "the other body." In 1962, this sentiment resulted in a legislative impasse. The meeting place of the Conference Committe for an appropriations bill was the issue. House members chosen to serve on the committee disputed the custom of holding the committee's meetings in the Senate building. They also protested the practice of appointing a senator, rather than a congressman, as chairman of the committee. They maintained that both the meeting place and the chairmanship must be open to both institutions. The Senate viewing these demands as an usurpation of rights would not comply. After fifteen weeks, a compromise was reached. Committee members would elect the chairman, and they would confer in a chamber located mid-way between the two Houses of Congress.

### Disagreement between the President and Congress

| Year | Presidential Proposals Submitted | Approved by Congress | Approval Score |
|------|------|------|------|
| 1954 | 232 | 150 | 64.7% |
| 1955 | 207 | 96 | 46.3 |
| 1956 | 225 | 103 | 45.7 |
| 1957 | 206 | 76 | 36.9 |
| 1958 | 234 | 110 | 47.0 |
| 1959 | 228 | 93 | 40.8 |
| 1960 | 183 | 56 | 30.6 |
| 1961 | 355 | 172 | 48.4 |
| 1962 | 298 | 132 | 44.3 |
| 1963 | 401 | 109 | 27.2 |

Source: Nelson W. Polsby, *Congress and the Presidency* (Englewood Cliffs, N.J.: Prentice-Hall, Inc., 1965), p. 101.

Source: *Congressional Quarterly Weekly Report*, January 24, 1964, p. 181.

Regarding the Senate as the recipient of an unjustified volume of publicity, many congressmen maintain that individual members of the House may exercise as much or more power as any senator. As one congressman remarked, "There are a great many people in the House who have substantially more real power than a great many senators . . . in terms of the legislative process, and in terms of the power of getting something done."[11] Senators, on the other hand, may view the House as more bound to particular interests, and hence less inclined toward broad and innovative action.

Although there are differences in tone and style, the two Houses of Congress strive to perform a common task. And despite institutional conflicts and complex demands, they fulfill their constitutional assignment of legislating for the nation.

[11] Clapp, *The Congressman*, p. 41.

# Glossary

**cloture**  Senate process by which the signatures of one-sixth of the Senate members and then a two-thirds vote of the senators can limit debate to one hour per senator.

**Committee of the Whole**  Committee comprised of 100 or more House members to debate and amend legislation after which the committee dissolves, and the entire House acts upon its recommendations.

**consent calendar**  Legislative agenda of the House listing noncontroversial measures that will entail little or no debate.

**discharge calendar**  Legislative agenda of the House listing motions to discharge a committee from further consideration of a bill.

**discharge petition**  Petition that must be signed by 218 House members in order to force a House committee to report a bill to the floor.

**filibuster**  Time-delaying tactic of unlimited speech making used by a minority to prevent a vote on a bill they do not favor.

**House Appropriations Committee**  Powerful House committee dealing with legislation funding government programs and operations.

**house calendar**  Legislative agenda of the House listing noncontroversial measures that will entail little or no debate.

**House Rules Committee**  Powerful House committee controlling the order in which legislation will come before the House for consideration.

**House Ways and Means Committee**  Powerful House committee dealing with revenue and tax proposals.

**impeachment**  The indictment of a President, Vice-President, federal judge, or Cabinet member by the House of Representatives on charges of grave misconduct in office.

**private calendar**  Legislative agenda for the House listing bills relating to the interests of individual citizens, such as land titles.

**record vote**  Type of vote, initiated in both Houses of Congress upon demand by one-fifth of the members present, in which the vote of a member on a bill is recorded next to his name, and becomes part of his public record.

**Senate Appropriations Committee**  Powerful Senate committee dealing with legislation providing funds for government programs and operations.

**Senate Finance Committee**  Powerful Senate committee dealing with proposals for revenue, taxes, tariff quotas, and other areas of finance.

**Senate Foreign Relations Committee**  Powerful Senate committee reviewing proposals for foreign aid, and other areas of international endeavor.

**special rule**  Concept that the House Rules Committee may at any time initiate a special rule regarding floor debate, which can be adopted by a majority vote of the House.

**standing vote**  Type of vote, initiated in both Houses of Congress upon demand by one of the members, in which those for and against a bill stand and are counted in place.

**union calendar** Major legislative agenda for the House, listing bills dealing with appropriations, revenue, and tax proposals.

**voice vote** Vote in which each congressman calls out his "aye" or "nay" to decide on a measure in which the votes are recorded as a total, rather than individually.

# Suggested readings

Anderson, Dennis, "The Effect of Senate Foreign Relations Committee Membership in Terms of Support of Foreign Policy, 1964–65 (Unpublished Ph.D. dissertation, University of Connecticut, 1968).

Bolling, Richard, *House Out of Order* (New York: E. P. Dutton and Co., Inc., 1966). Critical account of the legislative process in the House of Representatives by a liberal congressional reformer.

Carroll, Holbert N., *The House of Representatives and Foreign Affairs*, rev. ed. (Boston: Little, Brown and Co., 1965). Study of the role of the House of Representatives in making United States foreign policy.

Fenno, Richard F., Jr., *The Power of the Purse: Appropriations Politics in Congress* (Boston: Little, Brown and Co., 1966). Detailed analysis of the House Appropriations Committee by an eminent social scientist.

Galloway, George B., *History of the House of Representatives* (New York: Thomas Y. Crowell Co., 1962). History of the House of Representatives by a noted congressional scholar.

Leavel, Willard Hayden, "Congressional Variables and Presidential Leadership" (Unpublished Ph.D. dissertation, University of Washington, 1963).

MacNeil, Neil, *Forge of Democracy: The House of Representatives* (New York: David McKay Co., Inc., 1963). Descriptive portrait of the House of Representatives based on daily observations by a leading journalist.

Manley, John F., *The House Committee on Ways and Means* (Boston: Little, Brown and Co., 1970). Detailed account of the House Ways and Means Committee from the New Deal to the present, including its relationship with the President, Congress, and pressure groups.

Mathews, Donald R., *U.S. Senators and Their World* (Chapel Hill, N.C.: University of North Carolina Press, 1960). Detailed and influential analysis of the behavior of senators who served between 1947 and 1957.

Miller, Clem, *Member of the House: Letters of a Congressman*, ed. by John W. Baker (New York: Charles Scribner's Sons, 1962). Personal account of life in the House of Representatives by a then newly elected congressman.

Moreland, Lois B., "Notes on History of the House of Representatives, Galloway, George B.," *American Political Science Review*, LVI (1962):720.

Norton, Bruce Dwight Francis, "The Committee on Banking and Currency as a Legislative Subsystem of the House of Representatives" (Unpublished Ph.D. dissertation, Syracuse University, 1970).

Peabody, Robert L., and Nelson W. Polsby, eds., *New Perspectives on the House of Representatives* (Chicago: Rand McNally and Co., 1963). Selected essays on the functions of the House of Representatives.

Polsby, Nelson W., *Congress and the Presidency* (Englewood Cliffs, N.J.: Prentice-Hall, Inc., 1965). Examination of Congress and the President within the separation of powers system.

Ripley, Randall B., *Power in the Senate* (New York: St. Martin's Press, Inc., 1969). Study of political power in the United States Senate.

Robinson, George L., "The Development of the Senate Committee System, 1789–1950" (Unpublished Ph.D. dissertation, New York University, 1955).

Robinson, James A., *Congress and Foreign Policy Making: A Study in Legislative Influence and Initiative*, rev. ed. (Homewood, Ill.: Dorsey Press, Inc., 1967). Critical examination of Congress's influence on United States foreign policy, particularly in relation to executive power in this area.

Smeltzer, David Amos, "The Problem of Alternatives in Congressional Decision-Making: The Role of Committee Hearings" (Unpublished Ph.D. dissertation, University of Michigan, 1964).

# Topics of further study

Henderson, Thomas A., *Congressional Oversight of Executive Agencies* (Gainesville, Fla.: University of Florida Press).

Ripley, R. B., and C. O. Jones, *The Role of Political Parties in Congress* (Tucson, Ariz.: University of Arizona Press, 1966).

Schneier, Edward V., "The Politics of Anti-Communism: A Study of the House Committee on Un-American Activities and its Role in the Political Process" (Ph.D. dissertation, Claremont Graduate School, 1964).

Smeltzer, David A., "The Problem of Alternatives in Congressional Decision-Making: The Role of Committee Hearings" (Ph.D. dissertation, University of Michigan, 1964).

# 16 the bureaucrats

## the machinery of government

THE TERM "bureaucracy" often has a negative connotation, evoking feelings of resignation, helplessness, or outrage. An individual may feel utterly powerless to combat rules and regulations imposed by "big government"; an educator may resent being told how to run his school system by "those bureaucrats in the state capital"; and a sculptor, interlocking ribbons of steel, may remind himself, despairingly, to check the status of an application for a government grant that he submitted two years ago. In each case, bureaucracy is perceived as a vast, impersonal organization, manned by isolated officials, and strangled into inefficiency on reels of red tape and paper.

But the characteristics often attributed to "bureaucracy" do not reflect the word's true meaning. More accurately defined, a *bureaucracy* is a system of organizing activities characterized by specialization of roles on the part of its participants, by fixed rules, and by a hierarchy of authority. A bureaucratic system of organization is just one among many methods of doing things and, like all systems, has its own built-in advantages and disadvantages.

Most big companies, as well as some small ones, are bureaucracies. This is so because certain features of the bureaucratic system are generally thought to promote the most efficient management of public and private big business. For example, the specificity of tasks encountered in a bureaucracy is important to the smooth functioning of larger organizations. In a small office, the question of who is responsible for interviewing new employees is rarely an issue; the person who will supervise the newcomer will probably recruit and interview candidates. In the executive branch of the national government, with its work force of nearly 3 million civilian employees, this important function cannot be left to individual supervisors in diverse positions; specialists will recruit, test, and interview large numbers of prospective employees.

Despite some of the apparent strong points of bureaucratic systems, negative views of governmental bureaucracies are to some extent understandable. One complaint is that the bureaucracies have become so big, and wield so much power that the individual is left with little real control over his own existence. For example, whether or not one's favorite prized rose garden is rescued from the on-rushing path of a new interstate highway depends on surveys made by the state highway commission in cooperation with the Federal Bureau of Public Roads.

*John Kenneth Galbraith, "Who Needs the Democrats," Harper's Magazine, 241, no. 1442 (July 1970): 43–62.*

John Kenneth Galbraith traces the roots of America's present difficulties beyond narrow partisan accusations, and fixes upon the sprawling, powerful bureaucracy, which cannot be dismissed by any election.

According to Galbraith, a colossal bureaucracy becomes isolated and insulated:

[it] will develop a life and purpose and policy of its own. . . . A bureaucracy is governed not by the truth but by its own truth. It defends its truth against the reality. Those who question its truth are discounted for eccentricity. . . . A bureaucracy is a continuing congregation of people who must act more or less as one. Its major test of truth is forthright: it is that on which those of influence can agree. And whatever it agrees on, the public is expected to accept and believe. This expectation is evidently optimistic, but it is another mark of a too-extended association with the bureaucracy when this is not recognized.

Galbraith fears that exposure to bureaucratic truth is detrimental to policy-makers. "In foreign policy, exposure to bureaucratic truth makes a man dangerous. In domestic policy, it makes him obsolete, useless, and something of a bore."

The domestic civilian bureaucrats are most in touch with "the corrective influence of public opinion." Yet, Galbraith notes that they succumb to such bureaucratic truths as the belief that environmental problems are "cosmetic" and not related to our system of government; and the dogma that a severe monetary policy, although it may be "unpleasant" for the prospective home-owner and small businessman who must borrow money, "should be tolerated for the common good."

Those bureaucrats, however, who run the huge military-economic machine of foreign policy are the chief offenders in our system. Many of these men exemplify "the ghastly effect of long-continued association with bureaucratic truth." For example, in 1960, foreign policy formulation was ruled by the specter of the "all-pervading Communist conspiracy" based in Moscow and dedicated to expansion. Galbraith analyzes the effects of bureaucratic acceptance of cold war ideology:

It required reaction to seeming Communist aggression; it would not allow for the possibility that a Communist insurrection might arise from civil, not international causes; that there might be insurrection and revolt without Communists; and that the revolt might be beyond the civil and military power of the United States to suppress. Most of all, it could not admit this last —that a super-power might not, after all, have the power. Of course, it could not hold that the Communists were themselves plural and divisive and that with some of them we needed, at a minimum, to be friends.

The failure of American foreign policy in Cuba, the Dominican Republic, and Vietnam, illustrates the dangers of the bureaucracy's adhering to its own truth and acting in opposition to the public interest, according to Galbraith.

This example illustrates legitimate claims of excessive bureaucratic power over an individual's right of choice. However, the average citizen often fails to consider that a changed and changing American society has made large governmental bureaucracies necessary, and that the bureaucracies themselves are the result of the public's demand for different and better service. Bigger and more powerful automobiles, for example, have led to demands for improved and increasingly complex highway systems. The increase in the number of people traveling by air has led to more closely supervised air-traffic controls by the Federal Aviation Agency. The concern of ecologists and conservationists with the conditions of environment has given rise to the establishment of more governmental regulating agencies to control pollution. Competition among broadcasting companies for limited air space has necessitated the creation of the Federal Communications Commission to regulate the industry. The migration to the suburbs and population shifts in general have created "depressed areas" that the national government has endeavored to rescue by making funds available for the establishment of local small businesses. The civil rights movement has resulted in the establishment of desegregation guidelines to be followed by the states and enforced by the national government.

Because of these changes in our society, and the public's demand that the specific problems arising from them be dealt with effectively by a concerned and responsible government, a bureaucratic form of administration has developed.

# Characteristics of a bureaucracy

[1] The foregoing discussion is based on the description by Peter M. Blau, *Bureaucracy in Modern Society* (New York: Random House, Inc., 1956), pp. 28–32.

The "ideal-type" bureaucracy was defined by Max Weber, a German sociologist, as displaying six distinguishing features.[1] First, there is a high degree of specialization required to perform the duties of office. Second, positions are organized in a hierarchy in which the lower office is supervised by the higher. Third, operations are governed by a system of rules and regulations. Fourth, the ideal official conducts operations in "a spirit of formalistic impersonality"; he is detached, rational, and impartial. Fifth, employment qualifications demand technical expertise; promotions are determined by seniority and/or achievement. Sixth, the ideal type of bureaucracy is the most efficient system of administrative organization. Weber declared that the ideal type "compares with other organizations exactly as does the machine with non-mechanical modes of production."

## Specialization

Weber's characteristics of an "ideal-type" bureaucracy can be illustrated by following the career of a government employee as he climbs the bureaucratic ladder.

A recent college graduate holding a joint degree in sociology and psychology believes he can put his knowledge to work more effectively by serving in one of the national government's agencies. He takes a written civil service examination that is designed to measure his degree of competence. By passing the exam, he is qualified to be appointed to the position of employment interviewer in Unit 47 of Local Office 583 of the Field Operations Bureau of the Division of Employment in the Department of Labor. He is assigned a specialized role within the hierarchy and is responsible for performing that role's specific duties. Because he is qualified to do the job to which he is appointed, he is able to perform his duties with competence and relative ease.

## Selection

Originally, the college graduate was hired solely on the strength of the knowledge gained in his study of sociology and psychology. After a year's probation period, and as he becomes more efficient in performing the functions of an employment interviewer, he becomes qualified to be appointed employment counselor. He takes another examination that is designed to measure his qualifications for that position. He passes the exam, thus becoming eligible for appointment to a position one step higher in the bureaucratic structure. His appointment to that position has been based in part on his achievements in a lower-ranking position and in part on the results of the exam, which by established rule he is required to take at each level.

**Advancement**

The established rules, in the case of the hypothetical employment counselor, consist of both a merit system of exams and job descriptions and titles. In order to advance to another grade, to that of senior counselor, for example, he must qualify by taking an examination designed specifically to measure his qualifications for that particular job. The established rules assure the advancement of qualified personnel.

**Full-time salaried employees**

As the employment counselor continues to advance in rank, it becomes increasingly likely that he will become a career administrator. He receives the designated salary appropriate to each rank and the fringe benefits accruing from it. As he moves from worker to administrator, what was at first for him a job becomes his career. Ideally, he becomes dedicated not only to furthering his own career, but also to the effective administration of policies that he now has the authority to formulate and in which he believes. Because he has benefited from the bureaucracy, the bureaucracy benefits from his expertise and loyalty.

**Decision making**

Our civil service counselor has advanced from employment interviewer, with very little, if any, power of decision, to a career man, with considerable policy-making leeway. However, at every step of the way his decision-making power has been exercised only within the sphere of his particular operation. His decisions have been made according to guidelines issued by each of his superiors in turn. For example, an office manager must defer to policies formulated by a superintendent, and the superintendent must defer to guidelines established by his superior. At the top of the hierarchical structure is the Secretary of Labor, who has formulated the policies for his entire department in consultation with the President and members of Congress. Decision making based on a hierarchical set of relationships keeps the lines of communication open, makes for a high degree of coordination, and equalizes responsibility for performance.

# The working force of government

The bureaucracy is the working core of government. It employs approximately one out of every six people in the total work force of the United States, and has an annual budget of broad proportions. Its decisions can directly affect the welfare of individual citizens. In implementing government programs and policies, the activities of the bureaucracy can have a significant impact on daily life.

The traditional American political dictum of government by consent of the governed makes it imperative that the bureaucrat be responsive not only to the advice of his superiors, but to the public interest as well. But how can this be accomplished? How can bureaucrats, living in a highly political world, with its conflicting loyalties and pressures, continue to do their jobs

Source: Data: U.S. Departments of Commerce and Labor, Office of Management and Budget. Drawing: Copyright 1971, U.S. News & World Report, Inc.

## HOW BIG IS "BIG GOVERNMENT"?

| | |
|---|---|
| 1 out of every 6 civilian workers in the U.S. is employed by government—federal, state and local. | |
| Workers on public payrolls number 12.6 million. Ten years ago, there were 8.4 million. | |
| $1 out of every $4.30 of personal income in the U.S. is accounted for by direct government payments. | |
| Spending by public agencies totals 313 billion dollars a year—more than double the outlays of 10 years ago. | 313 billion $ in a year / 10 years ago |
| Of all spending for goods and services in the U.S., governments account for nearly $1 out of $4. | |
| Taxes at all levels of government take 35 cents out of each dollar of national income, up from 32 cents a decade earlier. | 35¢ out of each dollar |
| Of total outlays for construction in the U.S., governments account for $1 out of $3. | |

Basic data: U.S. Depts. of Commerce and Labor; Office of Management and Budget and yet remain servants of the people? Not being directly accountable to the electorate, how much power does and should the bureaucrat have? Who and where are the people behind the system? What kind of people pull the switches to make the system go?

These are the primary questions to be kept in mind as we discuss who the bureaucrats are, what they do, where they work, and how the delicate balance between bureaucracy and a responsive form of government is maintained.

"Let me put it this way—how many of you are NOT college presidents?"

Drawing by Berry; © 1969 by NEA, Inc.

Federal employees reflect the classic American profile, in their diversity of backgrounds. They are a melting-pot mixture of creed, social class, partisan, religious, and regional affiliation. They hail from many fields. They mirror the American public and reflect the representative character of the government's administrative system. There are nearly three million of them on the federal roster. The nation's capitol and its immediate environs see less than one tenth of this vast force which extends down to the county level.

# The levels of bureaucracy

A recognition of the size of the bureaucracy nearly always inspires important questions. How is it possible to get the right men for critical or complex tasks? How is it possible for bureaucrats to keep the government running smoothly and leave enough room to house an individual President's political philosophy?

To answer these questions, we must consider the classifications of the bureaucrats, the criteria of employment, and the specification and differentiation of function.

Bureaucrats fall into three basic categories: *civil servants, career civil service executives*, who act as professional administrators and who have permanent civil service status, and *political executives*, who hold their positions by right of presidential appointment, sometimes with and sometimes without the consent of the Senate.

The lower-grade civil servant, is rarely subject to political pressures. The political executive, on the other hand, must constantly make decisions that will satisfy congressmen, the heads of other agencies, interest groups, and the public at large. The career executive must aid his temporary presidentially appointed chief by bringing his managerial expertise to bear on any decision the political executive may make.

Especially at the top levels of the governmental hierarchy—it is almost impossible to isolate the bureaucracy from politics. For example, the non-partisan permanent career executive must work hand in glove with his politically appointed short-term boss. He must be constantly concerned with his staff's and his own competent performance, yet remain responsible to shifts in political philosophy and to his responsibilities as a public servant. Similarly, the politically appointed executive must be committed to the policies and programs of the administration in office, yet rely on the career official to implement these programs.

In any large organization, personal pressures and loyalties are factors that cannot be ignored in the process of reaching successful resolutions to problems of political importance and those involving the management of large numbers of people. Similarly, variances of personality, political attitude, education, and professional background complicate the executive's tasks.

## Executives

The total force of approximately 6,000 administrators is divided into two distinct types of executives: career civil service executives and presidentially appointed political executives. Career executives are those who have climbed up the bureaucratic hierarchy and plan to remain in the civil service for most of their working lives. Within this hierarchy, career executives are immediately below *political executives*, men who are appointed by and directly responsible to the President. The level at which political appointments end and career positions begin depends on the department and the administration in power. In most parts of the bureaucracy the top three positions are filled by political executives.

Administrators, career or political, are appointed to perform one of three functions: some hold responsibility for a specific program or operation (the director of the Peace Corps, for example). Others provide specialized skills in management, budgeting, personnel, and general administration (an under-secretary or a personal assistant to the Secretary of Labor, for example); and still others serve in highly professional and technical areas, such as law, economics, physics, and biology (a lawyer in the Federal Trade Commission, or a chemist in the Food and Drug Administration, for example).

**Career executives**

The career executive is the master-administrator within the bureaucracy. He is responsible for hiring, assigning, and directing the members of his staff, and for implementing government policies and programs.

Contrary to common stereotype, the permanent career executive does not resemble a long-time staff member who is content to let the younger members of the firm do the work. Neither does he reflect the common image of a highly placed influential—but somewhat ineffectual—specialist. He may have served the government through several presidential administrations and concentrated his interests and talents on the business of one particular bureau or agency; but it is his length of service and specialized expertise that, ideally, give him the expert knowledge of specific programs and of the political climate; thus he can greatly assist his politically appointed chief in accomplishing the business at hand.

Theoretically, the career executive is a political neutral. On the assumption that both political parties serve the public interest, he is expected to serve loyally all presidential administrations and his different political chiefs, regardless of the party to which they belong or the programs and policies they represent. Because of their substantial knowledge of the political environment, however, career executives cannot avoid becoming involved in political matters. In fact they may be "better politicians—in the best sense of the word —than are their political supervisors."[2] A career executive's real dilemma is to make use of his considerable political skill without undue involvement in political partisanship.

In his dealings with his political boss and the presidential staff, the career executive has several options open to him. He may either resist presidential influence, or defer to it. He may adopt a cooperative attitude, or find imaginative means of overriding policy procedures imposed by the presidential executive staff. By marshalling political support from various interest groups or from the heads of congressional committees, he may fight either for or against pressures from the White House.

Regardless of how he expresses his political "nonpartisanship," his knowledge and familiarity with party programs and policies give him a great deal of freedom in establishing and realizing the objectives his particular agency has formulated. So long as the career executive does not openly or vehemently violate public policy, the President and his staff of advisers and appointees ordinarily find it in the interest of political peace and progress to allow the career executive to do his job without undue interference.

[2] Richard M. Paget, "Strengthening the Federal Career Executive," *Public Administration Review*, 17 (Spring 1957), p. 93.

## Political executives

The political executives are the top officials who are appointed by the President and who are directly responsible to him. They include all Secretaries of the Cabinet departments, such as Labor, Treasury, and Agriculture, all undersecretaries, and the heads of the various government regulatory agencies. Most political executives serve only one presidential administration. Their average tenure is three years. Some have had previous government experience as career civil service executives. (Note, therefore, that political and career executives' positions are not mutually exclusive.) Some have been recruited from the fields of law, political science, business, education, science, and engineering.

The job of the political executive is simply to govern within his particular sphere. The public nature of the political executive's position requires that he be an "on-the-job magician." He must operate in two different areas: internally with his subordinate career executives and their staffs in meeting day-to-day administrative problems, and externally with Congress, interest groups, and other agencies.

Internally, he must utilize the technical and political skills of his agency staff of specialized administrators, advisers, and their assistants. At times he must modify his own evaluations in deference to those of the experts on his staff. For example, the Secretary of Treasury is neither an accountant, mathematician, nor financial wizard. To plan policy effectively, he must rely on the highly specialized knowledge of those working under him.

In instituting a certain policy within his organization, the political executive may encounter resistance from staff members. For example, the political executive may find that his subordinates are not receptive to the new ideas he may propose, and he may encounter opposition to policies that command not only his own support, but that of the President and the general public as well. A particular agency or service may be bound by the methods of a previous administration, and changing the routine may require all the determination, ingenuity, and political support-building skills that the political executive can muster.

The political executive must be effective not only within his own organization, but also with outside forces, such as the congressional committees, the President, the Office of Management and Budget, and other departments and agencies. Thus he must satisfy Congress that the money he requests from the Office of Management and Budget will be spent advantageously or that new twists and turns that he may wish to give his agency's program will solve specific problems. For example, the Secretary of State may wish to add ten men to the embassy staff in Nepal. He must convince Congress that the men are really necessary; he must convince Congress that the department budget should be increased for that purpose.

The political executive may find himself of one mind with other department secretaries or agency chiefs, or at complete loggerheads. Important matters of policy are only rarely the concern of a single department or agency, and the political executive does not often have final decision-making authority. He is expected to consult with other officials who may have different, if not conflicting, constituencies. For example, the Secretary of Transportation may wish to construct a highway through a stretch of virgin forest, which the Secretary of the Interior promised would be saved, in deference to an interest group of ecologists.

To carry out this strong mandate, the political executive must first meet and deal with strong personal pressures. A crushing work load may play havoc with his health. If he has formerly been in big business, he will doubtless have to adjust to a cut in salary. He will also be confronted with the possible loss of promotion prospects and fringe benefits accrued in the practice of his private career. However, his biggest personal problem may be the assault made on his private life. As he is expected to be accountable to the public for all that he does and does not do, his every statement will be a measure of his sincerity, integrity, or suitability for the job.

The political executive may be left relatively free from harrassment by his Chief Executive, or he may be subject to nagging reminders that he is not doing his job either quickly enough, or well enough. His vulnerable position as a presidential appointee leaves him without the protection from excessive presidential pressures that elected officials enjoy. The political executive has the power to carry out the policies of the administration in office, and if he follows orders, he will be encouraged. If he becomes troublesome, he can be summarily fired.

## The civil service

For years, officials and other employees of the federal government were hired and fired solely on the basis of appointment. All positions were subject to *patronage*—that is, appointments to office by the party in power in return for partisan favors, such as campaign support or membership in a local party organization. Qualification was not a primary consideration. It was perhaps natural that a victorious party's leaders and followers felt that they had the right to fill the most desirable government jobs. Today, however, fewer positions are subject to political partisanship. For example, in 1970, 63,000 postmasterships were dropped from the patronage rolls. Over 75 percent of all federal employees are included in the Civil Service Commission's merit system; and only by passing a competitive examination can a person qualify for appointment. Unlike political executives, persons holding such positions are not the products of the patronage system; they are permanent employees, holding graded positions, who form the bulk of qualified personnel within the national government. They include top career executives, lawyers, doctors, engineers, scientists, social workers, teachers, dentists, nurses, accountants,

[3] Of the remaining positions, some are subject to patronage; most, however, are not. Some are covered by the merit systems of agencies not under the Civil Service Act (the Atomic Energy Commission, the Veterans' Administration, and the Federal Bureau of Investigation, for example); some are temporary positions to which no existing examination procedure applies; and some are positions held by foreign nationals working in various government offices overseas.

draftsmen, and thousands of stenographers, secretaries, clerks, messengers, janitors, and telephone operators.

Civil service positions are regulated by the Civil Service Commission, which has a working force numbering over 5,500. The commission acts as a kind of employment agency, and is responsible for the enlistment, testing, classification, and assignment of qualified personnel to specific civil service positions.

The general outline for this organized bureaucratic system was first prepared in 1883 by the Pendleton Act. This act initiated a competitive means of selection, administered by a Civil Service Commission composed of three members, not more than two of whom could be of the same party.

The original act related to only about 10 percent of the total number of federal positions, but the President could extend the system by executive order. Today, over 75 percent of all federal positions are classified by the Civil Service Commission as the result of gradual presidential action since 1883.[3]

"Children cry for it."
Grant: "If you can stand it, I can."

Drawing by Thomas Nast;
© 1938 *Harper's Weekly.*

Today, the civil service system is characterized by three basic methods of organization: *appointment based solely on merit-examination results; a specific method of job grading;* and *the use of job descriptions for classifying positions.*

**Merit examinations**

Within the civil service, there are two methods of examination: At the lower grades, appointment and promotion are based solely on the results of a written examination. In the higher grades, the examination includes, in addition, a review of the candidate's training and background, an appraisal of his previous experience and competency on a similar job, and an evaluation of his personality, judgment, and character. The individual's military status, too, is a major factor in ranking civil servants. The Veterans' Preference Act of 1944 provides for "special treatment" for veterans within the civil service grading system by boosting their test ratings. Today, veterans make up approximately 50 percent of the civil service work force.

The merit system has not been totally free from criticism and debate. Critics argue, for example, about how the competency of a candidate for civil service should be measured. Some people hold that examinations should test the aptitude to fulfill complex administrative functions; others contend that examinations should test the acquired experience necessary to do the job.

Another criticism of the merit system has been that some positions in the higher grades are "closed"—that is, reserved to the few who joined the civil service as young men—and are not open to qualified older persons who might otherwise be appointed had they "come up through the ranks."

**Appointment and staffing**

Despite these criticisms, the merit examination system has usually prevented the employment of the outright incompetent, and reserves positions for those who are able to do the job, irrespective of their political background. After a candidate successfully passes an examination, the Civil Service Commission places his name on a roster or "register" of persons qualifying for appointment. When an agency wishes to fill a vacant position or staff a new one, it asks the commission for the names of available candidates. The commission then submits three names for the agency's consideration, from among which one is selected.

The criteria for selection is often a subject of debate. Because an administrator may seek staff unity on policy, he may support the idea of appointment according to time in service or party affiliation. Other administrators support a nonpartisan approach to government staffing.

**Job grading and job description**

After successfully passing an examination, candidates for civil service positions are ranked by grades from GS-1 to GS-18. The grading system assigns a specific salary to each position on the scale, and a description of tasks pertaining to that grade. At the lowest levels (grades 1–11) on the gradation scale are file clerks, typists, secretaries, and stenographers; the top "super grades" (GS-16, GS-17, GS-18) include career executives, administrators, engineers, and lawyers. Each position on the scale is classified according to its rank in the organizational structure, the degree of specialization, and the scope of responsibility.

Source: Data: House-Senate Joint Committee on Reduction of Federal Expenditures: 1971 dollar estimate by USN & WR Economic Unit. Drawing: Copyright 1971, U.S. News & World Report, Inc.

## CHANGE IN FEDERAL PAYROLL UNDER NIXON
### (Although the number of workers is less, the expenditures have increased.)

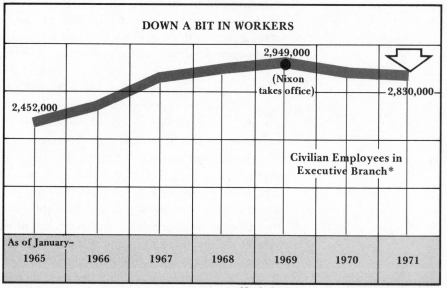

**DOWN A BIT IN WORKERS**

2,949,000
(Nixon takes office)
2,452,000
2,830,000

Civilian Employees in Executive Branch*

As of January–
1965 | 1966 | 1967 | 1968 | 1969 | 1970 | 1971

*Includes temporary and part-time workers.

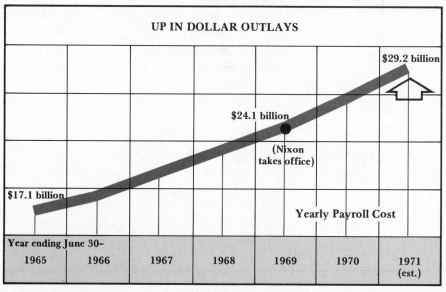

**UP IN DOLLAR OUTLAYS**

$29.2 billion
$24.1 billion
(Nixon takes office)
$17.1 billion

Yearly Payroll Cost

Year ending June 30–
1965 | 1966 | 1967 | 1968 | 1969 | 1970 | 1971 (est.)

**Recruitment: drawbacks and advantages of government services**

Specific descriptions of tasks and a system of job classification according to grade are necessary for effective recruitment and examination, especially within a bureaucracy as large and as complicated as that of the federal government.

In its recruiting efforts, the federal civil service has usually been content to use the "soft-sell" method, and to limit recruitment to those candidates who voluntarily apply for the job. For some, service in the federal government proves attractive and offers rich opportunities. However, the civil service has had a difficult task recruiting and retaining top talent, especially at the higher levels. One troublesome factor has been its unfavorable image as a collection of minor clerks pushing sets of paper from desk to desk and from office to office.

Another factor has been the tough competition from private industry with its usually higher pay scales for administrators and technical personnel, less rigid personnel rules and regulations, and more easily available incentives —pension plans, stock options, liberal vacation allowances, and the like. The traditionally low salary standards are perhaps the biggest obstacle confronting the civil service in its efforts to attract executive talent: even the most recent pay increases for top executives do not equal the salaries with those of many individuals in private industry.

For all these reasons—poor image, competition from industry, low salaries, countless rules and regulations governing morality and ethics—the civil service has experienced a high turnover rate in personnel. It must be noted here that because of the rigidity of personnel rules and the high degree of specialization of function within the civil service, the high turnover rate does not necessarily affect the stability of the government apparatus. A quite specific task can usually be performed just as easily by one qualified employee as another. In other words, the results do not change even though the person holding the position may.

Steady efforts have been made to improve the quality of the civil service. To attract to government service highly qualified personnel who may otherwise wish to continue to sell their talents in a comparatively attractive labor market, Congress has authorized several pay increases, as well as other incentives.

In addition to salary increases, other incentives for employment in the civil service have been inaugurated. Career-development programs provide on-the-job training for qualified college graduates, and special educational courses are offered at the university level to enable college graduates to qualify for faster movement up the civil service grade scale. Liberal pension benefits, vacation and sick-leave allowances, low-cost insurance and hospitalization plans have also been established.

Security of employment is perhaps the most attractive aspect of public

[4] *Statistical Abstract of the U.S. 1970* (Washington, D.C.: Department of Commerce, 1970) p. 395. *Humphrey's Executor* v. *United States*, 295 U.S. 602 (1935) substantiated the civil servant's right to protection against executive removal.

service in the federal government. By law, no civil service employee can be fired except in extreme cases of inefficiency or open and violent rebellion against administration policy. When agencies or jobs are abolished, or when a congressional cut in a department's funds forces a staff reduction, the civil servant is not protected, of course. However, he holds a priority and normally will be appointed to another position in a short period of time. Also, the procedure for dismissal is regulated by the Civil Service Commission under the provisions of the Veterans' Preference Act of 1944, which take into account an employee's length of service and quality of performance in dismissal cases.[4]

"It takes real concentration"

Drawing by Alexander in the Philadelphia *Bulletin*.

Evidence proves that the great majority of civil servants are honest and loyal. They are reasonably secure in their jobs for life if they are competent and avoid excessive involvement in political activity. Federal employees' political activities are curtailed by the *Hatch Acts* passed by Congress in 1939 and 1940.

Under the provisions of these acts, the right of civil servants to vote and engage in political discussion is guaranteed. But they are forbidden from engaging in political action such as campaigning for a candidate, or party, or particular office.

# Bureaucratic structure

With the increasing complexity of the problems involved in matters of defense, health, education, welfare, transportation, environmental control, communications, and foreign affairs, there has been simultaneous growth within the governmental bureaucracy of a number of agencies to deal with these problems. Each agency has its own special interest and its own staff of technical experts. Each is empowered by Congress to issue rules and regulations pertaining to its interest. Because Congress lacks the technical expertise required to solve specific technical problems (what makes smoke black or what causes infertile soil, for example), it has been increasingly willing to delegate more policy-making power to the bureaucracy.

From its earliest beginnings in 1789, when it was composed of only three major departments (State, War, and Treasury), the executive bureaucracy has grown into an interlocking, overlapping organization of 11 Cabinet departments, more than 50 agencies, and over 1,800 bureaus, branches, corporations, administrations, commissions, and authorities. Most of these agencies are responsible to the President. Some are partly independent of him.

## Cabinet departments

The principal organizations within the executive branch are the 11 *Cabinet departments*. Each department is headed by a secretary who is appointed by the President, and who is a member of the President's Cabinet. The one exception is the Department of Justice, which is headed by the Attorney General. Until July 1971, when the Post Office Department became a government corporation, its head, the Postmaster General, was also a Cabinet member.

Below the secretary, there is usually an undersecretary who bears part of the administrative responsibility. He, in turn, has anywhere from one to several assistant secretaries to supervise the enactment of far-reaching policies. Undersecretaries and their assistants are appointed either by the secretary himself or by the President and are directly responsible to the secretary.

Although all departments are organized along the same general structural lines, they differ considerably in their scope and functions. For example, the Department of Health, Education and Welfare has a working force of over 106,481, whereas the Department of Commerce is only 25,000 strong.

## Bureaus

Approximately 85 to 90 percent of all federal employees work in bureaus and agencies of government. Each department is divided into *bureaus* headed by bureau chiefs who may be either career executives or political executives. The bureaus are the real working agencies of the Cabinet departments and have quite definite and clear-cut duties. The burdens, like the departments over them, differ widely in their functions; they are the most basic units in the organizational hierarchy. The bureaus may also be organized according to whom they serve (Bureau of Minority Business Enterprise), what they do (Bureau of the Census), or the area they encompass (Bureau of International Commerce).

Often, the bureaus have been established prior to their departments, and have gathered power by legislative and interest group support. Control over them by temporary politically appointed officials who may be further up in the organizational hierarchy may be difficult to maintain. The controversy surrounding the continued service of J. Edgar Hoover as director of the FBI illustrates this point. The Federal Bureau of Investigation, as an operating arm of the Department of Justice, is so powerful and has so much congressional and public support that no President has taken the political risk of imposing his will too strongly on its structure and operation.

Generally, however, with each new administration there is an accompanying change in the political leadership of the departments and the bureaus subordinate to them.

## Branches and field offices

There is considerable decentralization within the organizational structure of the operating bureaus. Central bureau offices, with relatively small staffs, are located in Washington where policies are established. However, the major portion of bureau employees are located in field offices scattered across the country and in foreign nations. The *field services* of the operating bureaus are themselves composed of hundreds of branches, sections, and other subunits, and are responsible for even more specialized tasks. Typical examples of field offices are the local social security office and the local draft board.

These bureau subunits are bound by the same rules and regulations as those governing bureau headquarters in Washington, and are often the targets of demands by regional groups to change federal guidelines. For example, a local mail-order house may be requesting special considerations from the local postmaster in the matter of rates for bulk postage. These pressures sometimes cause conflict between the local office and the Washington bureau, and may also present problems in working with local offices of another bureau that answers to another department.

Because bureaus usually wish that all citizens, regardless of their location, have access to their services, they normally set up general guidelines to be followed in specific situations. Although frequent checks and inspections of local offices are made by headquarters personnel, the central office in Washington usually leaves it up to local citizens managing the field offices to apply general directives in individual cases. For example, *how* someone is drafted into the armed services is the responsibility of the Department of Defense; the decision as to who gets drafted is left to the local draft board.

## Federal agencies

Federal agencies are organizations that are headed by one administrator and that, although separated from the Cabinet departments, are subject to upper-level executive control. The United States Information Agency, and the Office of Economic Opportunity are examples of federal agencies. Such agencies are usually characterized by a higher degree of functional specialization than that typical of the Cabinet departments.

Federal agencies have often been formed more for political reasons than for purposes of administrative efficiency. In some cases, the sole justification for their existence is the desire of particular lobbies and legislators to restrain the influence of powerful Cabinet departments, and to make the administration more receptive to their demands. However, some of these agencies (NASA, for example) are engaged in unique programs, which necessitate freedom from the restraints imposed by the rigid rules of hiring and management.

## Corporations

The third major type of governmental organization is the government-owned corporation. These corporations are combinations of private business enterprises and regular government agencies established to operate more freely from some of the controls imposed on other agencies. The St. Lawrence Seaway Development Corporation and the Export-Import Bank are corporations. As noted earlier, the Post Office Department was transformed on July 1, 1971, into a government corporation.

Even though the government corporations are headed by presidential appointees who can be removed from office, they have a certain amount of autonomy in the financial realm. Once given their yearly funds, they may, like a private business corporation, reinvest funds according to their own judgment.

Government corporations are especially useful when the government is preparing to provide a private type of service, such as insurance or power, national services that are best achieved by an independent corporation, free from excessive presidential and congressional interference.

They are, however, far from being completely free agents. Although they are excluded from some controls of the Office of Management and Budget and the Comptroller General, they are still subect to yearly legislative appropriations—appropriations that have been subjected to increasingly stringent reviewing procedures and are given less freely by Congress. Government corporations are, in addition, subject to many regulations peculiar to their quasi-business-type operation. They are subject to prescribed procedures for hiring and firing, and executive review of their policies and programs. And if the corporations are to realize their goals, accommodation to various federal programs is often imperative.

"If we can get men to the moon . . . Who knows? We may even learn to get the mail across town."

Drawing by Haynie in *The Courier-Journal*; © 1969 *Los Angeles Times* Syndicate.

## Independent regulatory commissions

Who gets a license to operate a radio or TV station, whether or not an American registered freighter is safe for ocean travel, whether or not an airline can lower or raise its fare rates—all such considerations fall within the province of the government regulatory commissions and boards.

The commissions primarily serve to control business in the economic sector, and have been given lawmaking and judging powers to be subject to congressional directives. The commissions and boards are run, usually, by three or more commissioners holding long overlapping terms, and who must be, under the law, politically bipartisan.

Typical commissions are the Interstate Commerce Commission, the Federal Communications Commission, the Federal Aviation Administration, and the Federal Maritime Commission.

The regulatory commissions were created originally under pressure from politically powerful interest groups who wanted to be assured of fairer treatment by business interests that had authority over who performed certain public services. Because of the detailed technical issues involved, decision-making authority in cases involving competing interests was delegated to the commissions by Congress. In addition, because of the inability of the courts to handle quickly cases involving technical subject matter, the commissions were also authorized to exercise quasi-judicial powers, the precedent and pattern of which were set by the Interstate Commerce Commission.

The commissions are empowered, by statute, to issue rules and regulations that have the effect of law as far as the private citizen is concerned. They are also empowered to decide cases arising between the government and particular parties, or between citizens and other nonpublic interests.

The commissioners are appointed by the President for three-year overlapping terms, but presidential removal power has been considerably curbed by Congress. In fact, the boards, with their commission form of administration, were deliberately established by Congress in such a way as to keep them relatively free from presidential influence and political pressures.

The commissions are often criticized for falling too heavily under the influence of the groups they are supposed to regulate. The Federal Trade Commission has been criticized by Ralph Nader for this reason. For example, a particular commission is assigned the authority to regulate a certain private economic enterprise. Because of the interchange of personnel between the commission and the private business, and their mutual interest in technical matters, the commission and the business often become close allies—perhaps to the detriment of the public.

# Policy making and the bureaucrat

Because of their specialized knowledge in many fields and the pressing necessity for quick decisions, especially at the local level, bureaucrats have become more and more directly involved in the total governmental process: legislative, judicial, and executive. The executive branch of the federal government is so large and its members so scattered that the official down the line may be the key element in the formation of public policy. Obviously, major decisions are made in Washington in consultation with the President and members of Congress, but often the bureaucrat is required to make specific decisions that determine the effectiveness of the law.

Until recently, political theorists advocated sharp distinctions between the administrative and policy-making powers of the executive branch. In fact, some *traditionalists* still hold that the job of Congress is to formulate policy by the legislative process, and that the job of the executive branch is to administer it. This view is based on the principle that policy making and administration are two separate processes. Today, however, this view has been rejected by most students of government in favor of the belief that policy making and administration are simply different aspects of one government process. Congress not only creates a new agency to administer a law; it says how that law is to be enforced. The President acts not only as Chief Administrator; he is also the government's foremost policy-maker, especially in the areas of military activity and foreign affairs. Federal judges not only hand down rulings in cases of dispute; they review agency decisions and procedures that concern matters of broad political importance. Similarly, the bureaucracy not only implements governmental programs; it has become a full partner with the other branches of the government in the decision-making process. Its activities include servicing and enforcing, legislating, and adjudicating, as well as administrating. In short, the executive branch bureaucracy not only administers, but it makes rules and regulations, puts these rules into operation, and hears, tries, and judges cases as well. For example, Congress has outlawed deceptive advertising. The Federal Communications Commission sets up criteria for advertisers to follow, ascertains that the standards are being met and if an investigation proves otherwise, charges, tries, and judges a company accused of deceptive advertising.

A. *Lee Fritschler*, Smoking and Politics: Policymaking and the Federal Bureaucracy (*New York: Appleton-Century-Crofts, 1969*), *pp. 130–143.*

A. Lee Fritschler describes the policy-making function of the bureaucracy in producing legislation that would require manufacturers and advertisers of cigarettes to warn the public about the possible danger of cigarettes to their health. While several bureaucratic agencies actively supported health warnings, many members of Congress, under pressure from the tobacco industries, opposed the passage of "health warning" legislation; and, until 1965, Congress was successful in its attempt to block the enactment of any such bill. During this time and subsequent to it, bureaucratic agencies—notably the Federal Trade Commission—were avidly exerting pressure for its passage. (The FTC was joined in its fight by the Public Health Service of the Department of Health, Education and Welfare and the Federal Communications Commission.)

After publication of a lengthy report by the Advisory Committee on Smoking and Health, the first of three major breakthroughs occurred. The Trade Regulation Rule on Cigarette Labeling and Advertising, passed in June, 1965, and effective on January 1, 1966, provided that all cigarette labels contain health warnings.

Three additional reports were issued by the Federal Trade Commission and Public Health Service, while the tobacco industries attempted to discredit their findings. These reports produced the second breakthrough, the "fairness doctrine," which was instituted dramatically in June, 1967, by the Federal Communications Commission. This doctrine required that each television or radio station airing cigarette advertisements also allocate air time for health hazard information. During the eight months after the decision, the American Cancer Society had produced and aired almost five times as many antismoking commercials as it had aired in the three-and-a-half years before the FCC decision.

The third and most significant piece of legislation—completely banning radio and television cigarette advertising—was proposed in the early sixties by the FTC and, again, in February, 1969, by the FCC, just before the expiration of the 1965 Labeling Act.

The President signed the bill on January 2, 1971. Attached to this bill were provisions to strengthen "warning labels." Effective July 1, 1971, was a further measure to include health warnings in other cigarette advertising.

Fritschler, in a general evaluation of the bureaucracy's policy-making power in relation to the present legislative structure and procedure, concludes that

the initiation and continuation of the cigarette controversy were possible because of both the political power and delegated authority possessed by bureaucratic agencies. Had the decision on cigarettes and health been left to Congress alone, it is safe to assume that the manufacturers would have triumphed and no health warning of any kind would have been required. The cigarette labeling controversy is a clear example of agencies' powers to influence and even formulate public policy.

By right of the powers delegated to it by the Constitution, the executive branch is most directly involved in law-enforcing activities. As law enforcer, the bureaucracy acts as presidential deputy.

In the arsenal of the bureaucracy, the most effective instrument is its *license-issuing powers.* For example, a standard radio station or television channel cannot operate legally unless it has a license granted by the Federal Communications Commission. A bus company cannot go into business without a license from the Interstate Commerce Commission.

Another highly effective weapon is the bureaucracy's right to enforce federal laws, nationwide, by the use of authorized FBI agents, narcotics agents, treasury agents, and federal marshals and attorneys. The law-enforcing activities of such agents may be directed against violations of the federal anti-kidnapping statute and the various narcotics laws, for example. Law enforcement in criminal law cases is normally reserved to the states.

*Cease and desist* orders are another means whereby the administration makes sure that companies, groups, and individuals amend their ways and adhere to decisions handed down by a given agency. For example, the Food and Drug Administration may send a "cease and desist" order to a pill manufacturer if that manufacturer makes a claim unsupported by evidence that his pill will, once and for all, cure the common cold.

Finally, law-enforcing activities also include person-to-person confrontations between citizens and personnel of government agencies. For example, if a citizen fails to file a federal income-tax return or pay the amount he owes, he will inevitably come into personal contact with agents of the Internal Revenue Service. These government officials will, in all fairness, try to bring about a settlement. If the decision is in the government's favor, its agents will require that all due taxes be paid forthwith. Failure on the part of the taxpayer to do so will provoke a levy of fines or even indictment in the courts.

## Information gathering

If violators of the law are to be brought to heel by any of these means, there must be evidence to support an agency's claims. The ways an agency goes about gleaning information vary. Usually, however, the agency assumes either an active or passive role.

The active investigators and supervisors are most often concerned with cases involving federal criminal law. The FBI agents and other federal law-enforcement officers are all involved in the active investigation of violations. The Food and Drug Administration is another "active investigator." It may demand that cosmetic companies substantiate their claims about their products. The FDA then makes the decision as to whether or not a product should be sold.

Sometimes, however, an agency simply gleans its evidence from complaints submitted by parties in a dispute. For example, the Civil Rights Division of the Department of Justice may receive from an individual a request to act on his behalf in a matter of racial segregation or discrimination. The individual supplies the evidence, and the agency decides the case.

In addition, policy-making and administrative duties take place among merging lines of authority, in overlapping areas of responsibility, and in an atmosphere of constant change. Several government agencies may be concerned with the problem of pollution or with the building of an interstate highway. Similarly, new agencies and regulatory commissions to deal with the problems imposed by new industries are being established regularly. For example, the *United States Government Organization Manual* is published yearly. By the time it comes off press, however, twenty-five new agencies may have been created or eliminated, and the *Manual* is immediately out of date.

## Government services

Another important function of the government agencies is to perform countless services for the citizenry. These services include such activities as the handling of all the routine detail and paperwork involved in social security collections and payments. They also include making available to private citizens free expert advice in the preparation of income tax returns, for example. Agencies also actively engage in many health, school, and park services directly beneficial to the public at large. In addition, they provide federal monies for housing construction and the promotion of local businesses and colleges.

## Legislating

Increasingly, congressional legislation is less detailed and is concerned with stating only general purposes and guidelines that are to be followed in applying the law in specific cases. Rule- and regulation-making authority has been delegated by Congress to over one hundred agencies, most of which are regulatory commissions, such as the Interstate Commerce Commission and the Federal Communications Commission. These agencies not only interpret the laws passed by Congress; they issue regulations and rules pursuant to the general laws in individual circumstances. As no law can cover all contingencies, the agencies are assigned the responsibility for making policy decisions applicable at the local level.

Congress can guard against agency misuse of its policy-making authority by exercising its legislative power of amendment. Congress is also empowered to conduct investigations of the agencies and can, in most instances, withhold or reduce appropriations if agency abuses are not corrected.

## Adjudicating

The independent regulatory agencies, such as the Interstate Commerce Commission and the Federal Communications Commission, have been empowered by Congress to judge cases involving particular parties and the administration, or conflicts between nonpublic interests. Most cases are negotiated privately and informally, and rarely necessitate the formal procedures of the agency's top-level hearings.

Prior to 1946, attorneys often complained that the regulatory agencies had too much judicial power, and that the procedure of informal hearings contradicts due process of law. The agencies, they contended, did not grant all parties equal voice and did not conclude cases on substantial information to warrant a judgment.

The *Administrative Procedures Act of 1946* seeks to curtail such practices. The act specifies that agencies must make public how they are organized and how they operate. Other provisions of the act permit wider review of agency decisions by the federal courts. Under these provisions, the courts are empowered to review factual matters (the chemical analysis of a product, for example) as well as legal issues (whether or not the Federal Trade Commission has misinterpreted the fair trade statutes, for example).

# The bureaucracy vis-a-vis Congress and the President

The President, as Chief Executive, is accountable for the entire executive branch bureaucracy and is empowered by Congress to make changes in the bureaucracy, subject to congressional veto. Often Congress adopts presidential plans, or portions of them. Sometimes, however, it does not, suspecting that the President is merely seeking to increase his own power.

Several Presidents have appointed commissions to study the problem of executive branch reorganization and to recommend improvements, primarily to increase efficiency and reduce costs.

In 1937, the President's *Committee on Administrative Management* dealt with the problem of administrative responsibility, and established the Executive Office of the President. The *Hoover Commission* made recommendations for a reorganization of the executive branch in 1949, as did another Hoover commission in 1955.

The latest of these formal attempts to diagnose the ills of the bureaucracy was made by President Nixon's *Advisory Council on Executive Branch Reorganization.* The presidentially appointed commission presented a plan whereby the number of Cabinet posts would be cut from eleven to eight and the various parts of the Cabinet departments reshuffled according to specific function. The Departments of State, Treasury, Defense, and Justice would remain unchanged. The Departments of Agriculture, Labor, Commerce, Housing and Urban Development, Transportation, Interior, and Health, Education and Welfare would be eliminated and replaced by the four new Departments of Natural Resources, Human Resources, Economic Affairs, and Community Development.

> *John Fischer, "The Easy Chair: Can the Nixon Administration be Doing Something Right?"* Harper's Magazine, 241, no. 1446 (November 1970): 22–37.
>
> John Fischer commends President Nixon for decentralizing the federal bureaucracy, and, thus, helping to straighten out the tangle of red tape that clogs up our governmental process.
>
> President Johnson's effort at bureaucratic change had failed. When appointing a "coordinator of the month" proved unsuccessful, he organized a secret task force headed by Ben W. Heineman, a successful railroad

executive. In September, 1967, the Heineman team urged reorganization of the Cabinet and White House Staff "to get a grip on the runaway bureaucracy." They proposed that the country be divided into ten federal regions. Washington should concentrate on making policy while "responsible federal officials—men who can make decisions and make them stick," handle the day-to-day responsibilities through the states and local communities. The report suggested that local problems should be handled within each region by "field representatives of the President's Office of Program Coordination." This "decentralization of operational program decisions" was modeled after the system of organization used by big business.

The plan was not instituted, but it became the genesis for President Nixon's reforms, announced in May, 1969, and begun in the fall of 1970. Ten federal regions have been formed, with boundaries varying somewhat from the Heineman proposals.

The people in the Budget Bureau who worked out the nuts-and-bolts of the new arrangement do not regard it as ideal. They would have preferred to give special status to certain great metropolitan areas, such as New York, Philadelphia, Chicago, and St. Louis, which sprawl across state lines—making them, in effect, the modern equivalent of the ancient Greek city-states.

To begin with, the new regional system will apply only to three departments—HEW, HUD, and Labor—and two agencies—the Office of Economic Opportunity and the Small Business Administration. These are the outfits responsible for nearly all the welfare and social programs, and they handle by far the biggest chunk of the federal budget after the Department of Defense. Eventually, other agencies dealing with economic and development problems—the Farmer Home Administration, for instance, and the Economic Development Administration—are expected to rearrange their field operations to conform to the new setup. It is unlikely, however, that the provincial scheme will ever embrace all federal operations; there is no logical reason why the Coast Guard or the Forest Service, to name only a couple, need be fitted into the pattern.

According to the author, the change is working to make the government "more responsive and less inhuman." Half the time is now required to process a loan application for federal money. One agency, Housing and Urban Development, has cut the time for a response to a mayor's request for a rehabilitation loan from ninety-six to five days; and HUD and HEW have eliminated reams of superfluous paper work.

Fischer credits the Nixon administration with the traditional conservative inclination for the art of management. "They make things work better, they find the flaws and patch and tinker and overhaul the clanking machinery of government." Bureaucratic reforms do not excite the public, but "in the end, they may be far from negligible."

No doubt through this and other studies, improvements will be made, but critics of the present system contend that there are still too many people directly and personally responsible to the President, that Congress has established too many agencies with some degree of independence, that the President's power over the executive branch has been weakened by Congress.

"I'm sorry I said what I did. Why, if it weren't for dedicated public servants like you, our government would be in real trouble."

Drawing by Stevenson; © 1969 The New Yorker Magazine, Inc.

## The bureaucracy and the President

Constitutionally, the President has ultimate authority over every department of the executive bureaucracy. He can make his authority felt by appointing top executives and department heads who will be guided by his views in their particular spheres of responsibility. Often, department and agency heads are sympathetic to a President's policies and goals and endeavor to implement them in a spirit of cooperation. But the bureaucracy's checks on the presidential authority are strong, and sometimes administrators make concerted drives to exercise maximum independence and autonomy.

Although the President exercises a great deal of control over the bureaucracy through his White House Staff, the Office of Management and Budget, and the Cabinet, his influence is weakened by his need to rely on executive or civil servants further down the line to promote and defend his policies. Often, these people—including Cabinet members—have the powerful political support of interest groups and members of Congress, and may promote interests other than the President's.

## The bureaucracy and Congress

Congress is not only a deterrent to absolute control of the bureaucracy by the President; it keeps a watchful eye on the bureaucracy itself. Individual congressmen and senators have a major interest in retaining control over the agencies. In addition to upholding congressional power, they endeavor to mold agency policies that may significantly affect their constituents. By constant investigation and informational inquiry, and particularly by their power to control the purse-strings and review agency budgets, congressional committees in charge of policing a particular group of agencies keep a running check on agency activity.

# The bureaucracy—to whom is it responsible?

Given the tremendous power of the bureaucracy, and its influence on policy making, the question arises as to whether or not it is politically responsible. The bureaucracy is not completely self-governing; nor is it *fully* responsible to either the executive, legislative, or judicial branch of the government. Yet it administers programs of vital interest to millions of citizens—even those of peace and war. How, then, is a bureaucracy of such far-reaching authority and power kept responsive to the electorate whose interests it is supposed to serve?

*Norton E. Long, "Bureaucracy and Constitutionalism,"* American Political Science Review, 46 *(September 1952)*: 808–818.

Norton Long notes that formal and informal tradition has always dictated that Congress as a representative body should rule over the bureaucracy. But service to the public, according to Long, stems from the bureaucracy as well as from elected representatives. It is on the basis of service, and not merely tradition, that our entire political process should be investigated. Long agrees with J. A. Corry's assessment of the bureaucracy as the "mainspring" of government: the fourth branch of government. Long contends that:

The bureaucracy is in policy, and major policy, to stay; in fact, barring the unlikely development of strong majority party legislative leadership, the bureaucracy is likely, day in and day out, to be our main source of policy initiative. The role of the legislature and of the political executive may come to consist largely of encouraging, discouraging and passing on policy which wells up from the agencies of administration. All of this is because the bureaucracy is not just an instrument to carry out a will formed by the elected Congress and President. It is itself a medium for registering the diverse wills that make up the people's will and for transmuting them into responsible proposals for public policy.

According to Long, the power of the bureaucracy is incorrectly seen as a "menace to constitutionalism," while the power of the legislature is generally accepted. In actuality, dominance of neither branch is desirable.

To meet our needs, we have worked out a complex system in which the bureaucracy and legislature perform complementary and interlocking functions. Both are necessary, and the supremacy of either would be a constitutional misfortune. We sometimes forget that the authors of the Federalist and Jefferson alike were aware of the danger of legislative tyranny.

Long emphasizes the value of the bureaucracy by noting that, because of the diverse abilities and backgrounds of its members, it represents that part of our pluralistic society that Congress fails to represent. In addition, he notes that

responsible behavior in the sense of sensitivity to long-range and broad considerations, the totality of interests affected, and the utilization of expert knowledge by procedures that ensure a systematic collection and analysis of relevant facts, is more characteristic of the executive than of Congress. Despite the exceptions, and there are many, this kind of responsible behavior is more expected, more politically feasible, and more frequently practiced in the administrative branch.

The bureaucracy, Long continues, guards against the overrepresentation of the rural areas that exists in Congress and gives qualitative representation to professions, science, educational institutions, and the "conscience of society as it is expressed in churches, civil liberties groups and a host of others."

According to Long, America's diversity is best represented by its civil servants, who are more likely to be responsible to the public than are congressmen who must concentrate on pleasing their campaign-backers.

Long argues, moreover, that administrative agencies, unlike congressional committees, are continuing institutions and, thus, self-corrective. In congressional committees, the shifting of affiliations that results from partisan politics prevents stability, and works against the kind of learning that results in the correction of earlier mistakes. Administrative agencies are continuing, and are able to assess their own performance on a long-term basis—by conducting surveys, for example. Long, therefore, concludes that the bureaucracy, because of its long-term responsibilities and stability, is the institution best able to improve and increase the efficiency of the government operation.

Democracy has been defined as that method of government in which the majority of citizens select officials to represent them and make policy for them. The United States has been shown to be a constitutional democracy, in which the powers of government are subject to checks and balances. With these definitions in mind, we must determine whether or not the bureaucracy is responsible and responsive to the American population, or more responsive to special interest groups inside and outside Congress. On the one hand, bureaucrats are not elected by the people. Since they do not owe their jobs to the public, bureaucrats are not technically responsible to them. On the other hand, however, the bureaucracy belongs to the executive branch of government, which is obviously under the President's control. In addition, the agencies, bureaus, and departments of the bureaucracy are established by congressional acts and are dependent upon Congress for appropriations.

Thus, we can conclude that the bureaucracy is indirectly, through Congress and the President, responsible to the people. Is this responsibility, however, carried out? Can Congress or the President oversee and control the myriad details of the bureaucracy's work? Although constitutional democracy contains imbalances, and the bureaucracy is often most strongly influenced by the interest groups with which it has direct contact, major policy decisions affecting the nation will remain a combined interaction of political forces within a government which must ultimately reflect the will of the American public.

# Glossary

**administrative adjudication** The process of decision making in disputes between two or more parties characterized by court-like proceedings, that is, the hearing of witnesses, the presentation of evidence, the study of briefs, and judgments in accordance with the law based on the evidence presented.

**administrator** In government, a top official who is either a career executive or political executive and who has responsibility for a department, bureau, agency, or government corporation.

**bureau** The largest working subunit of a department that performs specific functions.

**bureaucracy** A system of administrative organization characterized by specialization of function, adherence to fixed rules, and a hierarchy of authority.

**career executive** A top official in government service who has permanent civil service status.

**civil service** The system of administration of government personnel characterized by the appointment to positions based on merit, the use of a specific method for grading jobs, and the use of job descriptions for the classification of positions according to the specific tasks applicable to those jobs and to their place in the graded hierarchy.

**department** The major administration unit of organization within the federal bureaucracy, which is headed by a secretary who is a member of the President's Cabinet.

**federal agency** An organization within the federal bureaucracy that is headed by a single administrator and that performs specialized functions and does not have departmental status; for example, NASA.

**field service** The regional, state, county, and local subunits of the federal bureaucracy.

**government corporation** A federal organization that provides a national service through a system that combines elements of private business and government agencies.

**Hatch Acts (1939 and 1940)** Congressional legislation giving civil servants the right to vote and engage in private political discussion, and forbidding their participation in political activities, such as their working for a party or running for office.

**Independent Regulatory Commission** A government agency responsible for the regulation of a major area of the economy. It is headed by several commissioners, who are appointed for specified overlapping terms and exercise both legislative and judicial powers.

**patronage** The distribution of government positions to those who are active political party members or who have supported an elected government official.

**political executive** A high-level official in government service, who is appointed to his position by the administration in office, and who serves at the discretion of the Chief Executive. Political executives are usually replaced when another administration comes into office.

**United States Government Organization Manual** Annual publication that lists the existing federal departments, bureaus, commissions, and agencies, their organization, and their responsibilities.

# Suggested readings

Appleby, Paul H., *Big Democracy* (New York: Alfred A. Knopf, Inc., 1945). Discussion of giant bureaucracies as permanent aspects of contemporary American society, by a well-reputed administrator.

Bernstein, Marver H., *Regulating Business by Independent Commissions* (Princeton, N.J.: Princeton University Press, 1955). Critical study of the politics of the regulation of American business by means of the independent federal regulatory commissions.

Bernstein, Marver H., *The Job of the Federal Executive* (Washington, D.C.: Brookings Institution, 1958). Description of the role of high-level administrators, both political appointees and career men, and the political environment in which they work.

Blau, Peter M., *Bureaucracy in Modern Society* (New York: Random House, Inc., 1956). Brief discussion of the problems of bureaucracy in contemporary society.

Corson, John J., and R. Shale Paul, *Men Near the Top: Filling Key Posts in the Federal Service* (Baltimore: Johns Hopkins University Press, 1966). Analysis of the functions and skills of the civil servants who serve directly under the political appointee.

Dimock, Marshall E., and Gladys D. Dimock, *Public Administration*, 4th ed. (New York: Holt, Rinehart and Winston, Inc., 1969). Standard text of the institutions, people, operations, and objectives of bureaucracies.

Downs, Anthony, *Inside Bureaucracy* (Boston: Little, Brown and Co., 1967). Description of the role of bureaucrats and the environment within which their agencies function.

Gawthrop, Louis C., *Administrative Politics and Social Change* (New York: St. Martin's Press, 1970). Analysis of administration at the national level, with a focus on current policy issues.

Gawthrop, Louis C., ed., *The Administrative Process and Democratic Theory* (Boston: Houghton Mifflin Co., 1970). Readings on contemporary issues in administration, especially in relation to democratic theory.

Hyneman, Charles S., *Bureaucracy in a Democracy* (New York: Harper and Row Publishers, Inc., 1950). Interesting study of American bureaucracy, its role and control, with emphasis on legislative and executive duties.

Jacob, Charles E., ed., *Policy and Bureaucracy* (New York: Van Nostrand-Reinhold Books, 1965). Description of policy formulation in administration.

March, James G., and Herbert A. Simon, *Organizations* (New York: John Wiley and Sons, Inc., 1958). Study of the theory of organizations.

Millett, John D., *Government and Public Administration* (New York: McGraw-Hill Book Co., 1959). Study of the problem of the controlling of bureaucracy in order to achieve higher standards of performance.

Mosher, Frederick C., *Democracy and the Public Service* (New York: Oxford University Press, Inc., 1968). Study of the relationship between democracy and administration and an attempt to reconcile the requirements of the democratic and administrative states.

Parkinson, C. Northcote, *Parkinson's Law* (Boston: Houghton Mifflin Co., 1957). Partly humorous, partly serious theory of bureaucratic expansion.

Powell, Norman J., *Responsible Public Bureaucracy in the United States* (Boston: Allyn & Bacon, Inc., 1967). Study of the growth, power, and control of American bureaucracy.

Presthus, Robert, *Organizational Society* (New York: Random House, Inc., 1962). Political, psychological, and sociological analysis of large oragnizations and their influence on the individuals who work within them.

Redford, Emmette S., *Ideal and Practice in Public Administration* (University, Ala.: University of Alabama Press, 1958). Study of the environment and values of the administrator.

Redford, Emmette S., *Democracy in the Administrative State*, ed. by Roscoe C. Martin (New York: Oxford University Press, Inc., 1969). Discussion of the practicality of democracy in modern society, which requires a strong executive branch of government.

Rourke, Francis E., *Bureaucracy, Politics, and the Public Policy* (Boston: Little, Brown and Co., 1969). Analysis of bureaucrat's role in formulating public policy and the politics involved in this role.

Rourke, Francis E., ed., *Bureaucratic Power in National Politics* (Boston: Little, Brown and Co., 1965). Readings on the power of bureaucrats, the strategies by which they maintain power, and the forces that control their use of power.

Seidman, Harold, *Politics, Position, and Power: The Dynamics of Federal Organization* (New York: Oxford University Press, Inc., 1970). Analysis of the factors that influence the structures and functioning of the national administrative organization, as seen by the Bureau of the Budget.

Simon, Herbert A., *Administrative Behavior*, 2nd ed. (New York: The Free Press, 1957). Classic analysis of decision making within the bureaucracy.

Stanley, David T., *Changing Administrations: The 1961 and 1964 Transitions in Six Departments* (Washington, D.C.: Brookings Institution, 1965). Study of bureaucratic continuity and change during two important transition administrations.

Townsend, Robert, *Up the Organization* (New York: Alfred A. Knopf, Inc., 1970). Serious analysis of large corporations and the problems of organization and distribution of power.

Tullock, Gordon, *The Politics of Bureaucracy* (Washington, D.C.: Public Affairs Press, 1965). Analysis of political relationships within a bureaucracy.

Wildavsky, Aaron B., *The Politics of the Budgetary Process* (Boston: Little, Brown and Co., 1964). Description of budget formulation in the political process, emphasizing the strategies of the participants.

Woll, Peter, *American Bureaucracy* (New York: W. W. Norton and Co., Inc., 1963). Study of the impact of bureaucratic growth on the delegation of powers and responsibilities in the federal system.

# Topics of further study

Craft, James P., "Public Employee Negotiations Legislation: The Paradox of Labor Divided," *Quarterly Review of Economics and Business*, Winter 1969, pp. 29–37.

Henderson, Keith M., *Emerging Synthesis in American Public Administration* (New York: Asia Publishers, 1966).

# 17 the judges

## guardians
## of
## the law

THE QUALITY of justice depends in large measure on the work of the courts.
In the operation of democratic government, law is binding on both the
governed and those who govern. "My freedom to swing my arm,"
Justice Holmes once remarked, "stops where the other man's nose begins."
It is unrealistic to expect, at least to this point in the history of mankind,
that individual men generally could settle their own serious differences
without the aid of an objective and disinterested third party. It is this third
party function that our courts attempt to fulfill.

The major objective of the judiciary in our society, then, is to adjudicate
disputes—that is, to serve as an impartial tribunal for the peaceful
adjustment and resolution of conflicting claims. The courts operate within
the context of social dynamics and change; laws are formulated or repealed
and traditions are created or discarded. The judiciary must endeavor to
transcend immediate social and political currents, striving always for
objectivity and impartiality in adjusting the conflicting claims of the
members of the society.

The existence of a court system presupposes that conflict will arise
naturally in a democratic society—whether it be between private citizens or
between government and the governed. The function of the courts is to
determine the facts of the case and then to apply the correct legal
principle to that particular case, and thereby achieve a resolution of
the conflict.

# The law

Before we can discuss the courts and the system under which they operate, we must explain the subject of their work, the law, and the kind of laws that comprise the American judicial system.

We are born and we die under the umbrella of rules and regulations. From our first contact with the state's compulsory education law—through our contact with the policeman who tells us that we were speeding and to the making of our last will and testament—we are in constant contact with the laws of government.

In the study of government, we are concerned with the laws that regulate behavior within the political system. Law, then, for our purposes, may be defined as the *principles and regulations established by a government, applicable to a people, and enforced by judicial decision.*

American law can be divided into specific types: common law, equity, statutory law, constitutional law, and administrative law.

## Common law

*Common law,* often called "judge-made" law, is an accumulation of judicial precedents. The history of common law harks back to legal practice in twelfth-century Britain. Designated officials were empowered by the king to circulate about the country and adjudicate local disputes. Their decisions were based initially upon common sense and custom in relation to the conditions of the case; but the various decisions of the judges grew ultimately into a body of judicial rulings that constituted common law.

With the establishment of British colonies in the New World, American common law evolved, adding its own body of "bench-made" decisions to those of the English common law. Judicial practice in every state, with the exception of Louisiana, now is guided by common law.[1]

When a judge is confronted with a case for which there is no statutory legislative law, but for which there are similar cases in common law, he may choose to apply the principle of *stare decisis.* The term literally means "let the decision stand," and involves a reference to the previous common law cases of the state for a judicial principle applicable to the case at hand. If the cases are sufficiently similar to warrant a similar decision, he allows the rule of precedent, *stare decisis,* to determine judgment of the case.

The major drawback to common law, however, is that in no case does it provide measures to deter an action. In other words, a case comes to court only after the act has been committed. If an individual knows in advance that an offense will be perpetrated against him, he can seek no remedy under common law until after it has been committed. For this reason, another type of law—equity—was developed.

[1] Louisiana has a civil law system, based more on legal statutes than on judicial precedents. The origins of this system are to be found in French law.

## Equity

2 Henry J. Abraham, *The Judicial Process* (New York: Oxford University Press, Inc., 1968), p. 17.

*Equity*, which evolved as a result of the inability of English common law to avert an illegal act, may be properly said to have begun "where the law ended."[2] Frustrated by the limitations of common law, citizens in England directed cases toward one of the king's officers, the chancellor, for help in preventing an illegal deed from occurring. For example, assume that A owned a plot of land upon which he was carefully nurturing his favorite type of tree, and he became aware that B was planning to construct a path which would involve eliminating his tree. Under common law, A could only wait until the act occurred before bringing B to court for the damages done. But, with the king's chancellor taking a role in preventative action, the chancellor's office itself developed into a separate type of court—an equity court—with a separate body of legal codes. Like common law, equity was based on rules made from prior judicial decisions.

One of the major weapons to effect equity law is the *injunction*, a court order requiring the person or persons to whom it is directed to perform a particular act, or to refrain from doing a particular act. A writ of injunction can thereby prohibit an action that threatens or has begun harm to the complainant seeking protection under equity law. If the writ is violated, the offender can be punished for contempt of court.

Today, in the United States, there are no separate federal courts of equity; the regular federal courts handle equity matters. However, a few state court systems do maintain separate equity courts (chancery courts). Whatever the arrangement, equity can avert potentially harmful acts, thereby performing a vital role in our legal system.

## Additional categories of law

*Statutory law*, a third type, differs from both common and equity law. A statute is a law made by a legislature. The fact that it is formally declared by a legislative body differentiates it from "judge-made" or common law. The tendency in the twentieth century has been toward more statutory law and less common law; much of what was originally common law has been converted to statutory law.

Statutory law allows the judges a great degree of latitude. The laws are formulated in general terms. Their interpretation and application to specific cases is an important function of the judiciary.

*Constitutional law* is yet another form of American law. It consists of the body of statements from lower federal courts and, most important, by the Supreme Court interpreting specific provisions of the Constitution. The American Constitution is a relatively brief and succinct document of some six thousand words. Because many provisions are general, and their meaning often ambiguous, clarification is necessary in order to apply them. The Supreme Court, through its decisions, defines the Constitution. The meaning of the Constitution is, therefore, to a great degree, the interpretation that the Supreme

Court of the United States has given to it. For example, in the First Amendment to the Constitution is the phrase "Congress shall make no law respecting an establishment of religion," applicable to prayers in public schools? Does it allow government to spend money for the construction of religious schools? The Constitution does not specify the meaning of this and other terms.

*Administrative law* includes the regulatory orders enacted by the government administrative agencies, such as the Securities and Exchange Commission, or the Interstate Commerce Commission. It is largely a twentieth-century product and is of importance in the economic life of the United States. The rulings of administrative agencies are now codified by the federal government. Cases involving application of the administrative law of our federal government are decided by administrative agencies and are reviewable by the federal courts.

## Stare decisis

The principle of *stare decisis*, explained in relation to common law, applies also to statutory, constitutional, and administrative law. Reliance on precedent, however, is not a compulsory practice that a judge must follow in all cases. He may simply ignore precedent by noting even the slightest difference between the case at hand and the earlier case, or he may choose specifically to overturn the precedent. The principle of *stare decisis* in the United States does not mean that legal principles reign supreme for all times. A wise judge is aware of the necessity for adopting judicial rulings to the demands and conditions of social change.

## Criminal and civil law

Law may also be categorized according to the type of case to which it applies. There are two broad categories: criminal and civil. *Criminal law*, which is statutory law, deals with acts or deeds jeopardizing the public welfare or order. It is enforced by the government. Therefore, in criminal cases, the government is always the original *plaintiff* (the party that brings the suit into the court), and the accused is the *defendant*. Breaches of criminal law can vary from the *misdemeanor*, a minor crime such as prostitution, to a *felony*, such as armed robbery, a much more serious offense. Conviction of a felony can result in a prison term, heavy fine, or both. Some crimes are federal in nature—violation of national tax laws, for example—and others, such as perjury, are defined by state laws. Still others—such as bank robbery or drug abuse—can be a violation of both federal and state law.

*Civil law* deals with cases involving conflicts between individuals (or corporations) and clarifies the rights of the parties in dispute. A suit for divorce, for example, is a civil case; or the illegal use of a trademark or material protected by copyright would be settled according to the applicable principles of civil law. Even though civil law cases involve individuals more often than not, the government may also be involved, either as the defendant or the plaintiff. The Sherman Antitrust Act, for instance, empowers the government to bring both civil and criminal charges against a corporation that enters into a "contract, combination, or conspiracy in restraint of trade."

# The adversary process

Courts are not active institutions that reach out for disputes to resolve. They must wait for cases to be brought to them before they can exercise their authority. Unlike the executive and legislative branches of government, the judiciary is largely passive. If a law is unconstitutional, nothing can be done about it by the courts until a case is brought before them. The courts cannot "initiate policy actions. Rather, they must wait until a case that raises the question they would like to settle is brought before them."[3]

[3] Herbert Jacob, *Justice in America* (Boston: Little, Brown and Co., 1965), p. 5.

When a case is brought to the court, it takes the form of a conflict of two parties. The court itself is considered to be an impartial observer witnessing the struggle between the government and a citizen, or between two citizens involved in a legal battle. In this process of presenting adverse interests, each party vies to win the favorable decision of the court. For this reason, the American judicial procedure has been described as an *adversary process.*

The courts, as required by Article III of the Constitution, thus hear only "cases and controversies," that is, instances involving real conflicts of interest between the parties to a dispute. In *Muskrat* v. *United States* (1911), the Supreme Court unanimously upheld this provision. The case involved an appeal by the Cherokee Indians who maintained that their constitutional property rights had been violated by a congressional law that redistributed Cherokee lands. The Court refused to hear the appeal on the grounds that the issues were not within the Court's jurisdiction as defined by "cases and controversies." Justice Day, in delivering the opinion of the Court, declared: "by the express terms of the Constitution, the exercise of the judicial power is limited to 'cases' and 'controversies.' . . . The term implies the existence of present or possible adverse parties, whose contentions are submitted to the court for adjudication. . . . It is true the United States is made a defendant to this action, but it has no interest adverse to the claimants."[4] The Court maintained that they lacked the constitutional authority to consider the case.

[4] *Muskrat* v. *United States* 219 U.S. 346 (1911).

Also, American federal courts, because of the case and controversy requirement, will not give advisory opinions. Congress, before it passes a law, or the President, before he issues an executive order, cannot seek an opinion from the Supreme Court on the act's constitutionality; the law must be passed or the order issued before the Court will consider the matter. In addition, there must be a legitimate dispute on the legality of the act.

## Judges and lawmaking

The "principles and regulations" that are enforced by judicial decision cannot be tailored exactly by the lawmaking bodies to the particularities and peculiarities of each situation that may arise regarding them. Thus, laws are often general, while cases involve specific applications. Many people view the judge as someone similar to an umpire: he applies the given law to the given situation as an umpire would declare whether a batted ball is fair or foul by carefully observing on which side of the white line it happens to drop. However, the role of the judge is not so clearly delineated. He often meets with situations in court that require interpretation of a law in order to apply it to a particular situation. This role of interpreter exists throughout all levels of the judicial hierarchy, whether it be a local judge defining what is meant by "automotive negligence," or the Supreme Court justices clarifying the constitutional concept of "freedom of assembly."

It is not surprising, therefore, that the judicial power to interpret and apply statutes to particular cases is considered by many to be lawmaking. Because of the ambiguity of the law, judges do not mechanically state the law that applies to a particular case. If that were so, the outcome would be preordained and judicial action would be entirely predictable. Judges, therefore, in interpreting and applying a law, actually possess a degree of choice. Some criticize this element of freedom as judicial lawmaking—a violation of separation of powers.

On the other hand, however, the choice open to judges inevitably raises the question of whether or not a given judge can be impartial in all situations. In each case, the individual before the court is, for the moment at least, pending possible appeals of his case, at the mercy of the presiding judge (and the jury, if it is at a trial level), all of whom are by no means equal in judicial capacity. "When a lawyer becomes a judge," states Howard James, "he does not simply shed his old opinions and wiggle into a robe of objectivity. Instead, he brings with him a viewpoint developed by his experiences. These include such influences as his economic, religious, and ethnic background."[5]

[5] Howard James, *Crisis in the Courts* (New York: David McKay Co., 1971), p. 9.

## Who becomes a federal judge

Although, today, all our federal judges have had legal backgrounds before coming to the bench, there are, in fact, no constitutional or statutory requirements that a federal judge be a lawyer or even have experience in the law. All federal judges are appointed by the President, with the consent of the Senate; the President usually bases his appointments on such factors as prior experience, geography, religion, and general political orientation. The Constitution requires presidential appointment for Supreme Court appointments only, but the Judiciary Act of 1789 extended it to apply to all federal judgeships. The process of selection is a fairly complex one, involving not only the constitutionally required President and Senate, but also the Attorney General, the Federal Bureau of Investigation, the American Bar Association, and party politics. The presidential nominee will usually be, first of all, a member of the President's party, or at least will share his political points of view. This is so for two reasons: 1. because the federal judiciary is an extension of the President's political influence insofar as the judges are "makers" of the law; and 2. because judgeships are commonly, although not always, a political reward for individuals who have supported the party in power in the White House.

Drawing by Pebin; © 1970 the Philadelphia Inquirer.

"Courage, judge! We feel humble too, by now . . ."

When there is a vacancy, particularly in federal district courts, the Attorney General's office will present the President with a list of possible appointees drawn from names submitted by the senior senator from the state in which the appointment is to be made, if that senator is a member of the President's political party. The unwritten rule of senatorial courtesy (discussed in Chapter 12) provides that if the senator declares a nominee to be personally "obnoxious" to him (he need give no other reason than that), the rest of the Senate will vote against the appointment. If neither senator from the state in which the appointment is to be made is a member of the President's party, then the President ordinarily will not consider the senator's preferences regarding a nominee, and is free to make his own selection.

*Joel B. Grossman,* "Social Backgrounds and Judicial Decision-Making," *Harvard Law Review,* 79 (1966): 1551–1564.

Joel Grossman writes that premises for judicial action are not solely related to the courtroom; every judge carries with him into his magistrate career his own personal values and attitudes. Grossman has presented and evaluated the findings of six studies in this area (by Stuart S. Nagel, John R. Schmidhauser, Sheldon Goldman, John D. Sprague, David J. Danelski, and Don R. Bowen) in order to determine to what extent these prejudicial attitudes and values affect judicial decisions. All the studies utilized similar techniques and are based on the same criterion—for example, judicial behavior in the form of votes. In addition, they accept the usefulness of isolating variables for evaluation, while still considering institutional factors. They reject absolute relationships between cause and effect that would imply that background characteristics account for all types of decisions.

Rather, they argue that evidence of a highly significant statistical relationship between a background variable and a decisional pattern is both relative and associational.

Each of the studies concentrated on a different area. Nagel, clarifying fifteen areas of law, concluded that:

In these areas of decision, Democratic judges were *more likely than* Republican judges to support the designated liberal position.

Schmidhauser, focusing on Supreme Court justices, distinguished regional voting patterns, and hypothesized that extreme decisions on regionally divisive issues were reinforced by party and sectional background, and moderate judges were influenced more by party than by regionalism. In another study, Schmidhauser discovered that those judges with experience on lower courts were more likely to abandon stare decisis. Dissenting judges were found to be traditionalists, rather than innovators.

Goldman studied all nonunanimous decisions of the United States Court of Appeals between 1961 and 1964.

He found, like Nagel, that the Democratic judges had significantly higher liberalism scores in economic cases; but he found no differences between Democrats and Republicans in criminal cases or general civil liberties categories. And he found that the marked differences Nagel noted between Catholic and Protestant judges—the former being more liberal—disappeared when party affiliation was controlled.

Sprague, unlike his colleagues, examined voting blocs on the Supreme Court, or groups of judges who consistently voted together, and he dealt only with cases involving federalism. His results seem to agree with Goldman's. He found that prior judicial experience was a better discriminator between blocs than any background variables.

In contrast to Nagel, he found that political party did not effectively discriminate between blocs except in the very limited area of property disputes.

Danelski's study, dealing with a single Supreme Court justice, Pierce Butler, differed from the other studies in the introduction of the intermediate variable of values between the judge's background characteristics and his eventual voting behavior. He attributed the values of morality, patriotism, and *laissez-faire* championship to Butler, painting him as a man who saw only "black and white" and who refused to sacrifice principle for expediency.

Relating these values to Butler's work on the Supreme Court, Danelski finds significant areas of agreement or correlation, with the exception that Butler proved much more sensitive to procedural *due process* claims—than his prior speeches and activities would have indicated.

It is Bowen who, in his study of state and appellate judges, considered the overall problem: how often does the relationship between background characteristics and voting behavior account for "the variance in judicial vote patterns?"

Bowen found that none of the variables most significantly "associated" with judicial decisions explained more than a fraction of the total variance among judges. No single variable accounted for more than 16 per cent of the variance in any particular area, and most were in the 1 to 8 per cent range.

Bowen concludes that background alone does not determine judicial behavior. "Intervening variables"—such as the traditions of courts, the interactions of forceful and intelligent individuals, and complex intellectual and motivational factors—also affect behavior.

In assessing the cumulative findings of all six experts, Grossman concludes:

There is no doubt that preliminary attempts to isolate particular background variables have initially and necessarily overlooked the essentially cumulative and often random nature of human experience, as well as slighting the impact of institutional influences on the judicial mind.

Since the Eisenhower administration, a more powerful role in nominations has been played by the *Committee on the Federal Judiciary*, a twelve-member committee of the American Bar Association, which considers itself particularly qualified to give an opinion in that it represents the nation's largest and most influential organization of lawyers. Although the committee has no formal veto power in the selection process, it can rate the nominees as to their qualifications on a scale running from "Not Qualified" to "Exceptionally Well Qualified," and the President, although he is not bound by the committee's views, will usually take that evaluation into consideration. Once the list has become made up, the Attorney General's office will instruct the Federal Bureau of Investigation to look into the backgrounds of the potential nominees in order to bring to light anything that might disqualify them for the appointment. The investigation also serves to save the President the embarrassment of a damaging revelation of such information after he has nominated an individual.

Traditionally, the President has a broader freedom of choice when the nomination concerns a circuit court judge or a member of the Supreme Court. Since these nominations involve no particular state, he need not seek favorable names from any senators. Presidents also consider other factors when considering a judicial nomination—factors such as age, religion, geographic area, political views, ethnic background, judicial experience, and philosophy. For example, President Nixon's appointment of Warren E. Burger as Chief Justice was based on his desire to add "strict constructionists" to the Court.

All presidential appointments to the federal courts require the consent of a majority in the United States Senate. The Senate usually gives its consent, but on occasion has refused to confirm a President's nominee to the Supreme Court. Only twenty-four times in the history of the Senate have nominees been rejected. The reasons were usually political. For example, in the 1850s when regional hostilities were surging, the Senate would not confirm the southerners nominated by President Fillmore. Senate consent was also withheld from President Grant's nomination of Attorney General Ebenezer Hoar, who had antagonized senators by ignoring senatorial courtesy. During the late 1950s and 1960s, the southern senators held long hearings on presidential nominations to the Supreme Court, thereby delaying confirmation. President Nixon's attempts to appoint Clement Haynesworth and G. Harrold Carswell to the Court were successfully blocked by the ninety-first Congress.

A federal judge's appointment is for life, or, according to the Constitution and the Judiciary Act of 1789, during "good behavior." A federal judge can be removed by impeachment for such offenses as treason or bribery, but impeachment is rare. The major shortcoming of a lifetime appointment is that the judges may lose some of their acuity because of old age and ill health. However, many of our greatest judges—John Marshall, Louis Brandeis, and Hugo Black, for example—had served well into their eighties, marshaling the knowledge accumulated from years of judicial experience.

## Service of Supreme Court Justices

| | |
|---|---|
| Less than 5 years | 12 |
| 5–9 years | 24 |
| 10–19 years | 29 |
| 20–29 years | 19 |
| 30 years and over | 8 |

Note: This list does not take into account the justices currently serving on the Supreme Court.

*Alexander Hamilton,* The Federalist Papers, *ed. by Clinton Rossiter (New York: The New American Library, 1961), Paper No. 78, pp. 464–472.*

Alexander Hamilton, writing in defense of the Constitution in essay No. 78, directs his attention to the tenure of federal judges, especially Supreme Court justices. Hamilton begins by noting that, by 1788, tenure "during good behavior" either had been adopted by or approved at the state level.

The standard of good behavior for the continuance in office of the judicial magistracy is certainly one of the most valuable of the modern improvements in the practice of government. In a monarchy it is an excellent barrier to the despotism of the prince; in a republic it is a no less excellent barrier to the encroachments and oppressions of the representative body. And it is the best expedient which can be devised in any government to secure a steady upright, and impartial administration of the laws.

Hamilton noted that since the judiciary holds only the power of judgment, it will always be "least dangerous to the political rights of the Constitution." Thus, the people should recognize the advantages of life tenure: First, to insure the permanence of the judiciary as an independent branch, permanency in office is considered "indispensable." Second, the appointment or election of judges for temporary periods of time would inevitably detract from "that inflexible and uniform adherence to the rights of the Constitution, and of individuals."

If the power of making temporary appointments was committed either to the executive or legislature there would be danger of an improper complaisance to the branch which possessed it; if to both, there would be an unwillingness to hazard the displeasure of either; if to the people, or to persons chosen by them for the special purpose, there would be too great a disposition to consult popularity to justify a reliance that nothing would be consulted but the constitution and the laws.

Third, Hamilton contends that judges are compelled to learn a "voluminous (and evergrowing) code of laws," one that delineates strict rules and precedents for "every particular case"—"a very considerable bulk." Certainly, "long and laborious study" is necessary for its mastery.

Hence it is that there can be but few men in the society who will have sufficient skill in the laws to qualify them for the station of judges. And making the proper deductions for the ordinary depravity of human nature, the number must be still smaller of those who unite the requisite integrity with the requisite knowledge. These considerations apprise us that the government can have no great option between fit characters; and that a temporary duration in office which would naturally discourage such characters from quitting a lucrative line of practice to accept a seat on the bench would have a tendency to throw the administration of justice into hands less able and less well qualified to conduct it with utility and dignity.

The last and most significant of Hamilton's arguments—the argument for the independence of the courts—is, in actuality, the first major argument for judicial review. Because the Constitution is simply a document specifying limitations on the legislative branch of government, Hamilton felt that a strong court system would be necessary for the preservation of these limitations. This, however, does not mean that the courts are to be considered superior to the legislature, but rather that the legislature alone cannot interpret the extentions or limitations on its power as provided by the "fundamental law," the Constitution. The courts, as intermediaries between the legislature and the people, should interpret this fundamental law in relation to legislative action.

If, then, the courts of justice are to be considered as the bulwarks of a limited Constitution against legislative encroachments, this consideration will afford a strong argument for the permanent tenure of judicial offices, since nothing will contribute so much as this to that independent spirit in the judges which must be essential to the faithful performance of so arduous a duty.

# The dual court system

The United States has a dual system of courts—federal and state. Each system has its own hierarchy of organization. This dual system, which reflects the federal nature of our governmental system, sometimes creates confusion and complexity in the courts. In certain areas, the state courts have exclusive jurisdiction (the power to hear a case). In other situations, the federal courts may have exclusive jurisdiction. In still other cases, both state and federal courts have jurisdiction.

Under this dual system, it is possible for an individual to violate simultaneously the federal and the state criminal laws. A kidnapper, for example, who takes his victim across state boundaries, violates both a state and a federal law, and may be prosecuted in either the state or federal courts, sometimes depending on whether it is federal or state officials who capture him. He can be legally prosecuted in both courts, for he has committed, in effect, two crimes—one in violation of state law and the other in violation of federal law.

The primary source of the division of jurisdiction between federal and state courts is the Constitution (Article III, Section 2), which gives the federal courts authority over cases involving national laws. This includes all cases in law and equity arising under the Constitution and the laws and treaties of the federal government; all cases involving ambassadors, other foreign ministers and consuls; all cases of admiralty and maritime jurisdiction; and controversies to which the United States shall be a party. The Constitution also gives federal courts jurisdiction over disputes that go beyond state boundaries. This includes controversies between two or more states; controversies between a state and citizens of another state, wherein, according to the Eleventh Amendment, the state initiates court action; controversies between citizens of different states; controversies between citizens of the same state claiming lands under grants of different states, and cases involving a state or a citizen of a state and a foreign state or a citizen thereof.

A legal dispute must fall within one of these areas, in order to be considered in federal court. But jurisdiction in these areas is not absolutely required by the Constitution; Congress can limit this potential federal jurisdiction. For example, in cases between citizens of different states, Congress has fixed in law that the dispute must involve a sum above $10,000. Cases involving lesser amounts must be heard in the state courts.

The Constitution and practice have established the Supreme Court as the highest and final authority in cases involving federal law, treaties, and the national Constitution. In cases affecting ambassadors, other foreign agents and consuls, and those in which a state is a party, the Constitution specifically assigns the Supreme Court *original jurisdiction*. (The Supreme Court sits as a trial court and determines the facts as well as the law.) In all other cases, the Supreme Court exercises *appellate jurisdiction* (review of a case that has already been decided by a lower court). The United States Supreme Court accepts only a small percentage of all the cases in which appeals are made.

Appeals generally go from a federal-district court to a United States court of appeals and then to the Supreme Court—or directly from the highest state court having jurisdiction over the case to the Supreme Court, if the case deals with a matter arising under the national Constitution, a treaty, or congressional law.

The enormous power of the United States Supreme Court, then, is self-evident. At the top of the judicial hierarchy, it is the final authority on constitutional questions; and what the Constitution says—or more precisely, what it is interpreted to say—is the backbone of the American federal system, the ultimate circumscription of the valid spheres of activity within which the federal and state governments must operate and of the extent of freedom possessed by individual citizens.

The power of the Supreme Court is, however, not absolute; its appellate jurisdiction, like that of all federal courts, is subject to alteration by Congress. In other words, Congress is given the power to define the jurisdiction of the Supreme Court, as well as of the lower federal courts, for those few items fixed by the Constitution. It may assign those powers to the other federal courts alone, to the state courts solely, or to the state and federal courts concurrently.

# The structure of the state court system

The court systems of the different states are arranged in a hierarchical fashion. The lowest rung on the ladder is occupied in some states by the justice of the peace, but more frequently by county or municipal courts. (Large cities frequently have a different type of court organization.) Above these may be the state district or circuit courts and, then, two levels of appellate courts. The higher of these two courts is generally the supreme court of the state, which exercises final jurisdiction on cases that cannot be appealed to the Supreme Court of the United States.

There has been some attempt toward centralizing the somewhat loosely structured court systems. In some cities, municipal courts have been established to replace the random assemblage of lower local courts, such as that of the justice of the peace (or magistrate). A number of states have adopted New Jersey's system, which empowers the chief justice of the state supreme court to reassign judges to courts that have a heavy backlog of cases.

Although some critics claim that the state court system, because of the delays and confusion that occur, is "suited better to the horse and buggy past than to the contemporary space age,"[6] it is within this system that most legal disputes are settled in America today.

[6] Jacob, *Justice in America*, p. 131.

# The structure of the federal court system

The federal court system consists of three levels of courts, the highest of which is the Supreme Court of the United States. The Supreme Court is the only court specifically established by the Constitution, but Article III, Section 1, extends judicial power to "such inferior courts" as the Congress may from time to time ordain and establish. Exercising this constitutional power in a series of judiciary acts, beginning with the Judiciary Act of 1789, Congress has fashioned a system that consists of over one hundred courts throughout the land. This federal court system is made up of district courts, appeals courts, and a number of special courts.

*District* courts, established in 1789, are the trial courts of the federal system. Within a given district, there may be as many as twenty judges or more, each hearing a separate case.

Congress has divided the fifty states, Washington, D.C., and the Territory of Puerto Rico into ninety-three districts, with over three hundred district judges, thus giving some states more than one such court (New York, for example, has four). Congress has required that no district cross state boundaries.

The district courts have *original* jurisdiction only, and hear cases only as trial courts. It is in the district courts that all criminal cases are begun by the government and all civil disputes within federal jurisdiction are initiated.

Appointed by the President to each district court is a United States *marshall* and his deputies, whose functions include moderate law enforcement activities, such as halting unruly conduct in the courtroom or enacting an order for arrest. The staffs of the district courts also include United States magistrates, probation officers, and bailiffs.

The district courts are the only federal courts to make use of juries, of which there are two types; grand and regular (petit or petty). A *grand jury* is empowered to hear the evidence against the individual concerned and, if the evidence warrants it, to *indict* and *arraign* that individual, bringing a formal accusation of guilt against him. The *regular* or *petty jury*, which is the trial jury, will then be convened to consider the facts.

## United States Circuit Courts of Appeals

While the district courts are exclusively trial courts, the *United States Circuit Courts of Appeals* are solely appellate courts. An 1891 act of Congress created a system which today encompasses eleven circuits and ninety-five judges for the fifty states and the District of Columbia. A court of appeals is empowered to hear appeals from the district courts within its circuit and also to review the decisions of administrative tribunals (government commissions performing judicial functions). The judges of the courts of appeals, like those of the district courts, are appointed for life by the President, with the Senate's consent.

A United States Court of Appeals consists of from three to nine judges —depending on the size of the particular circuit—who generally sit in panels of three on a case. The attorneys for the disputants in the suit appear before the judges with *briefs* (written arguments submitted to the court), and are allowed a limited time for oral argument of their cases. The judges, after hearing the arguments and studying the briefs, confer privately before announcing their decision.

A court of appeals does not decide which cases it will review and which it will not. According to federal law, every individual involved in litigation has the right to at least one appeal in his case. Thus while the Supreme Court has wide discretion in its choice of granting appeals, the courts of appeals have little.

## Specialized courts

Congress has also established, for certain special types of cases, various special courts: a court of claims, a customs court, a court of customs and patent appeals, and the United States Court of Military Appeals.

The *court of claims* sits as a trial court in cases brought against the federal government for tax and contract claims. It has seven judges, and is located in Washington, D.C. The *customs court*, composed of nine judges, is empowered to hear appeals from decisions of customs collectors involving import duties and the evaluation of imported goods. The *court of customs and patent appeals*, with five judges, reviews decisions of the customs court and the United States Patent Office. Appeals from decisions of this court can be taken to the United States Supreme Court.

The *United States Court of Military Appeals* hears appeals dealing with the interpretation of military law and, in this area, is the highest court of appeals. Presiding are three civilian judges serving overlapping terms of fifteen years. The President, with Senate confirmation, designates the judges, who consider all cases involving the death penalty for a member of the armed forces and all cases involving high-level military personnel. It has power, also, if it sees fit and if it is petitioned by the defendant, to review certain cases appealed by members of the armed forces.

# Lower courts in operation

In the administration of justice, the work of the lower courts is of vital importance to the life, liberty, and property of citizens seeking protection under the law.

## Trial courts

Federal district courts and many state courts of original jurisdiction are trial courts and hear cases in both civil and criminal cases. The right to trial by jury in criminal cases is guaranteed by the Sixth Amendment to the Constitution; but that right can be waived by the individual before the bench, if he so wishes. The Constitution does not, however, guarantee trial by jury in all civil cases, and certain states sometimes limit the right to a jury trial in civil disputes.

Procedure in the trial courts is prescribed by law. In civil cases, the initiator of the suit first files a complaint explaining the injustices or injuries to which he feels himself subjected. The accused is ordered by the court to reply. After these preliminaries, the case comes before the court, which may or may not have a jury. Now the adversary process, discussed earlier, is apparent as the lawyers for the contending parties substantiate conflicting positions. If the trial is by jury, it is the judge's function to clarify the laws involved and inform the jury. More often than not, however, the trial is by judge alone.

Criminal cases employ a type of trial early in the legal process. Following the arrest of the individual, a hearing is usually held; if there appears to be ground for legal action, the suspect is indicted and *arraigned* (informed of the terms of the indictment and asked to respond with his pleas). While awaiting trial, the subject may be released temporarily through bail (money provided for the release of a prisoner and guaranteeing his appearance at the proper time).

## The jury

The grand or indicting jury consists of from twelve to twenty-three people chosen from the population at large, while the regular or trial jury usually consists of twelve citizens. (In states where grand juries have been eliminated, a *bill of information*—whereby the public prosecutor simply presents his evidence to a court of original jurisdiction—is used.) The grand jury determines whether or not an indictment is warranted; the trial jury assesses the information presented in court and then passes judgment. In some states, the decision of the trial jury must be unanimous; in others, two-thirds or three-quarters is sufficient.

*Howard James*, Crisis in the Courts (*New York: David McKay Co., Inc., 1971*), Chap. XIV, *pp. 191–205.*

Howard James describes our system of trial by jury as the particular segment of our judicial system that belongs distinctly to the people. A jury, composed of twelve men or women of differing backgrounds and interests, is more likely to give an objective, fair opinion than is one man. A judge has only his own experience of legal expertise on which to rely.

Says Jacob D. Fuchsberg, former president of the American Trial Lawyers Association, a member of the President's Commission on Civil Rights and on the legal services advisory board of the Office of Economic Opportunity:

"Judges have no monopoly on intelligence, insight, or fairness. They are ordinary human beings like anyone else. I believe the opinions of 12 people are better than the opinions of one—and I don't care whether they are 12 lawyers, 12 judges, or 12 laymen."

James argues that juries may be freer of political pressure than is a judge. In metropolitan areas, for example, where local judges are appointed by the mayor, the judge may be subjected to a conflict of interests; he owes his position to a city official, but one-fourth of his cases are directed against the city government.

James further points out that juries tend to be more humane than judges. Not bound by "the letter of the law," as a judge is, it can, so to speak, "bend the law."

Although the jury system has these advantages, critics argue that its disadvantages result in greater threats to public justice. Among the problems are the lengthiness of jury trials (and the resulting delays incurred), plus the high cost of such trials. As James has noted,

In Philadelphia and in a number of other cities I visited it can take days and even weeks to select a jury. This is especially true where a criminal case has made headlines for several days running. Or when the prosecutor intends to ask for the capital penalty and prospective jurors who oppose capital punishment are excused.

Other problems include the unfamiliarity of jurors with the law, and the lack of popular representation among jurors.

In some cases, for example, doctors, clergymen, teachers, justices of the peace, dentists, and government officials are exempted from jury duty.

In many instances, lawyers, when selecting a jury, will refuse to accept business executives or others holding responsible positions. And they reject jurors for other reasons that are not always explained—in a way that makes citizens feel that the system must be wrong.

What makes the twelve people who are finally chosen especially capable of deciding controversies? One critic has gone so far as to call the jurors a "group of twelve people of average ignorance."

Despite all the drawbacks of the jury system, juries and judges agree 80 percent of the time, and leading lawyers maintain that intelligent juries keep lawyers alert and competent.

**The judge**

When the jury is ready to deliberate, it does so in a locked room. It may take a second look at the evidence or it may ask the judge to clarify a legal question, but its deliberations are otherwise kept in the strictest of privacy.

The judge, that black-robed, silver-haired dignitary so often portrayed in the media, is the presiding figure in a court of law. Most judges are former lawyers with substantial legal experience. Many have had or plan to have political careers.

In the courtroom the judge's function is that of maintaining a legal atmosphere in which testimony and argument may be fairly presented according to accepted judicial procedures. The judge also instructs the jury in difficult points of law, discusses the alternative verdicts that the jury might reach, and, finally, pronounces a judgment on the case, a sentence on the accused.

*Herbert Jacob,* Justice in America *(Boston: Little, Brown and Co., 1965), pp. 123–127.*

Herbert Jacob contends that the mass media "encourages widespread vicarious participation in the judicial process." It does so by its extensive coverage of "spectacular criminal trials," as well as its weekly dramatizations of courtroom scenes on television.

This widespread coverage by the media is primarily a result of the American public's great interest in criminal proceedings. And because of the manner in which these trials are presented by the media, the public has developed a strong feeling of confidence in the judicial system.

The degree to which Americans are interested in criminal proceedings has not been exaggerated. In Wisconsin, 59 percent of all respondents in a statewide survey followed criminal news in the press or watched television courtroom dramas as often as once a week; only 19 percent did so rarely or never. These proportions varied little between city dwellers and county people, between one occupation group and another, between the rich and the poor. Nevertheless, the high degree of vicarious participation in court trials through media exposure had little or no effect on the respondent's view of the court system. Both those who were highly exposed and those who paid little attention in Wisconsin thought that the judicial process was fair; they both thought highly of judges, and both favored jury trials over judge trials.

While the media have been useful in inspiring public confidence in the courts, they have presented some problems for the effective operation of this system. For example, it is often difficult to obtain impartial jurors because of the common practice of broadcasting accusations, confessions, and evidence before a trial begins—as in the case of Charles

Manson's trial for the murder of six California residents. Jury selection may be further complicated by the media's biased exposure, as when 96 percent of all prospective jurors saw Jack Ruby murder Lee Harvey Oswald (President John Kennedy's alleged assassin) on television. As actual witnesses to the crime, almost every possible juror could be thought to be partial in this case.

The danger, then, of "contaminating" future jurors is high and, as long as the public craves press coverage, the fair selection of jurors will remain a difficult task.

The media, besides affecting selection of jurors, may also disrupt courtroom procedures (if allowed to be present). Thus, most states bar television cameramen and photographers from courtrooms. A few states, however, do not; and studies in Colorado have indicated that the effect of broadcasting has not been so harmful as anticipated.

A justice of the Colorado Supreme Court reported that in Colorado the experiment with televised trials had been entirely successful. Such evidence has reinforced the media's determination to gain entry into courtrooms. Most judges and lawyers, however, have continued to oppose their entrance.

The publicizing of trials was originally intended to be a means of making judges and juries accountable to the public. However, only a few cases have been subject even to media coverage. Even cases of the United States Supreme Court receive relatively little attention. Some claim, however, that the Supreme Court is affected by the media. These critics note that the Court assigns an opinion to a particular justice based on the positive press reception he will receive. "For instance, the generally conservative Justice Clark wrote the Court's opinion in 1963 declaring unconstitutional the reading of the Lord's Prayer or verses from the Bible as class devotionals."

Jacob concludes that the protection of individuals in our courts and the freedom of the press are two fundamental American values that often clash in the judicial process of our nation.

## Appellate courts

The fundamental question before an *appellate court* is whether the law has been properly applied in a lower court. An appellate court will not reverse the decision of a lower court unless it is determined that the lower court mishandled the case—by following improper procedures or by misconstruing the nature of the offense or the laws that apply to it, for example. Appellate courts generally use no juries. The decision is rendered by the judge or judges presiding over the court.

# The Supreme Court

The Supreme Court is the final interpreter of the law on all matters involving the application of the federal Constitution, federal laws, and treaties, whether the case began in a lower federal or in a state court.

## Current Supreme Court Justices

| | Age | State | Appointed | President |
|---|---|---|---|---|
| William Douglas | 73 | Connecticut | 1939 | Franklin Roosevelt |
| William Brennan, Jr. | 65 | New Jersey | 1956 | Eisenhower |
| Potter Stewart | 54 | Ohio | 1958 | Eisenhower |
| Byron White | 54 | Colorado | 1962 | Kennedy |
| Thurgood Marshall | 63 | New York | 1967 | Johnson |
| Warren Burger | 64 | Virginia | 1969 | Nixon |
| Harry Blackmun | 63 | Minnesota | 1970 | Nixon |

## The Supreme Court: setting and procedures

The business of the Supreme Court is carried out in a setting highly appropriate to the important role it plays in the governing of our nation. The court is held within a classic, white-pillared edifice, and a sumptuous and imposing interior, set off by red velvet drapery. Court proceedings begin at precisely 10:00 A.M. At that time, the justices emerge from the robing room where they have donned their regal dress and have, traditionally, exchanged handshakes. At their entrance, the room resounds with the knock of the gavel, the audience and all other individuals in the Court stand, and the traditional declaration is heard:

> The Honorable, the Chief Justice and Associate Justices of the Supreme Court of the United States, Oyez, Oyez! All persons having business before the Honorable, the Supreme Court of the United States are admonished to draw near and give their attention, for the Court is now sitting. God save the United States and this Honorable Court.

The Supreme Court is in session every Monday through Thursday from October through late June of each year. Fridays are reserved for conferences. The Court ordinarily hears cases for two weeks of each month and then retires for two weeks to consider, debate, and vote on the cases at hand. Its Court sessions on any given day are limited to four hours, so that, during the weeks when it is hearing cases, it does so for sixteen hours a week.

When the Supreme Court is sitting, it reserves Mondays and sometimes Tuesdays to announce recent decisions and opinions. For the remainder of the week the Court hears oral arguments of the cases before them. The litigants are represented before the Court by attorneys, who submit briefs of their cases in advance of their appearance so that the justices will have a chance to familiarize themselves with the cases before they actually come into Court. The briefs submitted to the Court are carefully written explanations of the cases, citing, in detail, legal precedent, pertinent history, and points of law.

In addition to the briefs submitted by the attorneys involved, *amicus curiae* briefs may also be submitted (see Chapter 9). It is a matter for the court to decide whether or not a brief from an *amicus curiae* is to be accepted. While appearing before the Court, the attorney for each litigant is limited to a specific time for oral argument. The time can be as little as twenty minutes and is usually limited to a maximum of one hour. In that time, he must plead his case before the nine imposing justices. Whatever the time limit set upon the attorney by the Court, it is strictly enforced, even to the point of stopping an argument in the middle of a sentence. A system of lights on the attorney's stand before the bench warns him when he has little time left, and signals him again when his time is up. If they have questions, the justices are allowed to interrupt the attorney whenever they feel the need, often to the chagrin of the attorney, who, depending on his self-possession and knowledge, or lack of it, may be thrown entirely off-balance by the question. Some justices are more gentle than others in questioning the attorney. Others, however, are less kind, and are more inclined to fire inquisitional broadsides at the man on the stand. Felix Frankfurter, an associate justice of the Court from 1939 to 1962, interrupted the arguments so often that the phrase "the Felix problem" came into being among those who had to argue cases before him.

## Oral arguments

"If you please, Mr. Justice, would you mind not saying, 'Of course, we could be wrong'?"

Drawing by Wren; © 1971 The New Yorker Magazine, Inc.

**Conferences**

After they have studied the briefs and heard the oral arguments for some of the pending cases, the justices retire for private conference on Fridays and during the alternate two-week conference periods. The conference is presided over by the Chief Justice, who sums up the important matter in each case under consideration and then asks the other justices, in order of their seniority, to give their opinions and conclusions. A vote is then taken in order of reverse seniority, the newest members of the Court voting first, so that the votes of the older members will not influence theirs. Each case is decided by majority vote, and one of the justices voting with the majority is assigned the important duty of writing the decision. The Chief Justice, if he votes with the majority, is the individual who either assigns the job of writing the majority opinion or writes the opinion himself; or, if the Chief Justice votes with the minority, the senior justice among the majority assigns the writing of the opinion.

**Opinions**

Opinion writing is a demanding and difficult task, because it requires the writer not only to declare the opinion of the Court, but to create a statement that will satisfy all the members of the Court who voted for that opinion. Often, one justice will come to the same decision as another, but for somewhat different reasons; in those cases, the writer of the opinion may have a subtle and troublesome job reconciling the differences.

Besides the majority opinion, two other types of opinions may be written: concurring and dissenting opinions. *Concurring opinions* are written when one of the justices who voted with the majority feels that the written majority opinion has not fully explained his own reasons for voting as he did. He may have voted with the majority, for example, but may have arrived at that conclusion through a different path of legal logic; and so, he may decide to write a concurring opinion.

A *dissenting opinion* is one written by a justice whose vote was in the minority. The justice or justices in the minority decide whether or not a dissenting opinion is to be written. These dissenting opinions are by no means simply an exercise in discontent. Though they may have no immediate effect, they are records for the future. In the oft-quoted words of former Chief Justice Hughes:

[7] C. E. Hughes, *The Supreme Court of the United States* (New York: Columbia University Press, 1928), p. 68.

> A dissent in a court of last resort is an appeal to the brooding spirit of the law, to the intelligence of a future day, when a later decision may possibly correct the error into which the dissenting judge believes the court to have been betrayed.[7]

When the opinion or opinions have been completed, they are printed and copies are distributed to the press. The written opinion is basically the means by which the Court communicates to the public, to members of the bar in general, and to the judiciary.

## The Chief Justice of the Supreme Court

Although the Chief Justice, like the other members of the Court, has only one vote, some of his extra power stems from his right, if he votes with the majority, to designate the opinion writer. Also, in his role as presiding justice in Court, and in his function of presenting the case to the members in conference, the Chief Justice may greatly influence the outcome of the proceedings. Ultimately, however, the power he will wield depends a great deal upon his personality. The position of Chief Justice does not ensure authority, but it offers a man who is respected by colleagues a forum to exercise far-reaching powers.

## Methods of bringing a case before the Supreme Court

The Constitution assigns the Supreme Court a very limited original jurisdiction. Of the categories under original jurisdiction, those that involve ambassadors and other public ministers are rare; and those to which a state is a party—such as a state boundary dispute—are limited in number by the Eleventh Amendment, which adds the provision that the state must be the plaintiff in the case.

Most cases heard by the Supreme Court fall within its appellate, rather than original, jurisdiction. In functioning as a court of appeals, the Supreme Court receives cases primarily in one of two ways: appeal or *certiorari*.

In particular types of controversies—for instance, when a special district court issues an injunction—*appeal*, according to congressional law, is a matter of right for the litigant. Cases involving questions of civil rights are frequently referred to the Supreme Court through this route. An appeal may also be made if a federal court declares a federal law or treaty unconstitutional, assuming that the national government is involved. Theoretically, the Supreme Court must hear appeals in all such cases; in fact, however, many of them are not considered by the High Court on the basis that they do not present an important enough federal question. Only 10 percent of the Supreme Court's case load is based on appeal.

A *writ of certiorari* is a writ issued by the Supreme Court directing a lower court to send up a case record for review. It is a discretionary writ, the means by which the Court can decide to hear those cases that it feels are important because they present "a substantial federal question." The appellant in a federal court of appeals, or in the highest state court having jurisdiction over the case, petitions the Supreme Court for the writ. The Court may then issue a writ, if four of the justices feel that the claim has sufficient merit. Every year, the Court reviews over two thousand of these petitions, and issues writs of *certiorari* in only about 10 percent of the cases. This number, however, represents almost 90 percent of the Court's work.

## Statutory interpretation

The two main functions of the Supreme Court are *statutory interpretation* (that is, determining meaning and intent of legislation) and *judicial review*, which is also a function of lower federal courts. Statutory interpretation makes up a significant part of the Court's work. The Court will, however, sometimes avoid questions of a constitutional nature, if they can be decided on grounds other than the Constitution. For example, in *Cole* v. *Young*,[8] the Court avoided declaring the Summary Suspension Act of 1950 unconstitutional. The Act had authorized, in the interests of national security, summary suspensions and unreviewable dismissals of disloyal federal employees by agency heads. Rather than raise the constitutional question of due process, the Supreme Court chose instead to interpret the statute. The Court held that the act did not authorize the government to fire employees as security risks if they were employed in "non-sensitive" areas. By deciding in this way, "the Court effects a gain . . . for individual civil rights while retaining the generally popular and politically desirable law" in the loyalty and security area of our government.[9]

[8] *Cole* v. *Young*, 351 U.S. 356 (1956).

[9] Abraham, *The Judicial Process*, p. 372.

## Judicial review

*Judicial review*—the power of a court to decide whether a legislative act, executive order, or other official act conflicts with the Constitution, and if so to declare it void—is an extraordinary power of the American judiciary. All courts possess the power of judicial review, but the Supreme Court is the final arbiter in matters of the national Constitution, treaties, and laws. The power of the Supreme Court specifically extends to acts of Congress and the President, state laws and acts of governors, and decisions of state courts. Review of state court decisons has been an instrument for insuring the supremacy of the national government.

The legal basis of the Supreme Court's power to review state court decisions is Article VI of the Constitution, which provides that the Constitution and federal statutes and treaties "shall be the supreme law of the land" and that "judges in every state shall be bound thereby, anything in the Constitution or laws of any State to the contrary notwithstanding."

The legal basis for judicial review of acts of Congress or the President was established by the Supreme Court decision in *Marbury* v. *Madison* (1803), which is described in detail in Chapter 4. Chief Justice Marshall declared Section 13 of the Federal Judiciary Act of 1789 unconstitutional, thereby setting the precedent for judicial review of national acts.

In his decision, Marshall used an argument similar to that presented by Alexander Hamilton in *The Federalist* No. 78. He reasoned that the Constitution is the supreme law and that any act that violated it should be voided. According to Marshall,

> It is emphatically the province and duty of the judicial department to say what the law is. Those who apply the rule to particular cases, must of necessity expound and interpret that rule. . . . A law repugnant to the Constitution is void; . . . courts as well as other departments are bound by that instrument.

*John Marshall, third Chief Justice of the Supreme Court, whose decision in* Marbury v. Madison *was crucial to the future of judicial review.*

Critics of judicial review noted, however, that the Constitution did not assign this power to the Court; that errors made by the legislative and executive branches of the government are best corrected by those two branches of government, if not of their own will, then through the will of the majority of the people at election time; that the power of judicial review contradicts the principle of the will of the majority, because it puts what amounts to supreme power over the Constitution in the hands of a life-appointed judiciary. To Thomas Jefferson, for example, "the doctrine of judicial review, with its inherent possibilities of leading to judicial supremacy, was both elitist and antidemocratic."[10]

10 Abraham, *The Judicial Process*, p. 318.

The Supreme Court, after establishing the precedent in *Marbury* v. *Madison*, did not again exercise its power of judicial review over a federal law until the *Dred Scott* decision of 1857. The Court, although it refused jurisdiction on the grounds that Scott was not a citizen and, therefore, not entitled to sue in a federal court, ruled on other issues, among them, the constitutionality of the Missouri Compromise. The Compromise, which outlawed slavery in Illinois, was declared unconstitutional because, depriving those who owned slaves of their property, it violated the Fifth Amendment.

In the period between the *Marbury* and *Dred Scott* rulings, the Supreme Court, for the first time, in 1810, held a state law to be unconstitutional.[11] By the time of the outbreak of the Civil War, the Court had declared only two federal statutes and twenty state statutes to be unconstitutional; and it was not until after the Civil War that judicial review came into somewhat regular use by the Court, with respect to both state and federal law.

The decisions of the Court tend to follow certain patterns within given periods. For example, from 1920 to 1937, the justices declared legislative statutes increasing government control of the economy unconstitutional on the grounds that they violated property rights protected by the "due process" clauses of the Fifth and Fourteenth Amendments. In nine decisions between 1935 and 1937, the Supreme Court struck down New Deal statutes for government programs in the industrial and agricultural sectors of the economy.

After 1937, the Court changed its constitutional philosophy, and came to accept the constitutionality of government regulation of the nation's economy. For example, in 1939, the Supreme Court declared the Second Agricultural Adjustment Act,[12] although it had invalidated the first A.A.A. in a previous decision.[13]

[11] *Fletcher* v. *Peck,* 6 Cranch 87 (1810).

[12] *Mulford* v. *Smith,* 307 U.S. 38 (1939).

[13] *U.S.* v. *Butler,* 297 U.S. 1 (1936).

"Too much judicial pressure on the Scales of Justice"

Drawing by Jerry Doyle; © 1968 in the Philadelphia *Daily News.*

In response to some Supreme Court rulings, there have been various proposals, from time to time, to modify the Court's power by changing the rules under which it operates. Some have suggested, for example, that a two-thirds vote of the Court be required to declare national acts unconstitutional. Still others claim that Congress should have the right to legislate a law which has been invalidated by the Court.

One of the more famous and sweeping moves to curb the Court occurred in 1937, when President Franklin Roosevelt made his attempt to pack the Court through legislation which provided for the addition of one member to the Court for every sitting member older than seventy, up to a maximum of fifteen judges (from the original nine). Roosevelt's plan to minimize the Supreme Court's opposition to New Deal legislation was opposed by Congress. But his proposal does illustrate the possibility of limiting judicial power by congressional statute.

The impeachment process is, in theory, a legislative check on the Court. According to Article II, Section 4, of the Constitution, impeachment of civil officers of the government can be for "Treason, Bribery, or other High Crimes and Misdemeanors." The House of Representatives votes by a majority to impeach or not, and conviction is by a two-thirds vote of the Senate. The only Supreme Court justice ever to be impeached by the House was Samuel Chase in 1804; he was acquitted by the Senate in 1805. Thus, the impeachment process, despite the occasional efforts of some legislators, remains a device of rhetoric, rather than reality.

The most effective limitation on the power of the Supreme Court is imposed by the justices themselves. The nine members, aware of their responsibility to the democratic body politic, exercise judicial self-restraint. Judicial self-restraint is a philosophy as to the role of the Court in the political and legal system. This code is comprised of practices and attitudes developed over the past two centuries. The idea of self-restraint was best expressed by Mr. Justice Brandeis in 1936, when he stated that the Supreme Court:

1. will not pass upon the constitutionality of legislation in a friendly, non-adversary proceeding . . .

2. will not anticipate a question of constitutional law in advance of the necessity of deciding it . . .

3. will not formulate a rule of constitutional law broader than is required by the precise facts to which it is to be applied . . .

4. will not pass upon a constitutional question, although properly presented by the record, if there is also present some other ground upon which the case may be disposed of . . .

5. will not pass upon the validity of a statute upon complaint of one who fails to show that he is injured by its operation . . .

6. will not pass upon the constitutionality of a statute at the instance of one who has availed himself of its benefits . . .

7. And when the validity of an act of Congress is drawn in question, and even if a serious doubt of constitutionality is raised, it is a cardinal principle that this Court will first ascertain whether a construction of the statute is fairly possible by which the question may be avoided.[14]

[14] *Ashwander v. Tennessee Valley Authority*, 297 U.S. 208 (1936).

LUX · VERITAS · JUSTITIA

"These steps are killing me. I say we settle out of court."

Drawing by Richter; © 1968 The New Yorker Magazine, Inc.

Whatever may be the future of judicial review, and despite the past and present controversies over some of the Court's decisions based on this power, at this point in our history, the principle of judicial review is solidly established in the tradition of the Court, and it is an important aspect of our constitutional system. The Supreme Court functions in our political system as "the balance wheel of our whole constitutional system . . . a vehicle of the Nation's life" and "the collective conscience of a sovereign people."[15]

[15] Abraham, *The Judicial Process*, pp. 377–378.

## Theories of constitutional interpretation

One point of view regarding interpretation of the Constitution is that of literal or strict construction. According to this philosophy, the Court should seek out the intent of the Framers and literally apply the language of the text to issues before the Court. Chief Justice Roger B. Taney, an exponent of strict construction maintained that constitutional interpretation must not be determined by current popular sentiment. The constitution, he declared,

[16] *Dred Scott* v. *Sanford*, 19 Howard 393 (1857).

> speaks not only in the same words, but with the same meaning and intent with which it spoke when it came from the hands of its framers, and was voted on and adopted by the people of the United States.[16]

By and large, the Supreme Court has chosen to apply a more flexible interpretation to the Constitution. The proponent of loose constitutional construction is less concerned with the intent of the Framers or with judicial precedent. Justice William O. Douglas, defending the loose construction view stated:

[17] Justice William O. Douglas, "Stare Decisis," *The Record* of the Association of the Bar of the City of New York, April 1949.

> the decisions of yesterday or of the last century are only the starting points . . . a judge looking at a constitutional decision may have compulsions to revere past history and accept what was once written. But he remembers above all else that it is the Constitution which he swore to support and defend, not the gloss which his predecessors may have put on it. So he comes to formulate his own views, rejecting some earlier ones as false and embracing others. He cannot do otherwise unless he lets men long dead and unaware of the problems of the age in which he lives do his thinking for him.[17]

The flexible constructionist approach interprets the Constitution as it relates to the conditions of the times. The provisions are applied to adjust conflicting interests in society; and some are given more weight than others, according to their viability in the contemporary system. It has been stated by adherents to the flexible constructionist view that if the Supreme Court does not register the changing relevance of the constitutional provisions, dozens of new constitutional amendments might be necessary each generation. President Woodrow Wilson once characterized the Supreme Court as "a constitutional convention in continuous session."

# Glossary

**administrative law**  Rules and regulations promulgated by agents of the executive branch of government (such as the Federal Trade Commission).

**adversary process**  Term characterizing the Anglo-American judicial process as the conflict of two opposing parties before an impartial third party, the court.

**appellate courts**  Courts that review cases already decided by a trial court, to determine whether or not the law has been correctly applied.

**appellate jurisdiction**  Authority of a court to review a case on appeal, which has already been decided by a lower court.

**arraignment**  In a criminal case, the formal announcement of the terms of an indictment to which the defendant responds with his plea of guilt or innocence.

**bill of information**  Method of obtaining an indictment in which the public prosecutor presents in writing his evidence to a court of original jurisdiction.

**briefs**  Written arguments submitted to the court by attorneys of the disputants.

**civil law**  Law that defines the legal rights of citizens and thereby provides rules to resolve disputes between individuals and/or corporations, and also between individuals and/or corporations and government.

**Committee on the Federal Judiciary**  Twelve-member committee of the American Bar Association established in 1946 to investigate and evaluate presidential nominees for federal court judges; it has no veto power, but its ratings are important to the initial stages of the nominating process.

**common law**  Law established by past judicial decisions, often referred to as "judge-made" law.

**concurring opinion**  Written explanation by a judge who agrees with the decision of the majority, but feels that the majority opinion does not adequately express his own reasoning in the case.

**constitutional law**  Law based on the provisions of the Constitution, as interpreted by the federal courts and especially by the United States Supreme Court.

**court of claims**  Federal court, having original jurisdiction in cases brought against the national government involving such matters as contract and tax claims.

**court of customs and patent appeals**  Federal court, which reviews the decisions of the customs court on the duties placed on imported items, and the United States Patent Office on matters relating to copyrights, patents, and trademarks.

**criminal law**  Law that defines those acts that constitute a violation of the public order, and that provides stated punishment of those acts.

**customs court**  Federal court, having the power to review the decisions of customs officials regarding the evaluation of imported goods.

**defendant**  Party against whom court action is commenced, or legal suit is brought.

**dissenting opinion**  Opinion written by a judge to register his disagreement with the majority decision, and to express his reasons for casting his vote with the minority.

**district court**  The federal trial court possessing only original jurisdiction, and established by the Judiciary Act of 1789.

**dual system of courts**   Court system in a federal form of government in which the state and federal governments each have separate court systems.

**equity**   System of law exercised by certain courts, which provides relief in situations where ordinary courts are unable to act, especially through the issuance of injunctions.

**federal court system**   National judiciary system consisting of district courts, courts of appeal, the Supreme Court, and special courts.

**felony**   A serious crime, punishable either by death or imprisonment in a penitentiary.

**grand jury**   In a criminal case, a jury of twelve to twenty-three persons, which decides whether there is sufficient evidence to indict and bring to trial a person accused of a criminal act.

**indictment**   In a criminal case, the formal accusation by a grand jury charging a named individual with specific criminal acts.

**injunction**   A court order issued by a court of equity forbidding a person from committing an act, which he is threatening or attempting, or restraining him from continuing to commit such an act.

**judicial review**   Power of a court to decide whether or not laws of the legislatures or actions of the executive are constitutional.

**misdemeanor**   Minor violation of criminal law, less serious than a felony.

**original jurisdiction**   Authority to decide a case "in the first instance," exercised by trial courts.

**petit (regular) jury**   Trial jury of twelve people in civil and criminal cases, which decides the questions of fact present in a dispute.

**plaintiff**   The party who brings suit, or initiates court action.

**precedent**   A judicial decision that establishes a legal principle upon which future cases of a similar nature can be decided.

**stare decisis** (let the decision stand)   A policy followed by courts of adhering to precedent.

**statutory interpretation**   Judicial function of determining the meaning and intent of a legislative statute.

**statutory law**   Law written and enacted by a legislative body.

**United States Circuit Courts of Appeals**   The eleven federal appellate courts empowered to hear cases appealed from district courts within their circuits, and from some administrative agencies of the federal government.

**United States Court of Military Appeals**   Military equivalent of the Supreme Court, consisting of three civilian judges who have appellate jurisdiction over all decisions involving the death penalty for a soldier and all decisions involving a general or a flag officer.

**United States magistrate**   District court official, serving an eight-year term, responsible for preliminary court matters, such as issuing arrest warrants, or setting bail.

**United States marshal**   District court official, appointed by the President, to enforce summonses and other court proceedings.

**writ of certiorari** ("made more certain")   Discretionary writ granted by the Supreme Court directing a lower court to send up a case for review.

**Supreme Court decisions**

*Barron* v. *Baltimore*   1833 Supreme Court decision that the Bill of Rights applied only to the national government and not to the states.

*Dred Scott* v. *Sanford*   1857 Supreme Court decision that declared the Missouri Compromise unconstitutional and stated that Dred Scott, whose ancestors "were sold as slaves," was not entitled to the rights of an American citizen.

*Marbury* v. *Madison*   1803 Supreme Court decision which declared a congressional act unconstitutional, thus setting the precedent for judicial review of the laws of Congress.

*Muskrat* v. *United States*   1911 Supreme Court decision confirming that the judicial power is united to "cases" and controversies.

# Suggested readings

Abraham, Henry J., *The Judicial Process: An Introductory Analysis of the Courts of the United States, England, and France*, 2nd ed. (New York: Oxford University Press, Inc., 1968). Comparative study of the three judicial systems, illustrating common traditions in practice and philosophy as well as differences.

Asby, John B. "Supreme Court Appointments Since 1937" (Unpublished Ph.D. dissertation, Notre Dame University, 1972).

Bickel, Alexander M., *The Least Dangerous Branch: The Supreme Court as the Bar of Politics* (Indianapolis, Ind.: Bobbs Merrill, Co., Inc., 1962). Critical discussion of the work of the Supreme Court and its role in the American political system.

Calihan, David S., "Series and Practices of Bail in Four Ohio Municipal Courts" (Master's thesis, Columbus: Ohio State University, 1970).

Cardozo, Benjamin N., *The Nature of the Judicial Process* (New Haven, Conn.: Yale University Press, 1921). Classic study of the forces that influence the decisions of judges, by an important Supreme Court justice.

Carp, Robert Arthur, "The Function, Impact and Political Relevance of the Federal District Courts: A Case Study" (Ph.D. dissertation, Iowa City: University of Iowa, 1969).

Carr, Robert K., *The Supreme Court and Judicial Review* (New York: Holt, Rinehart and Winston, Inc., 1942). Analysis of the Supreme Court's use of judicial review.

Cole, Stracy, "The Politics of Prosecution: The Decision to Prosecute" (Ph.D. dissertation, Seattle: University of Washington, 1968).

Danelski, David J., *A Supreme Court Justice Is Appointed* (New York: Random House, Inc., 1964). Conflict involved in the 1922 appointment of Pierce Butler as justice of the Supreme Court.

Drury, Douglas S., "Earl Warren: The Warren Court, 1952–1958" (Master's thesis, Dallas, Tex.: Southern Methodist University, 1958).

Dunham, Allison, and Phillip B. Kurland, eds., *Mister Justice*, 2nd ed. (Chicago: University of Chicago Press, 1964). Brief studies of nine eminent Supreme Court justices, including their pre-Court experience and notable work while on the Supreme Court.

Eulau, Heinze, and John D. Sprague, *Lawyers in Politics: A Study in Professional Convergence* (Indianapolis, Ind.: Bobbs Merrill Co., Inc., 1964). Analysis of the role of lawyers and bar associations in the political process.

Frank, Jerome, *Law and The Modern Mind* (New York: Brentano's, Inc., 1930). Provocative and perceptive psychological analysis of the role of law in modern society.

Frank, Jerome, *Courts of Trial* (Princeton, N.J.: Princeton University Press, 1949). Critical analysis of the American judicial system, with emphasis on the trial courts.

Holmes, Oliver Wendell, *The Common Law* (Boston: Little, Brown and Co., 1881). Classic study of the growth of the common law as a response to the changing needs of society, by one of America's foremost jurists.

Jackson, Robert H., *The Supreme Court in The American System of Government* (Cambridge, Mass.: Harvard University Press, 1955). Concise and comprehensive essays on the Supreme Court by a former justice of that court.

Jacob, Herbert, *Justice in America: Courts, Lawyers, and the Judicial Process* (Boston: Little, Brown and Co., 1965). Discussion of the political forces that influence the American judicial system, the factors involved in judicial decision making, and the consequences of judicial decisions.

Jahnige, Thomas P., and Sheldon Goldman, eds., *The Federal Judicial System: Readings in Process and Behavior* (New York: Holt, Rinehart and Winston, Inc., 1968). Essays and articles on the federal judicial system.

Krislov, Samuel, *The Supreme Court in the Political Process* (New York: The Macmillan Co., 1965). Politically oriented study of the Supreme Court.

Mason, Alpheus T., *Brandeis: A Free Man's Life* (New York: The Viking Press, Inc., 1956). Biography of a noted Supreme Court justice who served on the Court from 1916 to 1939.

Mason, Alpheus T., *Harlan Fiske Stone: Pillar of the Law* (New York: The Viking Press, Inc., 1956). Biography of a noted Supreme Court justice who served between 1925 and 1941.

Mason, Alpheus T., *William Howard Taft: Chief Justice* (New York: Simon and Schuster, Inc., 1965). Biography of a noted Supreme Court Chief Justice who earlier had served as President of the United States.

McCloskey, Robert G., *American Supreme Court, 1789–1960* (Chicago: University of Chicago Press, 1960). Brief historical account of the Supreme Court.

Mendelson, Wallace, *Justices Black and Frankfurter, Conflict in the Court*, 2nd. ed. (Chicago: University of Chicago Press, 1966). Study of the conflicting political and judicial ideas of two important Supreme Court justices.

Murphy, Walter F., *Elements of Judicial Strategy* (Chicago: University of Chicago Press, 1964). Analysis of the behavior of members of the Supreme Court, based on analysis of the writings of several of its justices.

Peltason, Jack W., *Federal Courts in the Political Process* (New York: Random House, Inc., 1955). Analysis of the role of lower federal court judges in the judicial system.

Porter, J. Sherman, "Hugo Black's Decisions," (Master's thesis, Lexington: University of Kentucky, 1941).

Pritchett, Charles H., and Alan F. Westin, *The Third Branch of Government: Eight Cases in Constitutional Politics* (New York: Harcourt Brace Jovanovich, Inc., 1963). Analysis of eight cases that illustrate the context in which Supreme Court decisions are made.

Pusey, Merlo J., *Charles Evans Hughes,* 2 vols. (New York: Columbia University Press, 1963). Biography of a noted Supreme Court justice, who served between 1910 and 1916, and was Chief Justice between 1930 and 1941.

Rackow, Felix, "The Right to Counsel: English and American Precedents, *William and Mary Quarterly,* XI (1954), 3–27.

Resnik, Solomon, "Black and Douglas: Variations in Dissent" (Ph.D. dissertation (New York: New York University, 1955).

Rohde, David W., "Comments on 'A Cost Theory' of Judicial Alignment," *Midwest Journal of Political Science,* XIV (1970), 331–36.

Rosenblum, Victor G., *Law as a Political Instrument* (New York: Random House, Inc., 1955). Study of the role of the judicial system in the formulation of public policy.

Schmidhauser, John R., *The Supreme Court* (New York: Holt, Rinehart and Winston, Inc., 1960). Interesting study of the manner in which personalities and procedures influence the work of the Supreme Court.

Schubert, Glendon, *The Judicial Mind: Attitudes and Ideologies of Supreme Court Justices, 1946–1963* (Evanston, Ill.: Northwestern University Press, 1965). Empirical study of the attitudes of eighteen Supreme Court justices who served between 1946 and 1967.

Schubert, Glendon, *Constitutional Policy* (Boston: Boston University Press, 1970). Study of the conflict between liberals and conservatives on the Supreme Court between 1922 and 1969.

Schubert, Glendon, ed., *Judicial Decision-Making* (New York: The Free Press, 1963). Studies by political scientists of judicial behavior, indicating that judicial decisions are not mere mechanical applications of legal rules.

Sigler, Jay A., *An Introduction to the Legal System* (Homewood, Ill.: Dorsey Press, Inc., 1968). Study of how the law operates within the political system.

Warren, Charles, *The Supreme Court in the History of the United States,* 2 vols. (Boston: Little, Brown and Co., 1960). Originally published in 1922. Standard general history of the Supreme Court.

Westin, Alan F., ed., *The Supreme Court: Views from Inside* (New York: W. W. Norton and Co., Inc., 1960). The judicial process as seen through the writings of Supreme Court justices.

# Topics of further study

Bartholomew, Charles P., "Supreme Court of the United States, 1959–1960," *Western Political Quarterly,* March 1961, pp. 5–16.

Becker, Robert Myron, "The Judicial Philosophy of Chief Justice Earl Warren Regarding Civil Rights and Civil Liberties" (Ph.D. dissertation in progress, New School for Social Research, 1972).

Charles, A. D., *Law for Business* (Cincinnati: South-Western Publishers, 1963).

Henderson, B. C., *The Selection of Judges in Texas* (Houston: University of Houston Press, 1966).

Itoh, Hiroshi, "The Delegation of the Legislative Power to the Supreme Court of the United States," *Journal of Political Studies,* February 1971.

Klein, Milton M., "Prelude to Revolution in New York: Jury Trials and Judicial Tenure," *William and Mary Quarterly*, October 1960, pp. 439–462.

Klein, Stanley, "A Study of Social Legislation Affecting Prisons and Institutions for the Mentally Ill in New York State, 1822–1846" (Ph.D. dissertation, New York University, 1957).

Spiegel, Fred, *Illinois Court of Claims: A Study of State Liability* (Urbana, Ill.: University of Illinois Press, 1962).

Woeffl, Paul A., S.J., *Politics and Jurisprudence* (Chicago, Ill.: Loyola University Press, 1966).

Wood, John W., "A Study of the Iowa Judiciary" (Ph.D. dissertation, University of Iowa, 1964).

# part four

# government in action

# 18 civil
# liberties

1 *West Virginia State Board of Education v. Barnette*, 319 U.S. 624 (1943).

A CHARTER of civil liberties, the Bill of Rights was designed to safeguard the individual against the arbitrary use of power by the national government. "If there is any fixed star in our constitutional constellation, it is that no official, high or petty, can prescribe what shall be orthodox in politics, nationalism, religion or other matters of opinion or force citizens to confess by word or act their faith therein."[1] The civil liberties guaranteed by the Bill of Rights include freedom of speech, press, assembly, and other protections against arbitrary government.

Civil liberty may be defined as "the liberty of an individual freely to exercise those rights guaranteed by the laws of a country, or the limitations on national government by the Constitution." These individual rights, such as freedom of speech, are listed in the Bill of Rights, the first ten amendments to the Constitution. The term "civil liberties" denotes personal freedoms; but it has a distinctly different meaning from the term "civil rights," which we will use later to signify the right to "equal protection of the laws," as guaranteed by the Fourteenth Amendment.

The interpretation of civil liberties and civil rights, and how they are to be applied, is an important function of the courts, especially the Supreme Court. As impartial third parties established to arbitrate conflicts between individuals and state and national governments, the nation's courts have played a significant role in determining, for example, the meaning of the First Amendment guarantee of free speech.

The United States Bill of Rights, which was added to the Constitution in 1791, was partly inspired, at least, by those of England and the early state constitutions. The Magna Charta (1215), the Petition of Rights (1628), and the English Bill of Rights (1689) are the major legal guarantees of English liberty. The English Bill of Rights, adopted during the reign of William and Mary, limited the power of the king of England; he could not suspend laws adopted by Parliament, nor could he enact laws without its consent. The king's right to keep a standing army was also limited; citizens were given the right to bear arms, and to petition the king for a change in law; and free elections and fair trials were guaranteed. In the colonies some state constitutions, particularly that of Virginia, included bills of rights that were another source of inspiration for our national Bill of Rights. Paralleling the English and state documents, the United States Bill of Rights provides for the protection of the individual from arbitrary acts of government.

## The states and civil liberties

At one time, the Supreme Court held that the limitations on government that are stated in the Bill of Rights applied only to the national government, and not to the states. This interpretation was established in the case of *Barron* v. *Baltimore* (1833). In the course of a city paving project, gravel and sand had filled up the channel near Barron's wharf, and made it useless for shipping. Barron contended that the city's action had violated the Fifth Amendment clause that forbids the taking of private property "for public use without just compensation." Barron won at the local level, but the decision was reversed by the Maryland State Court of Appeals.

When the case reached the Supreme Court, the justices rejected Barron's plea, and ruled that the Fifth Amendment applied only to the national government, not to the states. In his majority opinion, Chief Justice Marshall said that there was "no repugnancy between the several acts of the general assembly of Maryland . . . and the Constitution of the United States."[2] His decision was based on the view that the Bill of Rights had been added to the Constitution because of a general fear of the national government; it was not intended to regulate state actions.

2 *Barron* v. *Baltimore*, 7 Peters 243 (1833).

The Supreme Court decision that the Bill of Rights applied only to the national government has never been overruled. However, the Fourteenth Amendment, ratified in 1868, has served in the twentieth century as the vehicle through which nearly all the provisions of the Bill of Rights may be applied to the states. The Supreme Court has maintained that the rights guaranteed by the First Amendment are included in the liberties guaranteed in the Fourteenth Amendment, which declares that no state shall "deprive any person of life, liberty, or property, without due process of law."

It was not until 1925 that the due process clause was first interpreted as the basis for applying a part of the Bill of Rights to the states. The case of *Gitlow* v. *New York* (1925) was a major turning point in guaranteeing freedom of speech at the state level. Benjamin Gitlow, an active member of the Socialist Party, had been convicted under New York State's Criminal Anarchy Act of 1902. Gitlow argued that the state statute violated freedom of speech and denied due process. Although the Supreme Court's decision upheld the constitutionality of the lower court's decision, Justice Sanford's majority opinion set a historical precedent by declaring:

> Freedom of speech and of the press—which are now protected by the First Amendment from abridgment by Congress—are among the fundamental personal rights and "liberties" protected by the due process clause from impairment by the States.[3]

Since the Gitlow case, the Supreme Court has applied, case-by-case, all but a few of the guarantees of the Bill of Rights to the states; so that today, the United States has a nearly uniform standard of rights applying to both the national and state governments. It is the Supreme Court that has served as the interpreter and champion of these protections.

# Freedom of religion

The paramount importance of religious liberty to the Framers of the Bill of Rights is reflected by the fact that they included this guarantee first in the Bill of Rights. "Congress shall make no law respecting an establishment of religion or prohibiting the free exercise thereof." Two distinct limitations are placed on government regarding religion. The first limitation, the *establishment clause*, prohibits many forms of association between church and state. The second, the *free exercise clause*, prohibits the government from restricting the right to religious belief.

## The free exercise clause

In interpreting the free exercise clause of the First Amendment, the Supreme Court has maintained that religious beliefs are inviolate, but that some religious practices are subject to government controls. The first major case dealing with freedom of religion, after the adoption of the First Amendment, was *Reynolds* v. *United States* (1878). Reynolds, a Mormon residing in Utah, had violated a congressional statute that outlawed polygamy in that territory. The Supreme Court upheld the conviction of Reynolds and the constitutionality of the statute, despite the fact that Mormon doctrine at that time sanctioned the practice of polygamy. The Supreme Court concluded that religious liberty does not include the right to commit unlawful acts.

The Court further refined this opinion in *Davis* v. *Beason* (1890), noting that religious freedom was allowed "provided always the laws of society, designed to secure its peace and prosperity, and the morals of its people are not interfered with."[4] Within this spirit, the Supreme Court has upheld, for example, certain state laws that forbid Sunday business activities, despite the fact that this imposed an economic burden on groups such as Orthodox Jews and Seventh Day Adventists, who observe a Saturday Sabbath.[5]

[3] *Gitlow* v. *New York,* 268 U.S. 652 (1925).

[4] *Davis* v. *Beason,* 133 U.S. 33 (1890).

[5] *McGowan* v. *Maryland,* 366 U.S. 420 (1961); *Kosher Super Market,* 366 U.S. 617 (1961); *Sherbert* v. *Verner,* 374 U.S. 398 (1963).

The right to believe or disbelieve, as opposed to the right to exercise a particular practice, has also been strongly defended by the Supreme Court. An example of the Court's absolutist view on religious freedom is the case of *Torcaso* v. *Watkins* (1961). Roy Torcaso, an atheist who was appointed a notary public in Maryland, has refused to obey the state constitution's requirement that he declare his belief in the existence of God as part of his oath of office. Consequently, Torcaso did not receive his commission to the office. The Supreme Court ruled that, in this case, the freedom of religion guaranteed Torcaso by the Constitution had been denied. Justice Black, in a unanimous decision, wrote that, in placing Maryland on the side of "one particular belief,"—namely the theist belief in the existence of God—the state's requirement imposed a burden on the free exercise of the faiths of nonbelievers, in violation of the free exercise clause. The Court declared:

> this Maryland religious test for public office unconstitutionally invades the appellants' freedom of belief and religion and therefore cannot be enforced against him. . . . Neither a State nor the Federal Government can constitutionally force a person "to profess a belief or disbelief in any religion." Neither can it constitutionally pass laws or impose requirements which aid all religions as against non-believers, and neither can it aid those religions based on a belief in the existence of God as against those religions founded on different beliefs.[6]

[6] *Torcaso* v. *Watkins,*
367 U.S. 488 (1961).

## Conscientious objectors

Since colonial times, various sects in American society have held that, in principle, it is wrong to participate in war. Although the first compulsory draft law was not passed until World War I, members of these sects, and other individuals, referred to as *conscientious objectors*, have resisted military service on the grounds of religious belief, conscience, or moral code. During World War I, conscientious objectors were not exempt from the draft, but they were granted exemption from combat duty and assigned to service in the medical or supply corps. Those who refused service often were sentenced to prison. In World War II, the Selective Service and Training Act of 1940 broadened the alternatives given above. But, conscientious objectors who rejected service in any branch of the armed services were dealt with severely; between 1940 and 1945, nearly 5,000 were imprisoned. More recent legislation has not resulted in more lenient judgments. Between 1948 and 1960, some 1,400 objectors were sent to jail.

*Charles S. Hyneman and George Carey, eds.,* A Second Federalist: Congress Creates a Government (*New York: Appleton-Century-Crofts, 1967*), *pp. 301–304.*

On January 17, 1814, Zebulon R. Shipherd, of New York, attempted to prevent passage of a bill authorizing President Madison to enlist additional troops to fight on foreign soil. He used the constitutional principles of religious and civil liberty to refute Tennessee Congressman Grundy's view that refusal to accept the bill on the floor was an act of moral treason. The annals of the House of Representatives contain Shipherd's argument:

One cannot be guilty of treason in law, without lifting his arm against the Government . . . if moral treason can exist, which is doubtful, certain I am that the sin of differing in opinion from the majority will not constitute the crime.

Shipherd believed that the Constitution was clear on the issue:

Sir, in the whole of this instrument there is not a word, by reasonable exposition, that imposes upon the citizen the least obligation to aid the Government in the prosecution of a war beyond our territorial jurisdiction, nor has the Government any power over its citizens in this respect, except the levying of taxes.

It is left to the feelings, discretion, and violation of every man whether, when solicited to lend his assistance, he will accept the invitation to engage in the war. Why this omission in the Constitution? It was undoubtedly omitted by design for two reasons:

1. To prevent the prosecution of foreign wars.
2. Because the power to drag forth the reluctant citizen to a war of conquest is wholly inconsistent with the principles of civil and religious liberty.

It seemed inconsistent to Shipherd that we should boast of a government that gives us freedom to choose or refuse if, in application, we are free only to choose one path. The Constitution certainly did not intend for the individual to be subject to a "proud Executive or corrupt majority of the Legislature."

Never let your country be mocked with the title of free, if the enjoyments and employments of domestic life are ever placed in the hands of any group of erring and perhaps wicked men.

Shipherd further notes that Grundy's allegation of moral treason not only encroaches on the individual's civil liberty, but also on his freedom of religion. According to the First Amendment to the Constitution, every citizen is free to abide by the rules of his religion, as long as they do not violate the law. And since there are those who oppose wars of revenge, as well as those who oppose any bloodshed, the government has no right to force war upon them.

> Shall it then be justified that such a man shall stand condemned as guilty of an odious violation of moral obligation because he obeys the dictates of conscience? Shall he have the liberty of judging for himself, from the lights of reason and revelation, or shall he be compelled to submit his conscience, his religion, and soul, to the arbitrament of a majority, who may scout the ties and obligations of the two former and deny the existence of the latter?
>
> An act of Congress, writes Shipherd, cannot absolve a religious man from guilt.
>
> The crime of a multitude is no less heinous in his sight than that of an individual . . . In his breast the laws of God are superior to the laws of men, and when he finds them opposed he obeys the former and disregards the latter.

Today, the exemption procedure requires that an individual seeking conscientious objector status must: a) have a letter from a religious leader in support of his religious beliefs, character, and integrity; b) testify before a panel of judges (more often than not, his own draft board, in the first stage); c) prove that he has previously advocated pacifist doctrines and lived in a manner exemplifying his beliefs; and d) spend the succeeding two years working in a Peace Corps, VISTA or similar type of social work, in which he is allowed to earn only a certain small sum of money.

At one time, Congress confined conscientious objector status to those "persons who by reason of religious training and belief are conscientiously opposed to participation in war." And "religious training and belief" were carefully spelled out:

> Religion and belief in this connection means an individual belief in relation to a Supreme Being involving duties superior to those arising from any human relation, but does not include essentially political, sociological or philosophical views, or merely a personal moral code.

In subsequent Supreme Court decisions, this provision was construed to encompass more diverse beliefs. In *United States* v. *Seeger* (1965), for example, the Supreme Court upheld Seeger's claim to exemption as a conscientious objector. The decision reversed the ruling of Seeger's draft board, which denied his claim on the grounds that his moral convictions did not include faith in a Supreme Being. The Court declared that there are "diverse manners in which beliefs . . . may be articulated," and that "the test of belief in a relation to a Supreme Being is whether a given belief is sincere. . . ."

The Selective Service Act of 1967 eliminated the requirement that conscientious objectors hold a "belief in relation to a Supreme Being" and provided exemption for those who, "by reason of religious training and belief," are "conscientiously opposed to participation in war in any form." This provision of the draft law was broadly interpreted by the Supreme Court in *Welsh* v. *United States* (1970). In the majority opinion, Justice Black wrote:

> If an individual deeply and sincerely holds beliefs which are purely ethical and moral in source and content, . . . such an individual is as much entitled to a religious conscientious objection as is someone who derives his conscientious opposition from traditional religious grounds.[7]

[7] *Welsh* v. *United States,* 398 U.S. 333 (1970).

A year later, the Supreme Court denied a claim based on this provision. The defendant sought conscientious objector status on the grounds that he was opposed to the war in Vietnam. The statute applies to individuals "who, by reason of religious training and belief" are "conscientiously opposed to war in any form." The Court ruled ". . . that persons who object solely to participation in a particular war are not within the purview of the exempting section, even though the latter objection may have such roots in a claimant's conscience and personality that it is 'religious' in character."[8]

[8] *Gillette* v. *United States* (1971).

In these recent decisions, however, beliefs based on exclusively moral, rather than established, religious convictions came to be included in the definition for exemption.

Mindful of recent precedents, the Supreme Court upheld the conscientious objector claim of Muhammad Ali, a heavyweight boxing champion. The decision invalidated the five-year prison sentence given to Ali in a lower court. It unanimously overruled the conviction on the grounds that Ali's request for exemption as a conscientious objector had been improperly handled. The Justice Department was "simply wrong as a matter of law in advising that the petitioner's beliefs were not religiously based and were not sincerely held." The Supreme Court maintained that the sincerity of Ali's beliefs, and their foundations in religious training as a Black Muslim, were beyond doubt.[9]

[9] *Clay* v. *United States,* 39 LW 4873, 783 (1971).

# The establishment clause

The establishment clause and its application have often evoked heated political controversy. There are two broad interpretations of this clause. The first is the *no-preference doctrine*, which holds that government can encourage religious activities on the condition that no preference is given to any particular faith. The second, more stringent view, the one most often accepted by the Supreme Court, is the *wall of separation doctrine*, which holds that the establishment clause outlaws any government aid or encouragement to any religion.

# Aid to parochial schools

Federal assistance to public schools has remained a highly controversial area of the church-state relations question. There has been a constant shifting in public attitudes on the question, as well as a high degree of uncertainty in the decisions of the Supreme Court.

The first major case to assert the wall of separation theory was *Everson v. Board of Education of Ewing Township* (1947). The case involved a New Jersey statute authorizing public funds for bus fare reimbursement to parents of students in public and private schools. Because the funds authorized were being used to pay the bus fare of children traveling to parochial, as well as public, schools, it was argued that the statute levied a tax to support religious activities and, therefore, violated the establishment clause of the First Amendment. By a 5–4 vote, the Court decided that the statute was valid, since the aid provided was in the category of a general public service, and not an aid to religion. The service in question was said to be no more forbidden than the furnishing of police and fire protection to all schools, public and parochial alike, or requiring local transit companies to carry all schoolchildren at reduced rates. The reasoning of the Court reflects the so-called "child benefit theory" formulated in an earlier decision which holds that in providing these benefits, the state is aiding the child, not the school or institution he attends.[10]

Although the Court's decision upheld the New Jersey statute, the wall of separation doctrine was strongly stated. In stating the majority opinion, Justice Black went to great pains in defining the establishment clause:

> Neither a state nor the Federal government can, openly or secretly, participate in the affairs of any religious organizations or groups and vice versa. In the words of Jefferson, the clause against establishment of religion by law intended to erect a "wall of separation between Church and State." . . . The First Amendment has erected a wall between church and state. The wall must be kept high and impregnable.[11]

Those judges who objected to the authorization of public funds for bussing of children in private school felt that the "wall" had not only been breached, but breached flagrantly and inexcusably . . . "that famous 'wall of separation' seems to be of rather different height depending on who is viewing it, be they Supreme Court justices, other jurists, or subjective or objective commentators, lay or professional."[12]

After the Everson decision upheld those state laws that allocated aid to parochial schools in the form of transportation subsidies, thirty-six states enacted programs involving aid to parochial schools in the form of bussing, free lunches, counseling services, and, most recently, salary supplements for teachers, and aid for school construction. In June, 1971, however, the Court ruled, by a vote of eight–to–one, that state programs to supplement the salaries of parochial school teachers with public funds constitute an establishment of religion.[13] In another case, the Court declared that a Pennsylvania state law supplementing parochial school teachers' salaries with the funds from cigarette taxes was invalid.[14] In these cases, the Supreme Court

[10] *Cochran v. Louisiana State Board of Education,* 281 U.S. 370 (1930).

[11] *Everson v. Board of Education of Ewing Township,* 330 U.S. 1 (1947).

[12] Henry J. Abraham, *Freedom and the Court,* 2nd ed. (New York: Oxford University Press, Inc., 1967), p. 210.

[13] *Early v. DiCenso,* 39, LW 4845, 569 (1971); *Robinson v. DiCenso,* 39, LW 4845, 570 (1971).

[14] *Lemon v. Kurtzman,* 39 LW 4845, 89 (1971).

took a firm stand against state laws that entangle the state with religion.

The 1965 Federal Aid to Elementary and Secondary Education Act marked the first time that a general aid to education bill which included parochial as well as public schools was passed by Congress. The act was carefully drafted to conform with the Supreme Court's wall of separation theory, by directing the aid to school children, rather than to the actual religious organizations. This bill extended federal aid to schools in poverty areas.

The legal foundation for challenging this act was set in 1968, when the Supreme Court ruled, for the first time, that taxpayers had the right to challenge the constitutionality of laws which violated the establishment clause of the First Amendment.[15]

The Supreme Court has yet to decide on the constitutionality of the 1965 federal aid to education law. However, in 1971, the Court did uphold the constitutionality of a 1963 federal law that provided grants to construct buildings for nonsectarian purposes on campuses of private and church-related colleges.[16]

## Released time

The term *released time* refers to special hours set aside from regular classroom study to allow children in public schools to receive religious instruction. In 1914, the system was first established in Gary, Indiana, in opposition to the supposed "Godless" education given in public schools. By 1947, over two thousand communities had adopted some form of released time. The practice, which many came to view as interfering with the separation of church and state, became a public and constitutional issue of heated debate. The Supreme Court ruled against released time in *McCollum* v. *Board of Education* (1948), a case that involved the right of an interfaith council to provide religious instruction for public school children on public school premises. In an eight-to-one decision, the Supreme Court declared the law a clear violation of the First and Fourteenth Amendments, in that it used the state-supported compulsory school system to provide students with religious training. In 1952, however, the Court distinguished between the McCollum case and another that challenged the released time system.

In *Zorach* v. *Clauson* (1952), the Supreme Court, by a vote of six-to-three, upheld a New York City school program that provided for public school children to be "released" from classes (at the request of their parents) to attend religious classes *outside* the school building itself, while nonparticipating students remained either in class or study hall. In his majority opinion, Justice Douglas declared:

> We find no constitutional requirement which makes it necessary for government to be hostile to religion and to throw its weight against efforts to widen the effective scope of religious influence. . . .[17]

## Prayer in school

In 1962, a storm of controversy arose over the Supreme Court's decision in

[15] *Flast* v. *Cohen*, 392 U.S. 83 (1968).

[16] *Tilton* v. *Richardson*, 39 LW 4857, 153 (1971).

[17] *Zorach* v. *Clauson*, 343 U.S. 306, 312, 313, 314 (1952).

*Engel* v. *Vitale,* a case dealing with the constitutionality of New York's so-called Regent's prayer, a short, nondenominational prayer approved by the New York State Board of Regents.[18] The prayer was "Almighty God, we acknowledge our dependence upon Thee, and we beg Thy blessings upon us, our parents, our teachers and our country." The Supreme Court, in a six–to–one decision, found that the prayer was an unconstitutional establishment of religion. Justice Black noted that by using the public school system to encourage recitation of the Regents' prayer, the State of New York had adopted a practice wholly inconsistent with the establishment clause.

The ruling sparked public indignation to the point that there was strong support in both houses of Congress to adopt a constitutional amendment to allow prayers in public school, though the amendment never received the necessary majority in Congress.

In still another case, the Court held Bible reading in public schools to be unconstitutional. In *Abington School District* v. *Schempp* the validity of a Pennsylvania law, requiring a daily reading in public schools of ten verses from the Bible, was challenged. The Supreme Court declared the Pennsylvania law unconstitutional on the grounds that it violated the establishment clause of the First Amendment.[19]

# First Amendment: freedom of speech and press

The Supreme Court has never interpreted the First Amendment guarantee of free speech as an absolute freedom. It has accepted the view that, in certain limited circumstances, government does have a right to curtail free expression. In Justice Holmes's classic example, screaming "Fire!" in a crowded theater when there is no fire is an exercise of free speech that must be prohibited, because it can result in panic and injury.

The First Amendment declares, "Congress shall make no law abridging the freedom of speech, or of the press." Unfortunately, people find it easier to tolerate controversial expression in theory, rather than in practice. They tend to advocate free speech as long as what is being said is in accord with their ideas.

## Tests of free speech

Under what circumstances can government restrict free speech? What statements can be labeled "seditious," "subversive," "dangerous," "obscene," "libelous," and so on? Depending on the times and public attitudes, such labels can lend themselves easily to the repression of freedom of speech in the name of public morality or patriotism. It is the role of the courts to determine when it is within the power of government to infringe on this freedom. In assessing the limits to free speech, the Supreme Court has used several criteria, or standards.

*Henry J. Abraham,* Freedom and the Court: Civil Rights and Liberties in the United States (*New York: Oxford University Press, Inc., 1967*), *pp. 167–171.*

Henry Abraham argues that "No other branch of our government is so qualified to draw lines between the rights of the individual and the rights of society as the Supreme Court of the United States." Because the majority of executive and legislative branches of government too often act on political experience or the desire for popularity, he contends that the Supreme Court is most able to determine whether or not freedom of expression should be restricted.

The question upon which Abraham focuses is the application by the Court of the "clear and present danger" theory. He finds this guideline imperfect, but contends that its sole alternative, legislation for or against free expression, is even less compatible with democratic principles, as it would lead to "an almost total absence of immunity in the face of legislation." No other protection but that of Supreme Court interpretation of the Constitution, seems possible.

Freedom of expression cannot, in the nature of things, be absolute; but it can be protected to the widest degree humanly feasible under the Constitution.

Rejecting absolute freedom, Abraham offers the view that clear and present danger, and its inherent tendency toward "balancing," is the most acceptable means of protecting individual liberty.

Of course, to support the "clear and present danger" doctrine, or that of "clear and present danger plus imminence," is not to ignore its inherent dilemmas. . . . The very adjectives "clear" and "present" raise problems of great magnitude—e.g. clear and present danger of what? Still, both in its basic philosophy and its application, the doctrine's overriding tenets are realistic in approach and reflect an attitude which is both liberal *and* conservative in the classic connotations of those two so often misunderstood and misapplied terms. It is simply not possible to get away from the concept of "balancing"—a contentious term in some quarters—liberty and authority, freedom and responsibility. But when "balancing" is called for, and in the absence of a danger clear, present, and imminent, we must presume the scale to be weighted on the side of the individual.

He suggests that free expression is a necessity, because a democracy must leave all political channels open in order that it can be replaced if it loses popular support. Yet the result of this freedom, to date, has not been the desire for an alternative government, but for a deeper loyalty to democracy.

> Surely the loyalty of the mass of men to liberal democracy has been immensely strengthened by the right to free expression and the consequent feeling of a genuine stake in society, a society that allows the expression of our deepest and most rankling grievances.
>
> Free expression, not absolute, but as protected and regulated by the Supreme Court which "draws a line steeped in constitutional common sense," is a "safety valve" that warns of dangerous pressures to our society.

## Clear and present danger

Justice Oliver W. Holmes was the first to use the phrase *"clear and present danger"* as the constitutional standard for determining when freedom of speech can be restricted. In *Schenck* v. *United States,* he noted:

[20] *Schenck* v. *United States,* 249 U.S. 47 (1919).

> The question in every case is whether the words are used in circumstances and are of such a nature as to create a *clear and present danger* that they will bring about substantive evils that Congress has a right to prevent.[20]

Thus, according to Holmes, the question of free speech is an issue of circumstances and immediacy.

In a later opinion, Justice Louis D. Brandeis further defined the difference between free speech (as guaranteed by the Constitution) and speech that is subject to restraint.

[21] *Whitney* v. *California,* 274 U.S. 57 (1927).

> No danger flowing from speech can be deemed clear and present unless the incidence of the evil is so imminent that it may befall before there is opportunity for full discussion.[21]

If the expression of an idea constitutes a "clear and present danger," it is not constitutionally protected under the free speech guarantee. However, precisely what constitutes a "clear and present danger" is difficult to define. Despite the ambiguity, the clear and present danger doctrine has been used as one criterion for judicial decisions on the constitutionality of laws and the legality of individual actions.[22]

[22] *Stromberg* v. *California,* 283 U.S. 359, 369 (1931); *Herdon* v. *Lowry,* 301, U.S. 242 (1937).

## Dangerous tendency

The *dangerous tendency doctrine* was another of the early tests of free speech used by the Court. This doctrine held that the expression of ideas having a tendency, however remote, to bring about acts in violation of the law, can be constitutionally restrained by the government. The dangerous tendency test became the determining criterion in the aforementioned case of *Gitlow* v. *New York* (1925). Benjamin Gitlow had published a Socialist manifesto supporting the destruction of the bourgeois state. Although no unlawful acts were caused by the manifesto, the Court ruled that restricting its publication was constitutionally justifiable. In the majority opinion, the Court declared that Gitlow's writings had a *"bad tendency"* to "corrupt morals, incite crime, and disturb the public peace." Justice Sanford, in delivering the opinion of the Court, said:

> A single revolutionary spark may kindle a fire that, smoldering for a time, may burst into sweeping and destructive conflagration. . . . the state may, in the exercise of its judgment, suppress the danger in its incipiency.[23]

[23] *Gitlow* v. *New York*, 268 U.S. (1925).

## Absolutist position

Several members of the Supreme Court, most notably Justices Hugo Black and William O. Douglas, have argued that the First Amendment should be interpreted literally, that the amendment makes all laws which restrict freedom of speech, press, or assembly unconstitutional. As Justice Black wrote in the Pentagon Papers case:

> The Solicitor General argues and some members of the Court appear to agree that the general powers of the Government adopted in the original Constitution should be interpreted to limit and restrict the specific and emphatic guarantees of the Bill of Rights adopted later. I can imagine no greater perversion of history. Madison and the other Framers of the First Amendment . . . wrote in language they earnestly believed could never be misunderstood: "Congress shall make no law . . . abridging the freedom of the press. . . ." Both the history and language of the First Amendment support the view that the press must be left free to publish views, whatever the source, without censorship, injunctions, or prior restraints.[24]

[24] *New York Times Co.* v. *United States* 91 S. Ct. 2140 (1971).

## Balancing of interests

The *balancing of interests doctrine* holds that in judging the constitutionality of an act or law, one must weigh the value of restriction against the First Amendment rights. In the case of a law that limits such rights, this gives the Court the latitude to declare such a law valid if that law is necessary to achieve a valid political objective. During the 1950s the Supreme Court used this approach in a number of cases to uphold the right of the government to regulate the political activities of Communists and Communist groups. For example, the Court used this approach to uphold a provision of the Taft-Hartley Act (1947), which denied to labor unions the protection of the nation's labor laws if their officials would not take a "non-Communist" oath. The Court accepted the contention of Congress that such a provision was designed to circumvent the danger of serious political strikes.[25]

Another advocate of the balancing of interests doctrine is Justice Harlan. In a case involving the power of government to investigate political beliefs and activities, he wrote:

[25] *American Communications Association* v. *Douds*, 339 U.S. 382 (1950).

[26] *Barenblatt* v. *United States*, 360 U.S. 109 (1959).

> Where First Amendment rights are asserted to bar governmental interrogative, resolution of the issue always involves a balancing by the courts of the competing private and public interests at stake in the particular circumstances shown. . . .[26]

These four tests of free speech—the clear and present danger, dangerous tendency, absolutist position, and balancing of interests—provide rough "rules of thumb" by which the Supreme Court decides cases. One area in which they have been applied is to settle the controversies arising from sedition legislation tests.

## Sedition

*Sedition* is defined in Webster's dictionary as "incitement of discontent or rebellion against a government, or any action, especially in speech or writing, promoting such discontent or rebellion." Whether the government can and should punish "seditious activities" has been a heated issue in several periods of national history. Sedition legislation has been enacted particularly in times of war—World Wars I and II, Korea—and prosecutions have taken place during times of national political stress, such as the "red scare" of the early 1920s, and the cold war period. For example, following World War II, "seditious" speech was suppressed in the name of national security. More and more, however, from the end of the 1950s until today, courts have come to support civil liberties, and the executive branch of government has made few attempts to enforce existing sedition legislation.

## The Sedition Act of 1798

At the close of the eighteenth century, when the United States appeared to be on the verge of war with France, the question of internal subversion became a major national issue. There were charges that many Americans were pro-France, and were involved in spying activities for France. It was against this inflammatory background that the *Sedition Act* was passed by Congress, on July 14, 1798. The stringent act, which outlawed any speech that tended to criticize the government, aroused public indignation, and was a major issue in the 1800 presidential campaign. When Jefferson assumed office, he pardoned all those who had been convicted under the Act. The law expired and was not re-enacted.

## The Sedition Act of 1918

One hundred twenty years elapsed before another such law was enacted by Congress. Like the 1798 law, The Sedition Act of 1918 made it a crime to criticize, verbally or in print, the Constitution, the government, or government policies. Under its provisions, hundreds were tried and convicted on the grounds of dangerous and seditious speech.

## The Smith Act of 1940

The *Smith Act* was passed just before the United States entered World War II, at a time of alarm over the rise of fascism. According to the Act, seditious behavior involved support of violent overthrow of the government, distribution of materials intended to promote overthrow of the government, or organizing or becoming a member of any group with such intentions. Like earlier sedition laws, the Smith Act restricted freedom of speech of those with unpopular beliefs.

*Dennis* v. *United States* (1951) was the first major test of the Smith Act. The Supreme Court ruled that the Act was constitutional, and that the leaders of the American Communist party could be validly convicted under its provisions. Chief Justice Vinson's majority opinion noted that the activities of the eleven defendants, as leaders of the American Communist party, constituted a serious danger to the government. "In this case we are squarely presented with the application of the 'clear and present danger' test." In applying this test, Chief Justice Vinson discarded the time element. Whether or not danger was imminent was immaterial. "It is the existence of the conspiracy which constitutes the danger."

The Court has since revised and refined its position on the Smith Act. In *Yates* v. *United States* (1957), Justice Harlan spoke for the majority in stating that the Smith Act did not prohibit supporting an abstract theory that promoted the overthrow of government. The Act outlawed only supporting overt actions to overthrow the government. The Supreme Court reversed the conviction of fourteen Communist party leaders on the grounds that they had advocated only the abstract doctrine of revolution, rather than direct action to overthrow the government. Four years later, however, the Supreme Court upheld the conviction of a citizen for "active membership in an organization [the Communist party] engaged in illegal advocacy."[27]

[27] *Scales* v. *United States,* 367 U.S. (1961).

## The Internal Security Act of 1950 (McCarran Act)

The escalation of the cold war, and the rising public fear of communism, led to the passage of additional sedition legislation. The *Internal Security Act* of 1950 (or "McCarran Act,") was passed over the veto of President Truman, who said the measure would "give government officials vast powers to harass all of our citizens in the exercise of their right to free speech." The measure had many provisions: it made the process of naturalization more difficult and deportation easier, it barred Communists from working for the federal government.

L. A. Nikolorić, "The Government Loyalty Program," The American Scholar, 19 (summer 1950): 285–298.

L. A. Nikolorić criticizes the loyalty program, the administration of oaths of loyalty to the United States, established by President Truman's Executive Order of March 1947. He notes that the program, in the name of "national security and loyalty," denies "most of the basic tenets of Anglo-American jurisprudence and legal philosophy traditional since the seventeenth century."

The Order, says Nikolorić, is a violation of two basic concepts, particularly: the right of innocence until proven guilty, and the right of protection from bills of attainder. In the first case, it holds one guilty who is only "potentially disloyal." In the second, it dismisses the concept of equal justice under the law by singling out specific people, such as government employees, and requiring special standards of them.

The accusation of "potential disloyalty" necessitated a more specific definition for those who had to execute the oaths. Membership in communist or fascist organizations, showing "sympathy" to communism or fascism, being friendly with people or organizations who were sympathetic to the two theories of government, and being "unduly talkative" in the presence of sympathetic individuals or organizations, all provided grounds for dismissal or refusal to hire. Most distressing to Nikolorić was the fact that the Loyalty Boards did not need to prove anything; they merely had to have a "reasonable doubt."

Although employers were required to present charges to a rejected employee, the charges were often unsubstantiated, and lawyers and employees found it impossible to acquire complete explanations.

Nobody in the United States, writes Nikolorić, can be convicted of a crime as petty as pickpocketing, nor as serious as treason, without proof of having committed the crime. To entertain thoughts of a criminal act is not sufficient proof for a court of law; therefore, it should not be proof of disloyalty either. This position was defended by Justice Hugo Black, who held that, along with proof of disloyal acts, the only legal proof for dismissal from a job was inefficiency. Advocates of the government program, however, chose another line of reason entirely:

Those who would defend the program argue that the government is not required to secure to its employees procedural safeguards when it fires them. It is said that no citizen has an inherent right to government employment. Thus the government may fire arbitrarily—because it does not like the color of the employee's hair, because he is inefficient, or because the government fears that the employee may become a security risk. The procedural safeguards that are provided—charges and a hearing—are a matter of the sovereign's largess. They do not accrue to the employee as a matter of constitutional right. Therefore, the employee may not ask for other safeguards as a matter of constitutional right.

After all the debate and controversy, the program was found to be a total failure. The FBI did not find one spy, or one security violation. In effect, the FBI was forced to do the impossible, to determine who will be the spies of the future. The results of the purge were self-imposed limitation on personal freedoms, refusals to serve in public office, the impossibility of obtaining employment for those hastily branded as traitors by the Boards, and a body of government officials constantly in fear of losing employment. Nikolorić contends that "all Americans suffer" when this is the result.

The suppression of opposition can only mean the retention of outmoded and useless institutions, and impossibility of compromise and adjustment.

To enforce the law, the McCarran Act established a Subversive Activities Control Board. Its job was to judge, by order of the Attorney General, which groups were Communist-inspired or controlled. Upon such a determination, the organizations were required to register with the Attorney General, and to list the names and addresses of the members. Those on the list were prohibited from working "in any defense facility."

In 1965, the Communist party refused to register on the grounds that the Act violated freedom of assembly under the First Amendment, and the protection against self-incrimination under the Fifth Amendment. Speaking for the five–four majority in *Communist Party* v. *Subversive Activity Control Board* (1965), Justice Frankfurter upheld the registration requirement of the McCarran Act, and said that "on its face and as here applied, it does not violate the First Amendment."

[28] *Aptheker* v. *Secretary of State*, 378 U.S. 500 (1964).

[29] *Albertson* v. *Subversive Activities Control Board*, 382 U.S. 70 (1965).

[30] *United States* v. *Robel*, 19 L. ED. 2d 508 (1967).

In the 1960s, however, the Supreme Court declared several provisions of the McCarran Act unconstitutional. In 1964, the Court outlawed the provisions denying passports to members of the United States Communist party and its "front" organization, as an indiscriminate restriction of travel in violation of the Fifth Amendment right to due process of law.[28] In 1965, the Supreme Court ruled that registration could not be forced on individual Communist party members, since this would violate the self-incrimination prohibition of the Fifth Amendment.[29] In 1967, the Court declared unconstitutional the section prohibiting the employment of Communist group members in a United States defense facility.[30]

## The Communist Control Act of 1954

In 1954, with anti-Communist sentiment in the United States still high, and election time approaching, Congress passed the *Communist Control Act*. The Act denied the Communist party the basic rights and privileges enjoyed by other political parties under the laws of the United States. Although the Act did not make party membership a federal crime; it did restrict the rights of unions with Communist officers and employers who hire Communists to represent them by denying them benefits granted by the nation's labor laws.

## Government employment and loyalty

Post-World War II charges that spies and subversives had infiltrated the government, and given classified information to the "enemy" prompted President Truman to institute a national loyalty-security program by executive order in 1947.

A 1950 act of Congress, the *Summary Suspension Act*, stipulated that key federal employees in vital jobs bearing on national security could be summarily dismissed on the strength of evidence bearing on their security status. Such individuals were granted a hearing, but the government was not required to reveal either their accusers or the specific charges against them.

[31] *Cole* v. *Young*, 351 U.S. 536 (1956).

During the Eisenhower administration, the Act's provisions were broadened to apply to *all* federal employees; however, the Supreme Court held that the Act's provisions applied only to individuals in "sensitive positions."[31]

## Symbolic free speech

The individual's right to free speech is not restricted solely to words; it also includes some acts that dramatize the spoken principle, such as flying a revolutionary banner.

An interesting case involving the issue of symbolic free speech as in *United States* v. *O'Brien* (1968), a case that centered on the burning of draft cards. The defendant claimed that burning a draft card was constitutionally protected "symbolic speech." The Supreme Court held that the First Amendment guarantee of freedom of speech does not protect the individual against a conviction for violating a provision of the Selective Service Act. The Court held that the government, in the interest of maintaining a workable Selective Service System, could prohibit the burning of draft cards. Thus, card burning was denied the status of symbolic "free" speech.

## Free speech and public order

A variety of cases have arisen concerning "reasonable" limits on free speech and the use of sound-amplifying devices. In *Saia* v. *New York* (1948), the Supreme Court upheld the right of a Jehovah's Witnesses minister to broadcast the gospel in Lockport, New York, despite a local ordinance outlawing the use of sound systems without first obtaining permission from the Chief of Police. Speaking for the majority, Justice Douglas said that the ordinance was "unconstitutional on its face, for it establishes a previous restraint on free speech," with the minister's right to be heard at the "uncontrolled discretion of the Chief of Police."

The Court, however, in *Kovacs* v. *Cooper* (1949), upheld a Trenton, New Jersey, law forbidding the use on the city's "public streets, alleys or thoroughfares" of any "device known as a sound truck, loudspeaker or sound amplifier" that ". . . emits there from loud and raucous noises." In this case, freedom of speech was limited in the interest of community welfare.

Another free speech issue involves the question of whether or not government can refuse to grant a permit for the use of public streets to persons giving speeches with unpopular ideas. In *Kunz* v. *New York*, the defendant was a minister given to inflammatory speeches berating Jews and Catholics. Denied a license to speak in Columbus Circle, he was arrested and fined ten dollars for violating the New York City ordinance that made it unlawful to hold public worship meetings on the streets without first obtaining a permit from the City Police Commissioner. The Supreme Court declared the ordinance invalid. The majority opinion centered on the prior suppression of free speech and concluded:

> New York cannot vest restraining control over the right to speak on religious subjects in an administrative official where there are not appropriate standards to guide his action.[32]

32 *Kunz* v. *New York*, 340 U.S. 290 (1951).

# Prior restraint and the press

The principle of "no prior restraint" has been stated in relation to several of the free speech criteria; but perhaps its most significant application is in maintaining free press. In this sense, *prior restraint* is the restraining or censoring of material before it is published. The Supreme Court has elevated the principle of no prior restraint to a nearly absolute criterion. Prior government censorship constitutes a particular threat to First Amendment guarantees by narrowing public access to ideas and information.

Although the Supreme Court has not found all prior censorship unconstitutional, the majority of its decisions has been against such practices. In *Near* v. *Minnesota* (1931), the Supreme Court enunciated the "no prior restraint" doctrine when it declared a state law restricting freedom of the press unconstitutional. The statute, dubbed the "Minnesota gag law," was invalidated because it exercised prior restraint. "Liberty of the press," said Chief Justice Hughes, "has meant . . . immunity from previous restraints or censorship."

Drawing by Frasconi; © 1970
The New Yorker Magazine, Inc.

## The Pentagon Papers

Yet, with regard to movie censorship, the Supreme Court has allowed some exercise of prior restraint. In *Freedman* v. *Maryland*, for example, the decision set forth standards for movie censorship procedures. But these were designed as "safeguards against undue inhibition of protected expression—that is, the freedom of expression guaranteed by the First Amendment. For example, to prevent lengthy and costly litigation, the Court required that the censor either promptly issue a license to show the film, or promptly go to court to restrain showing the film. This procedure was intended to minimize the burden of delay that falls on the distributor. Moreover, the Court specified that "the burden of proving that the film is unprotected expression [that is, not guaranteed by the First Amendment] must rest on the state."

Formerly titled *"History of the U.S. Decision-Making Process on Viet Nam Policy,"* this classified, forty-seven-volume study was the recent subject of heated controversy. The government sought court injunctions against certain newspapers in order to halt the further printing of classified documents. The case came before the Supreme Court, which subsequently ruled that the prior restraint sought by the government was unjustified. By a vote of six–to–three, they upheld the newspapers' right to publish the Pentagon Papers. In one of the six separate opinions for the majority, Justice Black declared, "the press must be left free to publish news, whatever the source, without censorship, injunctions, or prior restraints."[33] He added:

[33] *The New York Times* Co. v. *United States*, 91 S. Ct. 2140 (1971).

> Paramount among the responsibilities of a free press is the duty to prevent any part of the government from deceiving the people and sending them off to distant lands to die of foreign fevers and foreign shot and shell. In my view, far from deserving condemnation for their courageous reporting, the *New York Times*, and *Washington Post*, and other newspapers should be commended for serving the purpose that the Founding Fathers saw so clearly. In revealing the workings of government that led to the Viet Nam war, the newspapers nobly did precisely that which the Founders hoped and trusted they would do.

Justice Douglas, in another opinion, said, "As we stated only the other day in *Organization for a Better Austin* v. *Keefe*, 'any prior restraint on expression comes to this Court with a heavy presumption against its constitutional validity.'" Thus, the government's attempt to halt publication in the interests of national security was not upheld by the majority of the Court, because "grave and irreparable" damage to the nation would not result from publication. Justice Stewart noted, "an informed and critical public opinion . . . can here protect the values of democratic government."

In a dissenting opinion, Chief Justice Burger decried the "frenetic haste" of the proceedings. "A great issue of this kind," he said, "should be tried in a judicial atmosphere conducive to thoughtful reflective deliberation." In another dissenting opinion, Justice Harlan stated, "if . . . with

*Pressmen applaud as prepared page of Pentagon series is wheeled from a guarded storage area.*

**Modern media and censorship**

the Court's action today, these newspapers proceed to publish the critical documents and the results there from," the results will be "the greatly increased difficulty of negotiation with our enemies . . . then the Nation's people will know where the responsibility for these sad consequences rests." When freedom of speech and press were written into the First Amendment of the Constitution, motion pictures did not yet exist. Before World War I, they still were not a major medium for conveying information. They were limited to portraying slapstick comedies, highway robberies, and other light topics. Reflecting the state of the industry, the Supreme Court in *Mutual Film Corporation* v. *Ohio Industrial Commission* (1915) ruled that motion pictures, like plays, were not protected by the Constitution because they were essentially a means of entertainment. Pictures did not constitute any part of "the press of the country." With this decision, state and local censorship boards had the power to ban the showing of any film.

In the late twenties, talking pictures were invented; and with them came newsreels, documentary films, and other forms that made film a media of public opinion. Not until 1952, however, did the Court conclusively rule that films were safeguarded under the First and Fourteenth Amendments, but "not necessarily subject to precise rules governing any other particular method of expression."[34]

[34] *Burstyn* v. *Wilson,* 343 U.S. 495 (1952).

Rather than bar all prior censorship, the Court has allowed it to exist, requiring, instead, increasingly difficult standards to justify the practice of prior censorship. In *Burstyn* v. *Wilson,* for example, the Court struck down a ruling by the New York State Board of Regents banning a film called "The Miracle." Yet, it did not rule that all prior censorship of motion pictures was invalid. Instead, it held that such censorship was constitutional, if sufficiently definite standards can be drawn by state and local censors.

In 1959, for example, the Court prohibited New York from banning the showing of "Lady Chatterley's Lover," because such an action violated free press. "What New York has done . . . is to prevent the exhibition of a motion picture because that picture advocates an idea. . . . Yet the First Amendment's basic guarantee is the freedom to advocate ideas. The State, quite simply, has thus struck at the very heart of constitutionally protected liberty."[35]

[35] *Kingsley Pictures Corp.* v. *Regents,* 360 U.S. 684 (1959).

[36] In Maryland, a state censorship system still operates, but in accordance with the standards set in *Freedman* v. *Maryland.*

[37] *National Broadcasting Company* v. *United States,* 319 U.S. 190 (1943).

Today, most state and local censorship boards have either disappeared, or ceased to exercise any real power. Prior censorship of the motion picture media has been curtailed, and the First Amendment guarantee of liberty of expression has been given broad scope by the Supreme Court.[36]

Radio and television are in an unusual position with regard to government control. Only a certain number of broadcast frequencies is available, and a chaotic situation would develop if the government did not regulate the airways. Here, the regulating agency is the Federal Communications Commission (FCC), which grants or renews licenses to broadcast. It can also cancel a license to broadcast, if it decides that the public interest is not being served by a particular station. In practice, however, the power to revoke licenses is seldom exercised. Nevertheless, the Supreme Court has ruled that the unlicensed use of radio air waves is not protected by the First Amendment.[37]

[38] Vice-President Spiro Agnew addressing the Mid-West Regional Republican Committee at Des Moines, Iowa, on November 14, 1969.

[39] *The New York Times, Magazine Section,* May 16, 1971, p. 78.

Freedom of the air waves is of great importance. "Where the *New York Times* reaches 800,000 people, N.B.C. reaches twenty times that number on its evening news."[38] The difficulty lies in the fact that radio and TV stations, though free, must be licensed. "Nobody yet has figured out a way to make licenses and freedom of the press compatible."[39]

## Obscenity

Another area of government control concerns the publication of allegedly obscene materials. The Supreme Court decisions that uphold these restraints rest on the proposition that "obscenity is not protected by the Freedoms of

40 *Roth* v. *United States,*
354 U.S. 476 (1957).

speech and press."[40] However, a clear-cut, standard definition of obscenity is difficult to construct, for what is obscene to one person is not necessarily so to another. As a consequence of the subjectivity of the term, and of ever-changing public tastes, application and enforcement of the ban on obscene material has been extremely difficult.

"So much for *my* version of the news. And now over to my colleague for the same news but with a different set of biasses, hangups, and axes to grind."

Drawing by Donald Reilly; © 1970
The New Yorker Magazine, Inc.

The Supreme Court has attempted to establish criteria for judging whether or not a film, book, play, and other material might be obscene. In *Roth* v. *United States,* the Court defined obscene material as that "which deals with sex in a manner appealing to the prurient interest" and, therefore, not protected by the First Amendment. In addition to the social importance criterion, the Roth case put forth another test for obscenity. This test asked whether or not the average person (rather than those particularly suscep-tible), in applying "contemporary community standards," would be affronted by the material. The Court held that the material must be judged in its entirety; in other words, a book cannot be declared obscene because of a few isolated passages. The Court further declared that ". . . the portrayal of sex . . . in art, literature, and scientific works, is not itself sufficient reason to deny material the constitutional protection of freedom of speech and press."

Although the overall effect of the Roth ruling has been to limit the meaning of obscenity, it has caused problems in Court application. In *Jacobellis* v. *Ohio* (1964), the Court applied the Roth rule, and reversed the Ohio court decision that the movie *The Lovers* was obscene. However, only two justices agreed on the test to be applied. In affirming the Roth test, Justices Brennan and Goldberg stated that "community standards" referred to national, not local, standards. Supporting the Roth rule, but not the Court's decision, Justices Warren and Clark dissented on the grounds that "community standards" referred to local standards.

The Roth rulings were again applied in *Ginsburg* v. *United States* (1966). At issue was the manner in which the publication in question had been promoted and advertised to the public. The Court declared the material obscene because its advertising gave evidence of pandering to the prurient interest of the reader. The decision upheld the conviction of Ginsburg, the publisher, for violating a federal law that prohibits the mailing of obscene materials. The Court, however, was sharply divided in its thinking. The Supreme Court, in recent years, has accepted the constitutionality of precisely drawn statutes designed to protect minors from material which may or may not be obscene to adults.[41] In the light of these and past decisions in obscenity cases, it can be said that the Court has attempted to limit hard-core pornography, while maintaining freedom from censorship for all other forms of expression.

[41] *Ginsberg* v. *New York*, 390 U.S. 629 (1968).

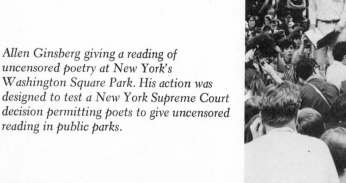

*Allen Ginsberg giving a reading of uncensored poetry at New York's Washington Square Park. His action was designed to test a New York Supreme Court decision permitting poets to give uncensored reading in public parks.*

The publication of pornographic materials is not only an issue in judicial, but also in legislative, debate. Declaring the traffic in obscenity "a matter of national concern," Congress proclaimed that it was government's "responsibility to investigate the gravity of this situation." The United States Commission on Obscenity and Pornography was established in 1968, to suggest national solutions. Submitting its long, voluminous report to President Nixon on September 30, 1970, the Commission, to the surprise and dismay of many, found that the traffic in obscenity and pornography was not "a matter of national concern." It noted a lack of evidence regarding the detrimental effect of pornography on minors, crime, and society. The majority on the Commission felt that "Public opinion in America does not support the imposition of legal prohibitions upon the rights of adults to read or see explicit sexual materials."[42] Commenting on the report, President Nixon said:

[42] *Report of the Commission on Obscenity and Pornography,* 1970.

> I have evaluated that report and categorically reject its morally bankrupt conclusions and major recommendations. . . . The Commission contends that the proliferation of filthy books and plays has no lasting effect on a man's character. . . . American morality is not to be trifled with. The Commission on Pornography and Obscenity has performed a disservice, and I totally reject its report.

## Libel and slander

Although freedom of speech and press is a broad term, it does not guarantee the freedom to use speech or language considered slanderous or libelous—that is, words used with malicious intent to publicly defame the character of an individual. *Slander* is defamation by the spoken word; *libel* refers to defamation by the written word, by pictures, or any form other than the spoken word. Specifically, what constitutes libelous or slanderous speech, however, is often a matter of controversy and dispute.

In general, the Supreme Court has ruled that criticism of public officials, if related to the performance of their official duties, cannot be considered slanderous or libelous.

The Supreme Court, in the famous case *New York Times* v. *Sullivan* (1964), ruled that the newspaper's advertisement criticizing officials of Birmingham, Alabama, for their treatment of blacks, was not libelous. To be libelous, a statement about public officials must be proven to be made with malicious intent (a knowledge that the statement is false, or a reckless disregard for the actual facts). Even though the advertisement did contain some factual errors, this was not sufficient grounds for libel.

[43] *New York Times Co.* v. *Sullivan,* 376 U.S. 254 (1964).

These modifications in the traditional definition of libel serve to protect the critics of government officials from prosecution for libel. Thus, the Supreme Court affirmed a "profound national commitment to the principle that debate on public issues should be uninhibited, robust, and wide-open."[43]

# Freedom of assembly and petition

44 *De Jong* v. *Oregon*, 299 U.S. (1937).

The "right of the people peaceably to assemble, and to petition the government for redress of grievances" is guaranteed by the First Amendment. The Supreme Court made this right binding on the states, through the due process clause of the Fourteenth Amendment. The decision declared that "The right of peaceable assembly is a right cognate to those of free speech and free press and is equally fundamental."[44]

The right to assembly can be subject to certain restrictions, such as traffic regulations. A meeting or "demonstration" that would block traffic, for example, can be prohibited by government, in the interests of public safety. Rules for meetings can be established to maintain the public order.

In *Feiner* v. *New York* (1951), the Supreme Court upheld the conviction of Feiner for disorderly conduct. The Court maintained that his street-corner speech constituted a clear and present danger because it could have caused a riot, if police had not stopped the speaker. The crowd was "pushing, shoving, and milling around," and one member of the crowd "threatened violence if the police did not act." Chief Justice Vinson said that the police were correct in arresting Feiner under the circumstances, because they were

45 *Feiner* v. *New York*, 340 U.S. 315 (1951).

> motivated solely by a proper concern for the preservation and protection of the general welfare, and there was no evidence which could lend color to a claim that the acts of the police were a cover for suppression of [Feiner's] views and opinions. The petitioner was thus neither arrested nor convicted for the making or content of his speech. Rather, it was the reaction which it actually engendered.[45]

The right to assembly became an important issue in the 1960s, when the movement for civil rights fostered demonstrations and marches in many parts of the country. In *Edwards* v. *South Carolina* (1963), the Court declared illegal the arrest of a group of black students who were holding a civil rights protest meeting in front of the South Carolina State House, on the grounds that "The Fourteenth Amendment does not permit a State to make criminal the peaceful expression of unpopular views . . ." Similarly in *Cox* v. *Louisiana* (1965), the Supreme Court upheld the right to demonstrate on public property. Cox, a civil rights leader, had been arrested and convicted for picketing near a courthouse. The Court reversed his conviction on the grounds that the state's breach of peace statute was unconstitutional.

In *Adderly* v. *Florida* (1966), however, the Supreme Court upheld the arrest and conviction of demonstrators. The case involved a group of Florida A & M University students who had marched to the town jail and refused to leave the area. They demonstrated to protest the arrest of a fellow student, as well as the segregated conditions within the jail. The Court ruled that

46 *Adderley* v. *Florida*, 385 U.S. 39 (1966).

to demonstrate on this particular property violated the state's trespass laws.[46] While everyone has a constitutional right to protest unequal treatment, this does not mean that they can exercise it "whenever and however and wherever" they please.

"My, what a beautiful day! I think I'll restore partial freedom of assembly."

Drawing by Donald Reilly; © 1971 The New Yorker Magazine, Inc.

## Right of association

47 *Sweezy* v. *New Hampshire*, 354 U.S. 234 (1957).

The Supreme Court has interpreted the First Amendment's guarantees to include the right of association. This right is not specifically stated in the Constitution, yet it has been recognized as fundamental to political freedom. As Chief Justice Warren once wrote:

> Our form of government is built on the premise that every citizen shall have the right to engage in political expression and association . . . Exercise of these basic freedoms in America has traditionally been through the media of political associations. Any interference with the freedom of a party is simultaneously an interference with the freedom of its adherents.[47]

The Supreme Court has struck down state attempts to infringe on this right. In *NAACP* v. *Alabama* (1958), for example, the Court ruled that the NAACP need not disclose its membership lists to the state of Alabama. This prohibition was necessary in order to protect the individual members of the National Association for the Advancement of Colored People from harassment, in the form of job loss, economic discrimination, and other such actions. In this decision, the Court held that "the right of association was guaranteed by the First Amendment of the Constitution."[48]

[48] *NAACP* v. *Alabama*, 357 U.S. 449 (1958).

# Protection of property

In protecting property rights from national government encroachment, the Fifth and Fourteenth Amendments guarantee that no person shall be deprived of life, liberty, or property without due process of law. The "due process" clause, a complex matter of interpretation, is explained in connection with individual rights described later in this chapter. Several other clauses safeguard the individual's property from the arbitrary activities of government.

## The contract clause

Article I, Section 10, of the Constitution prohibits the states from passing any law "impairing the obligation of contracts." Known as the *contract clause*, this provision originally was intended to prevent state legislatures from passing laws to free debtors of their contractual obligations to creditors. In actuality, the contract clause was interpreted by the courts as a constitutional prohibition against any state regulation of business activity. However, this interpretation changed with the growing complexity of the economy. In 1880, the Supreme Court ruled that the state legislature had the power to terminate a contract if that contract violated the public interest, (in this case the contract involved a lottery detrimental to the public interest).

In 1934, when the Great Depression necessitated government assistance, the case of *Home Building and Loan Association* v. *Blaisdell*, which held that a state law violated the contract clause, came before the Supreme Court. The law in question had declared a moratorium on the foreclosure of certain mortgages providing temporary relief to home owners, who, as victims of the Great Depression, were confronted with the prospect of losing their property. The Court upheld the constitutionality of the law on the grounds that states could make "reasonable" alterations in contracts between individuals when conditions warranted it. The legislation, passed during a time of economic emergency, was "for the protection of a basic interest of society." However, in contemporary America, the contract clause is no longer a significant restriction on government regulation of the economy.

| **Just compensation clause** | The Fifth Amendment safeguards private property by preventing the federal government from taking private property "for public use without just compensation." This *just compensation clause* restricts the power of *eminent domain*, which allows the governments (local, state, and national) to acquire property for public use—for parks, educational facilities, dams, reservoirs, and other purposes. Government must pay the owner of the property a fair price. If the owner refuses to sell, or if a dispute arises on the question of a fair price, the case is presented to the courts for settlement. |

# Law and civil liberties

The apprehension of criminals is always newsworthy. "Shortly before 3 A.M., the Nassau County police seized the burglary suspect . . . from four of his angry pursuers who were holding him at bay with a chair and sticks." But what will happen to the burglary suspect after his arrest is less apparent.

The main text of the Constitution contains certain provisions limiting the powers of government with relation to persons accused of crime. (For example, it prohibits the enaction of *ex post facto* laws.) However, the Bill of Rights and the Fourteenth Amendment provide for most of those rights invoked in encounters with the administration of justice. They reflect the accumulated wisdom and experience of English and American common law at the close of the eighteenth century.

| **Protection of rights in the original constitution** | The safeguards in the main text of the Constitution include the writ of *habeas corpus,* and the prohibition against *ex post facto* laws and bills of attainder. |

*Habeas corpus* is a fundamental right that protects the individual against arbitrary arrest and punishment. Issued by a court, the writ demands that the authorities holding the prisoner bring him before a judge and there state the reasons for his arrest. If they cannot establish a valid reason for the arrest, the accused is freed.

The Constitution states that the writ can be suspended only under conditions of rebellion or invasion, and then, only if it is essential to "the public safety." Since the Civil War, the writ has been suspended only once, in Hawaii during World War II.

The Constitution prohibits national and state governments from passing *ex post facto* laws, which impose a penalty on an act previously not considered criminal, or increase the punishment for a crime *after* it has been committed. This prohibition is a fundamental protection that has rarely been violated.

The enactment of bills of attainder is also forbidden under the Constitution. A *bill of attainder* is an act of Congress that singles out specific persons or groups and orders their punishment without a judicial trial. Bills of attainder have seldom been enacted. In 1943, however, a bill of attainder was actually passed in the form of a rider to an appropriations bill. Prompted by the House Committee on Un-American Activities, the rider singled out three government employees. It declared them subversive and unfit for government service, and forbade the payment of their salaries. The three men sued in the Court of Claims, and the case came before the Supreme Court. In *United States* v. *Lovett* (1946), the Court ruled, ". . . that legislative acts . . . that apply either to named individuals or to easily ascertainable members of a group in such a way as to inflict punishment on them without a judicial trial are bills of attainder prohibited by the Constitution."[49] The Supreme Court upheld the claim of the three, reasoning that Congress, by charging them with disloyalty and denying them money, had punished them without a judicial trial, in violation of the Constitution.

[49] *United States* v. *Lovett,* 328 U.S. 303 (1946).

## The Bill of Rights and due process of law

The procedural guarantees listed in the Bill of Rights were designed to protect the individual from unjust treatment by government law enforcement authorities, the police, and the courts. It has been said that the Bill of Rights makes it more difficult to apprehend those accused of crime. Yet, this was the purpose the provisions were to fulfill. They sought to insure that the innocent would not be wrongly convicted, even though a few of the guilty might go free. The Bill of Rights seeks to guarantee justice by ensuring the procedural rights of all persons.

The *due process* clause of the Fifth and Fourteenth Amendments prohibits the national and state governments, respectively, from depriving any person of "life, liberty, or property without due process of law."

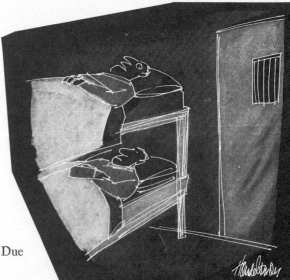

Drawing by Handelsman; © 1970 The New Yorker Magazine, Inc.

"What's so great about due process? Due process got me ten years."

Due process of law has two categories: substantive and procedural. *Substantive due process* of law has to do with the substance of the law and the protection it provides; *procedural due process* concerns rules of procedure and the manner in which the law is applied. From the end of the nineteenth century until the late 1930s, the Supreme Court invoked substantive due process as a criterion for determining the constitutionality of laws dealing with economic regulation. For example, the Court declared state minimum wage laws unconstitutional on the grounds that such economic controls were not within the power of government, and violated the right to property under the due process clause. Since 1937, however, the Supreme Court has abandoned substantive due process, and today, due process of law is primarily concerned with procedural guarantee. It is applied to insure that the government adheres to certain procedural standards in the administration of criminal justice.

## Search and seizure

The Fourth Amendment guarantees:

> The right of the people to be secure in their persons, houses, papers and effects, against unreasonable searches and seizures, shall not be violated, and no warrants shall issue, but upon probable cause, supported by oath or affirmation, and particularly describing the place to be searched, and the persons or things to be seized.

This provision reflects the common law principle that "a man's house is his castle." To secure evidence of illegal acts, the state must abide by certain rules of law. "Unreasonable" searches and seizures are prohibited. A search and seizure, under most circumstances, can be conducted only after a search warrant has been issued by either a judge or another judicial authority. The inspector, to justify the warrant, must show the judge evidence of "probable cause" that a law has been breached. He must also describe specifically the place to be searched and the things to be seized. This requirement was designed to prevent broad-scale searching of entire neighborhoods and indiscriminate searching of private homes.

Under common law, a court would accept the evidence presented, regardless of the legality of the methods used to obtain it. In 1914, however, the Supreme Court ruled that evidence obtained through illegal search and seizure could not be used against the accused in a federal criminal prosecution.[50] The exclusion of unconstitutionally seized evidence provided an effective deterrent against illegal searching. This rule (barring the use of unconstitutionally seized evidence), however, was not held binding on the states. In 1949, the Supreme Court held that while unreasonable searches and seizures by a state violated the Fourteenth Amendment, a state could use evidence obtained through an illegal search and seizure, if its own laws so

[50] *Weeks* v. *United States*, 232 U.S. 383 (1914).

51 *Wolf* v. *Colorado,*
338 U.S. 25 (1949).

permitted.[51] At that time, over half the states still adhered to the common law rule.

But in *Mapp* v. *Ohio* (1961), the Supreme Court, for the first time, applied the exclusionary rule to the states. In the majority opinion, Justice Tom Clark wrote, "We hold that all evidence obtained by searches and seizures in violation of the Constitution is, by that same authority, inadmissible in a state court."

Drawing by Dana Fradon; © 1971
The New Yorker Magazine, Inc.

## Electronic eavesdropping

When the Fourth Amendment was written in 1791, its authors, of course, could not foresee the development of electronic listening devices which would make a physical entry for search and seizure unnecessary. Such modern technological developments have given rise to new interpretations of classic guarantees. A case involving wiretapping first came before the Supreme Court in 1928, in *Olmstead* v. *United States.* Olmstead was the head of a huge complex of bootleggers (traffickers in illegal alcohol), which had an annual income of over two million dollars. It was the Prohibition Era, and Olmstead had an elaborate network of underground offices. Federal officers had tapped the telephone wires of this basement network. On the basis of evidence recorded from the conversations, the conspirators were convicted. The Supreme Court ruled that the recording of telephone conversations by secret electronic devices such as wiretaps did not qualify as unreasonable searches and seizures. The rationale was that, since the police had not actually entered the offices, no physical trespass had occurred and, therefore, no "unreasonable" search had taken place; and because spoken words were the subject, and only tangible objects can be seized, no unreasonable seizure had occurred.

After this rigid interpretation of the Fourth Amendment, Congress proposed several bills to prohibit wiretapping by the government. The Federal Communications Act of 1934 provided that "no person not being authorized by the sender shall intercept any communication and divulge or publish the existence, contents, substance . . . of such intercepted communication to any person." In *Nardone* v. *United States* (1939), the Supreme Court ruled that evidence obtained from wiretaps could not be used to prosecute in federal court, since it had been obtained in violation of a congressional law. But it was not until 1967 that the Supreme Court overturned the Olmstead decision and subjected all electronic surveillance to the procedures stated in the Fourth Amendment.[52]

In 1968, Congress enacted the *Omnibus Crime Control and Safe Streets Act*, which legalized wiretapping activities by federal, state, and local police. The law requires that officers obtain judicial warrants for wiretaps, as an instrument of law enforcement and criminal investigation.

President Johnson forbade both wiretapping and eavesdropping by federal officers, even after Congress had authorized their use. The only exception made was for cases of national security, which strictly meant espionage. Under President Nixon, Attorney General John Mitchell has applied the provisions of the 1968 Act to expand government wiretapping activities, and he has broadly interpreted the "nationality security" section to include surveillance of domestic organizations suspected of subversion, such as the Weathermen and the Black Panthers.

The issue of electronic eavesdropping was met squarely by the Supreme Court in 1969, when it declared that the Fourth Amendment "affords protection against the uninvited ear."[53] However, as the pace of discovery and invention increases, subtler and more far-reaching listening devices threaten "the sanctities of a man's home and the privacies of life."[54]

[52] *Berger* v. *State of New York*, 388 U.S. 41 (1967).

[53] *Alderman* v. *United States*, 394 U.S. 165 (1969).

[54] *Olmstead* v. *United States*, 277 U.S. 438 (1928).

## Freedom from self-incrimination

Another of the major procedural rights guaranteed by the Bill of Rights is the Fifth Amendment's guarantee that no person "shall be compelled in any criminal case to be a witness against himself." This protection applies not only to the accused, but also to the witnesses testifying in court, and individuals who appear before legislative or administrative investigatory bodies. Although the protection against *self-incrimination* had long been applied in federal courts, it was not made binding on the states until 1964. The Court's decision in *Malloy* v. *Hogan* announced, "The Fourteenth Amendment secures against state invasion the same privilege that the Fifth Amendment guarantees against federal infringement—the right of a person to remain silent."

*Richard A. Watson,* "Federalism v. Individual Rights: The Legal Squeeze of Self-Incrimination," *American Political Science Review, 54 (1960)*: 887–898.

Richard Watson argues that the two separate court systems, federal and state, do not have sufficient procedural safeguards to protect an individual from self-incrimination.

The dilemmas arise because the principles of federalism necessarily affect the right against self-incrimination in two distinct situations: one when the right is first asserted in national proceedings and its effect on a later state prosecution must be considered; and the other the obverse case, when the right is first claimed in state proceedings and its consequence for a federal prosecution is in issue.

While it has generally been assumed that all citizens have the right to protect themselves from self-incrimination by "claiming the Fifth Amendment," which states that no citizen may be a witness against himself, the application of this right in federal courts for future protection in state prosecution was unclear until the 1931 case of *United States* v. *Murdock*. The Supreme Court ruled that Murdock could not claim fear of self-incrimination leading to later state prosecution, because the "protection money he allegedly paid in connection with gambling operations" was being investigated under federal law in regard to federal matters. This case has been used subsequently as precedent for acquiring information from citizens. With the exception of Florida and Michigan, which have refused to allow federal evidence to be used in state embezzlement actions, most states do not hesitate to accept "windfall evidence," evidence revealed by other courts. Because of such state court actions, federal immunity statutes have been enacted to permit a witness to testify, without fear of further prosecution.

The use of limits on federal testimony in state courts was challenged in the cases of *Adams* v. *Maryland* and *Ullman* v. *U.S.* In both cases, the Supreme Court's ruling stressed the importance of testifying in federal court and obtaining total protection from ensuing state proceedings after revealing the compelled information.

The power of the national government to preclude state prosecutions is important to a witness appearing before a national agency for questioning. Equally important is the policy of Congress toward immunity against state prosecution. For example, the Murdock ruling allows federal inquiries for national purposes notwithstanding possible incrimination under state law. Yet in Ullman the Supreme Court construed the federal immunity statute of 1954 as granting witnesses complete protection from state prosecution, even though, in a national inquiry for an admittedly national purpose, they could have been legally required to answer regardless of the consequences for state criminal action.

Not until 1944 was the federal government faced with the obverse constitutional question of whether or not they should use evidence from state proceedings. In *Feldman* v. *United States*, evidence acquired by New York State's creditors' prosecution was considered admissible in a mail-fraud proceeding before the United States Supreme Court. The Court ruled that only in cases where federal authorities aided those of the state would the evidence be inadmissible.

Richard Watson argues that "cooperative federalism," or "new federalism," in which the national and state governments collaborate "can lead to serious inroads on individual liberties." Watson further argues that we must aim at weighing conflicting interests and seeking a balance of values in our system. He claims that collaboration on investigations and prosecutions should not occur. But neither should witnesses be granted total immunity. Rather, he submits a compromise:

Perhaps the most satisfactory solution is a compromise, namely, to say that testimony compelled by one jurisdiction should not be admissible as evidence in the courts of another, but that the second sovereignty should not be barred from prosecuting the witness on other evidence for matters related to those about which he was previously interrogated. This approach would certainly offer the witness more protection than the present rule affords, although it would still enable one jurisdiction to secure leads which another could follow in developing the other evidence. This risk seems preferable to that of foreclosing any action against the witness by the second jurisdiction, as a grant of complete immunity would do.

This could be achieved if the Supreme Court would rule to forbid the use of all nationally coerced confessions in state courts. The Court would also need to overrule *Feldman* v. *United States*, thereby prohibiting federal courts from using state-elicited confessions. Watson contends that since Congress finds that complete immunity is necessary in certain areas of "paramount national interest," it should legislate immunization specifically for these areas, and the Supreme Court should validate them.

Federal law has long required that no adverse interpretation be construed from the silence of an accused in a courtroom: the burden of proving guilt rests with the state. Moreover, in cases where defendants refuse to appear in their own defense, the jury must be warned by the judge not to misconstrue the defendants' refusal to take the stand.

## Right to counsel

"In all criminal prosecutions, the accused shall enjoy the right . . . to have the Assistance of Counsel for his defense." This Sixth Amendment guarantee was originally designed to ensure that the accused be represented in court by a counsel trained in law, so that the complexity of trial procedure would not frustrate his case.

The landmark case for applying this right in federal courts was *Johnson* v. *Zerbst* (1938). The Supreme Court held that if a federal court did not grant the right of counsel, then the court would not have the power to proceed with the case. In state courts, the right to counsel has gradually been extended since the early 1930s. In *Powell* v. *Alabama* (1932), the right was applied to the states through the Fourteenth Amendment with regard to cases involving the death penalty. Here, in the first of the famed Scottsboro cases, the Supreme Court reversed the death penalty conviction of seven young Negroes accused of raping two white girls on the grounds that the accused had been denied the right of counsel and, hence, due process of law.[55]

[55] *Powell* v. *Alabama*, 287 U.S. 45 (1932).

It was not until 1963, in *Gideon* v. *Wainright*, that the double standard for this right ended at last. The Court unanimously held that the Sixth Amendment's right to counsel applied to all state criminal trials.

While this case brought the right to counsel in line with federal practice, the problem of when to apply this right still remained unresolved. At what point in the criminal process—upon arrest, while awaiting trial, or at some other point—is the accused entitled to counsel?

Crimes may be solved by interrogating suspects; but, often, in their zeal to secure confessions, investigators may infringe upon the constitutional rights of suspects. The Supreme Court has been increasingly assertive in striking down convictions smacking of the least hint of police brutality. In 1964, for example, the Supreme Court ruled that an individual had the right to consult with a lawyer as soon as he is taken into custody by police as a prime suspect for questioning. In delivering the majority opinion on *Escobedo* v. *Illinois*, Justice Goldberg stated:

> We hold, therefore, that where, as here, the investigation is no longer a general inquiry into an unsolved crime but has begun to focus on a particular suspect, the suspect has been taken into custody, the police carry out a process of interrogations that lends itself to eliciting incriminating statements, the suspect has requested and been denied the opportunity to consult with his lawyer, and the police have not effectively warned him of his constitutional rights to remain silent, the accused has been denied "the Assistance of Counsel" in violation of the Sixth Amendment of the Constitution as

56 *Escobedo* v. *Illinois,*
378 U.S. 478 (1964).

"made obligatory upon the States by the Fourteenth Amendment" . . . and that no statement elicited by the police during the interrogation may be used against him at a criminal trial.[56]

Much criticism was leveled at the Court for this ruling, particularly by law enforcement officers, attorneys, prosecutors, and the police. It was claimed that the majority of criminal convictions were based on evidence obtained from confessions, rather than from other forms of police investigation. Critics often quoted the dissenting opinion of Justice John Harlan, who said the ruling "seriously and unjustifiably fetters perfectly legitimate methods of criminal law enforcement." Yet, despite public criticism, the Supreme Court reaffirmed and strengthened the Escobedo decision two years later in *Miranda* v. *Arizona.* The ruling in Miranda further clarified the procedural rules in the questioning of persons suspected of crime. The decision states that when an individual has been arrested or deprived of his freedom by the police, his protection against self-incrimination is threatened, and procedural safeguards must be followed to guarantee this right.

> He must be warned prior to any questioning that he has the right to remain silent, that anything he says can be used against him in a court of law, that he has the right to the presence of an attorney, and that if he cannot afford an attorney one will be appointed for him prior to any questioning if he so desires. Opportunity to exercise the rights must be afforded to him throughout the interrogation. After such warnings have been given, and such opportunity afforded him, the individual may knowingly and intelligently waive these rights and agree to answer questions or make a statement. But unless and until such warnings and waiver are demonstrated by the prosecution at trial, no evidence obtained as a result of interrogation can be used against him.[57]

57 *Miranda* v. *Arizona,*
384 W.S. 436 (1966).

The Miranda decision established new restrictions on the conduct of police interrogations. It has been criticized as unnecessarily hindering police use of an effective method for solving crime. Whether it has actually reduced the number of actual confessions, however, is not at all certain. But regardless of its effect on law enforcement, it cannot be doubted that the Supreme Court in the Miranda case made a bold and strong ruling in favor of the importance of protecting the constitutional rights of the criminally accused.

## Excessive bail

The Eighth Amendment guarantees that "Excessive bail shall not be required, nor excessive fines imposed." In determining bail, courts consider the seriousness of the offense. Bail can be denied in cases of major crime. When the granting of bail is proper, however, it must not be "excessive," though there is no fixed standard for determining these limits. Whether or not the excessive bail provision is binding on the states has not been declared as yet by the Supreme Court.

Crowded jails, lengthy courtroom dockets, and the financial difficulty of the poor in raising bail, led to the passage of the *Bail Reform Act of 1966*. The law gives federal judges greater leverage in granting men freedom, pending trial or appeal, but the new law applies only to federal criminal procedure. In the state court system, conditions are little improved. In some large metropolitan areas, conditions are often grim. In New York City, for example, where courts are jammed and prisons overflowing, obtaining bail is still a problem. There are many who cannot raise the required bail and who must go to prison. In 1971, it was reported that in the Tombs (the Manhattan House of Detention for Men), the population "now stands at 1,453 or 500 above its capacity."[58] A case was cited of a couple who were arrested five months ago and are still in prison awaiting trial.

[58] *The New York Times*, September 2, 1971, p. 37.

## Indictment by grand jury

The Fifth Amendment declares "No person shall be held to answer for a capital, or otherwise infamous crime, unless on a presentment or indictment of a Grand Jury . . ." This procedure was designed to ensure that a person would not be forced to stand trial unless there was sufficient evidence against him and this was to be determined by a body of men called the grand jury. The judgment of the group was to protect the accused from arbitrary prosecution by the government.

A "capital" crime is one punishable by death. An "infamous" crime has never been defined clearly. It does include major violations of the law, punishable by prison terms, or the revoking of political and civil privileges. When an act violating federal law is committed, a grand jury determines if the evidence warrants a trial. The jury has from sixteen to twenty-three members. The government prosecutor states the case and if the jurors view the evidence as insufficient, the accused must be released. A grand jury does not have the power to convict or punish. Its power is confined to deeming whether or not government should proceed with further prosecution by actual trial.

[59] *Hurtado* v. *California*, 110 U.S. 516 (1884).

In this country, indictment by grand jury is one of the few procedural guarantees of the Bill of Rights not binding on the states.[59] Instead of this procedure, the states have made increasing use of the "information affidavit," which is a simple affidavit filed by a prosecutor and presented to a court to show he has evidence to warrant a trial.

## Trial by jury

Trial by jury is guaranteed by the Sixth Amendment, which declares, "In all criminal prosecutions, the accused shall enjoy the right to a speedy and public trial by an impartial jury."

The stipulation "speedy" protects the accused from long pretrial waits; "public" prevents secret and arbitrary proceedings; and, most importantly,

*The Sixth Amendment to the Constitution gives every citizen the right to a speedy trial. A major problem of today's courts is overcrowded calendars, which inhibits this right and result in overcrowded jails (such as this one in Kentland, Indiana).*

"impartial" holds that the jury must judge the case objectively.

In practice, the guarantee to an impartial jury has been violated sometimes by the effects of sensational publicity, adverse, "pre-judging" newspaper headlines, and unruly courtrooms. In such cases, the Supreme Court has reversed convictions on the principle that the prevailing atmosphere hindered the jury from arriving at an unbiased verdict.[60] To conduct a trial where the climate of opinion is charged, denies the defendant due process of law.

The demand for fair trial involves not only atmosphere, but also the initial composition of the jury, and the objectivity of each prospective juror. By common law, the jury consists of twelve members, and the vote of the jurors usually must be unanimous. In the selection of the jury, discrimination due to race, creed, or sex, is forbidden. This principle was affirmed, for example, in *Hernandez* v. *Texas* (1954), where evidence proved that no one of Mexican or Latin-American extraction had been selected to serve on the county jury for twenty-five years.

[60] *Estes* v. *Texas,* 381 U.S. 532 (1965); *Shepperd* v. *Maxwell,* 384 U.S. 333 (1966).

The right to a jury trial in state criminal cases has recently been an issue before the Supreme Court. In several early cases, the Court had ruled that trial by jury is not required of the states by the Constitution.[61] However, in 1968, the Court reversed itself by holding that jury trial in criminal cases was required of the states by the due process clause of the Fourteenth Amendment. The decision stated, "a general grant of jury trial for serious offenses is a fundamental right, essential for preventing miscarriages of justice and for assuring that fair trials are provided for all defendants."[62]

[61] *Walker* v. *Sauvinet,* 92 U.S. 90 (1876); *Maxwell* v. *Dow,* 176 U.S. 581 (1900).

[62] *Duncan* v. *Louisiana,* 20 L. Ed. 2d 491 (1968).

## Double jeopardy

Protection against double jeopardy is guaranteed by the Fifth Amendment clause, "nor shall any person be subject for the same offense to be twice put in jeopardy of life or limb . . ."

This prohibition against double jeopardy means that once a person has been tried for a particular crime and the trial has ended in a decision, he cannot be tried again for the same crime. It bars the government from initiating further proceedings against him.

Double jeopardy is a complex guarantee. It defies a precise definition, because the circumstances from which the issue may arise are so varied. The double jeopardy clause does not prevent, for example, a defendant from being tried again for the same offense, if the jury cannot arrive at a verdict (a hung jury). Moreover, if the defendant is convicted, but released on appeal for a procedural error, he is subject to retrial for the same offense. If an act violates both state and federal laws, the individual who commits it may be tried separately in each court for the same act. In such cases, a single act entails more than one offense, in that it violates more than one law.

# Civil liberties and the democracy of justice

In the realm of *civil liberties* guarantees, practice is not always consistent with principle. Many criticisms have been made about our system of justice—the slowness of procedure, and the discriminations against minorities and the poor. Some of the criticism is valid. Judges, prosecutors, and the police sometimes behave arbitrarily; complex legal procedures prevent "speedy trial;" and if you are poor, it is difficult to obtain competent counsel. In regard to the Supreme Court's 1971 decision reversing Muhammad Ali's conviction for draft evasion, a reporter wrote:

[63] Robert Lipsyte in *The New York Times,* July 1, 1971.

> As one of his lawyers commented recently, Ali's case disproved those who claim the American legal system does not work. It works perfectly, he said, if you have the money and power to go all the way.[63]

Inconsistencies in the administration of the law contradict the underlying constitutional principles of equality and value of individual rights. Yet, in the realm of civil liberties, the Supreme Court, in upholding constitutional guarantees, has strengthened American constitutional democracy. In prescribing the limits of government power, the Court establishes the obligations of a government toward its people in a democratic society. As former Supreme Court Justice Arthur Goldberg once declared in respect to the right to counsel:

> We have . . . learned the . . . lesson of history that no system of criminal justice can, or should, survive if it comes to depend for its continued effectiveness on the citizens' abdication through unawareness of their constitutional rights. No system worth preserving should have to fear that, if an accused is permitted to consult with a lawyer, he will become aware of, and exercise these rights. If the exercise of constitutional rights will thwart the effectiveness of a system of law enforcement, then there is something very wrong with that system.[64]

[64] *Escobedo* v. *Illinois,* 378 U.S. 478 (1964).

This extension of civil liberty guarantees reflects changing times and the active strengthening of democratic principles. And yet it cannot be too greatly emphasized that the effectiveness of Supreme Court decisions in protecting civil liberties depends, to a tremendous degree, on the public will to comply. The Supreme Court has limited power of enforcement. If the lower courts, local officials, the police, and the public do not carry out and enforce the rulings of the Court, then its judgments and policies are ineffective, and the democratic process suffers accordingly. The widespread evasion of the Court's ruling in *Engel* v. *Vitale* (1962), which banned the reciting of prayers in public schools, illustrates this fact. To avoid the impact of the decision, school boards throughout the country devised means of evasion. Some authorized the students to recite prayers of their own choosing; others had adopted a "moment of silence" to be used voluntarily for silent prayer. Still others ignored the ruling altogether. The impact of Court decisions can be restricted by the reaction of the public. The liberties of a people ultimately depend on a reasoned commitment to individual freedoms by the members of that society.

# Glossary

**absolutist position**    View that the First Amendment should be interpreted literally, that it prohibits all laws which limit the freedoms guaranteed by the amendment.

**balancing of interests doctrine**    Supreme Court interpretation of First Amendment freedoms which requires that those freedoms be balanced against the needs of the government and the society. This view contrasts with that of "preferred position."

**child benefit theory**    Doctrine which holds that the government, in authorizing funds for aid to both public and private school children, are aiding the *child*, not the school or institution he attends.

**civil liberties**    Liberty of an individual to exercise those rights guaranteed by the laws of a country.

**clear and present danger theory**    A standard, or criterion, promulgated by the Supreme Court whereby free speech may be constitutionally restrained if the expression of ideas tends to constitute a real and/or immediate threat to the American system of government or its citizens.

**Communist Control Act of 1954**    Congressional act which denied to the Communist Party rights enjoyed by other political parties and which took away labor benefits from communist-dominated unions and from employers who hire communists to represent them.

**conscientious objectors**    Those members of American society who hold that it is wrong to participate in war, and who resist military service on the grounds of religious belief, conscience, or moral code.

**contract clause**    Provision in Article I, Section 10, of the Constitution which prohibits the states from passing any law "impairing the obligation of Contracts"; and which was once interpreted by the Supreme Court as a constitutional prohibition against state regulation of business activity.

**dangerous (bad) tendency**    A standard or criterion promulgated by the Supreme Court whereby free speech may be constitutionally restrained if the expression of ideas might tend to result in acts which constitute a threat to the American system of government and to the public welfare.

**double jeopardy**    Indicting and retrying someone for a crime of which he has already been acquitted; prohibited by the Fifth Amendment to the Constitution.

**eminent domain**    Doctrine of the Fifth Amendment to the Constitution, allowing the governments (local, state, and federal) to appropriate property required for public use, but only if just compensation is made for it.

**establishment clause**    Provision of the First Amendment to the Constitution, denying Congress the right to establish a church, thereby maintaining the separation of church and state.

**free exercise clause**    Provision of the First Amendment of the Constitution, that prohibits the national government from restricting the individual's right to the free exercise of religion, as long as the religious practices do not violate the law.

**Internal Security Act of 1950 (McCarran Act)**   Congressional act establishing a Subversive Activities Control Board to determine, at the request of the Attorney General, which organizations were "Communist-action" or "Communist front," and upon such a determination, made it mandatory that these organizations register with the Attorney General. The registration provision was later declared unconstitutional by the Supreme Court.

**just compensation clause**   Provision of the Fifth Amendment safeguarding private property, by preventing government from taking private property "for public use without just compensation," thus restricting the power of eminent domain.

**libel**   Written defamation with malicious intent to publicly defame the character of an individual.

**Omnibus Crime Control and Safe Streets Act** (1968)   Congressional act permitting restricted use of wiretapping by national, state, and local police.

**Pentagon Papers**   Classified government documents, formally called "History of U.S. Decision-Making Process on Viet Nam Policy—United States—1971," which were first made public by *The New York Times* and The Washington *Post*.

**prior restraint of the press**   Prohibiting or censoring material by government before it is actually released.

**procedural due process of law**   The rules of procedure proscribed by law, especially in the field of criminal law, as guaranteed by the Fourth, Fifth, and Sixth Amendments to the Constitution.

**released time**   Special hours set aside from regular classroom study to allow children in public schools to receive religious instruction.

**sedition**   "Act of rebellion against or attempt to incite such rebellion against a government."

**Sedition Act of 1798**   Congressional act outlawing any speech that tended to criticize the government or its officials.

**Sedition Act of 1918**   Congressional act that made it a crime to criticize, verbally or in print, the Constitution, the government, or governmental policies.

**self-incrimination**   Serving or tending to incriminate oneself by being compelled in a criminal case to be a witness against oneself. Prohibited by the Fifth Amendment to the Constitution.

**slander**   Oral defamation with malicious intent to publicly defame the character of an individual.

**Smith Act of 1940**   Congressional act, which made it illegal to advocate the violent overthrow of the government, to distribute materials intended to promote the overthrow of the government, or to organize any group with such intentions.

**substantive due process of law**   Due process of law pertaining to the substance or content of a law.

**Summary Suspension Act** (1950)   Congressional act stipulated that key federal employees in vital jobs bearing on national security could be summarily dismissed on the strength of evidence bearing on their security status.

**symbolic speech**   Acts that dramatize the spoken word.

**wall of separation doctrine**   Interpretation of the First Amendment which holds that the establishment clause outlaws government aid to religion and, therefore, requires complete separation of church and state.

## Supreme Court decisions

*Adderly* v. *Florida* (1966)   Declared that picketing before a jail house was not protected by the First Amendment.

*Alderman* v. *United States* (1969)   Ruled that the Fourth Amendment "affords protection against the uninvited ear," and that the government must reveal to the defendant all records of illegal electronic surveillance in order to determine whether evidence was derived from this source.

*Barron* v. *Baltimore* (1833)   Established that the Bill of Rights applied only to the national government and not to the states.

*Benton* v. *Maryland* (1969)   Held the prohibition against double jeopardy applicable not only to the national government, but to the states as well.

*Betts* v. *Brady* (1942)   Decision that "appointment of counsel is not a fundamental right" in noncapital cases and hence not applicable to the states by the Fourteenth Amendment.

*Blau* v. *United States* (1950)   Decision that the Fifth Amendment protection against self-incrimination protected an individual in refusing to testify about his employment by the Communist Party.

*Cox* v. *Louisiana* (1965)   Upheld the right to demonstrate peacefully before a court house.

*Dennis* v. *United States* (1951)   First major test of the Smith Act in which the Supreme Court decided that the act was constitutionally applicable to Communist Party leaders charged with advocating the violent overthrow of the government.

*Engle* v. *Vitale* (1962)   Outlawed the recitation in public schools of a religious prayer (the Regent's prayer, composed by the state government) as a violation of the First Amendment.

*Escobedo* v. *Illinois* (1964)   Held that the Sixth Amendment requires that all persons being held by the police be told of their right to counsel and that in the absence of this warning no statement elicited by the police during an interrogation can be used against the defendant at a criminal trial.

*Everson* v. *Board of Education of Ewing Township* (1947)   Upheld the right of the state to provide bus transportation to children attending parochial schools as not a violation of the First Amendment's establishment clause.

*Feiner* v. *New York* (1951)   Upheld the right of states to restrict street speeches where a "clear and present danger" of riot, interference with traffic, or threat to the public safety exists.

*Gideon* v. *Wainright* (1963)   Ruled that the Sixth Amendment's right to counsel applied to trials in state courts.

*Gitlow* v. *New York* (1925)   Ruling that allowed states to restrict writing that amounted to a *"bad tendency."*

*Johnson* v. *Zerbst* (1938)   Decision that the right to counsel must be offered to all defendants in criminal trials.

*McCollum* v. *Board of Education* (1948)   Decision that outlawed religious instruction for public school children on public school premises as a violation of the First Amendment's establishment clause.

*Malloy* v. *Hogan* (1964)   Held that the constitutional guarantee against self-incrimination was binding on the states as well as the national government.

*Mapp* v. *Ohio* (1961)   Decision that evidence obtained by searchers and seizures in violation of the Fourth Amendment is inadmissible in a state court.

*Miranda* v. *Arizona* (1966)   Established the constitutional procedures police must follow when they take a person into custody and before they begin to interrogate him.

*Mutual Film Corporation* v. *Ohio Industrial Commission* (1915)   Ruled that motion pictures, like plays, were not protected by the Constitution because they were essentially a means of entertainment. As a result of this decision, state and local censorship boards gained the power to ban the showing of films.

*NAACP* v. *Alabama* (1958)   Held a law which required the disclosure of the names of the members of an organization to the state government to be an illegal violation of the First Amendment.

*Nardone* v. *United States* (1939)   Decision that evidence obtained from wiretaps could not be used as evidence in federal court since the practice had been made illegal by the Congress in 1934.

*National Broadcasting Company* v. *United States* (1943)   Decision that the First Amendment right of free speech is not denied by the licensing system established by the Federal Communications Act of 1934.

*Near* v. *Minnesota* (1931)   Declared prior censorship of the press unconstitutional.

*New York Times* v. *Sullivan* (1964)   Decision that in order for a newspaper advertisement that berated public officials in Birmingham, Alabama, to be deemed libelous, it must be proven to be made with " 'actual malice'—that is, with a knowledge that it was false, or with a reckless disregard of whether it was false or not."

*Olmstead* v. *United States* (1928)   Decision that wiretapping did not violate the Fourth Amendment.

*Powell* v. *Alabama* (1932)   Landmark Supreme Court decision that the right to counsel in cases involving capital punishment, as guaranteed by the Sixth Amendment against federal encroachment, applied to the states through the Fourteenth Amendment.

*Reynolds* v. *United States* (1878)   Decision that religious liberty does not include the right to commit acts that violate the laws of society, in this instance the practice of polygamy.

*Roth* v. *United States* (1957)   Reasserted that obscene material was not protected by the First Amendment and that obscene material was that "which deals with sex in a manner appealing to the prurient interest."

*Times Film Company* v. *City of Chicago* (1961)   Upheld a Chicago ordinance calling for examination of all films by city authorities prior to the issue of permits for public showing.

*Trop* v. *Dulles* (1958)   Decision that the expatriation of an American citizen for the act of deserting from the armed services was a cruel and unusual punishment in violation of the Eighth Amendment.

*Ullmann* v. *United States* (1956)   Upheld the constitutionality of the Compulsory Testimony Act of 1954 as not a violation of the Fifth Amendment protection against self-incrimination.

*United States* v. *Lovett* (1946)   Declared unconstitutional an act of Congress that denied payment of salaries to three named federal employees because the law was a bill of attainder.

*United States* v. *The New York Times* (1971) and *United States* v. *The Washington Post* (1971)   Decisions that publication of the classified Pentagon Papers could not be prevented by the federal government.

*United States* v. *O'Brien* (1968)   Decision that burning a draft card was not protected by the First Amendment's guarantee of freedom of speech.

*Yates* v. *United States* (1957)   Interpreted the Smith Act to mean that only direct incitements to overthrow the government are illegal.

*Zorach* v. *Clauson* (1952)   Declared that religious instruction held outside a public school was not a violation of the establishment clause of the First Amendment.

# Suggested readings

Abraham, Henry J., *Freedom and the Court: Civil Rights and Liberties in the United States* (New York: Oxford University Press, Inc., 1967). Examination of the Supreme Court's role in the development and implementation of civil liberties.

Barker, Lucius J., and Twiley W. Barker, Jr., *Freedoms, Courts, Politics: Studies in Civil Liberties* (Englewood Cliffs, N.J.: Prentice-Hall, Inc., 1965). Examination of select civil liberties problems as evidenced in Supreme Court decisions.

Bickel, Alexander M., *The Supreme Court and the Idea of Progress* (New York: Harper & Row Publishers, Inc., 1970). Critical analysis of the work of the Supreme Court during the period that Earl Warren served as Chief Justice.

Chafee, Zechariah, *Free Speech in the United States* (New York: Atheneum Publishers, 1969). Originally published in 1941. Historical account testing right of free speech in the United States, emphasizing the period during and after World War I.

Commager, Henry S., *Freedom and Order: A Commentary on the American Political Scene* (New York: George Braziller, Inc., 1966). Essays dealing with civil liberties, political institutions, and political practices.

Cox, Archibald, *The Warren Court; Constitutional Decision as an Instrument of Reform* (Cambridge, Mass.: Harvard University Press, 1968). Lectures that provide an analysis and defense of the work of the Supreme Court under Chief Justice Warren.

Cushman, Robert Eugene, *Civil Liberties in the United States: A Guide to Current Problems and Experience* (New York: Johnson Reprint Corporation, 1969). General account of the entire field of civil liberties since World War II.

Emerson, Thomas I., *Toward a General Theory of the First Amendment* (New York: Random House, Inc., 1966). Essay that seeks to establish a general theory of freedom of speech that would guarantee absolute protection.

Fellman, David, *The Defendant's Rights* (New York: Holt, Rinehart & Winston, Inc., 1957). Study of the defendant's rights as stated in the bill of Rights of the Constitution, now partially dated by recent Supreme Court decisions.

Gellhorn, Walter, *American Rights: The Constitution in Action* (New York: The Macmillan Co., 1960). Examination of our civil liberties and how they evolved.

Hand, Learned, *The Bill of Rights* (New York: Atheneum Publishers, 1964). Series of lectures discussing the proper role of the Supreme Court in dealing with civil liberty questions.

Hymen, Harold M., *To Try Men's Souls: Loyalty Tests in American History* (Berkeley: University of California Press, 1959). Study of the history, use, and propriety of loyalty and security tests.

Konvitz, Milton R., *Fundamental Liberties of a Free People: Religion, Speech, Press, Assembly* (Ithaca, N.Y.: Cornell University Press, 1957). Critical and historical study of the First Amendment freedoms.

Konvitz, Milton R. *Expanding Liberties: Freedom's Gains in Postwar America* (New York: The Viking Press, Inc., 1966). Study of the expansion of civil liberties and civil rights since World War II, especially as a result of Supreme Court decisions.

Konvitz, Milton R., *Bill of Rights Reader: Leading Constitutional Cases*, 4th ed. revised (Ithaca, N.Y.: Cornell University Press, 1968). Annotated compilation of judicial cases dealing with the First Amendment.

Krislov, Samuel, *The Supreme Court and Political Freedom* (New York: The Free Press, 1968). An analysis of the Supreme Court and freedom of expression, from historical and practical viewpoints.

Kurland, Philip B., *Politics, The Constitution and the Warren Court* (Chicago: University of Chicago Press, 1970). Critical essays on the work of the Warren Court.

Lewis, Anthony, *Gideon's Trumpet* (New York: Random House, Inc., 1964). Popular account of the Supreme Court processes in the fight by C. E. Gideon to obtain the right of counsel.

Meiklejohn, Alexander, *Political Freedom: The Constitutional Powers of the People* (New York: Harper & Brothers, 1960). Reprint of a prior book (*Free Speech and Its Relation to Self-Government*), and a collection of papers dealing with questions of intellectual and political freedom.

Rutland, Robert A., *The Birth of the Bill of Rights*, 1776–1791 (New York: Collier Books, The Macmillan Co., 1962). Historical and political study of the amendments that form the Bill of Rights.

Shapiro, Martin, *Freedom of Speech: The Supreme Court and Judicial Review* (Englewood Cliffs, N.J.: Prentice-Hall, Inc., 1966). Analysis of the role of the Supreme Court in interpreting the First Amendment right of freedom of speech.

Shapiro, Martin, ed., *The Supreme Court and Constitutional Rights* (Glenview, Ill.: Scott, Foresman and Co., 1967). Readings on the major civil liberty and civil rights issues considered by the Supreme Court.

Simon, Yves R., *Freedom and Community*, ed. by Charles P. O'Donnell (New York: Fordham University Press, 1968). Six papers on the various aspects of freedom and civil society.

Spicer, George W., *The Supreme Court and Fundamental Freedom*, 2nd ed. (New York: Appleton-Century-Crofts, 1967). Analysis of the role of the Supreme Court in the development of the major individual rights guaranteed by the Constitution.

Wirt, Frederick M., and Willis O. Hawley, *New Dimensions of Freedom in America* (San Francisco: Chandler Publishing Co., 1969). Series of articles examining the meaning of freedom and liberty.

# Topics of further study

Auerbach, Jerold S., "La Follette Committee: Labor and Civil Liberties in the New Deal," *Journal of American History* (December 1964):435–459.

Bean, Barton, "Pressure for Freedom: The American Civil Liberties Union" (Ph.D. dissertation; Ithaca, N.Y.: Cornell University, 1954).

Bloss, Richard John, "The Right of Silence and Statutory Immunity: A Study of the Privilege Against Self-Incrimination with Particular Emphasis Upon the Immunity Act of 1954" (Ph.D. dissertation; Philadelphia: University of Pennsylvania, 1959).

Boyan, A. Stephen, Jr., "Defining Religion in Operational and Institutional Terms," *University of Pennsylvania Law Review*, CXVI (1971), 479.

Brenneman, Lynn D., "The Interpretation of the Commerce Clause During the Chief Justiceship of John Marshall, 1801–1835" (Master's thesis; Yipsilanti, Mich.: Eastern Michigan University, 1962).

Coyle, William Edward, "The Ninth Amendment and the Right of Privacy: The Griswold Case" (Ph.D. dissertation; Gainesville: Florida State University, 1966).

Enhorning, Norman A., "From 'Everson' to 'Zorach': The Triumph of Conservatism in Church-State Cases 1945–1952" (Ph.D. dissertation; Princeton, N.J.: Rutgers University, 1970).

Gray, C. Vernon, "The Impact of Federal Anti-Subversive Measures Upon Civil Liberties" (Master's thesis; Atlanta, Ga.: Atlanta University, 1962).

Haliby, Raymond N., "Problems of Loyalty of United States Personnel" (Ph.D. dissertation; Minneapolis: University of Minnesota, 1965).

Horton, David, *Freedom and Equality, Addresses by Harry S. Truman* (Columbia: University of Missouri Press, 1960).

McKenna, Robert J., "American Protestant Understanding of Catholic Church-State Doctrine" (Master's thesis; Catholic University at Washington, 1962).

Moore, Richter H., Jr., "Censorship: The Albatross of a Free Society," *Perspectives*, 2 (1965):5–7.

Nelson, Robert, "Judicial Interpretation of Freedom of the Press Since 1919" (Ph.D. dissertation; New York: Fordham University, 1959).

Pew, Mary, "Justice Jackson and the Religious Clauses of the First Amendment" (Ph.D. dissertation; Fordham University, 1961).

Pfeffer, Leo, *Church, State, and Freedom* (Boston: Beacon Press, 1967).

Stenshoel, M. Clayton, "Religious Neutrality under the Constitution: An Analysis of Alternative Rationales of the First Amendment Religious Clauses" (Ph.D. dissertation; Boulder: University of Colorado Press, 1965).

Voigt, Francis G. W., "The School Prayer Decision: A Study of Compliance" (Master's thesis; University of Iowa, 1968).

Willis, Paul G., "Political Libel in the United States, 1607–1948" (Ph.D. dissertation; Bloomington: Indiana University, 1949).

Womelsdorff, Clayton A., "The Federal Wire-Tapping Controversy" (Master's thesis; Dallas, Tex.: Baylor University, 1956).

# portfolio
# minority rights
# North/South

"The KKK welcomes you to Macon County," read the road signs. A Klan leader represented Macon County in the Alabama legislature. Yet, in the 1950s, well over 80 percent of the people of Macon County were black and the county seat, Tuskegee, was the home of Tuskegee Institute, a well-known black college. In Macon County, as in most of the rest of the Deep South, few blacks had voted since Reconstruction. They had been kept from voting, first, by violence and intimidation by the Ku Klux Klan and other white vigilante groups and, later, by state laws designed to sidestep the Fifteenth Amendment guarantee. These legal methods included literacy tests, poll taxes, gerrymandering, and "grandfather clauses." Until 1944, blacks could not join the Alabama state Democratic party—whose motto was "White Supremacy"—or vote in its primary although the party's nomination was tantamount to election in the one-party state. The periodic recurrence of violence—or the threat of it—also kept blacks from seeking political and social equality. Even in Tuskegee, with its potential for educated black leadership, few blacks dared, openly, to question this system until 1954 when, with the Brown decision, the Supreme Court began to knock down the elaborate legal structure that separated the races in the South. Blacks throughout the South took action directly and in the courts to demand their rights, including the right to vote, and in 1957 Congress passed a civil rights law to restore their right to vote. But civil rights advocates still ran into difficulties. Riot-equipped policemen patrolled their rallies. Other policemen physically barred blacks from registering. Blacks who got in to register found registrars "absent." Blacks who registered lost their jobs. Some were threatened with violence. In this situation it was difficult to convince blacks to register, but in some areas, including Tuskegee and the rest of Macon County, intensive registration campaigns were undertaken, potential registrants were instructed, and the number of black voters grew.

# PUBLIC NOTICE

If any voters or members of their family who are planning to vote Tuesday, are wanted by Law Enforcement Officials for the following offenses, information has been received that a list of voters has been drawn to be arrested after voting for the following offenses, committed in the past five years:

1. Traffic tickets
2. Speeding or negligent collision tickets.
3. Parking Tickets
4. Child Support Payments ordered by the Courts in divorce suits or child desertion.
5. Questioning by the Police for any offense.
6. Voters who have not appeared in Court as witnesses or Defendants in criminal or civil matters.
7. Voters who have not paid fines ordered by the Court.

Please take care of these matters before voting or else contact a Bail Bondsman or Lawyer before voting in order to be sure that you won't miss work or have to spend the night in jail by being arrested.

*(Harris County Negro Protective Association)*

Gaining access to the polls was not enough. A pattern of harassment prevailed throughout much of the area. On election day, black volunteers who were at the polls to help the new voters through the unfamiliar process were arrested for trespassing. Voters who had not paid traffic tickets were arrested. But by 1964, Tuskegee had registered 3500 blacks, 55 percent of the electorate, and two black men were elected to the city council. Three other blacks were defeated by white "moderates"—an indication that black voters in Tuskegee did not vote on strictly racial lines. After the Voting Rights Act of 1965 was passed, blacks moved quickly to political power in Macon County. In 1966, it elected the first black sheriff in Alabama since Reconstruction. A black was elected tax collector, another won a seat on the county Board of Revenue, and six were elected to the county Democratic executive committee.

Despite white fears, blacks did not "take over." Instead, the people of Tuskegee and Macon County have shown a willingness to vote on the issues and on the candidate's merits rather than according to race, and the pattern of moderation set in the city council election of 1964 has continued. That city council promised to show "no discrimination or favoritism," and for the most part that promise has been kept. The Tuskegee police department has been entirely integrated, as have the city planning commission and the county housing authority. Tuskegee has improved living conditions for both its black and white citizens by upgrading roads, water supply, light resources, and garbage collection. It has attracted new industry and integrated the public school system. As a result, a biracial government has brought to Tuskegee a lessening of tensions and a new confidence in the future of the town.

"Wherever the cities of America are going, Newark is going to get there first," said Kenneth Gibson, Newark's first black mayor. Newark, with a population of 375,000, of which 61 percent is black, is afflicted with every major urban ill in an extreme form. One-third of the people are getting public assistance. Fourteen percent of the labor force is unemployed. Newark has the highest crime rate in the country and the highest percentage of substandard housing. And with a diminishing tax base, it has almost no money. These problems, aggravated by problems of discrimination in hiring and housing, poor relations between the police and the black community, and the lack of black political power, were at the root of the riots that shook Newark in the summer of 1967. Understanding the causes of the riots but realizing their futility, black political groups began to unify to gain political power. Blacks, over half only recently from the South, were urged to vote and shown how to use voting machines. In 1970 they backed Gibson for mayor.

With blacks united behind him, Kenneth Gibson was elected mayor in 1970 by a large majority. Facing almost insurmountable financial obstacles, Gibson, like most residents of Newark, is skeptical concerning the city's future. Black-white disharmony has not lessened significantly as many political coalitions have weakened. Some of his black supporters criticized his appointments of white officials and his opposition to the 1971 school strike. Yet, a cautious optimism is being expressed by some residents, and the black political leadership is looking forward to gains in the 1974 election.

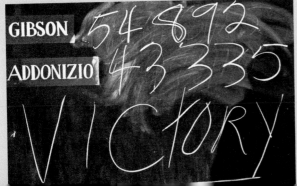

# 19 civil rights
## equal protection under the law

"CIVIL RIGHTS—here is an idea whose time has come . . . and it can't be stopped." Such was the pronouncement of Senate Minority Leader Everett Dirksen in 1964. Within the next seven years, the senator's prediction was to be substantiated.

It was all too clear that, indeed, the time had come for immediate and decisive action in guaranteeing the civil rights of all Americans. But the time had not come suddenly; for several decades, those who were denied their full rights had tried to shake the nation into realizing how great were the injustices, how numerous the hurts. In 1955, came the famous boycott of the Montgomery Bus Company; in 1960, the lunch counter sit-ins; and in 1970, the school bussing controversy, and numerous other questions that addressed themselves to the majority conscience.

The civil rights movement of the past generation has worked to eliminate poverty, injustice, and the shame of a history that inhibits individual and national progress. More specifically, different groups have addressed themselves to questions of legal, political, or economic discrimination. The National Association for the Advancement of Colored People, for example, has taken a legal approach, thus challenging discriminatory practices primarily through court action. The Urban League, on the other hand, has addressed itself mainly to questions of economic discrimination. Our purpose here will not be that of evaluating the philosophies of such groups, or of investigating the inequalities of wealth, social status, and region that prompted their formation. Rather, we will examine the legal rights of individuals as established by the Fourteenth and Fifteenth Amendments, and by acts of Congress and decisions of the federal courts, in order to show the evolution, meaning, and current status of civil rights under the Constitution.

We will evaluate, especially, the extent to which we have enforced the requirement of the Fourteenth Amendment, that "no state shall . . . deny to any person within its jurisdiction the equal protection of its laws." We will focus, too, on the Fifteenth Amendment, which extends to voting the stricture against denial of equal protection.

In short, we shall explore what has been done, and is still being done, to make the constitutional provision of equality for all citizens a reality.

# Civil rights of nonwhite Americans

The successful resolution of the struggle for equality, some observers contend, is the most critical challenge that has ever been posed to American democracy. W. E. B. DuBois, the black historian and founder of the NAACP, wrote almost seventy years ago that the racial issue was the major problem of the twentieth century. Gunnar Myrdal, the contemporary Swedish economist and observer of American institutions, has reached a similar conclusion in his exhaustive study of the white and black races in our country; however, he acknowledges that:

[1] Gunnar Myrdal, *Challenge to Affluence* (New York: Vintage Books, 1962), p. 67.

What has impressed the world more than the grave inferiority of status still inflicted on Negroes in America is the fact that such serious efforts have been directed to improving their status—legally, politically, socially and economically—and that so remarkable an improvement has taken place since the beginning of the Second World War.[1]

# A history of the problem: progress and futility

Racial prejudice in America began, naturally enough, with the encounter between the Indians and the Europeans in the seventeenth century. The Indian was the subject of many misconceptions and racial myths. Alternately viewed as a "noble savage," or as a lowly heathen, he was denied social access to the fledgling European culture that began to mature on American soil. William Byrd of Virginia, an eighteenth-century writer, remarked on the aloofness of the early settlers after their initial landing in 1607:

[2] Quoted in Alan P. Grimes, *Equality in America* (New York: Oxford University Press, Inc., 1964), pp. 42–43.

They had now made peace with the Indians, but there was one thing wanting to make that peace lasting. The natives could by no means persuade themselves that the English were heartily their friends, so long as they disdained to intermarry with them. . . .[2]

The situation was further complicated, and the sensitivities of the colonists further confused, by the arrival of another different racial group—the captive African black.

In 1619, twenty African laborers were brought to Virginia. At first they were treated like other indentured servants; but, two generations later, the Virginia House of Burgesses declared that all newly arrived Africans, and the children born to them, would be slaves forever. By the eighteenth century, slavery was an established institution in the southern colonies.

Slavery was not an exclusively southern institution. Blacks were brought to the northern colonies, but they were not a truly efficient labor force there: the smaller northern farms did not call for the kind of large work force required on southern plantations; moreover, it was impractical for the northern farmers to feed and clothe the slaves throughout the long winters, when there was virtually no work.

In general, in the South as well as the North, the colonial period was marked by a more tolerant attitude toward Negroes than was the pre-Civil War period. There were movements to check the slave trade, even from its beginning. Economic and humanitarian interests pressured the Virginia House of Burgesses to petition the Crown in 1772 to pay more attention to the legislation created to stop the importation of Africans:

> The importation of slaves into the Colonies from the coast of Africa, hath long been considered as a trade of great inhumanity, and under its present encouragement, we have too much reason to fear will endanger the very existence of your Majesty's American dominions.[3]

[3] Quoted in Alan P. Grimes, *Equality in America*, p. 45.

Despite such appeals, Congress, according to the Constitution (Article I, Section 9), could not legally forbid the importation of slaves until 1808.

## The fugitive slave law

In the first half of the nineteenth century, slavery was so well established in the United States that when the South came to consider a slave's removal from a state as equivalent to his emancipation, many northern states passed laws either forbidding the immigration of free Negroes, or severely curtailing their economic, political, and social activities. As a possible solution to the racial dilemma, Henry Clay, in 1816, chaired a meeting to help organize the return of free Negroes to Africa. The society established for that purpose purchased land in Liberia, but by 1821, fewer than fifteen hundred Negroes had returned to the continent of their ancestors.

The colonization plans were the first limited efforts to solve racial differences; but the method of solution, physically removing the black instead of solving the problem of the nation's new residents, was an initial mistake in the history of attempts to correct the racial problem.

## Slavery and expansion—from independence to civil war

The slavery question plagued the new nation at the outset. Even the most sensitive and intellectual of America's educated class were morally confused by the slavery issue. For example, in his *Autobiography* of 1821, Thomas Jefferson wrote:

4 Quoted in Alan P. Grimes, *Equality in America*, p. 48.

> Nothing is more certainly written in the book of fate, than that these people are to be free; nor is it less certain that the two races, equally free, cannot live in the same government. Nature, habit, opinion have drawn indelible lines of distinction between them.[4]

This feeling of innate separateness—coupled with the invention of the cotton gin, and the subsequent rise in the importance of cotton as the dominant southern crop, the gathering of which required a large, cheap supply of labor—transformed the slavery question from a moral to an economic one. Historians have speculated that, without the cotton gin, slavery might well have been eliminated peacefully and gradually, as it was in the British-held islands of the Caribbean. However, the invention of the cotton gin made all such speculation purely academic, because the economic motive for slavery had now become irresistible.

The northern economy, on the other hand, did not depend on slave labor; and its interests as an area of commerce and manufacturing often conflicted with the agricultural interests of the South. For example, the North, to protect its fledgling industries, favored tariffs on incoming goods, while the South, which relied heavily on favorable trade conditions with Europe, was steadfastly opposed to these duties. The black slave's future stood in the crossroads, while the nation's two major regions grew further and further apart; slavery became both the symbol and fact of sectional differences.

## The Missouri Compromise

As the new nation expanded westward, the question of whether slavery should be extended to the new territories quickly became a ground of contention between northerners who favored free labor and southerners who claimed the right to bring their property (their slaves) with them wherever they chose to settle.

The expansion question came to a head when, in 1819, a bill admitting Missouri as a state came before the House of Representatives. To the surprise and indignation of the southern members, James Tallmadge of New York offered an amendment prohibiting the further introduction of slaves into Missouri, and requiring that all children subsequently born therein of slave parents should be free at the age of twenty-five. Thus amended, the bill was passed in the House, but was defeated in the Senate.

After Congress adjourned in March, the question of slavery or freedom in Missouri went to the people. In state legislatures, in the newspapers, and at popular mass meetings, it was discussed and debated—not solely as a moral issue, but as an issue involving sectional power and prestige. Both sides uttered threats of separation.

When Congress took up the question again, in January, 1820, a compromise measure was finally achieved. Missouri was admitted as a slaveholding state, but slavery was prohibited in the territory of the United States north of Missouri's southern boundary. At the same time, Maine, which had just detached itself from Massachusetts, was admitted to the Union, making twelve free and twelve slave states. This was the famous *Missouri Compromise*, which put the question of the extension of slavery at rest for almost a generation. For its time, the solution was fair. Angry passions subsided and the sectional alignment dissolved; however, the veil had been lifted, and some saw the bloody prospect ahead.

The slavery issue was to be fought finally on the battlefields of the Civil War, and answered by the Emancipation Proclamation of 1863, which freed the slaves of the southern states, and the Thirteenth Amendment, which prohibited slavery permanently.

## The postbellum era

The northern victory in the Civil War established the North in its political, legal, and economic supremacy. The Thirteenth, Fourteenth, and Fifteenth constitutional Amendments, and supportive congressional legislation, were passed to abolish slavery and all forms of involuntary servitude, giving the black man the same rights as his white brother. But in the difficult period that followed the Civil War, these principles were not fully or immediately applied. The gains in human liberty were less certain than legislative gains: emancipation took place in a society that was not willing or able to adhere to the doctrine of equality under God and law.

The problem was further complicated, on the one hand, by the fanaticism of the radical Republicans, who were determined to punish and humiliate the South and, on the other, by the rise in the use of violence by southern whites to intimidate the black and keep him from exercising his newly won freedom in a meaningful way.

The northern political leaders, in effect, left the former slaves who still lived in the south to the devices of their former white owners. The year 1877, only twelve years after the end of the Civil War, marked the end of northern political and military presence in the South, for in that year federal troops were withdrawn. Their withdrawal had been a campaign pledge of President Rutherford Hayes, who, in effect, had promised the South that northern control of their land would end if he were elected.

This was, in many respects, a setback for the black man, for it brought to a halt the progress he had made during the Reconstruction Era, in such areas as voting and education. For example, the progress that had been hailed in the establishment of the Freedman's Bureau, set up to provide and maintain education for the newly freed slaves, and the legal, political, economic, and social gains of Reconstruction, were undone as the free blacks were no longer protected by the national government.

# The meaning of the Fourteenth Amendment

Neither President Grant nor President Hayes provided political and moral leadership on the race issue. In 1875 Congress passed the Civil Rights Act of 1875, the last such legislation until 1957; and in the Civil Rights Cases of 1883, the Supreme Court interpreted the Fourteenth Amendment in a way that invalidated important aspects of the Civil Rights Act. The Act of 1875 had made it a crime and a civil offense for any person to deny another person "the full and equal enjoyment of any of the accommodations, advantages, facilities and privileges of inns, public conveyances on land or water, theaters and other places of public amusement; subject only to the conditions and limitations established by law, and applicable alike to citizens of every race and color. . . ."

In the 1883 cases, the Supreme Court declared the Act unconstitutional. Although the Fourteenth Amendment stated that no state could deprive the individual of equal protection under the law, the state or national government did not have the power to prevent *individuals*, in the private use of their property, from so depriving each other. Of the Fourteenth Amendment, the Court said:

[5] 109 U.S. 3; 3 S. Ct. 18; 27 L. Ed. 835 (1883).

It is state action of a particular character that is prohibited. Individual invasion of individual rights is not the subject-matter of the Amendment.[5]

# Separate but equal

The 1896 decision in *Plessy* v. *Ferguson* was the next milestone in the constitutional interpretation of racial equality. The decision established the doctrine of "separate but equal" as a valid interpretation of the Fourteenth Amendment's statement that "no state could deprive any citizen of equal protection of the law." The case involved a Louisiana state law that required separate railway coaches for black and white passengers in Louisiana. The law was challenged on the grounds that the state, by legislative act, had violated the equal protection clause of the Fourteenth Amendment. The Supreme Court said that as long as accommodations were equal, the Fourteenth Amendment had not been violated.[6]

[6] *Plessy* v. *Ferguson*, 163 U.S. 537 (1896).

The states, therefore, could provide separate facilities for the races, as long as the facilities were equal.

As a result of the separate-but-equal doctrine, schools, accommodations, public transportation conveyances, and so on could be legally segregated in many parts of the country. The doctrine was carried to its ultimate absurdity when a law was passed in Birmingham, Alabama, making it a crime, punishable by six months in prison, for whites and blacks to dine together or to play any game of cards, dice, dominoes, or checkers together.

In the North, the black was restricted by custom rather than law, but the effects were the same. The intensity of antiblack feeling at the turn of the century was exemplified in a headline of the Peoria, Illinois, *Journal* of December 3, 1899, that proclaimed: RACE PROBLEM IS DISAPPEARING. STATISTICS SHOW NEGRO RACE WILL EVENTUALLY DISAPPEAR.

## World War I— migration and its effects

World War I represented a major breakthrough as many war-related jobs became available to blacks in this period of acute labor shortage.

The southern black, in search of new opportunities, began to migrate north to the major industrial centers—New York, Washington, Philadelphia, Boston, Chicago, Detroit—where there was a demand for cheap and unskilled labor. New York, for example, used its cheapest forms of labor (the Irish, Italian, and Jewish immigrant, and the migrating black) to its best advantage. The blacks, like many minority groups before them, were confined to crowded urban areas, such as Harlem.

The "peculiarly southern problem," as northern journalists were content to call white-black racial relations, had become a problem in the North by World War I, due, in part, to the decline of agriculture in the South. Black migration to northern metropolises also brought with it the changed attitudes of a transient population, eager to work and desiring the economic benefits that work could bring.

Of course, the Great Depression in 1929 hurt the black as well as the white; but the New Deal programs benefited the black, and agencies such as the Civilian Conservation Corps (CCC) and the Works Progress Administration (WPA) provided thousands of jobs for blacks. During this same period, some of the unions, particularly the newly formed Congress of Industrial Organizations (CIO), recruited large numbers of members without regard to race.

## World War II and later advances

World War II was another period of progress for the black, both in the military and civilian areas. In 1948, the armed forces were finally integrated, and blacks found that the military often provided opportunities denied to them in the civilian sector.

Since then, job and educational opportunities have improved steadily, if slowly, and never without a struggle. As will be seen, obtaining compliance in the area of equal job opportunities is very difficult and, in some areas (for example, in the construction trades), progress has been minimal. However, upward mobility continues, and there is now a solid, well-established black middle class.

## Black consciousness

Black fraternal and self-help organizations go back to the free black communities that existed before the Civil War. The first major modern organization to be formed was the NAACP, founded in 1909. The NAACP probably had, and still has, wider support than any other black organization. It has always attracted many white as well as black supporters and has worked mainly through the courts to achieve equality and justice. The three lawyers who argued and won the famous school desegregation cases of 1954 were NAACP men.[7]

There is, today, a broad range of organizations, reflecting the spectrum of black attitudes. These organizations range from the moderate Southern Christian Leadership Conference (SCLC)—formerly headed by Martin Luther King, Jr.—to the more militant Black Panthers. Many of these organizations have worked to strengthen racial consciousness. Thus, in the past few years, blacks have developed a tremendous interest and pride in their history, both in Africa and America. The movement toward increased racial pride has attracted blacks of all ages; black history courses, and African motifs in art and fashion are symbolic of the black's new interest in his past. Other nonwhite groups, such as Puerto Ricans, Mexicans, Chinese, and American Indians, have also become more vocal in their demands for equality.

[7] *Brown* v. *Board of Education of Topeka,* 349 U.S. 294 (1954).

*Stan Steiner*, The New Indians (*New York: Harper and Row Publishers, Inc., 1968*), *pp. 28–64.*

On August 10, 1960, ten Indian youths, recently graduated from college, met in Gallup, New Mexico, to form the National Indian Youth Council. Arriving from nine scattered and different tribes, the group, known as the Red Muslims and called together by Herbert Blatchford, a young Navajo, created an organization "in the Indian way," based on, but not bound by, the "high principles derived from the values and beliefs of our ancestors." Unlike earlier "talk" groups, the council took positive action to end what they considered the United States government's policy of divide-and-rule over American Indians. The first such action was a Fish-In in the state of Washington, which Blatchford described as

the first full-scale intertribal *action* since the Indians defeated General Custer on the Little Big Horn . . . .

Organized by the Council at the request of the tribal council of the Makeh Indians, the Fish-In represented the Indian's fight for his treaty rights and for human and civil rights as well.

The Fish-In was chosen as the Council's first act because fishing was of tremendous economic importance to the Indians, and because the state recently nullified an 1854 treaty which had specified Indian rights to fish in the Puget Sound. In the Puget Sound area approximately 75 percent of the Indians earned much of their food and livelihood from fishing. Some tribes earned only 25 percent of their income in this way, but depended solely on fish for their sustenance.

By hitting strategically, the small Indian population sought to keep the fishing rights which the state, ignoring federal treaties and laws, had long denied them. As a result of their action, more than fifty Indians were arrested for fishing in the Quillayute, Columbia, Puyallop, and other rivers of Washington. The women and children joined their fishermen husbands in demonstrations and riots on the new "political battlefield."

In addition to on-the-spot protests, the Indians went to the capital city of Olympia and demonstrated before the state capitol, performing "peaceable" war dances.

Instead of a feast of peace, there were speeches of protest. Robert Satiacum, Bruce Wilkie, Mel Thom—the Fish-In leaders—talked of the "Proclamation of Protest" that they had brought to the Governor. In it they said the State of Washington had "unconstitutionally assumed jurisdiction over Indian tribes and lands . . . without prior consent of the tribes involved." That, they said, was the source of most of the conflict. That, they said, had violated their treaty rights.

Governor Albert Rossellini met with the protestors and recommended a commission to study the clash of interests. He refused to let the Indians choose their own fishing grounds. The next governor, Daniel J. Evans, concurred that the laws had to be enforced.

The State of Washington, though shaken, was unmoved. Under the law of the Congress, known as Public Law 280, said the officials, they had the right to decide what fishing "rights" the tribes did, or did not, have. Nor did they have to ask the tribes. Indeed, Public Law 280 had given any state that wished it the right to assume control of law and order, jurisdiction on any Indian reservation—without prior consent of the Indians.

The Indians of Puget Sound formed the Survival of American Indians Association. They hired lawyers, including Jack Tanner, a distinguished lawyer of the Northwest Area of the NAACP, to defend the jailed fisherman. The young and old banded together. Even the old tribal chairmen who knew that the national government held Indian pursestrings sympathized with the Youth Council, although they could not expediently support them openly.

Nearly two and a half years after the fishermen cast their nets upon the waters, the Department of Justice, in Washington, D.C., declared it was ready to uphold "the solemn obligations of the government" in the defense of the fishing "rights" of the tribes of the Northwest. The federal government appeared before the Supreme Court of Washington State "in behalf of a tribe which had been enjoined from exercising its treaty fishing rights." In the long memories of the tribal elders there were no memories of such a thing. For the government to defend the tribes' rights in a treaty made with the government was unprecedented.

The increase in black consciousness, inevitably, has led to movements that encourage the voluntary separation of blacks from whites. Among the most recent is the program of the Black Muslims, who want an area of the United States in which they will be able to create a separate black nation. Despite this sporadic separatist sentiment, the trend among black leaders has been toward greater political and economic integration into the life of the nation. At the same time, younger blacks and other nonwhites stress pride in background and the retention of cultural identity.

# Racial equality in voting

The right to vote is basic to full participation in the life of a democracy. The history of federal intervention to secure voting equality for blacks began with the passage of the Fifteenth Amendment, adopted in 1870, which barred the states from denying any citizen the right to vote on the basis of race, color, or previous condition of servitude, and gave Congress the power to create legislation necessary to enforce this right.

While the Fourteenth and Fifteenth Amendments sought to guarantee the right to be free from discrimination, the reality of white power in the South made the battle for racial equality in voting long and exceedingly difficult. The white southerner was ingenious in his invention of subterfuges. These included the introduction of "legal" measures, such as the white primary, the "grandfather" clause, the poll tax, racial gerrymandering, literacy tests that often included interpreting the Constitution to the examiner's satisfaction, and practices such as the disqualification of otherwise eligible black voters for such reasons as underlining, instead of circling, the word "Mr." on the application form for new voters.

Although the Fifteenth Amendment specifically sought to assure black suffrage, the amendment was successfully skirted by many states until the late 1960s. Between 1866 and 1875, Congress passed five major civil rights acts; but by 1910, the provisions of these acts had either been declared unconstitutional, repealed, or so hobbled by judicial interpretation that they became virtually meaningless.

8 *Smith* v. *Allwright,* 321 U.S. 649 (1944).

## Open intimidation

For several decades after the Civil War, the black voter was kept from the polls by "intimidation, violence, and other irregular practices."[8] A major legal question that arose from these practices was whether or not national laws could punish private citizens who interfered with the right of a citizen to vote. Several provisions of post-Civil War civil rights have provided criminal and civil remedies for such interference.

In 1884, however, in *Ex Parte Yarbrough*,[9] the Supreme Court modified its position on voting rights. Yarbrough and other members of the Ku Klux Klan in Georgia had been tried and convicted in a federal district court for employing violence to intimidate Berry Saunders, a black who was attempting to vote in a congressional election. In an appeal to the Supreme Court, Yarbrough argued that Congress had no power over acts of intimidation by individuals. The Court disagreed. "Can it be doubted," said Justice Miller, "that Congress can by law protect the act of voting, the place where it is done and the man who votes, from the personal violence or intimidation and the election itself from corruption or fraud?"

Although *Ex Parte Yarbrough* temporarily, and on paper, protected the black voter against open intimidation, this ruling, like most others during Reconstruction, was essentially ineffective. The executive branch of the government did not make a sufficient effort to enforce federal civil rights laws, and Supreme Court decisions were inconsistent. The problem was so pervasive that enforcement by the national government would have been impossible, even if the desire were there. Thus, intimidators escaped prosecution and conviction. In addition, the black voter's rights continued to be infringed upon through several seemingly "legal" techniques, such as the white primary, literacy tests, poll taxes, and residency requirements mentioned previously.

## Literacy tests and the "grandfather clause"

*Literacy tests* date back to 1855 and 1857, when Connecticut and Massachusetts, respectively, substituted literacy tests for property-holding qualifications. These tests were a constitutionally valid requirement for voting; citizens merely had to demonstrate that they had some basic knowledge of reading and writing. But in practice, these tests could be used by registration officials to disfranchise citizens, especially when the literacy requirement was expanded to include technical interpretations of state and national constitutions.

The practice of using literacy tests for discriminatory purposes first occurred in 1892, when Mississippi reintroduced a form of the literacy test, the effect of which was to disfranchise black voters. By requiring that voters be able to read, understand, and interpret the state and national constitutions, Mississippi was able to deny the vote to a large proportion of its black population. Other southern states soon adopted literacy tests, and several million black Americans were kept from the polls. The literacy tests had one drawback: many illiterate whites also were unable to pass the simplest examination. Several states attempted to sidestep this problem by adding "grandfather clauses" to their voting laws.

[9] *Ex parte* means from one side only, or in the interest of one party.

"*Grandfather clauses*" in state law provided exemption from literacy requirements to individuals who had voted before a specified date (which was invariably a date preceding the ratification of the Fifteenth Amendment); it also exempted the descendants of such individuals. Illiterate whites, whose "grandfathers" had voted, were thus excused from taking literacy tests. Inasmuch as no black had voted before the ratification of the Fifteenth Amendment, all blacks were required to take the test. Oklahoma's "grandfather clause," typical of such clauses in many states, read: "No person shall be registered as an elector of this state or be allowed to vote in any election held herein, unless he be able to read and write any section of the constitution of the state of Oklahoma, but no person who was, on January 1, 1866, or at any time prior thereto, entitled to vote under any form of government, or who at that time resided in some foreign nation, and no lineal descendant of such person, shall be denied the right to register and vote because of his inability to so read and write sections of such constitution."[10]

[10] *Guinn* v. *United States,* 238 U.S. 347 (1915).

*Literacy Test*

Herblock gallery © 1965 Simon and Schuster.

In 1915, in the case of *Guinn* v. *United States,* the Supreme Court ruled that Oklahoma's "grandfather clause" was an unconstitutional violation of the Fifteenth Amendment. The Court stated that, although the "grandfather clause" did not mention race or color, the law was clearly discriminatory. The Court pointed out that the only possible reason for selecting a date prior to the adoption of the Civil War amendments to the federal constitution was to deny blacks the right to vote.

Although the "grandfather clause" was abolished in 1915, literacy tests were widely employed to block black suffrage until the 1960s. State registration officials simply passed illiterate whites, and failed many blacks, including those who were unquestionably literate. The widespread use of discriminatory literacy tests was ended by the passage of the 1965 and 1970 Voting Rights Acts.

## The white primary

Perhaps the most ingenious and effective legal tactic used to disfranchise the black in the first half of the twentieth century was the so-called *white primary*, a party nomination election in which only white citizens could vote to nominate candidates. A Texas law passed in 1923, for example, stated that "in no event shall a Negro be eligible to participate in Democratic party primary elections held in the State of Texas." Since Texas, in common with most Southern states, was largely a one-party state, the winners of the Democratic primary were virtually assured of election. The law clearly denied blacks a vote in the only significant part of the election process. In 1927, however, the Supreme Court ruled in (L.A.) *Nixon* v. *Herndon* that the Texas law was a "direct and obvious infringement" of the equal protection clause of the Fourteenth Amendment and, therefore, was invalid.

Shortly after *Nixon* v. *Herndon*, the Texas legislature attempted to bypass the Supreme Court's ruling by passing a law that authorized the state executive committee of a political party to rule on who may vote in its primaries. Immediately after the law was passed, the executive committee of the Texas Democratic party barred blacks from voting in its primaries. But, in 1932, the Supreme Court declared the second Texas law to be in violation of the Fourteenth Amendment, since the discrimination, although it was applied by the Democratic party, was authorized by the state.[11]

11 *Nixon* v. *Condon*, 286 U.S. 73 (1932).

Even after the second ruling, Texas did not abandon the white primary. No further laws were passed; but in 1932, the Texas Democratic party declared that "all white citizens of the state . . . shall be eligible to membership in the Democratic party and as such entitled to participate in its deliberations." In 1935, in *Grovey* v. *Townsend*, the Supreme Court ruled that a black who was denied the vote under this resolution was not protected by the Fourteenth Amendment, since the resolution was adopted by a private organization, the Democratic party, and was not the result of any state action, as it had been in the two earlier cases. With *Grovey* v. *Townsend*, the white primary became a legal means of blocking black suffrage.

In 1944, however, in *Smith* v. *Allwright*, the Court reversed its decision and overruled *Grovey* v. *Townsend*. In declaring the white primary a violation of the Fifteenth Amendment, Justice Reed, writing for the Court, stated: "When primaries become a part of the machinery for choosing officials, state and national, as they have here, the same tests to determine the character of discrimination or abridgement should be applied to the primary as are applied to the general election."

In 1946, South Carolina made one last effort to save the white primary. The state legislature repealed some 150 statutes that either authorized, regulated, or simply mentioned primary elections. Thus, any mention of primaries was deleted from the state constitution. The South Carolina Democratic party, supposedly acting as a private club, then barred blacks from voting in primaries, but the effort was futile. The law was declared unconstitutional by a federal district court, and the decision was affirmed by a circuit court of appeals. The Supreme Court refused to hear an appeal from this decision, and the lower court decision was affirmed and the white primary abolished.[12]

[12] *Rice* v. *Ellmore*, 333 U.S. 875 (1948).

## Poll taxes

Mississippi, the originator of the literacy test, also implemented another method of disfranchising the black man—the *poll tax*. Poll taxes, once widely employed in many southern states, presented an insurmountable obstacle to millions of poor black voters, as well as white. Some southern states repealed these laws in the mid-twentieth century, and in 1964, with the ratification of the Twenty-fourth Amendment, poll taxes were abolished in national elections. Several southern states, however, attempted to retain the poll tax requirement for state elections. These attempts were declared unconstitutional in 1966, when in *Harper* v. *Virginia Board of Education*, the Supreme Court ruled that the poll taxes abridged the individual's right to equal protection of the laws under the Fourteenth Amendment.

## Recent legislation

[13] *Political Participation* (Washington, D.C.: U.S. Commission on Civil Rights, 1968), pp. 227, 243, 246.

"The harsh fact is that in many places in this country men and women are kept from voting simply because they are Negroes," said President Johnson to a special session of Congress in 1965—a week after Alabama police officers had attacked black civil rights marchers on their way from Selma to the state capitol in Montgomery to appeal for full voting rights. President Johnson went on to say that, "No law we now have on the books . . . can ensure the right to vote when local officials are determined to deny it."

In 1964, almost three million voting-age blacks in the eleven southern states were not registered to vote. Only 32 percent were registered in Louisiana, 23 percent in Alabama, and 6.7 percent in Mississippi.[13] The 1964 *Civil Rights Act* further attempted to end voting discrimination by declaring that the equivalent of a sixth-grade education in an American school would qualify a person to vote. But this law, like its predecessors, suffered from an important weakness: judicial procedures were required for enforcement. State and local officials ignored the provisions of the Act, and the courts became tangled in complicated legal proceedings. Finally, in the wake of demonstrations and civil rights protests across the nation, Congress turned to a more direct means of eliminating discriminatory legislative barriers to black voting, by passing the Voting Rights Act of 1965.

| Black Elected Officials in the United States (by Region) | | | | | | |
|---|---|---|---|---|---|---|
| States | Total | U.S. Congress | State | County | City | School |
| New England | 54 | 1 | 10 | 0 | 29 | 14 |
| Middle Atlantic | 252 | 3 | 43 | 12 | 84 | 110 |
| Midwest+ | 373 | 6 | 75 | 11 | 173 | 108 |
| South | 580 | 0 | 50 | 52 | 363 | 115 |
| Southwest | 98 | 0 | 13 | 0 | 40 | 35 |
| Mountain | 9 | 0 | 4 | 0 | 3 | 2 |
| West Coast | 103 | 2 | 10 | 1 | 33 | 57 |
| Totals | 1459 | 12 | 205 | 76 | 725 | 441 |

Through this legislation, all literacy tests or other devices in states and counties, where less than 50 percent of the population had been registered to vote in the 1964 Presidential elections, could be suspended by the Attorney General without recourse to courts of law.[14] The executive branch of government was given the power to appoint federal examiners who could register voters; when he signed the Act, President Johnson stated that, "if it is clear that State officials still intend to discriminate, then Federal examiners will be sent in to register all eligible voters." The examiners also would be empowered to monitor election proceedings in areas affected by the new voting laws. The 1965 legislation, in addition, made it a federal crime for a private citizen or public official to violate a person's right to vote, and set the penalty at five years in prison and a $5,000 fine.

[14] Literacy tests were subsequently suspended in six states—Alabama, Georgia, Mississippi, Virginia, Louisiana, and South Carolina— and in forty counties in North Carolina.

# Racial equality in schools

After the Civil Rights Cases of 1883, and *Plessy* v. *Ferguson* in 1896, the Supreme Court kept aloof from racial disputes and made few stands related to discriminatory practices in schools, housing, places of public gathering, voting, and all other areas of American life. In the 1940s and 1950s, however, the Supreme Court resumed an active role in the civil rights issue.

What is most significant about this period is that it marked the beginning of the end for the "separate but equal" doctrine. For example, as early as 1938, the Supreme Court hinted at its changing point of view in its ruling in *Missouri ex. rel. Gaines* v. *Canada.*[15] In this decision, the Court held that the State of Missouri could not subsidize the tuition of a black at a law school outside the state in order to avoid admitting him to study law at the University of Missouri.

*The major struggle for better schooling for blacks has been at the college level. In 1963, Alabama's Governor, George Wallace, refused to allow Attorney General Nicholas Katzenbach to integrate the University of Alabama.*

Other significant breakthroughs, however, did not come until twelve years later, helped, in part, by the changed status of the black man after World War II and by the NAACP's impressive legal efforts in the courtroom. In *Sweatt* v. *Painter* (1950) and *McLaurin* v. *Oklahoma State Regents* (1950), the Supreme Court held that it was a violation of the equal protection clause of the Fourteenth Amendment to discriminate against students on the basis of color or race. In the first case, the University of Texas law school had violated the amendment by refusing admission to a qualified black man, simply on the grounds that there was a separate law school provided for blacks. In the latter case, the Court ruled that the state violated the equal protection clause by segregating a black graduate student in separate facilities after he had been admitted.

In these decisions concerned with higher education, the Supreme Court gradually undermined the "separate but equal" doctrine.

The next major hurdle to be cleared, one that would be far more significant and emotional in its impact, concerned the public education systems. As a result of the favorable 1950 decisions concerning students seeking advanced degrees, a court test challenging the segregation of public school systems was inevitable. It came when sixty-seven black parents and children filed suit in Charleston, South Carolina. Their historic action was joined with four other cases of a similar nature in 1952, under the title of *Brown* v. *Board of Education*.

In 1952, Oliver Brown sued the Board of Education of Topeka, Kansas, to gain entrance for his young daughter to a public school near his home, instead of sending her to a black school farther away. With the 1950 decisions as background precedents, the South Carolina and Kansas cases were heard together; it was realized that the Supreme Court decision would have a wide-ranging effect on more than three million black children attending segregated schools across the country.

By 1953, the Supreme Court, aware of how momentous its decision would be, had delayed its ruling for a year. Additional arguments on the case were heard by the Supreme Court during the following term. The final arguing of the case, incorporating the Charleston and Topeka challenges, was presented by Thurgood Marshall (now a Supreme Court justice), counsel for the NAACP. Finally, on May 17, 1954, the Supreme Court handed down its historic decision.

That morning, the courtroom was tense, as it filled with press and spectators two hours before the justices were scheduled to appear. The new Chief Justice, Earl Warren, read the majority decision, which changed the course of American history:

> In each of the cases, minors of the Negro race, through their legal representatives, seek the aid of the courts in obtaining admission to the public schools of their community on a non-segregated basis. In each instance, they had been denied admission to school attended by white children under laws requiring or permitting segregation according to race.

> We come then to the question present: Does segregation of children in public schools solely on the basis of race, even though the physical facilities and other 'tangible' factors may be equal, deprive the children of the minority group of equal educational opportunities? We believe that it does.

> We conclude that in the field of public education the doctrine of 'separate but equal' has no place. Separate educational facilities are inherently unequal. Therefore, we hold that the plaintiffs and others similarly situated for whom the actions have been brought are, by reason of the segregation

complained of, deprived of the equal protection of the laws guaranteed by the Fourteenth Amendment.[16]

Separate-but-equal had finally been ruled unconstitutional by the Supreme Court. The order to implement the decision was passed a year later, and it stated that "with all deliberate speed" all public school systems were to admit students without racial discrimination basis. Implementation of the decision was to be handled by the federal district court.

*Supreme Court Decision, Swann v. Charlotte-Mecklenburg Board of Education, 91 S.Ct. 1267 (1971).*

In the opinion handed down by the Supreme Court in the April 1971 case of *Swann* v. *Charlotte-Mecklenburg Board of Education*, the Court repeated its firm stand that all traces of dual school systems be abolished, thus making clear its position on the controversial bussing issue. Chief Justice Burger stated the aim of the Court in offering the unanimous opinion:

Today's objective is to eliminate all vestiges of state-imposed segregation that was held violative of equal protection guarantees by *Brown* v. *Board of Education.*

The Court gave considerable freedom to local federal courts to shape means that would accomplish this result, so long as the end of dual school systems was in fact accomplished.

On the main question of bus transportation the Court said:

The District Court's conclusion that assignment of children to the school nearest their home serving their grade would not effectively dismantle the dual school system is supported by the record, and the remedial technique of requiring bus transportation as a tool of school desegregation was within the court's power. . . . An objection to transportation of students may have validity when the time or distance of travel is so great as to risk either the health of the children or significantly impinge on the educational process; limits on travel time will vary with many factors, but probably with none more than the age of the students.

The Court thus approved of the use of bus transportation, but indicated that there were times when its use would not be valid.

## Difficulties in implementing the Supreme Court decision

Desegregation quickly took place in the border states, for example, in Delaware, Maryland, and Kentucky. But the Supreme Court's decision in *Brown* v. *Board of Education* provided local officials in the South with considerable leeway to make their own timetable for desegregation. The absence of a specific time compliance, beyond the notion of "all deliberate speed," and the judgment of cases by federal district judges who were to oversee the work of the local school officials, delayed the complete equalization of schools. Federal district courts in the deep South, often slow or unwilling to act, frequently reflected the biases of their areas.

Despite Supreme Court decisions in education and other public areas, segregation continued during the fifties and early sixties. Officials had assigned the two races to different schools, ostensibly for reasons other than race; schools to which blacks were sent by court order were shut down; the "possibility of violence" was used to justify other delays in desegregation.

## Distribution of Educational Level: 1969

| Black | Less than 4 years high school | High school, 4 years | College, 1 year or more |
|---|---|---|---|
| 20 and 21 years old | 42.1 | 36.6 | 21.2 |
| 22 to 24 years old | 43.9 | 37.1 | 19.1 |
| 25 to 29 years old | 44.3 | 40.1 | 15.7 |
| 30 to 34 years old | 49.8 | 36.7 | 13.5 |
| 35 to 44 years old | 62.8 | 26.8 | 10.5 |
| 45 to 54 years old | 70.8 | 18.9 | 10.3 |
| 55 to 64 years old | 85.2 | 8.7 | 6.2 |
| 65 to 74 years old | 89.7 | 5.5 | 4.9 |
| 75 years old and over | 92.4 | 4.1 | 3.5 |
| White | | | |
| 20 and 21 years old | 18.1 | 41.6 | 40.1 |
| 22 to 24 years old | 19.6 | 44.8 | 35.7 |
| 25 to 29 years old | 23.0 | 44.8 | 32.1 |
| 30 to 34 years old | 27.3 | 44.9 | 27.6 |
| 35 to 44 years old | 33.9 | 41.0 | 25.1 |
| 45 to 54 years old | 40.7 | 39.3 | 20.0 |
| 55 to 64 years old | 55.2 | 27.5 | 17.3 |
| 65 to 74 years old | 67.6 | 18.9 | 13.4 |
| 75 years old and over | 75.1 | 13.8 | 11.1 |

Source: U.S. Department of Commerce, Bureau of the Census in *Civil Rights: Progress Report 1970* (Washington, D.C.: Congressional Quarterly, Inc., 1971), p. 44.

The first major crisis in the battle to obtain complete school desegregation was the 1957 confrontation between Governor Faubus of Arkansas and President Eisenhower. When the governor had called out the National Guard to stop black children from entering a newly desegregated school, the President, in turn, sent federal troops to Little Rock, the state capitol, to carry out the mandate of the federal courts to desegregate the city schools.

Since then, the Supreme Court has been increasingly stern in demanding that federal judges oppose and eradicate all means of willful evasion of the law's mandate. In a famous rebuke of local officials who announced that their decisions could nullify a federal court order, the Supreme Court justices wrote:

> In short, the constitutional rights of children not to be discriminated against in school admission . . . can neither be nullified openly and directly by state legislators or state executive or judicial officers, nor nullified indirectly by them through evasive schemes. . . . Article 6 of the Constitution makes the Constitution the supreme Law of the Land. . . . The federal judiciary is supreme in the exposition of the law of the Constitution. . . . No state legislator or executive or judicial officer can war against the Constitution without violating his undertaking to support it.[17]

[17] *Cooper v. Aaron,* 358 (U.S. 1, 17 [1958]).

In 1963, another attempt to maintain segregation brought a severe rebuke from the Supreme Court. In *Watson* v. *Memphis*, the Court wrote that what had been "deemed sufficient" in 1955 was no longer sufficient: the extended time for desegregation granted eight years earlier was exhausted, and more positive moves were needed to carry out the law. In another case, Virginia's Prince Edward County, as a result of the *Brown* case, had closed its school in 1959 rather than comply with the order to integrate. From 1959 to 1963, pupils had attended school facilities built by a private organization, and tuition was provided by state and county funds. No black children in Prince Edward County were allowed to attend those private facilities. As a result, black children received no public education for four years. The Supreme Court, in *Griffin* v. *County School Board of Prince Edward County* (1964), held that to close the schools in one county, while maintaining them in others, was a denial of the equal protection clause of the Fourteenth Amendment.

Another evasion devised by parents and school boards unwilling to submit to integration was the "freedom of choice" plan. This tactic allowed children to choose the schools they wished to attend. In practice, white children chose to remain in white schools, and few blacks were willing to risk entering the white institutions. The Supreme Court's decision in *Green* v. *School Board of New Kent County* (1968) declared that the time for such tactics had ended.

While the Department of Justice increased its pressure in the area of enforcement of constitutional rights, the Chief Executives were more cautious in their actions and attitudes. President Eisenhower, in particular, hoped to avoid a confrontation that he felt would inflame the nation; nevertheless, he sent the troops to Little Rock. The Kennedy administration and, in particular, its Justice Department under Robert Kennedy, was more vocal in its opposition to segregation. When, in 1962, Governor Ross Barnett of

Mississippi refused to allow a black student, James Meredith, to be admitted to the University of Mississippi, President Kennedy sent in federal marshals to support those who were attempting to enforce a court directive ordering Meredith's admission, and later supplemented them with federal troops to halt mob violence. President Kennedy's efforts in other areas were limited, however, by a Congress that refused to take action that would effectively outlaw discrimination.

It remained for a southern President, Lyndon Johnson, to maneuver through Congress the broadest legislation in support of racial equality. Four factors in 1964 were decisive in gaining passage, in the next two years, of Johnson's civil rights proposals: first, the President's own insistence on concrete, decisive action; second, the sense of national shame that followed the televised brutality of the police chief of Birmingham, Alabama, Eugene "Bull" Conner, who turned fire hoses and dogs on black civil rights demonstrators; third, the firebombing of a black church in that same city, where four young girls were killed while attending Sunday school; fourth, the open defiance of Governor George Wallace of Alabama, who used state police to prevent school desegregation, and also aroused the anger of much of the nation. These factors enabled President Johnson to convince Congress to pass the most wide-ranging civil rights legislation in the nation's history, in 1964 and 1965.

The Nixon administration has supported the constitutional mandate for an immediate end to deliberate racial segregation of pupils by official action, but it has established a "rule of reason" in conducting the pace of desegregation; it has allowed local officials to act "in good faith," and formulate a plan of desegregation which "best suits the needs of their own localities." Whether this policy will facilitate or retard desegregation of schools remains to be determined. It is clear, however, that the federal courts, especially the Supreme Court, continues to press for a speedy end to the South's dual school system, and the actual pace of school desegregation has increased rapidly during the late sixties and early seventies.

While much court attention has been focused on the state-sanctioned segregation of southern schools, the North has been no less reprehensible in segregating minority groups. Northern segregation of blacks and other racial minorities has been based not on law but practice, in the form of *de facto* ("actually existing") *segregation*. Children must attend the school in their neighborhood, regardless of the racial composition of the school; and families are forced to live in ghettoes such as Harlem and Bedford-Stuyvesant in New York, Roxbury in Boston, and Watts in Los Angeles.

*De facto* school segregation is the inevitable result of segregated neighborhoods. Naturally, the children will attend the school in their neighborhood; and, naturally, the school will be all black, for, by definition, the black ghetto has no whites. The law neither forbids whites to attend these schools, nor blacks to attend a school that is predominantly white. Yet, an all–black school in a ghetto is, in effect, just effectively as segregated as it would be were segregation officially decreed.

# Racial equality in public facilities

To achieve equal access to public accommodation facilities, such as restaurants, buses, other means of public transportation, theaters, and restaurants, is another major goal of the civil rights movement.

We have noted that the 1896 *Plessy* v. *Ferguson* decision established the separate-but-equal rationale for segregation of public facilities.

In the wake of the *Brown* decision, however, the Supreme Court took several steps to integrate public facilities. In *Muir* v. *Louisiana* (1954) and *Baltimore* v. *Dawson* (1955), segregation in public recreation facilities was ruled illegal. In *Morgan* v. *Virginia* (1946), segregation in transportation, was held to be illegal.

It was not until 1955, when blacks in Montgomery, Alabama, boycotted the local bus company, that the segregation of public transportation was severely challenged. In 1955, Mrs. Rosa Parks dared to cross the color line, and took a seat in the front, instead of the back, of a bus in Montgomery, Alabama. This was the first incident in the long, active, and essentially pacifist movement led by Dr. Martin Luther King, Jr., head of the Southern Christian Leadership Conference (SCLC). The authorities removed Mrs. Parks from the bus and arrested her. To protest racial discrimination in public transportation in a nonviolent manner, the black population of Montgomery, led by Mrs. Parks and Dr. King, boycotted the buses for a year.

Car pools were organized to transport some black workers, others walked long distances to and from work. The bus company lost 65 percent of its business and was forced to cut schedules, lay off drivers, and raise fares. Finally, the Montgomery Bus Company and the civil rights group reached a settlement: the company agreed not only to end segregation on the buses, but to hire black drivers as well. At 5:55 A.M. on December 21, 1956, Dr. King and Reverend Glen Smiley, a white colleague, boarded a bus together near King's home. As Dr. King paid his fare, the bus driver said, "We are glad to have you this morning."

This breakthrough led to others. In that same year, the Interstate Commerce Commission prohibited segregation of interstate passengers, and the courts ordered that the terminal waiting rooms and restaurants were to be desegregated as well.

Protests against other forms of racial discrimination in public (but privately-owned) facilities followed the Montgomery victory. The first lunch counter "sit-in" demonstration took place in Greensboro, South Carolina, on February 1, 1960. A group of black students challenged the segregation of the races when they sat in a luncheonette that refused to serve blacks. Lester Maddox, who later became governor of Georgia, gained notoriety as a defender of white segregationist tradition when he wielded an ax handle, threatening to strike any black who dared to come into his restaurant.

In another case (*Burton* v. *Wilmington Parking Authority*, 1961), the Court ruled that refusal to serve blacks in a restaurant leased by the state of Delaware was a violation of the equal protection clause of the Fourteenth Amendment. The Supreme Court was empowered to adjudicate this decision, in that a state, and *not* a private individual, had condoned segregation of accommodation.

*State of New York Division of Human Rights, and State Human Rights Appeal Board, Case No. CE-20340-70, Appeal No. 388.*

The civil rights fight of Puerto Ricans living predominantly in American urban areas has, within the last decade, drawn much attention. In New York State, for example, 1,300,000 inhabitants are Puerto Rican, most of whom live in New York City. A breakthrough in the elimination of discrimination against them occurred on May 25, 1971 when the New York State Legislature passed an act, introduced by Assemblyman Vito Battista of Brooklyn, N.Y., to amend Section 296.4 of the executive law of the state by adding the words *or national origin* so that the law now reads as follows:

It shall be an unlawful discriminatory practice for an education corporation or association which holds itself out to the public to be non-sectarian and exempt from taxation pursuant to the provisions of article four of the real property tax law to deny the use of its facilities to any person otherwise qualified, by reason of his race, color, religion *or national origin.*

Partial impetus for this action was a case brought to the New York State Division of Human Rights on April 2, 1970 and later appealed to the State Human Rights Appeal Board on June 18, 1970. The decision, and most importantly the dissenting opinion (handed down on September 17, 1970) sheds light on the problems incurred by Puerto Ricans in trying to obtain equal rights. The dissenting opinion also lends insight into the manner in which individuals are protected by the interaction of federal and state laws.

The appellants in the case were Cesar Santos, Chairman of the Bilingual Student Association at Bronx Community College of the City University of New York, and eighteen other students. The respondents were the Board of Higher Education of the City of New York, the City University of New York and its chancellor, and the Bronx Community College and its President.

Cesar Santos submitted a complaint on February 24, 1970 and later filed an addendum on March 24 of that year which contained allegations of denial of facilities and a list of at least seven discriminatory practices toward Puerto Ricans in the Bilingual Program and at Bronx Community College. They included such acts as ethnic slurrs committed by the English faculty, subjection to "racism" in the library, the classroom and the bookstore, where they had to "stand in separate lines" to purchase the "worst textbooks" while being subjected to "vile," "rude" and "racial attitudes," scornful and humiliating language of the College Dean and English teachers directed at the Puerto Rican Director of the Bilingual Program and other nonteaching Puerto Rican staff in front of students, and refusal on the part of the administration to hire qualified Puerto Rican faculty for the program.

The Division of Human Rights ordered in April that it was without jurisdiction in the case. The Appeal Board ruled that the original order of the Board was valid and that as the college does not come under the jurisdiction of Section 296.4 as an educational corporation, "the Board is precluded from considering the arguments that the facilities are being denied to applicants and that Puerto Ricans are within the groups afforded protection by Section 296.4."

The majority opinion stated that Puerto Ricans are not a race, nor are they of one color, nor are they a religion. Finding it difficult to classify them, for legal purposes, the Board suggested that the complainants might further pursue their case as nonwhites and expressed that other agencies had jurisdiction over the matter. They added that perhaps joint jurisdiction, as exists with employment, would be helpful in such matters.

Of major interest is the dissenting opinion written by Irma Vidal Santaella, one of the three-member appeal board. Santaella traces the complaints and original decision carefully. In her opinion she clarifies several points. First she contends that no investigation of the *entire complaint* was made as required by the Human Rights Law.

Second, she ascertains that the bilingual program under discussion is funded by the federal government under Title VI of the Civil Rights Act of 1964 and that such federal acts and their accompanying regulations supercede state law. The Act specifies no person receiving federal government funds shall be discriminated against and the pursuant regulations include that discrimination shall not occur on the basis of national origin. The 1964 Civil Rights Act includes a section (No. 1104) that states that any state law inconsistent with the provisions of the Act shall be considered invalid. This, therefore, is a case in which state law must be invalidated in keeping with the Act. Santaella cites several court precedents in which the federal government has upheld similar stipulations in the allocation of its funds.

Third, this sole dissenter argues that state law forbids that anyone deny the privileges and advantages of a program conducted in a public accommodation on the basis of national origin, religion, or race or make participants feel unwelcome or their customs objectionable.

Fourth, Santaella states as follows:

It seems to me that Puerto Rican appellants (and the class of American citizens that they represent) are entitled to the same protection given to other American citizens in New York under Section 296.4 in the protection of their rights against discriminatory practices in educational facilities covered by Section 296.4. It would further appear that Puerto Rican appellants, as members of an "identifiable ethnic minority" should be accorded the same protection against racial discrimination available to "Negroes" under the Order of the Division.

Fifth, it seems that in this case Puerto Ricans have been denied their rights as specified in the Fourteenth Amendment of the Constitution of the United States and its application to the states through the supremacy clause. This led to Santaella's claim that the Order of the Division of Human Rights should be reversed.

Sixth, Herman Badillo, attorney for the appellants, argued that exclusion of Puerto Ricans from the state law is inequitable. Santaella concluded that if the Puerto Ricans are an ethnic group, which they are, they should accrue the rights applicable to other races. Not to insist on recognition on these grounds would be a rejection of their national ancestry.

It would . . . appear that the 296.4 statutory criteria of "race" is extensive to all racial or ethnic groups and that it accords no preferential treatment to one group *over* another . . .

In statistic after statistic, it is officially said that Puerto Ricans are neither Caucasian nor Black, but presumably that does not mean that they are also *invisible* or *inexistent*. Today, the racial myth of the so-called "two-race theory" has no place any more in a state with a visible identifiable ethnic group of over one million Puerto Ricans.

Although the other two members of the Board of Appeals did not concur on Santaella's dissention, her argument, in addition to other controversies over legal provisions for dealing with the Puerto Rican community and general sympathy for the issue, have since resulted in a change of the state law. The case of Cesar Santos, therefore, exemplifies for the Puerto Rican community and other minority groups, how individuals, if adamant, organized, and properly represented in legal and legislative branches of the system, can make impact which leads to winning their civil rights.

By 1963, direct action sit-ins and such had become the most popular and effective means of protesting against racial discrimination in public accommodations. The Supreme Court, in several cases, invalidated convictions of sit-in demonstrators at lunch counters and elsewhere.[18] In each of these cases, the state, or a state's official, was implicated in the perpetuation of discriminatory practices. Thus, the equal protection clause of the Fourteenth Amendment was violated.

[18] *Peterson* v. *Greenville, S.C.,* 373 U.S. 244 (1963), and *Lombard* v. *Louisiana,* 373 U.S. 267 (1963).

## The Civil Rights Act of 1964

The provisions of Title II of the Civil Rights Act of 1964 were perhaps the result of all the demonstrations, marches, sit-ins, and, most importantly, the 1963 civil rights march on Washington. Title II prohibited discrimination because of race, color, religion, or national origin in all public accommodations such as hotels, motels, gas stations, restaurants, theatres, and other large places of amusement. It included facilities such as barber shops in hotels, or lunch counters in stores, but did not specifically cover retail stores, barber shops, bars, and small places of amusement. The Justice Department was given broad powers to enforce the law.

The enforcement provisions made it possible for a person to sue for preventive relief through a civil injunction, and for the courts to call on the Attorney General to intervene, if necessary. Preventive relief means that, if the Attorney General has "reasonable cause to believe" that the person engaged in the action will not comply, he can bring suit against that party without a waiting period, and further request that a three-judge court hear the case, if the case is of "general public importance." The Supreme Court unanimously upheld Title II in decisions reached several months after the passage of the Act. The Court's rulings reaffirmed the prohibition of discrimination in public accommodations. It found that Congress had acted fully within its constitutional power to regulate interstate commerce in two decisions of critical importance.[19] Moreover, in December, 1964, the Court ruled to suspend all pending state prosecutions of the sit-in demonstrators who had been arrested while trying to desegregate facilities covered by the 1964 Act. They suspended these prosecutions, even though the arrests had been made prior to the passage of the Act.

[19] *Heart of Atlanta Motel* v. *United States,* 231 r. Supp. 393 (1964); *Katzenbach* v. *McClung,* 379 U.S. 294 (1964).

In general, the legislation to assure desegregation of accommodations has been effective. The fierce opposition of Governors Wallace of Alabama and Maddox of Georgia has been replaced by increased tolerance in the more urban areas of the South. "White" and "colored" signs, and the humiliation that they represent, have generally disappeared. The laws that were passed to right the grievances of the blacks are still resented by some; others have complied, although their traditions and ways of life are still vastly different from those demanded by the executive orders. Rural areas remain unchanged in many regions of the South and North, where the tenacity of custom holds both white and black in patterns of life that are generations old. However, substantial progress has been made.

# Racial equality in housing

Housing is probably the least-changed area in the battle to create a more equal society through civil rights legislation. Although many laws have been passed at all levels of government, results have not been significant. It seems fair to say that segregation is still the rule, rather than the exception, in housing.

Discrimination in housing is very difficult for the government to deal with for two reasons: first, it is *de facto* (in fact or actuality), rather than *de jure* (according to law); second, it is generally perpetrated by individuals, rather than by the state.

**Quality of Housing, 1960–1968** (in thousands)

| Number of housing units: | Not meeting specified criteria | | Meeting specified criteria | |
|---|---|---|---|---|
| | Blacks and other races | White | Blacks and other races | White |
| 1960 (53,022) | 2,263 (26)[1] | 6,210 | 2,881 (6)[2] | 41,668 |
| 1968 (60,693) | 1,550 (32)[1] | 3,151 | 5,001 (8)[2] | 50,991 |

Source: U.S. Department of Commerce, Bureau of the Census in *Civil Rights: Progress Report 1970* (Washington, D.C.: Congressional Quarterly, Inc., 1971), p. 44.

For example, a white homeowner in an all-white neighborhood may put up a "For Sale" sign on his front lawn. Scores of black buyers may inspect the house. But no one can force the owner to sell his house to a black family. And, because a single sale does not really prove a pattern of discrimination, it is quite difficult for anyone to prove that the homeowner was practicing discrimination against blacks.

Even when a house in an exclusively white neighborhood is sold to a black, the possibility exists that the whole neighborhood will disband. As soon as a black family moves into the area, "For Sale" signs appear, at first slowly, then with greater frequency, in part because whites fear that property values will decline and the school system will deteriorate. The result of such a panic, of course, is that the whites bring about the very conditions that they feared—*de facto* segregation. The prices of homes fall, as more people grow more anxious to sell; and as prices fall, lower–income families can afford to move in. Finally, the neighborhood turns, at first predominantly black, then all black. At this point, it became another segregated community.

Who could have prevented this? Case studies of successful integrated neighborhoods suggest that the community action groups are the best defense against *de facto* segregation. In such instances, the government has very little real power.

*The need for better housing and more reasonable rents is not confined solely to the urban dweller.*

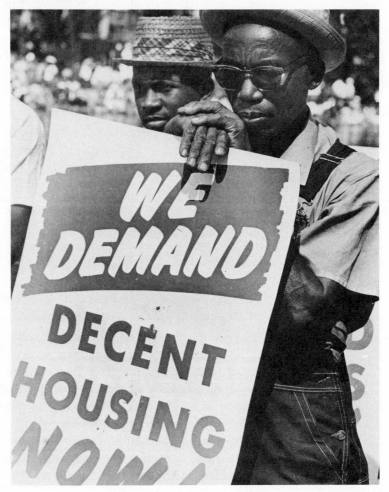

Rulings by the Supreme Court in 1917 and 1927 declared that all restrictions on the right of occupancy, when imposed by state statute or municipal ordinance, were discriminatory and thereby unconstitutional. To counter-act these rulings the "restrictive covenant" was used to maintain exclusively white neighborhoods. A *restrictive covenant* is a provision in a contract that bars the sale of a home to specific groups. Since such agreements were between private citizens, and did not involve state or local government, the court held that no constitutional violation was involved. The courts enforced the covenants, and blacks and other minority groups were "legally" excluded from living in many areas.

The turning point in civil rights' housing came in the case of *Shelley* v. *Kramer*, in 1948. Earlier rulings were overturned, and the Supreme Court held that the judiciary could no longer enforce restrictive covenants, because to do so would sanction illegal state actions and, thus, be in violation of the equal protection clause of the Fourteenth Amendment.

Later, in the 1968 case of *Jones* v. *Alfred H. Mayer*, the Supreme Court upheld the provision of the Civil Rights Act of 1866 which declares" All citizens . . . have the same right, . . . to inherit, purchase, lease, sell, hold, and convey real and personal property." Thus, this neglected provision of previous civil rights legislation was made available as a legal tool in the fight against discrimination in housing.

Since the early 1960s, presidential and legislative action have become increasingly important in the area of housing discrimination. President Kennedy issued an executive order in 1962 forbidding discrimination in federally assisted housing, as well as in public housing and urban renewal projects. The 1964 Civil Rights Act included a requirement (Title VI) that *any* program receiving federal aid—which included public housing and urban renewal programs—had to be free of discrimination.

President Johnson's signing of the 1968 *Civil Rights Act*, which was devoted largely to housing, was also an important breakthrough for the civil rights movement. A major provision of the law, Title VII, stated that there was to be no discrimination in the advertising, financing, sale, or rental of all housing in the nation. By 1970, 80 percent of the sale and rental of houses had come under the Act's provisions.

The Department of Housing and Urban Development (HUD) was given the responsibility of using "conference conciliation" to bring about compliance with the 1968 Act. Enforcement, however, has been weak: HUD has the power of persuasion, but it cannot order individuals or companies to observe the law. Further legal procedures slow down, the process of assuring compliance: the Department of Justice enters the situation only when a person or firm has been shown to pursue a "pattern of practice" of discrimination. Inasmuch as the "pattern of practice" does not cover one person's selling his home to another individual, meaningful enforcement is extremely difficult.

The ultimate force still lies within the government. Funds for federal programs of housing aid, urban renewal, and neighborhood development could be withheld, and disbursement and distribution of funds tightly controlled where discrimination is practiced. However, this power has not been used as yet to any great extent.

In 1970, the Civil Rights Commission acknowledged the strength of entrenched interests that have practiced discrimination in both industry and housing and, therefore, requested "vigorous enforcement and creative administration of fair housing laws."[20]

The Commission also noted that the government's willingness to correct noncompliance has been minimal. As a result, vast inequalities still exist in the area of housing. For example, of the 3,000 mortgage banking firms in America, only 16 black-owned companies were approved by the Federal Housing Administration and the Veterans Administration.[21] It is difficult for blacks to obtain financing from white-owned sources, and, because less than one percent of the home-financing sources in this country are black owned, it is difficult for them to obtain financing anywhere else.

[20] "Excerpts from the Commission on Civil Rights Report," *Civil Rights Progress Report 1970* (Washington, D.C.: Congressional Quarterly, Inc., 1971), 80.

[21] "Black Americans: Large in Numbers, Small in Wealth," *Civil Rights Progress*, 47.

# Racial equality in employment

The equal opportunity for nonwhites to secure employment that would promote self-respect and a decent living wage became a major issue in the early 1960s, but its roots are deeper in the American experience. In 1940, President Roosevelt issued an executive order forbidding discrimination in defense-related work. In 1945, President Truman issued an order forbidding discrimination in federal employment. In that same year, he requested the establishment of a *Fair Employment Practices Commission* (FEPC) in order to prevent discrimination by employers, labor unions, employment agencies, and employment bureaus, as well as the federal government.

It was not until the Civil Rights Act of 1964 that more comprehensive legislation was passed. The 1964 Act contains an equal employment section (Title VII) that forbids persons from discriminating against a prospective employee, or depriving him in any manner of equal employment opportunities because of his race, religion, sex, or national origin. Unions are similarly prevented from refusing or limiting membership, or discriminating in the assignment of apprenticeships.

The Civil Rights Act of 1964 also established the *Equal Employment Opportunity Commission* (EEOC). Like the Department of Housing and Urban Development (HUD), the EEOC is hindered from total effectiveness; both agencies can only seek resolutions of claims through voluntary conciliation. EEOC has no power to compel compliances. If conciliation fails, a civil suit may be begun by an individual, and the Attorney General is authorized to sue where there is a repetitive pattern of discriminatory practice in employment.

## Ratio of Black Income to White Income

### Median family income

| Year | White | Black | Ratio: Black to White |
|------|-------|-------|-----------------------|
| 1969 | $9,794 | $5,999 | 61 |
| 1968 | 8,937 | 5,360 | 60 |
| 1967 | 8,274 | 4,919 | 59 |
| 1966 | 7,792 | 4,506 | 58 |
| 1965 | 7,251 | 3,886 | 54 |

Source: U.S. Department of Commerce, Bureau of the Census in *Civil Rights: Progress Report 1970* (Washington, D.C.: Congressional Quarterly, Inc., 1971), p. 46.

Despite Lyndon Johnson's efforts to assure equal opportunities in hiring for federal jobs (1965), and President Nixon's authorization of program expansion within federal agencies in order to achieve equal employment opportunity within these agencies, progress is incomplete for the simple reason that most private employers and unions are not covered by these actions, and they control the great majority of available jobs in the country. Even when the jobs are in private companies that deal with the government, hiring practices sometimes do not satisfactorily meet the government's requirements. Yet, this has not resulted in the government's withholding of funds from these companies.[22] Thus, the "overwhelming majority of blacks" in federal jobs is concentrated in the lowest-level rungs, with relatively few blacks holding managerial or policy-making positions. For one thing, the Office of Federal Contract Compliance (OFCC), and the Department of Justice have not been able to coordinate their prosecution of delinquent employers and other hiring agents to successfully eliminate unfair employment practices; for another, some companies charged with discrimination claim that, by contract, men can only hire union members—very few of whom are black in some unions.

The Nixon administration has made an intensified effort to recruit blacks, Mexican-Americans, and other minorities for the civil service; but a long-term, continuing commitment, in a society that has a long history of discrimination, is still needed if any such program is going to be effective. A long-term commitment to equal employment involves a commitment to other areas of civil rights as well.

[22] "Excerpts," *Civil Rights Progress*, 78.

**Funds Available to Minority Businesses in 1969**

### Grants

| | |
|---|---:|
| Economic Development Administration | $6,350,000 |
| Department of HEW | 200,000 |
| Department of HUD | 350,000 |
| Department of Labor | 100,000 |
| Office of Economic Opportunity | 56,000,000 |
| SBA | 5,500,000 |
| Grant Total | 68,500,000 |

### Direct Loans

| | |
|---|---:|
| Department of Agriculture | 3,000,000 |
| Economic Development Administration | 5,000,000 |
| Bureau of Indian Affairs | 1,000,000 |
| Department of HUD | 4,000,000 |
| SBA | 74,300,000 |
| Direct Loan Total | 87,300,000 |

### Guaranteed Loans

| | |
|---|---:|
| Economic Development Administration | 400,000 |
| SBA | 144,400,000 |
| Guaranteed Loan Total | 144,800,000 |
| Grand Total | $300,600,000 |

Source: Commission on Civil Rights Report *Civil Rights: Progress Report 1970* (Washington, D.C.: Congressional Quarterly, Inc., 1971), p. 53.

Discrimination in housing almost always leads to racially segregated schooling, often characterized by inferior facilities and teaching personnel. Poor schooling, in turn, leads to poor training for employment. Clearly, discrimination in employment is, in part, a result of unequal access to opportunities in education and housing.

# Implications of civil rights for nonwhites

Steps taken by the President, Congress, the courts, and state and local governments in the generation since World War II have helped further fulfill the American ideal of social and economic equality of opportunity for all Americans. Achievements can be measured by looking at the numbers of nonwhites in previously all-white schools, the achievements of these children in school, their income opportunities and levels, their access to public facilities, their housing patterns, and so on.

While it is true that official segregation has not entirely disappeared from our nation's life, it cannot be denied that considerable progress has been made. More nonwhites are voting than ever before, and their wishes can no longer be ignored by politicians. Fayette, Mississippi; Gary, Indiana; Newark, New Jersey; and Cleveland, Ohio; for example, all have elected black mayors.[23] Alabama has a black sheriff. Many other cities have racially mixed city councils. These are major political accomplishments for the nonwhite voter, and for representative democracy in general.

[23] Charles Evers, mayor of Fayette, Mississippi, is the brother of Medgar Evers, slain leader of the NAACP in Mississippi; Carl Stokes, mayor of Cleveland, was the first black mayor to be re-elected.

Furthermore, economic and social conditions have improved in American society. Increasing numbers of blacks and other nonwhite minorities are being employed by banks, insurance companies, the telephone company, and so on. A generation ago, this would have been unthinkable. More nonwhites are in college and professional schools than ever before, and the incomes have been increasing steadily, although they still lag behind white incomes.

In general, we have learned that the concern and zeal of federal, state, and local officials in enforcing civil rights legislation is as important as the enactment of the laws themselves. The fact that a statute has been passed does not mean that the solution has been achieved. The recent conclusion of the Commission on Civil Rights is that "the great promise of the civil rights laws, Executive Orders, and judicial decisions of the 1950s and 1960s has not been realized. The Federal Government has not yet fully geared itself to carry out these legal mandates of equal opportunity." It further notes that "there is danger that the great effort made by public and private groups to obtain the civil rights law we now have will be nullified through ineffective enforcement."[24]

[24] "Excerpts," *Civil Rights Progress*, 91.

The *National Advisory Commission on Civil Disorders* (the Kerner Commission), created in response to the agitation in the urban ghettoes, and the expressed desire of the federal government to understand the deep causes of civil unrest in the last years of the 1960s, however, forecast an even bleaker picture. Regardless of the scores of federally operated agencies, the training programs, and the legislation to wipe out discrimination, the Commission noted that the basic conditions of unrest—poverty, ghetto life, poor school facilities, discrimination in hiring, and so on—had not been remedied; and that these inequities lead to violence when blacks see them as examples of the government's failure to respond to their needs.

It is certain that stopgap economic measures will not solve the racial problems of America, nor will the solutions come in immediate response to legislation or campaign promises. But, the role of moral leadership, the Commission on Civil Rights noted, lies with the President. The people of the urban and rural ghettoes—the blacks, Latin Americans, Indians, Mexican-Americans, Puerto Ricans—look to him for effective action on behalf of equal opportunity. The fulfillment of the American dream within the next decade would seem to rest with the American people, white and nonwhite, and with their leaders.

# Sexual equality

The vision of the civil rights movement—to attain equality before the law—has to some extent inspired in the late 1960s, an active drive to secure equal rights for the American woman. The leaders of the movement for sexual equality, also known as *"women's liberation,"* have pointed out that the same demand for equality and justice made by nonwhites must also be made by women. Women, too, have been discriminated against, assigned inferior roles in our society, and denied opportunities in education and employment. The leaders of women's liberation have stated that the quality of American life is determined by "sexist" policies: women, on the basis of sex alone, are systematically excluded from competing with men. Thus, the once largely unexamined role of woman in society has been brought under intense scrutiny by women who contend that their civil rights have been denied them by a male-oriented society.

## Employment and Income of Women

| | |
|---|---|
| Number of women in the United States | 108 million |
| Number of women who work | 31 million |
| Average income of college-educated women | $6,694/year[1] |

[1] Roughly equal to the income of a man with an eighth-grade education and less than the average amount earned by women in 1955.

Source: Bella S. Abzug (D. New York), "Power to the Majority—Women," *The New York Times* (August 26, 1971), p. 37.

Prior to the movement for women's suffrage, there had been little public protest over the place of women in society.

## Percentage of Women in Certain Professions

| Profession | Percentage[1] |
|---|---|
| Professor | 9 |
| Doctor | 7 |
| Lawyer | 3 |
| Legislator | 2 |
| Federal judge | 1 |

[1] Percentage of women in relation to the total number of people practicing the profession.

Source: Bella S. Abzug (D. New York), "Power to the Majority—Women," *The New York Times*, (August 26, 1971), 37.

While women played important roles in the various reform movements of the early nineteenth century (for example, prison reform and abolitionism), they were never able to apply the gains made for other groups to their own situation.

The Twentieth Amendment to the Constitution was the first legal breakthrough in the effort to equalize the status of women in America. The right to vote was a victory for civil rights, much as was the extension of suffrage to former slaves; it was a significant, but very incomplete, achievement. Today, women, as well as nonwhite citizens, are working for a more meaningful extension of civil rights.

## "Women's liberation"

[25] *The Gallup Opinion Index, Report No. 63,* September 1970 (Princeton, N.J.: The Gallup Opinion Index, 1970), p. 1.

The women involved in the women's liberation movement within the civil rights struggle are generally college educated and urban based. A recent poll of women indicated that 65 percent felt that they get "as good a break as men" in life; but only 53 percent of those women polled who had a college education agreed with that statement. Seventy-five percent of the college-educated women stated that they felt women were held back from top business positions just because of their sex.[25]

Drawing by Weber © 1971
The New Yorker Magazine, Inc.

In professional circles, women earn less than men in all kinds of jobs; the unemployment rate is higher for women. Contrary to common belief, women, like men, work because they need the money, not solely, as some men would believe, for "personal fulfillment," or to compete with men. A study by the United States Women's Bureau showed that money was found to motivate most of the 6.5 million single-women workers, who joined the labor force only for "compelling economic reasons."

One of the oldest, most powerful women's organizations, the *National Organization for Women* (NOW), protests that the provisions of the Constitution have little effect on the attitudes of the dominant males who control business and, indeed, most aspects of American life. They argue that they, in common with nonwhites, are oppressed, excluded, and discriminated against by the nation's institutions.

Women's caucuses, rights groups, and others have campaigned throughout the country with handbills and advertisements. They have threatened court suits against alleged discrimination; and they have succeeded in introducing an equal rights amendment to the Constitution (which failed to pass Congress).

It was not until 1967 that the first national conference on women's rights was held in Washington, D.C. NOW listed its demands in the form of a "Bill of Rights." This bill of rights was a protest against, as well as a formal declaration of, the manner in which women are denied their civil rights. The eight demands in the petition were for:

1. An equal rights constitutional amendment
2. An enforcement of the law banning sex discrimination in employment
3. Maternity-leave rights in employment and in social security benefits
4. A tax deduction for home and child care for working parents
5. Establishment of child day-care centers
6. Equal and unsegregated education
7. Equal job training opportunities and allowances for women in poverty
8. The right of women to control their reproductive lives.[26]

[26] Robin Morgan, *Sisterhood Is Powerful* (New York: Random House, Inc., 1970), pp. 512–514.

Inclusive as NOW's program is, the ultimate aims of today's feminists are more all encompassing. One manifesto, issued by a Chicago-based women's liberation group, for example, encompasses both the practical and spiritual goals of womanhood, in its effort to redefine the nature of being a woman in contemporary life.

[27] Morgan, *Sisterhood, op. cit.*, p. 531.

What does women's freedom mean? It means freedom of self-determination, self-enrichment, the freedom to live one's own life, set one's own goals, the freedom to rejoice in one's own accomplishments. It means the freedom to be one's own person in an integrated life of work, love, play, motherhood: the freedoms, rights and privileges of first class citizenship, of equality in relationships of live and work: the right to choose to make decisions or not to: the right to full self-realization and to full participation in the life of the world. That is the freedom we seek in women's liberation. [27]

**Equality of Women in Business**
**If a woman has the same ability as a man, does she have as good a chance to become the executive of a company, or not? (based on views of women only)**

|  | Yes % | No % | No Opinion % |
|---|---|---|---|
| All Women | 39 | 54 | 7 |
| Education |  |  |  |
| College | 22 | 75 | 3 |
| High School | 39 | 54 | 7 |
| Grade School | 54 | 36 | 10 |
| Occupation of Head of Household |  |  |  |
| Prof. & Bus. | 28 | 64 | 8 |
| White Collar | 30 | 67 | 3 |
| Farmers | 43 | 47 | 10 |
| Manual | 40 | 54 | 6 |
| Age |  |  |  |
| 21–29 years | 32 | 63 | 5 |
| 30–49 years | 33 | 59 | 8 |
| 50 & over | 49 | 45 | 6 |
| Religion |  |  |  |
| Protestant | 36 | 57 | 7 |
| Catholic | 46 | 46 | 8 |
| Jewish | X | X | X |
| Politics |  |  |  |
| Republican | 36 | 56 | 8 |
| Democrat | 43 | 52 | 5 |
| Independent | 35 | 58 | 7 |
| Region |  |  |  |
| East | 46 | 48 | 6 |
| Midwest | 38 | 56 | 6 |
| South | 31 | 60 | 9 |
| West | 40 | 53 | 7 |
| Income of Head of Household |  |  |  |
| $15,000 & over | 28 | 65 | 7 |
| $10,000–$14,999 | 31 | 64 | 5 |
| $ 7,000–$ 9,999 | 38 | 55 | 7 |
| $ 5,000–$ 6,999 | 43 | 49 | 8 |
| $ 3,000–$ 4,999 | 52 | 43 | 5 |
| Under $3,000 | 48 | 42 | 10 |
| Community Size |  |  |  |
| 1,000,000 & over | 38 | 57 | 5 |
| 500,000–999,999 | 38 | 54 | 8 |
| 50,000–499,999 | 38 | 55 | 7 |
| 2,500–49,999 | 38 | 55 | 7 |
| Under 2,500, Rural | 41 | 50 | 9 |
| Women/Children Under 21 | 33 | 60 | 7 |
| How Men Vote on This Question | 39 | 56 | 5 |

Source: *Gallup Opinion Index*, Report No. 63, September 1970 (Princeton, N.J.: Gallup Opinion Index, 1970), p. 10.

## Political action and women's liberation

The political activity that surrounds the women's liberation movement—for example, lobbying by NOW in Washington, D.C.—and the comprehensive drive toward attaining sexual equality for women have resulted in legislative achievements similar to those for nonwhites.

*Helen B. Shaffer, "The Status of Women,"* Editorial Research Reports, *vol. 2, no. 5, August 5, 1970, pp. 572–573.*

Helen Shaffer notes that a sign of the new feminist militancy is the reinvigoration of the drive for acceptance of an Equal Rights for Women Amendment to the Constitution and the increased number of bills being introduced to fight sex discrimination.

The Amendment, which has been introduced in every session of Congress since 1923, states simply:

Equality of rights under the law shall not be denied or abridged by the United States or by any state on account of sex.

Although it has not as yet been passed by Congress, the Amendment has progressed further in 1970 toward congressional approval than ever before. A female congresswoman, Rep. Martha W. Griffiths (D. Mich.), acquired 218 signatures on a discharge petition to draw the measure out of the House Judiciary Committee, the traditional "burial ground" of proposals. The Senate gave the Amendment hearings for the first time in fourteen years and it was subsequently approved by the Constitutional Amendment Subcommittee. Eighty-two senators sponsored the proposal and the chairman of the subcommittee Senator Birch Bayh (D. Ind.) predicted that the parent Senate Judiciary Committee would approve it, thus giving the proposal over to floor action. But the Amendment had not, as of July, 1971, passed from the committee to the Senate floor.

As of August, 1970, more than a dozen bills were pending in Congress to remove various forms of discrimination against women. In June, 1970, hearings were held on a measure introduced by Rep. Edith Green (D. Oregon). She would like to prohibit sex discrimination in any federally funded program, extend coverage of the Equal Pay Act of 1963 to executive, administrative and professional employees (which would aid many women) and extend jurisdiction of the Civil Rights Commission to include cases of sex discrimination. Another bill being considered would extend the enforcement power of the Equal Employment Opportunity Commission and the Civil Rights Act of 1964 to fight sex discrimination in academic and professional employment. Other bills would provide day-care centers for children of working mothers, remove inequities in the Social Security Act pertaining to working wives, and equalize the treatment of married women and married men in the federal service in regard to overseas benefits and survivorship benefits.

Legislative action then, according to Helen Shaffer, has recently been an active front in the battle for equal women's rights.

The inclusion of women in the 1964 Civil Rights Act is one example of the success of such activity. (To supplement this legislation, President Johnson issued an Executive Order on September, 1965, prohibiting discrimination, on the basis of sex, in federal employment.) The 1967 Equal Rights Amendment mentioned earlier is another example. The Citizen's Council on the Status of Women, apointed by President Nixon in 1969, recommended the passage of the Equal Rights Amendment proposed by NOW in 1967.

## Women in the 92nd Congress

| Name | Party | State | Age | First Elected |
|------|-------|-------|-----|---------------|
| Bella Abzug | D | N.Y. | 50 | 1970 |
| Shirley Chisholm | D | N.Y. | 46 | 1968 |
| Florence P. Dwyer | R | N.J. | 68 | 1956 |
| Ella T. Grasso | D | Conn. | 51 | 1970 |
| Edith Green | D | Ore. | 60 | 1954 |
| Martha Griffiths | D | Mich. | 58 | 1954 |
| Julia Butler Hansen | D | Wash. | 63 | 1960 |
| Margaret M. Heckler | R | Mass. | 39 | 1966 |
| Louise Day Hicks | D | Mass. | 51 | 1970 |
| Patsy T. Mink | D | Hawaii | 43 | 1964 |
| Charlotte T. Reid | R | Ill. | 57 | 1960 |
| Margaret Chase Smith | R | Maine | 73 | 1940 |
| Leonor K. Sullivan | D | Mo. | 67 | 1952 |

Source: "Women in Congress," *Current American Government* (Washington, D.C.: Congressional Quarterly, Inc., 1971), p. 25.

Although the civil rights amendment has not been passed, legislation against discriminatory practices in job hiring, salary compensation, and other areas, has led to the creation of licensed day-care centers, funded in part by federal funds totaling, in 1970, an estimated $125 million, an additional $26 million coming from state and private sources. Proposals also have been made to allow tax deductions for child care as an ordinary expense of business and to mandate maternity leaves which, at the present time, are only voluntarily given.

In addition to pressing for legislative action, women's liberationists have appealed to the executive branch of government. In one such action, two women's liberation groups—WEAL (Women's Equity Action League) and

NOW—filed complaints with the Department of Health, Education and Welfare against forty-three colleges and universities, charging that federal funds were being given in violation of Executive Orders No. 11246 and No. 11375, which forbid discrimination by federal contracts on the basis of sex. These groups stated that the schools cited discriminated against women through admissions quotas, in the allocation of financial aid for graduate study, in hiring practices, promotions, and salary differentials. Where there was resistance to the expected compromise between the groups and the schools, HEW officials took measures towards ending sex discrimination; they contacted deans of colleges and universities, asking them to list the measures they have taken to end this kind of discriminatory practice.

Several such executive orders issued by President Nixon are a response to the demands of women political activists for methods to obtain opportunities in their chosen fields.

## Civil rights and the homosexual

Homosexuality, once a carefully guarded secret, has now become a matter of concern to some civil rights organizations. Today's homosexuals are demanding more than mere acceptance; they also want full legal, social, and economic equality. Open homosexuality, for example, is still grounds for dismissal in most federal agencies. The American Civil Liberties Union is one of several organizations that is helping homosexuals to fight such instances of discrimination in the courts.

# Glossary

**Civil Rights Act of 1875**  Congressional act which sought to protect blacks against discrimination by private citizens in many areas including that of public accommodation.

**de facto segregation**  "Actually existing" segregation, although without lawful authority.

**de jure segregation**  Segregation according to or sanctioned by law.

**Equal Employment Opportunity Commission (EEOC)**  Commission established by Congress in 1964 to prevent discrimination in employment.

**Fair Employment Practices Commission (FEPC)**  Commission established by President Roosevelt in 1941 to investigate discrimination based on race. President Truman sought unsuccessfully to have Congress establish the Commission on a permanent basis in the years after the close of World War II.

**Fifteenth Amendment**  Constitutional amendment adopted in 1870, prohibiting states from denying the vote "on account of race, color, or national origin," and giving Congress the power to create legislation necessary to enforce the amendment's provision.

**"grandfather" clause**  Tactic designed to exempt illiterate whites from the literacy test by allowing all who had voted before the ratification of the Fifteenth Amendment (1870) and the descendants of those individuals to vote in future elections without having to pass the test.

**literacy test**  Legal tactic introduced by Mississippi in 1892 that successfully limited black suffrage by requiring voters to be able to read, understand, and interpret the state and/or national constitutions.

**Missouri Compromise**  Congressional act of 1820 admitting Missouri to the Union as a slaveholding state, and prohibiting slavery in the territory of the United States north of Missouri's southern border.

**National Advisory Commission on Civil Disorders (the Kerner Commission)**  1968 commission created by the national government to study agitation in the urgan ghettoes and report the causes of deep civil unrest to the federal government.

**National Organization for Women (NOW)**  One of the largest and most influential national organizations dedicated to women's liberation and to equality with men.

**poll tax**  A tax used primarily in the South to be paid by those who wished to vote, which resulted in the disfranchisement of many blacks and poor whites.

**restrictive covenant**  An agreement between property-owners specifying those to whom they will sell property.

**Voting Rights Act of 1965**  Legislation that suspended all literacy tests in all states and counties where less than 50 percent of the population had been registered to vote in the 1964 presidential election; it also provided for federal examiners to register voters and monitor election procedures in states covered by the Act.

**white primary**  Important device used in the one-party southern states to disfranchise the black citizen, by denying him the right to participate in Democratic primary elections, which were essentially the determining elections for local, state, and national officials.

**women's liberation** National movement demanding equal rights for women in education, employment, political, and social areas of American society.

## Supreme Court decisions

*Boynton* v. *Virginia* (1960) Decision which held that segregation by a restaurant in a bus terminal serving interstate travelers violated the Interstate Commerce Act.

*Brown* v. *Board of Education* (1954) Decision that "separate but equal" had no place in the interpretation of the Fourteenth Amendment guarantee of equal protection of the laws.

*Civil Rights Cases of 1883* Decision which declared the Civil Rights Act of 1875 unconstitutional on the grounds that the Fourteenth Amendment did not give Congress the right to make private discrimination illegal, only that it barred the state governments from engaging in discriminatory practices.

*Cooper* v. *Aaron* (1958) Decision that the constitutional rights of children not to be discriminated against in school admission could not be nullified by state legislators, state executives, or judicial officers, and that the decisions of the federal courts are the "supreme Law of the Land" within the meaning of Article V of the Constitution.

*Ex Parte Yarborough* (1884) Declared that Congress could protect the privilege of voting for members of Congress against state or individual aggression.

*Griffin* v. *County School Board of Prince Edward County* (1964) Held that to close the schools in one county, while maintaining them in others, was a denial of the equal protection clause of the Fourteenth Amendment.

*Grovey* v. *Townsend* (1935) Decision that temporarily legalized the white primary.

*Guinn* v. *United States* (1915) Declared Oklahoma's "grandfather" clause unconstitutional.

*Harper* v. *Virginia Board of Education* (1966) Declared poll taxes in state and local elections a violation of the equal protection clause of the Fourteenth Amendment.

*Heart of Atlanta Motel* v. *United States* (1964) Upheld provisions of the Civil Rights Act of 1964 making it illegal to discriminate in the interstate hotel and motel business.

*Katzenbach* v. *McClung* (1964) Upheld the provisions of the Civil Rights Act of 1964 making it illegal to discriminate in restaurants whose activities affect interstate commerce.

*Missouri ex. rel. Gaines* v. *Canada* (1938) Held that Missouri could not subsidize the tuition of a black at a law school outside the state in order to avoid admitting him to study at the University of Missouri.

*Nixon* v. *Herndon* (1927) Declared unconstitutional a 1923 Texas law that denied blacks the right to participate in a Democratic party primary election.

*Plessy* v. *Ferguson* (1896) Interpreted the equal protection clause of the Fourteenth Amendment as meaning "separate but equal."

*Shelley* v. *Kramer* (1948) Held that the judiciary could no longer enforce restrictive covenants, because to do so, would sanction illegal state actions and thus be in violation of the equal protection clause of the Fourteenth Amendment.

*Smith* v. *Allwright* (1944)    Declared the white primary to be a violation of the Fifteenth Amendment.

*Turner* v. *Memphis* (1962)    Decision which held invalid segregation established by an administrative regulation in airport restaurants.

# Suggested readings

Anderson, Walt, ed., *The Age of Protest* (Pacific Palisades, Calif.: Goodyear Publishing Co., Inc., 1969). Collection of probing the varied articles, essays, and studies pertaining to major protest movements, including civil rights, education, peace, and religion.

Berger, Morroe, *Equality by Statute: The Revolution in Civil Rights*, rev. ed. (Garden City, N.Y.: Doubleday and Co., Inc., 1968). Legalistic and historical treatment of government's role in the fight against discrimination.

Berman, Daniel M., *It Is So Ordered: The Supreme Court Rules on School Segregation* (New York: W. W. Norton and Co., Inc., 1966). Analysis of school segregation cases, particularly *Brown* v. *Board of Education*, which provides an outline of the Supreme Court and the judicial process.

Blaustein, Albert P., and Robert L. Zangrando, eds., *Civil Rights and the American Negro: A Documentary History* (New York: Washington Square Press, Inc., c/o Simon & Schuster, 1968). Collection of documents, each prefaced by the editors' comments, showing the history of the Afro-American and his relationship to United States citizenship.

Brisbane, Robert H., *The Black Vanguard: Origins of the Negro Social Revolution* (Valley Forge, Pa.: Judson Press, 1970). Summary of Negro movements in America, including the organization, history, and relationship to the political scene.

Brock, Jacobus Ten, *Equal Under Law*, rev. ed. (New York: The Macmillan Co., 1965). Originally published as *Antislavery Origins of the Fourteenth Amendment*. Analysis of the Fourteenth Amendment and its origins, thus providing a view of the role played by the Constitution in social reform.

Chambers, Bradford, ed., *Chronicles of Black Protest: A Background Door (or Young People Documenting the History of Black Power)*. (New York: Parents' Magazine Press, 1968). Collection of some forty-two documents with enlightening commentaries, mainly of an historical nature, dealing with the scope of racial problems.

Dorman, Michael, *We Shall Overcome* (New York: Dial Press, Inc., 1964). Integrationist's account of one of the critical years (1962–1963) in the civil rights revolution.

Dorsen, Norman, ed., *Discrimination and Civil Rights: Cases, Text, and Materials* (Boston: Little, Brown and Co., 1969). Text containing cases and materials dealing with racial discrimination, and organized in terms of problems, rather than legal doctrine.

Flexner, Eleanor, *Century of Struggle: The Woman's Rights Movement in the United States* (New York: Atheneum Publishers, 1968). Scholarly and absorbing account of the women's rights movement, with central attention given to the seventy-year struggle for suffrage and the personalities within the movement.

Goldwin, Robert A., ed., *100 Years of Emancipation* (Chicago: Rand McNally and Co., 1964). Series of essays offering a description of race problems in America.

Grimes, Alan P., *Equality in America: Religion, Race, and the Urban Majority* (New York: Oxford University Press, Inc., 1964). Succinct historical survey of religious and racial minorities in America.

Jacobs, Paul, *Prelude to Riot: A View of Urban America from the Bottom* (New York: Random House, Inc., 1968). Worthwhile examination of underlying conditions—welfare, housing, and jobs—that the author believes led to the Watts rebellion, and the police activity, and the McCowe Commission hearings on the Watts incident.

King, Martin Luther, Jr., *Where Do We Go From Here: Chaos or Community?* (New York: Harper and Row Publishers, Inc., 1967). Discussion and analysis of conflicts within the civil rights movement, and a view toward the future, stressing the constant need to influence the political process.

Krislov, Samuel, *The Negro in Federal Employment: The Quest for Equal Opportunity* (Minneapolis: University of Minnesota Press, 1967). Survey of civil rights in the civil service.

Lewis, Anthony, and *The New York Times, Portrait of a Decade: The Second American Revolution* (New York: Random House, Inc., 1964). Profile of the period of civil rights revolutions (1954–1964) and the role of law, supplemented by excerpts from *The New York Times*.

Lincoln, C. Eric, *Sounds of the Struggle: Persons and Perspectives in Civil Rights* (New York: William Morrow and Co., Inc., 1967). Eighteen previously unpublished articles that deal with various aspects of the civil rights struggle in the 1960s.

Lockard, W. Duane, *Toward Equal Opportunity: A Study of State and Local Antidiscrimination Laws* (New York: The Macmillan Co., 1968). Examination of various antidiscrimination laws, the political problems of enforcing these laws, and their actual and potential value to the American Negro.

Malcolm X, *By Any Means Necessary: Speeches, Interviews and a Letter*, ed. by George Breitman (New York: Pathfinder Press, Inc., 1970). Reflection of the changing views of Malcolm X in the last year of his life—that the struggle was between "haves and have-nots," rather than blacks and whites.

Malcolm X and Alex Haley, *The Autobiography of Malcolm X* (New York: Grove Press, Inc., 1966). Dictated to a friend, this book captures the presence and the agony of a man. No analysis is made of Malcolm X as a political leader, but his life as he traveled to "Islam" is humanly described.

Matthews, Donald R., and James W. Prothro, *Negroes and the New Southern Politics* (New York: Harcourt Brace and World, Inc., 1966). Comprehensive, analytical work pertaining to the southern Negro's political participation, its future, and its effects on both politics and race relations.

McKay, Robert B., *Reapportionment: The Law and Politics of Equal Representation* (New York: Twentieth Century Fund, Inc., 1965). Historical presentation of theories of representation, as well as the effect of reapportionment on a representative government.

Miller, Helen H., *The Case for Liberty* (Chapel Hill: University of North Carolina Press, 1965). Discussion of the colonial origins of our basic constitutional freedoms.

Miller, Loren, *The Petitioners: The Story of the Supreme Court of the United States and the Negro* (New York: World Publishing Co., 1967). Scholarly history of the Supreme Court and its changing attitude toward the Negro.

Morgan, Ruth P., *The President and Civil Rights* (New York: St. Martin's Press, Inc., 1970). Analysis of the civil rights policy making of five Presidents, from Franklin D. Roosevelt to Lyndon Johnson.

Myrdal, Gunnar, *An American Dilemma*, rev. ed. (New York: Harper and Row Publishers, Inc., 1962). Classic study of race relations and discrimination, emphasizing the disparity between American ideals and reality.

Perrucci, Robert, and Marc Pilisuk, eds., *The Triple Revolution: Social Problems in Depth* (Boston: Little, Brown and Co., 1968). Revealing analysis of the "triple revolution" in our society—warfare, cybernation, and human rights.

Proctor, Samuel D., *The Young Negro in America: 1960–1980* (New York: Association Press, 1966). Personal examination of the "present generation" of "disillusioned" blacks, projecting what lies in the future for the country and the young black.

Shapiro, Fred C., and James W. Sullivan, *Race Riots, New York 1964* (New York: Thomas Y. Crowell Co., 1964). Account of the 1964 race riots in the New York ghettoes of Harlem and Bedford-Stuyvesant.

Sterling, Dorothy, *Tear Down the Walls! A History of the American Civil Rights Movement* (Garden City, N.Y.: Doubleday and Co., Inc., 1968). Detailed account of the civil rights movement from the days of pre-Lincolnian slavery to post-World War II civil rights gains, including the organizations, people, and philosophies involved.

Sugarman, Tracy, *Stranger at the Gates: A Summer in Mississippi* (New York: Hill and Wang, Inc., 1966). Personal account of the southern civil rights movement, focusing on the summer of 1964 in Mississippi.

Wolff, Miles, *Lunch at the Five and Ten: The Greensboro Sit-ins: A Contemporary History* (New York: Stein and Day, 1970). Account of the 1960 sit-in movement, capturing the mood and characterization.

Woodward, C. Vann, *The Strange Career of Jim Crow*, 2nd rev. ed. (New York: Oxford University Press, Inc., 1966). Updated edition of his valuable 1955 study on slavery and segregation.

# Topics of further study

Breitbach, Richard C., "School Desegregation: An Analysis of Minority Rights and Majority Control" (Master's Thesis, Chicago: University of Chicago, 1970).

Carageorge, Ted, "Truman and Civil Rights: Political Expediency or Conviction?" (Master's Thesis; Coral Gables, Fla.: University of Miami, 1960).

Cheever, Herbert, "The International Politics of Apartheid in South Africa," Unpublished Ph.D. dissertation, University of Iowa, 1967.

Drake, Thomas E., *Quakers and Slavery in America* (New Haven: Yale University Press, 1965).

Drake, Thomas Mitchell, and D. G. Temple, eds., *Human Relations: A Reader for West Virginans* (Morgantown: University of West Virginia Press, 1968).

Goff, Kenneth, *Reds Promote Racial War* (New York: Roberts Publishing Corp., 1958).

Hemphill, Ralph W., "Civil and Criminal Enforcement of Civil Rights," Unpublished Ph.D. dissertation, University of Mississippi, 1970.

Otenasek, Mildred, "Women in an Elective Office—Women in an Appointed Office," in *Report of the Maryland Commission on the Status of Women* (Baltimore: The Maryland Commission, 1967).

Silznek, George Theodore, III, "The United States Commission on Civil Rights: A Study of Incrementalism in Policy-Making" (Ph.D. dissertation; Ann Arbor: University of Michigan, 1977).

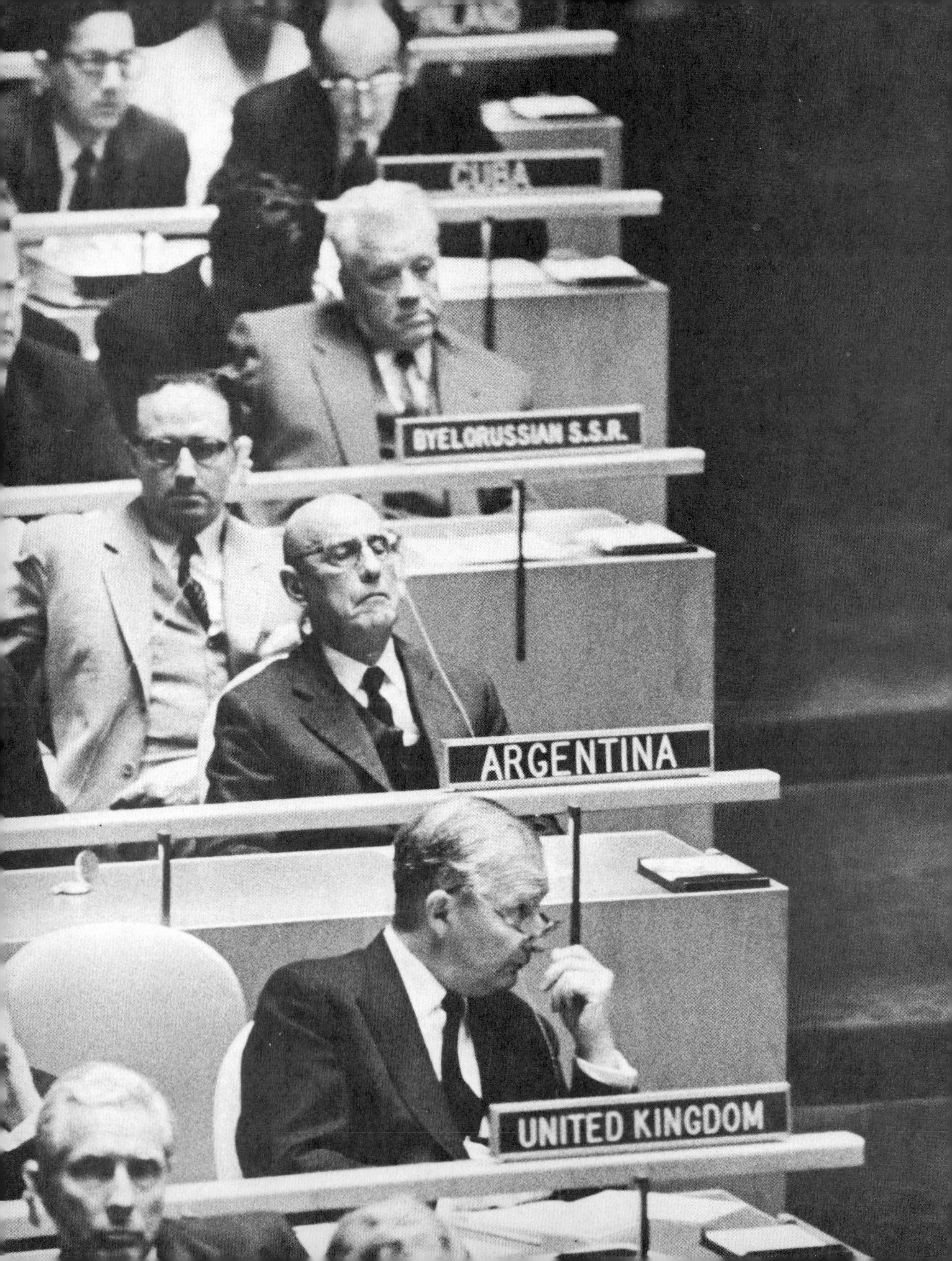
CUBA
BYELORUSSIAN S.S.R.
ARGENTINA
UNITED KINGDOM

# 20 foreign policy

## design and impact

ALMOST EVERYONE agrees that the purpose of foreign policy is to protect the national interest; and almost no one agrees on what the national interest is. It can mean anything from pursuing Communists in some remote corner of the world to raising the tariff on Italian pocketbooks. For many Americans, it simply means the maintenance of foreign relationships that are advantageous to the United States, and consistent with her principles as a world power. Yet, during various periods in our history, there has been considerable disagreement as to what is advantageous to us and consistent with our national principles and objectives.

In recent years, for example, some supporters of American policy in Vietnam have argued that military intervention is necessary, if we are to protect ourselves from the dangers of a Communist advance in Southeast Asia, and honor commitments to our allies. Critics of our policy have maintained that our interest would not be undercut by a Communist takeover in Southeast Asia, and that our interference is inconsistent with our stance as a nonaggressive nation. Both groups, however, justify their arguments in terms of the "national interest."

Although the debates on Vietnam are the most intense we have witnessed in years, similar controversies persisted throughout the Korean conflict, and prior to both World Wars I and II. Thus, as Senator Fulbright, chairman of the Senate Foreign Relations Committee, has stated:

> The major question of our time is not how to end these conflicts but whether we can find some way to conduct them without resorting to weapons that will resolve them once and for all by wiping out the contestants. A generation ago we were speaking of "making the world safe for democracy." Having failed of this in two World Wars, we must now seek ways of making

the world reasonably safe for the continuing contest between those who favor democracy and those who oppose it. It is a modest aspiration, but it is a sane and realistic one for a generation which, having failed of grander things, must now look to its own survival.[1]

# From isolationism to involvement

[1] J. W. Fulbright,
*Old Myths and New Realities*
(New York: Random House, Inc., 1964), pp. 77–78.

Many of the first American settlers were disaffected Europeans who had little interest in maintaining political bonds with the countries they had left. Instead, they sought to develop as an independent nation, free of European politics and diplomatic entanglements, and free, so far as possible, from economic domination. When George Washington, in his *Farewell Address*, stated, "we may safely trust to temporary alliances for extraordinary emergencies," and advised future leaders to "steer clear of permanent alliances with any portion of the foreign world," he was echoing the sentiments of his countrymen. For most of them, alliances implied taxation, exploitation, and corruption; international diplomacy seemed to demand compromises incompatible with the American conception of freedom.

*The United States adhered to an isolationist policy throughout the nineteenth century. This cartoon is an 1864 depiction of American foreign policy.*

Drawing by Hochstein from the Astor, Lenox and Tilden Foundations of the New York Public Library.

**OUR FOREIGN RELATIONS**

Washington's Address is often cited as the initial assertion of American isolationism, an attitude that began to dominate American policy and policy-makers early in the nineteenth century. True, there was a brief conflict with Britain and France in 1812 over interference with American shipping and conflicting desires for territorial conquests; but, in general, America managed to steer clear of foreign entanglements—and avoided involvement in the revolutions and rebellions that were shaking the aristocratic foundations of almost every major European nation throughout the nineteenth century. Although most Americans sympathized with these revolutions in spirit and principle, the overwhelming majority were content to follow the advice of John Adams, who, in 1775, had vehemently argued in favor of an isolationist policy—a policy that should guide all of America's relations with Europe.

## The Monroe Doctrine

America continued to assert her independence from nations and events outside her hemisphere, and throughout the nineteenth century, vowed that she would protect all North, Central, and South American countries from foreign intervention. This clarification of American isolationism became official in 1823, when President James Monroe declared that "American continents" were "not to be considered as subjects for future colonization by any European power." If the European powers should try "to extend their systems to any portion of this Hemisphere," the United States would view this as "dangerous to our peace and safety." Reciprocally, the United States promised not to interfere in European affairs. The *Monroe Doctrine*, as it came to be known, was prompted by a desire to keep America's borders intact by preventing foreign powers—France and Spain in Latin America, and Russia in North America—from setting up protectorates.

The doctrine, however, was not tested until 1865, when President Andrew Johnson sent American troops to help British and native Mexican forces expel Maximilian, the puppet-king of France's Napoleon III. The next major enforcement of the doctrine occurred during the Spanish-American War of 1898, when Teddy Roosevelt and his Rough Riders stormed through Cuba and drove out the Spanish colonialists.

By 1900, America was a great world power, committed throughout the world, and surpassing other nations in population, resources, and productivity. Nevertheless, she clung to her isolationist heritage. Farsighted statesmen and military men realized that this posture could not be maintained for long. They warned that the United States would soon have to take a leading role, perhaps even an aggressive role, in world affairs in order to preserve her autonomy and her power. Teddy Roosevelt stated in his vice-presidential inaugural address of 1901: "We stand supreme in a continent, in a hemisphere. East and West we look across two great oceans toward the larger life in which, whether we will or not, we must take an ever-increasing share."[2]

2 Quoted in Donald Brandon, *American Foreign Policy* (New York: Appleton-Century-Crofts, 1966), p. 33.

*Theodore Roosevelt blended a generous portion of the Monroe Doctrine into his "big stick" soup. The nutritional quality of the mixture is explained in this 1901 cartoon, in which Uncle Sam Rooster shelters the Latin chicks.*

Culver Pictures

## The great wars

[3] Quoted in William Henry Chamberlin, *America's Second Crusade* (Chicago: Henry Regnery Co., 1950), pp. 4–5.

Despite admonitions from men such as Theodore Roosevelt, Americans resisted entering what was to become World War I. Even after the Germans, in 1915, sank the British ship Lusitania, carrying 118 American passengers, Americans looked to the nonbelligerent leadership of President Wilson, who had declared: "There is such a thing as a nation being so right that it does not need to convince others by force that it is right."[3] When Wilson finally did involve America in the war in 1917, it was as a moral crusade to make the world "safe for democracy."

Upon the signing of the peace treaty in 1919, Americans returned to domestic matters—domestic jazz, domestic dance, and domestic booze—and vowed never to go to war again. By 1929, Americans had danced their way into the Great Depression. Besieged with domestic ills, haunted by breadlines on the streets, they were oblivious to rumors from Europe that a fanatical little man with a mustache was rearming Germany and packing trainloads of people off to strange places. Americans in the 1930s were still trying to recover their morale and their money. They refused to admit to the possibilities of becoming involved in another world war—even as Franklin D. Roosevelt warned in his "quarantine speech" of 1937:

> Let no one imagine that America will escape, that America may expect mercy, that this Western Hemisphere will not be attacked and that it will continue tranquilly and peacefully to carry on the ethics and arts of civilization.[4]

[4] Franklin D. Roosevelt's "Quarantine speech," Chicago, October 5, 1937.

Not until the Japanese bombed Pearl Harbor on December 7, 1941, did all Americans appreciate the significance of Roosevelt's vision. Pearl Harbor and the entry of the United States into World War II marked the end of a long history—one hundred fifty years—of isolationism. Americans, in 1946, finally realized that they could no longer afford the price of isolation. In order to make the world "safe for democracy," America would have to play an active role in world affairs.

## Containing communism

In February 1945, United States President Franklin Roosevelt, England's Prime Minister Winston Churchill, and the Soviet Union's Premier Josef Stalin met at Yalta to set the terms for German surrender, to determine the future of the occupied countries, and also to discuss a world organization for peace called the *United Nations*. Not long after the Yalta agreement, however, the Soviet Union had violated its peace pledges at Yalta, by turning Poland and Romania into satellite countries. The descent of Moscow's "iron curtain" on Albania, Bulgaria, Hungary, and Yugoslavia aroused the American people to the nature and extent of Communist expansion.

In the late 1940s, Americans sought to restrain Stalin's ambitions through a policy of *containment*. This policy, first propounded by American diplomat George Kennan, proposed to prevent the expansion of communism beyond its postwar boundaries. Kennan argued that the Communists would not risk a major war, since the development of atomic energy had made war as risky for the U.S.S.R. as it was for the United States. Instead, the Communists would seek to convert other countries through elections, economic aid and rehabilitation, infiltration, and propaganda.

Kennan urged the United States to watch these moves and to counteract them.

[5] Mr. X (*nom de plume* for George Kennan), "The Sources of Soviet Conduct," *Foreign Affairs* (July 1947).

> The Soviet pressure against the free institutions of the Western world is something that can be contained by the adroit and vigilant application of counterforce at a series of constantly shifting geographical and political points, corresponding to the shifts and maneuvers of Soviet policy.[5]

Kennan's policy of containment became the basis for postwar policy, and remains a principle in the conduct of American foreign relations.

## The Marshall Plan (1947)

In the aftermath of World War II, President Truman's Secretary of State, George Marshall, developed a plan to rehabilitate the war-torn and devastated European economy. Influenced, in part, by Kennan's theory, Marshall urged that the United States give financial aid to Europe to be used for economic recovery, arguing that such recovery was essential if Europe was to resist communism. Although many congressmen denounced the Marshall Plan as unnecessary and extravagant, they were shocked into compliance by the Communist military take-over of Czechoslovakia in February, 1948. This aggressive Soviet action convinced the western world that until Europe was restored economically and militarily, it would be vulnerable to attack and invasion. Six weeks later, Congress passed the *Foreign Assistance Act*, which appropriated $5 billion in European aid for a one-year period; smaller amounts of aid were to be continued until 1951.

This plan was so successful that, within two years, the economies of several western European countries equaled, and in some cases exceeded, that of the prewar years. Even more important, the Marshall Plan demonstrated to most European countries the economic and political advantages of a cooperative and unified economy. (Under the Marshall Plan, several European countries set up "payments unions" for the quick conversion of currency, and also dropped tariffs on goods being shipped within the countries involved.) In 1952, most European nations joined together to form the European Coal and Steel Community, which provided for the common production and supervision of all coal and steel; and in 1958, six nations (Luxembourg, Belgium, France, Italy, The Netherlands, and West Germany) formed the European Economic Community (commonly called the European Common Market), which provided for the removal of existing tariff barriers, the creation of a common tariff system, and free movement of capital and labor for all member nations.

## The Truman Doctrine (1947)

Shortly after the initiation of Secretary of State Marshall's economic plan for rehabilitating the depressed European economy, President Truman announced that the United States would assist Greece and Turkey to combat communism. Aid was later extended to any other nation in which the existing government was threatened by Communist overthrow. In 1950, this policy was again challenged when North Korean troops crossed the 38th parallel (the legal boundary between North and South Korea, which had been set up at the close of World War II), and attacked the Republic of South Korea. Under the aegis of the United Nations, Truman assigned United States troops to South Korea, appealed to other United Nations' members for help, and sent the Seventh Fleet to guard Taiwan (Formosa)—non-Communist China—from attack. Truman, however, resisted General MacArthur's subsequent request to expand the war into China, and held the fighting to the boundaries of Korea. In 1953, Eisenhower concluded the war.

## Pact for peace

The tragic aftermath of World War II not only committed America to an active economic and military role, but, in addition, prompted her to initiate and support "peacetime" alliances and organizations. The experience of World Wars I and II and the development of nuclear weapons made the major nations of the world as well as the smaller countries realize that survival could no longer be a private affair, but required the active cooperation of all nations.

## The United Nations (1945)

The most far-reaching venture in international cooperation is the *United Nations*, established in 1945 by the Allied powers (the United States, United Kingdom, and the Soviet Union) in order to establish a legal and diplomatic body through which world peace could be preserved. The United Nations has a number of goals that contribute to this major objective of maintaining international peace and security. These include: encouraging amicable relations among diverse nations; fostering international cooperation in cultural, economic, and social problems; increasing respect for human rights and individuality; and serving as an arena for the resolution of international disagreements.

The organs of major importance to the UN are the Security Council, the General Assembly, and the Secretariat. The Security Council consists of fifteen member nations, five of which are elected by the General Assembly for terms of two years. Each member nation has one vote, but each of the permanent nations—The People's Republic of China, the Soviet Union, the United States, France, and Great Britain—also have the power to veto decisions of the council; and all proposed actions require the consent of all permanent members.

The *Security Council* has the primary task of maintaining peace. It is empowered to investigate any dispute (threatened or actual), and recommend action on the basis of this investigation. It may, for example, enlist a unified response from member nations to economically boycott a country that commits an act of aggression, or it may request military aid to support a nation under attack. Although the Security Council has been effective in resolving minor conflicts, such as that between Holland and Indonesia between 1945 and 1949 it has been unable to resolve major crises, such as those that have occurred in the Middle East, in Hungary, Cuba, Berlin, and Vietnam.

The *General Assembly*, the central governing body of the UN, is today comprised of representatives from the 126 member nations. Every member has one vote, and a two-thirds majority is needed to approve a motion. The Assembly has the power to investigate any issue not before the Security Council, as long as it does not involve the internal politics of a nation.

The *Secretariat* provides administrative leadership for the many agencies of the UN. Heading it is the Secretary General, who is nominated by the

Security Council and elected by the General Assembly for a period of five years. Since he must deal with conflicts among the world's superpowers, he is generally a skillful negotiator from a neutral nation.

*The United Nations building in New York City and Security Council, where major debates are held and decisions made.*

The *International Court of Justice* is a separate yet significant arm of the UN. Situated in The Hague in Holland, this court is composed of fifteen judges, elected by the General Assembly and the Security Council for terms of nine years. The Court deals with disputes between nations, rather than between people.

The UN has been criticized primarily because of its inability to resolve

crises affecting the Soviet Union and the United States. Nevertheless, the UN provides an international forum where member nations can attempt to work out differences through communication and conciliation. As long as it exists, the possibility also exists that some day it will be utilized to its maximum.

# Foreign policy making

Despite the existence of the United Nations, and despite our commitments to numerous allies, most of United States foreign policy is determined in Washington. In making this policy, the government is seeking to promote American national interests abroad. It should be noted, however, that American domestic conditions can and do affect, for better or worse, the enaction of certain programs. The success of foreign policy, therefore, is not entirely under the control of the elected or appointed officials who specialize in foreign policy. How American blacks are treated by local school systems may be more important to African nations than what our statesmen say at the Paris peace conference table. Similarly, what we do to alleviate an economic recession is especially critical to the many nations that rely on American trade. American foreign policy, consequently, involves our successful resolution of domestic problems.

In sum, it is of prime importance for us to convey a national image that succeeds both in retaining the confidence of nations linked to us economically and militarily, and in winning the good will of neutral nations, such as India, and the African states. The formulation of foreign policy is a highly complicated and delicate endeavor involving psychological insight, money, skill, and patience. (Military aid and alliances, potent instruments of foreign policy, will be discussed in the following chapter on national defense.) Here, we will discuss the use of diplomacy, propaganda, and economic aid as instruments of foreign policy.

D. B. Schirmer, "My Lai Was Not The First Time," The New Republic, 164, no. 17 (April 24, 1971): 18–21.

Cloaks of secrecy and sparks of controversy accompanied government foreign policy and military operations abroad long before Vietnam. D. B. Schirmer, examining United States involvement in the Philippines at the turn of the twentieth century, underlines the parallels that exist between these two uneasy periods in our national history.

In the fall of 1899, President McKinley attempted to extend American sovereignty to the Philippine Islands. The United States succeeded in destroying the Islands' government, but full-scale guerilla warfare ensued, with forty thousand American soldiers battling the Filipinos, despite the protests of anti-imperialist politicians and voters. By January 1901, the disgruntled American soldiers were pressuring the government to send them home; they were replaced, in part, by enlisted Philippine troops.

An exposé of the extent of death in the central province of the country, which reported that 616,000 out of 3,727,488 natives were killed, roused further anti-imperialist opinion.

When Theodore Roosevelt became President after McKinley's assassination, a congressional investigative committee was established under the chairmanship of Senator Henry Cabot Lodge (father of the present-day statesman and ex-ambassador to Vietnam). When Secretary of War Root appeared before the committee, he deemed allegations of cruelty "unfounded or exaggerated" and declared that "humanity and self-restraint" was the prevalent mode of conduct among American soldiers in the Philippines.

Lodge attempted to isolate the committee from public opinion:

Lodge had refused to admit the public and the press to the hearings, giving out information solely to three or four selected newsmen. He had allowed only two categories of witnesses: high-ranking officials and military men who defended the Administration, and veterans of lower rank who testified to personal knowledge of various cruelties practiced. He had done his best to protect "friendly" witnesses from searching cross-examination by the Democratic minority and kept the witnesses put forward by the opposition down to a minimum.

Insofar as the investigation was an attempt to soothe the public, it backfired. Congressmen journeyed to the scene and reported massacres. Major Littleton W. T. Waller was court-martialed for shooting eleven defenseless Filipinos; a high–ranking official, General of the Army Nelson A. Miles, wrote Secretary Root to protest the cruelty, as did Governor Gardner, a United States official in the Philippine province.

These exposures and the public indignation they aroused brought the greatest embarrassment to the Roosevelt Administration. It was clear, at the very least, that Governor Gardner's report had been in Root's hands when he publicly denied charges of cruelty and praised the army for its exemplary humanity. The anti-imperialist *Springfield Republican* . . . accused both Root and Roosevelt of concealment and bad faith. Nor was the *Republican* alone in making such charges. There was talk in Washington of Root's resignation.

At this point, President Roosevelt abruptly changed his position, and soon championed the fight against war atrocities. But some militants were suspicious of this sudden reversal.

Boston anti-imperialist leaders . . . insisted that Roosevelt and Root had

> known all along the way the war was going, had kept it quiet as long as they could, and had only spoken out when forced by public opinion.
>
> The final result, despite all attempts to the contrary, was the temporary enlightenment of the public as to the nature of the war waged by the American army. When the question of responsibility arose, Herbert Welsh, a campaigner against army cruelties, suggested that the "ultimate responsibility lay with the highest authority of all, 'the people of the United States'."

## Diplomacy

[6] Sir Harold Nicolson, British diplomat and author, is best known for his work, *Peacemaking, 1919* (Boston: Houghton Mifflin Co., 1933).

*Diplomacy*—probably the oldest of all those arts concerned with foreign policy—is the most difficult to define. Most political scientists, however, accept the twentieth-century diplomat and writer Sir Harold Nicolson's classic definition of diplomacy as "the organized process of negotiations between sovereign states."[6] Diplomacy, which makes all other aspects of foreign policy possible, in and of itself, has little power or effect. A diplomat armed with a proposal for $3 million in foreign aid is always an important and well-received visitor; but a diplomat armed merely with a dinner invitation or a pleasant verbal repertoire may be pleasantly ignored.

While the phrase "diplomatic corps" still suggests glamorous images of romantic nights on the banks of the Seine, and glittering cocktail parties, the life of the diplomat is, in actuality, quite different. Not all diplomats live in Paris, London, or Rome; not all diplomats are involved in high-level strategic decisions; and not all diplomats are welcomed by the host country. Their lives, in fact, may be routine, frustrating, and difficult. High-level diplomats may have to make strategic decisions without adequate advice or information, and they may have to live with threats, hostility, and danger; low-level diplomats may spend most of their time tracking down lost American passports and appeasing distraught American tourists.

## Propaganda

Generally speaking, *propaganda* is anything designed to influence public opinion in a certain way. In foreign affairs, it is the manipulation of words and symbols by government to influence the thinking and action of foreign governments and peoples. Although propaganda was used to secure foreign commitments as early as the Revolutionary War, propaganda agencies were not organized until World War I. At that time, under the direction of George Creel, the Committee of Public Information was established. The committee engaged professional people of academic and artistic backgrounds to provide a wealth of material proof of America's unfailing morality as opposed to the cruelty of her enemies. During World War II, the government created the *Office of War Information*. Although this office was disbanded after the war, the United States replaced it with a permanent propaganda agency, *the United States Information Agency* (USIA). Its purpose is to spread favorable American propaganda and to perpetuate a benevolent American image abroad.

"A quick pat on the head and a bit of the old Special Relationship mullarkey for Wilson, and then the big hello and glad hand for the General."

© Punch, London, n.d.

## The power of propaganda

During both World Wars, propaganda was a critical factor in eliciting the support of Americans at home and allies abroad. Since most Americans were poorly informed about what was happening overseas and ill-equipped to understand what they were told, large-scale propaganda efforts were undertaken to rouse them. Most of the wartime movies, for example, included a romanticized view of the war as part of their themes. More often than not, these films celebrated a handsome, rugged and idealistic American hero who managed to earn his manhood, the girl back home, and a Purple Heart or two by overcoming insurmountable odds in the shell-shocked trenches of Verdun or at the Battle of the Bulge. When Gregory Peck, wounded, tired, and hungry, looked the Germans in the eye and spat "nuts" to their offer of surrender (as did General MacAuloff in World War II), he enlisted not only the support of his exhausted troops, but the support of the millions of Americans who were watching him in moviehouses throughout the country. And in "Casablanca," when Humphrey Bogart gave up Ingrid Bergman for the "cause," thousands of Americans prided themselves on the very real husbands, lovers, and sons whom they had sacrificed. While movies such as

"Buck Private," "Anchors Aweigh," and "You're in the Army Now" were crude in technique, simplistic in their view of war, and unrealistic about the virtues of American soldiers overseas, they were necessary to raise the vast amounts of money and extravagant moral support needed to win the war.

While American movie-makers were winning the American public at home, millions of boys overseas were listening to the sultry and seductive tones of Tokyo Rose and AXIS Sally, who warned them daily that the Germans were really winning the war. If competing American propaganda were not confirmed by supportive letters from home, frequent food packages, encouraging news reports, and secondhand tales of "conquering" heroes, the morale and, thus, the effectiveness of American soldiers might have lessened.

The information released to foreign countries is usually directly related to our goals in foreign policy. To understand just how effective propaganda is as an instrument of foreign policy, we need only recall some recent examples. In the early 1960s, the United States, having interviewed Juana Castro, who had defected to this country from Chile, released that interview to Chilean papers shortly before the elections in Chile were scheduled. This, presumably, was an attempt to influence voters to reject Salvador Allende, a Marxist candidate for President of Chile who actually won the election. Similarly, the manner in which Svetlana Alleluyeva's (Stalin's daughter) defection was publicized was intended to demonstrate to undecided nations the advantages of the United States over the Soviet Union.

## Economic aid

Economic aid in the form of financial assistance, technological advice, and material goods (such as military hardware and soil fertilizer) is another important instrument of foreign policy; yet, it is less influential than either diplomacy or propaganda, because it is often dependent upon propaganda for success. For example, if an underdeveloped nation is unaware of the full extent of American aid, one of the purposes of that aid—to develop an ally in that nation—is not achieved: propaganda identifies economic aid.

Theoretically, economic aid should enable a country to build up its inner resources, and establish a relatively independent economy; such aid is preventive, in that it is supposed to help a fledgling nation resist any threat of foreign invasion or subversion. In practice, foreign aid has been successful only in nations with already developed economic systems. West Germany and Japan, for example, prospered as a result of post-World War II economic aid. Although the United States, in 1969, authorized $1.9 billion in aid to underdeveloped nations such as India, Africa, Thailand, and Southeast Asia,[7] it is questionable how successful this aid has been in promoting economic growth.

Some critics maintain that our efforts have met with little success because we are careless and often imperious in our methods of giving aid. They

[7] "National Diplomacy 1965–1970," *Congressional Quarterly* (Washington, D.C.: Congressional Quarterly, Inc., 1970), p. 18.

point to the blundering example of the "ugly Americans" who set themselves up in the rice paddies of Southeast Asia as miniature culture-kings, ridiculing and scorning the very natives they were trying to "Americanize" and educate. Men like these alienated many more people than they won, and taught us that "how to give" is just as important as "how much to give." While the State Department has tried to correct these abuses, the hostile attitudes that they engendered are difficult to overcome.

## Breakdown of all United States Foreign Aid between 1946 and 1968 (*in billions of dollars*)

### Economic Aid

| | |
|---|---|
| AID and Predecessor Agencies: | |
| Economic Cooperation Act (European Recovery Program—1949–1952) | $ 14.5 |
| Mutual Security Act (Mutual Security Agency—1953–1961) | $ 16.5 |
| Foreign Assistance Act (Agency for International Development—1962–1968) | $ 15.7 |
| Total | $ 46.7 |
| Food for Freedom (Disposal of U.S. agricultural surplus under PL 480 since 1954) | $ 16.4 |
| Export-Import Bank (Long-term loans—1946–1968) | $ 10.7 |
| Other Economic Programs (Primarily postwar relief aid—1946–1952) | $ 20.8 |
| Total economic aid | $ 94.7[1] |

### Military Aid

| | |
|---|---|
| Military Assistance Program | $ 35.6 |
| Other Military grants | $ 1.7 |
| Export-Import Bank Military Loans | $ 1.4 |
| Total military aid | $ 38.8[1] |
| Grand Total | $133.5 |

[1] Totals do not add due to rounding.

Source: Agency for International Development.

Still other critics maintain that the major problem with foreign aid is that we do not give enough of it to the nations that need our support most. Since many Americans are not in favor of giving aid to underdeveloped countries who are not committed to America or to democracy, it is often difficult to receive congressional support for the generous amounts of aid needed by such countries. Preventive aid is, therefore, difficult to implement.

**Administration Requests for Foreign Aid
Appropriations Compared to Actual Allocations**

| Fiscal Year | Request | Author- ization | Appropri- ation | Percent Cut[1] |
|---|---|---|---|---|
| 1948–49 | $7.37 | $6.91 | $6.45 | 12.5% |
| 1950 | 5.68 | 5.59 | 4.94 | 13.0 |
| 1955 | 3.48 | 3.05 | 2.78 | 20.1 |
| 1960 | 3.93 | 3.58 | 3.23 | 17.8 |
| 1961 | 4.87 | 4.69 | 4.43 | 9.0 |
| 1965 | 3.52 | 3.50 | 3.25 | 7.7 |
| 1968 | 3.23 | 2.68 | 2.30 | 28.8 |
| 1970 | 2.71 | 1.97 | 1.81 | 33.2 |

[1] Appropriation below request.

Source: *National Diplomacy 1965–1970* (Washington, D.C.: Congressional Quarterly, Inc., 1970), 52.

A recent and striking example was India's request for aid at the beginning of the 1960s. Because the funds were not to be used in a manner agreeable to many American politicians, the request was denied. Today, India is one of the largest and most important neutral governments in the world, and she has managed to develop an impressive constitutional government. Many critics believe that had we given aid to India when she requested it, she would have made firm commitments toward the United States.

Preventive aid generally is difficult to appropriate, not only because of adverse public opinion, but because appropriations often take months to go through Congress, and are not likely to be processed quickly except in clear-cut crisis situations.

# Policy makers

The most important foreign policy-maker is the President, who is empowered by the Constitution to act in this capacity. The President, although theoretically given a great deal of autonomy, must count on the support of Congress and work with a highly specialized group of advisers to achieve his policy objectives. Any President who disregards the intentions of Congress in his policy-making decisions will have difficulty achieving success in the international field.

Yet recent Presidents have been vigorous leaders in world affairs and, since the outbreak of World War II, Congress has usually followed their initiatives. It is believed that one man can act with far greater swiftness, secrecy, and precision than can 535 men in Congress, particularly because the President has access to information not available to any others. "Presidents Truman, Eisenhower, Kennedy and Johnson were all reared in the conviction

[8] *The New York Times,*
July 6, 1971, p. 1.

that only Presidents and their experts can have the perspective and knowledge needed to define the national interest in a hostile world. . . ."[8]

*James A. Robinson,* Congress and Foreign Policy-Making (*Homewood, Ill.: Dorsey Press, Inc., 1967*), *pp. 145–170.*

James Robinson has applied basic communications analysis to a study of "the exchange of information" between the 85th (1957–1958) and 87th (1961–1962) Congresses and the Department of State. He found that most legislators have weekly contact with the department; moreover, he noted a rising number of contacts related to policy questions. For example, of the legislators interviewed in 1959, 70 percent reported weekly contact related to their constituents' problems (such as procurrance of passports), while 30 percent stated that their communication involved foreign policy matters. By 1963, only 46 percent of the legislators had contacts related to constituents' matters, while 34 percent had communications related to foreign policy. In 1959, 21 percent said they had no contacts about foreign policy legislation; in 1963, only 2 percent reported no policy communications.

Robinson found that certain members of Congress have more contact than others with the State Department. Members of the Foreign Affairs and Foreign Relations Committees had far more frequent communication than did members of the Appropriations and Government Operations Committees. On matters of foreign policy not necessitating legislation, members of the majority party of Congress are contacted more often than those of the minority party.

The level of communication between Congress and the State Department was raised between 1959 and 1963. By 1963, 25 percent of the congressmen dealt with the secretary or undersecretary, 64 percent with an assistant secretary, 11 percent with less important officials. Although there is a congressional liaison office, it is rarely used by those with an "in" elsewhere; in fact, some congressmen confessed that they did not even know such an office existed.

Robinson could not find a definite correlation between frequency of communication and approval of policy. Members of the 85th Congress—especially those on foreign policy-making committees—who were satisfied with the voluntary efforts of the department to keep Congress abreast of policy, *were* more likely to approve of policy than other congressmen were. But approval of the information process, argues Robinson, is more a function of party affiliation than anything else.

It appears that the information process may be more important for the "out-of-executive" party than for the "executive" party. Republican legislators, by identifying with the Republican Administration, may reach policy conclusions irrespective of the information, or they may receive their facts and evaluations from other sources, such as through the President's weekly conference with his party's Congressional leaders. Democrats, on the other hand, who do not identify with the Department and who do not have similarly ready access to the President, may depend more heavily on the communications channels to the Department.

Because of the Vietnam war, the Chief Executive's power to determine foreign policy has been severely criticized recently by Congress and the press. The publication of the "Pentagon Papers," classified documents detailing United States involvement in Indochina, rekindled the controversy over presidential authority in foreign affairs. Max Frankel, columnist, wrote:

> The Pentagon papers . . . mark the end of an era in American foreign policy—a quarter of a century of virtually unchallenged Presidential management and manipulation of the instruments of war and the diplomacy bearing on war . . . the Pentagon papers are . . . an insider's study of the decision-making processes of four administrations that struggled with Vietnam from 1945 to 1968. . . . It was and is a Greek tragedy. [The Pentagon Papers reveal] this was a war not only decreed but closely managed by the civilian leaders of the United States. . . . The American Presidents . . . were unrestrained in both their public and private rhetorical commitments "to stay the course." Gradually, some of the leading advocates of the war lost their enthusiasm for it, but even in disillusionment they felt a higher duty of loyalty to the President and his policy than to the public that had become deeply divided and tormented by the war.[9]

[9] *The New York Times*, July 6, 1971, p. 14.

## The Secretary of State

Next to the President, the most prominent policy-maker is the *Secretary of State*. Better known at home and abroad than most other officials, he advises the President on policy, represents the United States at international conferences, administers the large and unwieldly Department of State, and receives foreign diplomats. The Secretary of State also defends the President's foreign policy statements to the public and Congress, and negotiates with foreign ministers, heads of governments, and chiefs of states. Under a presidential executive order of 1966, the secretary was given the further power to manage all operations overseas, besides strategic military forces, and he was also given two interdepartmental committees to assist him.

Despite the manifold responsibility delegated to the Secretary of State, the actual importance of his office is a highly individual and varying matter. The secretary cannot exercise any powers that the President chooses to deny him. Cordell Hull was denied almost all power by Franklin Roosevelt, while John Foster Dulles was virtually omnipotent under Dwight Eisenhower.

Some Secretaries of State have initiated important foreign policies, which were subsequently named after them. Included in the past forty years are the

(Henry) Stimson Doctrine of 1932 (in which the United States refused to recognize any acts by the Japanese that violated American treaties), and the (George) Marshall Plan of 1948 (which provided for large amounts of American aid to be given to Europe after World War II)—major acts by Secretaries of State under Herbert Hoover and Harry Truman, respectively.

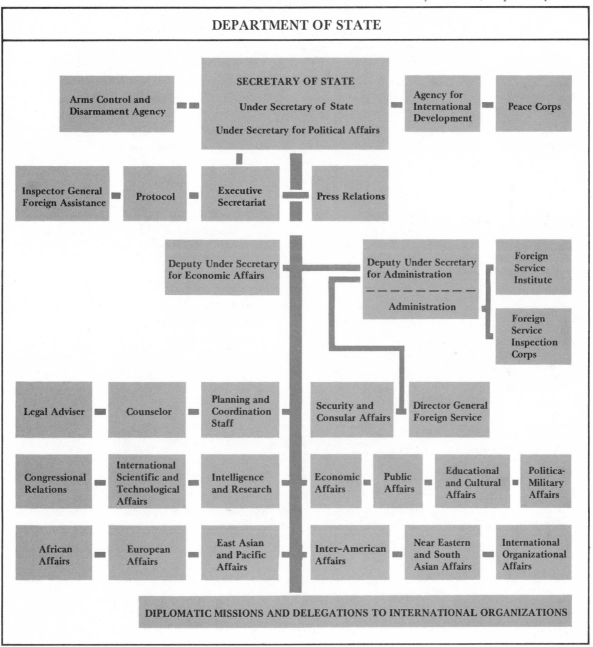

In addition, some Secretaries of State have enjoyed the full confidence of their Presidents and have been almost completely responsible for making policy. For example, Presidents such as Calvin Coolidge and Dwight Eisenhower gave very broad policy-making powers to their Secretaries of State, men of such stature as Frank Kellogg and John Foster Dulles, respectively. In recent years, however, most Presidents have followed the examples of Woodrow Wilson and Franklin Roosevelt, both of whom were far more concerned with foreign policy questions than were their predecessors. These Presidents have assumed a key role in the making of foreign policy and have relied on the advice of non-Cabinet members. President Kennedy, for example, drew heavily on the faculty of his alma mater, Harvard, for advice;[10] President Johnson consulted frequently with his friend and later Supreme Court Justice Abe Fortas, former Secretary of State Dean Acheson, and presidential adviser Clark Clifford; and President Nixon relies more closely on the direction of Henry Kissinger, the chairman of the National Security Council, than he does on that of Secretary of State William Rogers.

[10] In his *A Thousand Days* (Boston: Houghton Mifflin Co., 1965), Arthur M. Schlesinger, Jr. discusses the ineffectiveness of the Secretary of State during John F. Kennedy's administration.

## The Department of State

## The State Department abroad

The *Department of State* is chiefly responsible for administering and carrying out the foreign policies of the United States. Although it is only one of forty agencies concerned with international affairs, it employs twenty-five thousand people (one-fifth of the agencies personnel). While ten thousand are citizens of the countries in which embassies or consulates are located, the remaining fifteen thousand are American citizens, who work both at home and abroad. Those State Department officials assigned to overseas duty constitute the *diplomatic corps,* or *foreign service.* While their main duties are to collect relevant "political information" and interpret it for the authorities in Washington, they perform a variety of duties, which range from helping tourists with minor personal problems to dealing with foreign representatives on major international issues.

An *ambassador* is the most important representative overseas, in that he is the official and personal representative of the President. Ambassadors are expected to interpret the internal and international policies of the country they represent, and to recommend policy on the basis of that evaluation. Since the President often prefers to deal directly with the officials of foreign nations, an ambassador is often forced to play a subordinate role. Like the office of the Secretary of State, an ambassadorship is a highly flexible position that can be important or irrelevant, depending on the skills of the ambassador and his relationship with the President and Secretary of State. Some ambassadors have been prominent figures and have played key roles at critical times in history. These include Averill Harriman in the Soviet Union during World War II, Clare Booth Luce in Italy from 1953 to 1955, David Bruce in West

Germany and France, and Charles Bolen who succeeded Harriman to the Soviet Union post.

An ambassador is in charge of all the members of his embassy, and must coordinate the diverse and often-conflicting staff of CIA employees, military officers, psychologists, and Peace Corps staff. This coordination may involve more diplomatic skills than those required to maintain friendly relations with the host country, and it often takes more time.

## The State Department at home

Foreign service officers, at one time, spent all their time abroad, and disliked the "home" duty officers. Today, however, as a result of the *Wristonization* of the Department of State (a plan of reform proposed in 1954 by Henry Wriston), all foreign officers, which is about three-quarters of the executive staff of the department, now spend a third of their careers in Washington. While in this country they are responsible for maintaining contacts with the Secretary of State, the CIA, and other agencies, receiving and interpreting information from consulates and embassies overseas, and making certain that overseas requests, recommendations, and policies are carried out.

### THE GREAT SEAL OF THE UNITED STATES

*As part of his job, the Secretary of State must visit countries where the United States has ambassadors. Here Secretary of State Rogers visits with United States envoy Bunker in Vietnam.*

Each of these home officers is responsible to a *country director*, and each country director is responsible to one of the 5 *assistant Secretaries of State*, who direct the regional bureaus for Africa, Europe, East Asia and the Pacific, the Western Hemisphere, and the Near East and Southeast Asia. In addition to these top-level country directors and assistant secretaries, there are two interdepartmental committees—the Junior and Senior Committees—which assist the Secretary of State. The *Senior Committee* reviews general policy statements, and is headed by the undersecretary of state. Members include the Deputy Secretary of Defense, the chairman of the Joint Chief of Staff, a White House representative, and the regional directors. The *Junior Committee* is composed of five groups, each headed by an assistant Secretary of State. Other representatives come from the Defense Department, the Agency for International Development (AID), the CIA, the Joint Chiefs of Staff, the USIA, and the White House.

Major criticism of the Department of State has been directed at its administrative setup, as shown on the organizational chart. A *New York Times*

## National Security Council

study on the State Department, conducted in January, 1971, indicated that the appointment of an ambassador may require twenty-seven signatures, and a cable may take at least one week to send. The same study indicated that because of this cumbersome structure, the State Department is losing power and effectiveness. Its traditional policy-making powers have been usurped primarily by the smaller and more cohesive National Security Council.

Created in 1947 by the *National Security Act*, today the *National Security Council* is a major advisory body to the President on foreign and defense policy. Its members include both the President and Vice-President, the Secretary of State, the Secretary of Defense, and the director of the Office of Emergency Planning; the head of the CIA and the chairman of the Joint Chiefs of Staff often attend meetings. It is presently chaired by Henry Kissinger, who has been called the "pivotal figure" of Nixon foreign policy.[11] These men work closely with a permanent staff of research assistants and analysts to evaluate the present state of affairs and define the alternate courses of action available to the President. Although the council may recommend one policy over another, the final choice still belongs to the President. In order to assess information properly, the National Security Council depends on the information services of the *CIA* (which will be discussed in Chapter 21).

[11] Hedrick Smith, "Foreign Policy: Kissinger at Hub," *The New York Times*, January 19, 1971, p. 12.

*The new United States Embassy in Saigon.*

# Foreign policy and public opinion

Public opinion is the most intangible factor in the determination of foreign policy, but one that every President must consider. While few Presidents make specific policy in response to the direct reaction of the public, all Presidents know that they must defend their policies to Congress and the voters. Consequently, a President may be encouraged or discouraged by the anticipation of the public's reaction to a given policy. American entrance into both World Wars was checked until unavoidable. And in 1951, President Truman was deterred from sending an ambassador to the Vatican because he received harsh criticism from America's majority Protestant population. Consequently, while the public may not make foreign policy, it can certainly influence it.

*Kenneth N. Waltz*, Foreign Policy and Democratic Politics: The American and British Experience (*Boston: Little, Brown and Co., 1967*), *pp. 286, 291.*

Kenneth Waltz notes that the American President has a considerable independence from the vagaries of public opinion in conducting foreign policy.

The chances that a President will be unable to carry out a controversial policy are slight, nor is it at all likely that he will be dissuaded from pursuing a difficult and possibly unpopular line of policy by the fear that he and his party will thereby be electorally punished.

The reasons for this presidential independence lie with the voter himself. Studies indicate that an individual does not usually vote on the basis of how foreign policy is conducted. The public does not appear to see the complex and delicate matter of protecting the national interest in a particularly partisan light; both parties are believed capable of managing foreign policy.

Recently, this executive independence from public reaction has drawn strong criticism, mainly because of the course of events in Vietnam. Although polls revealed that President Johnson's "consensus" on the war was steadily evaporating in 1965–1966, he continued on his course, increasing the number of United States troops in Vietnam tenfold during that period. This ignoring of public opinion has been cited as a prominent example of "the arrogance of power"; however, Waltz, writing during Johnson's administration, sees the President's lack of responsiveness to the public as admirable because it reflects a transcendence of expediency.

If the public standing and moral authority of the administration should gravely weaken, it will be time for a change, whether or not blame has been justly accorded. Obviously President Johnson has been keenly aware of the domestic political risks he was running. To have changed policies because of electoral fears for the future would not have been honorable.

## Public opinion

Despite the large number of daily newspapers, news broadcasts, and news magazines that pervade our society, many Americans are uninformed about the world beyond their neighborhood. *The New York Times* brought to light that 40 percent of the American population during the Berlin crisis of 1959 did not know Berlin was situated inside East Germany.

Studies have also shown that during times of national crisis and war, most of the uninformed public unanimously support the actions of the President. While they might resist the idea of war, once the President takes definite action toward that end, they approve and support his action.

Sometimes, however, public opinion is not supportive, and in such cases, the press and interest groups may encourage an examination of foreign policy that results in opposition to the President. Our commitment in Vietnam probably affects fewer people in 1971 than it did in previous years, when expenditures and draft inductions were higher. But because of constant public debate over the war, most people have formulated generally negative views concerning American involvement in Southeast Asia.

While the Department of State seeks to influence public opinion through agencies such as Public Information Service, through press releases and news conferences with the President, and through testimony before Congress by State Department personnel, there are other forces within American society that have an equal, if not greater, effect on public opinion. These include the mass media and the national, more powerful interest groups.

# Glossary

**ambassador**  Highest ranking official representing the United States in a foreign nation.

**assistant Secretary of State**  Department of State official who directs one of the five regional bureaus for Africa, Europe, East Asia and the Pacific, the Western Hemisphere, and the Near East and Southeast Asia.

**Central Intelligence Agency (CIA)**  Agency established by the National Security Act of 1947 to coordinate strategic information and espionage activities; discussed in detail in Chapter 21.

**containment**  Policy of prohibiting the expansion of communism beyond its post-World War II boundaries.

**country director**  Officer in the diplomatic corps who oversees the activities of foreign service officers when they are on duty in the United States.

**Department of State**  Government agency that administers and enacts United States foreign policy.

**diplomacy**  Organized process of negotiations between sovereign states, a key instrument of foreign policy.

**diplomatic corps (foreign service)**  Division of the State Department comprised of officials assigned to overseas duty.

**Foreign Assistance Act**  1949 Congressional legislation that appropriated six billion dollars for European economic recovery.

**isolationism**  Policy of noninvolvement in international affairs.

**Junior Committee**  Interdepartmental committee in the Department of State composed of five divisions, each headed by an assistant Secretary of State, and including representatives from the Department of Defense, the Agency for International Development (AID), the CIA, the Joint Chiefs of Staff, the USIA, and the White House.

**Marshall Plan**  Post-World War II program formulated by Secretary of State George Marshall in 1947, to provide financial aid to Europe.

**Monroe Doctrine**  An early statement of the United States isolationist policy, introduced by President John Monroe in 1823.

**National Security Council**  Chief foreign policy and national defense advisory body of the President, created in 1947 by the National Security Act, and including the President, Vice-President, Secretary of State, the Secretary of Defense, and the director of the Office of Emergency Planning.

**propaganda**  Manipulation of words or symbols to influence public opinion in a certain direction, frequently used as an instrument of foreign policy.

**Secretary of State**  Top-ranking Cabinet official, head of the Department of State, adviser to the President on foreign policy; often, the most influential foreign policy-maker next to the President.

**Senior Committee**   Interdepartmental committee to review overall foreign policy, headed by the undersecretary of state, and including the deputy Secretary of Defense, the chairman of the Joint Chiefs of Staff, a White House representative, and the assistant Secretaries of State.

**Truman Doctrine**   President Truman's 1947 proposal to Congress to provide economic and military aid specifically to Greece and Turkey so that they might combat communism; later extended to include other countries in need of similar help.

**United Nations**   International legal and diplomatic organization, established in 1945, ideally to provide a forum where the member nations could attempt to work out differences through communication and conciliation.

**United States Information Agency (USIA)**   Government agency that distributes information and propaganda to foster a favorable American image abroad.

**Wristonization**   Reforms proposed by Henry Wriston in 1954, by which foreign service officers were to spend one-third of their careers in Washington.

# Suggested readings

Adler, Selig, *The Isolationist Impulse: Its Twentieth-Century Reaction* (New York: The Free Press, 1966). Clearly written study of isolationism from World War I to the late 1950s.

Almond, Gabriel Abraham, *The American People and Foreign Policy* (New York: Harcourt Brace and World, Inc., 1950). Analysis of the relationship between public opinion and the conduct of foreign affairs.

Alperovitz, Gar, *Atomic Diplomacy: Hiroshima and Potsdam* (New York: Random House, Inc., 1965). Controversial account of American diplomacy from March to August 1945.

Badeau, John S., *The American Approach to the Arab World* (New York: Harper and Row Publishers, Inc., 1968). Analysis of the history of American-Arab relations.

Bartlett, Ruhl, *Policy and Power: Two Centuries of American Foreign Relations* (New York: Hill and Wang, Inc., 1963). Brief history of American foreign relations, with emphasis on the major issues.

Bemis, Samuel F., *A Diplomatic History of the United States*, 5th ed. (New York: Holt, Rinehart, and Winston, Inc., 1965). Originally published in 1936. Classic study and interpretation of the diplomatic history of the United States.

Brandon, Donald, *American Foreign Policy: Beyond Utopianism and Realism* (New York: Appleton-Century-Crofts, 1966). Overview of major American foreign policies of the twentieth century.

Crabb, Cecil V., Jr., *American Foreign Policy in the Nuclear Age* (New York: Harper and Row Publishers, Inc., 1965). General study of the formulation and conduct of American foreign policy.

Fulbright, J. William, *Old Myths and New Realities, and Other Commentaries* (New York: Random House, Inc., 1964). Stimulating analysis of national security, NATO, de Gaulle, and the cold war.

Fulbright, J. William, *The Arrogance of Power* (New York: Random House, Inc., 1967). Lectures critical of American foreign policy. Author argues that communism is no longer "an evil," poses an eight-point solution to the Vietnam War, and discusses foreign aid and government priorities.

Goldwin, Robert A., Ralph Lerner, and Gerald Stourzh, *Readings in American Foreign Policy* (New York: Oxford University Press, Inc., 1970). Selected articles on American foreign policy, arranged in groups, so as to give the sense of a debate.

Hammond, Paul Y., *The Cold War Years: American Foreign Policy Since 1945* (New York: Harcourt Brace Jovanovich, Inc., 1969). Examinations of postwar foreign relations, organized by presidential administrations, with main issues examined in relation to each President and the prevailing political strategy.

Hoopes, Townsend, *The Limits of Intervention* (New York: David McKay Co., Inc., 1970). Personal account on the change in strategy for the Vietnam War and the debate (October 1967–March 1968) that led to President Johnson's March 21, 1968 announcement not to run for President and to impose a limited halt on the bombing of North Vietnam.

Jones, Joseph Marion, *The Fifteen Weeks* (New York: Harcourt Brace and World, Inc., 1964). Historical analysis of the fifteen weeks in 1947 encompassing the Truman Doctrine and the Marshall Plan.

Kahin, George McTurnan, and John W. Lewis, *The United States in Vietnam* (New York: Dell Publishing Co., Inc., 1967). An account of United States involvement in Vietnam.

Kennan, George F., *American Diplomacy, 1900–1950* (Chicago: University of Chicago Press, 1951). Series of essays on American diplomacy from 1900 to 1950, by the author of the United States policy of containment, who sees American foreign policy as "a problem in positive power relationships, with a workable and tolerable balance of power as its objective."

Kennan, George F., *Realities of American Foreign Policy* (New York: W. W. Norton and Co., Inc., 1966). Presentation of the author's philosophy of foreign policy, based on a 1954 lecture series.

Kissinger, Henry A., *American Foreign Policy: Three Essays* (New York: W. W. Norton and Co., Inc., 1969). Three essays on the impact of domestic structures and leadership on foreign policy, the central issues of today's foreign policy, and the Paris peace talks on Vietnam.

Lerche, Charles O., *Foreign Policy of the American People* (Englewood Cliffs, N.J.: Prentice-Hall, Inc., 1967). Analytic textbook on United States foreign policy, including the relationship between the democratic system and the responsibilities of a major international power.

Lieuwen, Edwin, *United States Policy in Latin America* (New York: Praeger Publishers, Inc., 1967). Historical analysis of the United States in Latin America, focusing on the twentieth century and recent problems.

Morgenthau, Hans J., *A New Foreign Policy for the United States* (New York: Praeger Publishers, Inc., 1969). Analysis of American foreign policy, emphasizing the need for a drastic revision of that foreign policy.

Osgood, Robert E., *Alliances and American Foreign Policy* (Baltimore: Johns Hopkins Press, 1968). Examination of American alliances, including the suggestion that these policies must be adjusted to meet the changing forces of the world.

Perkins, Dexter, *Foreign Policy and the American Spirit*, ed. by Glyndon G. Van Deusen and Richard C. Wade (Ithaca, N.Y.: Cornell University Press, 1957). Collection of essays by Dexter Perkins, emphasizing his theories ". . . that there is a uniquely American approach to foreign affairs, and that 'revisionist' writing on the two world wars . . . is . . . often misleading and dangerous."

Rosenau, James M., *Public Opinion and Foreign Policy* (New York: Random House, Inc., 1961). Analysis of the creation and development of foreign policies, including the role of national leaders in this process.

Sapin, Burton M., *The Making of United States Foreign Policy* (Washington, D.C.: The Brookings Institution, 1966). Clearly written and detailed analysis of United States foreign policy.

Shulman, Marshall D., *Beyond the Cold War* (New Haven: Yale University Press, 1966). Discussion of Soviet-American relations since 1945, based on a 1965 lecture series.

Skolnikoff, Eugene B., *Science, Technology, and American Foreign Policy* (Cambridge, Mass.: M.I.T. Press, 1969). Study of the relationship between scientific technology and the making of foreign policy, concentrating on the peaceful use of atomic energy, outer space, arms control, armaments, alliances, international organization, and economic aid.

Spanier, John W., *American Foreign Policy Since World War II* (New York: Praeger Publishers, Inc., 1968). Analysis of American foreign policy in the postwar period.

Stevenson, Adlai, *An Ethic for Survival: Adlai Stevenson Speaks on International Affairs, 1936–1965*, ed. by Michael H. Prosser (New York: William Morrow and Co., Inc., 1969). Edited collection of speeches by Adlai Stevenson, which provide a vivid portrayal of the man and his views on foreign affairs.

Swomley, John M., *American Empire: the Political Ethics of Twentieth Century Conquest* (New York: The Macmillan Co., 1970). Personal view of American foreign policy since 1939.

Whitworth, William, *Naive Questions About War and Peace; Conversations with Eugene V. Rostow* (New York: W. W. Norton and Co., Inc., 1970). Unedited and thought-provoking tape interviews with Eugene Rostow.

Williams, William Appleman, *The Tragedy of American Diplomacy* (New York: Dell Publishing Co., Inc., 1962). Controversial revisionist analysis of our foreign policy since the Open Door Notes of 1848.

# Topics of further study

Anderson, Betty J., "A Study of Tanganyika as a Mandate and a Trust" (Master's thesis, Bryn Mawr College, 1958).

Anderson, Dwight, "Are Democracy and Responsible Foreign Policy Compatible?" (Master's thesis, Uiversity of California at Berkeley, 1963).

Andripoulos, Angelo Theodore, "The United Nations' Peace-Keeping Force in Cyprus and the Changing Greek Regimes" (Ph.D. dissertation; New York: Fordham University, 1969).

Appleton, Sheldon Lee, "The Question of Representation of China in the United Nations" (Ph.D. dissertation; Minneapolis: University of Minnesota, 1960).

Arcilesi, Salvatore A., "Development of U.S. Foreign Policy in Iran, 1949–1960)" (Ph.D. dissertation, University of Virginia, 1966).

Banett, John W., "A Study of British and American Foreign Relations with Spain, 1942–1945" (Ph.D. dissertation, Georgetown University, 1970).

Bradley, E. R. (ed.), *Selected Readings in Modern World History* (New York: M. S. S. Educational Publishing Co., 1970).

Brandon, W. R., "United States–British Relations in the Far East, 1898–1921" (Master's thesis; University Park: Pennsylvania State University, 1948).

Brown, Michael Baratt, *After Imperialism* (Hillary House Publishers, Ltd., 1966).

Butler, G. L., *Beyond Arabian Sands: The People, Places and Politics of the Arab World* (New York: Devin Adair Co., 1964).

Chambers, Craig M., "Diplomacy and Prejudice: A Seventy-One Year Survey of Japanese–American Relations" (Master's thesis; Charleston: Eastern Illinois University, 1966).

Chenoweth, Gene, *Politics in Guatemala* (Lexington, Ky.: University of Kentucky Press, 1964).

Dressler, James B., "The Diplomacy of the Teheran Conference" (Master's thesis, University of Tennessee, 1970).

Druks, Herbert, "Harry S. Truman and the Russians, 1945–1953" (Ph.D. dissertation, New York University, 1966).

Elder, Charles D., and Roger W. Cobb, *International Community: A Regional and Global Study* (New York: Holt, Rinehart and Winston, Inc., 1970).

Fergusen, E. H., Jr., "The Yalta Conference" (Master's thesis, University of Texas, 1950).

Fishburne, Charles Carroll, Jr., "United States Policy Toward Iran, 1959–1963" (Ph.D. dissertation; Gainesville: Florida State University, 1965).

Goodwin, Crawford D., "Commonwealth and the U.N.," *International Organization* (summer 1965): 678–694.

Guannu, Joseph Sey, "Liberia and the League of Nations: The Crisis of 1929" (Ph.D. dissertation in progress, Fordham University, 1972).

Henderson, William, "Diplomacy and Intervention in the Developing Countries," *Virginia Quarterly Review* (winter 1963): 26–36.

Johnson, Richard J., "The Okhrana Abroad: 1885–1917: A Study in International Police Cooperation" (Ph.D. dissertation, Columbia University, 1970).

Kim, Tai Sung, "Japanese Foreign Policy Orientation since 1952: A Study of the Relationship between Japanese Public Opinion, Decision-Makers' Perceptions and the United States-Japanese Alliance" (Ph.D. disertation in progress, Michigan State University, 1972).

Knedler, Michael L., "Japanese Propaganda in the United States, 1931–1941," Master's thesis, Iowa State University, 1970.

Kolb, Eugene J., "Political Demands and Consensus in the United Nations Security Council and the General Assembly" (Ph.D. dissertation, Yale University, 1967).

Koontz, Earl L., "The United Nations Special Fund" (Ph.D. dissertation; Chapel Hill: University of North Carolina, 1972).

McDonald, Joyce Townsend, "The United States' Role in the Economic Development of Tunisia" (Master's thesis; Norman: University of Oklahoma, 1969).

Miles, E., "Organizations and Integration in International Systems," *International Studies Quarterly*, XII (1968): 196–224.

Miller, Eugene H., "Canada's Role in the Origin of NATO," *Statesmen and Statecraft of the Modern West*, Gerald Grob (ed.) (Barre, Mass.: Barre Press, 1967).

Miller, Eugene H., "India Revisited: A Study of American Decision-Making in the Sino" (Case #27), *Cases in American National Government and Politics*, Rocco Tresolini and Richard Frost (eds.) (Englewood Cliffs, N.J.: Prentice-Hall, Inc., 1966).

Myers, J. T., "Aid in a New Format," *Africa Report* (May 1970): 15–30.

Noyes, Lillian Frances, "The United States–United Kingdom Reciprocal Trade Agreement" (Master's thesis; Dallas, Tex.: Southern Methodist University, 1939).

Peeler, John A., "The Politics of the Alliance for Progress in Peru" (Ph.D. dissertation, University of North Carolina at Chapel Hill, 1969).

Richardson, Channing B., "The U.N. and Arab Refugee Relief, 1948–1950: A Case Study in International Organization and Administration" (Ph.D. dissertation, Columbia University, 1963).

Sabota, Leo Marcel, "United States–British Arbitration:. A Case Study of the Settlement of International Disputes by Judicial Means" (Ph.D. dissertation; Knoxville: University of Tennessee, 1968).

Samra, C. S., *India and Anglo-Soviet Relations, 1917–1947* (New York: Asia Publishing House, 1959).

Selzer, Will Joseph, "The Trusteeship Council of the United Nations and Self-government with Particular Reference to British East Africa, 1947–1951" (Ph.D. dissertation, University of Pennsylvania, 1959).

Shapiro, Harry Hersh, "The United States and the Principle of Absolute Non-Intervention in Latin America with Particular Reference to Mexico (1933–48)" (Ph.D. dissertation; Ann Arbor: University of Michigan, 1949).

Silverburg, Sanford R., "Domestic Pressures Affecting United States Foreign Policy in the Middle East," *Proceedings of the Sixteenth World Affairs Conference* (Greensboro, N.C., 1969).

Smith, Paul A., "Opinions Publics and World Affairs in the United States," *Western Political Quarterly* (spring 1961): 698–714.

Tune, George, "The United States–Filipino Relations, 1945 to the Present" (Master's thesis, University of Michigan, 1951).

# 21 national defense

As AMERICA developed from an isolated power to one involved in world affairs, the nature of her foreign policy changed, primarily because of the explosion in technology. The development of the jet airplane, oceanliner, and intercontinental communication made her "far and distant shores" only hours away from Europe and Asia; while the far more awesome development of submarines, missiles, and space satellites made the United States as vulnerable to attack as her overseas neighbors.

Ironically, America was a leader in all these technological developments, as well as in those which made her and the rest of the world susceptible to instant destruction. During World War II, President Roosevelt called together a group of eminent scientists—J. Robert Oppenheimer and Niels Bohr, to name two—to see if atomic energy could be used for military purposes. Their research was provided to Roosevelt's successor, President Truman, who, after extended deliberation and debate, decided to use the atom bomb (power equivalent to 20,000 tons of TNT) in order to persuade the Japanese to sign the surrender ultimatum that they had previously rejected. After United States bombers dropped one of these atomic bombs on Hiroshima on August 6, 1945, and another on Nagasaki, on August 9, 1945, the Japanese surrendered and the war in the Pacific came to an abrupt end.

Not until the ashes and bodies were cleared away, did America and the rest of the world comprehend the awesome implications of the bomb. In a temporary attempt to make the world safe and at peace, they had created an ultimate threat to human life. The atom bomb that concluded the war not only destroyed seventy-eight thousand lives, it replaced the former "balance of power" with a new and more precarious "balance of terror." In 1946, America was defined as the leading world power by virtue of her proven ability to destroy more people more quickly than any other nation. In 1949, the Soviet Union challenged this exclusive power by exploding an equally forceful atomic bomb. Thereafter, both nations became world powers by virtue of their monopolistic control of superior destructive capacities.

While this Soviet-American "balance of terror" has dominated and dictated world events since 1945, it has been modified recently due to shifts of power within the once-monolithic Soviet bloc, the rift between the People's Republic of China (Red China) and the Soviet Union (at one time close allies), and the emergence of the People's Republic of China as a nuclear power. Because of these developments, there are now five major world powers, all of whom possess nuclear weapons, and all of whom have competing goals and interests. While smaller nations, such as France and Great Britain, have also developed nuclear weaponry, their strike capabilities are still very limited. The balance of power, thus, rests on the responsibility, tolerance, and moderation of each of the major powers. As Senator J. William Fulbright has stated:

> Extreme nationalism and dogmatic ideology are luxuries that the human race can no longer afford. It must turn its energies now to the politics of survival. If we do so, we may find in time that we can do better than just survive. We may find that the simple human preference for life and peace has an inspirational force of its own, less intoxicating perhaps than the sacred abstractions of nation and ideology, but far more relevant to the requirements of human life and human happiness.[1]

[1] J. W. Fulbright, *Old Myths and New Realities* (New York: Random House, Inc., 1964), pp. 77–78.

# Preparing for the national defense

The advent of nuclear weapons not only changed the balance of power in the world, but it elevated defense into a permanent peacetime preoccupation. Before World War II, America had a relatively small standing army, a relatively small military budget, and relatively little military preparedness. The development of nuclear weapons delivery systems, and ballistic and antiballistic missiles, however, changed this, as it forced America to carry on wartime policies in times of peace. It provoked the need for peacetime forces, peacetime strategy, and peacetime research devoted to the production of weapons. The United States has engaged in two major ground wars, and at least twenty major foreign crises since 1945; and a large portion of her energies and resources since that time has been devoted to the production of weapons and delivery systems for those weapons. While her soldiers have been fighting in Korea and in Southeast Asia, her scientists, technicians, and engineers have been fighting an equally intensive and expensive "arms race" in the laboratories, universities, and deserts of the United States.

Broadly defined, an *arms race* is a "progressive, competitive peacetime increase in armaments by two states or [a] coalition of states resulting from con-

## The arms race

[2] Samuel P. Huntington, "Arms Races: Pre-requisites and Results," in Carl J. Friedrich and Seymour E. Harris, eds., *Public Policy* (Cambridge, Mass.: Harvard University Press, 1958).

flicting purposes or mutual fears."[2] While the arms race has always been a conventional method of power politics, the arms race of today involves the production of weapons and delivery systems (submarines, intercontinental ballistic missiles, and so on) so costly, complicated, and destructive, that they make all former weapons look like toys. Each new weapon elicits the development of an even more deadly weapon by the opposing nation.

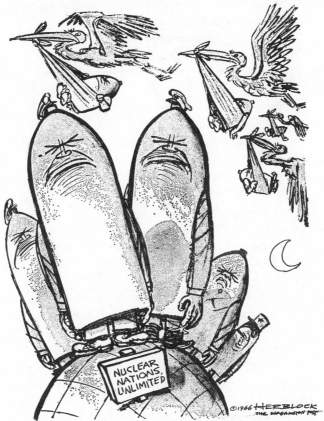

The Explosion Population

From *The Herblock Gallery* (Simon & Schuster, 1968).

Until 1945, when the first atomic bomb was dropped over Hiroshima, the largest bomb used by any nation was the "blockbuster," which had an explosive power slightly less than ten tons of TNT. The 1945 atomic bomb was two thousand times more powerful than this. Present hydrogen bombs are measured in megatons, a megaton being equal to one million tons of TNT. Bombs in the lower-megaton class can expose people in a 200–2,000 square mile area to radiation; and the rocket and multimissile delivery systems being produced can reach almost any delivery range desired. In fact, the total weapons system of the United States or the Soviet Union, if ever used in warfare, could easily destroy our planet; even a limited use of them by either side could destroy a large portion of civilization.

## The strategies of national defense

Because of these weapons developments, the present purpose of foreign defense policy is not to prepare for war, but to prevent its occurrence through deterrence; to prepare for partial retaliation and survival in the advent of occurrence; and to carry out the policy of containment by utilizing the threat of deterrence.

### Deterrence

The theory behind *deterrence* is not new. Governments (and parents) have been using similar theories for years in order to force citizens (and children) into obedience. For example, citizens are thought to be "deterred" from robbing banks, embezzling large sums of money, and shooting other citizens because of the penalties they must face as a consequence of their actions.

Deterrence in nuclear warfare works on the same principle. It seeks to prevent the enemy from attacking, by making it known that the attacked nation has a weapons system that will survive the attack and be able to strike back. Involved in deterrence is the establishment and advertisement—but, hopefully, never the demonstration—of a weaponry system that after surviving an unexpected assault can effectively counterattack.

The theory and goals of "deterrence" have changed slightly as our weapons have changed. During the sixties, "effective retaliation" meant the total destruction of an opponent's civilization. Today, the goal of deterrence is "controlled response," or the effective destruction of military centers, rather than cities. To understand just how deterrence can or should work, we might ask ourselves—would the United States have dropped an atomic bomb on Hiroshima if Japan had possessed one and had the capacity to attack American cities in retaliation?

### Retaliation and survival

Although most policy-makers believe that the threat of deterrence has made planned war a remote possibility, the very real possibility exists that an attack will occur through poor judgment or accident. Since our weapons system is so highly automated and synchronized, pushing the wrong button, sounding the wrong alarm, or putting the wrong person in charge might initiate a chain reaction that would lead to disaster for both sides. While the chance of this happening may be negligible, the "accidental" war envisioned in the popular movie entitled "Dr. Strangelove, or How I Learned to Stop Worrying and Love the Bomb" is still a consideration.

Another probability is that a supposedly limited conflict, such as that between Israel and the Arab nations, might develop into a full-scale war, with each nation requesting aid from one of the major powers. As the major powers supply more and more aid, in the form of weapons and eventually fighting men, the conflict might develop into a contest between them— the issue between the smaller nations having become totally insignificant.

Because the possibility of armed conflict is real, the United States has to be prepared to retaliate in the event of an attack. Retaliation might consist of destroying enemy bombers in the air or while still at their bases or of destroying apparent or yet uncommitted enemy forces and installations such as missile sites on the ground. On American soil, preparation for attack involves the buildup of defense systems for civilians, such as radiation decontamination methods and bomb shelters. During the fifties, when the scare of nuclear war seemed more immediate than it does today, many citizens and institutions built bomb shelters in their homes or buildings, and stores began to design special equipment to be used in case of attack. This activity has subsided since the Nuclear Test Ban Treaty was signed in 1963, and we can only hope that the causes for it have subsided as well.

**Containment by deterrence**

Since shortly after World War II our policy has been to "contain" communism, primarily by deterrence—that is, by publicizing the potential use of nuclear weapons in areas where communist advances appear threatening. Containment and deterrence are thus closely related, the former being a policy and the latter a method. Certainly, deterrence has succeeded in Western Europe, where the possession of nuclear weapons by NATO forces has served to deter the Soviet Union from staging a full-scale invasion.

Containment in Southeast Asia, however, is a more difficult and delicate matter; it is questionable whether or not containment in this area has succeeded. While the threat of nuclear retaliation has served to keep the war "limited," it has not served to keep the peace. The United States and, indirectly, the Soviet Union are involved in an explosive conflict and the possibility of a massive nuclear attack has not "deterred" either side from escalating. While it is unlikely that either side will resort to nuclear force, the development of nuclear weapons by the mainland Chinese may change the nature of our policy in this area as well as others.

# Methods of national defense

While most military and nonmilitary officials agree that nuclear deterrence is currently the major instrument of American defense policy, they disagree on how to make it effective. Many people, notably air force and navy personnel, insist that the maintenance of conventional weaponry is just as important as the development of nuclear weaponry. Those who favored nuclear deterrence seemed to hold sway during the fifties, when most of our energy and money went into the production of nuclear systems; however, in the last decade, those who favor the development of superior conventional weaponry predominated. Recent Presidents and their advisers, such as Presidents Kennedy, Johnson, and Nixon, former Secretary of Defense McNamara, and National Security Adviser Kissinger, have sought to build up America's conventional military powers and have made efforts to "get the nuclear genie back into the bottle."

Even when administrators reach an agreement on how much money and manpower should be devoted to the development of nuclear weapons, they disagree over the kind of weapons to be produced. Should we be primarily interested in developing powerful offense, or defense, weapons systems? Should we develop systems to protect ourselves from a possible nuclear holocaust or should we concentrate on the development of weapons that might administer such a disaster on a potential enemy? Charles Schultze, former director of the Bureau of the Budget, and presently a member of the Brookings Institution, has summarized the problem:

> Primarily what we buy in the military budget is an attempt to protect the nation and its vital interests abroad from the danger and risks posed by hostile forces. We seek either to deter the hostile force from ever undertaking the particular action or, if worst comes to worst, to ward off the action when it does occur. Similarly, in designing particular weapons systems, the degree of complexity and the performance requirements built into the systems depends in part on an evaluation of the various kinds of contingencies which the weapon is expected to face. Now there are almost an unlimited number of 'threats' that can be conceived. The likelihood of their occurrence, however, ranges from a significant possibility to a very remote contingency.[3]

[3] Charles L. Schultze, "Re-examining the Military Budget," *The Public Interest*, 18 (winter 1970): 15–16.

Once the contingencies are identified, once priorities are established, there remains the equally great problem of financing these weapons systems. These systems are complicated to produce and maintain, and their cost represents a substantial portion of the national budget: the present defense budget is 40 percent of the budget. Congress, because of the continuing high cost of the war and the need to expand domestic programs in Vietnam and of the military in general is becoming increasingly reluctant to vote for appropriations requested for sophisticated weapons systems.

Once appropriations are settled, it may take months, and even years, to develop and produce the weapon and a system for delivering it. The B-52 bomber required over six years to travel from a concept on paper to the take-off field. Furthermore, the production of these weapons requires large amounts of materials, produced by industries which must be able to stay in business financially whether or not their war materials are currently being used. Finally, by the time a new weapon is produced, it may have been made obsolete by the production or plan of a superior weapon by the opposing nation. Producing weapons is, therefore, an activity fraught with very special kinds of problems.

## The human element

Although much military energy and discussion today centers around the building of superior nuclear weapons, an equally great amount centers around

## The standing military

the maintenance of conventional air, sea, and land forces. It is these forces that we have relied on to fight the ground wars of Korea and Vietnam.

The army, navy, marines, and air force of today are a far cry from the ragged, poorly equipped citizenry that staved off the British in 1776. Each branch employs a number of engineers, technicians, translators, and even writers, as well as infantrymen, sailors, and pilots. Together, the army, navy, marines, and air force employ some 3.5 million men, 1.2 million of whom are stationed abroad. Of this number, 224,000 are stationed in South Korea, Japan (primarily Okinawa), and West Germany, to protect American interests there. It would be useless to give a current figure for South Vietnam, since the number of men stationed there changes daily; it can be noted, however, that in 1968, 540,000 (half the soldiers overseas) troops were stationed there.

*Contrast this to the glamour and excitement of war portrayed in the movies.*

## Ready reserve units

In addition to the *standing* military, there is a large corps of *ready reserves* who back these men in times of war and national emergency. The reserves consist of the National Guard, the army, navy, air force, marine, and Coast Guard reserves. These troops take part in weekly drills, weekend retreats once a month, and two-week summer camps in order to maintain military alertness. They may be called into active duty by the President. Reserves were called up during the first invasion of Cambodia in 1970, and remained in a state of readiness until the use of extra military was determined to be unnecessary.

### U.S. Military Forces Abroad[1] (as of September 1969)

| | |
|---|---:|
| Asia and Pacific | |
| Korea | 56,000 |
| Okinawa | 45,000 |
| Japan | 40,000 |
| Philippines | 30,000 |
| South Vietnam | 508,000 |
| Thailand | 49,000 |
| Nationalist China | 10,000 |
| TOTAL | 738,000 |
| Latin America | |
| Panama, Canal Zone, Puerto Rico, and Guantanamo (Cuba) | 23,000 |
| Other | 1,000 |
| TOTAL | 24,000 |
| North America | |
| Canada, Greenland, Iceland | 10,000 |
| Western Europe | |
| West Germany | 228,000 |
| Other NATO Countries | 82,000 |
| Spain | 10,000 |
| TOTAL | 320,000 |
| Middle East and Africa | 10,000 |
| United States Fleets | |
| Western Pacific, Vietnam | 95,000 |
| Mediterranean | 25,000 |
| TOTAL | 120,000 |
| GRAND TOTAL | 1,222,000 |

[1] Note that these figures are subject to constant change, particularly those for Southeast Asia.

Source: Defense Department, 1969.

The *National Guard* differs from the other reserve units, because it was originally created as a state, rather than a national unit. The National Guard is the result of the *Second Amendment* to the Constitution, giving each state the right to organize its own militia; and the guard is immediately responsible to the governor. However, it is financed by the national government and operates under national standards. The President has the power to call the guard into service during domestic or international crises. Although the training of National Guardsmen is less rigorous than the training of regular army, navy, and air force personnel, the guardsmen are on constant call for a period of six years. They have been particularly active during the domestic disorders in Detroit, Watts, and Newark, and in the strike of postal employees in 1970.

## Weapons of war

While conventional weapons have been used to carry on recent ground wars, a superior weapons system is necessary to fulfill the goal of containment through deterrence. Most nuclear weapons come under the jurisdiction of the *Strategic Air Command* (SAC), which was created in 1946 to supervise atomic air strategy. SAC began with 250 World War II propeller-driven B-17, B-25, and B-29 bombers, and now has 1,054 intercontinental missiles (1,000 Minutemen and 54 Titan-II missiles), and about 500 long-range jet bombers. It provides about 85 percent of American strike capability.

### Major Strategic Air Command Forces in the U.S.

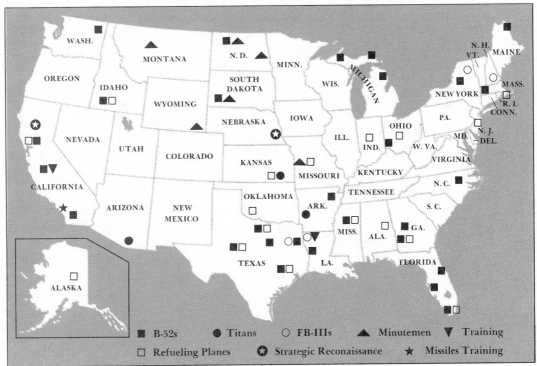

## B-52 bombers

Today's long-range bombers, the *B-52's*, are able to fly long distances without refueling or stopping. Most of them are equipped to carry atomic bombs, with the explosive power equal to 170,000 tons of TNT. They operate out of twenty-nine inland SAC bases and twelve non-SAC bases.

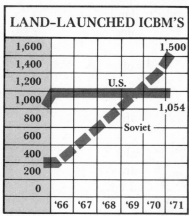

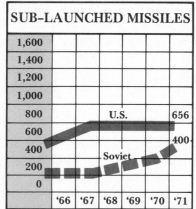

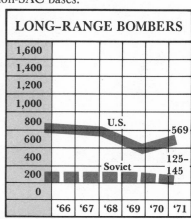

© 1971 by The New York Times Company. Reprinted by permission. May 21, 1971.

## Missiles

*Missiles*, a more advanced, more recent development than long-range bombers, are weapons that can be fired from a land or water base to hit a specified target many thousands of miles from the launching site. At the present time, there are two varieties of missiles—ballistic and guided. A *ballistic missile* is self-guided and self-propelled. After being shot, it forms its own free-falling path. A *guided missile* can be more accurately directed by electronic devices operated from the ground to hit predetermined targets. Specialists estimate that a missile fired from a land base in Greenland will be able to hit a target in the U.S.S.R. within a matter of minutes.

Most American missiles are called *Minutemen* and they are equipped with MIRVs, or "multiple individually targeted re-entry vehicles." This means that each missile has a number of warheads in its nose, each of which carries a separate bomb with a separate target goal. Consequently, each missile has the potential to destroy several targets; and even if one warhead is intercepted, the total destructive might of the MIRV is not completely lost.

In addition to the missiles operated by SAC, the navy operates nuclear submarines, which constitute the remaining 15 percent of our nuclear equipment. Each of these submarines is equipped with missiles, either *Polaris* (single warhead) or *Poseidon* (multiple warhead), which can be fired from submarine at any time in any area of the world. The navy is presently arguing that it should have more (or, at least, equal) control over nuclear weapons than SAC, inasmuch as submarines have more mobility and long-range capabilities than SAC bases, and are more difficult to track and locate.

## Defense systems

Since the Soviet Union possesses equally powerful and accurate weapons (currently 1,440 land-based intercontinental missiles and 350 submarine-based missiles), it is crucial for the United States to have a comprehensive warning system that will detect and intercept incoming missiles. At the present time, we have an elaborate radar system, primarily along the Canadian border, as well as the tracking systems known as Spartan and Sprint. *Spartan* is designed to track missiles and intercept missiles at a hundred-mile range. In the event that Spartan misses, *Sprint* will intercept the incoming missile as it nears its target.

There are also plans now for the installation of a new "647" infra-red satellite that will warn us approximately one minute after a missile has been fired from the Soviet Union, or from a submarine at sea. Our present warning systems do not sound alarms until several minutes after the attacking missile has begun its flight.

## The ABM controversy

Although the present radar system can detect missiles, there is considerable support for the installation of a more comprehensive *Anti-Ballistic Missile System* (ABM) around strategic missile centers and cities to defend them if attacked.

*The controversial ABM is being launched here. Note that several missiles are fired at the same time.*

Supporters of the ABM insist that such a system is necessary to protect America, while critics argue that the cost (about $12 billion), is exorbitant, especially for a system whose effectiveness is questionable. Equally important, they argue that such a system will encourage the arms race, in that the Soviet Union would respond by working to expand its nuclear attack system. ABM supporters respond that the development of multiple warheads (MIRVs) with more accurate and diverse target ranges, and the development of an effective ABM system, would reduce the possibility of a nuclear victory for either side and, thus, the installation of ABM is consistent with the strategy of deterrence.

## Alliances

The United States not only has the resources of her own troops and nuclear weapons, but, through treaties and alliances, she has the military support of nations in Europe, Latin America, and Asia.

### Military Forces of the NATO and Warsaw Pact Countries

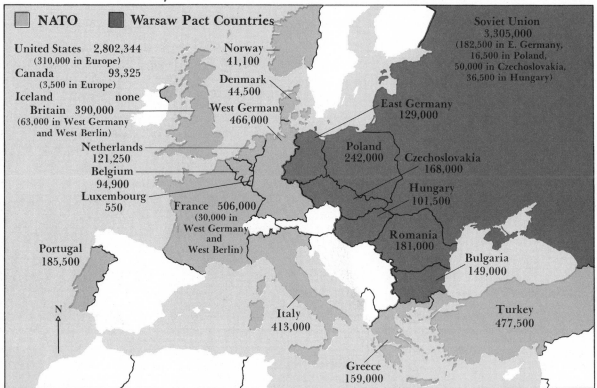

NATO — Warsaw Pact Countries

United States 2,802,344 (310,000 in Europe)
Canada 93,325 (3,500 in Europe)
Iceland none
Britain 390,000 (63,000 in West Germany and West Berlin)
Netherlands 121,250
Belgium 94,900
Luxembourg 550
Portugal 185,500
France 506,000 (30,000 in West Germany and West Berlin)
Norway 41,100
Denmark 44,500
West Germany 466,000
Italy 413,000
Greece 159,000
Turkey 477,500

Soviet Union 3,305,000 (182,500 in E. Germany, 16,500 in Poland, 50,000 in Czechoslovakia, 36,500 in Hungary)
East Germany 129,000
Poland 242,000
Czechoslovakia 168,000
Hungary 101,500
Romania 181,000
Bulgaria 149,000

## NATO (1949)

The major defense organization that emerged from the debris of World War II was *NATO,* or the *North Atlantic Treaty Organization.* Stimulated by the same seizure of Czechoslovakia that jolted Congress into passing the Marshall Plan, and by the Berlin Blockade of 1948, twelve North Atlantic nations banded together and formed a pact in 1949 through which they agreed, among other things, "that an armed attack against one or more of them in Europe or North America shall be considered an attack against them all." Today, NATO is composed of the United States, Belgium, Canada, Denmark, France, Greece, Iceland, Italy, Luxembourg, the Netherlands, Norway, Portugal, Turkey, the United Kingdom and West Germany. Each nation has committed itself to resisting attacks as well as to giving mutual aid that assists the other members to do the same.

Although NATO has been effective in uniting European defense resources, and in serving as a deterrent to the use of power by the Soviet Union and its allies, its power has been undercut by disagreements over the distribution and control of nuclear weapons and, since 1966, by the withdrawal of French military forces from NATO control.

## Organization of American States

Created in 1947, the OAS is a defense agreement made by the United States with twenty-four other American Republics (Canada and Cuba are not members). According to this defense pact, a threatening act toward any member nation is cause for action by the other members. While the approval of only two-thirds of the foreign ministers of each nation is necessary to establish an action that is binding on all members, each country must itself consent to contributing armed forces. In addition, the OAS provides for inter-American conferences once every five years for the purpose of establishing general hemispheric policy.

### United States Aid to Treaty Allies 1946 through 1968 (in millions of dollars)

| Treaty | Economic | Military | Total |
|---|---|---|---|
| Rio Pact-OAS | $11,239.6 | $ 1,147.2 | $12,386.8 |
| NATO | 27,940.5 | 18,760.2 | 46,879.0 |
| SEATO | 20,557.0 | 12,716.6 | 26,749.5 |
| Australia and New Zealand | 169.2 | 576.5 | 745.7 |
| Republic of China | 2,291.1 | 2,796.3 | 5,087.4 |
| Japan | 3,076.5 | 1,065.5 | 4,141.5 |
| Korea | 4,630.6 | 2,825.3 | 7,455.9 |
| Philippines | 1,487.3 | 535.9 | 2,023.2 |
| Total[1] | $56,635.8 | $33,218.6 | $89,854.4 |

[1] Figures take into consideration the fact that certain countries are members of more than one defense treaty.

Source: Agency for International Development, 1968.

## SEATO (1954)

Shortly after the 1953 cease-fire and armistice in Korea, the United States initiated the formation of *SEATO*, the *Southeast Asia Treaty Organization*. Patterned after NATO, SEATO was designed to protect certain independent nations (Pakistan, Laos, Vietnam, Cambodia, Malaysia, Australia, New

Zealand, and the Philippines) from external aggression. Today, it includes the United States, the United Kingdom, France, Australia, New Zealand, the Philippines, Thailand, and Pakistan. The protocol creating the organization extends protection to Laos, Cambodia, and the Free Territory under the State of Vietnam, although Cambodia has expressed disinterest in SEATO, and Laos has refused to recognize its protection. Furthermore, it lacks the support of important "nonmember" Southeast Asian nations such as Afghanistan, India, Ceylon, Burma, and Indonesia.

In the case of aggression against a member, members are committed "to meet the common danger in accordance with their constitutional processes." While they must "consult immediately," no action can be taken without the permission and invitation of the threatened nation. Although SEATO's organizational structure is similar to NATO's (both have policy-making bodies comprised of the foreign ministers of member nations), SEATO is not as unified, nor has it joint armed forces at its disposal. Because of its military weakness and the looseness of its organization, SEATO has not been an important force in the affairs of Southeast Asia. At the present time, it is little more than a paper organization with little military or political muscle.

**Defense Commitments of the United States**

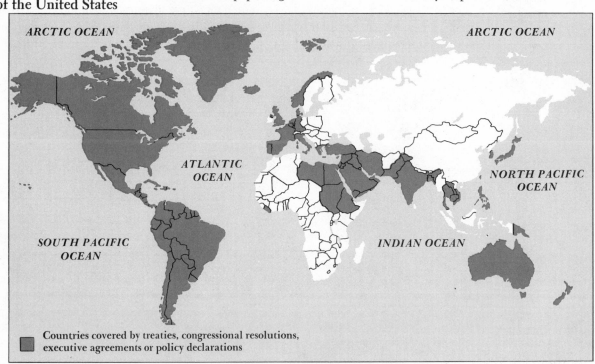

Source: *Congressional Quarterly*, 1969.

In addition to these major organizations, the United States has independent bilateral treaties with the Republic of Korea (South Korea), Japan, the Philippines, the Republic of China (Formosa), and a separate defense pact with Australia and New Zealand (ANZUS). Currently committed to the defense of 48 countries on various continents, despite the absence of a single treaty with any African nation, America supports, at a cost of about $5 billion a year, 429 major bases out of a total of 2,500. Clearly, America has broken with her isolationist past.

**Disarmament**

Recognizing the dangers inherent in the development of superior weapons with assured destructive capacities, and the possibility of war through plan, accident, or miscalculation, most people agree that the arms race may lead to international disaster. Disagreements occur, however, over whether the solution should be a defense buildup or *disarmament*, and, if the latter, whether disarmament should be *total* or *partial*. Supporters of total disarmament argue that this is the only way to insure peace; they envision a world that does not rely on military threat, fear, and force for survival. Supporters of partial disarmament argue that while total disarmament is desirable, it is unrealistic, and even dangerous. Total disarmament would require that all nations guarantee that they will not manufacture, produce, or maintain any kind of weapon (nuclear or conventional); and it appears that such a guarantee would be impossible to obtain, let alone enforce. Partial disarmament, on the other hand, is a more practical goal, one which would provide at least a degree of security, while it would prevent use of the most destructive weapons.

**Nuclear test bans**

During the 1950s, the Soviet Union and the United States agreed that some kind of arms control and, at least, partial disarmament are necessary to limit the possibility of war and/or nuclear conflict. Since arms control and total disarmament were unlikely first steps, nuclear testing was selected as the first objective. In 1958 talks began between the United States, the United Kingdom, and the Soviet Union (then the three nuclear powers) and nuclear testing was voluntarily halted. France, however, refused to accept the moratorium, and exploded a nuclear bomb in 1960. The agreement ended in 1963, after the Soviet Union resumed testing. Following this, both the United States and Great Britain initiated further tests, although conferences continued to proceed in Geneva, Switzerland.

> *"The 'Military Lobby'—It's Impact on Congress, Nation,"* Congressional *Quarterly (March 24, 1961), pp. 463–478.*
>
> President Eisenhower in 1960 warned of a rising "military-industrial complex" that was placing "pressure-group inducement" before the needs of the nation. Deeply committed to the goal of disarmament, and opposed to the pressure tactics of this "complex," he was determined not to be awed by the military or weapons manufacturers, a hundred of

which received contracts amounting to 73.4 percent of the total $21 billion defense budget.

Eisenhower's statements were based on the 1959 Hébert probe into the activities of retired military officers, and the role of Congress in allocating military expenditures. In the first case, a study was conducted in 1959 by the House Armed Services Special Investigations Subcommittee, chaired by F. Edward Hébert (D. Louisiana), to assess the extent of employment of retired military officers in defense industries. The committee, after interviewing seventy-five witnesses, indicated a lack of objectivity of some government contract decisions. The witnesses' testimonies were often inconsistent in relation to the influence of retired officers and the coincidences of contract and personal contact with firms employing these retired officers. The committee, therefore, proposed that a law be passed to regulate sales to these companies.

The investigation of congressional activities was also conducted by the Hébert Subcommittee. It was found that congressmen zealously represent district and state interests, and many want for their area a "fair share" of contracts and military installations.

Summing up the cumulative impact of these varied expressions of Congressional interest, Representative Jamie L. Whitten, Democrat, of Mississippi, a member of the House Appropriations Defense Subcommittee, testified as follows Jan. 29, 1960, before the Joint Economic Committee's Defense Procurement Subcommittee:

I am convinced defense is only one of the factors that enter into our determinations for defense spending. The others are pump priming, spreading the immediate benefits of defense spending, taking care of all services, giving all defense contractors a fair share, spreading the military bases to include all sections, etc. There is no State in the Union and hardly a district in a State which doesn't have defense spending, contracting, or a defense establishment. We see the effect in public and Congressional insistence on continuing contracts, or operating military bases, though the need has expired.

A classic example of Congress's influence on the defense budget and the awarding of contracts is the conflict over the building of the Nike-Zeus antimissile. Eisenhower had allocated $287 million for production systems, but Congress wanted to add $137 million. When the President refused, lobbies in and out of Congress were formed to exert pressure on the President. Pressure began with the publication by *Army* magazine of seven articles praising the Zeus, as well as nine full-page advertisements by the missile's prime contractor, Western Electric, and its subcontractors. Senator Strom Thurmond (R. South Carolina), joined by the senators from North Carolina and Kansas, whose states were to receive $36 and $8.5 million, respectively, then urged production of the Zeus.

Congress continued to lobby for an expanded budget—for regional reasons and in fear of the Soviet threat—until 1961, when John Kennedy, the newly elected President, agreed to allocate an additional $100 to $200 million for construction of the missiles.

The extent of congressional influence on this decision can be summed up as follows:

Proponents of the Nike-Zeus, it should be noted, base their case squarely on the national interest—the touchstone of debate, pro and con, concerning the merits of every proposal made in the name of defense. It is never clear, however, where the national interest begins and self-interest leaves off.

All of the persons questioned by CQ agreed that an element of self-interest pervades relationships among the services, their contractors and Members of Congress. There was no consensus, however, regarding the extent to which decisions affecting the national interest are influenced by the self-interest of persons and organizations involved.

In Moscow, a few months later (on August 5, 1963) the United States, Britain, and the Soviet Union signed the Nuclear Test-Ban Treaty. This treaty, however, banned nuclear explosions only in places where there was danger of radioactive fallout; it did not apply to underground testing. It also included a clause enabling any participating nation to withdraw from the treaty provided it gives the other nations three months' notice. Despite the escape clause, the original three signatories and more than one hundred other nations have adhered to the test-ban. The withdrawers have been France and the People's Republic of China; both of them have continued nuclear testing by exploding bombs above ground.

In recent years, several treaties have been signed, each of which moved a step further toward barring the use of nuclear weapons. The *International Treaty on the Peaceful Uses of Outer Space* was created in 1967. Its limitations include prohibiting the dispatch of nuclear devices from satellites. In 1968, the nuclear powers signed the *Nonproliferation Treaty* and, consequently, the nations with nuclear weapons guaranteed for at least twenty-five years not to give these weapons to those who do not already have them; the "have-not" nations reciprocally promised not to attempt to acquire nuclear weapons. Although this treaty has also been rejected by the nuclear powers, France and the People's Republic of China, it has succeeded in limiting the possession of nuclear weapons and energy to a few countries.

Having achieved some initial success with nuclear weapons treaties, the United States and the Soviet Union have embarked on a series of conferences

## Strategic Arms Limitations Talks (SALT)

[4] "Disarmament—Saving on Salt," *Time*, 97, no. 5 (February 1, 1971): 26–27.

devoted to the limitation of strategic arms production. The decision to hold these conferences, the *Strategic Arms Limitations Talks* (SALT), was made at a meeting in December, 1969, in Helsinki, Finland; the conferences themselves, held in Helsinki, Vienna, and Geneva, entered their fourth round in 1971.[4] Current debates center around the reduction of offensive missiles, the limitation of an ABM system to the defense of capital cities (Washington and Moscow), a halt in the development of MIRVs, and the inclusion of American air bases in Europe under the restrictions of a disarmament pact.

While it remains to be seen whether or not the two nations will come to an agreement on these matters in the near future, it is at least encouraging that they are trying to solve these major issues at the conference table. Also encouraging is the development of more sophisticated detection systems, which will make it less likely that nations will succeed in violating the resultant treaties.

# Providers for the national defense

Although our Founding Fathers did not foresee the development of American nuclear power, they did foresee the danger of military influence on the affairs of a republic. To prevent military control, they established the principle of civilian supremacy over the military, and designated the President as Commander-in-Chief of the armed forces.

## The President and defense

As indicated in Chapter 20, the Constitution delegates ultimate responsibility for military decisions to the President. By virtue of his designation as Commander-in-Chief of the armed forces, he has the ability to disperse troops anywhere in the world at any time. While his action ultimately must be sanctioned and supported by Congress, the President has often used this power first, and obtained congressional approval later. In 1846, for example, President Polk ordered troops into the United States territory that was feuding with Mexico. Since the Mexican government had made it clear that any such action would be regarded as an act of war by Mexico, Mexico declared war on the United States, and Congress accepted its challenge. Similarly, in the 1960s, Congress appropriated the money needed by Presidents Kennedy, Johnson, and Nixon to conduct an undeclared war in Vietnam.

During times of declared war, the powers of the President increase. Because of the need for immediate action and reaction, one man with expert advisers can better provide national leadership than can a Congress of 535 men with varying and often conflicting viewpoints. How the President uses that power depends on the man and the situation. He may become directly involved in planning strategy and directing campaigns, or he may prefer to rely more on the advice of others in such matters, and make only major decisions. He can also end hostilities by agreeing to an armistice, setting up military governments in conquered territories, and negotiating treaties to establish the terms of peace. His powers over domestic policy can also increase during wartime, since several statutes gave him the power to harness civilian and industrial support, create and/or take over industrial plants, and do whatever he feels is necessary to carry out a successful war effort.

**Congress and defense**

Although the President has the power to initiate action, Congress alone can make a formal declaration of war. It does this through a *joint resolution* of Congress, which the President usually requests and always signs.

Congress also has the sole power to "raise and support armies" and to "provide and maintain a navy." It decides upon the numbers and kinds of troops that are to be enlisted, the limits and standards of the draft, and—if there is to be conscription at all—the pay scale of military men, the authorization of war materials, and the appropriation of funds for the building, development, and maintenance of military forces. No appropriation for military use may extend longer than two years; it must be renewed by subsequent legislation. In recent years, congressional concern aboùt the armed forces has centered about the size of military appropriations, the terms and existence of conscription, and the control of the Pentagon.

*Paul Jacobs, "Precautions Are Being Taken by Those Who Know,"* The Atlantic, 227, 2 *(February 1971)*: 45–56.

Paul Jacobs expresses his concern over the vast powers of the AEC:

The Atomic Energy Commission has total and exclusive control over every aspect of nuclear energy, including both its military and peaceful uses. It has at its disposal more than $2 billion a year, its own security force, the right to police its own activities, and the authority to classify any data which the Commission judges might threaten the national interest if they were to be released. In effect, the AEC is a government within the government.

More than $3 billion ($300 million annually) has been invested in research facilities. Approximately 53 percent of the Commission's budget is allocated to military spending. More than 500 nuclear devices have been detonated, plus an unpublished number of secret ones. Eight plants produce weapons components, and the estimated number of weapons stock-piled reaches into the thousands, though the exact figure is a secret.

Despite the signing of test-ban treaties, production and testing of nuclear weapons continues today. Most of the limitations on testing are established by the AEC itself, as it is the sole guardian of the public safety from dangers of radiation. As a major influence on the administration of international nuclear energy agreements, the Commission with its congressional and industrial allies, is an important formulator of foreign policy and national defense.

A major suspicion of Jacobs is the inability of the Commission to guard the safety of the public health in this area. The doubts about AEC operations stem primarily from the period of the 1950s, when the United States conducted extensive nuclear testing. A report prepared by the Public Health Service on the Commission's testing in 1953

revealed that while the AEC was saying publicly that there was no health hazard from the Nevada tests and that radiation levels were being adequately monitored and recorded, in fact there was great uncertainty within the Public Health Service over the effects of the tests. The report also indicated that the spread of fallout had been unpredicted in many cases, simply because the wind had shifted in a way that the AEC had not expected. The result of the wind shift was that large numbers of people had received doses of radiation in differing amounts.

By tracing down pilots who monitored low-level radiation fallout, the author discovered that many people involved in the tests and living in areas near the test sites contracted leukemia. The occurrences of the disease were so many in Fredonia, Utah, that a Salt Lake City radiologist who was treating the patients called it an epidemic.

Jacobs discovered that a report written by Dr. Harold Knapp pointed to high levels of I-131, a radioactive iodine, near St. Louis, Missouri. I-131, taken in dairy products in large quantities by children, affects the thyroid gland. Knapp found data hard to come by:

Not only did he point out that, until 1962, "no systematic effort had been made to obtain fallout levels and milk levels at the same time," but also he concluded that, on the basis of the 1962 data, heavy doses of iodine 131 had been ingested by children in Utah from at least one earlier test and perhaps from others as well.

His employer, the AEC, pressured him not to publish his findings.

A further study, by Doctors John Gofman and Arthur Tamplin in California, blamed four thousand infant and fetal deaths and many cancer deaths on the fallout of the tests of the fifties. Most significant was this finding:

On the basis of their studies, they believed that the federal standard for acceptable radiation exposures was ten times higher than it ought to be and that it should be cut back; failure to do so would result in 32,000 additional cancer and leukemia deaths, they said.

According to Jacobs, the AEC cannot accurately claim, but does, that illnesses are not due to nuclear tests. No one knows how much radiation people have been exposed to, nor how low-level radiation affects an individual.

Jacobs concludes that the AEC must increase the level of efficiency and face facts. It must take into account the public safety. The Commission, along with its congressional and industrial allies, must face political and moral issues responsibly.

Congress may choose to invest the President with more extensive powers through special resolution. For example, during the Middle East crisis of 1958, a special congressional resolution gave the President the power to deploy troops in the area as he saw fit. Similarly, during the Cuban crisis of 1962, Congress adopted a resolution giving President Kennedy the power to call on the ready reserves to "permit prompt and effective responses, as necessary to challenges which may be presented in any part of the free world." And after American air strikes in North Vietnam in 1964 in retaliation for alleged North Vietnamese attacks on American destroyers, Congress passed the Gulf of Tonkin Resolution, approving and sanctioning President Johnson's action: *Resolved by the Senate and House of Representatives of the United States of America in Congress assembled*, that the Congress approves and supports the determination of the President, as Commander-in-Chief, to take all necessary measures to repel any armed attack against the forces of the United States and to prevent further aggression."[5]

[5] Quoted in "Global Defense: U.S. Military Commitments Abroad," *Congressional Quarterly* (Washington, D.C.: Congressional Quarterly, Inc., 1969), 23.

## The Department of Defense

While Congress and the President may be jointly responsible for military and defense policies, the Department of Defense is responsible for assisting the President in executing these policies. Because of the enormity of its job, the Department of Defense has become the largest and most expensive department in the government. The *Pentagon* alone (the headquarters of the Department of Defense) employs around 25,000 persons; 350 are generals and admirals, and over 170 are security guards who keep constant surveillance on the building. There are 1,262,800 people involved in defense work of some form or another (exclusive of active military personnel and individuals working on defense contracts). The Department of Defense is even more expensive than it is populous. In 1970, it spent over $77 billion in a national budget of $215 billion.

Before World War II, the organization of the military was divided between the Department of War and the Department of the Navy. (The Coast Guard was and still is attached to the navy during war.) Experience in World War II indicated the need for more integration and coordination of the military. Thus, in 1947, Congress passed the *National Security Act*, which created a unified Department of Defense. The Act provided for "three military departments for the operation and administration of the Army, the Navy (including Naval Aviation and the Marine Corps) and the Air Force . . . for their authoritative co-ordination and unified direction under civilian control . . . and for the effective strategic direction of the armed forces and for their operation under unified control and for their integration into an efficient team of land, naval, and air forces." Although designed to unify the three departments, the Act was only nominally effective in centralizing control. Further legislation, in 1949 and 1953, respectively, also failed to accomplish this integration.

When the Soviets launched Sputnik in 1958 and impressed the world with their military and scientific strength, Congress, upon the urging of President Eisenhower, passed new legislation designed to centralize control over the three branches of the military. The *Defense Department Reorganization Act of 1958* gave the Secretary of Defense increased power and control over the three armed services.

## The secretary of defense

The Secretary of Defense has a number of major responsibilities, including the management of a large and often secretive department and the giving of advice to the President on important military matters. The Defense Reorganization Act of 1958 gave the Secretary the right to communicate directly with field operational commands; it also gave him more authority to control the military services of his department. While the Act increased the Secretary's powers substantially, it also preserved the right of individual officers to complain to Congress and the right of Congress to veto the Secretary's decisions to transfer, merge, or abolish established functions of the military. It also protected the navy's flight corps, the Marine Corps, and the National Guard against alteration by any administration.

## Unification under McNamara

Important changes took place in the Department of Defense following the appointment by President John Kennedy of Robert McNamara as Secretary of Defense in 1961. McNamara, a former president of Ford Motor Company, believed that the department badly needed nonmilitary minds to examine its problems, and he brought in a number of highly trained economists, planners, and analysts to unify and streamline it. These men, commonly known as McNamara's "whiz kids," introduced programmed budgeting and systems analysis (PBS) for the dual purpose of determining the department's budget priorities and evaluating weapons. They also established unified military commands and coordinated the intelligence and supply services.[6] McNamara and the economists also raised provocative questions about military strategy and stressed funds to build up conventional forces. While McNamara was sharply criticized by many, he emerged as a most powerful and influential Secretary of Defense.

[6] A. Enthoven and K. W. Smith, former "Whiz Kids" describe in *How Much Is Enough* (New York: Harper and Row Publishers, Inc., 1971), the process of decision-making while McNamara was Secretary of Defense.

## Defense advisory agencies

The *Armed Forces Policy Council* and the *Joint Chiefs of Staff* are the two top advisory agencies in the Department of Defense. The Council, which functions as the general advisory board for all military operations, is composed of the Secretary of Defense, the Deputy Secretary, the director of defense research and engineering, the secretaries of the army, navy, and air force, the chief of staff of each branch of the military, and the chairman of the Joint Chiefs of Staff.

The Joint Chiefs of Staff stands as the highest military advisory body. It is composed of the chiefs of staff of the army, navy, and air force, the commandant of the Marine Corps, and a chairman, who are all appointed for two years by the President and in peacetime are eligible for only one reappointment. The Joint Chiefs generally advises the Secretary of Defense and the President on matters of strategy and military policy. The chairman of the Joint Chiefs, selected on a rotating basis from each branch, is particularly important, since he acts as the key military adviser to the President. In this role, he regularly sits on several key advisory committees, including the National Security Council.

In addition to their advisory duties, the Joint Chiefs of Staff are directly responsible for all military operations. Specifically, they must plan for all contingencies and for control of certain special or joint operations. It is this group that must be ready with answers to such questions as "What should the American response be if the Vietcong rebuild their supply bases in Cambodia within the next month or two? What should the United States do if the North Vietnamese enter Thailand."

During their frequent, and often heated, meetings, the Joint Chiefs plan military strategy, decide, or at least recommend, what weapons to build and develop, discuss personnel and supply needs, recommend what unified commands to establish in strategic areas, and represent the United States in the military commissions of NATO and SEATO. The Joint Chiefs often disagree over the adoption of plans and the distribution of resources, for each seeks priority and autonomy for his service. The navy, for example, argues that the air force has too much control over strategic nuclear weapons; the army often insists that more money be allocated to ground forces, and the air force argues for the continued development of long-range bombers.

## Intelligence agencies

There are presently three major intelligence agencies, which spend a total of $5 billion yearly, and employ some 200,000 persons. The *Defense Intelligence Agency* (run by the Department of Defense) is the largest and most expensive of these. It spends about $1.9 billion yearly, and employs well over 100,000 people. The *National Security Agency*, located at Fort Mead, Maryland, and also run by the Department of Defense, employs some

110,000 persons and spends more than $1 billion devising and cracking codes and intercepting radio broadcasts. It provides information of great value to the Central Intelligence Agency.

The *Central Intelligence Agency* (CIA), created in 1947 by the National Security Act, is smaller than either of these two agencies. (Although statistics on the CIA are secret, it is estimated that it employs 15,000 Americans; estimates on its spending range from slightly less than $600 million annually to $2 billion annually.) Its job as coordinator of the work of the other intelligence agencies makes it the most critical of the three agencies.

## Central Intelligence Agency

*"Cooper Acts to Force CIA to Report to Congress,"* The New York Times *(July 8, 1971), p. 14.*

The Central Intelligence Agency's coordinating and evaluating role makes it the mastermind of United States intelligence. But the CIA's burgeoning and conveniently undefined power has provoked public fear; and Congress, feeling its own power in foreign policy and defense matters threatened, is acting to regulate the once-untouchable agency.

Senator John Sherman Cooper (R. Kentucky) has initiated a bill to require the CIA to regularly report "detailed intelligence information" to Congress. It is felt that the lack of such information, until now available only to the executive branch, has limited the legislative role in enacting foreign policy. The publication of the "Pentagon Papers" has given an impetus to this legislation, which had been under consideration for three years. Among those supporting Senator Cooper is Senator Stuart Symington (D. Missouri), the only senator serving on both the Armed Services and the Foreign Relations Committees.

Mr. Symington said that it was "no secret that we on various committees have not been entirely satisfied with the intelligence information we have obtained."

"If the proper committees are not acquainted with what we're doing," Mr. Symington went on, "how can we function properly?"

The proposal would require the CIA to report to the Foreign Relations and Armed Forces Committees of both the House and the Senate, with the provision that any request by a committee for a special report would also be honored. Considering Senator Cooper's influential position, congressional hearings, and even floor debate, may well take place before the end of the year.

In addition to Cooper's bill, George McGovern (D. South Dakota) has proposed that expenditures and appropriations for the agency be listed independently in the budget, instead of being concealed in other budget areas. And Senator Clifford P. Case (R. New Jersey) said that he would "offer measures" that prohibit CIA activities, such as the financing of Thai troops fighting in Laos.

The information that flows daily into the CIA comes from three major sources: published matter, technical collectors (such as spy satellites), and personal agents. Although the "secret agents" get the most televised credit for gathering information (*I Spy; The Man From UNCLE*), the agent is probably the least informative source. As one Senate member remarked recently: "On a clear day we get as much from a satellite as we get from an agent in a year." Once the information (which may have a direct bearing on American policy) comes in, CIA experts—at least 50 percent of whom have advanced degrees and 30 percent of whom have their doctorates—spend hours in research facilities evaluating it. For example, a team of geologists and research assistants helped convince President Kennedy that the Soviets could not be hiding missiles in the Cuban caves after the 1962 crisis, since their compendious and exacting reports on the location of Cuban caves showed that such an action was impossible.

In addition to these functions the CIA itself engages in a variety of covert activities. *Covert* activity involves work that the CIA, for political reasons, cannot do publicly. Such work can involve dangerous and glamorous excursions into the back alleys and cafés of Middle Eastern capitals; more often, it entails such routine tasks as passing funds to foreign ministers, bugging hotel rooms, and gathering technical information on military installations by spy satellites and U-2's (high-altitude surveillance planes). In addition, the CIA often becomes involved in the support or subversion of foreign governments, and it is in this area that the agency has received the most criticism. The CIA has been accused, for example, of aiding in the overthrow of the Mossadegh government in Iran in 1953, the Arbenz government of Guatemala in 1954, and it currently finances the operations of Laotian military forces which oppose the Communist Pathet Lao.

The secrecy and independence of the CIA make it suspect to many Americans who seriously question the desirability of having such an agency in a democratic society. Because of the CIA's surprisingly influential role in some major policy moves, such as the unsuccessful attempt to invade Castro's Cuba and the successful overthrow of the Guatemalan government in 1954, many Americans feel that it is performing "un-American" activities. Yet, most of these same critics realize that some form of "undercover" work is necessary to protect America and promote its national interest. In addition, the CIA operates in a world where to advertise its successes would be self-defeating, while its failures become news in a matter of days.

# Space and the national defense

When the Soviet Union launched the first earth satellite, Sputnik I, in October, 1957, America's belief in its technological superiority was shaken. The Soviet achievement gave major impetus to the creation of a comprehensive space program in the United States. The controversy over how to meet the Soviet challenge became a prime issue in the 1960 presidential campaign. In his "State of the Union Message" in January, 1961, President Kennedy called for a national commitment to land a man on the moon and return him safely to earth "before the decade is out." That year, "Mercury," the first American satellite, was launched, and astronaut Alan Shepherd successfully orbited the earth. Since that time, there have been numerous space programs, such as Gemini in 1965, and the Apollo series in 1968.

Federal expenditures for space research and technology have soared within the past decade. Budget appropriations in 1960 totaled $401 million, and by 1971, allocations had risen to $3 billion 400 million.

While Mercury, Gemini, and Apollo were under the direction of the civilian control of the National Aeronautics and Space Administration (NASA), the "space race" is, in part, related to military considerations. For example, the space satellites that we have sent into orbit are often used to "recruit" information from other nations.

While for the present, our space explorations are connected with our defense developments on earth, hopefully, both terrestrial and extraterrestrial defense efforts will someday channel man's aggressions and his energies into purposeful adventure. The "race for space" may turn into a cooperative "race in space" for knowledge, wisdom, and solitude.

# Democracy and defense

Although most Americans have come to accept the need for a strong and stable military force, some fear the danger of military authority. A powerful military may not lead to a dictatorship, but it does eventually affect the lives and fortunes of all the citizens it is designed to protect. The *draft*, for example, affects almost every young man between the ages of eighteen and twenty-six, as well as those people intimately associated with him. Moreover, it may also affect the industries that lose the talent of such men, temporarily or permanently. In 1971, for example, the nation was shocked to discover that the military had been observing the political activities of civilians. This revelation dramatically demonstrated the possible threat to individual freedom from the presence of the military in civilian affairs. The practice, however, was quickly discontinued by the army.

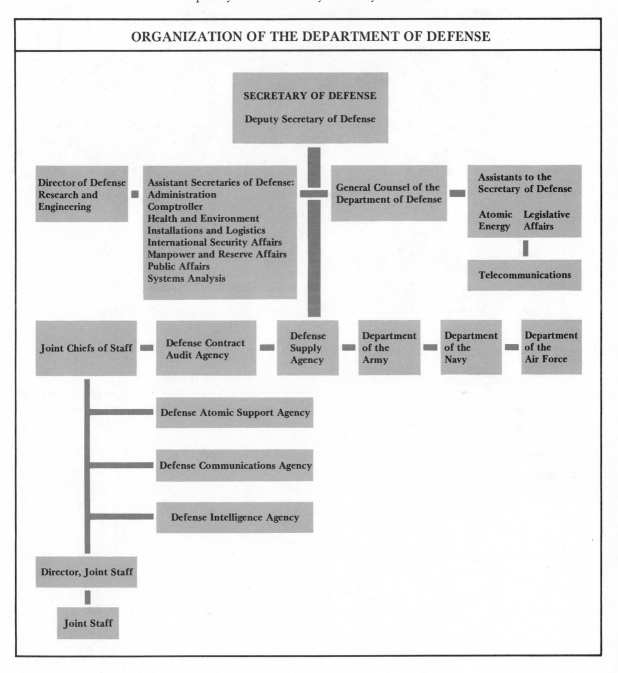

ORGANIZATION OF THE DEPARTMENT OF DEFENSE

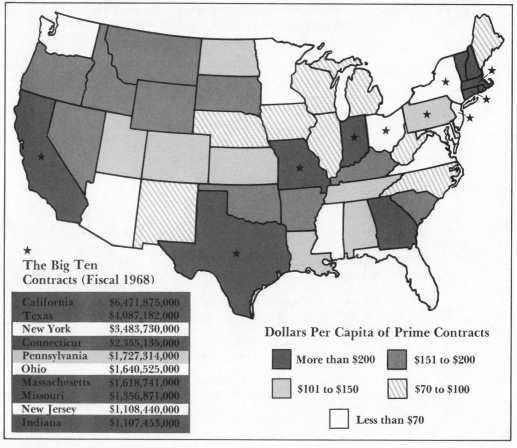

**The Big Ten Contracts (Fiscal 1968)**

| California | $6,471,875,000 |
|---|---|
| Texas | $4,087,182,000 |
| New York | $3,483,730,000 |
| Connecticut | $2,355,135,000 |
| Pennsylvania | $1,727,314,000 |
| Ohio | $1,640,525,000 |
| Massachusetts | $1,618,741,000 |
| Missouri | $1,356,871,000 |
| New Jersey | $1,108,440,000 |
| Indiana | $1,107,453,000 |

**Dollars Per Capita of Prime Contracts**

More than $200

$151 to $200

$101 to $150

$70 to $100

Less than $70

**Contracts between the National Government and Individual States for Defense Production**

Source: U.S. Department of Defense, 1968.

## A defense economy

Even more inclusive in its effect than the draft or military eavesdropping, however, is the high cost of defense—to every citizen who pays taxes. In recent years, the military budget has consumed over one-third of the national budget. If we include indirect expenses in the defense budget (veterans' payments, space agencies and research, atomic energy projects), the total becomes almost one-half the national budget.

In addition to using taxpayers' money, these costs have a number of effects on the economy that are less noticeable, but more serious. When the government suddenly cuts back its defense contracts (as it did in 1971), it creates serious manpower readjustments and unemployment. Our economy is now facing difficulties because we have trained so many men (engineers, scientists, technicians) and designed so many industries (aerospace, research, and production) for defense projects which are either no longer necessary or are being reduced.

It is primarily the fear of excessive military influence on domestic affairs that motivated our Founding Fathers to introduce a system of checks and balances into the Constitution by establishing the doctrine of civilian supremacy and separating control over military affairs between the executive and legislative branches of government. Amendments III and IV also speak to the issue of military intrusion and surveillance of private citizens. Despite these precautions, the threat of war and the pressure for more reliable defense measures have had and will continue to have an impact on society. While it is to be hoped that we can sustain such measures within a democratic and open society, we must recognize the dangers inherent in the growth and development of a military nation. Alexander Hamilton warned of this danger in *The Federalist* No. 8:

> Safety from external danger is the most powerful director of national conduct. Even the ardent love of liberty will after a time give way to its dictates. The violent destruction of life and property incident to war, the continual effort and alarm attendant on a state of continual danger, will compel nations the most attached to liberty to resort for repose and security to institutions which have a tendency to destroy their civil and political rights. To be more safe, they at length become willing to run the risk of being less free.[7]

[7] Alexander Hamilton, James Madison, John Jay, *The Federalist Papers,* ed. by Clinton Rossiter (New York: The New American Library, 1961), p. 67.

# Glossary

**anti-ballistic missile system (ABM)**  Proposed defense system that would surround strategic missile centers and cities with defensive missiles to be fired against approaching enemy missiles.

**ANZUS**  Defense pact among the United States, Australia, and New Zealand, created in 1951.

**Armed Forces Policy Council**  Advisory agency on military operations, composed of the Secretary of Defense, the deputy secretary, the secretaries of the army, navy, and air force, the director of defense research and engineering, the chairman of the Joint Chiefs of Staff, and the chief of staff of each of the military services.

**arms race**  Concurrent increases in armaments by rival nations.

**ballistic missile**  Self-guided missile.

**B-52 bombers**  Long-range bombers used for nonrefueling missions.

**Central Intelligence Agency (CIA)**  Key government agency for gathering and integrating information from all intelligence sources, established by the National Security Act of 1947.

**containment**  Policy of preventing the expansion of communism beyond post-World War II boundaries.

**Defense Department Reorganization Act (1958)**  Legislation to consolidate the Defense Department by granting the defense secretary increased power and control over the armed services, and by establishing direct lines of command between his offices and the field.

**Defense Intelligence Agency**  Government information agency, which correlates material from the agencies of the uniformed services.

**deterrence**  Policy designed to prevent military attack, which involves the existence of sufficient military power to discourage military action.

**disarmament**  Program of national military reduction or elimination, established on either a unilateral or multilateral basis.

**draft**  Conscription of citizens into military service.

**guided missile**  Missile that is not self-directing, but requires guidance to hit a specific target.

**International Treaty on the Peaceful Uses of Outer Space**  1967 treaty signed by sixty nations banning the use of satellites in outer space as vehicles or platforms for the launching of nuclear weapons.

**Joint Chiefs of Staff**  Key military advisory body to the Secretary of Defense and the President, including the chiefs of the army, navy, and air force, the commandant of the Marine Corps, and the chairman of the Joint Chiefs.

**Minutemen**  American missiles equipped with MIRVs.

**MIRV (multiple individually-targeted re-entry vehicles)**  Warheads on the nose of a missile, each of which carries a separate bomb capable of being targeted for different goals.

**missile**  Weapon fired from a land or water base, to explode on contact with a designated distant target.

**National Guard**  Military force organized on a state basis, financed by the national government, which is responsible to the governor, but which can be called into service by the President.

**National Security Agency**  Agency run by the Defense Department to create and decipher codes and intercept radio broadcasts, and which furnishes the CIA with material for its evaluation.

**Nonproliferation Treaty**  1967 agreement among Britain, the Soviet Union, and the United States, in which they pledged not to distribute nuclear devices to non-nuclear nations for at least twenty-five years, and which pledges non-nuclear powers not to develop such devices.

**North Atlantic Treaty Organization (NATO)**  Organization of nations, formed in 1949 for mutual defense, composed of the United States, Canada, the United Kingdom, Italy, Belgium, Denmark, Iceland, Luxembourg, the Netherlands, Norway, Portugal, Greece, Turkey, France, and West Germany.

**Nuclear Test-Ban Treaty**  1963 agreement among the United States, Great Britain, and the Soviet Union to limit the testing of atomic weapons, and which now includes over a hundred nations.

**Organization of American States (OAS)**  Organization of nations, formed in 1947 for mutual defense, now including the twenty-four American republics.

**Polaris**  Missile with a single warhead that can be fired from a nuclear submarine.

**Poseidon**  Multiple warhead missile that can be fired from a nuclear submarine.

**ready reserve units**  Nonregular armed forces units, including the National Guard, the army, navy, air force, and Coast Guard reserves, which are constitutionally under state control, but may be called up by the President in times of war or emergency.

**Second Amendment**  Constitutional amendment guaranteeing to each state the right to organize its own militia.

**Southeast Asia Treaty Organization (SEATO)**  Organization of nations, formed in 1954, designed to protect independent governments in Southeast Asia, and including the United States, Great Britain, France, Australia, New Zealand, the Philippines, Thailand, and Pakistan.

**Spartan system**  System for tracking down and intercepting incoming missiles.

**Sprint system**  System for tracking down and intercepting incoming missiles, deployed in the event that Spartan fails.

**standing military**  Regular active units of the army, navy, and air force.

**Strategic Air Command (SAC)**  Air force command established in 1946 to administer and execute atomic air strikes.

**Strategic Arms Limitations Talks (SALT)**  Talks initiated in 1969, and continuing to the present, between the Soviet Union and the United States on limiting the use and production of strategic arms.

# Suggested readings

Baldwin, Hanson W., *Strategy For Tomorrow* (New York: Harper and Row Publishers, Inc., 1970). A survey of United States defense needs in the 1970s, and 1980s, by a *New York Times* correspondent.

Barnet, Richard J., *The Economy of Death* (New York: Atheneum Publishers, 1969). Documentary on the military-political-industrial complex.

Berkowitz, Morton, and P. G. Bock, eds., *American National Security: A Reader in Theory and Policy* (New York: The Free Press, 1965). Collection of essays, with introductory notes, on national security policy.

Chayes, Abram, and Jerome B. Weisner, eds., *ABM: An Evaluation of the Decision to Deploy an Anti-ballistic Missile System* (New York: Harper and Row Publishers, Inc., 1969). Collection of essays assessing the value of the ABM system and emphasizing a negative view of its deployment.

Clark, Keith C., and L. J. Legere, eds., *The President and the Management of National Security: A Report* (New York: Praeger Publishers, Inc., 1969). Study of the organizational structures of national security under the administrations of Presidents Truman, Eisenhower, Kennedy, and Johnson.

Fox, William T. R., and Annette B. Fox, *NATO and the Range of American Choice* (New York: Columbia University Press, 1967). Study of the United States policy toward NATO, including key political and strategic issues.

Gilpin, Robert George, *American Scientists and Nuclear Weapons Policy* (Princeton, N.J.: Princeton University Press, 1962). Technical study of the "role of the scientist in policy-making decisions since 1944."

Goldwin, Robert A., ed., *America Armed: Essays on United States Military Policy* (Chicago: Rand McNally and Co., 1963). Six essays on American military policy in a nuclear world.

Goulding, Phil G., *Confirm or Deny: Informing the People on National Security* (New York: Harper and Row Publishers, Inc., 1970). Vivid depiction of the difficulties involved in informing the American public of national security matters from 1965–1969, including discussions on the Israeli attack on the American warship Liberty, the Pueblo Incident, the loss of an H-bomb in Spain.

Holst, Johan J., ed., *Why ABM? Policy Issues in the Missile Defense Controversy* (Elmsford, N.Y.: Pergamon Press, Inc., 1969). Collection of essays assessing the value of the ABM system and emphasizing a positive view of its deployment.

Huntington, Samuel P., *Soldier and the State: The Theory and Politics of Civil-Military Relations* (Cambridge, Mass.: Harvard University Press, 1957). Study of the relationship between professional officers and the state, with an examination of the most efficient means of maintaining civilian control and national security.

Huntington, Samuel P., *The Common Defense: Strategic Programs in National Politics* (New York: Columbia University Press, 1961). Study of American military policy between 1945 and 1960, emphasizing strategic programs.

Janowitz, Morris, *The Professional Soldier: A Social and Political Portrait* (New York: The Free Press, 1969). Sociological and political analysis of the American professional soldier.

Kissinger, Henry A., *Nuclear Weapons and Foreign Policy* (New York: Harper and Brothers, 1957). Reappraisal of American war and defense policies, including an analysis of the effect of nuclear weaponry on military strategy and foreign policy, by President Nixon's personal adviser on national security affairs.

Lapp, Ralph E., *Arms Beyond Doubt: The Tyranny of Weapons Technology* (New York: Cowles Book Co., Inc., 1970). Detailed historical account of the arms race, stressing the need for establishing checks on the weapons industry.

LeMay, Curtis E., *America Is In Danger* (New York: Funk and Wagnalls Co., 1968). Statement of a military position on Vietnam, by former chief of staff of the air force and vice-presidential candidate with George Wallace in 1968.

Proxmire, William, *Report From Wasteland: America's Military-Industrial Complex* (New York: Praeger Publishers, Inc., 1970). Valuable compilation of Senate subcommittee hearings on military budgets, national priorities, and the so-called military-industrial complex.

Ries, John C., *The Management of Defense* (Baltimore, Md.: The Johns Hopkins Press, 1964). Analysis of the American defense organization and defense strategy, including the use of military force, the decision-making process, and the effectiveness of centralization.

Russett, Bruce M., *What Price Vigilance? The Burden of National Defense* (New Haven, Conn.: Yale University Press, 1970). Methodological and quantitative study of the causes and consequences of military spending.

Schilling, Warner R., Paul Y. Hammond, and Glenn H. Snyder, *Strategy, Politics, and Defense Budgets* (New York: Columbia University Press, 1962). Three studies of national security policy dealing with three phases of policy transition since 1948—warning, reaction, and change.

Tyrrell, C. Merton, *Pentagon Partners, the New Nobility* (New York: Grossman Publishers, Inc., 1970). Discussion of the relationships among congressmen, businessmen, and the military in the development of American national defense.

York, Herbert, *Race to Oblivion: A Participant's View of the Arms Race* (New York: Simon and Schuster, Inc., 1970). An insider's analysis of the arms race, providing rare insight into the political decision-making process on matters of national defense.

# Topics of further study

Bright, Samuel R., Jr., "Confederate Coast Defense" (Ph.D. dissertation; Durham, N.C.: Duke University, 1961).

Burd, Frank A., "United States Policy in Laos, 1959–1961" (Master's thesis; Chicago: University of Chicago, 1962).

Close, Richard Bernard, "Nuclear Weapons and West Germany" (Ph.D. dissertation; Amherst: University of Massachusetts, 1967).

Courtney, Robert, "Disarmament: Dream or Necessity?" *La Salle Quarterly*, 10 (spring 1966): 8–10.

Gassner, Julius S., "The Origins of the Rome–Berlin Axis" (Master's thesis (New York: Fordham University, 1940).

Harkavy, Robert E., "The International Arms Trade: A Comparison of the Interwar and Postwar Period," (Ph.D. dissertation; New Haven: Yale University, 1971).

Henderson, Larry W., *Vietnam and Countries of the Mekong* (Camden, N.J.: Thomas Nelson, Inc., 1967).

Johnson, Earl B., "The Political Aspects of the United States Intervention in Lebanon," (Master's thesis; Washington, D.C.: George Washington University, 1966).

Joiner, Harry, "NATO and MLF," (Ph.D. dissertation; Kent, Ohio: Kent State University, 1971).

Malik, Charles, *Man in the Struggle for Peace* (New York: Harper and Row Publishers, Inc., 1963).

McLain, Ralph E., "Standardization: A Difficult Road for NATO" (Master's thesis; Delaware: University of Maryland, 1963).

O'Sullivan, Thomas C., "Weapons and Technology, 1964" (*Current History*, XXXXVII, 1964, 6–11, 50–51).

Pilant, Denny Eugene, "A Peacetime Dilemma: The Legal Status of American Civilians Accompanying the Armed Services Abroad" (Ph.D. dissertation; Durham, N.C.: Duke University, 1963).

Ruff, Robert M., "Interpretations of the Origins of the Cold War: A Historiographical Approach" (Ph.D. dissertation; Eugene: University of Oregon, 1971).

Silverburg, Sanford R., "Insurgency in the Middle East," (*International Problems*, VII, 1969, 56–59).

Walker, Ralph H., "United States and International Space Cooperation," (Master's thesis; Kent, Ohio: Kent State University, 1967).

Waters, Harold, *Adventure Unlimited: My Twenty Years of Experience in the United States Coast Guard* (Englewood Cliffs, N.J.: Prentice-Hall, 1955).

# 22 the economy
## management and regulation

[1] See Adam Smith, *Wealth of Nations: Representative Selections*, ed. by Bruce Mazlish (Indianapolis, Ind.: Bobbs Merrill Co., Inc., 1961) for a description of this economic philosophy.

PEOPLE OFTEN have the same attitude toward the government that they have toward their parents: when things are going well they want to be left alone, but when things are going badly, they seek help. The American government, for many years, tried to behave like a noninterfering parent; but it soon discovered that this strategy hurt many more people than it helped. Even those citizens who adhered to a "laissez-faire" philosophy ("let the economy run itself")[1] came to realize that unregulated self-interest could work against them, as well as for them. Consumers complained about the high costs of inferior goods; shopkeepers complained about the high costs of suppliers; suppliers complained about the high rates of producers; and producers complained about heavy rains, ruined crops, and the high rates of the railroads. Not until the Great Depression of the 1930s, however, did masses of people fully realize that an economy that largely ran itself could also ruin itself. As millions of people lost jobs, homes, and fortunes, government leaders came to advocate government intervention.

Although our Founding Fathers recognized the dangers of unbridled self-interest, they had little reason to legislate against it. In 1800, America was a rural and agrarian society. Ninety-five percent of the population lived in self-sustaining farming communities where everyone knew the local storekeeper, the local doctor, the local sheriff, the local prostitute, and the local thief. Women baked their own bread, churned their own butter, sewed their own clothes, and often taught their own children. Men milked their own cows, built their own houses, rode their own horses, and fired their own guns. Few people wanted, or needed, the government to regulate their daily lives.

With the coming of cities and factories after the Civil War, however, this pattern of life changed. And as society became more "urbanized" and "industrialized," the people became less self-sufficient. Farm workers and immigrants who came to the cities often became employees of ungenerous factory owners. Mothers had to buy groceries in unfamiliar shops, send their children to unfamiliar schools, and rely upon unfamiliar and often remote authorities for advice and help. Paradoxically, as Americans became more sophisticated in their tastes, secluded in their private lives, and specialized in their skills, they became more reliant on the government for protection and assistance.

[2] James Anderson, *Politics and the Economy* (Boston: Little, Brown and Co., 1966), p. 20.

The framework for the expansion of government activity has been provided by technological development, economic growth, and the evolution of the United States from a rural, agrarian society to a complex urban, industrial society. As a society becomes more complex and industrial, and people become more interdependent, and less self-sufficient, the needs, conflicts, and demands which give rise to government action multiply.[2]

As the United States became more industrialized, it also became more productive. Today, the United States has the highest standard of living in the world; more people enjoy more goods than at any time in history.

*John Kenneth Galbraith,* The Affluent Society *(Boston: Houghton Mifflin Co., 1958), pp. 253–331.*

Analyzing the American economy, John Galbraith suggests that our burgeoning affluence is in general being put to poor use. He observes that in the United States, there is an acceptance of the "paramount position of production" and a suspicion of government expenditure; such expenditure is assumed to be linked to the problems of inequality, and those who must pay more taxes to equalize the society rarely enjoy their role. The public today, trapped by modern advertising, believes that the surrender of money through taxes is not as independent an act as the choice between two privately produced goods such as a car and a television. Americans must come to realize that this distinction is false, according to Galbraith.

Galbraith, viewing the result of an economy shaped by misconceptions, sees an imbalance: there is an abundance of privately produced products and a lack of good public services.

The family which takes its mauve-and-cerise, air-conditioned, power-steered, and power-braked automobile out for a tour passes through cities that are badly paved, made hideous by litter, [that have] blighted buildings, billboards, and posts for wires that should long since have been put underground. They pass on into a countryside that has been rendered largely invisible by commercial art. The goods which the latter advertise have an absolute priority in our value system. Such aesthetic considerations as a view of the countryside accordingly come second. On such matters we are consistent. They picnic on exquisitely packaged food from a portable icebox by a polluted stream and go on to spend the night at a park which is a menace to public health and morals. Just before dozing off on an air mattress, beneath a nylon tent, amid the stench of decaying refuse, they may reflect vaguely on the curious unevenness of their blessings. Is this, indeed, the American genius?

An equilibrium between the two must be attained:

It is scarcely sensible that we should satisfy our wants in private goods with reckless abundance, while in the case of public goods, on the evidence of the eye, we practice extreme self-denial. So, far from systematically exploiting the opportunities to derive use and pleasure from these services, we do not supply what would keep us out of trouble.

Goods have remained supreme in our society because, Galbraith believes, it is so much simpler than to substitute the other tests—compassion, individual happiness and well-being, the minimization of community or other social tensions. He suggests that:

. . . a widely affluent society must change its philosophical attitude toward the poor in its midst: an affluent society, that is also both compassionate and rational, would, no doubt secure to all who needed it the minimum income essential for decency and comfort. . . . It would help insure that poverty was not self-perpetuating. . . . When poverty was a majority phenomenon, such action could not be afforded. A poor society . . . had to enforce the rule that the person who did not work could not eat. An affluent society has no similar excuse for such rigor. It can use the forthright remedy of providing for those in want. Nothing requires it to be compassionate. But it has no high philosophical justification for callousness.

According to Galbraith, any direct remedy is beyond reasonable hope. But Americans can act indirectly to prevent the self-perpetuation of poverty by providing first-rate schools, good food, sound health services, opportunity for advanced education, and enforced law and order.

Educational deficiencies can be overcome. Mental deficiences can be treated. Physical handicaps can be remedied. The limiting factor is not knowledge of what can be done. Overwhelmingly it is our failure to invest in people.

While the standard of living has improved for almost every member of society, the costs of maintaining this standard are extremely high. And because the national government provides a large percentage of the financial aid—through welfare, school subsidies, and housing construction, for example—government costs have soared. In 1913, national government expenditures were $2.5 billion, and these rose each year until 1970, they were $215 billion. In addition to the rising costs of all governmental operations (local, state, and national), the costs of the national government alone have risen phenomenally. In 1913, the national government spent 29 percent of the total government revenues; by 1970, it was spending over 60 percent.

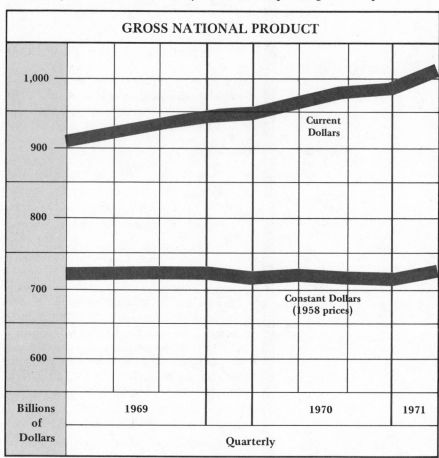

The reasons for these increases are complex, but certainly one major cause can be attributed to the improved standard of living that has affected almost all Americans. Today, the national government provides a vast number of services, social goods, and securities which a vast number of Americans demand. The national government regulates giant interstate corporations, maintains interstate highways, provides health, education, and welfare for the population, assists in times of national disasters (floods and earthquakes), and provides grants-in-aid to the states and cities. Furthermore, the national government alone established military and defense policies necessary to protect this country. We are still paying off the huge World War II debt incurred in order to defeat Germany and Japan. And as the threat of nuclear war remains, the government, even in peacetime, must continually seek ways to prepare for it and prevent it. While taxpayers often complain about these high defense costs (43 percent of the 1970 national budget went into defense and security), they also generally support programs designed to maintain America's military defense.

# Financing the economy

When people complain about taxes, they usually complain about the income tax form they must file on April 15. Few of them realize that almost everything we buy throughout the year involves a "hidden" government tax. When we buy a refrigerator, for instance, we pay not only the state sales tax that the salesman computes on the sales slip, but we also pay the corporate, customs, and property taxes that the original supplier, manufacturer, and retailer included in their estimation of costs and expenses. Many goods, such as liquor, cars, and gasoline, are expensive because of the high "excise" taxes that the dealer who sells these goods must pay. Consequently, in one way or another, about a quarter of every dollar we spend goes to the government.

**Taxation**

In 1787, the Constitution gave Congress the power to levy "indirect" taxes on its citizens in the form of "duties, imposts, and excises." While these taxes supplied government with a substantial sum of money, the sum was insufficient to finance the rising costs of government. Consequently, in 1913, Congress adopted the Sixteenth Amendment, which gave Congress the power to "lay and collect taxes on incomes, from whatever source derived, without apportionment among the several states, and without regard to any census or enumeration." Since that time, Congress has used the income tax to raise needed government revenues.

> *Michael D. Reagan, "The Expanding Economic Role of the Government," The Managed Economy (New York: Oxford University Press, 1963), pp. 159–189 (Sec. III, Chap. 8).*
>
> Michael Reagan emphasizes the necessity of governmental intervention in the economy; in fact, he insists that the "limits of . . . intervention have not yet been reached."
>
> Presently, the national government's economic role takes the form of income protection programs, personal income taxes to redistribute income, federal welfare payments, and automatic stabilizers such as unemployment compensation and agricultural price-supports. In addi-

tion, the national government has allocated its own resources to meet social need, thus incurring the wrath of many citizens, who object to governmental use of their tax money for "welfare" purposes.

The issue of resource allocation goes to the heart of the current division of opinion over the role of government in the economy. Free enterprise ideologists contend that the private competitive market can satisfy all wants, except defense, education, and the maintenance of order. They believe that market allocation is the "democratic" way, and that every dollar taxed by government to pay for a collective service is a dollar less that the consumer is free to allocate as he wishes. Thus, in the ideologists' minds, public allocation is "arbitrary" and "undemocratic," because the citizen pays the tax to supply a particular service, whether he wishes to or not. In contrast, socialists and liberals believe that many public needs are better met by government than by private action and that public allocation does not involve a net loss of freedom or democracy so long as the political process is open, free, and democratic.

In an effort to cut through the verbiage surrounding the topic of resource allocation, Reagan offers a concise defense of public allocation as consistent with the principles of freedom and democracy.

It is not correct to assume that one's freedom diminishes in exact proportion to the level of taxation. Better roads and schools, for instance, can only be built with tax money. Similarly, the theory of majority rule gives a legitimate political basis for contribution whether or not one approves of a public program. Equal "votes" in the market place can only be a reality if every individual has the same amount of money at his disposal. This is obviously untrue. Finally, public allocation of goods and services must exist as long as personal wealth is unequally distributed.

Reagan concludes that more public planning and management is a necessity for democratic control over economic development.

The pace may be agonizingly slow, but the secular trend is surely toward increased public sector services. . . . When opponents of government action charge that we are moving toward a planned or managed economy, they are quite right. Their error is in supposing that this is an arbitrary development rather than a necessary response to modern economic structure, technological forces, and humanistic values. They are also wrong in assuming that the managerial role of the national government will produce a trend toward dictatorship or at least a less democratic system.

At the present time, *personal income taxes* account for about 52 percent of the national tax revenue; *corporate taxes* (taxes levied on the profits of corporations) account for about 18 percent; *excise* taxes (taxes on items

[3] Internal Revenue Service,
Washington, D.C.,
December 12, 1970.

such as tobacco, gasoline, automobiles and telephone) comprise 8 percent.[3] In addition to these major taxes, the national government receives revenues from *customs duties* (taxes on goods brought into this country from abroad) and *employment* taxes (social security, for example). States raise most of their revenue from either personal and corporate income taxes, or from *sales taxes* (taxes on certain goods sold in stores), and from excise taxes, and *estate* or *death taxes* (taxes on inherited property and money). Local governments receive most of their revenue from *property taxes* (taxes on land), but are increasingly resorting to a variety of other taxes to meet their financial needs.

"For want of a better word, I call my idea 'taxes'. And here's the way it works."

Drawing by H. Martin © 1969
The New Yorker Magazine, Inc.

Congress enacts tax legislation, often according to the President's proposals; the Internal Revenue Service, as branch of the Treasury Department, is responsible for collecting them. In 1970, the federal government received $195,722 million in taxes. Of this amount, $103,652 million was from personal income tax, $35,037 million from corporate income tax, and the remainder from all other tax sources.

**Borrowing**

When federal taxes do not produce enough revenue in a fiscal year to meet expenditures, the national government borrows money from banks, corporations, and individuals by selling bonds to them. The rate of interest and time of refund of government bonds are fixed at the time of sale.

"Are you sure you've examined all the
loopholes? Mineral depletion? Municipal
Bonds? Capital gains? . . ."

Drawing by Oliphant
© 1969 in The Denver *Post*.

During World War I, the government borrowed $23 billion from cor-
porations, individuals, and foreign governments to help pay for the war effort.
During the thirties, it borrowed $18.4 billion in an attempt to speed the na-
tion out of the Great Depression. And during World War II, the government
borrowed an additional $183 billion. Since the end of World War II (more
than a quarter of a century), the national government frequently has had
annual budget deficits. The debts have continued to accumulate, and the
present *national debt* amounts to some $374 billion.[4] The interest on this
debt has become so sizable (about $18 billion annually), that it has become
a significant item in the national budget.

Although this sounds like an overwhelming sum, most economists maintain that a national debt does not indicate a great weakness in the economy.
Instead, it is believed that the government, which is borrowing from its population to offset the cost of the debt, is exhibiting a sign of flexibility in a time
of financial stress. Nevertheless, many citizens do not favor any measures that
will increase the national debt (including tax cuts), and Presidents almost
always seek to establish a balanced budget each year in order to prevent an
increase.

[4] *Statistical Abstracts for
the United States, 1970*
(Washington, D.C.:
Department of Commerce,
1970), p. 377.

## Spending

These vast taxes and revenues are used for equally vast expenditures on the part of the government. In 1932, total government expenditures represented approximately 5.5 percent of the *gross national product* (the sum of goods and services produced and marketed in the United States), and the government spent about thirty dollars per person. In 1970 the national government's expenditures represented over 20 percent of the gross national product, and the government spent more than a thousand dollars per person. This same year, 43 percent of these national expenditures went into national security and defense; about 40 percent went into providing domestic services and paying salaries, including the payrolls of national government employees, who number some twenty million; and about 20 percent went into "transfer" payments (payments collected from individuals in the form of taxes, and paid back to other individuals in the form of social security, unemployment compensation, and interest on the national debt).

## The budget

Because the national government spends such large sums of money, the planning of the annual budget is a complicated and difficult process that usually goes on throughout the year. The budget that finally emerges is not only a financial plan, but a political document. In it, one can determine the scope and direction of current administration policies on domestic and foreign affairs. For example, a budget with increased appropriations for national defense and smaller appropriations for housing may demonstrate an administration's belief that there is a greater immediate need for defense than for housing.

## Preparation of the budget

Before 1921, there was no central review of department and agency budgets by the President or his advisers. The Treasury Department merely sent the agency and departmental request to Congress for approval. These procedures were disorganized and nonsystematic, and did not result in a concerted administration program or an overall philosophy of government. In order to centralize the budget process and make the budget more responsible to national needs, Congress passed the *Budget and Accounting Act* in 1921. This act authorizes the President to formulate the budget and present it to Congress. It also created a Bureau of the Budget (now the Office of Management and Budget—OMB) to assist the President in preparing the budget.

Early in the fall of each year—well before the following July, when the new budget goes into effect—the President confers with his budget director and establishes how much he wants to spend in various areas. While the President is setting up these guidelines and ceilings (spending limits), the various government agencies and departments determine how much money they will need in order to run their departments for the coming year. In preparing their estimates, the agencies must anticipate the probable reactions of Congress (which must finally approve the budget appropriations), the overall policies of the President, and the general and specific needs of the country. When these agencies have completed their estimates, they send them to OMB, where expert examiners check them for accuracy and see that they are in line with the President's policies. The OMB then holds hearings in which representatives from the various agencies have an opportunity to explain more fully why the amounts of money requested are actually needed.

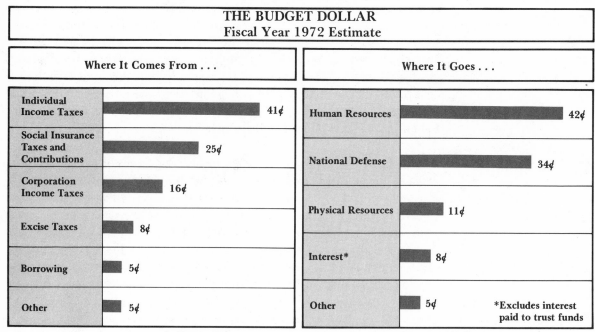

## THE BUDGET DOLLAR
### Fiscal Year 1972 Estimate

**Where It Comes From . . .**

| | |
|---|---|
| Individual Income Taxes | 41¢ |
| Social Insurance Taxes and Contributions | 25¢ |
| Corporation Income Taxes | 16¢ |
| Excise Taxes | 8¢ |
| Borrowing | 5¢ |
| Other | 5¢ |

**Where It Goes . . .**

| | |
|---|---|
| Human Resources | 42¢ |
| National Defense | 34¢ |
| Physical Resources | 11¢ |
| Interest* | 8¢ |
| Other | 5¢ |

*Excludes interest paid to trust funds

After the hearings, the examiners prepare a final set of recommendations and submit them to the budget director, who makes a final determination on how much money he can request for each department in order to keep below the maximum set by the President. The director then brings his report to the President, and sits with him for several days while the President reviews it. After final decisions are made, the President prepares a "budget message" and delivers it to Congress soon after it convenes in January. In this address, the President explains the reasons for his various expenditures, showing how they promote the national welfare.

The budget is then referred to the Appropriations Committee of the House of Representatives, where subcommittees assess the various department estimates and conduct additional hearings on them. After the committees approve the budget as submitted or as revised, it is presented to the House floor for a vote; and after the House approves it, the budget is passed on to the Senate, where it goes through a similar process. After Senate approval, the budget is returned to the President who may veto any of the various bills, but not the separate items (he may reject the bill for housing, but he cannot reject one or two items in that bill). After final presidential approval, the budget goes into effect on July 1, by which time, plans for the next year's budget are already in the making.

**Accounting for budget expenditures**

Expenditures by the federal government are watched by the *General Accounting Office*. The GAO was established by the Budget and Accounting Act of 1921, in order to make certain that the money would be spent in accordance with law. The GAO is headed by a comptroller general who is appointed by the President, with Senate approval, for fifteen years. His office staff conduct *pre-audits* (reviews before the money is spent, to make certain that funds have been totaled correctly, and that funds for intended appropriations exist) and *post-audits* (reviews after the money is spent to make certain that it has been spent as designated by law).

# Fiscal and monetary policies

In the twentieth century, government has increasingly assumed positive responsibility for controlling the state of the nation's economy. In particular, it seeks to guard against the occurrences of periods of inflation and recession.

During an *inflation*, prices generally go up, because people spend more than they can produce; the value of the dollar declines. During a *recession*, prices fall off, jobs become scarce, production decreases, and spending generally declines. Recessions may lead to depression, a more extreme form of economic slowdown. Both inflations and recessions may be "normal" irregularities (some economists state that a slight inflation is healthy), but they can become disastrous if allowed to continue without check.

**Employment Act of 1946**

While many people in 1946 still valued individual independence and initiative, they placed even greater value on security and stability. The Great Depression of the 1930s resulted in millions of lost jobs, fortunes, and homes. Government expenditure during this trying period and during World War II had taught the population that public spending could stimulate the economy and bring about an economic upturn. In 1946, the prospect of peace was as frightening as it was desirable: without the wartime activity that had resurrected the depressed economy of the thirties, many people feared that the economy would collapse once again. Consequently, in 1946, Congress passed the Employment Act which, for the first time, dedicated the national government to the goal of maintaining full employment and a healthy economy.

*The Employment Act of 1946* committed the national government to the goal of achieving a "maximum" employment economy. The Act stated that the government should fulfill this goal by promoting the free and competitive system on which our economy is based, and by sharing the responsibility with industry, agriculture, and labor; but it avoided committing itself to any particular policy.

The Act also stipulated that the President submit an annual economic report to Congress at the start of each legislative session, in which he analyzes the state of the economy and recommends legislation that would make full use of the nation's resources. The law also created the *Council of Economic Advisers* to help the President with this task.

Drawing by Orsin © 1970 in
The Cleveland *Plain Dealer*.

"Eeny, meeny, miny, moe . . ."

The *Council of Economic Advisers* (CEA) was created to "develop and recommend to the President national economic policies." The CEA is composed of three economists, appointed by the President, to collect data on past and present economic performance and advise the President on constructive and rehabilitative programs. During the Kennedy and Johnson administrations, for example, this Council recommended tax cuts and deficit spending.

# Fiscal policy

## Fiscal legislation

[5] Wilfred Lewis, Jr., *Federal Fiscal Policy in the Postwar Recessions* (Washington, D.C.: The Brookings Institution, 1962), provides a clear description of the use of fiscal policy since 1945.

## Deficit spending

[6] See John Maynard Keynes, *General Theory of Employment, Interest, and Money* (New York: Harcourt Brace Jovanovich, Inc., 1936).

## Automatic stabilizers

One direct result of the Employment Act of 1946 was the adoption of *fiscal* measures that would help the government achieve its goal of maximum employment and increasing production.[5] Fiscal controls involve the use of taxation, borrowing, and spending to encourage increased spending by private individuals, corporations, and government agencies.

In times of inflation or recession, Congress, based on recommendations from the President, can initiate legislation to increase or decrease the spending potential of the consumer. The most common, and familiar, of these acts are tax cuts or tax hikes. During recessions, when individuals are hard pressed for cash, Congress can increase the spending potential of the consumer by cutting his taxes. Conversely, during inflations, Congress may raise taxes in order to restrict the spending power of the individual. Congress can also increase government spending during recessions by initiating more federal spending programs. All these measures will make more money available to the consumer. During an inflation, the government can follow the reverse of these policies: reduce government spending and raise taxes.

Government fiscal policy has been strongly influenced by the theories of English economist John Maynard Keynes.[6] Writing during the 1930s, Keynes argued that when private enterprises and private individuals could not spend enough money to increase production and employment, the government should increase its spending through contracts, loans, and employment. The government should do this even when it did not have sufficient funds to pay for the cost of the spending program. Keynes argued that the government could run a deficit (debt) and pour money into the economy during periods of economic depression. The increased production and incomes resulting from tax cuts and government spending would eventually allow the national government to balance its budget or create a surplus, because of the higher taxes that would be paid in the restored economy.

Although Keynes's theory does not always work this well, it is still used as a general guideline to boost the economy in times of economic slowdown, or to slow it down (the more recent trend) in times of inflation.

In addition to legislative measures, there are certain stabilizers that will automatically regulate the amount of money in circulation in times of prosperity and adversity. The most familiar of these stabilizers is the *graduated income tax*, introduced in 1913. Since income taxes increase in proportion to one's earnings, the income tax *automatically* restricts spending habits in times of prosperity by taking large cuts of income. In times of adversity and/or low earnings, taxes will drop automatically, and the consumer will have proportionately more money to spend.

More recent stabilizers are the *welfare payments*, introduced during the Depression in order to provide minimal economic security for individuals during times of private or public difficulty. These payments, such as social security, unemployment compensation, and old-age pensions, increase during recessions (when many people depend upon unemployment insurance for income); and they decrease during prosperity, when most people are employed. Consequently, government welfare payments help to control the amount of money the recipients have.

Since these automatic stabilizers naturally reduce the national income in times of hardship, and increase it in times of economic growth, they apply Keynes's theory without direct congressional action.

## Monetary policy

While *fiscal* policy is designed to redistribute the amount of money in circulation through taxation, borrowing, and spending, *monetary policy* serves to increase the amount of money in circulation by making more money available to banks. Since banks are the major source of credit for investors, businessmen, and manufacturers, the government can control large-scale spending by making it easy or difficult to borrow money from banks.

*Scene from the United States Mint in Philadelphia, Pennsylvania. The thin metal strip shown on the right is fed to a blanking press, which shapes the coins seen on the left.*

# The Federal Reserve System

The Federal Reserve Board (FRB) was created in 1913 to regulate the nation's supply of money through its power to control the amount of money commercial banks can lend. The board now has twelve regional federal reserve banks; and over 5,740 private banks belong to this system. Even though the federal reserve banks represent less than 50 percent of the banks in the nation, they control about 85 percent of its bank assets and deposits.

At the top of the FRB is a seven-man Board of Governors, appointed by the President, with Senate approval, for overlapping terms of fourteen years. The board controls the volume of funds that member banks have available for lending through three principal instruments: open market operations, the discount rate, and the reserve ratio requirement. The most often used is *open market operations*, a process in which the federal reserve buys or sells government bonds in the "open market"—that is, from or to commercial banks, big business, insurance companies, dealers in government securities, and the general public. The buyer generally pays for the bonds by a check to the federal reserve drawn on his bank account. The federal reserve will present this check to his bank, which, in making payment, reduces its deposits and its reserves. Unless the commercial bank has considerable excess reserves, they are prompted to reduce the amount of loans they make to business. Open market sales, thus, are a potent means of monetary regulation.

The *discount rate* is the interest rate charged by federal reserve banks on loans made by them to the commercial banks. It is usually slightly lower than the interest rate that banks charge on their loans. Therefore, when the discount rate is raised, commercial banks borrowing from federal reserve banks must likewise increase their rates to private borrowers to cover this raise, and thereby reduce borrowing. The measure is considered anti-inflationary because it decreases borrowing and, hence, the level of business and consumer spending.

The *reserve ratio* is the percentage of deposits (in the form of cash or cash equivalents) that the Federal Reserve System requires its member banks to maintain. Although the upper and lower limits of the reserve requirement are set by congressional law, the Federal Reserve Board has the power to alter the reserve ratio within these statutory boundaries. Raising the reserve ratio tightens credit; banks find themselves deficient in excess reserves, so they must sell bonds, call in loans, and decrease investments. This leads to higher interest rates, and restricts available credit. Changing the reserve requirements is a means of regulation that is used sparingly, because even a one-percent change in the reserve ratio would have a substantial effect on economic activity.

Although the government uses both monetary and fiscal policy to regulate the flow of money in the economy, there are difficulties with each. It is not always possible, or feasible, to cut government spending in a period of inflation, inasmuch as the government is committed to projects of national defense and welfare. Furthermore, changes in laws take months of planning and debate, and then may not have the desired effect on the economy. But if the timing is good, changes in tax laws have a fairly rapid effect. Monetary policy, in contrast, has a less immediate impact; many months may pass before a change in monetary policy will begin to take effect.

# Regulating business

Most Americans are as ambivalent about "big business" as they are about "big government." For most of them, "big business" is synonymous with General Motors, dehumanization, tranquilizers, and Mrs. Robinson. Yet, most people also recognize that without big business they could not enjoy the luxuries of color TV sets, four-ply durable napkins, no-iron crease-resistant sheets, and frozen "fresh" vegetables. Their dependence upon big business is even more profound than their distrust.

When large corporations and industries developed after the Civil War, there were few laws designed to protect laborers from employers and small businessmen from larger businessmen. In fact, there was almost no legislation protecting big businessmen from each other. As a result of this "laissez-faire" environment, businesses engaged in fierce and cut-throat price wars that threatened to drive them out of existence. This competition became so intense that businessmen soon realized they would have more opportunity to make profits if they consolidated resources. In 1882, John D. Rockefeller initiated this process by forming the Standard Oil Company from forty different oil companies. These various oil captains handed over their stocks to a board of trustees (directed by Rockefeller), who gave them "trust" certificates in return. The board then established the "price" of oil, and all the companies agreed to sell at this price.

As the advantages of this trust became apparent, other industrial leaders followed Rockefeller's example. By 1900, twenty-six corporations controlled over 80 percent of the output in their respective fields; market operations were monopolized. These trusts were able to vanquish any and all competitors by buying up resources, producing more goods for less money, and discriminating against markets that might sell to nontrust members. Trusts injured the small businessmen who had higher operating costs and fewer resources, and exercised control over consumer prices. They absorbed basic industries, such as meat packing, steel, petroleum, lead, coal, and tobacco. While the public may have benefited from the increased supply of available goods they were compelled to accept the noncompetitive selling scales of the trusts. They had to buy at the prices dictated by these large companies, or do without.

Although trusts were maintained well into the twentieth century, their excesses have been mitigated by the passage and enforcement of "antitrust" laws. Generally speaking, these laws have tried to create what economist Edward Mason calls a state of "workable competition"—a state characterized by "a fairly large number of buyers and sellers, no one of whom occupies a large share of the market, the absence of collusion among either group, and the possibility of market entry by new firms."[7]

[7] Anderson, *Politics and the Economy*, p. 6.

*Characterization of the public's fear of the strong influence of trusts over the Congress.*

Joseph Keppler in *Puck* (January 23, 1889).

Strictly speaking, our present economy is characterized by "oligopoly" (competition among the few), rather than competition among the many. Large corporations are still the rule, rather than the exception, and most major areas of the industrial economy are dominated by several huge corporations. The United States Department of Commerce cited that, in 1966, the output of the four largest companies in each field in this country accounted for over 90 percent of electric bulbs and flat glass; for over 75 percent of linoleum, breakfast cereals, cigarettes, typewriters, and automobiles and their parts; for over 70 percent of household refrigeration, soap and detergents, tires and tubes, and tin cans. In each case, then, over two-thirds of business

[8] See George Leland Bach, *Economics: An Introduction to Analysis and Policy* (Englewood Cliffs, N.J.: Prentice-Hall, Inc., 1971), p. 417.

## Sherman Anti-Trust Law

### Rule of reason

[9] *United States* v. *Standard Oil Co.*, 251 U.S. 417 (1911).

## United States Steel Corporation

[10] *United States* v. *United States Steel Corp.*, 251 U.S. 417 (1920).

## Clayton Act

conducted in these fields is in the hands of only four corporations.[8] Although these corporations are enormous, they are prohibited from making price-fixing agreements with competitors, pooling their resources, or creating any situation that the law can define as "monopolistic" and anticompetitive.

The first federal antitrust legislation was passed in 1890, with the enactment of the *Sherman Anti-Trust Act*. Stimulated by the growth of trusts and the publicity about their practices, the Act made illegal "every contract, combination in the form of trust or otherwise, or conspiracy in the restraint of trade or commerce. . . ."

Soon after the Sherman Act was initiated, however, much controversy developed because of its unclear and ambiguous wording. By "restraint of trade," did the law mean *all* restraint of trade, or only *unreasonable* restraints of trade? Could the Act be used to outlaw manufacturing concerns that did not engage in, or affect, trade? These controveries were settled by cases involving the two largest monopolies to be affected by the Act.

In 1911, Standard Oil of New Jersey controlled 91 percent of its industry. Not only did it have almost complete domination over its products, but it had used price-cutting, industrial bribery, threats, and exclusive agreements with subsidiaries to eliminate competition. The Supreme Court ruled in that same year that Standard Oil had used "unreasonable" methods to restrain trade, and ordered the company to dissolve into several smaller, independent corporations.[9] (Standard Oil is now regionalized into various independent companies.) Most important, however, the Supreme Court applied the "rule of reason" as a guide for judging the legality of monopolies: only unreasonable restraints of trade were to be considered illegal by the courts.

The "rule of reason," in practice, served to lessen the power of the Sherman Act. For example, in 1912, a suit was brought against United States Steel, because it controlled over 50 percent of the steel assets in the United States. When the case was finally decided in 1920, the Supreme Court ruled that the corporation had not engaged in unreasonable behavior and, therefore, had not violated the Sherman Act. The Supreme Court declared: "The law does not make mere size an offense. It . . . requires overt acts and trusts to enforce its prohibition of them and its power to repress or punish them. It does not compel competition nor require all that is possible."[10]

Although the decision in United States Steel cautioned other big monopolies to proceed with "reason" in their activities, the Supreme Court had weakened the effectiveness of the Sherman Act. The next major enforcement of the Sherman Act did not occur until 1945.

The ambiguous wording of the Sherman Act led to clamors for more concrete antitrust legislation. Therefore, in 1914, Congress passed the *Clayton Anti-*

*Trust Act*, which was intended to prevent and prohibit activities which could result in curtailing free competition or establishing a monopoly. The act specifically outlawed the following practices:

1. Price discrimination. Such as granting concessions to certain buyers in order to restrict their markets, or underselling to other buyers in order to obtain their markets.

2. Exclusive agreements. Selling goods to a dealer on the basis that he not buy goods from another company.

3. Contingent sales. Selling a company item X, only if it will also buy Y and Z.

4. Interlocking directorates. Individuals seated on the board of directors of two or more competing firms.

5. Horizontal mergers. The common ownership of two competing companies.

## The DuPont-General Motors case

The Clayton Act was responsible for breaking up the merger between Du-Pont and General Motors. In 1919, DuPont acquired 23 percent of the stock of General Motors, to whom it sold automotive fabrics and paints. Because DuPont was such a large shareholder, it was able to obtain from GM its business for the sales of fabrics and paint. In 1957, the government brought suit against DuPont, and the company was convicted of violating the Clayton Act. As a result, the Supreme Court ordered DuPont to divest itself of all GM stock.[11]

11 *United States* v. *DuPont*, 353 U.S. 586 (1957).

In 1967, a similar case occurred when the Supreme Court ordered Procter & Gamble to divest itself of Clorox stock. Procter & Gamble had such vast resources, it was argued, that the corporation could make Clorox monopolize the field of liquid bleach by "lending" its advertising people and store display space to Clorox. Other intended mergers, such as that between Youngstown and Bethlehem Steel (1958), and Chrysler and Mack Truck (1964), have also been blocked by enforcement of the Clayton Act prohibition against mergers that substantially reduce competition or tend to create a monopoly.

## Federal Trade Commission Act

In 1914, the same year that Congress passed the Clayton Act, it also passed the *Federal Trade Commission Act*. This act set up a five-member *Federal Trade Commission* (FTC) to work with the Department of Justice in carrying out the provisions of the Clayton Act. It also included special provisions to protect the consumer from "deceptive acts or practices in commerce" as well as disadvantageous commercial competition. In order to stop illegal business practices, the FTC was given the power to file a complaint based on its findings, notify the company, and hold a hearing. If evidence is substantial enough, the FTC may issue a "cease and desist" order to those engaged in the illegal practice. The FTC, however, has relied more on voluntary compliance than on court orders; it prefers to obtain the manufacturer's agreement to alter its activities before instituting formal procedures.

The provisions of the Federal Trade Commission Act were extended by the *Truth-in-Packaging Act* of 1966 and the *Truth-in-Lending Act* of 1968, both of which were specifically designed to protect the consumer against false or misleading advertising, packaging, or consumer credit terms. In May, 1971, for example, the Federal Trade Commission applied the standards of Truth-in-Packaging to false or misleading advertising of grocery "specials" that never appeared on the grocer's shelves.

# Government projects

In addition to regulating large businesses, the government owns and operates a small number of enterprises, the largest and most important of which is the famous Tennessee Valley Authority.

**Tennessee Valley Authority (TVA)**

During World War I, the United States government developed an area, located by the Tennessee River, for the purpose of changing nitrate deposits into explosives. When the war ended, the government did not give up the land, but retained it in order to produce electric power. The fight for this development of the Tennessee Valley was championed by Senator George Norris of Nebraska. In 1933, the federal government established its own corporation, the *Tennessee Valley Authority*. Although the TVA was, in part, an "antidepression" measure, the Authority was so successful that it has become a world-famous model for other river projects.

Using the direction and resources of the government, the TVA has been able to develop inexpensive electricity for all the residents in the area. In addition, the TVA has controlled flooding, reforested many of the wooded areas in the vicinity, developed related agricultural and industrial projects, and provided employment for many people in the area.

Most people agree that the TVA has been run efficiently and effectively at great benefit to the people in the surrounding area. However, there is still reluctance to institute "TVAs" on a nationwide basis because many people and groups, especially the private utilities of the nation, oppose any further extension of this form of public ownership of a basic economic activity.

# Transportation

Another important area of American business regulated by the national government is that of interstate transportation. The high rates charged by the railroads following the Civil War stimulated the first attempts at regulating the railroads. While the Grangers (a political group of midwestern farmers) had succeeded in securing a number of state regulatory laws aimed at curbing the high and discriminatory rates charged by the railroads, the Supreme

*The Tennessee Valley Authority provides power and employment for residents in parts of Tennessee, Kentucky, Alabama, and Georgia.*

Court voided these by upholding, in 1886, the constitutional provision that Congress and not the states had the power to "regulate commerce with foreign nations, and among the several States. . . ." Shortly after this decision, Congress passed the Interstate Commerce Act, which was designed to prevent railroads from charging high and discriminating rates and engaging in other deceptive business policies. The act also created the *Interstate Commerce Commission* (ICC).

The ICC is headed by a board of eleven commissioners (appointed for seven-year terms); it employs about 2,400 persons. The ICC controls railroad rates, costs, and proposals for corporate mergers. It also regulates interstate ground transportation, domestic water transportation, and specified pipeline systems.

**Air regulation**

Since the airplane has become a major mode of transportation for personal and business travel, it has been the subject of governmental supervision. This supervision is channeled through the *Civil Aeronautics Board* (CAB), the *National Transportation Safety Board* (NTSB), and the *Federal Aviation Administration* (FAA). The main purpose of these agencies is to protect the public from monopolistic airline practices, faulty equipment, and careless operators and mechanics.

The CAB, a five-man independent commission, issues licenses to airlines, controls price rates, mergers, and other market activities, and establishes the fees to be paid by the government to the airlines for letter carrying. The FAA is chiefly concerned with air safety, and the supervision of the air traffic systems that direct planes on take-off, in flight, and on landing. The NTSB investigates air accidents, conducts hearings on the evidence and hears appeals from FAA decisions. It conducts similar investigations and hearings regarding railroad, automobile, and interstate pipeline accidents.

**The Department of Transportation**

In 1967, Congress established a Department of Transportation, in an attempt to centralize the various agencies concerned with transportation, and put them under common supervision. Most transportation industries, however, have objected to this centralization, because they feel it will restrict their autonomy and preferential treatment. Consequently, the Department of Transportation has limited power. While some national agencies are under its administrative control (Federal Highway Administration and Urban Mass Transportation Administration, for example), the most important regulatory commissions—the CAB, ICC, and Maritime Commission—remain independent.

# Labor and management

Although, for many years, labor was an unprivileged and unprotected group, unions have gained so much economic and political power that present legislation must protect not only labor from industry, but industry from labor. Government regulates the relationship between labor and management in order to carry out its responsibilities toward the large masses of people who are dependent upon the continued and efficient production of goods and services.

Current labor legislation has two goals: it seeks to prevent management from exploiting laborers, as it had throughout the nineteenth and early twentieth centuries, and it also seeks to restrict organized labor from making excess use of its power.

When business and industry became large and powerful in the mid-nineteenth century, there were few protective laws for the average worker. Although labor unions were organized as early as 1790, these unions had virtually no power. The courts, by nature conservative and pro-management, refused to recognize the legality of labor unions. At the close of the nineteenth century, they accepted the application of the Sherman Act to labor unions as illegal conspiracies to restrain trade.

Throughout the nineteenth century and into the early decades of the twentieth, business took advantage of all available manpower, including very young children, women, and elderly men. It was not until 1842 that the first child labor law was passed; Massachusetts then declared that children under twelve, who worked in manufacturing establishments, could not work more than ten hours per day. Although seven more states passed child labor laws in the next twenty years, these laws were largely ineffective. Child labor laws did not become effective until the early twentieth century; and it was not until 1938 that children under sixteen were prohibited by national law from working in manufacturing plants. Today, there are national as well as state laws that regulate and restrict child labor.

Adults were also mistreated and abused by factory owners in the early twentieth century. A normal workday for men and women was a twelve- or fourteen-hour day. In 1847, New Hampshire passed a law limiting the hours a woman might work to ten hours per day; but ten-hour work laws for women did not become effective in many other states until much later. Wages were as low as hours were long. Finally, in 1938, when Congress passed the *Fair Labor Standards Act*, a national system of minimum wages was established in the United States. This law originally provided a minimum wage of twenty-five cents and limited the working week to forty-four hours. These provisions have since been extended so that, today, the minimum wage (set by Congress in 1971) is $2.00, and the maximum working week is forty hours (before over-time is paid).

Congressional legislation has also fostered the growth of organized labor by guaranteeing the right to organize and bargain collectively—that is, the right to deal with an employer as a group rather than as individuals. This right was granted first by the *National Industrial Recovery Act* in 1933 and, then, by the National Labor Relations Act in 1935.

Today, about 75 percent of all American workers belong to some form of union. In the manufacturing, mining, transportation, and construction industries, 80 percent of the members belong to unions. The three largest unions in the country—the International Brotherhood of Teamsters, Chauffeurs, Warehousemen and Helpers of America; the United Automobile, Aerospace and Agricultural Implement Workers of America, International Union; and the United Steelworkers of America—have close to, or more than, one million members apiece. The next eight largest unions have between 350,000 and 750,000 members each. The total membership of these eleven unions equals eight million members, or nearly one-half the total labor force.

## The right to strike and join unions

Despite the growth of the American Federation of Labor craft unions during the end of the nineteenth century and the first quarter of this century, employers managed to prevent the development of industrial unions primarily by employing court injunctions and the so-called "yellow-dog" contracts. A *yellow-dog contract* was a contract between an employer and employee guaranteeing that the worker would not join a union during the period of his employment. If union organizers tried to make the employee join the union, the employer could order an *injunction* (court order) to stop the organizers. Court injunctions were also used by employers to break up actual or threatened strikes.

This coercive employer action continued until 1932, when Congress passed the *Norris-LaGuardia Act*. This act freed labor from judicial interference, as it prohibited the national courts from enforcing yellow-dog contracts and from issuing injunctions against strikes, peaceful picketing, and union membership. The Norris-LaGuardia Act restricted court action to labor situations in which it was necessary

> to prevent damage to tangible property and to preserve public order; otherwise, the disputants should be left to their own resources to work out their own problems. Both labor and business would now be free to promote their own interests in the field of labor policy through self-help without interference of the courts.[12]

[12] Anderson, *Politics and the Economy*, pp. 237–238.

## The right to organize

During the thirties, the power and influence of the unions continued to grow. The Congress of Industrial Organizations was formed in 1935, and during the next ten years, successfully organized a large number of major industries (steel, automobiles, and rubber, for example) into a cohesive unit. The *National Industry Recovery Act* (NIRA) of 1933 helped to foster the growth of industrial unions by providing, in law, for the first time that labor had the "right to organize and bargain collectively through representatives of their own choosing." Although this was a major breakthrough for labor, the NIRA was declared unconstitutional by the Supreme Court in 1935.

Congress, however, quickly enacted the *National Labor Relations Act*, more commonly known as the *Wagner Act* after its initiator, Senator Robert Wagner of New York. The Wagner Act declared that unequal bargaining power between employers and employees was economically dangerous, and in order to produce a better balance, labor was guaranteed the right to form unions and bargain collectively through unions of their own choosing. The law also spelled out certain illegal business practices. Specifically, it forbade employers from restraining employees in their right to organize, establishing company unions (management-run unions), discriminating against workers because of their union membership, and refusing to engage in collective bargaining.

"Gentlemen, nothing stands in the way of a final accord except that management wants profit maximization and the union wants more moola."

Drawing by Alan Dunn © 1970
The New Yorker Magazine, Inc.

**Rights of management**

As a result of favorable labor legislation such as the Wagner Act, the sympathy of the Roosevelt administration, and the effect of World War II (which created a demand for increased industrial production and, hence, more workers), the number of union members soared from four million in 1935 to over fifteen and one-half million in 1947. As their membership increased, so did their strength, and businessmen as well as the general public began to complain that labor had been given special privileges, rather than equal rights. This growing hostility toward unions was bolstered by the flagrant corruption that existed in several of the largest unions, and by several nationwide strikes called by large labor unions. Consequently, in 1947, Congress passed a second *Labor-Management Relations Act*, generally known as the *Taft-Hartley Act*, to protect management and the nation from the growing power of unions.

This act retained labor's right to organize and bargain collectively, but it also prohibited certain labor practices, namely:

1. The *closed shop*. A shop in which an employer is permitted to hire only union members. A *union shop*—a shop in which new employees must join a union within a specified length of time—was allowed, provided that the majority of workers vote for a union shop, and provided also that union shops are not outlawed by a state "right to work" law.

2. *Jurisdictional strikes*. Strikes caused by disputes between unions as to which is to represent a certain category of laborers.

3. *Featherbedding*. Requiring employers to retain union employees, even though their jobs have become superfluous.

4. Using union funds to support political candidates.

5. Using *secondary boycotts*. A strike by workers, designed to have their employer bring pressure on another company which is in dispute with the union.

6. *Sympathy strikes*. Strikes by workers not having grievances against an employer, but engaged in as a means of helping another group of workers who are on strike.

7. *Refusal to bargain in good faith* with an employer.

8. *Strikes by federal employees*, although they still retained the right to join a union and bargain with the government.

The Act also reintroduced a limited use of the injunction in major labor-management disputes. It permits the President to obtain an eighty-day injunction against strikes that threaten the national health or safety. During the last twenty days of this "cooling-off" period, the employees must vote on whether or not to accept the employers' last contract offer. If the offer is not accepted and the dispute not settled, the President gives Congress his recommendations for a solution.

**Rights for union members**

Although most unions are law-abiding and honestly administered, the scandals in several unions during the 1950s, widely publicized in the mass media, led Congress to enact the *Labor Reform Act of 1959*, more commonly known as the *Landrum-Griffin Act*. The main provisions of the act are:

1. It gave union members a "bill of rights" by which they are guaranteed the right to vote secretly in union elections, obtain public hearings in disci-

plinary situations, have equal say in union meetings, testify before a government body without union pressure, and bring suit in a federal court if the union abridges any one of these rights.

2. It attempted to create more responsible and trustworthy union leadership by making the misuse of union funds a federal crime, requiring union leaders to submit detailed financial reports to the Secretary of Labor, and requiring local elections every three years, and national elections every five years.

3. Since union assets run into billions of dollars, it attempted to control further the misuse of union funds by requiring the bonding of union officials, and by barring from office persons with competing financial interests.

# Agriculture

Although most groups in our society have benefited from technology, technology has been both a blessing and a hindrance for those engaged in agricultural activities. By increasing production, technology aided the bigger, more successful farmer, but hurt the smaller farmer. The large farmer could afford new equipment that doubled or quadrupled his production; now he could produce as much as many small farmers had produced in the nineteenth century. Many small farmers, unable to compete with the larger producers, continued to add their crops to the market until farmers began to overproduce in relation to demand. Farm prices declined, and during periods of stress the small family farmer was often forced to leave his land and move to the city.[13]

[13] Geoffrey Shepherd, *Farm Policy: New Directions* (Ames: Iowa State University Press, 1965).

Not only did technology make it possible for fewer farmers to produce more goods, but it created wasted surpluses of goods. While farm production increased significantly, in proportion, farm consumption increased relatively slightly. Even though more people began to earn more money than at any time in history, they continued to buy a proportionally similar amount of milk, eggs, meat, cheese, and vegetables. They spent their "extra" money on luxury items, such as automobiles, theaters, trips, houses, and clothing, rather than farm products. As a result, when farmers produced an excess of a particular crop, they were forced to sell it at extremely low prices in order to sell it at all.

## Farm programs

In an attempt to remedy the problem of overproduction and make it possible for farmers to survive, the government has established programs designed to regulate the supply of farm goods available to the consumer and the cost of these goods on the market. These programs began during the 1930s, when the farmers, as well as the society in general, were suffering the consequences of the Great Depression. In order to make farm goods available to the public at prices that the consumer could afford, and which would maintain the price of farm produce at a level high enough to sustain the farmer, Congress passed the *Agricultural Adjustment Act* of 1933. This act was designed to increase farm incomes by reducing the supply of goods on the market. Farmers were paid for not producing farm products. Although the act was declared unconstitutional by the Supreme Court in 1936, it was quickly replaced by a second Agricultural Adjustment Act, which utilized the concept of "parity."

## Parity

In a program for implementing farm price supports, *parity* is the relationship between the prices farmers are paid for their produce and the prices they must pay for the goods and services they require. In simple terms, "parity" means that the price paid the farmer for vegetables should have the same purchasing power today that it had during a base period. Usually, 1909–1914 is used because it was a prosperous period for farmers. Or, as a farmer stated more bluntly, "If a man could take a bushel of corn to town in 1912 and sell it and buy him a shirt, he should be able to take a bushel of corn to town today and buy a shirt."[14] Government programs since the 1930s have tried to guarantee farm income from major crops at some percentage of parity, 75 percent being a typical figure.

[14] Quoted in Clair Wilcox, *Public Policies Toward Business* (Homewood, Ill.: Richard D. Irwin, Inc., 1960), p. 471.

## Price supports

In order to maintain prices for major farm commodities and thus sustain farm incomes, the national government has instituted a variety of *"price support"* policies. These policies set a support price on "basic" commodities, and also determine the amount of particular crops the farmer can produce and market. (If he exceeds the legal quota, he is not eligible for government support and has to pay a penalty tax.) Before these production controls are established, a majority of farmers who raise a particular crop must approve the system in a referendum. If the market price falls below the support price set by the government, the government will reimburse the farmer for the difference; if the price rises above the support price, the farmer is free to pocket the difference. For example, if the support price of corn is $1.50 a bushel, and corn sells for $1.35 a bushel on the market, the government will give the farmers up to fifteen cents per bushel to make up the difference. At the present time, there are government price support programs for such basic commodities as cotton, corn, wheat, tobacco, rice, peanuts, dairy products, wool, oats, barley, and honey.

Price supports and parity ratios are flexible, so that they can accomplish their immediate purpose of raising or lowering the rate of production. Low or medium price supports, with the government's agreeing to pay 75 percent or less of parity, are established in times of potential overproduction, in order to discourage farmers from producing large crops. Conversely, high price supports (90 percent of parity) are usually instituted during periods of underproduction, in order to encourage production and increase the supply of a particular commodity at lower prices. High price supports were established during the Korean War, when there was a great demand for food supplies. However, the recent tendency has been to authorize lower price supports, thus encouraging less production of the protected commodity.

Another program for implementing farm price support and adjusting the supply of basic commodities is administered by the *Commodity Credit Corporation*. The CCC was set up in 1933 and is headed by a board of directors, which includes the Secretary of Agriculture and six presidential appointees. Its main function is to help maintain the farm price supports designated by law.

The CCC purchases certain commodities directly in the open market at the support price; however, it generally makes nonrecourse (nonrepayable) loans to farmers equal to the price of their crops. When a farmer intends to sell his produce, he applies to the CCC for a loan based on the support price of his crop. (If the support price of wheat is two dollars per bushel, and the farmer wants to sell a thousand bushels, he will ask the government for a two-thousand-dollar loan.) If the market price exceeds the support price, the farmer will sell his wheat, pay the loan, and profit the difference. If, however, the market price falls below the support price (if wheat sells at $1.50 per buhsel) and the loan is due, the farmer will give the wheat to the CCC and use the loan as payment. Thus, the farmer receives a "guaranteed" price for his product, regardless of market conditions.

**Surplus food**

Even though attempts have been made to discourage and restrain production, the American farmer is still producing more than can be consumed. In order to dispose of these surplus crops, Congress passed the *Agricultural Development and Assistance Act* in 1954 (*Public Law 480*), in order to use these surpluses in a beneficial way.

This law allows the government to give away or sell this surplus food to underdeveloped foreign countries. India, for example, had at one time received one-fifth of American wheat production. When the government "sells" this food to poor countries, however, she allows the country to pay in local currency. The United States then deposits this money in American banks in the foreign country, and lends it to persons or organizations wishing to use it for development or educational projects in that nation. Consequently, the more food that these countries buy from Americans, the more money they have at their disposal to develop the land and country. This program has become one of our chief methods for foreign aid. Since its inception, the government has sold over $20 billion in surplus food to underdeveloped nations.

In addition to the food that goes overseas, much surplus food is used for domestic programs, such as school lunch programs, food stamp plans, and emergency relief.

# Looking forward

In this chapter, we have seen that government regulation is largely a twentieth-century phenomenon. At present, at least, it seems necessary in order to maintain a healthy economy. Such regulation can assume many forms—legislation designed to control the amount of money in circulation, to regulate the relationship between labor and business, to assist the farmer in securing a decent income, and to guard against the natural hazards of the environment. In a few instances, it takes the form of government ownership of enterprises, such as the Tennessee Valley Authority and the postal service.

The general purpose of such legislation is to make the economy work more effectively and efficiently, and to provide an economic environment that will encourage individual incentive, ambition, and creativity, and eliminate the exploitation, imbalances, and insecurity that existed prior to 1933. Strictly speaking, we live in an economy that tries to sustain "capitalistic" incentive by protecting it. Whether or not we have succeeded in that is, of course, a controversial subject among political scientists.

# Glossary

**Agricultural Adjustment Act** (1933)   Legislation designed to increase farm income by reducing the supply of goods on the market; declared unconstitutional in 1936 by the Supreme Court.

**Agricultural Development and Assistance Act** (Public Law 480) (1954)   Legislation that provides for governmental distribution of surplus food to foreign countries or depressed areas within the United States.

**Budget and Accounting Act** (1921)   Legislation assigning the President the task of preparing the national budget and presenting it to Congress; the Act also created a Bureau of the Budget (now Office of Management and Budget) to assist the President in the preparations.

**Civil Aeronautics Board**   Commission that grants airline licenses, regulates airline fares, rates, and mergers, and establishes fees to be paid to airlines for air mail.

**Clayton Anti-Trust Act** (1914)   Legislation that prohibited interlocking directorates, price discrimination, and other practices that lead to the creation of industrial monopoly.

**Commodity Credit Corporation**   Governmental agency that maintains farm price supports by issuing loans to farmers on crops.

**Council of Economic Advisers**   Agency in the executive office of the President, composed of three economists, appointed by the President to advise him on economic matters.

**Employment Act** (1946)   Legislation that committed the national government to the goal of a full employment economy, and set up the Council of Economic Advisers.

**excise taxes**   Taxes on goods and services, such as tobacco, gasoline, and telephones; used by both federal and state governments.

**Fair Labor Standards Act** (1938)   Legislation that set a national minimum wage and maximum work-hour week, and regulated child labor.

**Federal Aviation Administration**   Agency concerned with enforcing air safety standards.

**Federal Reserve System**   National banking system established in 1913, which employs monetary policy to regulate the amount of credit available in the country. Composed of a central national bank and twelve district banks throughout the United States.

**Federal Trade Commission Act** (1914)   Legislation that included provisions to protect the consumer, and set up a five-member Federal Trade Commission to enforce the Clayton Act against monopolies and combinations in restraint of trade.

**fiscal policy**   Economic policy designed to regulate the amount of money in circulation through taxation, borrowing, and spending.

**General Accounting Office**   Office of national government that reviews the allocating and spending of monies to ensure that such monies are appropriated in accordance with law.

**graduated income tax**   Form of taxation in which the individual pays in proportion to the amount of money he earns.

**gross national product**   The sum of goods and services produced and marketed in the United States.

**inflation**   Economic condition characterized by rising prices and wages, resulting in a decrease in the value of the currency.

**injunction**   Court order requiring a person to perform an act, or to restrain him from performing an act.

**Interstate Commerce Commission**   Organization established by Congress in 1887 to regulate railroad rates and services, and whose authority has been extended to include regulation of interstate motor and water carriers and some pipelines.

**"laissez-faire"**   Economic philosophy advocating a capitalistic economy free of government interference, which will regulate itself according to certain basic economic laws.

**Landrum-Griffin Act** (1959)   Legislation regulating the management of the labor union by providing a "bill of rights" for union members.

**monetary policy**   Government economic policy designed to regulate the amount of money in circulation, primarily by controlling the interest rate on bank loans.

**national debt**   The money that the government owes to individuals, corporations, and foreign governments, especially for refunds on bonds.

**National Industry Recovery Act** (1933)   Legislation that set up a system of industrial codes to regulate business, and also established the right of workers to organize the bargain collectively. Declared unconstitutional by the Supreme Court in 1935.

**National Transportation Safety Board**   Agency that investigates air accidents and safety hazards in railroads, automobiles, and natural gas pipelines, and also hears appeals from the Federal Aviation Administration concerning air safety.

**Norris-LaGuardia Act** (1932)   Legislation limiting the use of injunctions in labor disputes to situations in which property and public order were endangered, and prohibiting courts from enforcing yellow-dog contracts.

**parity**   The relationship between a farmer's purchasing power and prices he must pay for the goods and services he requires, maintained by national government through a system of price supports for farmers.

**price supports**   Amount paid by the national government to a farmer in order to maintain the price of certain basic commodities.

**recession**   Economic condition of decreased economic activity, characterized by a decrease in consumer spending, a high rate of unemployment, and decreased production.

**Sherman Anti-Trust Act** (1890)   Legislation that declared illegal all "contracts, combinations and conspiracies in restraint of trade."

**Taft-Hartley Act** (1947)   Legislation that outlawed such labor practices as the closed shop, featherbedding, and jurisdictional strikes, and gave the President the power to obtain an injunction against strikes that threaten the national health or safety.

**Tennessee Valley Authority** (1933)   Governmental authority set up during the Depression, which was given the power to develop the resources in the Tennessee Valley. By controlling the rivers there, TVA has been able to provide inexpensive electric power, to control floods, reforest, and increase employment opportunities.

**trust**   An illegal combination of companies in which the stock of these organizations is controlled by a single board of trustees.

**Truth-in-Lending Act** (1968)   Legislation designed to protect the consumer against false credit terms.

**Truth-in-Packaging Act** (1966)   Legislation designed to protect the consumer against false or misleading packaging or advertising.

**yellow-dog contract**   Contract between employee and employer in which the employee agreed not to join a union during the term of his employment.

# Suggested readings

Anderson, James E., *Politics and the Economy* (Boston: Little, Brown and Co., 1966, paper only). Survey of government economic policy, its form, substance, formation and implementation, and the political factors affecting such policy.

Anderson, Walt, ed., *Politics and Environment: A Reader In Ecological Crisis* (Pacific Palisades, Calif.: Goodyear Publishing Co., 1970). Collection of articles on ecological problems and issues.

Buchanan, James M., *Public Finance In Democratic Process; Fiscal Institutions and Individual Choice* (Chapel Hill: University of North Carolina Press, 1967). Advanced text on the effects of public finance and taxation on individuals and businesses.

Carson, Rachel, *The Silent Spring*, rev. ed., (New York: Fawcett World Library, 1970). Influential "indictment" of the use of insecticides, the book that first drew public attention to ecological problems.

Cary, William L., *Politics and the Regulatory Agencies* (New York: McGraw-Hill Book Co., 1967). Series of lectures discussing the role and effectiveness of the regulatory agencies in a political context.

Dahl, Robert A., and Charles E. Lindblom, *Politics, Economics, and Welfare: Planning and Politico-Economic Systems Resolved into Basic Social Processes* (New York: Harper and Row Publishers, Inc., 1953). Comprehensive account of "social policy," emphasizing the necessary integration of economic and political theories and the general welfare.

Drucker, Peter F. *The Age of Discontinuity: Guidelines to Our Changing Society* (New York: Harper and Row Publishers, Inc., 1969). Thought-provoking look at the technological generation of new industry.

Ecker-Racz, L. L. *The Politics and Economics of State-Local Finance* (Englewood Cliffs, N.J.; Prentice-Hall, Inc., 1970). An explanation of the political and economic aspects of twenty-four major issues in national state and local finance.

Friedman, Milton, and Walter W. Heller, *Monetary vs. Fiscal Policy: A Dialogue* (New York: W. W. Norton and Co., Inc., 1969). Two divergent views on how to establish economic prosperity. Friedman is critical of fiscal policy, whereas Heller believes that the government's budget can be used to aid economic growth.

Galbraith, John K., *The New Industrial State* (Boston: Houghton Mifflin Co., 1969). Examination of the contemporary industrial state and the forces that are shaping its future development.

Grossman, Mary Louise, Shelly Grussman, and John N. Hamlet, *Our Vanishing Wilderness* (New York: Grosset and Dunlap, Inc., 1969). Consideration of current ecological questions.

Heller, Walter W., *New Dimensions of Political Economy* (Cambridge, Mass.: Harvard University Press, 1966). Examination of the changes that occurred in United States economic policy during the 1960s.

Jewkes, John, *The New Ordeal By Planning: The Experiences of the Forties and the Sixties* (New York: St. Martin's Press, Inc., 1968). Critical analysis of the means and machinery of central economic planning.

Krislov, Samuel, and Lloyd D. Musolf, eds. *The Politics of Regulation; A Reader* (Boston: Houghton Mifflin Co., 1964). Series of articles pertaining to the politics of administrative regulation.

Redford, Emmette S., *American Government and the Economy* (New York: The Macmillan Co., 1965). General survey of the roles of state and national government in the American economy.

Rostow, Eugene V., *Planning For Freedom: The Public Law of American Capitalism* (New Haven: Yale University Press, 1959). Description and evaluation of various aspects of monetary and fiscal policy and the American capitalistic system.

Sharkansky, Ira, *The Politics of Taxing and Spending* (New York: Bobbs Merrill Co., Inc., 1969). Analysis of the politics involved in spending decisions, and the relationship between state and local expenditure and government output.

Sirkin, Gerald, *The Visible Hand: The Fundamentals of Economic Planning* (New York: McGraw-Hill Book Co., 1968). Examination of governmental economic planning.

Stein, Herbert, *The Fiscal Revolution In America* (Chicago: The University of Chicago Press, 1969). A study of the history of fiscal policy emphasizing the changes in American fiscal policy that occurred between the administrations of Presidents Hoover and Johnson.

Theobald, Robert, ed., *Committed Spending: A Route To Economic Security* (Garden City, N.Y.: Doubleday and Co., Inc., 1968). Collection of essays and commentary dealing with contemporary social problems, especially including a discussion of the guaranteed income and "committed spending"—income maintenance plans.

Wildavsky, Aaron, *The Politics of the Budgetary Process* (Boston: Little, Brown and Co., 1964). Discussion of the nature of budgets and the politics involved in the budgetary process.

Wogaman, Philip, *Guaranteed Annual Income: The Moral Issues* (New York and Nashville, Tenn.: Abingdon Press, 1968, paper). Examination of the arguments for and against the guaranteed annual income.

# Topics of further study

Anderson, Paul S., "Apparent Decline in Capital Output Ratios," *Quarterly Journal of Economics* (November 1961): 615–634.

Elder, Charles R., "Explaining the Increase in Public Employee Unionization" (Ph.D. dissertation; Madison: University of Wisconsin, 1972).

Goodwin, R. M., *Socialism, Capitalism and Economic Growth* (New York: Cambridge University Press, 1967).

Grubbs, D. H., and Richard D. Sheridan, eds., *Tennessee Water Resources Conference Proceedings, May 1–2, 1961* (Knoxville: University of Tennessee Bureau of Public Administration, 1961).

Henderson, Gordon D., and Robert A. Mundheim, "Applicability of the Federal Securities Laws to Pension and Profit Sharing Plans," *Law and Contemporary Problems* (summer 1964): 795–841.

Hodges, Wiley E., "Laissez-Faire in Virginia, 1789–1836," *Southern Political Science Journal* (1956).

Holcombe, David M., "The Western North Carolina Railroad and the State Democrats: An Era of Changing Philosophy," Unpublished Master's thesis, Wake Forrest University, 1966.

Kaiser, Richard D., "A Comparison of the Workingman in England and the United States in the 1890's," Unpublished Master's thesis, Western Michigan University, 1970.

Lybbert, Jay. "Automatic Data Processing in the Intergovernmental Tax Information Exchange Program," Unpublished Master's thesis, Florida State University at Tallahassee, 1966.

Massey, Sarah S., "The Financial Policies of Alexander Hamilton," Unpublished Master's thesis, Jacksonville State University, 1962.

Nagley, Philip, "Reaction of the Union Labor Press to the NIRA," Unpublished Master's thesis, Columbia University, 1968.

Somers, Herman, and Anne R. Somers, "Health Insurance: Are Cost and Quality Controls Necessary?" *Industrial and Labor Relations Review* (July 1960): 581–595.

Tucker, G. S. L., "Ricardo and Marx," *Economica* (August 1961): 252–269.

Vaughn, James Abbott, "The Economic Policies of the Last Royal Governor of Massachusetts, Thomas Hutchinson," Unpublished Ph.D. dissertation, Boston University, 1950.

# 23 national welfare

## human and natural resources

UNTIL THE late nineteenth century, there was no apparent need for public welfare. While local governments and private charities provided some minimal welfare measures for the disabled and orphaned, almost all people belonged to a family unit that provided them with the necessities of life. Those people who had no immediate family found lodgings with other families. People with severe diseases and/or mental disorders were cared for in private hospitals, asylums, and parish houses.

With the growth of industry and the large-scale immigration to the cities, however, the number of small, self-reliant family units gradually decreased. The thousands, and eventually millions, who moved to the cities had to depend more and more on outside assistance. This expanding urbanite population could not grow its own food or manufacture its own clothing, nor could it, in many cases, find the work or housing necessary for survival. Many of the immigrants, whether from rural America or Southern and Eastern Europe, were unskilled and uneducated, while many others were endowed with skills inappropriate to city life. Consequently, more and more Americans were forced to rely on government for social and economic assistance.

Today, there are 204 million individuals living in the United States. In 1970, more than 12 million of these people, because of age or lack of education or skills, were on welfare. Because of the increasingly large number who need help, national, state, and local governments have become increasingly active in providing for citizens who are unable to support themselves because of physical disabilities, death, or desertion of the family breadwinner, sickness, or inadequate training.

# Providing for the national welfare

The welfare legislation that exists today developed out of the Great Depression of the 1930s. The depression pointed out that the majority of people had no way of providing for themselves in the event of a national disaster. Even the most ambitious and industrious citizens could do little in the face of the overpowering economic forces that wiped out homes, fortunes, and careers.

In 1932, the national government attempted to alleviate these troubles by issuing limited loans to state and local governments to aid the needy. However, this money was soon used up, and more lasting and sweeping national reforms were needed. When Franklin Roosevelt was inaugurated President in 1933, he proposed to provide those reforms through extensive welfare legislation.

The *Public Works Administration* (PWA), established in 1933, initiated permanent work projects, such as dams, bridges, housing, and tunnels to provide employment opportunities for those who were out of work. The PWA was complemented by the *Works Progress Administration* (renamed the *Works Project Administration* and known as WPA) which was initiated in 1935 to provide additional work on other public projects, such as airports, public buildings, and roads.

The PWA and the WPA, however, were only two of the many temporary reforms instituted by Roosevelt between 1933 and 1935. He also established grants-in-aid programs for local communities, and he instituted legislation to aid depressed farm and industrial areas. The Railroad Retirement Act of 1934, for example, was designed to provide benefits to retired railroad workers. By 1935, he had achieved the start of a permanent national welfare system—a system that has gradually been extended over the years.

## The Social Security Act

While some of Roosevelt's reforms were temporary "depression" measures designed to alleviate large-scale unemployment, they demonstrated both the need and the effectiveness of government intervention in such situations. The most important and permanent act to provide government assistance was the *Social Security Act* of 1935.

## OASDHI

The most important and widely publicized section of the Social Security Act was that which created a system of retirement benefits based on a national insurance program. Currently known as *OASDHI* (Old-Age, Survivors, Disability, and Health Insurance), the program originally was directed toward the aged. In 1939, the Act was extended to provide *survivors' insurance* for the family of a deceased breadwinner. In 1960, insurance was extended to people with physical handicaps; and in 1965, *health-care benefits* were extended to people over sixty-five. Today, the retirement program protects almost all Americans. Exempted are federal employees and railroad workers who have their own insurance programs, some state and local employees, and some employees of tax-free, nonprofit organizations. However, many of these organizations have refused to be tax exempt in order to obtain the benefits of OASDHI. OASDHI, which is administered by the national government alone, taxes a predetermined percentage of one's income every year, and puts the taxes into *a national trust fund*, to be returned to the payee, or his dependents, in the event of disability, retirement, or death. At the present time, OASDHI taxes are established on the basis of annual earnings up to $7,800. Presently, employers and employees pay a 4.8 percent tax on their earnings under $7,800. This amount is scheduled to be increased to 5.65 percent in 1973. Self-employed persons pay 6.9 percent, which is scheduled to be increased to 7.65 percent in 1973.[1]

In order to be paid in full, a person must be fully insured for a predetermined time; the required time is presently set at five years. Exceptions are made for persons over the age of seventy-two who are eligible regardless of prior earnings; they receive a minimum of $40, a maximum of $60 per month. Retirement payments are made on a monthly basis and range from a minimum of $70 to a maximum of $483, depending on the amount the individual has paid into the fund over the years and on the number of people in his family who must rely on additional so-called *secondary benefits*. Men and women become eligible for full retirement payments at the age of sixty-five, providing they are not earning more than $1,680 annually from jobs covered by OASDHI. A percentage of the full payment may be acquired at an earlier age. At age seventy-two, any person, regardless of earnings, may collect full benefits. Permanently disabled workers may receive full benefits at any time; these benefits are equal to the amounts they would receive as old-age benefits.

Secondary benefits provide for payments to the insured for family members. Among those for whom these benefits are paid are disabled children, dependent children less than eighteen years of age, dependent husbands, elderly wives, and the elderly widowed. In 1970, the maximum amount paid to a family member was $434.

## Unemployment insurance

The Social Security Act of 1935 also set up a system of *unemployment insurance,* to alleviate the effects of economic recessions, layoffs, and cutbacks. While some state-sponsored unemployment programs existed prior to 1935 (Wisconsin had passed one in 1932, with benefits due in 1936), many states were reluctant to establish provisions for unemployment. They feared that businesses in those states that did not initiate similar programs would not have to bear their costs and would thus be at an advantage.

The Social Security Act, however, induced the states to adopt an unemployment system by levying a payroll tax (now 3.2 percent) on all employers

## How OASDHI works

[1] *Statistical Abstracts of the US for 1970* (Washington, D.C.: Department of Commerce, 1970), p. 288.

## How OASDHI pays

(now of four or more persons) on the first $3,000 earned annually by the employee. (*The Employment Security Amendments of 1970* provide for an increased amount in 1972: 3.2 percent of $4,200.) The act, however, stipulated that the employer could forward this amount to a state employment program approved by the federal government, and could deduct up to 90 percent of his contributions to the state program from his national payroll tax. In other words, the national government would collect only 10 percent of the payroll tax—which would be used for administrative costs—if the employer contributed to a nationally approved state program. Although states were free to refrain from using the national program, it was pointless to do so, because they must pay the tax regardless of participation. By 1937, all states had passed unemployment laws.

Drawing by Wright in The Miami *News* (March 21, 1971).

## Who is eligible for unemployment compensation

The Social Security Act allowed each state to administer the program and to decide who is eligible, when they are eligible, and how much compensation they should receive. While all states levy a tax on management, some also levy a tax on labor. The Social Security Act does not cover migrant workers, domestics, the self-employed, state and local government employees, and employees of nonprofit organizations. Twenty-five states now extend coverage to firms with fewer than four employees and twenty states extend the coverage to state and local government workers. But only a few states have deviated from the national government's practice and provided compensation for nonprofit organizations, farmers, and domestics. Today, approximately 59 million people are protected by unemployment compensation.

Financial payments vary from state to state. Although the federal law requires that a tax be levied on the first $3,000 an employee makes, twenty-two states have broadened the initial salary stipulation. In Alaska, for example, the base is set at $7,200. Present compensation payments range from $152 per month in Tennessee to $235 in Connecticut.

Conditions for payment also vary from state to state. In most states, an eligible person must be able and willing to work, but unable to obtain a job. If the worker is unable to work because of sickness (or becomes sick during his period of unemployment), he is not eligible for payments. However, Rhode Island, California, New Jersey, and New York do provide compensation for illness or injury suffered off-the-job. Although unemployment payments are hardly enough to allow a person to live at the level provided by regular employment, they at least provide minimal economic security in times of hardship.

## Other insurance and assistance programs

### Veterans

Groups not covered by the Social Security Act—veterans, railroad workers, and federal employees—are covered by special insurance and assistance programs that are also sponsored by the national government.

Veterans and their dependents are considered eligible for government insurance benefits because of their military service to the nation. Inasmuch as almost 28 million Americans are veterans, a great number of people enjoy special veterans' benefits, including educational assistance, medical treatment, various forms of job training, housing loans, and pensions. Payments for disability vary according to the seriousness of the injury. Veterans who incur disabilities in service during war receive between $25 and $450 per month; veterans in peacetime receive between $20 and $360 per month. The survivors of veterans who died in service, or due to an injury or condition resulting from service, are eligible to receive the payments due the deceased.

Veterans may also qualify for treatment in Veteran's Administration hospitals. Some may receive home nursing care, while others receive care in VA physical rehabilitation centers, for example—at no cost, if the disability is service-connected, or if the veteran cannot personally defray the costs. The VA offers other economic assistance, such as job placement, low-cost insurance, and loans for a variety of purposes. In 1970, $8 billion was spent on veterans benefits, of which $5.4 billion was paid out for compensation and pension plans.

### Railroad workers

The system that provides national insurance and assistance to railroad workers is financed by equal contributions from employers and workers, and it is administered by the *Federal Railroad Retirement Board*. Under this system, railroad workers may receive up to twenty-six weeks' unemployment compen-

## Public employees

sation (also payable during periods of illness or disability), retirement payments, survivor payments, and disability payments. In 1970, about 623,000 railroad workers were covered by this broad system.

Almost all public employees are covered by insurance programs which include retirement, disability, and survivors' payments. Those civilians who are employed by the national government are included in the *Civil Service Retirement System*, which provides health insurance, in addition to pensions. Under this system, employees may retire at fifty-five, after thirty years of employment. However, civil servants are forced to retire at the age of seventy (except for certain elected and appointed officials and federal judges). A 6.5 percent deduction is levied on their annual salary, and the national government contributes matching funds.

Nearly 75 percent of all government employees are covered by some form of retirement program. Most of those who are not covered by such programs have been made eligible for OASDHI through special amendments to the Social Security Act.

## Public assistance

Despite the wide coverage of social security insurance and private pension plans, there are millions of needy people not eligible for payments, or not able to survive on the payments they receive. These include the unemployable who lack essential skills, old people who must rely solely on social security benefits, and those with young children whose fathers are absent from the home. Consequently, the Social Security Act established *public assistance programs*, to be financed out of general tax revenues. These programs currently include: Aid to Families with Dependent Children (AFDC), Old-Age Assistance (OAA), Aid to the Blind (AB), and Aid to the Permanently and Totally Disabled (APTD), initiated in 1950.

*John A. Hamilton, "Welfare: It May Soon Be Known As 'Workfare,'"* The New York Times *(June 27, 1971), Section 4, p. 4.*

In June, 1971, the House of Representatives passed a bill that could change welfare into the "workfare" urged by President Nixon. Whether the Senate will pass the proposal remains uncertain; nonetheless, the bill, termed by President Nixon "the most important social legislation in 35 years," indicates the trend toward a guaranteed annual income for all Americans rather than just for the jobless—as well as the trend toward creating jobs for those currently unemployed, but employable.

The legislation calls for subsidization of working as well as nonworking poor and requires employable recipients to take jobs. It also provides for an increase in Social Security benefits, a tightening of Medicare and Medicaid provisions, and, most significantly, sets a new minimum national income of $2,400 for a family of four. The government would give some aid to families earning up to $4,320. Supplementary amounts may be added by state governments.

The legislation attempts to standardize benefits. Up to now, each state has been free to establish its own income floor as the national government had none, and discrepancies have resulted. Some families of four in the category of aid to dependent children, and living in industrial states, receive as much as $4,000 annually, while other families of the same size in nonindustrial states receive only $2,000.

But the most novel aspect of the legislation is its emphasis on employment. The House bill would assign families with temporarily unemployed members to the Opportunities for Families Program run by the Department of Labor. Only those who are too young, ill or incapacitated, or who have very young children will be excluded from the employment requirement. If there are no employable members in the family, the family would be assigned to the Family Assistance Plan run by the Department of Health, Education and Welfare. Paradoxically, opposition to the omnibus bill came from two extremes—from (1) the left, which objected to the sweeping work requirement and to the benefit levels, which it considered too low; and from (2) the right, which objected to the income floor in principle as "a guaranteed annual wage."

Unemployment may also pose a problem for the program. In New York for example—where unemployment is currently estimated at 40 percent among urban black teen-agers—it may be difficult for state employment officials to find jobs on the open market for welfare recipients. Many liberals stress this fact, since the inability to find suitable jobs for the recipients could lead to harsher measures by conservatives.

[2] James C. Vadakin, *Children, Poverty, and Family Allowances* (New York: Basic Books, Inc., 1968) provides a complete analysis of family assistance programs and their future role.

# Aid to Families with Dependent Children (AFDC)

While the individual states are responsible for enacting and supervising these programs, the national government sets definite guidelines, as it assumes, in the end, well over 50 percent of the total cost paid to states through a variety of matching-grant programs. The state programs vary regarding the amount of payments granted to individuals and the persons who are eligible for payments. Though average monthly payments to the elderly are about $70, some states may pay as little as $40, while others pay over $100.

AFDC, which is administered by the states and funded by both state and national governments, provides economic assistance for families in which the father has left, either voluntarily or involuntarily.[2] In certain large urban areas, such as Detroit, New York, and Chicago, the number of families eligible for these payments has increased sharply in the past decade due to the increased number of illegitimate births, desertions by the breadwinner, divorces, and separations. Consequently, in 1970, AFDC gave aid to over six million mothers and children, and spent $3.5 billion.

Because of the unexpectedly large rise in the number of people eligible for AFDC, some critics are questioning whether or not the program is too lenient in its administration. They argue that not only does AFDC fail to keep families together, but it also encourages welfare dependence. Since most states decree that in order to be eligible for benefits, the husband must be absent from the home, they suggest that a father who cannot find work may desert his family in order to make them eligible for payments.

In order to combat what many consider to be the abuses of the act, Congress passed amendments in 1967 requiring that mothers and children age sixteen and over must join a vocational training program to be eligible for payments. It also provided that welfare benefits continue to working mothers. In addition, the amendment also provided for day-care centers to be established for children of working mothers.

Programs such as AFDC have become volatile political issues. Some are opposed to AFDC because they feel that the government has assumed too much responsibility for its citizens and has encouraged idleness, while others feel that government has not assumed enough responsibility and they point to Sweden, Great Britain, and Australia, where welfare systems are more generous and widespread.

# Providing for the national health

While the Social Security Act of 1935 provided the elderly with several forms of social welfare protection, the Act originally contained no special provisions for health care. Yet, it is precisely in the area of health that the elderly needed help the most. Since the medical expenses of the aged often exceeded the money allotted to them from social security benefits, many were forced to rely on relatives, charity, and voluntary groups of many sorts for assistance. Even though other western nations, such as Great Britain, Sweden, France, and West Germany, had already instituted national coverage, national health insurance was a controversial issue in the United States for many years, and did not become a reality until 1965.

For some one hundred seventy years prior to 1965, however, the national government had been involved in some aspects of the nation's health. In 1798, the national government set up the *Public Health Service* to provide in-hospital medical treatment for merchant seamen. By 1946, the Public Health Service had extended its services to other special groups, including the Coast Guard and armed forces veterans. Presently, the Public Health Service —which is in the Department of Health, Education and Welfare—provides medical care for 800,000 individuals. In addition, the government provides

## The National Institute of Health (NIH)

health services for members of the armed forces, and dependents of army personnel. Today, some thirty million individuals receive health benefits directly from the national government.

The Public Health Service conducts its research activities through the *National Institutes of Health*, which was established in 1948 (and reorganized in 1968) for the purpose of conducting medical research. Although the NIH is only one of many institutions conducting research on medical problems, it is the largest. Working in conjunction with many other institutions, universities, and hospitals, the NIH, in 1957, supplied $250 million for medical research; in 1962, it spent $738 million; the current expenditure is about $1.4 billion.

In recent years, the main concentration has shifted from communicable diseases (viruses, polio, malaria) to chronic diseases and disabilities (cancer, heart disease, arthritis, and mental illness). In addition, research is being conducted on environmental health problems, such as radiation, water and air pollution. In the last few years, Congress has consistently increased appropriations for the NIH.

"It says here the economy needs cooling off."

© 1969 by Herblock
in The Washington *Post*.

## Personnel and hospital programs

In addition to providing for extensive research, the national government has also been active in building new hospitals and establishing needed training programs for hospital personnel. In 1946, Congress passed the *Hill-Burton Act*, which has since granted over $5 billion for hospital construction. And in 1963, the *Health Profession Education Assistance Act* authorized grants for medical and dental schools, while the *Nurse Training Act* of 1964 authorized grants for the construction of nursing schools, student loans to nurses, and the expansion of nurses' training programs.

In recent years, the government has also authorized scholarships for medical students who need financial assistance to complete their training. Because of the high cost of medical training in the United States, only those students with substantial financial resources are able to complete medical studies. Because of this situation, and because of the limited number of openings in the nation's medical schools, there is still a critical shortage of doctors in the United States.

## Medicare health insurance for the old

Despite the extensive provisions for medical research, hospital construction, and supplementary health training, national health insurance for the old and the poor was the focus of intense debate for many years. While President Truman had urged Congress to pass legislation to create health insurance as early as 1949, the American Medical Association (AMA) waged such a strong fight against national insurance that until *Medicare* was passed in 1965 all proposals were defeated. The AMA, which represented some two hundred thousand practicing doctors in the United States, argued that such a program would "socialize" medicine, that private insurance plans were sufficient, and that the centralization of medicine under federal control would lower medical standards.

However, no arguments could conceal the fact that most of the elderly could not afford health insurance, and even those who could afford it found it difficult to obtain because of their status as "high-risk" clients. Most of all, no argument could conceal the fact that over one-fourth of the nation's hospital beds were occupied by people over sixty-five.

The first step toward government health insurance was finally taken in 1960, with the passage of the *Kerr-Mills Bill*. Authorizing the national government to match state grants in defraying the cost of medical expenses for the needy elderly, the bill also provided separate federal matching-grant programs to help older people with insufficient incomes to meet necessary and extra medical expenses. The bill, however, did not provide uniform nationwide coverage, as participation of states was not mandatory and less than half availed themselves of the national grants. As a result, pressure for new legislation continued, until in the summer of 1965, when Congress, prodded by President Johnson's persistent interest in national health care for the aged, finally passed a health bill.

The resulting *Medicare* (medical care insurance for the aged) provided basic hospital coverage and supplementary medical services for people over sixty-five. This bill initially included predominantly persons who were covered by social security. However, since the year 1968, all persons over sixty-five qualify for health insurance, if they have paid the Medicare tax for a determined period of time.

Today, basic Medicare coverage includes 90 days' hospital care, 100 days' convalescent care, and 100 home health-care visits. This care is financed by an increase in social security taxes. The social security money for Medicare is put into a separate *Federal Hospital Insurance Trust Fund*, the money of which is used for all those persons covered by social security. The persons not covered are supported by general tax revenues.

There is also a voluntary and supplementary health insurance program used by most Medicare participants which pays for 80 percent of other medical services, such as doctors' bills, home visits by medical personnel, outpatient diagnostic tests, X-ray treatments, and mental hospital care. These benefits can be obtained by an additional premium paid by each participant. To date, 3 million claims have been filed with Medicare and $30 billion has been spent on it.

## Medicaid health insurance for the poor

While Medicare covers only people over sixty-five, *Medicaid* which is also included in the Medicare Law of 1965, provides coverage for the poor. Medicaid is basically an extension of the Kerr-Mills program, since it increases national grants to the state. Federal grants from general tax revenues are supplied to the states' social services or welfare department for the purpose of giving medical assistance to all persons who qualify—that is, persons of any age, who qualify for public assistance. Medicare and Medicaid now cover some thirty million persons and may eventually lead to more comprehensive medical programs for persons of all ages and incomes.

## Food and drug programs

In addition to programs of national health and medical service, measures have been instituted by Congress in order to prevent the health disorders and diseases that may result from faulty foods and drugs. This legislation began with the *Pure Food and Drug Act* of 1906, which outlawed the interstate sale of impure or mislabeled drugs. In 1938, the *Food, Drug, and Cosmetic Act* gave consumers further protection by prohibiting the sale of misbranded foods, drugs, and cosmetics. The responsibility for the supervision of these programs is charged to the *Food and Drug Administration* of the Department of Health, Education, and Welfare.

Further protective drug legislation was passed in 1962 as a result of the damage done to newborn children whose mothers had been treated with the drug "thalidomide." This drug had not been properly tested in America before it was administered, and when taken by pregnant women it caused severe deformities in the fetuses of some of these women. Consequently, the *Kefauver-Harris Amendment* to the Food, Drug, and Cosmetic Act was passed, requiring that before a drug could be marketed, it had to be registered with the Food and Drug Administration, its effectiveness had to be properly tested, and any possible negative consequences had to be weighed against its positive effects. Only after the drug had been approved by the Federal Drug Administration (FDA) would the company receive a license to sell its product. In addition, the amendment required that a drug had to achieve what it was advertised to do.

# Providing for national housing

The urbanization of American society not only created economic and health problems, but also problems of housing. Attempts by the national government to alleviate the problems in this area were first directed at the middle classes. Since poor people had few resources when they moved to central cities, they were forced to live together in small and crowded quarters in areas that were soon identified as either city slums or ghettoes. While these slums began to develop as far back as the late nineteenth century, the national government did not attempt to alleviate the housing situation until the 1930s. At that time, however, most of the legislation passed was directed at the middle classes and not the poor who had to remain in the ghettoes. For example, the government attempted to help the citizen become a "homer" by extending the supply of mortgage money.

In 1932, the *Federal Home Loan Bank Act* encouraged people to build homes by issuing them loans. In 1933, the *Home Owner's Loan Corporation* made mortages available at low interest rates. And in 1934, the *Federal Housing Administration* (FHA) encouraged middle-income people to buy homes, by augmenting the supply of mortgage money and providing insurance for these mortgages: the government would insure the mortgage, and thereby encourage banking institutions to make loans to citizens.

After World War II, the national government aided servicemen to become home-owners by insuring loans that these men received for this purpose from private lending organizations. As of June, 1970, home loans, supervised by the *Veteran's Administration* (VA), have been made to more than 7 million veterans, 650,000 of whom have been aided since the Korean War.

## Housing for the poor

The urbanization problems of America have affected the lower classes even more severely than the middle classes. The poor had few resources when they moved to central cities, and were forced to live together in small and crowded quarters that became the slums and ghettoes of today. While these slums began to develop as far back as the late nineteenth century, the national government did not attack the slum problem until well into the Great Depression, with the *Housing Act of 1937*. This act encouraged the construction of low-rent housing by making federal loans and subsidies available to local housing authorities that wished to construct public housing facilities. Since that time, an average of 35,000 public housing units have been built annually.

The government determined, however, that the construction of low-rent housing projects was not sufficient to meet the needs of the urban poor. The new buildings might provide for some of the increasing number of low-income families in urban areas, but would not better the living conditions for those already entrenched in the overcrowded slum areas. With these problems in mind, Congress directed its attention to slum clearance and urban renewal. The *Housing Acts of 1949* and *1954* enabled local governments to undertake such programs by contributing two-thirds of the necessary funds for planning of projects and for the purchase and clearance of slum property to be repurchased and built on by public or private companies.

## Housing and Urban Development (HUD)

In 1965, the government created the Department of Housing and Urban Development to supervise the government's attack on the nation's housing problem, and to coordinate it with the overall attack on poverty. In 1968, the *Housing and Urban Development Act* was passed. Its objective is to build 6 million housing units annually over a ten-year period, and to make these units available to low-income groups through rent subsidies and mortgages. In order to be eligible for a rent supplement, a tenant must not earn more than a specific income (varying according to the region of the country and the type of housing in question). Rent supplements consist of the difference between 25 percent of the tenant's income and the rent he is to pay.

The Housing Act continued the 1965 policy of FHA mortgage insurance plans for low- and moderate-income families, while it also continued national subsidies to low-rent public housing. In addition, it provided grants to cover maintenance costs of urban homes. It also provided grants for the construction and development of local facilities, such as community centers, and parks and recreational centers.

Despite the high aims of the act, only limited funds have been appropriated for it in recent years, and housing in the large urban areas is deteriorating faster than it is being replaced.

Although the Housing Acts from 1949 through 1968 have resulted in 542 urban renewal projects, and another 1,181 under construction, 367 approved for planning, and 131 localities receiving annual aid for neighborhood renewal, critics claim that the government has not achieved enough. Unfortunately, slum clearance projects have created many new problems. In destroying shoddy and unsafe buildings, slum clearance has uprooted large groups of people who cannot find housing elsewhere because of economic or racial barriers, and who are forced to move into other slums. In many other instances, the new housing units are too expensive for the poor to afford. Furthermore, renewal projects often take a long time to institute, and authorities often object to the many regulations imposed by the national government. Both national and local governments, in an attempt to still the criticism, have been increasingly careful about the selection of sites and the use to which the buildings are put.

# Anti-poverty programs

While the Great Depression spurred the government to provide job, retirement, and housing security for the poorer members of society, little was done to modify the conditions that created poverty. Social security did not eliminate poverty, nor did it change the conditions that created poverty. While the number of poor declined from 47 million Americans (32 percent) in 1948 to 25.5 million (12.6 percent) in 1970 (poverty is set at a yearly income below $3,968 for an urban family of four), a substantial portion of Americans continue to live in substandard conditions, in the midst of rising incomes and improved standards of living.

As this fact became more apparent and noticeable to the public (the public that was earning substantial wages, and the public that was not), many social critics argued that the only lasting way to attack poverty was to make the mass of poor people able to support themselves by making them eligible, through education and training, for skilled and highly-paid jobs.

*William M. Blair, Food Stamp Plan Broadly Revised, The New York Times (July 23, 1971), p. 1.*

The national government's current Food Stamp Program enables the poor to purchase stamps from the government for below their face value and spend them at privately owned food stores. "Food stamps are sold at rates based on household monthly income. Bonus stamps are given to raise buying power in the grocery store."

On July 22, 1971, the plan was extensively revised. The now $2 billion plan, to be in full operation by January 1, 1972, will cover 12.5 million people by June 30, 1972, and will "retain the current provision that households in which all members get public assistance will remain eligible for stamps even if those households exceed new uniform national income standards."

Assistant Secretary of Agriculture, Richard E. Lyng, as spokesman for the revisions, explained that the revised rules will add 1.7 million people to the program and enable the poorest in the country, estimated at 900,000, to get food stamps. A family of four with an income of less than $30 a month would pay nothing for $108 in food stamps.

The revised plan has altered the requirements for eligibility, and the extent of payments to participating families. Because of these changes, 65,000 persons will be eliminated from the plan. A family of four with the highest income allowed to be eligible for food stamps will pay $99 for $108 worth of stamps.

It is expected that migrant farm workers will benefit from the new provisions, while those in communal living conditions and college students will find it more difficult to use the program.

The revised regulations also retained a hotly debated provision to require all able-bodied adults to register for and accept jobs in return for food stamps. This provision was amended, however, to exempt persons whose health or safety would be jeopardized by work.

President John F. Kennedy initiated the "poverty programs" with the creation of the *Area Redevelopment Administration* in 1961, and the coincident passage of the *Appalachian Program*. This program attempts to provide roads, sewers, water facilities, recreational opportunities, job training, and other rehabilitative measures for the rural poor in Appalachia (parts of West Virginia) through cooperation of the national, state, and local governments.

## "Anti-Poverty Act"

The most important law to have emerged from the "war on poverty" started by President Kennedy, and continued by President Johnson, was President Johnson's *Economic Opportunity Act* of 1964, commonly known as the "Anti-Poverty Act." Primarily designed to educate and train young people who were handicapped because of inadequacies in their environment and home, the Economic Opportunity Act also formed an *Office of Economic Opportunity* (OEO)—now a branch of the Executive Office of the President —to supervise the allocation of monies and to administer programs aimed at eliminating poverty. The act presently authorizes funds for five major poverty programs:

*Project Head Start*, administered by the Department of Health, Education, and Welfare, was created in 1965 to prepare underprivilged preschool chlidren to enter school on a level comparable with children from more privileged backgrounds. The project runs year-long as well as summer programs in which children receive a nutritious diet, medical care, and educational instruction. To date, Project Head Start has initiated projects in more than 2,500 urban and rural areas across the country and it has helped one-and-a-half million children.

For youngsters in need of training, two approaches have been initiated. One is the *Neighborhood Youth Corps*, which tries to motivate either potential or actual high-school dropouts by making supplementary work programs available to youth between the ages of sixteen and twenty-one. Under the aegis of the Department of Labor, it provides full-time summer work and part-time work during school months to students who stay in school. Jobs are arranged in community centers, libraries, and nonprofit organizations through contracts with the Department of Labor.

**Federal Aid to the Poor, 1970**

| | (Billions of dollars) |
|---|---:|
| Social Security | $10.0 |
| Welfare | |
|     Public assistance | 3.9 |
| Nutrition | |
|     Food stamps | 0.6 |
|     Child nutrition | 0.5 |
| Health | |
|     Medicare | 2.4 |
|     Medicaid | 2.1 |
|     OEO programs | 0.1 |
| Employment | |
|     Manpower development | 1.0 |
|     Unemployment insurance | 0.6 |
|     Employment services | 0.2 |
|     Work incentives | 0.1 |
| Education and Youth | |
|     Disadvantaged children | 1.1 |
|     Educational opportunity | 0.1 |
|     Other | 0.5 |
|     OEO programs | 0.5 |
| Housing | |
|     Public housing and rent supplements | 0.3 |
|     Model cities and other | 0.2 |
| Other | |
|     Veteran's Administration | 3.0 |
|     Other HEW programs | 1.3 |
|     Other agencies | 0.5 |
|     other OEO programs | 0.5 |
|     Indian affairs | 0.1 |
|     Rural poverty | 0.1 |
| Total | $29.7 |

Sources: U.S. Bureau of the Budget and Office of Economic Opportunity.

Another approach to aid youth is the *Job Corps*, currently an agency within the Department of Labor designed to aid the poorest and least-motivated students. To aid these students, the Job Corps sets up urban training centers, through contracts with manufacturers, businessmen, schools, and rural camps. In these centers, young people receive training that will enable them to work in industry and agriculture upon the completion of their two-year training. Throughout this period, they are also given food, clothing, shelter, medical care, and a small allowance. The Corps, however, is now being phased out. Supplementary programs that provide educational and training opportunities for residents of poverty areas are *Community Action Programs* (CAPS). Through federal grants, CAPS sets up community programs such as day-care centers, law services, educational programs, birth control clinics, and information centers to deal with consumer problems.

The last of the major programs is an organization whose purpose is to improve the quality of life in poverty areas. *Volunteers in Service to America* (VISTA) sends volunteers to the poorest communities of the United States—particularly the Indian reservations in the Southwest and the Appalachia region of the East—in order to rehabilitate residents through programs in areas such as education, housing, and health.

All these programs, however, have been severely criticized. Many critics claim that the programs do not make enough funds available to deal adequately with the problems of poverty on a large enough scale. Others charge that existing funds are misused, wasted, or diverted into unnecessary and irrelevant programs.

## Training for adults

The aforementioned programs have as one of their main goals the education of underprivileged youth; however, there are a great number of adults who are unable to find suitable work because they lack appropriate training or have been replaced by automation. The government, therefore, has initiated adult training programs, commonly called "manpower" programs, designed to give these adults skills that will equip them to handle specific jobs. Although manpower training has only recently become a significant government objective, such programs began as early as 1917, when the *Smith-Hughes Act* initiated grants to states for vocational training in the public schools. In 1956, the national government granted aid to states for the training of practical nurses; and in 1958, the *National Defense Education Act* (NDEA) established additional funds for the educating of teachers in science, math, and foreign languages, and for improving the vocational training facilities of states. The most important act of recent years is the *Manpower Development and Training Act* of 1962, which was directed toward retraining workers displaced by automation. The act authorized that general education programs be administered by state units, and that employers give on-the-job training to employees who lack precise skills, but have the potential for developing them. The national government agreed to bear 90 percent of the cost.

## Manpower Development and Training Act (MDTA)

In 1966, various amendments to this act were passed—so that workers who were forty-five years old and older could gain needed job skills and so that people serving prison terms could find work upon release. More attention was also given to courses that would upgrade the skills of already-employed workers who desired to raise their job levels.

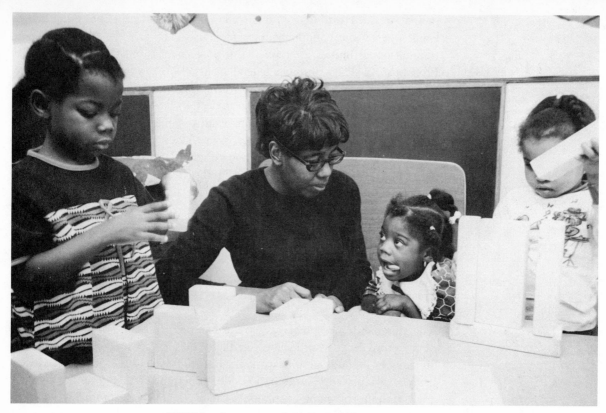

*VISTA volunteers work in depressed areas
of the United States to educate the children
and their parents.*

## Job Opportunity in Business Sector (JOBS)

In 1968, the National Alliance of Businessmen, a privately organized and funded association, formed *JOBS* in order to retrain the hard-core unemployed. While JOBS does receive some government aid, the major portion of expenses is paid by the participating companies, such as IBM, Chrysler Motors, and American Airlines.

Other manpower training programs include the "labor-mobility demonstration project" of 1963, which designated $5 million for the relocation of displaced workers. More recently, President Nixon authorized $42 million to be used for the retraining and relocation of engineers and scientists who are now out of work due to the recent decrease in defense production and the decline in aerospace spending.

## Educational programs

While training programs to make youth and adults capable of handling specific jobs are an immediate way of thwarting the unemployment and poverty problems, more lasting reforms must come through education. Although training programs can equip individuals with specific skills, only education—

that is, the development of more general and theoretical knowledge—can prepare individuals to go on to more specialized and challenging careers. The awareness that education is a prerequisite for personal advancement has encouraged government at all levels to appropriate more money for the financing of education.

The first wave of educational legislation took place during the Great Depression, when the New Deal extended the national government's involvement in education by allocating funds for educational facilities and programs from the nursery to the adult education level. Further aid came in 1940 and 1944 with the passage of the *Lanham Act* and the *Servicemen's Readjustment Act* respectively. The Lanham Act assisted local governments in building and running schools in areas where military bases had been very rapidly expanding. Known as the *GI Bill of Rights*, the Servicemen's Readjustment Act provided assistance to World War II veterans who wished to complete their education.

During the 1950s, legislation was enacted that was designed to promote the research and teaching of subjects considered vital to national defense, such as science, engineering, and foreign languages. In 1950, the National Science Foundation (NSF) authorized grants and loans for both applied and theoretical research in science and engineering. Similar projects were sponsored by the National Institutes of Health (NIH), the Atomic Energy Commission (AEC), and the National Aeronautics and Space Administration (NASA). The *National Defense Education Act* (NDEA) of 1958 was similarly designed to improve the teaching of subjects considered vital to national defense, such as the physical and social sciences, mathematics, and foreign languages. The NDEA encouraged the pursuit of studies in these fields by issuing low-interest loans and generous grants and fellowships to students who wished to study these subjects in graduate school.

While the legislation of the 1950s extended federal involvement in education, this involvement was related primarily to higher education. Bills that were introduced to provide general aid to education were defeated in Congress because of the church-state and race issues, as well as opposition to and fear of federal control over education.

Critics argued that parochial schools should not receive government aid, because it would violate the separation of church and state doctrine. Many maintained, too, that segregated schools were not entitled to such assistance. However, these arguments, like those opposing Medicare, could not conceal the fact that many school systems suffered from serious financial problems. Nor could critics of national aid to education conceal the fact that there was a direct relationship between the educational level of a child and the quality of the school system that had educated him. In the wake of President Johnson's landslide victory in 1964, Congress finally passed a general aid to education bill (the *Elementary and Secondary Education Act*), which Johnson signed outside the small elementary school that he had attended in Stonewall, Texas.

In order to bypass the church-state issue, the Act was offered as an "anti-poverty" bill that had as its main goal the education of poor children. Although it was designed to aid school districts with a majority of students from low-income families, funds have been assigned to practically all school districts, as well as to most parochial schools. In order to be eligible, a school district need only show that 3 percent of its students, or 100 of its children come from homes defined as poor. However, districts that have a high density of low-income families receive more financial assistance. Thus, the Act tries to apportion funds in such a way that children from deprived environments will have educational facilities comparable to those for children from wealthier districts.

Appropriated funds are used to build school and library facilities, establish special remedial and cultural programs, provide counseling services, edu-

## The Elementary and Secondary Education Act (1965)

cational radio and television programs, and special equipment and facilities. These funds are available to all schools, parochial or public, provided they have the required number of children from low-income families.

**The Higher Education Act (1965)**

Before 1965, federal aid to colleges and universities was given only for the construction of university buildings and classrooms, or for the funding of some graduate programs. The *Higher Education Act* of 1965 was a milestone, because it extended federal aid to undergraduate students who showed financial need and intellectual promise. The grants for undergraduates vary from $200 to $800 per year. Students whose families earn less than $15,000 per year can defer repayment of these loans until after college. This Act also set up and financed "work-study" programs that allowed a student to earn money while attending classes.

The Higher Education Act also provides funds, equipment, and library materials for new colleges that are often struggling; many small black colleges in the South have been the recipients of significant aid under this program. The law also makes available matching grants to states wishing to develop university-run community services that relate to the problems of metropolitan areas.

# Government and the natural resources

When Teddy Roosevelt proposed that conservation of our natural resources be a major consideration of government, many people shook their heads with mild amusement and considered it another one of his far-fetched schemes. Sixty years later, when President Johnson's wife, Ladybird, proposed that conservation of natural resources be a national preoccupation, people still shook their heads and considered the proposal visionary. But recently, President Nixon announced that the decade of the seventies must "absolutely be the years when America pays its debt to the past by reclaiming the purity of its air, its waters, and our living environment. It is literally now or never."[3] At the same time, he signed into law the *National Environmental Policy Act* of 1969, which made protection of the nation's environment federal policy, and created a three-man council to conduct studies and research on environmental protection systems.

[3] Congressional Quarterly, *Man's Control of his Environment* (Washington, D.C.: Congressional Quarterly, Inc., 1970), p. 1. This publication is the basic source for information on Government and Natural Resources. See pages 13–15, 18–20, and 36–38.

Today, the "environment" has become such an important part of the American conscience that ecology (the study of the relationship between organisms and their environment) has become a byword on college campuses, where special programs and institutes have been set up specifically for the purpose of protecting the environment. Publishers are printing on recycled paper in order to prevent waste and to preserve needed timber; children are collecting bottles and cans for recycling; cities and/or industries have organized campaigns to bring in used materials for reuse; and Earth Day has become an annual festival in many cities and towns.

Just why this concern for the environment should have developed so recently is difficult to explain. Certainly part of the reason for it lies in our increasing desire to protect man's environment against all kinds of natural and external disasters; part lies in an increasing sensitivity to the "evils" produced by technology; and part in our increasing belief that technology can relieve the very problems that it has created. While poets and writers have always objected to the ugliness of cities and the horrors of factories (Charles Dickens often compared the industrial parts of London to a biblical city of sin), it is only the massive technological advances of the present that have made these blights noticeable on a mass level. Even the most conscientious American has become, in some ways, a contributor to a situation that hurts him and others. One observer has noted that each American will "contribute his share to the 142 million tons of smoke and fumes, seven million junked cars, 48 billion cans and 26 billion bottles the overburdened environment must absorb each year."[4] Controlling the environment is, therefore, an important part of the battle against disease, bad health, and poverty.

[4] Congressional Quarterly, *Man's Control of his Environment*, p. 1.

## Purifying the water

Water has always been a symbol of purity, regeneration, and life; yet, its recent pollution by sewage, gases, and chemicals has made it a source of disease, dirt, and decay. In January, 1969, an oil slick burst from oil well drilling on the coast of Santa Barbara, California, and created $1.3 million in damages, blackening thirty miles of southern California beaches. In March, 1969, the Food and Drug Administration discovered that 28,150 pounds of Coho salmon contained high and dangerous DDT residues, as a result of the pesticides that enter waterways through waste and sewer systems. Later in 1969, Congressman Henry Reuss and Senator Gaylord Nelson (both Democrats of Wisconsin) introduced bills to ban the sale of detergents that contain phosphates; phosphates have been shown to stimulate plant life (mostly algae) in water, thereby removing needed oxygen, and making lakes into swamps and then into dry land before their natural dying age.

## Water Quality Improvement Act (1970)

In an effort to purify the water that is so vital for the survival of mankind, Congress has passed several pieces of legislation designed to limit the output of contaminating material into lakes, streams, rivers, and oceans. The first of these was the *Water Pollution Control Act* of 1948, which allocated money for sewage plant construction loans, authorized the Justice Department to file suits against polluters after notices and hearings, and created a Water Pollution Control Advisory Board. In 1952, this program was extended for three years; and in 1956, additional grants amounting to $50 million yearly were allocated. These early laws, however, were relatively ineffective, because they were financially inadequate and socially unenforced.

In 1964, the *Federal Water Pollution Control Administration* was set up within the Department of Health, Education, and Welfare in order to supervise antipollution programs, and the Secretary was given authority to institute water quality standards for interstate waters. The following year, 1965, the *Water Quality Act* strengthened national antipollution legislation; it ordered states to create and enforce water quality standards for interstate bodies of water by 1967.

"So *that's* where it goes! Well, I'd like to thank you fellows for bringing this to my attention."

Drawing by Stevenson © 1970
The New Yorker Magazine, Inc.

The most comprehensive pollution act passed was the *Water Quality Improvement Act* of 1970. This Act, prompted by the oil spill in Santa Barbara, requires the owner of a ship or sea facility to pay for cleaning up oil spills, unless the operator can prove that he is not in any way responsible for the spill. In addition, the Act requires builders of nuclear power plants to accept state water pollution standards. Finally, this important Act renamed the Water Pollution Control Administration the Federal Water Quality Administration, and created an Office of Environmental Quality.

Lobbyists against water pollution, as well as individual legislators, are now urging Congress to consider additional measures that will: ban the production of all detergents containing phosphates; build large dumping reservoirs where needed along the Great Lakes to collect harmful sludge; tax industries that dump pollutants; and grant allocations for building municipal sewage treatment plants. While it cannot be ascertained how many of these measures will be passed, it is certain that, for the first time, the nation is attempting to make water safe for fish, fowl, and plants to live in, and for all human beings to drink. Several state and local laws have been passed and, more important, the national government has shown a greater willingness to enforce existing legislation.

## Purifying the air

While water pollution is caused by sewage and chemicals, most air pollution is caused by the unburned particles of coal, soot, lead, and gases (such as sulphur dioxide, hydrocarbons, and carbon monoxide) that are poured into the atmosphere from factories, mills, and automobiles. Intense pollution of this kind can cause severe damage to health. For example, a four-day fog in the small mill town of Donora, Pennsylvania, in 1948 caused numerous illnesses and twenty deaths as a result of the sulphur dioxide emitted by steel and chemical plants. Similar disasters occurred in the Neuse Valley in Belgium in 1930, and in London in 1952. Since a recent Task Force concluded that the only way to alleviate these situations is to shut down all heating and electrical units that cause such combustion, the challenge for air pollution control experts is to find ways that will limit the combustile materials in the air, and still sustain the electrical and generating services required for our existence and comfort.

## Cleaning the air

In 1955, national air pollution control legislation began with a bill authorizing the Public Health Service to conduct air pollution research, costing $5 million per year for a five-year period. Once again, however, the legislation was inadequate to combat air pollution problems. In 1963, the *Clean Air Act* increased appropriations for this research to $95 million for the fiscal years 1964–1967, and provided that legal action be taken against any state or city that did not attempt to combat air pollution. The following year, 1965, the Act was extended to establish exhaust-emission standards for new cars, buses, and trucks.

The most comprehensive piece of new legislation, however, has been the *Air Quality Act* of 1967, which strengthened the ability of the national, state, and local authorities to institute pollution control. This bill authorizes the Secretary of the Department of Health, Education, and Welfare to specify air quality regions in all fifty states; it provides for financing by the national government of regional control commissions to be created by state governors, and authorizes HEW to enforce air quality standards in cases of violation or

"Air pollution? Nonsense! It's just gloom . . ."

Drawing by Long in The Minneapolis *Tribune* (May 31, 1970).

refusal to adopt them. Recently, President Nixon has requested further air pollution measures, including: air quality standards for specific pollutants from immobile sources; state exhaust-emission standards for automobiles and industries; national emissions standards for stationary sources; federal regulation of fuels and fuel additives; and the strengthening of national enforcement in all these areas.

**Preserving the land**

Land conservation has been a concern of the national government since the late eighteenth century; but how to conserve this land has recently become a subject of great controversy. Although there are now about eleven acres of land for every person in the United States, most people live in relatively congested areas, where ten square feet of greenery is considered a luxurious Eden. Cities occupy only 8 percent of the nation's land area, while farm acreage accounts for 49 percent. Consequently, the great problem that faces the national government—which owns 770 million acres, or 34 percent of the United States land—is how to make it benefit the vast number of people who live in crowded urban areas, and how to meet the growing demand for rural recreation in the national parks. This involves a greater effort to make parks and recreational facilities available to urban residents; a greater effort to diversify the congested urban centers of America; and a greater effort to conserve the mineral, metal, and timber resources of this nation.

In 1964, the Land and Water Conservation Fund was established for the acquisition of land for parks and recreational areas near the urban areas of the nation. However, not until 1971 was adequate money ($327 million) appropriated for the acquisition of this land.

Drawing by Franklin © 1968
The New Yorker Magazine, Inc.

*"Coalition Blocks Bill to Increase Federal Timber Cuts," Man's Control of the Environment: To Determine His Survival . . . or To Lay Waste His Planet (Washington, D.C.: Congressional Quarterly, Inc., 1970), pp. 70–72.*

On February 26, 1970, the House of Representatives refused to consider a bill calling for increased cutting of timber in national forests. The bill,

The National Forest Timber Conservation and Management Act, was shelved because, in trying to increase the lumber supply needed for housing construction, it also stirred up the powerful anger of those working to preserve the environment.

Submitted to the House by the Subcommittee on Forests of the House Agricultural Committee, the bill proposed that the Secretary of Agriculture revise permissible forest harvesting rates, that the United States Treasury create a High Timber Yield Fund, and that one year from the bill's enactment, the Secretary of Agriculture submit to Congress a program to develop and manage all national forest resources and to ensure that small business acquire a fair proportion of the marketable timber.

The bill, initiated by the lumber industries as a result of pressure from the housing industry, was supported by the National Association of Home Builders, the National Forest Products Association, several home builder and urban lobbyists, Secretary of Agriculture Clifford M. Hardin, and Secretary of Housing and Urban Development George Romney. They argued that the housing shortage was due, in large part, to a lack of timber; and that unless more was available, the new housing that was critically needed could not be provided. They additionally noted that "almost any wood substitute required the development of depletable resources and the production of water and air polluting wastes in the manufacturing process."

Opponents of the bill, however, refused to accept this statement, arguing that the housing shortage was, instead, a result of high interest rates, high land prices, and high labor costs—not lumber.

Opponents argued that the timber industry, whose real worry is that wood will be displaced by lower-priced substitutes, was trying to hold on to the construction material market.

They formed an *ad hoc* Conservation Coalition (whose ten members included, among others, the Sierra Club, the Audubon Society, The Wilderness Society, and the National Rifle Association). The committee stressed the disproportionate emphasis on logging, as opposed to other uses of national forests—for example, parks and recreational areas. Led by the Sierra Club, the coalition canvassed Congress, providing information kits to its members and visiting their offices. It also sent information to members of the Sierra Club, urging that they write to their representatives to oppose the bill.

The Conservation Coalition in the House gained enough support in the House to produce a 228–150 roll call vote rejecting the rule under which the Act was to be considered.

While other acts were passed to beautify highways and to preserve wilderness and scenic rivers, little was done to enforce these bills. The most comprehensive legislation in the field of land preservation is the National Land-Use Policy Act, which is now under consideration in Congress. The bill calls for the annual allocation of $50 million in grants-in-aid for state development and implementation of land-use plans. The money would be used for hiring and training personnel in both planning and management, and in funding land-use planning agencies.

Although the future of this Act is as yet uncertain, it is certain that more and more attention must and will be given to the conservation of land and all our other natural resources. Governmental resources in the form of money and political power, supported by public opinion, can move our nation to meet the challenge of preserving our natural resources.

# Glossary

**Aid to Families with Dependent Children** (AFDC)   Federally aided program which establishes a system of making payments to families in which there are children without fathers.

**Air Quality Act** (1967)   Legislation providing for means to establish and enforce national air quality standards.

**Appalachian Program**   Federal program initiated in 1961 to aid the hard-core poverty area of West Virginia by providing job training, roads, and employment.

**Area Redevelopment Administration**   Government organization that administers the program of federal grants and low-income loans made to poverty areas for industrial development and improvement of public facilities.

**Civil Service Retirement System**   Established by the Civil Service Retirement Act of 1920, a program for federal employees, which provides disability, retirement, and survivors' insurance, as well as health insurance, workmen's compensation, and sick leave.

**Clean Air Act** (1963)   Legislation increasing federal appropriations for air pollution research, prevention, and control, and which also encourages interstate cooperation.

**Community Action Programs** (CAPS)   Part of the federal antipoverty program allowing the poor to plan and operate urban antipoverty activities, such as legal services and day-care centers.

**Economic Opportunity Act** (1964)   Antipoverty legislation authorizing funds for programs to educate disadvantaged youth.

**Elementary and Secondary Education Act** (1965)   Legislation providing federal funds to build school facilities, establish special remedial and cultural programs, and provide counseling services, educational radio and television programs, and special equipment and facilities.

**Employment Security Amendment** (1970)   Amendments to the Social Security Act raising the taxable payroll base from $3,000 to $4,200—the base annually taxed at 3.2 percent.

**Federal Home Loan Bank Act** (1932)   Legislation providing loans for housing construction.

**Federal Hospital Insurance Trust Fund**   Pool for social security monies used for persons who qualify for the Medicare program of social security.

**Federal Housing Administration** (FHA)   Government organization established in 1934 to increase the supply of mortgages, now a part of the Department of Housing and Urban Development, and serving to supervise housing construction programs.

**Federal Railroad Retirement Board**   Organization that administers social insurance benefits to railroad workers.

**Federal Water Pollution Control Administration**   Established in 1964 as part of the Department of Health, Education, and Welfare, to supervise antipollution activities. Renamed by the Water Quality Improvement Act of 1970 as the Federal Water Quality Administration.

**Food and Drug Administration**   Division of the Department of Health, Education and Welfare which administers protective food and drug laws.

**Food, Drug, and Cosmetic Act** (1938)   Legislation prohibiting the sale of misbranded foods, drugs, and cosmetics.

**GI Bill of Rights (Servicemen's Readjustment Act)** (1944)   Legislation providing educational benefits to veterans.

**Health Profession Education Assistance Act** (1963)   Legislation authorizing grants for medical and dental schools.

**Higher Education Act** (1965)   Legislation extending federal aid to promising undergraduate students and to colleges.

**Hill-Burton Act** (1946)   Legislation granting federal aid for hospital construction.

**Home Owner's Loan Corporation**   Government organization formed in 1933 to make mortgages available at low-interest rates to potential home-owners.

**Housing and Urban Development Act** (1968)   Legislation designed to provide new or rehabilitated housing available to low-income groups through rent subsidies and mortgages.

**Housing Act** (1937)   Legislation providing federal loans and rent subsidies for the construction of public housing.

**Housing Acts of 1949 and 1954**   Legislation enabling local governments to undertake urban renewal programs by providing two-thirds of the necessary funds for planning of projects and clearance of slum property.

**Job Corps**   Antipoverty agency to train disadvantaged youths for jobs in industry and agriculture.

**Job Opportunity in Business Sector** (JOBS)   Program initiated in 1968 by private industry, and funded primarily by them, for the retraining of hard-core unemployed.

**Kefauver-Harris Amendment** (1962)   Amendment to the Federal Food, Drug, and Cosmetic Act of 1938, requiring that all drugs be registered with the Food and Drug Administration, and that they be tested thoroughly for safety and effectiveness before marketing.

**Kerr-Mills Bill** (1960)   Legislation authorizing the national government to match state grants for medical care for the elderly.

**Lanham Act** (1940)   Legislation to increase federal aid to schools in areas affected by military and defense activities.

**Manpower Development and Training Act** (1962) (MDTA)   Legislation designed to train and counsel unemployed workers.

**Medicaid**  Federal grant-in-aid program that provides medical care to those who qualify for public assistance, and to those who pass state-imposed means tests.

**Medicare** ("medical care insurance for the aged") (1965)  Legislation providing basic hospital coverage and supplementary medical services for people over sixty-five and financed through social security payroll tax.

**National Defense Education Act (NDEA)** (1958)  Legislation granting funds for training teachers in science, math, and foreign languages, and expanding state facilities for vocational education.

**National Environmental Policy Act** (1969)  Legislation that created a three-man council to conduct studies and research on environmental protection systems.

**National Institutes of Health**  Division of the Public Health Service established in 1948 for conducting medical research.

**national trust fund**  Pool of OASDHI funds collected from taxes, later returned to the payee, or his dependents, upon retirement, death, or disability.

**Neighborhood Youth Corps**  Program providing full-time summer work and part-time winter work opportunities to students who pursue their high school educations.

**Nurse Training Act** (1964)  Legislation authorizing grants for the construction of nursing schools, loans to student nurses, and nurses' training programs.

**OASDHI (Old-Age, Survivors, Disability, and Health Insurance)**  That part of social security system that provides insurance payments for those over sixty-five, families of deceased workers and disabled persons.

**Office of Economic Opportunity (OEO)**  Government agency that supervises the various poverty programs and oversees the distribution of federal funds.

**Project Head Start**  Program started in 1965 to prepare preschool children who are economically disadvantaged to enter school on a level comparable with children from more affluent backgrounds.

**public assistance programs**  Programs financed by general tax revenues to aid those ineligible for social security benefits, or unable to survive on the payments received: *Old-Age Assistance, Aid to Families with Dependent Children, Aid to the Blind, and Aid to the Permanently and Totally Disabled.*

**Public Health Service**  Federal agency within the Department of Health, Education and Welfare, which operates clinics, quarantine stations, and hospitals, and supports and engages in health research.

**Public Works Administration (PWA)**  Government organization created in 1933, which initiated permanent work projects to provide employment during the Depression.

**Pure Food and Drug Act** (1906)  Legislation prohibiting the interstate sale of adulterated or misbranded drugs.

**Smith-Hughes Act** (1917)  Legislation authorizing grants to states for vocational training in the public schools.

**Social Security Act** (1935)  Law that created several major governmental programs: old age and survivors' insurance, public assistance, and unemployment insurance.

**unemployment insurance**  That part of the social security system that makes insurance payments to workers who have lost their jobs.

**Veteran's Administration (VA)**   Independent government agency that provides a wide variety of services to ex-servicemen.

**Volunteers in Service to America (VISTA)**   Volunteer program that sends teams of people into economically depressed communities in the United States to work on local programs such as health, education, and housing.

**Water Pollution Control Act** (1948)   Earliest legislation to provide environmental protection, by authorizing the Justice Department to file suit against polluters.

**Water Quality Act** (1965)   Legislation requiring states to enforce water quality standards by a 1967 deadline.

**Water Quality Improvement Act** (1970)   Act to control the pollution of water resources by penalizing industrial polluters, and by establishing an Office of Environmental Quality in the Executive Office of the President.

**Works Progress Administration (WPA)**   Renamed *Works Project Administration*, an organization established by President Franklin Roosevelt in 1935 to provide work on public projects.

# Suggested readings

Blake, Peter, *God's Own Junkyard; The Planned Deterioration of America's Landscape* (New York: Holt, Rinehart and Winston, Inc., 1964). Attack on the exploitation of our land.

Caldwell, Lynton K., *Environment: A Challenge for Modern Society* (Garden City, N.Y.: Doubleday and Co., Inc., 1970). Discussion of the importance of the ecology as a major concern of public policy.

Caudill, Harry M., *Night Comes To The Cumberlands: A Biography of a Depressed Area* (Boston: Little, Brown and Co., 1963). Description of the destruction of the environment in eastern Kentucky as a result of the methods of coal mining used in the region.

Derthick, Martha, *The Influence of Federal Grants: Public Assistance in Massachusetts* (Cambridge, Mass.: Harvard University Press, 1970). Qualitative analysis of the Massachusetts public assistance program designed to show the effect that federal grants have on state and local politics and administrations.

Dorst, Jean, *Before Nature Dies* (Boston: Houghton Mifflin Co., 1970). Discussion of man's effect on the environment.

Dubois, René, *So Human an Animal* (New York: Charles Scribner's Sons, 1970). Vivid description of the current ecological crisis.

Ehrlich, Paul R., and Anne H. Ehrlich, *Population Resources Environment: Issues in Human Ecology* (San Francisco: W. H. Freeman and Co., 1970). Analysis of overpopulation and its consequences on both food supply and the environment.

Galbraith, John K., *The Affluent Society* (Boston: Houghton Mifflin Co., 1958). Analysis of the consequences of affluence in America; also an early warning of the existence of widespread poverty in America.

Harrington, Michael, *The Other America: Poverty in the United States* (New York: The Macmillan Co., 1962). Study of poverty in the midst of affluence, emphasizing the need for federal programs to aid the poor.

Hook, Sidney, ed., *Human Values and Economic Policy: A Symposium* (New York: New York University Press, 1967). Collection of papers by philosophers and economists discussing the questions of human wants and needs, and economic policy as a means to satisfy them.

Miller, Herman P., *Rich Man, Poor Man: The Distribution of Income in America* (New York: Thomas Y. Crowell Co., 1970). Analysis of income distribution in the United States in relation to education, occupation, religion, race, age, and other factors.

Moynihan, Daniel P., *Maximum Feasible Misunderstanding: Community Action In the War on Poverty* (New York: The Free Press, 1969). Critical analysis of one aspect of the federal government's war on poverty—the Community Action program.

Moynihan, Daniel P., ed., *Toward a National Urban Policy* (New York: Basic Books, Inc., 1970). Collection of papers on poverty, education, transportation, housing, crime, pollution, and other urban problems.

Nash, Roderick, *Wilderness and the American Mind* (New Haven, Conn.: Yale University Press, 1967). Historical analysis of American public opinion toward the nation's wilderness areas.

Seligman, Ben B., ed., *Poverty as a Public Issue* (New York: The Free Press, 1969). Collection of essays analyzing the problems of poverty and the government's attempts to solve them.

Sherraed, Thomas D., ed., *Social Welfare and Urban Problems* (New York: Columbia University Press, 1968). Collection of papers emphasizing the importance of social welfare policies and practices in relation to today's urban problems.

Udall, Stewart L., *The Quiet Crisis* (New York: Holt, Rinehart and Winston, Inc., 1963). Concise analysis of the problem of conserving the land.

Udall, Stewart L., *1976: Agenda for Tomorrow* (New York: Harcourt Brace Jovanovich, Inc., 1968). Analysis and proposed solutions to some current social, political, and economic problems in the United States.

Wilcox, Clair, *Toward Social Welfare* (Homewood, Ill.: Richard D. Irwin, Inc., 1969). Analysis of governmental programs designed to eliminate poverty and inequality of opportunity in America.

# Topics of further study

Davis, William W., "A Proposal of Financing Public Education in Texas," Master's thesis, North Texas State University, 1947.

Hayhurst, Donald E., "Development of Consumer Welfare as a Function of the National Government in the Food and Drug Administration," Ph.D. dissertation, University of Pittsburgh, 1962.

Jensen, Daniel, "The Civilian Conservation Corps: Youth's Second Chance," Master's thesis, San Diego State College, 1964.

Moore, L. F., "County Health Units in Virginia," Master's thesis, Stanford University, 1931.

# appendix A

## The Declaration of Independence, 1776

When in the course of human events, it becomes necessary for one people to dissolve the political bands which have connected them with another, and to assume among the Powers of the earth, the separate and equal station to which the Laws of Nature and of Nature's God entitle them, a decent respect to the opinions of mankind requires that they should declare the causes which impel them to the separation.

We hold these truths to be self-evident, that all men are created equal, that they are endowed by their Creator with certain unalienable Rights, that among these are Life, Liberty and the pursuit of Happiness.—That to secure these rights, Governments are instituted among Men, deriving their just powers from the consent of the governed, That whenever any Form of Government becomes destructive of these ends, it is the Right of the People to alter or to abolish it, and to institute new Government, laying its foundation on such principles and organizing its powers in such form, as to them shall seem most likely to effect their Safety and Happiness. Prudence, indeed, will dictate that Governments long established should not be changed for light and transient causes; and accordingly all experience hath shown, that mankind are more disposed to suffer, while evils are sufferable, than to right themselves by abolishing the forms to which they are accustomed. But when a long train of abuses and usurpations, pursuing invariably the same Object evinces a design to reduce them under absolute Despotism, it is their right, it is their duty, to throw off such Government, and to provide new Guards for their future security.—Such has been the patient sufferance of these Colonies; and such is now the necessity which constrains them to alter their former Systems of Government. The history of the present King of Great Britain is a history of repeated injuries and usurpations, all having in direct object the establishment of an absolute Tyranny over these States. To prove this, let Facts be submitted to a candid[1] world.

He has refused his Assent to Laws,[2] the most wholesome and necessary for the public good.

He has forbidden his Governors to pass Laws of immediate and pressing importance, unless suspended in their operation till his Assent should be obtained; and when so suspended, he has utterly neglected to attend to them.

He has refused to pass other Laws for the accommodation of large districts of people, unless those people would relinquish the right of Representation in the Legislature, a right inestimable to them and formidable to tyrants only.

He has called together legislative bodies at places unusual, uncomfortable, and distant from the depository of their Public Records, for the sole purpose of fatiguing them into compliance with his measures.

He has dissolved Representative Houses repeatedly, for opposing with manly firmness his invasions on the rights of the people.

He has refused for a long time, after such dissolutions, to cause others to be elected; whereby the Legislative Powers, incapable of Annihilation, have returned to the People at large for their exercise; the State remaining in the mean time exposed to all the dangers of invasion from without, and convulsions within.

He has endeavoured to prevent the population of these States; for that purpose obstructing the Laws of Naturalization of Foreigners;[3] refusing to pass others to encourage their migration hither, and raising the conditions of new Appropriations of Lands.

He has obstructed the Administration of Justice, by refusing his Assent to Laws for establishing Judiciary Powers.

He has made Judges dependent on his Will alone, for the tenure of their offices, and the amount and payment of their salaries.

He has erected a multitude of New Offices, and sent hither swarms of Officers to harass our People, and eat out their substance.[4]

He has kept among us, in times of peace, Standing Armies without the Consent of our legislature.

He has affected to render the Military independent of and superior to the Civil Power.

He has combined with others to subject us to a jurisdiction foreign to our constitution, and unacknowledged by our laws giving his Assent to their acts of pretended legislation:

For quartering large bodies of armed troops among us:

For protecting them, by a mock Trial, from Punishment for any Murders which they should commit on the Inhabitants of these States:

For cutting off our Trade with all parts of the world:

For imposing taxes on us without our Consent:

For depriving us in many cases, of the benefits of Trial by Jury:

For transporting us beyond Seas to be tried for pretended offences:

For abolishing the free System of English Laws in a neighboring Province,[5] establishing therein an Arbitrary government, and enlarging its Boundaries so as to render it at once an example and fit instrument for introducing the same absolute rule into these Colonies:

For taking away our Charters; abolishing our most valuable Laws, and altering fundamentally the Forms of our Governments:

For suspending our own Legislature, and declaring themselves invested with Power to legislate for us in all cases whatsoever.

He has abdicated Government here, by declaring us out of his Protection and waging War against us.

He has plundered our seas, ravaged our Coasts, burnt our towns, and destroyed the lives of our people.

He is at this time transporting large armies of foreign mercenaries to compleat the works of death, desolation and tyranny, already begun with circumstances of Cruelty & perfidy scarcely parallelled in the most barbarous ages, and totally unworthy the Head of a civilized nation.

He has constrained our fellow Citizens taken Captive on the high Seas to bear Arms against their Country, to become the executioners of their friends and Brethren, or to fall themselves by their Hands.

He has excited domestic insurrections amongst us, and has endeavoured to bring on the inhabitants of our frontiers, the merciless Indian Savages, whose known rule of warfare, is an undistinguished destruction of all ages, sexes and conditions.

In every stage of these Oppressions We have Petitioned for Redress[6] in the most humble terms: Our repeated Petitions have been answered only by repeated injury. A Prince, whose character is thus marked by every act which may define a Tyrant, is unfit to be the ruler of a free People.

Nor have We been wanting in attention to our British brethren. We have warned them from time to time of attempts by their legislature to extend an unwarrantable jurisdiction over us. We have reminded them of the circumstances of our emigration and settlement here. We have appealed to their native justice and magnanimity, and we have conjured them by the ties of our common kindred to disavow these usurpations, which, would inevitably interrupt our connections and correspondence. They too have been deaf to the voice of justice and of consanguinity.[7] We must, therefore, acquiesce in the necessity, which denounces our Separation, and hold them, as we hold the rest of mankind, Enemies in War, in Peace, Friends.

We, therefore, the Representatives of the united States of America, in General Congress, Assembled, appealing to the Supreme Judge of the world for the rectitude of our intentions, do, in the Name, and by Authority of the good People of these Colonies, solemnly publish and declare, That these United Colonies are, and of Right ought to be Free and Independent States; that they are Absolved from all allegiance to the British Crown, and that all political connection between them and the State of Great Britain, is and ought to be totally dissolved; and that as Free and Independent States, they have full Power to levy War, conclude Peace, contract Alliances, establish Commerce, and to do all other Acts and Things which Independent States may of right do. And for the support of this Declaration, with a firm reliance on the Protection of Divine Providence, we mutually pledge to each other our Lives, our Fortunes and our sacred Honor.

# Notes to the Declaration of Independence

1. Unbiased

2. In some of the colonies, laws passed by the colonial legislature required the approval of the British Crown before they became effective.

3. Colonial laws which established the procedures by which immigrants could obtain the privileges and immunities of citizenship.

4. To deprive the American colonists of their possessions, means, and wealth, either by requiring their cooperation and support or by actual confiscation of material possessions.

5. Reference to the Quebec Act of 1774, which provided among other things the adoption of French law in civil trials, which meant no right to trial by jury, and the extension of the boundaries of the Province of Quebec to include western land, some of which was claimed by several eastern colonies.

6. The colonists repeatedly requested that the King repeal his arbitrary policies and, in so doing, correct the injustices to which the colonists had been subjected.

7. Relationship based on ancestry or descent, referring to the English background of many American colonists.

# appendix B

## The Constitution of the United States of America

We the People of the United States, in Order to form a more perfect Union, establish Justice, insure domestic Tranquility, provide for the common defence, promote the general Welfare, and secure the Blessings of Liberty to ourselves and our Posterity, do ordain and establish this Constitution for the United States of America.

### ( ARTICLE I )

#### Section 1

[GENERAL LEGISLATIVE POWERS]

All legislative Powers herein granted shall be vested in a Congress of the United States, which shall consist of a Senate and House of Representatives.

#### Section 2

[HOUSE OF REPRESENTATIVES, ELECTIONS, QUALIFICATIONS, OFFICERS, AND IMPEACHMENT POWER]

The House of Representatives shall be composed of Members chosen every second Year by the People of the several States, and the Electors in each State shall have the Qualifications requisite for Electors of the most numerous Branch of the State Legislature.

No Person shall be a Representative who shall not have attained to the Age of twenty-five Years, and been seven Years a Citizen of the United States, and who shall not, when elected, be an Inhabitant of that State in which he shall be chosen.

Representatives and direct Taxes shall be apportioned among the several States which may be included within this Union,[1] according to their respective Numbers, which shall be determined by adding to the whole Number of free Persons, including those bound to Service for a Term of Years, and excluding Indians not taxed, three fifths of all other Persons.[2] The actual Enumeration shall be made within three Years after the first Meeting of the Congress of the United States, and within every subsequent Term of ten Years, in such Manner as they shall by Law direct. The Number of Representatives shall not exceed one for every thirty Thousand, but each State shall have at Least one Representative; and until each enumeration shall be made, the State of New Hampshire shall be entitled to chuse three, Massachusetts eight, Rhode-Island and Providence Plantations one, Connecticut five, New-York six, New Jersey four, Pennsylvania eight, Delaware one, Maryland six, Virginia ten, North Carolina five, South Carolina five, and Georgia three.

When vacancies happen in the Representation from any State, the Executive Authority[3] thereof shall issue Writs of Election[4] to fill such Vacancies.

The House of Representatives shall chuse their Speaker and other Officers; and shall have the sole Power of Impeachment.

## Section 3

[THE SENATE: ELECTION, QUALIFICATIONS, OFFICERS, AND IMPEACHMENT TRIALS]

The Senate of the United States shall be composed of two Senators from each State, chosen by the Legislature thereof,[5] for six Years; and each Senator shall have one Vote.

Immediately after they shall be assembled in Consequence of the first Election, they shall be divided as equally as may be into three Classes. The Seats of the Senators of the first Class shall be vacated at the Expiration of the second Year, of the second Class at the Expiration of the fourth Year, and of the third Class at the Expiration of the sixth Year, so that one third may be chosen every second Year; and if Vacancies happen by Resignation, or otherwise, during the Recess of the Legislature of any State, the Executive thereof may make temporary Appointments until the next Meeting of the Legislature, which shall then fill such Vacancies.

No person shall be a Senator who shall not have attained to the Age of thirty Years, and been nine Years a Citizen of the United States, and who shall not, when elected, be an Inhabitant of that State for which he shall be chosen.

The Vice President of the United States shall be President of the Senate, but shall have no Vote, unless they be equally divided.

The Senate shall chuse their other Officers, and also a President pro tempore, in the Absence of the Vice President, or when he shall exercise the Office of President of the United States.

The Senate shall have the sole Power to try all Impeachments. When sitting for that Purpose, they shall be on Oath or Affirmation. When the President of the United States is tried, the Chief Justice shall preside: And no Person shall be convicted without the Concurrence of two thirds of the Members present.

Judgment in Cases of Impeachment shall not extend further than to removal from Office, and disqualification to hold and enjoy any Office of honor, Trust or Profit under the United States: but the Party convicted shall nevertheless be liable and subject to Indictment, Trial, Judgment and Punishment, according to Law.

## Section 4

[STATE REGULATION OF CONGRESSIONAL ELECTIONS]

The Times, Places and Manner of holding Elections for Senators and Representatives, shall be prescribed in each State by the Legislature thereof; but the Congress may at any time by Law make or alter such Regulations, except as to the Places of chusing Senators.

The Congress shall assemble at least once in every Year, and such Meeting shall be on the first Monday in December, unless they shall by Law appoint a different Day.[6]

## Section 5

[CONGRESSIONAL RULES AND PROCEDURES]

Each House shall be the Judge of the Elections, Returns and Qualifications of its own Members,[7] and a Majority of each shall constitute a Quorum to do Business; but a smaller Number may adjourn from day to day, and may be authorized to compel the Attendance of absent Members, in such Manner, and under the Penalties as each House may provide.

Each House may determine the Rules of its Proceedings, punish its Members for disorderly Behavior, and, with the Concurrence of two thirds, expel a Member.

Each House shall keep a Journal of its Proceedings,[8] and from time to time publish the same, excepting such Parts as may in their Judgment require Secrecy; and the Yeas and Nays of the Members of either House on any question shall, at the Desire of one fifth of the present, be entered on the Journal.

Neither House, during the Session of Congress, shall, without the Consent of the other, adjourn for more than three days, nor to any other Place than that in which the two Houses shall be sitting.

## Section 6

[CONGRESSIONAL PAY, PRIVILEGES, AND RESTRICTIONS]

The Senators and Representatives shall receive a Compensation for their Services, to be ascertained by Law, and paid out of the Treasury of the United States. They shall in all Cases, except Treason, Felony and Breach of the Peace, be privileged from Arrest during their Attendance at the Session of their respective Houses,[9] and in going to and returning from the same; and for any Speech or Debate in either House, they shall not be questioned in any other Place.

No Senator or Representative, shall, during the time for which he was elected, be appointed to any civil Office under the authority of the United States, which shall have been created, or the Emoluments[10] whereof shall have been encreased during such time; and no Person holding any Office under the United States, shall be a Member of either House during his Continuance in Office.

## Section 7

[LEGISLATIVE PROCEDURES]

All Bills for raising Revenue shall originate in the House of Representatives; but the Senate may propose or concur with Amendments as on other Bills.

Every Bill which shall have passed the House of Representatives and the Senate, shall, before it become a Law, be presented to the President of the United States; if he approve he shall sign it, but if not he shall return it, with his Objections to that House in which it shall have originated,[11] who shall enter the Objections at large on their Journal, and proceed to reconsider it. If after such Reconsideration two thirds of that House shall agree to pass the Bill, it shall be sent, together with the Objections, to the other House, by which it shall likewise be reconsidered, and if approved by two thirds of that House, it shall become a Law. But in all such Cases the Votes of both Houses shall be determined by Yeas and Nays, and the Names of the Persons voting for and against the Bill shall be entered on the Journal of each House respectively. If any Bill shall not be returned by the President within ten Days (Sundays excepted) after it shall have been presented to him, the Same shall be a Law, in like Manner as if he had signed it, unless the Congress by their Adjournment prevent its Return, in which Case it shall not be a Law.[12]

Every Order, Resolution, or Vote to which the Concurrence of the Senate and House of Representatives may be necessary (except on a question of Adjournment) shall be presented to the President of the United States; and before the Same shall take Effect, shall be approved by him, or being disapproved by him, shall be repassed by two thirds of the Senate and House of Representatives, according to the Rules and Limitations prescribed in the Case of a Bill.

## Section 8

[POWERS OF CONGRESS]

The Congress shall have Power

To lay and collect Taxes, Duties, Imposts and Excises, to pay the Debts and provide for the common Defence and general Welfare of the United States; but all Duties, Imposts and excises shall be uniform throughout the United States;

To borrow Money on the Credit of the United States;

To regulate Commerce with foreign Nations, and among the several States, and with the Indian Tribes;

To establish an uniform Rule of Naturalization, and uniform Laws on the subject of Bankruptcies throughout the United States;

To coin Money, regulate the Value thereof, and of foreign Coin, and fix the Standard of Weights and Measures;

To provide for the Punishment of counterfeiting the Securities and current Coin of the United States;

To establish Post Offices and post Roads;

To promote the Progress of Science and useful Arts, by securing for limited Times to Authors and Inventors the exclusive Right to their respective Writings and Discoveries,[13]

To constitute Tribunals inferior to the supreme Court,[14]

To define and Punish Piracies and Felonies committed on the high Seas, and Offences against the Law of Nations;

To declare War, grant Letters of Marque and Reprisal,[15] and make Rules concerning Captures on Land and Water;

To raise and support Armies, but no Appropriation of Money to that Use shall be for a longer Term than two Years;

To provide and maintain a Navy;

To make Rules for the Government and Regulation of the land and naval forces;

To provide for calling for the Militia to execute the Laws of the Union, suppress Insurrections and repel Invasions;

To provide for organizing, arming, and disciplining, the Militia, and for governing such Part of them as may be employed in the Service of the United States, reserving to the States respectively, the Appointment of the Officers, and the Authority of training the Militia according to the discipline prescribed by Congress;

To exercise exclusive Legislation in all Cases whatsoever, over such District (not exceeding ten Miles square) as may, by Cession of particular States, and the Acceptance of Congress, become the Seat of the Government of the United States, and to exercise like Authority over all Places purchased by the Consent of the Legislature of the State in which the Same shall be, for the Erection of Forts, Magazines, Arsenals, dock-Yards, and other needful Buildings;—And

To make all Laws which shall be necessary and proper for carrying into Execution the foregoing Powers, and all other Powers vested by this Constitution in the Government of the United States, or in any Department or Officer thereof.[16]

## Section 9

[RESTRICTIONS ON CONGRESSIONAL POWER]

The Migration of Importation of such Persons as any of the States now existing shall think proper to admit, shall not be prohibited by the Congress prior to the Year one thousand eight hundred and eight, but a Tax or Duty may be imposed on such Importation, not exceeding ten dollars for each Person.

The privilege of the Writ of Habeas Corpus shall not be suspended, unless when in Cases of Rebellion or Invasion the public Safety may require it.

No Bill of Attainder or ex post facto Laws shall be passed.[17]

No Capitation, or other direct, Tax shall be laid, unless in Proportion to the Census or Enumeration herein before directed to be taken.[18]

No Tax or Duty shall be laid on Articles exported from any State.

No Preference shall be given by any Regulation of Commerce or Revenue to the Ports of one State over those of another: nor shall Vessels bound to, or from, one State, be obliged to enter, clear, or pay Duties in another.

No Money shall be drawn from the Treasury, but in Consequence of Appropriations made by Law; and a regular Statement and Account of the Receipts and Expenditures of all public Money shall be published from time to time.

No Title of Nobility shall be granted by the United States: And no Person holding any Office of Profit or Trust under them, shall, without the Consent of the Congress, accept of any present, Emolument, Office, or Title, of any kind whatever, from any King, Prince, or foreign State.

## Section 10

[RESTRICTION ON THE POWERS OF THE STATES]

No State shall enter into any Treaty, Alliance, or Confederation; grant Letters of Marque and Reprisal; coin Money; emit Bills of Credit; make any Thing but gold and silver Coin a Tender[19] in Payment of Debts; pass any Bill of Attainder, ex post facto Law, or Law impairing the Obligation of Contracts, or grant any Title of Nobility.

No State shall, without the Consent of the Congress, lay any Imposts or Duties on Imports or Exports, except what may be absolutely necessary for executing its inspection Laws: and the net Produce of all Duties and Imposts, laid by any State on Imports or Exports, shall be for the Use of the Treasury of the United States; and all such Laws shall be subject to the Revision and Control of the Congress.

No State shall, without the Consent of Congress, lay any Duty of Tonnage,[20]

keep Troops, or Ships of War in time of Peace, enter into any Agreement or Compact with another State, or with a foreign Power, or engage in War, unless actually invaded, or in such imminent Danger as will not admit of Delay.

## ARTICLE II

### Section 1

[PRESIDENTIAL POWER, ELECTION, AND QUALIFICATIONS]

The executive Power shall be vested in a President of the United States of America. He shall hold his Office during the Term of four Years and, together with the Vice President, chosen for the same Term, be elected, as follows:[21]

Each State shall appoint, in such Manner as the Legislature thereof may direct, a Number of Electors, equal to the whole Number of Senators and Representatives to which the State may be entitled in the Congress: but no Senator or Representative, or Person holding an Office of Trust or Profit under the United States, shall be appointed an Elector.

The electors shall meet in their respective States, and vote by ballot for two Persons, of whom one at least shall not be an Inhabitant of the same State with themselves. And they shall make a List of all the Persons voted for, and of the Number of Votes for each; which List they shall sign and certify, and transmit sealed to the Seat of the Government of the United States, directed to the President of the Senate. The President of the Senate shall, in the Presence of the Senate and House of Representatives, open all the Certificates, and the Votes shall then be counted. The Person having the greatest Number of Votes shall be the President, if such Number be a Majority of the whole Number of Electors appointed; and if there be more than one who have such Majority and have an equal Number of Votes, then the House of Representatives shall immediately chuse by Ballot one of them for President; and if no person have a Majority, then from the five highest on the List the said House shall in like Manner chuse the President. But in chusing the President, the Votes shall be taken by States, the Representation from each State having one Vote; A quorum for this Purpose shall consist of a Member or Members from two-thirds of the States, and a Majority of all the States shall be necessary to a Choice. In every Case, after the Choice of the President, the person having the greatest Number of Votes of the Electors shall be the Vice President. But if there should remain two or more who have equal vote, the Senate shall chuse from them by Ballot the Vice President.[22]

The Congress may determine the Time of chusing the Electors, and the Day on which they shall give their Votes; which Day shall be the same throughout the United States.

No Person except a natural born Citizen, or a Citizen of the United States, at the time of the Adoption of this Constitution, shall be eligible to the Office of President; neither shall any Person be eligible to that Office who shall not have attained to the Age of thirty-five Years, and been fourteen Years a Resident within the United States.

In Case of the Removal of the President from Office, or of his Death, Resignation, or Inability to discharge the Powers and Duties of the said Office, the same shall devolve on the Vice President, and the Congress may by Law provide for the Case of Removal, Death, Resignation, or Inability, both of the President and Vice President, declaring what Officer shall then act as President, and such Officer shall act accordingly, until the Disability be removed, or a President shall be elected.

The President shall, at stated Times, receive for his Services, a Compensation, which shall neither be encreased nor diminished during the Period of which he shall have been elected, and he shall not receive within that Period any other Emolument from the United States, or any of them.

Before he enter on the Execution of his Office, he shall take the following oath or Affirmation:—"I do solemnly swear (or affirm) that I will faithfully execute the Office of President of the United States, and will to the best of my Ability, preserve, protect and defend the Constitution of the United States."

## Section 2

[POWERS OF THE PRESIDENT]

The President shall be the Commander in Chief of the Army and Navy of the United States, and of the Militia of the several States, when called into the actual Service of the United States,[23] he may require the Opinion, in writing, of the principal Officer in each of the executive Departments, upon any Subject relating to the Duties of their respective Offices,[24] and he shall have Power to grant Reprieves and Pardons for Offences against the United States, except in Cases of Impeachment.

He shall have Power, by and with the Advice and Consent of the Senate to make Treaties, provided two thirds of the Senators present concur; and he shall nominate, and by and with the Advice and Consent of the Senate, shall appoint Ambassadors, other public Ministers and Consuls, Judges of the supreme Court, and all other Offices of the United States, whose Appointments are not herein otherwise provided for, and which shall be established by Law: but the Congress may by Law vest the Appointment of such inferior Offices, as they think proper, in the President alone, in the Courts of Law, or in the Heads of Departments.[25]

The President shall have Power to fill up all Vacancies that may happen during the Recess of the Senate, by granting Commissions which shall expire at the End of their next Session.

## Section 3

[PRESIDENTIAL/CONGRESSIONAL RELATIONSHIP]

He shall from time to time give to the Congress Information of the State of the Union, and recommend to their Consideration such Measures as he shall judge necessary and expedient; he may, on extraordinary Occasions, convene both Houses, or either of them, and in Case of Disagreement between them, with Respect to the Time of Adjournment, he may adjourn them to such Time as he shall think proper,[26] he shall receive Ambassadors and other public Ministers; he shall take Care that the Laws be faithfully executed, and shall Commission all the Officers of the United States.

## Section 4

[IMPEACHMENT]

The President, Vice President and all civil Officers of the United States shall be removed from Office on Impeachment for, and Conviction of, Treason, Bribery, or other high Crimes and Misdemeanors.

# ( ARTICLE III )

## Section 1

[STRUCTURE OF THE JUDICIARY]

The judicial Power of the United States, shall be vested in one supreme Court, and in such inferior Courts as the Congress may from time to time ordain and establish. The Judges, both of the supreme and inferior Courts, shall hold their Offices during good Behavior,[27] and shall, at stated Times, receive for their Services, a Compensation, which shall not be diminished during their Continuance in Office.

## Section 2

[JURISDICTION OF FEDERAL COURTS]

The judicial Power shall extend to all Cases, in Law and Equity, arising under this Constitution, the Laws of the United States, and Treaties made, or which shall be made, under their Authority;—to all Cases affecting Ambassadors, other public Ministers and Consuls;—to all Cases of admiralty and maritime Jurisdiction;—to Controversies to which the United States shall be a party;—to Controversies between two or more States;—between a State and Citizens of another State;—between Citizens of different States;—between Citizens of the same State claiming Lands under Grants of different States, and between a State, or the Citizens thereof, and foreign States, Citizens or Subjects.[28]

In all Cases affecting Ambassadors, other public Ministers and Consuls, and those in which a State shall be Party, the supreme Court shall have original Jurisdiction. In all the other Cases before mentioned, the supreme Court shall have appellate Jurisdiction, both as to Law and Fact, with such Exceptions, and under such Regulations as Congress shall make.

The Trial of all Crimes, except in Cases of Impeachment, shall be by Jury; and such Trial shall be held in the State where the said Crimes shall have been committed; but when not committed within any State, the Trial shall be at such Place or Places as the Congress may by Law have directed.

## Section 3

[TREASON]

Treason against the United States, shall consist only in levying War against them, or in adhering to their Enemies, giving them Aid and Comfort. No Person shall be convicted of Treason unless on the Testimony of two Witnesses to the same overt Act, or on Confession in open Court.

The Congress shall have Power to declare the Punishment of Treason, but no Attainder of Treason[29] shall work Corruption of Blood, or Forfeiture except during the Life of the Person attained.

## ARTICLE IV

### Section 1
[FAITH AND CREDIT AMONG STATES]

Full Faith and Credit[30] shall be given in each State to the public Acts, Records, and judicial Proceedings of every other State. And the Congress may by general Laws prescribe the Manner in which such Acts, Records and Proceedings shall be proved, and the Effect thereof.

### Section 2
[PRIVILEGES AND IMMUNITIES]

The Citizens of each State shall be entitled to all Privileges and Immunities of Citizens in the several States.[31]

A person charged in any State with Treason, Felony or other Crime, who shall flee from Justice, and be found in another State, shall on Demand of the executive Authority of the State from which he fled, be delivered up to be removed to the State having Jurisdiction of the Crime.[32]

No person held to Service or Labour in one State, under the Laws thereof, escaping into another, shall, in Consequence of any Law or Regulation therein, be discharged from such Service or Labour, but shall be delivered up on Claim of the Party to whom such Service or Labour may be due.[33]

### Section 3
[ADMISSION OF NEW STATES]

New States may be admitted by the Congress into this Union; but no new State shall be formed or erected within the Jurisdiction of any other State; nor any State be formed by the Junction of two or more States, or Parts of States, without the Consent of the Legislatures of the States concerned as well of the Congress.

The Congress shall have Power to dispose of and make all needful Rules and Regulations respecting the Territory or other Property belonging to the United States; and nothing in this Constitution shall be so construed as to Prejudice any Claims of the United States, or of any particular State.

### Section 4
[THE STATES AS REPUBLICAN GOVERNMENTS]

The United States shall guarantee to every State in this Union a Republican Form[34] of Government, and shall protect each of them against Invasion; and on Application of the Legislature, or of the Executive (when the Legislature cannot be convened) against domestic Violence.

## ARTICLE V

[AMENDING THE CONSTITUTION]

The Congress, whenever two thirds of both Houses shall deem it necessary, shall propose Amendments to this Constitution, or, on the Application of the Legislatures of two thirds of several States, shall call a Convention for proposing Amendments, which, in either Case, shall be valid to all Intents and Purposes, as Part of this Constitution, when ratified by the Legislatures of three fourths of the several States, or by Conventions in three fourths thereof, as the one or the other Mode of Ratification may be proposed by the Congress; Provided that no Amendment which may be made prior to the Year One thousand eight hundred and eight shall in any Manner affect the first and fourth Clauses in the Ninth Section of the first Article; and that no State, without its Consent, shall be deprived of its equal Suffrage in the Senate.

## ARTICLE VI

[DEBTS, SUPREMACY, AND OATH]

All Debts contracted and Engagements entered into, before the Adoption of this Constitution, shall be as valid against the United States under this Constitution, as under the Confederation.

This Constitution, and the Laws of the United States which shall be made in Pursuance thereof; and all Treaties made, or which shall be made, under the Authority of the United States, shall be the supreme Law of the Land; and the Judges in every State shall be bound thereby, any Thing in the Constitution or Laws of any State to the Contrary notwithstanding.[35]

The Senators and Representatives before mentioned, and the Members of the several State Legislatures, and all executive and judicial Officers, both of the United States and of the several States, shall be bound by Oath or Affirmation, to support this Constitution; but no religious Test shall ever be required as a Qualification to any Office or public Trust under the United States.

## ARTICLE VII

[RATIFICATION]

The Ratification of the Conventions of nine States, shall be sufficient for the Establishment of this Constitution between the States so ratifying the Same.

Done in Convention by the Unanimous Consent of the States present the Seventeenth Day of September in the Year of our Lord one thousand seven hundred and Eighty seven and of the Independence of the United States of America the Twelfth. In Witness whereof We have hereunto subscribed our Names,

G:⁰ WASHINGTON—Presidt. and Deputy from Virginia

New Hampshire { JOHN LANGDON
             { NICHOLAS GILMAN

| Massachusetts | { | NATHANIEL GORHAM<br>RUFUS KING |
|---|---|---|
| Connecticut | { | WM SAML JOHNSON<br>ROGER SHERMAN |
| New York | | ALEXANDER HAMILTON |
| New Jersey | { | WIL: LIVINGSTON<br>DAVID BREARLEY<br>WM PATERSON<br>JONA: DAYTON |
| Pennsylvania | { | B FRANKLIN<br>THOMAS MIFFLIN<br>ROBT MORRIS<br>GEO. CLYMER<br>THOS. FITZSIMONS<br>JARED INGERSOLL<br>JAMES WILSON<br>GOUV MORRIS |
| Delaware | { | GEO READ<br>GUNNING BEDFOR JUN<br>JOHN DICKINSON<br>RICHARD BASSETT<br>JACO: BROOM |
| Maryland | { | JAMES McHENRY<br>DAN OF ST THOS. JENIFER<br>DANL CARROLL |
| Virginia | { | JOHN BLAIR —<br>JAMES MADISON JR. |
| North Carolina | { | WM BLOUNT<br>RICHD DOBBS SPAIGHT<br>HU WILLIAMSON |
| South Carolina | { | J. RUTLEDGE<br>CHARLES COTESWORTH PINCKNEY<br>CHARLES PINCKNEY<br>PIERCE BUTLER |
| Georgia | { | WILLIAM FEW<br>ABR BALDWIN |

# Amendments to the Constitution

The first ten amendments, known as the Bill of Rights, were ratified and adopted on December 15, 1791.

## AMENDMENT I

[FREEDOM OF RELIGION, SPEECH, PRESS, ASSEMBLY, AND PETITION]

Congress shall make no law respecting an establishment of religion, or prohibiting the free exercise thereof; or abridging the freedom of speech, or of the press; or the right of the people peaceably to assemble, and to petition the Government for a redress of grievances.

## AMENDMENT II

[FREEDOM TO KEEP AND BEAR ARMS]

A well regulated Militia, being necessary to the security of a free State, the right of the people to keep and bear Arms, shall not be infringed.

## AMENDMENT III

[QUARTERING OF SOLDIERS]

No Soldier shall, in time of peace be quartered in any house, without the consent of the Owner, nor in time of war, but in a manner to be prescribed by law.

## AMENDMENT IV

[SECURITY FROM UNREASONABLE SEARCHES AND SEIZURES]

The right of the people to be secure in their persons, houses, papers, and effects, against unreasonable searches and seizures, shall not be violated, and no Warrants shall issue, but upon probable cause, supported by Oath or affirmation, and particularly describing the place to be searched, and the persons or things to be seized.

## AMENDMENT V

[RIGHTS OF ACCUSED PERSONS IN CRIMINAL CASES]

No person shall be held to answer for a capital, or otherwise infamous crime, unless on a presentment or indictment of a Grand Jury, except in cases arising in the land or naval forces, or in the Militia, when in actual service in time of War or in public danger; nor shall any person be subject for the same offence to be twice put in jeopardy of life or limb; nor shall be compelled in any Criminal Case to be a witness against himself,[36] nor be deprived of life, liberty, or property, without due process of law; nor shall private property be taken for public use, without just compensation.

## AMENDMENT VI

[ADDITIONAL RIGHTS OF THE ACCUSED]

In all criminal prosecutions, the accused shall enjoy the right to a speedy and public trial, by an impartial jury of the State and district wherein the crime shall have been committed, which district shall have been previously ascertained by law, and to be informed of the nature and cause of the accusation; to be confronted with the witnesses against him; to have compulsory process for obtaining Witnesses in his favor, and to have the Assistance of Counsel for his defence.

## AMENDMENT VII

[CIVIL RIGHTS IN COMMON LAW]

In suits at common law, where the value in controversy shall exceed twenty dollars, the right of trial by jury shall be preserved, and no fact tried by a jury shall be otherwise re-examined in any Court of the United States, than according to the rules of the common law.

## AMENDMENT VIII

[BAILS, FINES, AND PUNISHMENTS]

Excessive bail shall not be required, nor excessive fines imposed, nor cruel and unusual punishments inflicted.

## AMENDMENT IX[37]

[RETENTION OF RIGHTS OF THE PEOPLE]

The enumeration in the Constitution, of certain rights, shall not be construed to deny or disparage others retained by the people.

## AMENDMENT X[37]

[RESERVATION OF POWERS TO THE STATES OR PEOPLE]

The powers not delegated to the United States by the Constitution, nor prohibited by it to the States, are reserved to the States respectively, or to the people.

## AMENDMENT XI[38]
[Ratified on January 8, 1798.]

[RESTRICTION OF JUDICIAL POWER]

The Judicial power of the United States shall not be construed to extend to any suit in law or equity, commenced or prosecuted against one of the United States by Citizens of another State, or by Citizens or Subjects of any Foreign State.

## AMENDMENT XII[39]
[Ratified on September 25, 1804.]

[ELECTION OF PRESIDENT AND VICE-PRESIDENT]

The Electors shall meet in their respective states, and vote by ballot for President and Vice-President, one of whom, at least, shall not be an inhabitant of the same state with themselves; they shall name in their ballots the person voted for as President, and in distinct ballots the person voted for as Vice-President, and they shall make distinct lists of all persons voted for as President, and of all persons voted for as Vice-President, and of the number of votes for each, which lists they shall sign and certify, and transmit sealed to the seat of the government of the United States, directed to the President of the Senate;—The President of the Senate shall, in presence of the Senate and House of Representatives, open all the certificates and the votes shall then be counted;—The person having the greatest number of votes for President, shall be the President, if such number be a majority of the whole number of Electors appointed; and if no person have such majority, then from the persons having the highest numbers not exceeding three on the list of those voted for as President, the House of Representatives shall choose immediately, by ballot, the President. But in choosing the President, the votes shall be taken by states, the representation from each state having one vote; a quorum for this purpose shall consist of a member or members from two-thirds of the states, and a majority of all states shall be necessary to a choice. And if the House of Representatives shall not choose a President whenever the right of choice shall devolve upon them, before the fourth day of March next following, then the Vice-President shall act as President, as in the case of the death or other constitutional disability of the President. The person having the greatest number of votes as Vice-President, shall be the Vice-President, if such a number be a majority of the whole numbers of Electors appointed, and if no person have a majority, then from the two highest numbers on the list, the Senate shall choose the Vice-President; a quorum for the purpose shall consist of two-thirds of the whole number of Senators, and a majority of the whole number shall be necessary to a choice. But no person constitutionally ineligible to the office of President shall be eligible to that of Vice-President of the United States.

## AMENDMENT XIII[40]
[Ratified on December 18, 1865.]

### Section 1
[ABOLITION OF SLAVERY]

Neither slavery nor involuntary servitude, except as a punishment for crime whereof the party shall have been duly convicted, shall exist within the United States, or any place subject to their jurisdiction.

### Section 2

Congress shall have power to enforce this article by appropriate legislation.

## AMENDMENT XIV[41]
[Ratified on July 28, 1868.]

### Section 1
[RIGHT OF CITIZENSHIP]

All persons born or naturalized in the United States, and subject to the jurisdiction thereof, are citizens of the United States and of the State wherein they reside. No State shall make or enforce any law which shall abridge the privileges or immunities of citizens of the United States;[42] nor shall any State deprive any person of life, liberty, or property, without due process of law;[43] nor deny to any person within its jurisdiction the equal protection of the laws.[44]

### Section 2
[REPRESENTATION IN CONGRESS]

Representatives shall be apportioned among the several States according to their respective numbers, counting the whole number of persons in each State, excluding Indians not taxed. But when the right to vote at any election for the choice of electors for President and Vice-President of the United States, Representatives in Congress, the Executive and Judicial officers of a State, or the members of the Legislature thereof, is denied to any of the male inhabitants of such State, being twenty-one years of age, and citizens of the United States, or in any way abridged, except for participation in rebellion, or other crime, the basis of representation therein shall be reduced in the proportion which the number of such male citizens shall bear to the whole number of male citizens twenty-one years of age in such State.[45]

### Section 3
[RESTRICTION ON ELIGIBILITY TO HOLD OFFICE]

No person shall be a Senator or Representative in Congress, or elector of President and Vice-President, or hold any office, civil or military, under the United States, or under any State, who, having previously taken an oath, as a member of Congress, or as an officer of the United States, or as a member of any State legislature, or as an executive or judicial officer of any State, to support the Constitution of the United States, shall have engaged in insurrection or rebellion against the same, or given aid or comfort to the enemies thereof. But Congress may by a vote of two-thirds of each House, remove such disability.

### Section 4

[DEFINITION OF PUBLIC DEBTS]

The validity of the public debt of the United States, authorized by law, including debts incurred for payment of pensions and bounties for services in suppressing insurrection or rebellion, shall not be questioned. But neither the United States nor any State shall assume or pay any debt or obligation incurred in aid of insurrection or rebellion against the United States, or any claim for the loss or emancipation of any slave; but all such debts, obligations and claims shall be held illegal and void.

### Section 5

The Congress shall have power to enforce, by appropriate legislation, the provisions of this article.

## AMENDMENT XV

[Ratified on March 30, 1870.]

### Section 1

[BLACK SUFFRAGE]

The right of citizens of the United States to vote shall not be denied or abridged by the United States or by any State on account of race, color, or previous condition of servitude.

### Section 2

The Congress shall have power to enforce this article by appropriate legislation.

## AMENDMENT XVI[46]

[Ratified on February 25, 1913.]

[PERSONAL INCOME TAXES]

The Congress shall have power to lay and collect taxes on incomes, from whatever source derived, without apportionment among the several States, and without regard to any census or enumeration.

## AMENDMENT XVII
[Ratified on May 31, 1913.]

[POPULAR ELECTION OF SENATORS][47]

The Senate of the United States shall be composed of two Senators from each State, elected by the people thereof, for six years; and each Senator shall have one vote. The electors in each State shall have the qualifications requisite for electors of the most numerous branch of the State Legislature.

When vacancies happen in the representation of any State in the Senate, the executive authority of such State shall issue writs of election to fill such vacancies: Provided, That the Legislature of any State may empower the executive thereof to make temporary appointment until the people fill the vacancies by election as the Legislature may direct.

This amendment shall not be so construed as to affect the election or term of any Senator chosen before it becomes valid as part of the Constitution.

## AMENDMENT XVIII
[Ratified on January 29, 1919.]

### Section 1

[PROHIBITION OF LIQUOR]

After one year from the ratification of this article the manufacture, sale, or transportation of intoxicating liquors within, the importation thereof into, or the exportation thereof from the United States and all territory subject to the jurisdiction thereof for beverage purposes is hereby prohibited.

### Section 2

[ENFORCEMENT POWER]

The Congress and the several states shall have concurrent power to enforce this article by appropriate legislation.

### Section 3

[PROVISION FOR RATIFICATION]

This article shall be inoperative unless it shall have been ratified as an amendment to the Constitution by the legislatures of the several states, as provided in the Constitution, within seven years from the date of the submission hereof to the states by the Congress.

## AMENDMENT XIX
[Ratified on August 26, 1920.]

[WOMEN'S SUFFRAGE]

The right of the citizens of the United States to vote shall not be denied or abridged by the United States or by any state on account of sex.

Congress shall have power, by appropriate legislation, to enforce the provision of this article.

## AMENDMENT XX
[Ratified on February 6, 1933.]

### Section 1
[TERMS OF PRESIDENTIAL AND VICE-PRESIDENTIAL OFFICE]

The terms of the President and Vice-President shall end at noon on the 20th day of January, and the terms of the Senators and Representatives at noon on the 3rd day of January, of the years in which such terms would have ended if this article had not been ratified; and the terms of their successors shall then begin.

### Section 2[48]
[TIME OF CONVENING CONGRESS]

The Congress shall assemble at least once in every year, and such meeting shall begin at noon on the 3rd day of January, unless they shall by law appoint a different day.

### Section 3
[DEATH OF PRESIDENT-ELECT]

If, at the time fixed for the beginning of the term of the President, the President elect shall have died, the Vice-President elect shall become President. If a President shall not have been chosen before the time fixed for the beginning of his term, or if the President elect shall have failed to qualify, then the Vice-President elect shall act as President until a President shall have qualified; and the Congress may by law provide for the case wherein neither a President elect nor a Vice-President elect shall have qualified, declaring who shall then act as President, or the manner in which one who is to act shall be selected, and such person shall act accordingly until a President or Vice-President shall have qualified.

### Section 4[49]
[PRESIDENTIAL SUCCESSION]

The Congress may by law provide for the case of the death of any of the persons from whom the House of Representatives may choose a President whenever the right of choice shall have developed upon them, and for the case of the death of any of the persons from whom the Senate may choose a Vice-President whenever the right of choice shall have devolved upon them.

### Section 5

Sections 1 and 2 shall take effect on the 15th day of October following the ratification of this article.

### Section 6

This article shall be inoperative unless it shall have been ratified as an amendment to the Constitution by the legislatures of three-fourths of the several States within seven years from the date of its submission.

## AMENDMENT XXI
[Ratified on December 5, 1933.]

### Section 1

[REPEAL OF LIQUOR PROHIBITION]

The eighteenth article of amendment to the Constitution of the United States is hereby repealed.

### Section 2

["DRY" STATES]

The transportation or importation into any State, Territory, or Possession of the United States for delivery or use therein of intoxicating liquors, in violation of the laws thereof, is hereby prohibited.

### Section 3

This article shall be inoperative unless it shall have been ratified as an amendment to the Constitution by conventions in the several States, as provided in the Constitution, within seven years from the date of the submission hereof to the States by the Congress.

## AMENDMENT XXII
[Ratified on February 26, 1951.]

### Section 1[50]

[LIMITATION ON PRESIDENTIAL TERM IN OFFICE]

No person shall be elected to the office of the President more than twice, and no person who has held the office of President, or acted as President, for more than two years of a term to which some other person was elected President shall be elected to the Office of the President more than once. But this Article shall not apply to any person holding the office of President when this Article was proposed by the Congress, and shall not prevent any person who may be holding the office of President, or acting as President, during the term within which this Article becomes operative from holding the office of President or acting as President during the remainder of such term.

### Section 2

This Article shall be inoperative unless it shall have been ratified as an amendment to the Constitution by the legislatures of three-fourths of the several states within seven years from the date of its submission to the States by the Congress.

## AMENDMENT XXIII
[Ratified on March 29, 1961.]

### Section 1
[ELECTORAL VOTES FOR THE DISTRICT OF COLUMBIA]

The District constituting the seat of Government of the United States shall appoint in such manner as the Congress may direct:

A number of electors of President and Vice-President equal to the whole number of Senators and Representatives in Congress to which the District would be entitled if it were a State, but in no event more than the least populous State; they shall be in addition to those appointed by the States, but they shall be considered, for the purposes of the election of President and Vice-President, to be electors appointed by a State; and they shall meet in the District and perform such duties as provided by the twelfth article of amendment.

### Section 2

The Congress shall have power to enforce this article by appropriate legislation.

## AMENDMENT XXIV
[Ratified on January 23, 1964.]

### Section 1
[POLL TAX ABOLISHED]

The right of citizens of the United States to vote in any primary or other election for President or Vice President, for electors for President or Vice-President, or for Senator or Representative in Congress, shall not be denied or abridged by the United States or any State by reasons of failure to pay any poll tax or other tax.

### Section 2

The Congress shall have power to enforce this article by appropriate legislation.

## AMENDMENT XXV
[Ratified on February 10, 1967.]

### Section 1
[PRESIDENTIAL SUCCESSION]

In case of the removal of the President from office or his death or resignation, the Vice-President shall become President.

### Section 2
[VICE PRESIDENTIAL SUCCESSION]

Whenever there is a vacancy in the office of the Vice-President, the President shall nominate a Vice-President who shall take the office upon confirmation by a majority vote of both houses of Congress.

### Section 3
[PRESIDENTIAL DISABILITY]

Whenever the President transmits to the President pro tempore of the Senate and the Speaker of the House of Representatives his written declaration that he is unable to discharge the powers and duties of his office, and until he transmits to them a written declaration to the contrary, such powers and duties shall be discharged by the Vice-President as Acting President.

### Section 4
[CONGRESSIONAL POWER TO DECLARE AND TO END PRESIDENTIAL DISABILITY]

Whenever the Vice-President and a majority of either the principal officers of the executive departments, or of such other body as Congress may by law provide, transmit to the President pro tempore of the Senate and the Speaker of the House of Representatives their written declaration that the President is unable to discharge the powers and duties of his office, the Vice-President shall immediately assume the powers and duties of the office as Acting President.

Thereafter, when the President transmits to the President pro tempore of the Senate and the Speaker of the House of Representatives his written declaration that no inability exists, he shall resume the powers and duties of his office unless the Vice-President and a majority of either the principal officer of the executive department, or of such other body as Congress may by law provide, transmit within four days to the President pro tempore of the Senate and the Speaker of the House of Representatives their written declaration that the President is unable to discharge the powers and duties of his office. Thereupon Congress shall decide the issue, assembling within 48 hours for that purpose if not in session. If the Congress, within 21 days after receipt of the latter written declaration, or, if Congress is not in session, within 21 days after Congress is required to assemble, determines by two-thirds vote of both houses that the President is unable to discharge the powers and duties of his office, the Vice-President shall continue to discharge the same as Acting President; otherwise, the President shall resume the powers and duties of his office.

## AMENDMENT XXVI
[Ratified on June 30, 1971]

### Section 1

The right of citizens of the United States, who are eighteen years of age, or older, to vote shall not be denied or abridged by the United States or by any state on account of age.

### Section 2

The Congress shall have power to enforce this article by appropriate legislation.

# Notes to the Constitution

1. The Sixteenth Amendment abolished the apportionment requirement.

2. A section of the Fourteenth Amendment modified this to include "the whole number of persons in each state, excluding Indians not taxed."

3. State governor.

4. Executive order calling for an election to be held.

5. Modified by the Seventeenth Amendment, which provided for direct election of Senators.

6. The Twentieth Amendment changed the date to the 3rd day of January each year.

7. Each house, acting as a judicial Tribunal can, by a two-thirds vote, bar a member-elect from taking his seat. It can call witnesses, issue warrants of arrest, and punish for perjury. But the Supreme Court has held that a member-elect can be banned only for failing to meet the requirements set forth in Article I, Sections 2 and 3 of the Constitution.

8. The Journals, in which are recorded each house's daily acts and proceedings are published at the end of each session of Congress. The Congressional Record, which is a daily record of the debates and proceedings of both houses and a calendar of events and committee meetings, is intended to make the legislators responsible to their constituents by publishing their opinions and actions.

9. Congressional immunity.

10. Fees or salaries paid for employment.

11. Presidential veto power (see Chapter 12).

12. Pocket veto (see Chapter 12).

13. Copyrights and patents (see Chapter 18).

14. Provision for establishing the federal court system, including district and circuit courts (see Chapter 17).

15. Commission given by a government to a private citizen to capture and confiscate the ships of a foreign nation.

16. Known as the necessary and proper or elastic clause (see the discussion of the powers of the national government in Chapter 5).

17. See Chapters 4 and 18 for definitions of these terms.

18. Tax of uniform size imposed on each person. Eliminated by the Sixteenth Amendment, which established the graduated personal income tax.

19. That which can be offered in payment of a debt or other obligation.

20. *Tax upon a vessel for entering, using, or leaving a port.*

21. *The Twenty-Second Amendment limits the President to two terms or ten years.*

22. *The Twelfth Amendment altered the Electoral College procedure to fit the party system by separating the candidates for President and Vice-President, but voting for them as a unit per their party affiliation.*

23. *Constitutional basis for President as Commander-in-Chief.*

24. *Constitutional basis for President as Chief Administrator.*

25. *Constitutional basis for President as Chief of State.*

26. *Constitutional basis for certain of the President's duties as Chief Legislator.*

27. *Life tenure.*

28. *Modified by the Eleventh Amendment, which limits judicial power over cases between a state and citizens of another state and between a state and foreign states.*

29. *Attainder of treason is the elimination of civil rights, which occurs as a result of conviction for treason. Under this clause the penalty imposed by Congress can only apply to the individual during his lifetime and not to his descendants.*

30. *Requirement that states accept the laws, public records, and certain court decisions of other states (see Chapter 5). This clause does not apply to criminal laws.*

31. *Known as the comity clause of the Constitution, it protects citizens of one state from acts of discrimination by other states in respect to a relatively few fundamental rights including the right to travel, to be protected against physical harm, to reside, marry, and engage in trade.*

32. *Extradition.*

33. *Repealed by the Thirteenth Amendment, which prohibited slavery.*

34. *This phrase has no specific meaning. Congress alone decides the Republican character of the states.*

35. *The national supremacy clause (see Chapter 4).*

36. *Self-incrimination clause (see Chapter 18).*

37. *Retained rights refers back to the Declaration's conception of a political organization.*

38. *Revision of Article III, Section 2.*

39. *Revision of the electoral college procedure in Article II, Section 1.*

40. *Repeals that part of Article IV, Section 2 which provided for the continuance of slavery.*

41. *Revision of the definition of citizenship and the right to vote in Article I, Section 2.*

42. *Privileges and immunities clause (see Chapter 5).*

43. *Due process clause, which, in combination with the Fifth Amendment, provides civil rights to all citizens.*

44. *Equal protection clause.*

45. *Revised by the Nineteenth and Twenty-Sixth Amendments to include women and citizens over eighteen years of age.*

46. *Revision of the type and method of collection of taxes in Article I, Sections 2 and 9.*

47. *Revision of senatorial election procedures in Article I, Section 3.*

48. *Revision of part of Article I, Section 4, so that the congressional session would begin at nearly the same time as the President's term in office.*

49. *Revision of presidential succession procedure in Article II, Section 1.*

50. *Limitation on presidential terms in office, not specified in Article II, Section 1.*

# illustration credits

*all photographs are listed top to bottom and left to right*

page *194*      United Press International, Inc.
*194-5*   Rhoda Galyn—Photo Researchers, Inc.
*195*     Wilfred Randall—Black Star
*200*     United Press International, Inc.
*224*     Norris McNamara—Nancy Palmer
*230*     United Press International, Inc.
*232*     Library of Congress
*254*     Myron Wood—Photo Researchers, Inc.
*270*     Brown Brothers
*280*     United Press International, Inc.
*284*     Wide World Photos
*286*     Patrick A. Burns—The New York Times Company, 1971, reprinted by permission
*289*     Dave Harvey—Black Star
*296*     Juliana Wang—Nancy Palmer
*306*     Library of Congress
*328*     Norris McNamara—Nancy Palmer
*334*     United Press International, Inc.
*334*     United Press International, Inc.
*336*     Bob Wands
*337*     Wide World Photos
*337*     Wide World Photos
*339*     Dennis Brack—Black Star
*355*     United Press International, Inc.
*355*     United Press International, Inc.
*358*     United Press International, Inc.
*359*     Leo Choplin—Black Star
*361*     Wallace Kirkland—Life Magazine © Time Inc.
*372*     H. Armstrong Roberts
*374*     Ken Heyman
*406*     © by White House Association. Photograph by National Geographic Society
*406*     © by White House Association. Photograph by National Geographic Society
*406-7*   © by White House Association. Photograph by National Geographic Society
*407*     © by White House Association. Photograph by National Geographic Society
*407*     © by White House Association. Photograph by National Geographic Society
*418*     Cornell Capa—Magnum
*423*     Wide World Photos
*428*     Library of Congress
*430*     Wide World Photos
*434*     Wide World Photos
*441*     Wide World Photos
*445*     Wide World Photos
*452*     H. Armstrong Roberts
*464*     United Press International, Inc.
*466*     United Press International, Inc.
*467*     United Press International, Inc.
*486*     Cornell Capa—Magnum
*495*     Edward Clark—Life Magazine © Time Inc.
*510*     Arthur Leipzig Photo
*546*     Wide World Photos

## portfolio

## campaigns then and now

## portfolio

## the presidency

## portfolio

## committees in action

## portfolio

## minority rights north/south

# index

# name index

## A

Abbott, David W., 185, 326
Abels, Rudolph, 397
Abraham, Henry J., 502, 503, 549$n$, 571$n$, 572$n$, 575$n$, 594$n$, 597
Acheson, Dean, 704
Adams, Abigail, 62
Adams, John, 62, 66, 70$n$, 101, 301, 303, 304, 409, 687
Adams, John Quincy, 501
Adams, Robert W., 185
Adams, Samuel, 59, 61
Adams, Sherman, 434, 435$n$
Adkins, Roscoe C., 22
Agnew, Spiro, 213, 409, 608$n$
Albert, Carl, 467
Alexander, Rudolph P., 221
Ali, Muhammad, 593, 626
Alleluyeva, Svetlana, 698
Allende, Salvador, 698
Amaru, Augustine, 326
Anderson, Betty J., 714
Anderson, Clinton P., 266
Anderson, Dwight, 714
Anderson, James, 756$n$, 771$n$, 778$n$
Anderson, Paul S., 789
Andress, Robert P., 22
Andripoulos, Angelo Theodore, 714
Appleton, Sheldon Lee, 714
Aquinas, Thomas, 201
Arcilesi, Salvatore A., 714
Aronfreed, Eva, 294
Auerbach, Jerold S., 634
Auerbach, Maurice S., 46
Aurand, Art R., 484
Ayres, Richard E., 234$n$

## B

Bach, George Leland, 772$n$
Bachrach, Peter, 46
Badillo, Herman, 470, 661
Bailey, Jess, 84
Bailey, Stephen K., 269$n$, 480, 489$n$, 491$n$, 503
Bain, H. M., Jr., 360$n$
Bair, F. H., 185

Baker, Robert, 283
Banett, John W., 714
Banfield, Edward C., 163, 164, 183
Barber, Bernard, 259$n$
Barber, Kathleen L., 326, 370
Barnes, Philip H., 22
Barnett, Ross, 656
Barth, Norman, 185
Bartholomew, Charles P., 581
Bartley, Ernest R., 185
Barton, Allen N., 13$n$
Bayh, Birch, 18, 363, 674
Beals, William, 370
Bean, Barton, 634
Beard, Charles A., 72, 430
Beaverbrook, William, 6
Beck, Dave, 264
Becker, Robert Myron, 581
Bennett, Thomas T., 22
Berelson, Bernard, 247, 248, 356
Bibby, John, 439, 440
Bierce, Ambrose, 4
Binkley, Wilfred A., 306$n$, 391, 427$n$, 431$n$, 434$n$
Black, Gordon S., 22
Black, Hugo, 557, 590, 593, 594, 596, 599, 602, 606
Blackstone, William, 53
Blair, Harry W., 252
Blair, William M., 806
Blank, Blanche, 326
Blatchford, Herbert, 644
Blau, Peter M., 514$n$
Bloss, Richard John, 634
Boggs, Hale, 468, 469
Bohr, Niels, 719
Bolen, Charles, 705
Bolling, Richard, 478
Bone, Hugh, 18
Bortz, Arnold, 277$n$
Bowen, Don R., 554, 555
Bowen, William G., 234$n$
Boyan, A. Stephen, Jr., 634
Boyd, Richard, 484
Bradley, E. R., 714
Brandeis, Louis, 557, 574, 598
Brandon, Donald, 687$n$
Brandon, W. R., 714
Breitbach, Richard C., 682

Brenneman, Lynn D., 634
Bricker, John, 431
Bright, Samuel R., Jr., 752
Brogan, D. W., 87, 297, 304$n$, 305$n$
Brown, H. Rap, 213
Brown, Michael Baratt, 714
Brown, Mike, 22
Brown, Oliver, 652
Brown, Stuart Gerry, 420$n$, 432
Bruce, David, 704
Bruner, Jerome S., 193$n$
Buchanan, James, 305, 420
Buckley, James, 143, 313
Bundy, McGeorge, 18, 380
Bunzel, John H., 269$n$
Burd, Frank A., 752
Burger, Warren E., 556, 606
Burke, Edmund, 301
Butler, G. L., 714
Butler, Pierce, 555
Byrd, William, 638

## C

Cabot, George, 227
Calhoun, John C., 495; on distribution of government power, 89–90
Campbell, Angus, 201$n$, 206, 207$n$, 233, 236$n$, 242$n$, 243$n$, 247, 258$n$, 365$n$
Cannon, Joseph, 463, 492
Cantril, Hadley, 214$n$
Carageorge, Ted, 682
Carey, George W., 95, 590
Carswell, G. Harrold, 272, 556
Cartwright, Dorwin, 201, 258$n$
Case, Clifford P., 743
Castro, Fidel, 5
Centers, Richard, 202$n$
Chamberlin, William Henry, 688$n$
Chambers, Craig M., 714
Chapman, Shirley, 370
Charles, A. D., 581
Charles, Joseph, 301$n$
Chase, Samuel, impeachment, 502–503, 574
Cheever, Herbert, 682
Chenoweth, Gene, 714
Childs, Harwood L., 271$n$

# subject index

appeal, 570
appellate court, 566
appellate jurisdiction, 559
appointment(s): presidential, 501; and staffing, civil service, 523
*Aptheker* v. *Secretary of State,* 603n
Area Redevelopment Administration, 807
"Are Regional Differences Diminishing?" (Glenn and Summons), 205n
"Are We a Nation of Cities?" (Elazar), 156–157
Armed Forces Policy Council, 741
arms race, 720–721
"Arms Race: Pre-requisites and Results" (Huntington), 721n
*Army* magazine, 734
arraignment, 563
*Arrangement of Names on the Ballot and Its Effect on the Voter's Choice* (Hecock and Bain), 360n
Articles of Confederation, 63–69, 118
*Ashwander* v. *Tennessee Valley Authority,* 575n
assembly and petition, freedom of, 612–614
Associated Press, 210
association, right of, 613–614
Association of Western Railways, 260–261
associations, national, by type, 260
Atomic Energy Commission, 405, 501, 737–739, 812
atomic testing and health, 738–739
atrocities, 694–696
attitudes, 193
Audubon Society, 819
*Autobiography* (Jefferson), 640
Automobile Manufacturers Association, 270

# B

bail, excessive, 623–624
Bail Reform Act of 1966, 624
Baker's Guild of New York City, 269
*Baker* v. *Carr,* 456, 482
balancing of interests doctrine, 599–600
ballots and balloting, 358–360
*Baltimore* v. *Dawson,* 658
*Barenblatt* v. *U.S.,* 599n
*Barron* v. *Baltimore,* 579, 588, 630
Baruch, Bernard, 424
behavioralism, 17
*Benton* v. *Maryland,* 630
*Berger* v. *State of New York,* 619n
*Betts* v. *Brady,* 630
bifactionalism, 311
Bilingual Students Association, 659
bill of attainder, 122, 615–616
bill of information, 563
Bill of Rights, 94–97, 122–123; and civil liberties, 587–588; and due process of law, 616–617
Binkley, Wilfred E., 391, 392

"Black Americans: Large in Numbers, Small in Wealth," 666n
black consciousness, 643–646
Black Panthers, 279, 619, 644
blacks: advances, 643; elected officials, by region, 651; interest groups, 278–279; population, cities and suburbs, 161; unemployment, 162–163; *see also* central cities; civil rights; racial equality
black vote in the South, 229
black voter, 229–231
blanket primaries, 332
*Blau* v. *U.S.,* 630
block grants, 139
*Book of the States,* 332n
borrowing to finance the economy, 761–762
bosses, political, 315, 318–320
Boston Tea Party, 59, 279
*Boynton* v. *Virginia,* 678
briefs, 562
*Brown* v. *Board of Education of Topeka,* 287, 293, 644n, 653–654, 678
"Buckley Calls His Two Rivals 'White Flag' Candidates on War" (Ronan), 143
budget: accounting for expenditures, 765; preparation of, 763–765
Budget and Accounting Act of 1921, 389, 402, 763
bureaucracy, 511–512; characteristics, 514–515; vs. Congress and President, 536–539; levels of, 517–527; political responsibility, 539–541; structure, 527–531
"Bureaucracy and Constitutionalism" (Long), 539
*Bureaucracy in Modern Society* (Blau), 514n
bureaucrat and policy making, 531–536
Bureau of International Commerce, 528
Bureau of Minority Business Enterprise, 528
Bureau of the Budget, 399, 439, 763
"Bureau of the Budget and Executive Agencies: Notes on Their Interaction, The" (Davis and Ripley), 402
Bureau of the Census, 154n, 156n, 528
bureaus, government, 528
*Burstyn* v. *Wilson,* 608
*Burton* v. *Wilmington Parking Authority,* 659
business: equality of women in, 673; interest groups, 269–271; regulating, 770–774

# C

Cabinet, 407–409; departments, 527; Secretariat, 408
campaign funding, regulations, 343–345

campaigning, presidential election, 342–357
"Campaign Management: Expertise Brings Dollars," 348n
campaign organizations, 354
campaign spending: reforms, 346–347; regulations, 344–345
campaign strategy, congressional, 354–356
candidates: and issues, 237–239; and political socialization, 205–208
capitalism and democracy, 42–43
*Capitol Hill: Studies in Legislative Process* (Bibby and Davidson), 438
career executives, government, 519
*Caucasians Only: The Supreme Court, the NAACP, and the Restrictive Covenant Cases* (Vose), 287n
caucus, 331
"Caught in a Crunch: Secretary Finch," 274n
cease-and-desist orders, 106
censorship and modern media, 607–608
"Census," 166n
Center for Law and Social Policy, 276
Center for the Study of Responsive Law, 276
central cities, 156; congestion and lack of planning, 158–161; national aid, 176–180; riots, 163–164; state aid, 176, 177; taxes and services, 163–165; transportation and poverty, 159–161; unemployment in, 161–163
Central Intelligence Agency, 705, 706, 707, 742–744
centralization: case for, 144–145; local government, 171; mass media outlets, 210
ceremonial head, President as, 396–397
*certiorari,* writ of, 570
*Challenge to Affluence* (Myrdal), 638n
Chamber of Commerce of the United States, 261, 271
change and development, constitutional, 94–107
"Characteristics of Members of the 92nd Congress," 454n
"Characteristics of Party Leaders" (Patterson), 316
charisma, 10, 446
charter colonies, 55
Chase Manhattan Bank, 9
checks and balances, government, 38, 92–93
*Chicago Sun-Times,* 218
chief administrator, President as, 386–389
*Chief Executive, The* (Koenig), 385n, 424n, 426n, 429n, 439n
chief of state, President as, 396–397
child labor, 777

1400 Governments (Wood), 156n
franking privileges, 460
Freedman v. Maryland, 606, 608n
Freedmen's Bureau, 641
freedom: of assembly and petition,
612–614; of religion, 589–596;
from self-incrimination, 619–622;
of speech and press, 596–604
Freedom and the Court: Civil
Rights and Liberties in the
United States (Abraham), 594n,
597
free speech: and public order, 604;
symbolic, 604; tests of, 596–598
fugitive slave law, 639
full faith and credit in interstate
relations, 123
funding, presidential campaigns,
342–343

# G

Gallup Opinion Index, Report No.
63, 671n
General Accounting Office, 765
General Assembly, UN, 691
general primaries, 331–332
General Theory of Employment, Interest, and Money (Keynes),
767n
gerrymander, 456–458
ghettos, 158
GI Bill of Rights, 811
Gideon v. Wainright, 622, 630
Gillette v. U.S., 593n
Ginsberg v. U.S., 610
Gitlow v. New York, 588–589, 598–
599, 630
"Global Defense: U.S. Military Commitments Abroad," 739n
government: activities at local
level, 178; aid to central cities,
176–180; and Articles of Confederation, 66–67; branches and
field offices, 528–529; bureaucratic structure, 527–531; bureaus,
528; Cabinet departments, 527;
centralized, 115; checks and balances, 92–93; concurrent powers,
state and national, 127; by consent, 75–76; constitutional amendments affecting powers of, 128;
constitutional distribution of
power, 88–93; control of interest-
group activity, 287–288; cooperation with cities and states,
140–143; corporations, 529–530;
defined, 10–11; and education,
131–133; first attempts at, 56–58;
foreign affairs, 120; limitations
on, 122–123; limited, constitutionalism and, 35–37; local, reorganizing, 171–173; and natural
resources, 813–820; obligations
to states, 125–126; political party as
organizer of, 300; vs. politics, 11;
powers of, 119–123; projects, 774;
separation of powers of, 38–39,

90–92; services, 535; and states,
cooperation, 137–143; stronger,
130–134; supremacy of, 127–128;
as trustee, 30; working force of,
515–517
Governmental Process: Political Interests and Public Opinion, The
(Truman), 13n, 256–257, 262n,
290n
government employment and loyalty, 603
"Government Loyalty Program,
The" (Nikoloric), 601
graduated income tax, 767
Grand Army of the Republic, 277
"grandfather clause," 647–649
grand jury, 561; indictment by, 624
grants-in-aid, 138–139
Great Compromise, 74, 453
Green v. School Board of New Kent
County, 656
Griffin v. County School Board of
Prince Edward County, 656, 678
gross national product, 763
Group Dynamics: Research and
Theory (Cartwright and Zander),
201n, 258n
"Group Pressures and Group Stand-
ards" (Cartwright and Zander),
201n
groups: political behavior, 13; po-
litical participation, 202; see also
interest groups
Grovey v. Townsend, 649, 650, 678
Growth of the American Republic,
The (Morison and Commager),
62n, 68n, 77n
Guinn v. U.S., 648–649, 678
Gulf of Tonkin Resolution, 739

# H

habeas corpus, writ of, 122, 615
Harper v. Virginia Board of Educa-
tion, 650, 678
Harris, Louis, Associates, 279
Hatch Acts, 344, 345, 527
Head Start, 132, 163, 807
health, national, providing for,
800–804
Health Profession Education Assist-
ance Act, 802
Heart of Atlanta Motel v. U.S.,
662n, 678
Herdon v. Lowry, 598n
Hernandez v. Texas, 625
Higher Education Act, 813
Hill-Burton Act, 801
History of Labor in the United
States (Commons et al.), 271n
History of the U.S. Decision-Mak-
ing Process on Viet Nam Policy,
606
History of the U.S. House of Rep-
resentatives, 460n, 462n
Holmes v. Jennison, 120n
Home Building and Loan Associa-
tion v. Blaisdell, 614

Home Owners Loan Act, 426
Home Owners Loan Corporation,
804
homosexual and civil rights, 676
Hoover Commission, 536
Hoovervilles, 423
hospital programs and personnel,
801–802
House Agricultural Committee, Sub-
committee on Forests, 819
House Appropriations Committee,
491, 493, 764
House Armed Services Special Investigations Subcommittee, 734
House Committee on Un-American
Activities, 616
House Judiciary Committee, 674
House of Representatives, 74; cal-
endars, 493; Committee of the
Whole, 493–494; major commit-
tees, 491; order of debate, 493–
494; Speaker, 462–464; see also
Congress
House Out of Order (Bolling),
478n
House Rules Committee, 99–100,
463, 491–492, 493
House Ways and Means Commit-
tee, 470, 491, 492–493
housing: cases and legislation, 665–
666; for the poor, 804–806; pro-
viding national, 804–808; quality
of, 663; racial equality in, 663–
666
Housing Acts, 804–805
Housing and Urban Development
Act, 804
How Much Is Enough (Enthoven
and Smith), 740n
"How the Farmers Get What They
Want" (Lowi), 266
Humphrey's Executor v. U.S., 388n,
413, 526n
Hurtado v. California, 624n

# I

impeachment, 502–503, 574
implied powers, 119; and McCulloch v. Maryland, 121–122
income: black vs. white, 667; and
employment, women, 670; and
political socialization, 203–204;
and voting behavior, 244
income tax, 760; as automatic sta-
bilizer, 767; Sixteenth Amendment on, 129
In Defense of Politics (Crick), 4n,
5n
independence, 59–63
independents and partisans, voting
behavior, 245–249
Indiana-type ballot, 359–360
indictment by grand jury, 624
"Indispensable Opposition, The"
(Lippmann), 41n
individual, political behavior, 11–
13

management: and labor, 776–781; rights of, 779–780

mandamus, writ of, 101

Manpower Development and Training Act, 809

*Man's Control of His Environment*, 813n, 814n

*Mapp* v. *Ohio*, 618, 630

*Marbury* v. *Madison*, 101, 102, 571, 572, 579

marshall, 561

Marshall Plan, 391–392, 394, 690, 703

Massachusetts-type ballot, 359

mass media: commercialism, 210–211; modern, and censorship, 607–608; and political opinion, 208–213; trends in, 210–213

*Maxwell* v. *Dow*, 626n

McCarran Act, 601–603

*McCollum* v. *Board of Education*, 595, 630

*McCulloch* v. *Maryland*, implied powers and, 121–122

*McGowan* v. *Maryland*, 589n

*McLaurin* v. *Oklahoma State Regents*, 652

*Measures of Political Attitudes* (Robinson et al.), 191n

Medicaid, 803

Medicare, 274, 802–803

megalopolis, 158

*Megalopolis: The Urbanized Eastern Seaboard of the United States* (Gottman), 158n

merit examinations, civil service, 523

Metro, Miami, 174

metropolis, modern, 156–158

metropolitan areas, 156; city-county consolidation, 173–174; largest, population of, 159; population increase, 157; search for solutions, 171–181

metropolitanism, 156–157

*Meyers* v. *U.S.*, 388, 413

military forces abroad, 726

"'Military Lobby'—Its Impact on Congress, The," 733–735

minorities: unemployment, 161–163; *see also* blacks; civil rights; racial equality

minority businesses, funds available to, 668

minority leaders in Congress, 466–469

minority rights, 33–34

minor parties, 312–315

Minutemen missiles, 728

*Miranda* v. *Arizona*, 623, 631

MIRV, 728

misdemeanor, 550

missiles, 728

Missouri Compromise, 640–641; constitutionality of, 573

*Missouri ex. rel. Gaines* v. *Canada*, 652, 678

*Missouri* v. *Holland*, 120n

"Mr. and Mrs. America: The All Union Family," 281n

"Mr. Kennedy's Calculated Risk" (Drummond), 382n

Model Cities Program, 109, 159

*Modern Political Analysis* (Dahl), 6n

*Modern Presidency, The* (McConnell), 385n, 445n

monetary policy, 768–770

"Money Talks for Well-Heeled Office-Seekers in 1970," 345n

Monroe Doctrine, 394, 687–688

Montgomery Bus Co., 637, 658

*Morgan* v. *Virginia*, 658

movie censorship, 606

*Muir* v. *Louisiana*, 658

*Mulford* v. *Smith*, 573n

multifactionalism, 311

multiparty system, 308, 310

*Muskrat* v. *U.S.*, 551, 579

*Mutual Film Corp.* v. *Ohio Industrial Commission*, 607, 631

"My Lai Was Not the First Time" (Schirmer), 694–696

# N

*NAACP* v. *Alabama*, 614, 631

Nader's Raiders, 276

*Nardone* v. *U.S.*, 619, 631

National Advisory Commission on Civil Disorders, 669

National Aeronautics and Space Administration, 503, 744, 812

National Aeronautics and Space Council, 405

National Alliance of Businessmen, 810

National Apple Institute, 267

National Association for the Advancement of Colored People, 261, 278, 614, 637, 644, 652, 653; Legal Defense Fund, 108; Legal Defense of Education Fund, 287

National Association of Counties, 179

National Association of Home Builders, 819

National Association of Manufacturers, 256, 262, 263, 270

National Association of Theatre Owners, 255

*National Broadcasting Co.* v. *U.S.*, 608n, 631

National Budget message, 383, 403

National Catholic Welfare Council, 278

national character, theories of, 309

national committee, 317

National Conference of Commissioners on Uniform State Law, 142

National Conference of State Legislative Leaders, 98

national convention, 317, 338–341; criticism and reform, 341–342

National Council of Churches, 278

National Council of Senior Citizens' Clubs, 107

national debt, 762

national defense, *see* defense

National Defense Education Act, 809, 812

"National Diplomacy, 1965–1970," 698n

National Environmental Policy Act, 813

National Farmer's Union, 268–269

National Forest Products Association, 819

National Forest Timber Conservation and Management Act, 819

national government, *see* government

National Governors' Conference, 179

National Grange, 258, 267–268

National Guard, 726–727

National Highway Safety Bureau, 100

National Indian Youth Council, 644, 645

National Industrial Recovery Act, 426, 427, 777, 778

National Institutes of Health, 99, 801, 812

nationalism, road to, 56–59

nationalists, and centralization, 144

National Labor Relations Act, 777, 778

National Labor Relations Board, 285

National Land-Use Policy Act, 820

National League of Cities, 107, 179

National Limestone Institute, 283

National Organization of Women, 278, 672, 676

National Recovery Act of 1933, 102, 387

National Republican party, 304

National Rifle Association, 255, 819

National Science Foundation, 812

National Security Act of 1947, 404, 739–740

National Security Agency, 741–742

National Security Council, 389, 399, 404–405, 433, 704, 707, 741

National Society for the Prevention of Cruelty to Animals, 255

National Transportation Safety Board, 776

national trust fund, 795

National Wool Growers Federation, 267

natural dualism theories of two-party systems, 309

Natural Gas Pipeline Safety Act, lobbying and, 285–286

natural laws, 28

natural resources, government and, 813–820

natural rights, 28–29

*Near* v. *Minnesota*, 605, 631

*Negroes and the New Southern Politics* (Mathews and Prothro), 230n

*Negro Political Leadership in the South* (Ladd), 278n

search and seizure, 617–618
secessionist parties, 313
secondary benefits, 795
*Second Federalist, A: Congress Creates a Government*, 95, 590
Secretariat, UN, 691–692
Secretary of Defense, 740
Secretary of State, 702–704
Securities and Exchange Commission, 99, 276
Security Council, UN, 691
sedition, 600–603
Sedition Acts, 600
segregation: *de facto*, 657–658, 663–664; Harris Survey on, 208; *see also* desegregation; racial equality
select committees, 470
Selective Service Act of 1967, 592, 604
Selective Service and Training Act of 1940, 590
Selective Service Commission, 604
self-incrimination, freedom from, 619–622
self-interest: and federalism, 144–145; and rationality, 28–29
*Selling of the President, The* (McGinniss), 281*n*, 351*n*
Senate: major committees, 490–491; norms of deliberation, 494–500; presiding officers, 464–465; *see also* Congress
Senate Appropriations Committee, 490
"Senate Faces Early Decision on Electoral Reform," 363*n*
Senate Finance Committee, 490–491
Senate Foreign Relations Committee, 471, 490, 503–504, 685
"Senate Votes to Limit TV-Radio Campaign Spending," 347*n*
Senatorial Campaign Committee, 318
senatorial courtesy on federal appointments, 386–387
senators, Seventeenth Amendment on election of, 129
separate-but-equal doctrine, 642–643; declared unconstitutional, 653–654
separation of powers: FTC and, 106; in national government, 90–92
Servicemen's Readjustment Act, 811
*1787: The Grand Convention* (Rossiter), 70*n*
sexual equality, 670–676
Shays's Rebellion, 68
*Shelley* v. *Kramer*, 665, 678
*Shepperd* v. *Maxwell*, 625*n*
*Sherbert* v. *Verner*, 589*n*
Sherman Anti-Trust Act, 772, 777
short ballot, 360
Sierra Club, 819
*Sisterhood Is Powerful* (Morgan), 672*n*
sit-in demonstrations, 659, 662

slander and libel, 611
slavery, 304, 305; and expansion, 639–640; Thirteenth Amendment on, 129
slave trade, 75
Smith Act of 1940, 600–601
Smith-Hughes Act, 809
*Smith* v. *Allwright*, 646*n*, 650, 678
*Smoking and Politics: Policymaking and the Federal Bureaucracy* (Fritschler), 532
social class: and party affiliation, 299–300; and political socialization, 201–203; and voting behavior, 244
social contract and right of revolution, 30
socialization and opinion, political, 197–208
Social Security Act, 794, 795–796, 797, 798
"Some Determinants of Political Apathy" (Rosenberg), 191*n*
"Sources of Soviet Conduct, The" (Mr. X), 689*n*
Southeast Asia Treaty Organization, 731–733
Southern Christian Leadership Conference, 278, 644, 658
Southern Pine Industry Committee, 260
*Southern Politics* (Key), 311*n*
Southwestern Peanut Shellers' Association, 260
space and national defense, 744
Spartan tracking system, 729
Speaker of the House, 462–464
*Speaking Frankly* (Agnew), 213*n*
special committees, 471
specialization in bureaucracy, 514
*Special Message to Congress* (Nixon), 363
special rule, 492
speech and press, freedom of, 596–604
spending: deficit, 767; national, 763
*Spirit Mound Township in 1960 Election* (Clem), 352
*Spirit of the Laws, The* (Montesquieu), 38
splinter parties, 313
spoils system, 105
*Sports Illustrated*, 210
Sprint tracking system, 729
stability of political opinion, 196
stabilizers, automatic, 767–768
staff apparatus, President, 398–410
Stamp Act Congress, 59
Stamp Act of 1765, 58–59
Standard Oil Co., 770, 772
standing committees, 470–471
standing military, 725–726
standing vote, 499
standpatters, 245
*stare decisis*, 548, 550
"Stare Decisis" (Douglas), 576*n*

*State and the Citizen, The* (Mabbott), 40*n*
State of the Union message, 383
State of the World address, 383
states: activities at local level, 177; aid to central cities, 176, 177; and cities, cooperation, 140–143; and civil liberties, 588–589; constitutional amendments affecting powers of, 128; constitutions of, 63–66; courts, 560; and federal government, cooperation, 137–143; national obligations to, 125–126; powers and limitations on, 123; relations between, 123–125
"Statesman, The" (Plato), 32
states' rights, 89, 90
*Statistical Abstracts of the United States, 1970*, 235*n*, 526*n*, 762*n*, 795*n*
"Status of Women, The" (Shaffer), 674–675
statutes, congressional, 99–100
statutory interpretation, 570–571
statutory law, 549
Stimson Doctrine, 703
stock market crash, 306
Strategic Air Command, 727, 728
Strategic Arms Limitation Talks, 735–736
"Strengthening the Federal Career Executive" (Paget), 519
strike, right to, 778
*Stromberg* v. *California*, 598*n*
substantive due process, 617
suburbs, 156; and cities, percentage of black population, 161; move to, 165–166; problems of, 166–171
Subversive Activities Control Board, 602–603
succession, presidential, 376–377
Suffolk Resolves, 59
suffrage: amendments on, 129–130, 226–227; black, 229–231; 18-year-olds, 231–233; qualifications, 226–227; white male, 227–228; women, 231
Sugar Act of 1764, 58, 59
Summary Suspension Act of 1950, 571, 603
supportive consensus, 215
supremacy, national, 127–128
supremacy clause, 74
Supreme Court: Chief Justice, 570; constitutional interpretation theories, 576; declaration of unconstitutionality of federal laws, 127; as final authority, 559–560; growth of power, 108; judicial review, 571–576; justices, 567; opinions, 569; Roosevelt's effort to pack, 428, 574; self-restraint, 574–575; setting and procedures, 567–569; statutory interpretation, 570–571

# W

Wagner Act, 778–779
*Walden* (Thoreau), 35–36
*Walker* v. *Sauvinet*, 626n
wall of separation doctrine, 593–595
war: and national defense, 133; weapons of, 727–729
ward leaders, 315
War Industries Board, 388
War Labor Board, 388
war on poverty, *see* anti-poverty programs
*Washington Lobbyists, The* (Milbrath), 8n, 283n
"Washington Pressures: American Legion's Influence Wanes on Capitol Hill" (Bortz), 277n
watchdog function, Congress, 503–505
Water Pollution Control Act, 814
Water Pollution Control Advisory Board, 814
Water Quality Act, 815
Water Quality Improvement Act, 814, 816
*Watson* v. *Memphis*, 656
*Wealth of Nations* (Smith), 755n
"We Are Embarked on a Great Mission of Reform" (Richardson), 179n

welfare, national, providing for, 794–800
"Welfare: It May Soon Be Known As 'Workfare' " (Hamilton), 798–799
welfare payments, as automatic stabilizers, 767–768
*Welsh* v. *U.S.*, 593
*Wesberry* v. *Sanders*, 457–458, 482
*West Virginia State Board of Education* v. *Barnette*, 587n
*What Country Have I: Political Writings by Black Americans*, 279n
"What Direction for Political Science?" (Bone), 18n
Whig party, 304
whip checks, 467
Whisky Rebellion, 279
White House Press Conference, 381–382
White House Staff, 399–401, 404
white male suffrage, 227–228
*Whitney* v. *California*, 598n
*Who Governs: Democracy and Power in an American City* (Dahl), 6n
"Who'll Get What from Tax Sharing," 179n
"Who Needs the Democrats" (Galbraith), 512
Wilderness Society, 819
wiretapping, 618–619

*Wolf* v. *Colorado*, 618n
women: in Congress, 675; employment and income, 670; equality in business, 673; interest groups, 278; voters, 231
Women's Equity Action League, 675
Women's International Terrorist Conspiracy from Hell, 278
women's liberation, 670, 671–673; political action and, 674–676
*Works* (Webster), 88
Works Progress Administration, 429, 643, 794
Works Project Administration, 794
Wristonization, 705
writ of *certiorari*, 570
writ of habeas corpus, 122, 615
writ of mandamus, 101

# Y

*Yates* v. *U.S.*, 601, 632
yellow-dog contract, 778
Young Men's Christian Association, 4
*Youngstown Sheet and Tube Co.* v. *Sawyer*, 398, 414, 447n

# Z

Zootsuit Riots, 279
*Zorach* v. *Clauson*, 595, 632